Borland® C++ 4.5
Object-Oriented Programming

Fourth Edition

Borland® C++ 4.5

Object-Oriented Programming

Fourth Edition

Ted Faison

SAMS PUBLISHING

A Division of Prentice Hall Computer Publishing • 201 West 103rd Street • Indianapolis, IN 46290

Dedication: To all the wonderful members of my family.

Copyright ©1995 by Sams Publishing

FOURTH EDITION

International Standard Book Number: 0-672-30605-0

Library of Congress Catalog Card Number: 95-67160

98 97 96 95 4 3 2 1

Interpretation of the printing code: the rightmost double-digit number is the year of the book's printing; the rightmost single-digit, the number of the book's printing. For example, a printing code of 95-1 shows that the first printing of the book occurred in 1995.

Composed in AGaramond and MCPdigital by Macmillan Computer Publishing

Printed in the United States of America

Trademarks

Publisher
Richard K. Swadley

Acquisitions Manager
Greg Wiegand

Managing Editor
Cindy Morrow

Acquisitions Editor
Gregory S. Croy
Grace Buechlein

Development Editor
Phillip W. Paxton

Production Editor
Susan Christophersen
James Grass

Editorial Coordinator
Bill Whitmer

Editorial Assistants
Carol Ackerman
Sharon Cox
Lynette Quinn

Technical Reviewer
Greg Guntle

Marketing Manager
Gregg Bushyeager

Assistant Marketing Manager
Michelle Milner

Cover Designer
Tim Amrhein

Book Designer
Michele Laseau
Alyssa Yesh

Director of Production and Manufacturing
Jeff Valler

Imprint Manager
Kelly Dobbs

Manufacturing Coordinator
Paul Gilchrist

Production Analyst
Angela D. Bannan
Dennis Hager
Mary Beth Wakefield

Graphics Image Specialists
Tim Montgomery
Dennis Sheehan
Susan VandeWalle

Production
Lissa Auciello
Katy Bodenmiller
Jama Carter
Charlotte M. Clapp
Mary Ann Cosby
Terri Edwards
Aleata Howard
Cheryl Moore
Brian-Kent Proffitt
Erich Richter

Indexers
Greg Eldred
Craig Small

0

Overview

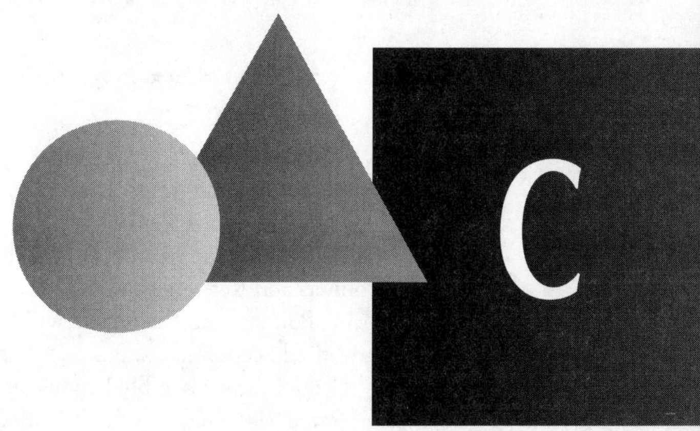

Contents

Part II OWL

Preface

Object-oriented programming (OOP) is a hot topic today. To many, C++ itself is synonymous with OOP, much the way many people implicitly associate LISP programming with artificial intelligence. The truth is, OOP is not so much a consequence of this or that language, but rather the result of the particular methods used. It is entirely possible to develop OOP applications with languages such as Pascal, Ada, BASIC, and assembly language, albeit with increasing difficulty.

What this book emphasizes is the OOP aspect of C++, using a particular implementation—Borland C++—as the vehicle. Given the recent explosion of interest in Microsoft Windows programming, the book covers selected topics of Windows programming, but only within the framework of OOP. The reader will learn to understand and reason in OOP terms when writing Windows applications, developing a methodology different from the traditional one presented in the Microsoft Windows Software Development Kit.

This is a "hands-on" book, because there are frequent programming examples and projects throughout. All sample programs and all code that appears with a listing number can be loaded and compiled immediately from the companion disk to test the various features of OOP shown. Much attention was given to such practical issues as functionality and efficiency. The reader is assumed to have experience with the C programing language. A minimum of two years is recommended. Advanced users will also find interesting material toward the end of each chapter.

Acknowledgments

A book like this is useful only if the information it contains is accurate, but it is very difficult to guarantee absolute correctness. I would like to thank all the people who provided corrections, suggestions, and input for this book. C++ streams are a particularly detailed field, and I am grateful to Lori Benner of Borland International for checking selected portions of Chapter 6. I also thank Borland's Nan Borreson, Phil Rose, Pete Becker, Carl Quinn, Richard Landsman, and Bruneau Babet, among the many others, for their cooperation and help. Last, but certainly not least, I thank my editor Greg Croy for being so helpful, friendly, and professional during the many months it took to write this book.

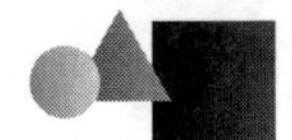

Introduction

During the 1980s, C emerged as one of the world's premier and universal programming languages. It made it possible and efficient to write code that was portable to a wide class of computers. Software could be written faster and projects on the average grew in size. With size came complexity, leading to increased development times. Today development time and effort for software is a major issue in many companies. AT&T developed the C++ language as an extension of ANSI C, in an attempt to bring many of the advantages of object-oriented programming to the world of C without losing the many desirable features—such as simplicity and runtime efficiency—that made C so popular.

C++ was developed to make programming easier. To make this possible, the language had to be more complex than its predecessor. All the added features of C++ are aimed at reducing levels of difficulty. Obviously, the mere adoption of C++ doesn't automatically guarantee better or simpler software. To reap the benefits of C++, you must adopt a new programming methodology commonly referred to as *object-oriented programming,* or *OOP.*

Why Object-Oriented Programming?

Several years ago computer science researchers noted that programmers can write and debug pretty much the same amount of code no matter what language they use. The amount of work is roughly the same, but the results are not. Writing 100 lines of code in C is about as difficult as writing 100 lines of code in assembly language, but the C code accomplishes much more. With this in mind, researchers sought to develop higher-level languages that multiply the power of a single programmer, thus reducing project development time and costs.

In the 1970s, the concept of the *object* became popular among programming language researchers. An object is a collection of code and data designed to emulate a physical or abstract entity. Objects are efficient as programming items for two main reasons: They represent a direct abstraction of commonly used items, and they hide most of their implementation complexity from their users. The first objects developed were those most closely associated with computers, such as Integer, Array, and Stack. Some languages (such as Smalltalk) were designed as orthodox languages in which everything is defined as an object.

Object-oriented programming is a methodology that gives great importance to relationships between objects rather than implementation details. Relationships are ties between objects and are usually developed through genealogical trees in which new object types are developed from others. Hiding the implementation of an object results in the user being more concerned with an object's relation to the rest of the system rather than how an object's behaviors are implemented. This distinction is important and represents a fundamental departure from earlier "imperative" languages (such as C) in which functions and function calls were the center of activity.

In C++, few objects are part of the language itself. The burden and responsibility for devising objects is on the user. Borland C++ is bundled with a number of object types, but to make any real use of the language requires developing many more types. The power of OOP is exploited if groups of interrelated object types are developed. These groups are usually called *class hierarchies.* Developing these class hierarchies is a central activity in OOP.

The Structure of This Book

This book describes the new methodology required to develop class hierarchies based on Borland C++ 4.0, using the object types furnished by Borland International. Before doing so, the book covers the basic features of C++. The main OOP features of C++ are introduced in separate chapters.

This book is divided into two parts. The first part, "C++," describes the C++ language in general, with particular attention to Borland C++ and the features that make it an object-oriented language. This book is not intended to be a complete reference on Borland C++, but it shows how to use the language features in an object-oriented sense.

The second part of the book, "OWL," beginning with Chapter 10, shows how to use OWL in ways not described in the Borland documentation. Much attention is given throughout the book to the program examples, which also are available in source code on the companion disk. Each of the examples has been tested and can be compiled and tried immediately.

The structure of this book is somewhat unusual. Although on the surface it is straightforward, in reality you sometimes are referred to material in later chapters. This is because I chose to describe C++ systematically rather than gradually. This makes it easier to find information in the book. For example, the section on class destructors in Chapter 2 has all the information on destructors, citing virtual destructors, even though virtual functions are described in detail only in Chapter 5. This order of presentation differs from that of most other C++ books; however, I believe the advantages outweigh the disadvantages.

Book Description

This book deals with C++ programming in general and Borland C++ 4.5 in particular. Frequently I refer to C++ rather than Borland C++ when a specific topic is general to the proposed ANSI C++ standard. Because Borland C++ is essentially a superset of AT&T C++ release 2.1, the distinction is necessary.

Chapter 1, "Basics," summarizes the main constructs of Borland C++ without making any formal definitions or presentations, giving space to topics in which C++ differs from ANSI C. Although C programs can be compiled with a C++ compiler, it is not true that C++ always uses the same techniques as C programs. Some C features considered obsolete in C++ are pointed out.

Chapter 2, "Objects and Classes," is the real beginning of the object-oriented extensions to ANSI C, introducing the new concepts of objects and classes. This chapter shows how code and data are used together to build an object, how objects are used, and what properties they have.

Chapter 3, "Inheritance," illustrates how objects can be built starting with other objects rather than from scratch. This enables the objects to inherit characteristics from the parent classes, reducing the amount of coding and debugging necessary to accomplish a task. Inheritance allows classes to be used repeatedly as *black boxes,* increasing programmer productivity. Both single inheritance and multiple inheritance are discussed.

Chapter 4, "Overloading," deals with function and operator overloading. Experienced programmers may yawn initially here, but don't even *think* of skipping this chapter. Overloading is an important characteristic that allows different classes to use a uniform notation for actions that are conceptually similar. This is another C++ simplification that comes to the aid of the programmer, helping you manage large projects better.

Chapter 5, "Polymorphism," covers one of the most touted features of C++. Polymorphism is described and shown as a concrete way to simplify programming through the use of virtual functions. Advantages and disadvantages of virtual functions are shown, including explanations of the runtime features of virtual functions.

Chapter 6, "Exception Handling," deals with a new feature added to the preliminary ANSI draft proposal of C++. Exceptions allow programs to deal with unusual situations in a very straightforwsard manner, allowing once-complex programs to be simplified considerably.

Chapter 7, "Streams," deals with input and output (I/0). All programs have to produce results to be useful, so they must have a means for outputting information. In general, programs need both input and output. Chapter 6 describes input and output in terms of the new C++ constructs of *streams.* I/O streams are described for both files and hardware devices. The concept of the stream is also applied to in-memory operations.

Chapter 8, "The Object-Based Container Library," describes each of the classes in the library that was first released with Borland C++ 2.0. The class library is based on a Smalltalk-like hierarchy, with the class `Object` at the root.

Chapter 9, "The Template-Based Container Library," also called the BIDS (Borland International Data Structures) library, is a library of class templates that form the basis of the new containers in Borland C++ 4.5. Using template-based containers, you can handle both scalar and class variables in containers, with ease of expression and complete type safety.

Chapter 10, "ObjectWindows Library Classes," covers a number of interesting OWL programming examples that are not described in the Borland documentation.

Chapter 11, "MDI Applications," shows how to take a basic OWL MDI program and enhance it through a detailed series of custionizations. If you use MDI, you'll definitely find this chapter useful.

Chapter 12, "Variations on a ListBox," shows a number of ways in which the standard Windows ListBox can be enhanced to satisfy a wide range of programming scenarios, by using classes derived from `TListBox`. Using techniques similar to those shown, you can customize other standard Windows controls.

Chapter 13, "OLE Programming with OWL," is a fast-forward view of the extensions Borland added to its C++ package to support OLE programming. Readers should be familiar with essential OLE concepts, like reference counting, the Component Oject Model, and interfaces before approaching this chapter. I have tried to describe some of the more important aspects of the ObjectComponent Frameworks that aren't covered in the Borland documentation. This chapter attempts to give readers some sense of how various pieces of ObjectComponents Framework code, BOCOLE code, and OWL code work together to give OLE support to applications.

Notational Conventions

A few basic conventions have been adopted throughout the book to increase readability:

1. When Borland C++ keywords are used in a sentence, they are printed in a special monospace type. This increases the clarity of the text, as in the following example:

   "When returning a `void` from a function..."

2. File names are printed in *italics,* as in the following example:

   "The definitions in *stdio.h* are used..."

3. Function names are printed in monospace and end with parentheses. When a file accepts parameters, three dots are used inside the parentheses to denote generic parameters:

   "The arguments of `printf(...)` are unknown at compile time..."

4. Variable names are printed in monospace:

   "Assigning a value to variable `arg` is allowable if..."

Requirements

You don't need a computer to study programming, but it sure helps! To master the material in this book, you not only need to study the source code of the various examples, but you should try making changes and compiling on your own. You will need the following items:

- An IBM PC AT or compatible computer
- MS-DOS 3.31 or later version
- A Microsoft-compatible mouse
- EGA, VGA, or better
- Borland C++ version 4.5
- Borland Application Frameworks (for chapters 10 through 13)
- Windows 3.1 or later version

The project files for the sample programs in chapters 8 through 13 were created using Borland C++ 4.5. If you are using prior versions of the compiler, you may not be able to successfully use these project files.

The Microsoft Software Development Kit (SDK) for Windows is not required. If you have Turbo C++, or a version of Borland C++ prior to 4.5, you can still compile most of the code in Chapters 1 through 6, but you won't be able to try the container classes in Chapter 7—or you might have to make changes to the code.

The Windows code in Chapters 8 through 11 requires Borland C++ 4.0. If you have Borland C++ 3.0 with Windows 3.0, you might need to make changes to the source code or the project files.

Note

The programming information in this book is based on information for developing applications for Windows 95 made public by Microsoft as of 9/9/94. Since this information was made public before the final release of the product, there may have been changes to some of the programming interfaces by the time the product is finally released. We encourage you to check the updated development information that should be part of your development system for resolving issues that might arise.

The end-user information in this book is based on information on Windows 95 made public by Microsoft as of 9/9/94. Since this information was made

public before the release of the product, we encourage you to visit your local bookstore at that time for updated books on Windows 95.

If you have a modem or access to the Internet, you can always get up-to-the-minute information on Windows 95 direct from Microsoft on WinNews:

On CompuServe: `GO WINNEWS`

On the Internet:
`ftp://ftp.microsoft.com/PerOpSys/Win_News/Chicago`
`http://www.microsoft.com`

On AOL: keyword `WINNEWS`

On Prodigy: jumpword `WINNEWS`

On Genie: `WINNEWS` file area on Windows RTC

You can also subscribe to Microsoft's WinNews electronic newsletter by sending Internet e-mail to `news@microsoft.nwnet.com` and putting the words `SUBSCRIBE WINNEWS` in the text of the e-mail.

C++

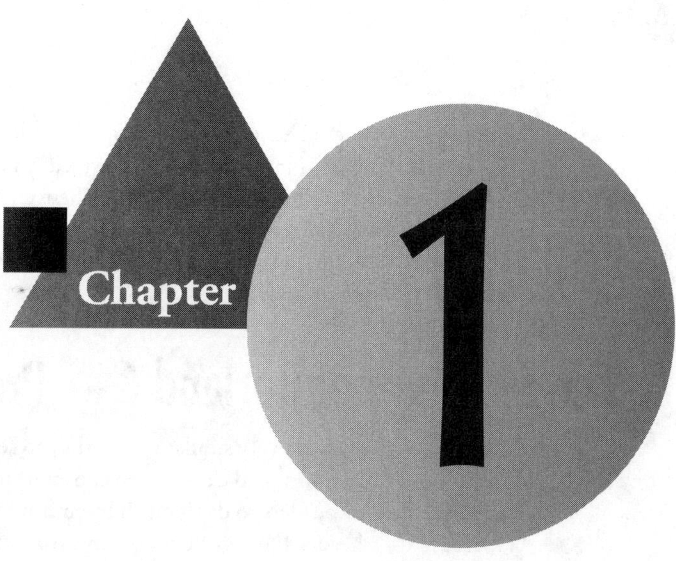

Basics

This chapter explores the main features of C++ that are extensions of or derivations from ANSI C, but the chapter doesn't deal with objects or other object-oriented constructs. I have tried to dedicate more space to those features of C++ that are less understood, avoiding lengthy discussions of trivial issues. For more elementary topics, I suggest reading the *Borland C++ Programmer's Guide*, supplied with the standard Borland documentation.

C++ is classified as a hybrid object-oriented language, as opposed to a pure or orthodox object-oriented one, because it is built on top of a more traditional procedural language. Other languages (such as Eiffel or Smalltalk) are pure languages, but that doesn't necessarily make them better. What constitutes "better" depends on how a language is to be used and on what task is to be solved.

C++ source code must be compiled before being executed. The programming process therefore entails a development cycle of editing, compiling, linking, and running. Although the iteration through this cycle is a slow process, the code produced is very fast and efficient. C++ represents an excellent balance between power of expression, runtime speed, and code size. Moreover, the Borland C++ Integrated Development Environment (IDE) automatically connects all phases of the development cycle, speeding up the cycle dramatically.

Because C++ was designed as an improvement to and as an extension of C, it is full of the traditional features of ANSI C. However, as with any new version of software, some changes have occurred even with rather basic items. These changes are highlighted in this chapter as the basic C language features are shown. C programmers won't find too many changes here, but that shouldn't encourage them to skip to Chapter 2, because some of the changes described are very important.

The Structure of Borland C++ Projects

Borland C++ projects are very similar to ANSI C projects in terms of structure. You set up declarations of structures (and classes) and constants in header files. The file suffix **.hpp* is often used for C++ headers to distinguish them from regular **.h* headers used with ANSI C, because C++ header files may contain constructs that don't compile under ANSI C. The actual C++ source code is contained in one or more source files that are compiled and linked in the same manner as ANSI C compiles and links them.

Header Files

A class identifier must be entered into scope before being used. Normally this is done in a class declaration. To use the `public` members of a class, the class identifier must not only be in scope, but the class must also be fully declared. Because each class has its own declaration, and many different modules can use it, the declaration is normally put in a header file that is included in every module that uses the given class.

The Multiple Inclusion Problem

Given the large number of classes and header files that make up typical programs, there is the risk of including a header file more than once in the same file. Consider the following files:

```
// file HEADER.HPP
class EssentialClass { /* ... */ };

// file DESKTOP.HPP
#include "HEADER.HPP"
class DeskTop { /* ... */ };

// file DRAWER.C
#include "HEADER.HPP"
#include "DESKTOP.HPP"            // file HEADER.HPP included
                                  // twice !
class Drawer { /* ... */ };
```

To prevent this all-too-common occurrence, C++ header files typically use some preprocessor directives to produce the following simple but effective trap:

```
// file HEADER.HPP
#ifndef HEADER.HPP
#define HEADER.HPP

class EssentialClass { /* ... */ };
...
...
#endif
```

All header files use the same mechanism. Usually the header's file name, or an abbreviated version of it, is used in the `#define` statement. Subsequent attempts to include the same file again are caught and handled by the preprocessor: If a file that has already been included is included again, the preprocessor will skip over everything between the `#ifndef` and `#endif` macros.

Precompiled Header Files

One of the complaints C++ users have is the lengthy time necessary to load the multitude of included header files into typical source files. Sometimes it can take longer for the compiler to load and scan the header files than to compile the source file. Often the same headers are loaded over and over again with different modules. It seems like such a waste of time.

Fortunately the people at Borland International are of the same opinion, and they came up with a solution, called *precompiled headers.* When Borland C++ scans through all the header files included in a source file, it saves a "precompiled" version of them on disk. The next time you need to include the same header files, the compiler reads the precompiled one instead, dramatically improving overall compilation speed. The difference in speed is particularly significant when many or large header files have to be included. Among the largest commonly used headers are *windows.h*, *dos.h*, *iostream.h*, and *graphics.h*.

To use precompiled headers, you need to enable the Precompiled Header option, via the Options | Project | +Compiler | Precompiled header. When using the option, the compiler scans the header files that are included in your source file and stores an image of them on disk in a file called *bcwdef.csm.* Only one precompiled header file is managed by the compiler at a time, but you can override the default file name to create different precompiled headers. Because these files have a tendency to get rather large, make sure you have enough disk space before starting. If the system runs out of disk space while making a precompiled header, you can get some really strange error messages or results.

A Complete Sample Program

Most books on C or C++ begin with the usual "hello, world!" program, consisting of a trivial `main()` function that prints a message on the computer screen and then terminates. Because this book is not an introductory one, I start with a more involved program that embodies most of the basic constructs at once. This method gives you an immediate feel for the procedural part of the language, without having to read three quarters of the book.

The example program in Listing 1.1 reads a line of text typed by the user, computes how much white space it contains, and then reports the results.

Listing 1.1. A complete C program.

```
// Count the number of spaces in a line of text

#include <stdio.h>          // These header files are supplied
#include <string.h>         // in the Borland C++ package.
#include "example.hpp"      // This is a user-defined header,
                            // which contains declarations
                            // necessary to compile the
                            // program. For this example, the
                            // header might contain the single
                            // statement:
                            // "const int TAB_SIZE = 8;"
int main()
{
     char words [80];

     // get a string From the user
     gets(words);

     int spaces = 0;
     // count the amount of white space
     for (int i = 0; i < strlen(words); i++) {
       switch (words [i]) {
         case ' ':
           spaces++;
           break;
         case '\t':
           spaces += TAB_SIZE;
           break;
         default:
           break;
       }
     }
     // report the results back
     printf("\nThe number of spaces was %d\n", spaces);
     return 0;
}
```

This short example uses the following C++ constructs (in order of appearance):

- Comments
- `include` files
- A `main()` function

- Variables
- Statements
- Functions

I describe each of these according to their order of appearance.

Comments

C++ introduces a new format for comments, designed to speed up things when writing single-line comments, which occur often in a program. The new format requires comment lines to start with the two characters `//`, and the comment is assumed to be confined to that one line. Multiple-line comments require the `//` characters on each line. The old formats

```
/* old style comments */
and
/* a
   multiline
   comment
*/
```

are still supported and are used mostly for multiline comments. Comments can occur almost anywhere in a program, but good style recommends keeping them on separate lines where they stand out.

C++ does not allow comments of either style to be nested, but Borland C++ allows some flexibility. It allows `/*...*/` style comments to be nested if the Nested Comments option is checked in the Options | Project | +Compiler | Source menu. Comments of type `//` can be nested inside a `/*...*/` comment. For example:

```
/*
     // a single line comment
     // another comment
*/
```

At times during program development, large sections of code need to be commented out. Using the `/* */` comment to block the code out works only if no other `/*...*/` comments appear inside the block. An alternative is to use the preprocessor directives, as shown here:

```
#if 0
     while (TRUE) {
       // wait here until the user types something
       printf("\nType a series of words. ");
       gets(words);
       if (strlen(words) )
         break;
     }
#endif
```

Using preprocessor directives can be taken one step further to allow different versions of code to coexist in the same file, with only one active:

```
#if 0
     while (TRUE) {
       // wait here until the user types something
       printf("\nType a series of words. ");
       gets(words);
       if (strlen(words) )
         break;
     }
#else
     // attempt to read user text only once
     printf("\nType a series of words. ");
     gets(words);
#endif
```

include Files

The example in Listing 1.1 shows two methods of including files in C++. C++ states that the search algorithms for the two methods are implementation-dependent. I describe the Borland C++ approach. The first `include` method takes the form

```
#include <filename.ext>
```

This tells the compiler to use a predefined search path when looking for the file. You set up the path via the Options | Project | Directories menu. The directories are searched in the order they appear, and the current directory is *not* searched. Note that spaces are considered part of the file name if they appear inside the angle brackets, so the two include statements

```
#include <stdio.h>
#include < stdio.h >
```

refer to two different files. The second statement is likely to cause the compiler to complain about not being able to locate the file, and you get the error message

```
Unable to open the include file ' stdio.h '.
```

This `include` method is normally used for standard header files, such as *stdio.h*, *string.h*, and so on, which are part of the Borland C++ package.

The second kind of file inclusion is meant to be used with a user header file, and takes the form

```
#include "filename.ext"
```

This causes Borland C++ to search the current directory first, then the standard directories as in the previous method. Here again, avoid spaces inside the quotes, because they will cause errors.

The *WinMain()* Function

Every Windows application program must have a function called `WinMain()`. This function is declared of type **`int PASCAL`**. The **`int`** indicates that on exit, `WinMain()` returns an integer value to Windows, indicating the application's exit status. A zero indicates normal or successful completion; any other value indicates abnormal termination. The **`PASCAL`** modifier indicates that `WinMain()` uses the Pascal calling sequence, as described in the section "Understanding the Pascal Calling Sequence" at the end of this chapter. The complete declaration for `WinMain()` looks like the following:

```
int PASCAL WinMain(HINSTANCE instance, HINSTANCE prevInstance, char
far* cmdLine, int cmdShow);
```

in which

> `instance` is the instance handle of the program being run. Each time a new program is run, Windows considers it a new instance. Multiple running copies of the same program are distinguished by their instance handle.
>
> `prevInstance` is the instance handle given to the last running copy of the same program. If no other copies are currently running, `prevInstance` will be 0.
>
> `cmdLine` is a pointer to the command line used to launch the application. Using the `File ¦ Run` command from the Program Manager, if you ran a program called PLEASE by typing the command
>
> ```
> PLEASE Fix this problem
> ```
>
> then the `WinMain()` function in the program PLEASE.EXE would receive a `cmdLine` parameter pointing at the string `Fix this problem`.
>
> `cmdShow` is a parameter that tells your application how to display itself initially. If your program is run from the Program Manager by double-clicking its icon, or by typing its name in the File Run dialog box, `cmdShow` will have the value `SW_SHOWNORMAL`, indicating a *normal* mode. Most programs *normally* come up in the restored mode, in which their main window occupies part of the screen. If you run the program from the Program Manager by selecting its icon and pressing Shift + Enter, `cmdShow` will have the value `SW_SHOWMINNOACTIVE`, in which case your program should run in an iconized window.

OWL 2.5 applications are not required to have a `WinMain()` entry point, because OWL supplies one for you that processes the `WinMain()` parameters, initializes OWL, and then calls the function `OwlMain()`. See the section "The Entry Point of OWL Applications" in Chapter 10 for a complete description of `OwlMain()`.

The *LibMain()* Function

Every Windows DLL must have an entry point called `LibMain()`, and OWL 2.5 supplies a default `LibMain()` function for you. This function creates a `TModule` object (actually a

TModule-derived object called TObjectWindowsLibrary), to which you can later gain access in your DLL using the global pointer Module, as follows:

```
HINSTANCE instance = Module->hInstance;
```

LibMain() is called from the Borland C++ DLL startup code, and is passed a few parameters. LibMain() is actually declared like this:

```
int FAR PASCAL LibMain(HINSTANCE hInstance, WORD wDataSeg, WORD
cbHeapSize, char far* lpCmdLine);
```

Like WinMain(), LibMain() uses the Pascal calling sequence, and is expected to return an integer value to Windows. This value indicates whether the DLL was able to initialize itself or not. If the value 0 is returned, Windows will immediately unload the DLL. A return value of 1 indicates successful initialization.

The hInstance parameter is the instance handle assigned to the DLL. This handle is used when loading resources contained in the DLL file. Windows doesn't run multiple instances of the same DLL, so LibMain() is called only once for a given library, and a DLL can have only a single instance handle—no matter how many applications are using the DLL at a given time.

wDataSeg is the value of the Data Segment used by the DLL. All global and static DLL data is stored in this Data Segment. Local (stack) data is stored on the stack of the calling applications. DLLs don't have their own stack.

cbHeapSize indicates the size of the DLL's local heap, as specified in the DLL's .DEF file.

cmdLine is the command line used to load a DLL. Most of the time, cmdLine will be 0, but a DLL can be loaded explicitly by a program using the LoadModule() function. LoadModule() allows you to pass a command string to the DLL.

Variables

Variables are nothing more than named areas in memory that are used for storing data. Variables are characterized by *scope*, *type*, and *storage class*. Each of these characteristics is treated in a separate section.

Variables can be declared in the usual ANSI C way, by putting them at the beginning of a function before executable statements appear. C++ also allows variables to be declared almost anywhere in the middle of a function. For example,

```
for (int i = 0; i < 10; i ++)
  // ...

int i = GetValue();
```

```
char* cp = NextString();
```

Embedding variable declarations in C++ code makes it harder to spot them, but it makes more sense to declare a variable at the moment you first need it rather than at the beginning of a function.

Scopes

When a variable is declared, it is also given a scope, that is, a realm of validity. Scope depends on *where* the declaration of a variable appears in a program. I describe all the C++ scopes in the following paragraphs, except class scopes, which are treated in Chapter 2.

Block Scope

C++ generalizes the concept of local scope, introducing the *block* concept. A block is an area enclosed between braces, like this:

```
{    // beginning of block
     // area inside a block
}    // end of block
```

In C++, variables declared at the beginning of a function have block scope, where the block coincides with the entire function body. It is possible to nest blocks, and variables can be declared inside the nested blocks. A declaration can appear anywhere a C++ statement can, such as

```
void some_function()
{
     int number;

     for (int i = 0; i < 10; i++) {
       int half_number;
       if (i & 1)
         number += 1;
     }

     // this will cause an error
     half_number = number / 2;

     // this is okay
     number = i;
}
```

In this example, `number` has scope from its point of declaration to the end of the function. Integer `i` also has the same scope, because it was declared before entrance into the `for` block. The variable `half_number` is defined only inside the `for` loop block, so the use of this variable outside that block results in an `undefined identifier` error.

Attention must be paid when declaring variables with the same name in nested blocks, because the compiler uses the variable in the innermost possible block. A variable declared in a block obscures all other variables with the same identifier in outer blocks. Consider the case

```
{
  int x, y;
  x = 3;
  {
    int x;
    x = 5;
    y = x;      // y = 5
  }
  y = x;        // y = 3
}
```

Here the results of using variable x change depending on which block you are in.

Function Prototype Scope

Variables declared inside a function prototype have a special scope, which goes from the point of declaration to the end of the function prototype, as shown in the following code:

```
int some_function(int x, int y);

int foo()
{
  // this won't work
  x = 5;
}
```

The first statement is a function declaration. The second is a function definition. The variable x can't be used in the function `foo()` because it is out of scope. The only place you can use the identifier x is inside the parentheses in which it is declared.

File Scope

Variables with this scope are declared outside of all blocks and classes. They may have internal linkage (in the case of static variables) or external linkage (in all other cases), in which case they are called *global variables*. In the fragment

```
int number;
static int value;
main()
{
  number = 0;
  value = number + 1;
  return number;
}
```

the variable `number` is `global` and has external linkage. In other words, `number` can be referenced in other modules. After the point in the file at which a variable is declared, it can be used by any other function in that file. To use a `global` variable before the point at which it is declared, the `extern` declaration must be used. The same goes when using a `global` variable that is defined in a different file.

In the preceding example, the variable `value` also has file scope, but with internal linkage only. It cannot be referenced by other modules.

Types

When you declare a variable, you have to indicate what kind of data it stores. C++ doesn't allow you to change the type of a variable after it has been declared. Borland C++ allows the same built-in types as ANSI C:

- `char`
- `short`
- `int`
- `long`
- `float`
- `double`

Types `char`, `short`, `int`, and `long` can be modified with the keywords `signed` and `unsigned`. The user can also create compound types that are derived from the built-in types by declaring the following items:

- Arrays
- Pointers
- Structures
- Unions

C++ doesn't introduce significant changes over ANSI C in this area, so I won't go into further details here. Note that arrays are usually called *vectors* in C++.

Storage Classes

The storage class of a variable indicates how the compiler is to allocate storage space for the variable. The following storage classes are defined

- `auto`
- `register`
- `extern`
- `static`

along with the modifiers

- const
- volatile

C++ introduces virtually no changes over ANSI C for the `auto`, `register`, `extern`, and `static` storage classes, so I won't give further details on them. The modifiers `const` and `volatile` are less known and deserve some attention.

The *const* Modifier

Declaring a variable to be `const` makes that variable read-only. The variable *must* be initialized when defined, and any attempts to subsequently modify it result in a compile-time error. Some compilers that generate ROMable code (code destined to be placed in ROMs) sometimes react to the `const` modifier by placing a variable in ROM memory space, where even the hardware prevents modifications to the variable. This practice usually works, but as shown in the next section, may lead to problems when a `const` variable is initialized with the value returned by a function. Because a `const` variable must be initialized when defined, the following code is wrong:

```
// this is wrong !
const int i;
```

The `const` modifier can be applied only to variables of `static` duration. `register` and `auto` variables can never be declared `const`. In C++, the following declaration sets up a `const` variable for internal linkage only:

```
// internal linkage only
const int i = 5;
```

Any attempts to reference this variable from another linked file results in an undefined identifier error when the linker is run. To provide external linkage, use the following declaration:

```
// this will be visible to the linker
extern const int i = 5;
```

To declare a `const` in a file other than the one it is used in, use the following declaration:

```
// variable is in another file !
extern const int i;
```

Note that it has the same form as the original variable declaration, but without the initialization. If a `const` variable is defined inside a file like this:

```
foo()
{
     const int i = 5;
     ...
     ...
}
```

it can *only* have internal linkage. Applying the `extern` modifier to it results in an error. If the variable has to have external linkage, declare it outside all functions.

C++ `const` objects are slightly different from ANSI C, because in the latter, the default linkage type is external.

Using *const* Rather Than *#define*

In C++, the old style of declaring program constants with `#define` is considered obsolete. The `const` method should be used instead. This allows the compiler to perform type checking, because it knows more about the items being handled. The compiler is also smart enough to avoid allocating storage to a `const` when unnecessary. As a standard practice, I use all uppercase letters for constants, just as for macros, to make it clear which variables can be changed and which can't. Consider the following code:

```
// these items have internal linkage
const int TRUE = 1;
const int FALSE = 0;

while (TRUE) {
  ...
  int a = FALSE;
  ...
}
```

Because `const` objects default to internal linkage in C++, use the `extern` notation if you define constants in one file that needs to be visible in another.

```
// these items have external linkage
extern const int TRUE = 1;
extern const int FALSE = 0;
```

The compiler recognizes that the constants `TRUE` and `FALSE` do not require storage. They are identifiers that the compiler replaces with actual values at compile time. The identifiers `TRUE` and `FALSE` are not included in the link map, because they cease to exist after compilation. There are occasions in which storage is actually allocated to a `const` object:

```
const int& number = 9;
```

This statement creates a constant reference and allocates storage to it. The identifier `number` is in the symbol table, and `number` behaves just like any other reference variable (with the proviso that it can't be modified).

Initializing a *const* with a Function Call

A `const` can be initialized pretty much like an ordinary variable, including initializing by assigning to `const` the value returned by a function. Consider the code:

```
int NewValue();
```

```
void main()
{
     // initialize a const through a function call
     const int i = NewValue();
}

// function returning an integer
int NewValue()
{
     return 4;
}
```

This type of `const` initialization is perfectly acceptable in Borland C++. The preceding code may however cause a problem on compilers generating code for ROMs: the `const i` needs to be placed in the code segment, but the value of `i` is not known until runtime. A partial solution may be to use a reference to a `const`, initializing the reference at runtime like this:

```
const int& i = NewValue();
```

The compiler places the reference in the data segment, but prevents the reference from pointing at anything other than a `const`.

The *volatile* Modifier

In certain cases you don't want the compiler to produce optimizations. When dealing with variables that are accessible both from an interrupt servicing routine (ISR) and by the regular code, the compiler must not make any assumptions about the value of a variable from one line of code to the next. In a multiprocessing environment, there may be other processors that have access to shared memory variables, thereby making changes to them without warning. In these cases and others that involve memory-mapped hardware devices, you need the `volatile` modifier.

The following example accesses a variable that is also managed by an ISR. The code loops until the ISR indicates that a character is available. The variables `character` and `ready` are declared `global` and `volatile`. They must be `global` so that the ISR has access to them and `volatile` so that the compiler doesn't get too creative in optimizing the code. In this example, I could have omitted the `volatile` declaration for variable `character`, but because I knew that it is accessed also from an ISR, I knew it was better to make it `volatile` beforehand.

```
volatile char character;
volatile int ready;

char get_character()
{
     // wait for a character
```

```
    while (!ready)
      ;

    // read the next character
    return character;
}
```

Statements

Statements are what control the flow and execution of a program. C++ introduces no new statements over ANSI C. The following is a list of the allowed simple statements in Borland C++:

- expression statement
- `if else`
- `switch`
- `case`
- `default`
- labeled statement
- `while`
- `do while`
- `for`
- `break`
- `continue`
- `goto`
- `return`

A *compound statement* consists of a series of statements enclosed in braces, like this:

```
{  // beginning of a compound statement
  simple_statement;
  simple_statement;
  ...
  ...
  simple_statement;
}
```

A compound statement can also have only one statement,

```
{  // a short compound statement
  simple_expression;
}
```

or can even consist of a null statement, which does nothing at all:

```
{ // do nothing
  ;
}
```

The following paragraphs describe briefly the simple statement types listed in the preceding bulleted list. For further information, consult the *Borland C++ Programmer's Guide* in the standard Borland documentation.

Expression Statements

C++ doesn't change the ANSI C definition of expressions, so I won't go into much detail here. Expressions are among the most common statements in typical C++ programs. The following are examples of expression statements:

- `x = a + b;`
- `foo();`
- `;`
- `a + b;`

Some of these may not look much like expressions, but they are. The idea of an expression usually suggests a sequence of arithmetic or Boolean operators, such as

```
(x + y / z) / (x - z & w)
```

because in mathematics an expression can always be reduced to a single value. It is convenient to consider the assignment statement as an expression, because this allows multiple assignments back-to-back, as in

```
x = y = z;
```

The value of `z` is first assigned to `y`, then to `x`. Technically, the value of the expression `y = z` is assigned to `x`.

Given the definition of expression, it becomes possible to abuse it as well. For example it would be rather confusing, although correct, to write code such as

```
a = b + c = d * e / f = g;
```

I don't recommend it, unless you're participating in the Annual Obfuscated C Contest.

The *if* Statement

All languages must have a method for conditional branching. Some languages (like Pascal) have `if then else` constructs for this purpose. The basic decision-making statement in C++ is the `if else` statement. Its complete format is the following:

```
if (condition)
  // if condition is non-zero
```

```
  simple_statement;
else
  // condition is false
  simple_statement;
```

There is no `then` keyword in C or C++, because the language implementors favored brevity. The expression following the condition expression is the `then` part of the `if else` statement. Moreover, the simplest form of `if` doesn't even require the `else` part.

```
if (condition)
  simple_statement;
```

The `condition` is considered true if it is nonzero and false otherwise. This means that even negative values are considered true. The condition tested must be a *scalar*, meaning that it must be reducible to a single value that can be tested for zero. The following values represent false for the basic C++ variable types:

type	false value
`char`	'\0'
`short`	0
`int`	0
`long`	0L
`float`	0.0
`double`	0.0
`pointers`	null or 0

It is not recommended in general to use `floats` or `doubles` as test conditions, because it is sometimes difficult to determine whether certain expressions evaluate to true or false. Consider this code:

```
{
     float a, b;

     a = 0.123456780;
     b = 0.123456784;

     if (a == b) {
       // this test will evaluate to true !
       ...
       ...
     }
     else
       ...
}
```

As you can see, the condition tests true, due to the lack of the necessary precision for `float` variables. If the variables `a` and `b` are declared `double`, the test fails. Moreover, if the code is compiled on a machine that uses more than 32 bits to hold a `float`, the code would execute correctly even with `floats`. The lesson: Beware of `floats` in conditional expressions!

Often a program needs to test a variable for a variety of conditions. This can be achieved by multiple `if` statements, using the `if...else if` construct, which is shown in the following example:

```
{
  char command [80];
  gets(command);
  if (command [0] == 'A')
    // ... process the A command
  else if (command [0] == 'D')
    // ... process the D command
  else if (command [0] == 'S')
    // process the S command
  else
    // default condition
    RejectCommand(command [0]);
}
```

The same results can be obtained with the `switch` statement, described in the next section. The `if...else if` form is typically used when you are testing for only a few conditions.

The *switch* Statement

This type of statement is designed to facilitate the handling of multivalued branching. It is preferred over the `if...else if` construct when there are several values to check for. Its general form is the following:

```
switch (expression) {
  case constant_1:
     simple_statement;
     simple_statement;
     break;
     ...
  case constant_2:
     simple_statement;
     simple_statement;
     break;
     ...
  default:
     simple_statement;
     simple_statement;
     ...
}
```

The expression must be reducible or convertible to type `int`. The values for `constant_1`, `constant_2`, and so on, must be all integers or must be unambiguously convertible to integers.

The following code fragment illustrates the use of a `switch` statement, showing a few of the possible variants:

```
int some_function(char command)
{
     switch (command) {

       case 'a':
       case 'A':
         StartMotors();
         WaitForCompletion();
         break;

       default:
         return 1;

       case 'H':
         return 1;

       case 'Z':
         StopMotors();
     }
     return 0;
}
```

The example illustrates the following points:

1. More than one `case` statement can refer to the same `switch` selection.
2. When a `break` expression is encountered in the processing of a `case` or `default` statement, the `switch` block is exited.
3. The `default` and `case` statements can be arranged in any order, as far as the selection process is concerned.
4. Execution of the statements in a `case` statement, in the absence of a `return` or `break` statement, continues into the next `case` statement (if any).

Labeled Expressions

More than an expression, a label is an identifier. Labels are not executable statements but are used to indicate the destination of a `goto` statement, like this:

```
{
  switch (character) {
    case 'A':
      ProcessCharacter(character);
      goto post_process;
```

```
    case '\n':
      ProcessNewLine();
      goto post_process;
    default:
      RejectCharacter(character);
  }
post_process:
  length++;
  CompleteProcessing(character);
}
```

Labels are not intended to be overused, because their use makes a program difficult to follow, debug, and maintain. A label is the only entity in C++ to enjoy function-wide scope. A label can be referenced anywhere within the function it is declared in, even before the line it is declared on (see the preceding example).

The *while* Statement

Iteration—the capability of repeating the execution of a block of statements—is a fundamental programming construct. Most structured high-level languages have the equivalent of the `while` statement. The `while` statement is one of the major constructs for iteration in C++. The general format is

```
while (condition)
  statement;
```

The `condition` must be convertible or reducible to a type that can be tested for zero. The statement can be replaced by a block of statements enclosed in braces. A `while` construct allows the execution of its associated `statement` zero or more times. The condition is first tested. If the condition is found to be nonzero (that is, true), the statement (or block of statements) is executed. The condition is then tested again, and the process repeats until a false condition is found. Here is an example:

```
long factorial(int number)
{
     long total;
     total = number;
     while (number--)
       total *= number;
     return total;
}
```

The usual care must be exercised when using `float` or `double` types in the following condition:

```
{
  double epsilon, interval;
```

```
  epsilon = 0.0000012345678;
  interval = 10.0;
  while (interval != epsilon) {
    area *= interval * 4;
    interval /= 2;
}
```

The test condition used will probably never be false, so the loop executes forever and hangs the computer. If the condition is changed to

```
while (interval >= epsilon)
```

the loop executes a finite number of times, but the exact number of times depends on the precision of the machine, leading to machine-dependent results. A `while` loop can also use a pointer as a condition, like this:

```
// print out the command line arguments

#include <stdio.h>

main(int argc, char **argv)
{
     while (*argv)
       printf("\n%s", *(argv++) );
}
```

The *do while* Statement

The `do while` construct is similar to the `while` statement. The main difference is that the loop is always executed at least once. The general form is

```
do
  statement;
while (condition);
```

The `statement` can be replaced by a block of statements enclosed in braces. The `condition` expression must abide by the same rules as are in the `while` statement.

The *for* Statement

The most common iteration construct is probably the `for` statement. The `for` statement is used heavily because it is concise. The loop condition can be initialized, tested, and updated in a single construct. Here is the general form:

```
for (init_statement; condition; control_statement)
  loop statement;
```

The sequence of events for the various parts is as follows:

1. The `init_statement` is executed.
2. The `condition` is tested.
3. The loop statement is executed (if `condition` tested true).
4. The `control_statement` is executed.

The `for` statement has a number of anomalies from typical C++ constructs. The `init_statement` and `control_statement` can each consist of more than one simple statement, each separated by commas. The `control_statement` does *not* have the usual semicolon after it. The implementors of the original C language chose this inconsistency for some obscure reason, possibly conciseness. Here is an example of the `for` construct:

```
{
     for (int total = 0, i = 1; i < 10; i++) {
       if (i == 5) continue;
       total += i;
       if (total == 13) break;
       if (total == 15) return total;
     }
}
```

The preceding example illustrates a number of features. The `for` loop has two initialization statements. Note that the variables `total` and `i` are both declared and initialized in the `for` construct. The loop can be exited prematurely through the use of the `break` and `return` statements. The `continue` statement interrupts the loop in progress, causing the iteration control variable to be updated before the next iteration starts.

The *break* Statement

The `break` statement can be used in different kinds of constructs, but always with the same net result. The `break` statement is used to exit either from an iteration loop or from a `switch` statement. Iteration loops are those that utilize the `for`, `while`, and `do while` constructs. Use of the `break` statement anywhere else in your program results in a compile-time error. The following code shows some examples of usage:

```
#include <stdio.h>
#include <string.h>

main(int argc, char **argv)
{
     // ask for input not more than 10 times
     for (int i = 0; i < 10 ; i++) {
       puts("\nType a few words ");
       char response [80];
       gets(response);
       if (!strlen(response) )
         // when no more input given, stop asking
         break;
```

```
        // process the last input command
        switch (response [0]) {
          case 'A':
            puts("\nYou typed an A command");
            // go get another command
            break;
          case 'Z':
            puts("\You typed a Z command");
            // exit back to DOS
            return 0;
        }
      }

      // print out the command line arguments
      char *cp;
      while (cp = *argv++) {
        puts(cp);
        // stop if the argument "stop" is found
        if (!strcmp(*argv, "stop") )
          break;
      }
      return 0;
}
```

The preceding program doesn't really do much. The first part shows `break` statements in a `for` statement and in a `case` statement. This part of the program uses a loop to ask the user for input, ensuring that the user won't be queried more than 10 times. If the user responds only with the Enter key, the loop is aborted. Otherwise the program checks to see whether the response begins with the letters `A` or `Z`. If the response begins with the letter `A`, a message is printed and another command is requested. If the response begins with a `Z`, the entire program is exited. The first `break` statement

```
if (!strlen(response) )
  break;
```

forces the `for` loop to be exited when the user presses the Enter key without typing anything else. The second break statement appears inside a `switch` statement, which is nested inside the `for` statement. Thus the code fragment

```
case 'A':
  puts("\nYou typed an A command");
  // go get another command
  break;
```

makes only the `case` statement terminate. The `for` loop is not affected.

The second part of the example illustrates the `break` statement in a `while` loop. The loop scans the command line arguments, printing them out until the argument `stop` is encountered.

The *continue* Statement

The `continue` statement is similar to the `break` statement. However, instead of forcing an iteration to terminate, the `continue` statement causes the current iteration to be skipped, and the next one to be started immediately. A `continue` statement can be used exclusively in iteration statements. Here are some quick examples:

```
// add up the even numbers under ten
for (int total = 0, i = 0; i < 10 ; i++) {
  if (i & 1) continue;
  total += i;
}
```

The `continue` statement causes the next statements inside the iteration loop to be skipped, and the next iteration is started with a new value for the variable `i`.

When multiple iteration constructs are nested, the `continue` statement affects only the nearest iteration block it is inside.

The *goto* Statement

As for labeled statements, `goto`s should be used sparingly, if at all. Many purists of structured programming argue that the `goto` statement should not be used at all. In any event, typical C and C++ programs rarely use `goto`s. To use a `goto`, you must have a labeled statement to jump to. `goto` is not allowed to jump to a statement in a different function, because labeled statements are visible only inside the function in which they are declared.

An interesting (although rather dangerous) characteristic of the `goto` statement is that it allows you to go from almost anywhere to anywhere inside a function, ignoring all block constructs. Caveats abound regarding the `goto` statement; I don't recommend abusing it. Using it at all may indicate that your program is not structured correctly or that it is not completely thought out.

Use `goto`s as a last resort, or where matters of code efficiency prevail over elegance.

The *return* Statement

When the end of a function is encountered at runtime, the function is exited, its local variables are destroyed, and the function returns to its caller. A `return` statement allows you to force this process to happen before the terminating brace of a function is reached. The `return` statement is another one of those unusual C and C++ constructs. In fact, the `return` statement allows you the following two styles:

```
return;
return expression;
```

The first is used in functions of type `void`, which return no value to the caller. The second is used in typed functions to return a specific value. The expression is converted to the function's type before the function returns. A `return` statement can be used in multiple places within a function. The following program shows some examples:

```
// Using the return statement

#include <stdio.h>
#include <string.h>
#include <math.h>

main(int argc, char **argv)
{
     float value;

     puts("\nThis program computes square roots.");
     for (int i = 0; i < 10 ; i++) {
       puts("\nEnter a number.");
       char answer [80];
       gets(answer);
       if (!strlen(answer) )
         return 0;
       else if ( (value = atof(answer) ) < 0)  {
         puts("\nCan't compute root of negative number.");
         return 1;
       }
       else
       printf("\nIts square root is %lf", sqrt(value) );
     }
     return 0;
}
```

The example computes the square root of numbers. The program prompts the user up to 10 times for a number. If the user types no number (and just presses the Enter key), the program terminates immediately and returns a successful status to DOS. If a negative value is entered, the program prints an error message, aborts, and returns an error status to DOS. If the user responds with non-negative numbers, the program asks for up for 10 numbers and prints their square roots. Then the program returns a normal exit status to DOS.

Omitting an expression from the `return` statements in the preceding section of code would have been an error, because the compiler must know what expression to return from the function (which is declared `int`). Conversely, it is an error to return an expression for `void` functions. If the end of a `void` function is reached without encountering a `return` statement, the function is said to have "run off the end," and the function implicitly executes a `return` statement. `void` functions commonly run off the end in typical C++ programs.

Functions

C++ functions are the equivalent of subroutines and procedures in other high-level languages. C++ functions accept a number of parameters, execute a body of code, then return to the caller. `void` functions return nothing, whereas other typed functions return one object of the given type.

A function must always be declared in a function prototype before being used. Declaring the function this way is no longer optional, as it was in ANSI C. The language implementors decided that the compiler needed to perform more thorough checking in function calls. Although it takes a little more effort to write function prototypes when coding a module, the subsequent benefits are considerable. The following example shows the declaration, invocation, and definition of a function called `CharactersInBuffer()`:

```
// declare the function before using it
int CharactersInBuffer(char* buffer);

int main()
{
     char InMessage [80];
     int count;

     // setup some data
     strcpy(InMessage,"A message");

     // invoke the function
     count = CharactersInBuffer(InMessage);
     ...
     ...

}

// define the function
int CharactersInBuffer(char* buffer)
{
     if (!buffer) return 0;
     return strlen(buffer);
}
```

Passing Parameters to Functions

If a function is invoked with an argument list, the arguments are pushed onto the stack. This is the way most procedural languages are implemented on general-purpose computers. Borland C++ is no different from most procedural languages in this respect. Three ways to pass parameters to a function exist in C++:

1. By value. The complete variable or structure is copied onto the stack. Parameters are always passed on the stack, instead of using machine registers, in Borland

C++. Passing by value prevents the called function from modifying the original copy of a parameter, because the called function receives only a copy of the parameter.

2. By address. A pointer to the parameter is passed. Most programmers elect to pass structures by address rather than by value for runtime efficiency. Arrays can only be passed by address.
3. By reference. A reference (pointer) to the structure is passed, allowing the reference to be used syntactically as a pointer and as a value. Changes made to a parameter passed by reference affect the original copy of the parameter in the calling function.

When passing large objects by value to a function, care must be exercised to ensure that the size of the data passed into a function does not use more stack than is available. Because of the difficulty in locating code that leads to stack overflows, Borland C++ has an option to enable warnings if structures are passed by value.

Passing *const* Parameters to a Function

C++ allows you to declare a function parameter to be `const` like this:

```
void some_function(const int);
```

Why would you want to declare a function in that manner? Because the function receives a copy of the original variable, the caller really doesn't care whether the function modifies its copy. That can be the case when passing a parameter by value, but things change if you pass a pointer to something. You may want to ensure that the called function doesn't use the pointer to modify the entity referenced. Consider the following code:

```
// declare a function with a const parameter
void NewValue(const char*);

void main()
{
     // call a function with a const char string
     NewValue("123456789");
}

void NewValue(const char* cp)
{
     // big trouble here
     *cp = 'A';
}
```

Function `NewValue()` is declared to take a pointer to a constant character string. Thus, the pointer can be used at will, except as a means to modify what it points to. The preceding example causes an error, because `NewValue()` attempts to modify what it points to.

Declaring functions to take `const` parameters is a way of allowing the compiler to trap undesirable side effects of function calls.

Using Default Arguments

The C++ language implementors sought ways to reduce the complexity of coding, making the compiler do more work to check for errors. C++ introduces a new type of argument in function calls: the *default argument.* The default argument is an argument that the programmer is not required to supply, because the compiler adds it automatically, if necessary. In such a case, the compiler assigns a default value to the argument. If the programmer wishes to pass a specific value, the value must be indicated explicitly. Default arguments are specified in a function's prototype.

```
int SaveName(char* name, char* last_name = "");
```

More than one default argument can be used, but all defaults must be at the end of the argument list, as shown in the following code:

```
int SaveName(char* first,
             char* second = "",
             char* third = "",
             char* forth = "");
```

This code indicates that in the actual invocation of the function `SaveName()`, the caller *can* omit parameters `second`, `third`, and `fourth`. If a particular default is specified, all the preceding defaults must also be. In the preceding example, to specify a value for `third`, you must also specify the value for `second`, as follows:

```
status = SaveName("Alpha", "Bravo", "Charlie");
```

Returning a Value from a Function

When a function is declared to be typed, it must return something to the caller. This something can be either a *scalar* or *compound* object. Scalar objects are those that are declared with one of the built-in types and returned in machine registers. Arrays can be returned only by address. Compound types are either structures or classes. Returning a class object is treated in Chapter 2. When a structure is returned, it is copied byte-by-byte, as shown in the following code fragment. The mechanics of returning structures by value are explained in more detail in the "Advanced Section" in this chapter.

```
// returning a structure from a function

// define a big structure
struct symbol {
       int i;
       long l;
       char name [4000];
};
```

```
// define two structured variables
struct symbol s = {
  1, 2, "one"
};

struct symbol s1 = {
  100, 200, "two"
};

// return a structure to the caller
symbol foo()
{
     // copy the struct out of the function
     Return s1;
}

main()
{
     // the object s1 will be copied over object s
     // when the function returns
     s = foo();
}
```

Returning *const* Items

It is legal to declare a function that returns a `const`, such as

```
const int foo();
```

Thus, the value returned can be used only as you would use a `const int`. In this example

```
const char* GetName();

void main()
{
     const char* cp = GetName();
}

const char* GetName()
{
     return "George";
}
```

the variable `cp` points to a constant string. Any attempt to modify the constant string through `cp` causes a compile-time error.

Problems When Returning Values

There is an important case to avoid when returning a pointer or reference from a function: the referenced entity must continue to exist after the function returns. As a result, you can't return a pointer or reference to an auto variable.

```
// this code is incorrect and will compile with errors
int& bad_function()
{
     int i;
     i = 3;
     // this is not allowed
     return i;
}
```

The preceding function is declared to return a reference to type int. When compiling this function, Borland C++ detects the problem correctly and issues the error message

```
     attempting to return a reference to local name i in function
     bad_function()
```

If the function is declared instead to return a pointer to int, as in the following code, the compiler is not able to detect the problem.

```
// this is incorrect, but it compiles without errors
int* another_bad_function()
{
     int i;
     i = 3;
     // you can't do this
     return &i;
}
```

Returning either a pointer or a reference to a local static variable is allowable in Borland C++, but it is not recommended. If the two preceding code fragments are modified

```
int& bad_function(int data)
{
     static int i;
     i = data;
     return i;
}

int* bad1_function(int data)
{
     static int i;
     i = data;
     return &i;
}
```

they both compile without errors. They may even execute correctly, but problems can occur. Calling these functions repeatedly results in the last call overwriting the data of any previous calls. Consider the following code:

```
// this may be a difficult bug to spot
{
     int& i = bad_function(2);
     int& j = bad_function(3);
}
```

After the first call is executed, `i` references value 2. After the second one is executed, both `j` and `i` reference value 3.

Using Function Modifiers

Borland C++ introduces a few function modifiers over C++. They are needed for compatibility with other high-level languages and for interrupt handling. The modifiers are

- `cdecl`
- `pascal`
- `interrupt`

Why declare a `pascal` or `cdecl` function if you're writing in Borland C++? Well, Borland International sells both Turbo Pascal and Borland C++, and you can write a single function that works with both languages. This compatibility can be really convenient for functions built into libraries, where the library user doesn't know how the library was implemented. Even Borland has implemented the Borland C++ libraries in this way.

The *cdecl* Modifier

The `cdecl` modifier is used to specify a C calling sequence for a function, which is the default calling method used in Borland C++. If you don't tell the compiler otherwise, it compiles each function with the C calling sequence.

When the `cdecl` modifier is used with a function, the compiler treats the function in the following way:

1. The calling sequence is set to the C method. (The details of this operation are described in the advanced section).
2. The function's name is preserved in the symbol table with its original upper- and lowercase letters. `cdecl` functions are more flexible than `pascal` functions, because they allow a variable number of parameters to be passed. The actual number can be determined at runtime. When the Borland C++ calling convention option is set to C, all functions are implicitly set to `cdecl` unless otherwise specified.

The *pascal* Modifier

You can declare a C++ function to be of type `pascal`. This statement sounds like a contradiction, but it's not. Declaring a `pascal` function has nothing to do with the language used to write the function, but rather with the convention used in passing parameters to the function. Most C programmers don't mix Pascal and C code in a single project, except possibly through libraries. Borland C++ changes all that. With Borland C++'s support for Microsoft Windows, `pascal` functions gain importance. Any function that is designed to be called directly by Windows must be declared of type `pascal`. Microsoft probably decided to require the `pascal` declaration because the Pascal sequence is slightly more efficient than the C sequence. When you are developing a project for Windows, only those functions called directly by Windows need to be of the `pascal` type.

The `pascal` modifier causes the following variations in function handling:

1. The calling sequence is set to the Pascal standard. (The details of this operation are described in the advanced section).
2. The function's name is converted to all lowercase letters in the symbol table. Name mangling is disabled for the function's identifier, allowing traditional C and Pascal functions to reference the identifier without problems.

The *interrupt* Modifier

An `interrupt` function is invoked directly by hardware via the 80x86 interrupt-handling mechanism. Regular functions must not be declared `interrupt`. Moreover, functions invoked by `interrupt` functions must not be declared `interrupt` themselves.

An `interrupt` function cannot be invoked with arguments and cannot return anything to the caller. The caller is a built-in hardware mechanism and would not be generally capable of handling returned values. Normally an `interrupt` function has to be installed before it can be used. This installation process utilizes the Borland C++ library function `setvect(...)`. The following shows an example of an `interrupt` function:

```
interrupt SystemTick()
{
     // handle the DOS system tick
     ...
     ...
}
```

This function is executed only if it is called by the DOS tick interrupt, which requires installing the `interrupt` function at the appropriate vector with the `setvect(...)` function.

An `interrupt` function transparently handles all the details of register-saving and restoring. See the Advanced Section of this chapter for implementation details.

Pointers and References

C++ uses two constructs for referring indirectly to a variable: pointers and references. The two are quite similar in concept, but references can be considered to be the evolution of pointers. A pointer variable simply contains the address of some entity. Using the address, you can indirectly access that entity. C++ accepts two notations for declaring a pointer variable, which are

```
char      *name;
char*     name;
```

The two are completely equivalent, but the second form is commonly used in function prototypes, where only types—not variables—are usually shown.

```
// a sample function prototype
void some_function(char*, int, char, int*, float*);
```

Pointers are not required to be initialized at the time of declaration, but they must be initialized before being used. Borland C++ has an option to flag any attempts to use uninitialized pointers. Once a pointer has been declared to point to a given type of C++ object, it is an error to attempt to point the pointer at a different type.

```
{ int* k;
 int j;
  char c;

  j = 5;
  c = 'S';

  // this is okay
  k = &j;

  // but this will cause a compiler error
  k = &c;
}
```

There is a special kind of pointer that can be used to point at any kind of C++ object, effectively turning off compiler-type errors regarding the pointer. Pointers of type `void*` can be used for any purpose.

```
{ void* k;
  int j;
  float f;
  char c;

  // these are all okay
  k = &j;
  k = &f;
  k = &c;
}+
```

`void` pointers have an important characteristic: a typed pointer may be assigned to a void pointer, but not vice versa. To assign a void pointer to a typed pointer, you must use an explicit typecast, otherwise the compiler produces an error. The following code illustrates the point:

```
void main()
{
        int* ip;
    int i = 5;
        char* cp;
    char c = 'A';
        void* vp;

        ip = &i;                    // okay
        vp = &i;            // okay

        cp = &c;            // okay
        vp = &c             // okay;

        ip = vp;            // oops: can't do this
        cp = vp;            // wrong again

        vp = ip;            // this is okay !
        vp = cp;            // and so is this
}
```

Reference variables also contain the address of some entity, but they obey slightly different rules. References require initialization when they are declared.

```
int& i = 3;
```

Thus, the reference variable `i` points to the value 3; the reference variable *references* the value 3. Although a reference is a pointer, it can be used as if it were the value itself.

```
#include <stdio.h>
#include <string.h>

main()
{
    int& i = 3;
    int j;

    if (i == 3) {
      i--;
      j = i;
    }
    i = strlen("title");
    printf("\nThe value referenced by i = %d", i);
}
```

You can't declare a general-purpose reference, such as with `void` pointers. The following declaration is wrong:

```
// this isn't valid
void& a_reference = 3;
```

There is no such thing as a `void&` type. The compiler may need to perform implicit type conversions, so it needs to know at all times what type of object is referenced. References are better to use because the compiler does more work for you, which ensures consistency to a greater extent. A reference can be changed at any time during its life, unless it is declared `const`.

```
// this reference can't be changed afterwards
const int& number = 9;

// you can forget doing this now
number = 5;

// you can't even do this
number = 9;
```

The compiler traps the last assignment as an error, even though the compiler wouldn't have actually changed the value of the reference. The compiler complains because it simply doesn't permit assignments to a `const` object—regardless of runtime values.

When returning references from a function, special rules apply. Attempting to return a reference to a local value causes Borland C++ to generate an error. References are widely used in C++, particularly in conjunction with overloaded operators, as is shown in Chapter 4.

Using Pointers and References with *const*

Some C++ constructs frequently seem to be the source of confusion. One of them is the use of `const` with pointers and references. Sometimes it isn't clear whether the item referenced, the pointer, or both are constant. The following examples should help clarify things:

```
/************** pointers to integers *******************/

// declare some data
const int nine = 9;
int number;

// the pointer is constant
int *const n1 = &number;

// the value pointed at is constant
const int *n2 = &nine;
```

```
// both are constant
const int *const n3 = &nine;


/****** pointers to characters *******

// the text is constant
const char *s1 = {"text"};

// the pointer is constant
char *const s2 = {"text"};

 // both are constant
const char *const s3 = {"text"};

/****** arrays of pointers to characters ******/

// the characters are constant
const char *text1 [] = {"line1", "line2", "line3"};

// the pointers are constant
char *const text2 [] = {"line1", "line2", "line3"};

// both are constant
const char *const text3 [] = {"line1", "line2", "line3"};
```

Advanced Section

So far I have treated the essential parts of C that are common to C++. In this section, I go into C++ implementation details that are mostly of interest to experienced programmers. You can go on to Chapter 2 even without reading this section, with no loss of continuity.

Using Inline Assembly Language

One of the best things about C and C++ is that you can do almost anything without using assembly language. You can access machine registers with Borland C++ pseudo variables. You can access specific locations in memory or registers in I/O devices with pointers. The main use of assembly language in the Borland C++ context is to gain speed—not features. Recognizing the importance of speed, Borland allows you to embed assembly language right in your C++ source file. The use of inline assembly language is also allowed in the proposed C++ ANSI standard; however, this use is declared implementation-dependent.

I don't recommend spreading assembly language statements around in your source files. The best practice is to isolate all the functions that require assembly language and group them together in a single module by themselves. At this point, you may want to consider writing the module entirely in assembly language, using Turbo Assembler instead of embedding assembly language in C++ functions. Whether to use embedded assembly language or only assembly language depends on how much assembly language is needed.

The following code illustrates many of the features of inline assembly language:

```
/* mix C++ and assembly language together */
int some_function(int number)
{
     unsigned int reg_ax, reg_bx;

     if (number == 1) {
       asm cli               /* disable interrupts       */
       asm mov ax, reg_ax    /* use a local variable     */
       asm mov number, bx    /* use a function parameter */
       asm sti               /* enable interrupts        */
     }
     else {
       /* use local variables in a block expression */
       asm {
         mov ax, reg_ax
         mov bx, reg_bx
       }
     }
     return reg_ax;
}
```

One of the most interesting features of inline assembly language is the capability of using C++ identifiers directly, including function arguments, `global` and local variables. Stack frame offsets are computed automatically where necessary, and that's really a big plus. The preceding code generates the necessary code to access correctly local variables and function arguments. The following shows the executable code as disassembled under Turbo Debugger:

```
; some_function: int some_function(int number)
          push bp
          mov  bp, sp
          sub  sp, 4
     ;if (number == 1) {
          cmp  word ptr [bp + 4], 0001
          jne  #TEST#22
     ;asm cli
          cli
     ;asm mov ax, reg_ax
          mov  ax, [bp - 2]
     ;asm mov  number, bx
          mov  [bp + 4], bx
     ;asm sti
          sti
          jmp  #TEST#26
```

```
#TEST#22:
     ;asm mov ax, reg_ax
          mov  ax, [bp - 2]
     ;asm mov bx, reg_bx
          mov  bx, [bp - 4]
#TEST#26:
     ;return reg_ax
          mov  ax, [bp - 2]
          jmp  #TEST#27
#TEST#27:
     ;}
          mov  sp, bp
          pop  bp
          ret
```

A slight inconvenience with inline assembly language is in error reporting. When the compiler discovers something wrong inside an `asm` block, it reports an error but doesn't tell you exactly what is wrong or where the error was found. If you put extensive amounts of code in a block, locating the precise statements at fault may take some effort. Notice how comments are embedded inside an `asm` block using the `/* */` comment style.

Name Mangling

An important objective of the C++ language is to increase the number and types of errors that are detectable during compilation and linkage. Calling a function with the wrong type or number of parameters was a frequent error with ANSI C. To avoid this error, C++ requires functions to be declared before being used. This requirement allows the compiler to do the necessary checking, but with C++ comes an additional problem: function names can be overloaded, allowing the same name to be used for more than one function. How do the compiler and the linker keep the various function names under control? The answer is a procedure called *name mangling*.

When a function is declared, the compiler modifies its name according to the following things: the number and types of parameters passed to the function and the class the function belongs to (if any). The function's name is therefore mangled by the compiler, and saved in its altered form in the object file. The modifications made to the function's name allow the linker to verify that function calls across module boundaries are correct in number and type of parameters. This process gives rise to what is called *type-safe linkage*, because the linker guarantees correctness in linking function calls with the proper function.

In Borland C++, mangled names are normally hidden from the user. When you inspect the symbol table, you see the unmangled names, because the linker unmangles names before saving them in the map file. The Turbo Debugger and the integrated debugger also hide the mangling from you. Because mangled names always seem to be hidden from the user, why worry about them at all? There is a good reason.

If you do any mixed-language programming, for example with assembly language, you need to know about name mangling so that a C++ function can correctly call an assembly language function and vice versa. The details of Borland C++ name mangling are fully described in Chapter 4.

Using C and C++ Together

C++ is an improvement over C. C++ is designed to accept C constructs as a subset. Thus, you can implement some modules in C++ and some in C, and then link them together. You can also `#include` ANSI C standard header files, such as *stdio.h*. How does the linker handle the mixing of C and C++? If name mangling were not controlled somehow, you would wind up with unresolved references. To solve this problem, C++ introduces a special linkage specification. Its basic format is as follows:

```
extern "C" {
     function declaration
}
```

Multiple function declarations can appear inside the braces. When the C++ compiler finds this declaration, the compiler saves the subsequent function names unmangled in the object file. For example, consider the following declaration:

```
extern "C" {
     int  putc(const int _ _c, FILE _FAR *_ _fp);
}
```

This declaration tells Borland C++ to save the identifier `putc` in the symbol table so that it can be accessed normally by other modules written in C. The preceding declaration is valid only in C++, so compiling it in the C mode would produce errors. To avoid these errors, Borland C++ has a macro that indicates whether it is running in the C or C++ mode. The macro is called *_ _cplusplus*. Its value is 1 when generating C++ code and undefined otherwise. You can use this macro to write code that can be linked with both C and C++ modules. The file *stdio.h* declares `putc()` as follows:

```
#ifdef _ _cplusplus
extern "C" {
#endif

int      _Cdecl putc(const int _ _c, FILE _FAR *_ _fp);

#ifdef   _ _cplusplus
}
#endif
```

This code forces the `extern` C linkage if compiling for C++, and maintains the regular C linkage otherwise. The macro *_Cdecl* is another macro defined in *stdio.h*. If the ANSI compatibility option is selected, its value is set to ""; otherwise it is defined as `cdecl`. The function putc() is therefore defined as using the C calling sequence and can be called both from C++ and C modules.

When declaring functions with C linkage, no overloaded functions can be specified because names are no longer mangled and the functions would collide in the symbol table. The following code is wrong and generates a compile-time error:

```
// this will cause an error
extern "C" {
     int foo(int);
     int foo(float);
}
```

Returning Large Structures by Value

When a typed function returns data, the types involved are often the built-in types: char, int, long, float, or double. Pointers are the preferred method of returning arrays and structures. It is possible, however, to return a structure by value. When a pointer or normal built-in type is returned, Borland C++ uses an 80x86 register. For large structures, this method won't work unless the structure is small enough to fit into registers. It follows that the compiler must be doing something unusual to achieve the correct result.

Fortunately, things don't get too complicated. When you call a function that is supposed to return a large structure, Borland C++ passes the function an extra pointer to a suitable storage location. Before the called function returns, it must copy the structure to be returned into this storage area. The following example shows a C++ function that passes structures by value and by reference:

```
// define a big structure
typedef struct {
  int i;
  char name [800];
  long values [500];
} FIELD;

FIELD GetStructure(FIELD);
FIELD *GetStructurePointer(FIELD*);

void main()
{
     FIELD field1, field2, *fp;
     field2 = GetStructure(field1);
     fp = GetStructurePointer(&field1);
}

FIELD GetStructure(FIELD field)
{
     return field;
}
```

```
FIELD* GetStructurePointer(FIELD* fp)
{
    return fp;
}
```

The code actually generated for this example can be examined with Turbo Debugger, and is shown here with some additional editing.

```
; main() {

        push      bp                ; setup local frame
        mov       bp, sp
        sub       sp, 0x15E6        ; make room for locals
                                    ; field1, field2, fp

; field2 = GetStructure(field1);

        lea       ax, [bp-0xAF4]    ; get address of field1
        mov       dx, ss
        mov       cx, 0xAF2
        call      N_SPUSH@          ; copy field1 onto the
                                    ; stack
        push      ds
        lea       ax,[bp-0x15E6]    ; get address of field2
        push      ax                ; put it on the stack.
                                    ; GetStructure will have
                                    ; to copy the return
                                    ; structure into this
                                    ; area.
        call      GetStructure      ; call the function
        add       sp, 0xAF6         ; clean up the stack

; fp = GetStructurePointer(&field1);

        lea       ax, [bp-0xAF4]    ; get address of field1
        push      ax                ; put address on stack
        call      GetStructurePointer
        pop       cx                ; clean up stack
        mov       [bp - 02], ax     ; save return value in fp
        mov       sp, bp            ; delete local frame
        pop       bp                ; restore previous frame
        ret
; }


; FIELD GetStructure(FIELD field) {

        push      bp                ; setup local frame
        mov       bp, sp
```

```
; return field;
                                    ; put address of field
                                    ; on the stack
          push      word ptr [bp + 06]
          push      word ptr [bp + 04]

          lea       ax, [bp + 08]   ; get address of the
                                    ; variable into which to
                                    ; store the struct field
          push      ss              ; put it on the stack
          push      ax
          mov       cx, 0xAF2       ; size of field
          call      N_SCOPY@        ; copy field into the
                                    ; destination variable
          mov       ax, [bp + 04]
          jmp       #TEST#20
#TEST#20: pop       bp              ; restore old frame
          ret

; }


; FIELD* GetStructurePointer(FIELD* fp)

          push      bp              ; set up local frame
          mov       bp, sp
          mov       ax, [bp + 04]   ; load ax with the passed
                                    ; parameter fp, so it can
                                    ; be returned to caller
          jmp       #TEST#25
#TEST#25: pop       bp              ; restore old frame
          ret
```

In function `main()`, calling `GetStructure()` requires the variable `field1` to be copied onto the stack. The library function `N_SPUSH@` is used for this purpose. `GetStructure()` is also passed a pointer to `field2`, into which it copies the return structure, using the library function `N_SCOPY@`.

It is important to realize the runtime overhead of passing and returning large structures. Not only is the process slow, but it is also expensive in stack consumption. The preferred method—when applicable—is to pass structures by address rather than by value.

Using Enumerations

In many cases, you need not one constant value but a whole series of constant values. For example, say you want to make a list of colors like this:

```
#define BLACK 0
#define BLUE 1
#define GREEN 2
```

```
#define RED 4
#define YELLOW 6
#define WHITE 7
```

ANSI C recognizes the importance of this series of constants and defines the keyword `enum` to declare them. The preceding sequence can be defined as follows:

```
enum COLORS {
  BLACK,
  BLUE,
  GREEN,
  RED = 4,
  YELLOW = 6,
  WHITE
};
```

This declaration is not only simpler than the previous one, but it also gives more power to the compiler. Although the values for the various colors are integers, they are considered to be restricted integers: those in the `enum COLORS`. This knowledge enables the compiler to perform some additional type checking, which is not possible with the `#define` method. The identifiers in the enumeration are assigned consecutive integer values starting from zero. Any or all of the identifiers can be assigned specific values to override the default identifiers. When no value is specified, the compiler assigns one automatically. The value used is that of the previous entry incremented by one. More than one identifier in the enumeration can have the same value. At a limit, all the values could be assigned the same value.

Using enumerations enables that extra amount of type checking in the compiler. Consider the following code:

```
#define BLACK 0

void PaintColor(int color);

void foo()
{
     int color;
     // this is all right
     color = BLACK;                          // no problem
     PaintColor(color);
     color = 55;                             // no problem
     PaintColor(color);
}
```

This code shows how the old `#defines` could be used to indicate constant values. The compiler is not capable of seeing any problems in the value of the variable `color`. The improved version of the preceding code, using an `enum`, is this:

```
enum COLOR {
  BLACK
};
```

```
void PaintColor(COLOR color);

void foo()
{
     COLOR color;
     // this is all right
     color = BLACK;                          // okay
     PaintColor(color);
     color = 55;                             // compiler issues warning
     PaintColor(color);
}
```

The compiler issues a warning when you assign a constant integer value to the `enum` variable color, just to flag a possible error in the code. The code may actually be correct, but the compiler is not sure.

Using Memory Management

In ANSI C, functions like `malloc()` and `free()` allocate and release blocks of memory from the heap. This sort of memory is usually referred to as *dynamic storage*, because it is created and destroyed during program execution. When dealing with objects, it is often necessary to create items dynamically. In fact, the C++ language implementors thought it was so important that they added three built-in operators to the language.

```
new
delete
delete[]
```

The operator `new` is similar in function to `malloc()`, but it is an operator, not a function. `new` is part of the C++ language itself, just like `delete` is, so no header files need to be included to use it. Moreover, `new` allocates memory from the global heap, using `GlobalAlloc()`, whereas `malloc()` allocates memory from the local heap, using `LocalAlloc()`. Because of this difference, `new` has access to much more memory than `malloc()`. One of the nicest features of `new` is that typecasting is never necessary. Say that you want storage for an array of 10 integers. All you need to write is

```
int* ip;
ip = new int [10];
```

or even more succinctly

```
int* ip = new int [10];
```

This code declares and sets the pointer `ip` to the value returned by `new`. Operator `new` returns a pointer to the beginning of a block of storage of the requested size, if one is available. If there isn't enough dynamic storage to satisfy a request, `new` throws an `xalloc` exception. If your program doesn't catch this exception, the program will make a call to the last function installed with the `set_new_handler()` function. If you installed no handler of your own, your program will be terminated. See Chapter 6 for a complete discussion of exceptions and exception handling.

When memory is requested with new, the exact size must be indicated. The size doesn't have to be known at compile time, but it must be known at runtime.

```
// declare and initialize a variable
int i = 5;

// request a block of "i" integers
int* ip = new int [i];
```

Requesting a block of memory results in a piece of memory being allocated from global memory. The size of the block reserved is slightly larger than the block requested. The additional storage is used internally by the heap manager to keep track of the blocks. In Borland C++, operator new uses the function `GlobalAlloc()`.

A few differences exist between new and `malloc()`. Although the functions are both designed to return a pointer to a block of data, their behavior is not identical. Consider the following code:

```
// include file when using malloc()
#include <alloc.h>

void main()
{
        // this returns a valid pointer !
        int* ip = new int [0];

        // this returns a null pointer
        int* ip1 = (int*) malloc(0);
}
```

Operator new returns a nonzero pointer even when you request zero bytes. If you start using this pointer that is returned from new, you're in for some big trouble, because there is no actual storage allocated to the block referenced. The function `malloc()` correctly returns a null pointer. Note that the old ANSI C style

```
// this is incorrect in C++
int *ip;
ip = malloc(size);
```

is no longer acceptable. The function `malloc()` is declared to return a `void*`. This pointer type was used in ANSI C to indicate that a pointer could be assigned to any pointer type, such as `int*`. The C++ language implementors consider this practice to be not only dangerous, but also incorrect. In C++, you must always explicitly typecast the `void*` pointer into the desired type, just like you do any other type. Operator new allows the dynamically allocated data to be optionally initialized to a given value, as shown here:

```
// initialize the array with the value 17
int* ip = new int [10] (17);
```

```
// initialize the character array with zeroes
char* cp = new char [10] (0);

// initialize a dynamic integer with the value 10
int* value = new int (10);
```

Unless an initialization parameter is given, you'll find garbage in the allocated blocks returned by new. Unfortunately, the initialize notation is quite awkward. Adding the parentheses after the square brackets is really bizarre, but that's the way it is.

Once you create an object from the global heap, you also take on the responsibility for destroying it. This operation is more complex for the compiler than the operation of creating an object. Why? Consider the following code:

```
int* ip = new int [10];
delete ip;
```

How much storage is going to be given up with the `delete` operation? The new operator is passed information on the number of typed elements to make room for. The `delete` operator is given only a typed pointer. In Borland C++, the heap manager uses the pointer to find the allocated block of storage. The heap also maintains additional information regarding the size of each allocated block. Using this hidden data, the manager can determine how much storage to relinquish.

A new operator has been formally added to the C++ draft by the ANSI committee to handle deletion of arrays. The operator is called `delete[]`, and should be used to delete arrays. The following code shows its usage:

```
char* cp = new char [10];
delete[] cp;
```

Understanding the C Calling Sequence

Whenever a function is declared with the `cdecl` keyword, it is compiled to use the C calling sequence. This sequence defines the order in which parameters are pushed onto the stack, and specifies whose responsibility it is to clean up the stack. The C sequence prescribes the following:

1. Parameters are pushed in reverse order. The last parameter in the function call is pushed first.
2. The calling function is responsible for balancing the stack after a function call.

Consider the following code:

```
int some_function(int first, int second, int third)
{
          int i;
          i = first + second + third;
          return i;
}
```

```
void main()
{
        int i = some_function(1, 2, 3);
}
```

The function call in `main()` generates the following code:

```
mov     ax, 0003                        ; push the last argument
push    ax
mov     ax, 0002                        ; push the second argument
push    ax
mov     ax, 0001                        ; push the first argument
push    ax
push cs                                 ; push cs for a FAR call
call    some_function
add     sp, 0006                        ; rebalance the stack
...
...
```

Note the `cs` register push. This push occurred because the preceding code was generated in the medium memory model, resulting in a *far* call. If you need to access the parameters using assembly language inside `some_function()`, it is best to use inline assembly language and use the parameter names `first`, `second`, and `third` directly. Borland C++ substitutes the names for the proper stack frame entries. Using C++ identifiers in the assembly language code also guarantees that the function continues to work if the function is later declared `near` or even `pascal` (unless an ellipsis is used).

Understanding the Pascal Calling Sequence

To force a function to be compiled using the Pascal calling sequence, use the `pascal` keyword in its declaration. This keyword causes the following variations in the compiled code:

1. Function parameters are pushed in their order of appearance, from left to right.
2. The called function is responsible for balancing the stack before returning to the caller.

Consider the following code:

```
int pascal some_function(int first, int second, int third)
{
        int i;
        i = first + second + third;
        return i;
}

void main()
{
        int i = some_function(1, 2, 3);
}
```

This code causes the compiler to generate code like this:

```
mov     ax, 0001                    ; push the first argument
push    ax
mov     ax, 0002                    ; push the second argument
push    ax
mov     ax, 0003                    ; push the last argument
push    ax
push    cs                          ; push cs for a FAR call
call    some_function
...                                 ; stack is already balanced
...
```

At the end of function `some_function()`, the stack is cleaned up with a single assembly language instruction.

```
retf    0006
```

This instruction returns to the caller and adjusts the stack up by six bytes.

Using Interrupt Handling Functions

When interrupts occur, whether software or hardware, the CPU looks in its exception table to find the address of a function to call to handle the interrupt. Because interrupts are asynchronous with respect to the main program, interrupt service routines need to preserve the contents of all the machine registers. The Borland C++ `interrupt` keyword specifies a function as an interrupt handler. `interrupt` causes the following changes in compiled code:

1. All registers are saved on entry.
2. All registers are restored on exit.
3. An `iret` instruction is used to exit.

Consider the following example:

```
void interrupt some_function()
{
// body of function
}
```

This function generates the following compiled code:

```
some_function:

        push    ax                  ; save all registers
        push    bx
        push    cx
        push    dx
        push    es
        push    ds
```

```
push      si
push      di
push      bp

... body of function ...

pop       bp                              ; restore all registers
pop       di
pop       si
pop       ds
pop       es
pop       dx
pop       cx
pop       bx
pop       ax
iret                                      ; return from interrupt
```

Although Borland C++ allows you to return a value from an `interrupt` function, doing so really doesn't make any sense. Attempting to return a value from an `interrupt` function is just a waste of time, because Borland C++ uses the `ax` register for returned values, and the register is restored to its original value on exit. It is also illegal to use `cdecl` or `pascal` concomitantly with the `interrupt` keyword.

Using Functions with Variable Argument Lists

Sometimes it is convenient to implement functions that can be applied to any number of arguments. Declaring such functions requires a special notation to indicate that they take an argument list of variable length. The standard library function `printf()` is one such function. To declare functions with argument lists of variable length, the special ellipsis notation is used.

```
// this function may have one or more arguments
int some_function(int i, ...);

// this function has at least two arguments
int another_function(int i, char c, ...);
```

The comma before the dots is optional. Here is a short, but complete, example:

```
#include <stdarg.h>
#include <stdio.h>

// declare a function with a variable argument list
void varg_function(int count...)
{
          // prepare to access parameters
          va_list parameters;
          va_start(parameters, count);
```

```
        // use the parameters
        for (int i = 0; i < count; i++) {
          int value = va_arg(parameters, int);
          printf("Parameter %d = %d\n", i, value);
        }

        // clean up before exiting
        va_end(parameters);
}

void main()
{
        varg_function(3, 4, 5, 6);

}
```

C++ uses a few macros to access the parameters inside `varg_function()`. The macros `va_list`, `va_start`, `va_arg`, and `va_end` do the actual work. These macros are declared in the header file *stdarg.h*. In Borland C++, a function with a variable argument list is required to have at least one named formal parameter. There are two reasons for this requirement:

1. The function has no way of knowing how many parameters were actually passed to it. At least one named parameter must be passed to convey this information.
2. The macro `va_start` expects two parameters: the first is the name of the variable argument list used with the macro `va_list`; the second must be the name of a formal parameter in the function's argument list.

You can use any kind of parameter you want to indicate the number of parameters actually passed to a function with a variable argument list. The function `printf()` uses a formatting string, where arguments are denoted with the `%` character. The function `varg_function()` received the number of parameters directly in the argument `count`. You can use any method you want in practice.

When you use the preceding macros, heed a few warnings. First, you must use them in the correct order. Using `va_arg` before `va_start` is disastrous. Failing to use `va_end` at the end of the function normally causes no problems in Borland C++, but is recommended for portability.

Second, the macro `va_arg` doesn't know when it has reached the end of the actual parameter list or what types the arguments have. It is your responsibility to tell `va_arg` the type you expect. If you tell the macro to fetch a `char*`, but the argument was an `int`, your program will not work, although it will compile without errors.

Third, watch for problems with default promotions for function parameters. If you pass a `char` (`signed` or `unsigned`), it is converted to `int` before being passed to a function. `Float`s are converted into `double`s. Therefore, don't attempt to access `char`s or `float`s with `va_arg`.

Objects and Classes

In computer science, an object is an abstract entity that embodies the characteristics of a real-world object. It doesn't take an object-oriented language or C++ to create and manipulate objects. Object-based programming has been around for some time, and is used with languages as diverse as FORTRAN, LISP, and Assembler. Objects are the result of a programming methodology rather than a language.

In C++, objects assume even more importance. With this new methodology, everything you manipulate in a program can be considered an object. Objects are created and deleted during program execution. Objects interact with other objects, and can be put together in groups, collections, arrays, lists, and so on. Some languages (such as Smalltalk) are completely based on objects. Anything you manipulate in a Smalltalk program is some kind of object. This uniform approach endows the language with great elegance, but not without drawbacks. The main one is efficiency. The use of objects sometimes imposes runtime penalties that can at times seriously degrade the performance of a program. The C++ language was designed to take advantage of the most desirable features of objects, avoiding the runtime disadvantages and overhead as much as possible. In C++, many (but not all) the things you manipulate in a program are objects, and for this reason C++ is said to be a *hybrid object-oriented programming language.*

Objects are programming constructs that are molded out of things called *classes.* Defining a variable of a class is also known as *class instantiation.* The programmer is entirely responsible for creating his own classes, but also may have access to classes developed by others, such as those in the Borland C++ container library or the stream library.

Defining a Class

C++ is touted everywhere as an exciting new language. But judging from what was covered in the previous chapter, C++ seems to be just another version of C. What is so different about C++? *Classes* are the main difference. In C terms, a class is the natural evolution of the structure. The existence of classes is the single most significant feature that makes C++ an object-oriented language. Classes are structures that contain not only data declarations but also function declarations. The functions are called *member functions* and indicate what kinds of things a class can do.

To use a class, you first have to declare the class, just as you do for structures. The full declaration for a class can appear only once in a program, just as it can for structures. Here's the declaration of a simple class:

```
class Counter {

  long count;

public:

  void SetValue(long);
  long GetValue();
};
```

This notation is new in C++. The keyword `class` introduces a class declaration. Next comes the name of the class. The body of a class must be enclosed in braces, followed by a semicolon. Classes can contain not only function declarations, but also entire function definitions. Functions inside classes can be as long and as complex as you want them to be. The variables declared inside a class are considered to belong to that class. Under certain circumstances, variables can be shared between the various instantiations of a class. The identifiers for variables and functions inside a class are guaranteed not to clash with the identifiers used in other classes. Essentially, a class is a world with its own unique identifiers, as far as the rest of the system goes.

Class Identifiers

For class identifiers, the same rules apply as for any other type or variable name. In C++ there is no maximum length defined for identifiers; however, in Borland C++ the maximum length is 32 characters. The number of characters that are significant can be adjusted via the Options ¦ Project ¦ +Compiler ¦ Source menu. The default is

32 characters. Case is significant in Borland C++ identifiers. A convention adopted throughout the Borland classes is to use names beginning with an uppercase letter to denote classes and global structures. The class

```
class counter {

   long count;

public:

  void SetValue(long);
  long GetValue();
};
```

defines a second class that is identical (except in name) to class `Counter`. Declaring two classes with the same name is an error, whether the declarations are identical or not.

The Class Body

The variable `count` is defined inside the body of the class. `count` is therefore called a *member variable* of the class. Any variables defined in a class have class scope. Class scope is unavailable in ANSI C and goes from the point of declaration of a variable to the end of the class declaration. Attempting to access a member variable after the class declaration is an error, as shown in the following code:

```
class Counter {

  long count;

public:

  void SetValue(long);
  long GetValue();
};

count = 3;            // error: count is undefined here
```

A class can have as many variables as it needs. These variables can be of any type, including other classes, pointers to class objects, and even pointers to dynamically allocated objects.

The class `Counter` declares the functions `SetValue(long)` and `GetValue()`. These are called *member functions* of the class. These functions are not defined yet; they are only declared. The missing part is the actual definition. Here's the definition for class `Counter`:

```
void Counter::SetValue(long value)
{
          count = value;
}
```

```
long Counter::GetValue()
{
        return count;
}
```

When defining member functions, after the return type you always have to indicate of which class the function is a member. The notation requires a class name followed by two colons. As for all functions in C++, member functions must be declared before being used. The declaration must be complete, including the function return type and the argument types. In C++, the function argument types must be declared at the same time as the member functions, using the notation

```
// function arguments must be declared immediately
int foo(int parm1, long parm2);
```

When defining a function, the old ANSI C style of declaring arguments is considered obsolete.

```
// Borland C++ will complain about this, because
// the notation is considered obsolete
int foo(parm1, parm2)
int parm1;
long parm2;
{...}
```

Using a Class

So, now I've defined a class. To use a class, an object must be defined with it. You define class variables just like structure variables or scalar variables. To define the class variable `people` of type `Counter`, you use this notation:

```
Counter people;
```

In some object-oriented languages, Smalltalk in particular, defining a class variable is also called *class instantiation.* An instantiation is simply an instance of a class in the form of a specific variable. I use the term *instantiation* extensively in this book.

> **NOTE**
>
> Classes can be considered shells containing a template of how data and code are used when the class is instantiated. Remember, classes are not objects.

The variables instantiated from classes are the objects. In general, using a class directly is impossible. The few exceptions to this rule are illustrated later in the chapter. Getting back to the `people` object, here is how a program might use it:

```
void main()
{
        Counter people;

        // initialize the object
        people.SetValue(0);

        // verify that it is cleared
        long value = people.GetValue();
}
```

The code doesn't do much, but it illustrates two important points: declaring an object inside a function and invoking member functions of an object. Member functions can take arguments and return values.

Class objects declared inside a function use the same notation as other typed variables. These objects enjoy block scope, extending from the point of declaration to the end of the block. In the preceding example, `people` is in scope from the end of the line it is declared on until the end of function `main()`. The object `people` has `auto` storage class, and it is stored in the stack frame.

Invoking a member function for a class object involves using the same notation you would use to access a structure member: a dot followed by the member's name. Other than that, using member functions is normally no different than using traditional C functions. With member functions you have to add the parentheses. With member variables you don't.

Encapsulation

The preceding code illustrates an important feature of C++, usually referred to as *encapsulation.* The class encloses both data and code. Access to the items inside the class is controlled. This control goes not only for the data, but also for the code. When a class is to be used, its declaration must be available. The user of a class is therefore presented with a description of the class, but not necessarily with its implementation. As far as the user is concerned, the internal details of a class are not essential, and need not be known. In fact the less a user needs to know about the internals of a class, the better. This concept is often referred to as *information hiding.*

To use a class, you must know something about it. You need to know what functions you can use, and what data is accessible. The set of usable functions and accessible data is called the *user interface* of the class. The interface is like the surface of a three-dimensional object; the interface is the boundary between the object and the world. Knowledge of a class's user interface is what a mathematician would call a *necessary and sufficient condition* to use the class. The user interface tells you how a class behaves, not how the class is made. You don't need to know how a class is implemented, which reduces the amount of information you have to keep track of while developing a project. Once a class has been implemented and debugged, it is finished and can be used repeatedly. As far as users are concerned, a class is a black box with a characterized behavior.

Control of Access to a Class

The job of a class is to hide as much information as possible. Thus it is necessary to impose certain restrictions on the way a class can be manipulated, and on how the data and code inside the class can be used. There are three kinds of users of a class:

1. The class itself
2. Generic users
3. Derived classes

Each kind of user has different access privileges. Each level of access privilege is associated with a keyword. Because there are three levels, there are three keywords:

1. `private`
2. `public`
3. `protected`

Every declaration inside the body of a class implicitly defines an access privilege by appearing in a section preceded by one of these three keywords. If none of the keywords is used, everything is `private` by default. The following example illustrates the various possibilities:

```
class AccessControlExample {

          int       value_1;          // private by default
          void      f_1(long);        // private by default

private:

          int       value_2;          // still private
          int       f_2(char*);       // private

public:

          char*     value_3;          // public
          long      f_3();            // public

protected:

          int       value_4;          // protected
          void      f_4(long);        // protected
};
```

Any declarations appearing before an access control keyword are `private` by default. Such is the case for the variable `value_1` and the function `f_1(long)`. In the preceding example, there is an explicit `private` declaration right after a `private` section. This example

illustrates an interesting point: sections with different access privileges can be declared in any order, and in any number. Class AccessControlExample could have been declared like this:

```
class AccessControlExample {
private:            int       value_1;        // private
private:            void      f_1(long);      // private
private:            int       value_2;        // private
private:            int       f_2(char*);     // private

public:             char*     value_3;        // public
public:             long      f_3();          // public

protected:          int       value_4;        // protected
protected:          void      f_4(long);      // protected

};
```

The preceding notation is perfectly acceptable in C++; it is so verbose, however, that it is generally not used.

private Class Members

private class members have the strictest access control. Only the class itself (or classes declared friend, as shown later) can access a private member. Derived objects discussed in the next chapter have no access to a parent class's private members. Note that the use of private makes a member inaccessible to the outside world, but not invisible. The concept of information hiding is implemented only partially, to prevent the inadvertent access of internal class variables or functions. I said *inadvertent* because it is always possible to intentionally gain access to any part of a class member by bypassing the normal channels.

For example, if you cast a pointer to a class object into a pointer to an unsigned char, you have gained access to the entire contents of the object, including its private and protected parts. This kind of tampering should be done only in the most exceptional cases—for example, when implementing a class browser or debugger—but not for ordinary coding.

In an extreme case, you could edit the declaration for a class to specify that everything is public and then manipulate the class internals to your heart's content. Access control in C++ has the purpose of reducing the likelihood of bugs and enhancing consistency. Preventing hacking is beyond the scope of the language.

Because a class needs to be usable in a program, it follows that the class must have at least one member that isn't private. Listing 2.1 shows what happens when all of the class's members are private.

Listing 2.1. A class with all `private` members.

```
// no one can use this class: everything is private
class PrivateClass {

        long value;
        void f1();
        void f2();
};

void main()
{
        // create a PrivateClass object
        PrivateClass object;

        // you can't do anything to the class !
        long l = object. value;       // invalid access
        object. f1();                 // invalid access
        object. f2();                 // invalid access
}
```

public Class Members

To use an object of a given class inside a function, you must be able to access member data, member functions, or both. To make members accessible across the board, you need to declare a `public` section in the class declaration, as shown in Listing 2.2.

Listing 2.2. A class with `public` members.

```
class PublicExample {

public:

        int variable;
        void function();
};
// define the member function PublicExample::function()
void PublicExample::function() {}            // do nothing

void main()
{
        // create a class object
        PublicExample object;
```

```
        // use the object's public parts
        int i = object. variable;           // this is okay
        object. function();                 // and so is this

}
```

Anything declared in the `public` section allows unlimited access to anyone. Often `public` members are used to access `private` data in a controlled manner, and invoke `private` member functions to carry out the work. How the interface to a class is designed is completely up to the programmer. In later chapters I describe techniques for designing classes from scratch and deriving new classes from old ones.

protected Class Members

When you define a class that is subsequently used as a base class for other classes, you can make members accessible only to functions in the derived classes by using the `protected` keyword. Consider a hierarchy of objects, as shown in Figure 2.1.

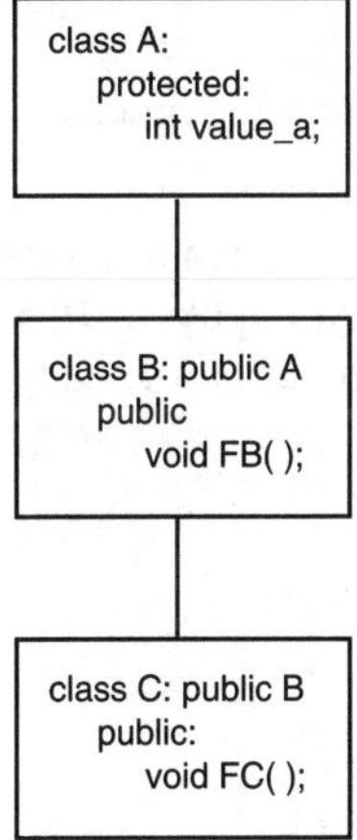

Figure 2.1. An inheritance tree with a `protected` *data member in the base class.*

The hierarchy in Figure 2.1 can be expressed with code like this:

```
class A {
protected:
  int value_a;
};
```

```
class B: public A {
public:
  void FB();
};

class C: public B {
public:
  void FC();
};
```

The property of being `protected` extends indefinitely down an inheritance tree, as long as derived classes are declared to have `public` base classes. With this fact in mind, any member functions in class `C` or `B` can access the `protected` data member `value_a` of their base class `A`, but only through the `this` pointer. For example, the following code is acceptable:

```
void B::FB()
{
  value_a = 0;      // accessed through this pointer
}


void C::FC()
{
  value_a = 0;      // also accessed through this pointer
}
```

The access of `protected` data in a base class is allowed only when accessed as shown in the preceding code, using the implicit `this` pointer. If a member function receives a pointer or a reference to a different object, the rules are different. Consider modifying class `C` like this:

```
class C: public B {
public:
  void FC(A&);
};


void C::FC(A& a)
{
  value_a = 0;      // Acceptable access: uses the this pointer.
  a.value_a = 0;    // This uses the A& reference: access violation.
                    // Now we are considered an external
                    // user of class A, and hence can only
                    // use the public interface class A.
}
```

The access to `value_a` through a reference to an `A` object is illegal, even though the function attempting the access is inside a class derived from `A`, which has access to the `protected` members of `A`. The `protected` keyword is discussed further in Chapter 3.

Storage Classes for Class Objects

You can consider a class to be a kind of structure, as far as storage allocation goes. As with structures, classes can be declared with `auto`, `register`, `extern`, and `static` storage. You can create as many objects as you want with the same class, as long as you have sufficient memory and you use unambiguous identifiers for the objects. Everything that was said about storage classes in Chapter 1 is still valid for class objects.

Class Scope

C++ introduces the new class scope for identifiers declared inside a class. Such identifiers are in scope only when used in conjunction with an object of the class. When ambiguities could arise, the scope resolution operator `::` must be used. The `::` scope resolution operator is described more fully in Chapter 3, but the following code illustrates its salient points:

```
class Counter {
public:
          GetValue() {return 1;}
};

void main()
{
  Counter counter;
  Counter* pointer = new Counter;

  GetValue();                 // not in scope: unknown function
  counter. GetValue();        // this is ok
  pointer->GetValue();        // and so is this
}
```

Empty Classes

Although the purpose of a class is to encapsulate code and data, a class also can have an empty declaration.

```
class Empty {};
```

Of course you are not going to be able to do much with the class, but you can create objects of class `Empty`.

```
void main()
{
          Empty object;
}
```

Why would you ever create an empty class? Often in the development of a large project you need to test early implementations in which some classes are either not fully identified or not fully implemented yet. These are often called *stubs* and are designed to get your code to compile without errors, allowing you to test some part of it.

Nested Classes

The power of abstraction of a class can be increased by including other class declarations inside the class. A class declared inside the declaration of another class is called a *nested* class, and can be considered something like a member class. Here is an example of nested class:

```
class Outer {
public:
     class Inner {
     public:
          int x;
     };
};
```

Class `Inner` is called a nested class, with respect to `Outer`. Just declaring a nested class doesn't automatically allocate storage for a class object. A nested declaration merely affects the scope of the nested class's name. Storage is allocated to classes only on instantiation.

Access Rules for Nested Classes

In AT&T release 3.0 and Borland C++ 4.5, a nested class has no special access privileges regarding the members of the enclosing class. Conversely, an enclosing class has no special access privileges regarding the members of the nested class. Nesting affects only the scope of a class's name.

The identifier of a nested class is subject to the same access rules that all other data members are subject to. If a nested class is declared in the `private` section of the enclosing class, the nested class will be usable only by data members of the enclosing class. The enclosing class may access the nested class's name without scope resolution. If a nested class's name is accessible to a nonenclosing class or function, the scope resolution operator must be applied to use the name. Listing 2.3 shows some dos and don'ts with nested classes and the scope resolution operator.

Listing 2.3. Accessing nested and enclosing class members.

```
class Outer {
  int privateOuter;
  void UseInner() {
    Inner obj;
```

```
//    int i = obj.privateInner;       can't do this:
// Outer::Inner::privateInner is unaccessible !
  }
public:
     class Inner {
       int privateInner;
       void UseOuter() {
        Outer a;
//         int i = a.privateOuter;     can't do this:
Outer::privateOuter is unaccessible !
       }
     public:
          int x;
     };
};

void main()
{
     // instantiate an Inner object
     Outer::Inner value;
     int v = value.x;
}
```

A Short Example

Listing 2.4 shows how a nested class is accessed by member functions of the enclosing class under Borland C++ 4.5.

Listing 2.4. A nested class.

```
class OuterClass {

public:

 // declare and define a nested class
  class InsideClass {
  private:
    int* value;
  public:
    InsideClass() {value = new int [100];}
    ~InsideClass() {delete value;}
  };

 // declare a pointer
  InsideClass *p;

public:
```

continues

Listing 2.4. continued

```
  OuterClass() {p = new InsideClass;}
  ~OuterClass() {delete p;}
};
```

`OuterClass` accesses `InsideClass` the same way it would access a non-nested class. Nesting a class only affects the scope of the nested class's name, giving no special access privileges to the enclosing class. For example, in the previous listing, class `OuterClass` is not allowed to access the `private` data member `InnerClass::value`. Only `public` members of the nested class are available to the enclosing class, unless the enclosing class is also declared a `friend` of the nested class.

The main reason for using nested classes is to reduce the number of identifiers in the global name space. If a class is used exclusively in the implementation of another class, it could be advantageous to make the class a nested class to avoid adding another identifier to the global names. For example, a linked list class might declare the list nodes as a nested class, because only the list manager would be likely to use the list nodes.

A nested class can access the regular non-`static` members of the enclosing class only through pointers or references. Listing 2.5 shows how a nested class is accessed outside the scope of the enclosing class.

Listing 2.5. Using the scope resolution operator to access the name of a nested class.

```
// use a nested class in another class
class New {
public:
       New() {OuterClass::InsideClass* p =
            new OuterClass::InsideClass;}
};


// use a nested class in a nonmember function
void f()
{
         OuterClass::InsideClass* p =
           new OuterClass::InsideClass;
}
```

Notice the use of the syntax

```
OuterClass::InsideClass
```

to access the name `InsideClass`. The syntax is the same as that used to access a `typedef` or `enum` declared inside a class.

Class Instantiation

A class is not a physical entity in storage. Being akin to a structure declaration, storage is allocated only when the class is used to create an object. I refer to this creation process as *instantiation.* The term is widely used in OOP circles and indicates the act of *making an instance,* or a physical entity, of a class. In some languages, objects are called *instances.* This is generally not the case in C++; however, instantiation is still a handy word that I use extensively.

Incomplete Class Declarations

A class *must* be declared before any of its members can be used. However, you sometimes need to use a class as a whole, without accessing its members. Declaring a pointer to a class is such a time, as shown in the following code:

```
// incomplete class declaration
class MembersOnly;

// define a global pointer to the class
MembersOnly* club;

void main() { /* ... */ }

// finally declare the full class
class MembersOnly {
public:
          MembersOnly();
          MembersOnly* AMember();
};
```

The first statement is called an *incomplete class declaration.* The incomplete class declaration is used to allow forward referencing to a class that is yet to be fully defined, such as a class appearing in another file. The `global` pointer `club` can be declared because the class identifier `MembersOnly` was introduced into scope with the incomplete class declaration. When the compiler reaches the statement in which the pointer is declared, the compiler doesn't actually know anything about the type pointed at, other than the fact that the type is a class named `MembersOnly`.

An incompletely declared class may not be instantiated. Attempts to do so cause a compiler error. Incomplete declarations are allowed only with classes and structures. Attempting to access members of an incompletely declared class causes compiler errors.

Using Data Members

Encapsulation indicates that some form of data is enclosed inside a class. There can be as much data as necessary in a class, memory permitting, including none. Data can be declared `private`, `protected`, or `public`. Here is an example:

```
class Counter {
private:
          static long count;
          char* name;
public:
          int identifier;
protected:
          unsigned char status;
          int value;
          float increment;
};
```

The preceding example is rather unusual because it declares only data and no functions. Having no member functions would prevent the `private` data from being accessed entirely. What is shown is that you can declare data in any section, in any order, and in any quantity.

It is an error to attempt to initialize a data member inside a class declaration. A class is not an object, and no storage is allocated to a class until it is instantiated. The data members declared in the class should be considered equivalent to structure fields, not variables. Just as for structures, you must declare an object of a class type, then initialize its data members. If a data member is a class member, it is a special case, which is described later in this chapter.

static Data Members

When a data member is declared `static` in a class, all instantiations of the class share the same member, much like a `static` variable in a regular C function. A `static` data member is allocated a fixed area of storage at link time, like a `global` variable, but the variable's identifier is in scope only using the scope resolution operator with the class name.

Data members are generally allocated with the same storage class. If an object is declared `auto`, all its data is `auto`; `static` objects have `static` data members. `static` data members are an exception to this rule: when an object with `static` data members is created, the `static` members are *not* allocated storage because this would cause multiple copies of the `statics` to appear. To declare or initialize a `static`, you use pretty much the same notation as you would with a `global` variable. Consider the code in Listing 2.6.

Listing 2.6. A class with a `static` data member.

```
class Example {
public:
        static int value;    // declare the static member
        int identifier;
};


int Example::value;          // define the static member

void main()
{
        Example object1;     // define some auto objects
        Example object2;

        object1.value = 1;   // use the static data member
        object2.value = 10;
}
```

If you omit the definition

```
int Example::value;
```

the code compiles, but the linker generates an undefined symbol error for the `static` member. No other way to define a `static` exists.

> **NOTE**
>
> In the older Turbo C++ 1.0, `static` data members were not required to be explicitly defined. When the linker found undefined `statics`, it would automatically define them and allocate storage for them instead of generating errors.

When a data member is declared `static`, the linker allocates storage to the data member only once, and only if the data member is defined. The storage class for `value` is `static`, even though `object1` and `object2` are declared to have `auto` storage class. `statics` are always `static`. You can also initialize a `static` member variable when you define it.

```
// define and initialize a static data member
int Example::value = 3;
```

Access privileges for `static` data members are different than for non-`static` members. It is always legal to access a `static` data member using the scope resolution operator, whether or not the data member is `private`, `protected`, or `public`. For example, the preceding statement that defines and initializes the variable `Example::value` is valid even if `value` is declared `private` or `protected` inside class `Example`. The rationale is that `static` data members accessed this way are essentially global data.

Using `static` members may cause unforeseen side effects. The two assignments in `main()` use the same location in memory, thus the second statement overwrites the first one. This is not obvious by just looking at the code in `main()`. You need to see the declaration of the class `Example` to tell. `static` data members can be accessed in one of three ways:

1. Using the `.` (dot) operator, as shown in Listing 2.6. When doing so, the compiler does not need to evaluate the expression on the left side of the dot, because there is only one storage location defined for the `static` member being accessed. Regular access privileges apply.
2. Using the `->` operator, if the left side is an object pointer. Again the compiler does not evaluate the left side's expression, but regular class member access privileges apply.
3. Using the class identifier itself without referencing an actual object. This action gives unrestricted access to all class data members, `private`, `protected`, and `public`. Using this method, the `static` value could be accessed like this:

```
// this is only an assignment statement, not a definition
// of storage
Example::value = 1;
```

The preceding code also makes it clear that the member being accessed is `static`, because the notation is allowed only for `statics`.

`static` variables act like a bridge between objects created from the same class. The linker allocates storage for a `static` member when the variable is defined, even if no objects are actually created from the class. A simple use for a `static` data member could be to count how many instances of a given class exist.

```
class Counter {
        static long count;
public:
        Counter() {count++;}
        long GetInstanceCount() {return count;}
        ~Counter() {count--;}
};
```

Each time a `Counter` object is created, whether it is `auto`, `global`, or `static`, the `static` member `count` is incremented. `statics` are initially set to 0 if they are defined but not initialized. `static` data members must be initialized to nonzero values explicitly. You can't initialize `static` data members to nonzero values in the class declaration. To initialize `count`, you need a statement like

```
// define and initialize a static data member
long Counter::count = INITIAL_VALUE;
```

For correct results, the preceding statement would have to occur before the first `Counter` object was created. Listing 2.7 is a complete program using `statics` in the class `Counter`.

Listing 2.7. An example of using `static` members.

```
#include <stdio.h>

class Counter {
public:
          static long count;
          Counter() {count++;}
          long GetInstanceCount() {return count;}
          ~Counter() {count--;}
};

// define and initialize the count
long Counter::count = 5;

// define three Counter objects
Counter c1, c2, c3;

void main()
{
  printf("\nThe object count is currently %d",
             Counter::count);
}
```

The sequence of events is important. The definition and initialization of `Counter::count` must occur before the three global `Counter` objects are created. This order is guaranteed if the statements appear in the same file in the order shown. However, a general problem exists in C++ regarding the order of execution of definitions when they appear in different files. There is no guaranteed order. The best way to solve the problem (although it's not a perfect solution) is to confine all the global objects of class `Counter` and the definition of `Counter::count` to the same file.

Note that `static` data members of a class can be defined, initialized, and used, even if no objects of that class are created.

private static Data Members

`static` data members don't always have to be `public`. Declaring a `static` member `private` can have some interesting applications. Consider the following class:

```
class Example {
private:
          static int value;        // declare a private static
};
```

```
// define the static member
int Example::value = 1;             // valid access

void main()
{
        Example object1;            // define an auto object

        // attempt to access the static data member
        object1.value = 1;          // error: illegal access
}
```

To access a `private static` data member you need to use the scope resolution operator. Using the scope resolution operator is completely new notation for member access. The only other ways to access a `private static` data member are

1. Through a member function of the class.
2. Through a class declared a `friend` to the class.

Using the dot operator with class objects or the `->` operator with pointers to class objects results in compiler errors.

Class Objects As Data Members

You can declare a data member that is, in turn, a class. If the data member has only a default constructor, or a constructor that takes no arguments, you don't need to do anything special (see Listing 2.8).

Listing 2.8. Class objects as data members.

```
class First {
public:
        int value;
        First() {value = 0;}
        int GetValue() {return value;}
};

class Second {
        int id;
public:
        First object;
        Second() {id = 0;}
        int GetName() {return id;}
};

void main()
{
        First one;
        Second two;
}
```

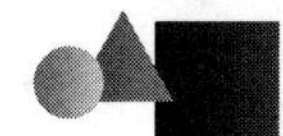

The constructor for class `First` requires no arguments. When object `one` is created, its constructor is invoked as usual. When object `two` is created, its constructor is also invoked, but before the body of this constructor is executed, the constructor for class `First` is executed. This sequence of constructor calls is generated automatically by the compiler and allows the final object `two` to contain a correctly constructed subobject of class `First`.

If a class data member needs to be initialized with specific parameters, you need a special notation. The data member's constructor needs to be called with arguments, which is done by passing the parameters just before the constructor body for the enclosing class is entered. Consider modifying the two classes as shown in Listing 2.9.

Listing 2.9. Initializing member objects.

```
class First {
public:
     int value;
     First() {value = 0;}
     First(int i) {value = i;}
     int GetValue() {return value;}
};

class Second {
     int id;
public:
     First object;
     Second() {id = 0;}
     Second(int v) : object(v) {id = v;}
     int GetName() {return id;}
};

void main()
{
     First one;
     Second two;
     Second three(10);
}
```

Now you can create an object of class `First` with an initialized value other than 0. The value is passed to the constructor by the expression

```
Second(int v) : object(v) {id = v;}
```

Notice the colon after the constructor parameter list. The colon serves to indicate that the `First` object is initialized before the body of the `Second` object is executed. Using the same notation, you can initialize multiple class data members. You can pass as many parameters to them as needed, as long as their values are known *before* the `Second` constructor is executed. When passing data to more than one subclass, the initializers must be separated with commas, like this:

```
BigClass::BigClass(int w, char* title) :
                    Class1(3),
                    Class2("Hello", title, 5),
                    Class3(w),
                    Class4()        // this takes no arguments

// constructor body for BigClass
{...}
```

A subclass can include subclasses of its own. The compiler recursively invokes the subclass constructors automatically. The subclasses are initialized in the sequence shown in the initializer line. If some of the subclasses require no arguments, they don't have to be specified in the initializer line, in which case they are initialized last. If you wish to impose a certain order of initialization even for these subclasses, you have to include them in the initializer statement with the other subclasses to initialize. You can include as many subobjects as you want in a class, and Borland C++ takes care of the details for you.

Note that the same notation used to initialize subclasses is used also with derived classes to initialize their base classes. Initialization of base classes is covered fully in Chapter 3.

References As Data Members

Instead of including a complete subobject into another object, it is usually more efficient to include a reference to the subobject. Consider including a reference to a `First` object in class `Second`. The declaration of `First` doesn't change in any way, but class `Second` does require a few minor modifications, and looks like this:

```
class Second {
     int id;
public:
     First& object;
     Second() : object(*new First) {id = 0;}
     Second(int v) : object(*new First(v)) {id = v;}
     ~Second() { delete &object;}
     int GetName() {return id;}
};
```

The two constructors for `Second` now initialize the data member `object` using a dynamically allocated item. A destructor also was added, to eliminate the item referenced by `First`. You don't have to necessarily create a new entity to initialize reference data members. If a `First` object were passed as a parameter in the constructor for `Second`, you could use it to initialize the `object` data member, as follows:

```
     Second(First& f) : object(f) {id = 0;}
     Second(First* f) : object(*f) {id = 0;}
```

Now the caller of the constructor is responsible for creating a `First` object somewhere. The following code is an example:

```
void f()
{
     First one;
     Second two(one);

     First* op1 = new First;
     Second three(op1);        use a pointer-to-First

     First& op2 = *new First;
     Second four(op2); use a reference-to-First
}
```

If the constructor creates a new object to initialize a data member, then the destructor will normally need to delete that object. If a reference data member is initialized with an object passed to the constructor as a parameter, you may or may not want to delete the object in the destructor. On one hand, you want to be sure the object gets deleted. On the other hand, you don't want to delete the same object more than once!

Pointers As Data Members

Data members also can be pointers. Pointers cannot be initialized inside a class declaration. If a data member points to a class type, the pointer is *not* initialized, nor are any constructors called automatically. Consider changing the declaration of class `Second` as follows:

```
class Second {
          int id;
public:
          First* object;
          Second();
          int GetName() {return id;}
};
```

Here the member is declared to point to an item of class `First`. When an object of class `Second` is created, its constructor `Second::Second()` no longer invokes the constructor for class `First`. In the constructor for class `Second`, storage is allocated for the pointer object, but the pointer is left uninitialized. Normally pointers like these are initialized in the code of the derived class's constructor, but that is not a C++ requirement. You may choose not to initialize pointer members in a class constructor, but all pointers must be initialized before being used.

Pointers to Class Data Members

Classes are not objects, but sometimes you can use classes almost as if they were. Declaring a pointer to a class member is an example. Consider the code in Listing 2.10.

Listing 2.10. Pointers to class data members.

```
class Example {
public:
          int value;
          int identifier;
};

void SetValue(Example& object)
{
          int Example::*ip = &Example::value;
          object.*ip = 3;
}

void main()
{
          Example object1;
          Example object2;
          SetValue(object1);
          SetValue(object2);
}
```

The function `SetValue()` has the unusual declaration

```
int Example::*ip = &Example::value;
```

This statement declares the variable `ip` to point to an `int` data member value in an object of class `Example`, without indicating a specific object. What is actually stored in `ip` is the offset of the variable `value` in an object of class `Example`. Actually, the offset is incremented by one to prevent pointers to data members from having an offset of 0. Zero offsets are reserved for pointers to `virtual` functions and are handled differently by the compiler. In any event `ip` is set to the value 1.

When `SetValue()` is invoked, it doesn't know on what object it is acting. `SetValue()` assumes it is working with a reference to an `Example` object. You can really mix up things by calling `SetValue()` with a non-`Example` object that is cast into an `Example&`. `SetValue()` silently takes the reference, indexes off of it, and changes the computed memory location. Your program can easily crash if the wrong object is intentionally passed to `SetValue()`. However, there may be legitimate uses for functions that use pointers to class data

members, such as in a debugging function that accesses the first two bytes of storage of any object and displays them. The example in Listing 2.11 is a little more explicit.

Listing 2.11. Using pointers to class data members.

```
class Pointer {
public:
  int private1, private2;
  void Private1() {}
  void Private2() {}
public:
  int public1, public2;
  void Public1() {}
  void Public2() {}
};

void main()
{
                                                  // offset
  int Pointer::*ip1 = &Pointer::private1;     // = 1
  int Pointer::*ip2 = &Pointer::private2;     // = 3
  int Pointer::*ip3 = &Pointer::public1;      // = 5
  int Pointer::*ip4 = &Pointer::public2;      // = 7

  // define an auto object
  Pointer object;

  // access two private data members
  object.*ip1 = 5;
  object.*ip2 = 5;

  // access two public data members
  object.*ip3 = 5;
  object.*ip4 = 5;
}
```

Although the values saved in each of the four pointers is an integer, C++ knows how to use these integers to look up the address of the correct data members. Also, note that both `public` *and* `private` members are accessible through pointers.

Pointers to Object Data Members

You can have a pointer that references a data member in a specific object. A pointer to an object data member is a more traditional pointer, and is similar to an ANSI C pointer. Listing 2.12 is an example with class `Example`.

Listing 2.12. Pointers to data members.

```
void SetValue(int* member)
{
        *member = 3;
}

void main()
{
        // make a couple of objects
        Example object1;
        Example object2;

        // create two pointers to object members
        int* pointer1 = &object1.value;
        int* pointer2 = &object2.value;

        // pass the pointers to SetValue()
        SetValue(pointer1);
        SetValue(pointer2);
}
```

Here the function `SetValue()` is an ordinary function taking a pointer to integer. When `SetValue()` is called, it has absolutely no idea what its argument points to, except that it presumably points to an `int`. The same function can be used to set `int` members of any class or nonclass object.

Using Member Functions

Inside a class declaration, you specify data and code. The code is contained in a series of functions, or more precisely, *member functions.* The access rules for member functions are the same as for data members. Here is an example that uses all kinds of possible member functions:

```
class AllKinds {
private:
        int value;
public:
        void f1();
        static int f2();
        const int f3();
        volatile int f4();
        int f5() {return value;}
        int f6() const;
        int f7() volatile;
        virtual int f8() {}
```

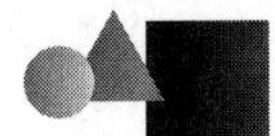

```
          AllKinds();
          ~AllKinds();
};

int identifier;

void AllKinds::f1() {value = 100;}
int AllKinds::f2() {return identifier;}
const int AllKinds::f3() {return 3;}
volatile int AllKinds::f4() {return value;}
int AllKinds::f6() const {return value;}
int AllKinds::f7() volatile {return value;}
AllKinds::AllKinds() {value = 0;}
AllKinds::~AllKinds() {}
```

Each of the basic member types is discussed in a separate section. `Virtual` functions are discussed separately in Chapter 5.

In the preceding code, note the use of the global variable `identifier`. `identifier` was added for the function `AllKinds::f2()`, which is declared `static`. A `static` member function cannot access non-`static` data in its own class without specific provisions. You also can combine declarations to provide additional variations in declaring functions. For example, you also could declare these member functions:

```
class AllKinds {
private:
          int value;
public:
          const int f8() const;
          static volatile int f9() const;
};

int identifier;

const int AllKinds::f8() const {return value;}
volatile int AllKinds::f9() const {return identifier;}
```

Member functions enjoy external linkage, unless their class is a nested class or declared inside a function. In these cases, the class is said to be *local* to a class or function, and the member functions are in scope in the enclosing class or function.

Simple Member Functions

I use the word *simple* rather loosely here, just to indicate member functions declared without the `const`, `volatile`, or `static` keywords. Function `AllKinds::f1()` is an example. Member functions can be declared to return typed values, including class objects, pointers, or references. They also can be declared to accept any number and type of arguments, just like normal ANSI C functions. Default arguments are allowed in member functions, and so is the ellipsis notation. Passing class objects to a function is considered a special case; it is described in the section "Constructors for Copying Objects" later in this chapter. Here are some examples of simple member function declarations:

```
class Simple {
private:
        char* name;
        void simple1(int, long, char* = 0);
        long simple2(char*);
protected:
        int value;
        char* simple3(unsigned char, long, int);
        void simple4(void);
public:
        long v1, v2, v3;
        simple5(int, long...);
        char* simple6(Simple&);
};
```

Note that function `simple5()` defaults to return an `int`. Function `simple6()` is declared to accept a reference to class `Simple`. Using a class inside the declaration of the same class is acceptable and is often used in list-processing and recursive classes.

static Member Functions

Declaring a `static` member function is very similar to declaring a `static` data member. `static` functions differ in the following ways from ordinary member functions:

1. They can be used without referring to a specific object, using only a class name.
2. They have no `this` pointer, so they cannot access class member data unless they are passed a `this` pointer explicitly.

Note that `static` member functions have external linkage, like all other member functions. This is different from ANSI C `static` functions, which have internal linkage. The following code shows how a `static` member function might be used:

```
// define some global variables
int v1, v2, v3;

class Simple {
public:
        static void sum();
};

void Simple::sum() {v1 = v2 + v3;}

main()
{
        Simple s1;
```

```
        s1.sum();
        Simple::sum();
}
```

Function `main()` invokes the `static` member function `sum()` using two possible methods. You can also access `static` member functions through a pointer to member function, like this:

```
main()
{
        // define a pointer to member function
        void Simple::(*fp)() = &Simple::sum;

        // define a Simple object
        Simple s1;

        // invoke the sum() member via a pointer
        (*fp)();
}
```

If a `static` function needs access to a class's member data, it needs to be passed an explicit `this` pointer. This is how `sum()` would be declared and used in this case:

```
class Simple {
        long v1, v2, v3;    // declare some private data
public:
        static void sum(Simple*);
};

// use member data
void Simple::sum(Simple* s) {s->v1 = s->v2 + s->v3;}

main()
{
        Simple s1;
        s1.sum(&s1);        // pass an explicit object
                            // pointer in the function call
}
```

Note that you can't declare constructors to be `static`. If a constructor was allowed to be `static`, it could be invoked without a `this` pointer and, therefore, would not be able to build specific objects from raw storage.

const Member Functions

A `const` member function returns a `const` object, which can be used like any `const` object. A `const` member function is used as shown here:

```
class ConstFunction {
public:
```

```
        const int f3();
};

const int ConstFunction::f3() {return 3;}

void main()
{
        ConstFunction s;
        const int i = s.f3();          // use f3() to initialize a
                                          const
        int y = s.f3();                // use f3() with an int
}
```

volatile Member Functions

`volatile` member functions simply return a `volatile` object to be used as any other `volatile` object. The compiler is less aggressive about optimizations, because the returned value is not assumed to remain unchanged from one instruction to the next. Here is an example of usage of `volatile` member functions:

```
class VolatileFunction {
public:
        int value;
        volatile int f4();
};

volatile int VolatileFunction::f4() {return value;}

void main()
{
        VolatileFunction s;
        volatile int i = s.f4();
}
```

inline Member Functions

`inline` is a common kind of member function in C++. The `inline` member function was designed to allow high-efficiency calls to member functions, giving the language the class approach without overhead in member function calls. `inline` functions are declared and defined in the class declaration without using any special keywords.

`inline` functions are treated by the compiler almost as a macro: the function call is immediately replaced by the function body. For short functions, this is extremely efficient because there is no function call or function return. Consider the following code:

```
class InlineClass {
public:
        int value;
```

 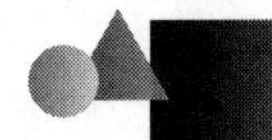

```
        int get_value() {return value;}
};

void main()
{
        InlineClass s;
        int i = s. get_value();
}
```

The function call `s.get_value()` is replaced at compile time by the contents of variable `s.value`, resulting in no overhead in the function call. Borland C++ has an option to modify this behavior. If you enable the `out-of-line inline functions` option in the Options ¦ Project ¦ +Compiler ¦ Debugging menu, `inline` function calls are treated just like ordinary member function calls. The normal function call overhead is incurred.

Every time an `inline` member function is called, the call is replaced with the function's body. This is referred to as *inline expansion.* It only makes sense to use `inline` members if they are short, otherwise you wind up with large (or even huge) programs unnecessarily.

The complexity of an `inline` function is restricted. Declaring a function `inline` doesn't automatically guarantee that Borland C++ uses it as such. If the compiler judges the function to be too big or complex, it treats it as a regular member function. The Advanced Section shows how an `inline` function is treated by the compiler.

Member Functions with *const this*

C programmers are familiar with the `const` keyword, which is used to indicate access restrictions on variables. The `const` modifier also can be applied to the body of a class member function to indicate a restriction on the function's capabilities. Member functions declared this way with `const` are new in C++. The `const` keyword in this case does not refer to the function's return value, but to the `this` pointer used in the function's body. To declare a function with `const` you can use the following notation:

```
class Example {
        int value;
public:
        int GetValue() const;                   // out-of-line
        int ReadValue() const {return value;}   // inline
};

int Example::GetValue() const {
        return value;
}
```

The `GetValue()` function shows the normal declaration style. The notation is highly irregular and can be confusing, so make sure you get the keyword `const` in the right place. The `const` keyword also has to be repeated in the definition of the function. Not doing so would make the compiler think you're defining a different function. You would get the error message

```
"GetValue() is not a member of Example".
```

What does it mean to declare a function in this way? It has to do with the type of the `this` pointer passed to the member function. C++ always passes an invisible `this` pointer to non-`static` member functions. Members then can use the pointer to access member data. Member functions of a class `Example`, declared without the `const` keyword, have the following declaration for `this`:

```
// usual implied this
Example *const this;
```

This statement indicates a `const this` pointer, referencing a non-`const` object of class `Example`. If you could see the invisible pointer passed into a normal member function called `Normal()`, the function's declaration would look like this:

```
class Example {
public:
        int Normal(Example *const this);
};
```

Of course you can't declare the `this` pointer explicitly, so the preceding class would give a compilation error. The reason for putting a `const` in front of the body of a function such as in functions `GetValue()` and `ReadValue()` is to allow you to change the type of the `this` pointer passed to the member function. The `const` makes `this` assume the following invisible declaration:

```
// the modified this
const Example *const this;
```

Now the `this` pointer is defined to reference a `const Example` object. The implications are that the member function is not allowed to make any changes to the class data members. The ability to declare a member function in such a restrictive manner can be useful with base classes, where a member function can be overridden in a derived class. Declaring the member with the `const` keyword in front of the body prevents any overriding functions from making changes to class data members. The Borland C++ class library uses this kind of declaration frequently. For example, in class `Bag` you see the member function

```
classType Bag::isA() const
{
    return bagClass;
}
```

The preceding declaration prevents any overriding `isA()` functions in derived classes from making changes to objects of which they are a part. The reason is that an `isA()` function is meant only to retrieve data, not to make changes. The `const` keyword gives more error-checking power to the compiler and should be used where possible.

> **NOTE**
>
> The `const` keyword put after the function name has nothing to do with a `const` placed before the name. The former use modifies the declaration of the `this` pointer for the member function; the latter regards the function's return value.

It also is possible to use functions declared with `const` with objects that are not declared `const`. The following code is an example:

```
class Example {
        int value;
public:
        int ReadValue() const {return value;}
};

void main()
{
        Example e;
        int i = e.ReadValue();          // use auto object

        volatile Example e1;
        int y = e1.ReadValue();         // use volatile object
}
```

Declaring a `static` member function with the `const` keyword doesn't make sense.

```
class Example {
public:
        int value;
        static int GetValue() const {return value;}
};
```

The reason is that member functions are not passed an invisible `this` pointer when they are called, and the purpose of the `const` keyword is to modify the type of `this`. Borland C++, however, doesn't complain about the preceding syntax, and doesn't even issue a warning.

In C++ it is illegal to declare a constructor or destructor with the `const` keyword, but here again Borland C++ doesn't issue errors.

Member Functions with *volatile this*

The syntax used to declare a `const this` pointer also can be applied to the `volatile` keyword. Member functions with `volatile this` are declared in the following way:

```
class Example {
        int value;
```

```
public:
        // out-of-line declaration
        void SetValue(int) volatile;
        // inline declaration
        void WriteValue(int v) volatile {value = v;}
};

void Example::SetValue(int v) volatile {
        value = v;
}
```

The notation has the same structure as for functions declared with `const`, as shown in the previous section. Declaring a function to be `volatile` entails the following declaration for the `this` pointer passed to it:

```
volatile Example* const this;
```

The function thus considers all data members of the class to be `volatile`, and the compiler disables certain kinds of optimizations. Here are some examples:

```
void main()
{
        Example e;
        e.SetValue(3);              // use with auto object

        const Example e1;
        e1.SetValue(4);             // can't use with const object

        volatile Example e2;
        e2.SetValue(4);             // use with volatile object
}
```

Invoking `SetValue()` with object `e1` causes the compiler to issue the warning

```
"non-const function Example::SetValue(int) volatile called for const
object in function main()"
```

Declaring functions to be `volatile` is often used when an object is expected to be handled by multiple independent agents. These agents might be different processors or the background and foreground (interrupt service) code in the same program. You can declare a function with the `volatile` and `const` keywords together as follows:

```
class Example {
        static int value;       // declare the static member
public:
        int identifier;
        int GetValue() volatile const {return value;}
};
```

What does this code mean? There seems to be a contradiction of terms. Is `GetValue()` volatile or constant? The compiler sees no conflict whatsoever in `GetValue()`, because

the function is declared `volatile` only to indicate that the member function may be used with `volatile` objects. The `const` keyword tells the compiler that `GetValue()` is used in objects that have data that cannot be altered. The order of appearance of `volatile` and `const` could be inverted without changing the semantics, like this:

```
int GetValue() const volatile {return value;}
```

In C++ release 2.1, it is illegal to declare a constructor or destructor with the `volatile` keyword; however, Borland C++ doesn't complain about it.

Special Class Functions

Classes can have any number of member functions, but two special functions can be declared: the *constructor* and the *destructor.* Although these are optional functions, they provide certain performance features to the class that are often indispensable. These two functions are different from the other member functions because they can be invoked automatically by the compiler on certain events. This built-in behavior frees the programmer from having to remember certain details, which in turn reduces the probability of bugs.

Constructors

As the name implies, a constructor is a function used to build an object of a given class. You don't have to define a constructor unless you need one, and you can even define more than one. C++ guarantees that if a class has a constructor, the constructor is called before any other function of the class. Consider the object definition

```
void main()
{
          Counter counter;
}
```

using the `Counter` class described earlier. What does the compiler do? First of all, an `auto` variable is being defined. The variable is allocated storage space in the stack frame, just as if a structure had been declared. At this point the compiler checks the declaration of class `Counter`, looking for a class constructor. If the compiler finds a class constructor that takes no arguments (because the example code doesn't provide any), the compiler generates code to invoke the constructor. Although constructors are always written to create new objects, this can involve different scenarios:

1. Creating objects with default initialization.
2. Creating objects with specific initialization.
3. Creating objects by copying another object.

Each of these involves a different kind of constructor and is discussed in a separate paragraph. A constructor has a special reserved name, which is the same as the class to which the constructor belongs. A constructor for class `Counter` could be defined as follows:

```
class Counter {

public:
        Counter();             // a constructor declaration
};
```

The various kinds of constructors have different declarations, but they have one thing in common: they are declared with no return type. It is an error to declare a constructor to return a value of any type, including `void`. The constructor's task is to build an object in memory, which doesn't entail returning values.

Constructors cannot be declared `static` or `virtual`. The possibility of making constructors `virtual` has been the subject of recent debate, and future releases of C++ just might support `virtual` constructors some day. The ability to declare a `virtual` constructor would add considerable flexibility to the language, although this ability isn't feasible in C++ in its current form.

Constructors for Classes with Subobjects

A subobject is a class object declared inside another class. When a class is instantiated, its constructor must create an object of that class. If the class has subobjects declared in it, the constructor has to invoke the constructors for these objects. Consider the example in Listing 2.13.

Listing 2.13. Constructors with subobjects.

```
class Counter {
  int value;
public:
  Counter() {value = 0;}
};


class Example {
  int value;
public:
  Counter cars;                // a subobject
  Example() {value = 0;}
};

void main()
{
  Example e;
}
```

When object `e` is created in `main()`, the constructor for class `Example` is called, in this case, function `Example::Example()`. Before executing its own body, function `Example::Example()` invokes the constructor `Counter::Counter()` for subobject `cars`. When this constructor completes, the body of `Example::Example()` is executed. The constructors for subobjects are invoked in the order in which the subobjects appear in the class declaration.

When an instantiation is made of a class derived from another class, the base class constructor is invoked automatically. This process is described in detail in Chapter 3.

private Constructors

Note that the preceding constructor appears in the `public` section of the class. This is not an absolute requirement, but it normally is the case. A `private` constructor would prevent generic users from creating objects from that class and force one of the following conditions to be met before an object is allowed to be created:

1. A static member of the class invokes the constructor.
2. A `friend` of the class invokes the constructor.
3. An existing object of the class has a member function that creates new objects by invoking the constructor.

`static` members and `friend` classes are treated later in this chapter. A class with a `private` constructor also has another interesting behavior: it doesn't allow you to create a `static`, `global`, or `auto` object, because the constructor would have to be invoked. The following code shows some examples:

```
class Counter {
        Counter();                        // constructor is private
};


// attempt to create a global object
Counter object;            // this will cause a compiler error

// attempt to create a static object
static Counter counter;    // another compiler error

void main()
{
        // attempt to create an auto object
        Counter object; // wrong again
}
```

Default Constructors

When a constructor is declared to accept no arguments, it is called a *default* constructor. Here's a modified declaration of the class Counter that was introduced earlier:

```
class Counter {

  long count;

public:

  Counter();
  void SetValue(long);
  long GetValue();
};
```

The constructor Counter() is a default constructor. Since a default constructor takes no arguments, it follows that each class can have only one default constructor. The code in a default constructor typically initializes data used subsequently by other member functions. Here is an example:

```
// define the default constructor
Counter::Counter()
{
          // notify user of new object
          printf("\nCreating a Counter object");

          // initialize some internal data
          count = 0;
}
```

If you don't specifically declare a default constructor, Borland C++ declares one automatically. This default constructor simply allocates storage to build an object of its class. A constructor that has all default arguments is similar to a default constructor, because it can be called without arguments. In fact, it is so similar that it might cause an error. Examine the following example:

```
class Counter {
  int value;
public:
  Counter(int i = 0) {value = i;}
  Counter() {value = 0;}
};

void main()
{
  Counter c;        // this will cause a compiler error
  Counter c1(4);    // this is ok
}
```

Declaring the first object in `main()` makes the compiler complain, because two different functions could be called. If the default constructor is removed from the declaration, everything works again.

Constructors with Arguments

Most constructors in typical C++ classes take arguments. The basic function of a constructor is to initialize an object before using the object. This initialization may entail calling functions, allocating dynamic storage, setting variables to specific values, and so on. The following could be a constructor for class `Counter`:

```
// put this in the class declaration
Counter(long);      // declare a constructor

// definition of constructor
Counter::Counter(long value)
{
          count = value;
}
```

The preceding code allows you to initialize the object while creating it. In this case, you would create a `Counter` object like this:

```
void main()
{
          Counter object(5);
}
```

Note the parentheses after the variable name, which make the object definition resemble a function call. The object definition is indeed a function call—with arguments. The variable `object` is both defined and initialized on the same line. Given the declaration of the constructor, you must supply an argument to the constructor. Default arguments should be used if the constructor can be called with no arguments.

Multiple constructors can be declared for a class, as long as they take different types or numbers of arguments. This is handy, because now you can create objects differently depending on how they are used. Defining multiple functions with the same name is treated in detail in Chapter 4.

Assume that you want to create a `Counter` class that is flexible enough to accept any kind of initialization, using `float`s, `long`s, `int`s, character strings, or even no arguments. Here's which constructors must be declared:

```
// put inside the class declaration
Counter(int = 0);   // take an integer, or default to zero
Counter(long);      // take a long
Counter(double);    // take a double
Counter(char*);     // take a character string
```

Here is how the constructors might be defined:

```
Counter::Counter(int initial_value)
{
        count = initial_value;
}

Counter::Counter(long initial_value)
{
        count = initial_value;
}

Counter::Counter(double initial_value)
{
        count = initial_value;
}

Counter::Counter(char* initial_value)
{
        count = atol(initial_value);
}
```

Here's how the constructors might be used:

```
void main()
{
        Counter object("5");     // use char* constructor
        Counter object1(5);      // use int constructor
        Counter object2(5L);     // use long constructor
        Counter object3(5.0);    // use double constructor
        Counter object4;         // use int constructor with
                                 // default
}
```

The compiler is capable of determining automatically which constructor to call in each case by examining the arguments. The argument-matching rules for overloaded functions described in Chapter 4 are used. Of course, a constructor can have as many arguments as it needs, not just one. You also can pass more complicated arguments, such as structures, arrays, pointers, or even entire classes. The use of multiple constructors makes it easy to build classes that are flexible and user-friendly. C++ again lives up to its goal of simplifying programs and reducing the likelihood of bugs.

Constructors for Copying Objects

When you are creating an object, you often don't want to initialize any values specifically; you simply want an object "just like" another one. This implies making a copy of a preexisting object, which requires a special type of constructor, usually called a *copy initializer* or a *copy constructor.* Listing 2.14 shows how such a constructor would be used.

 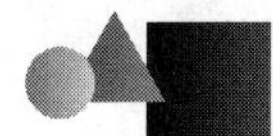

Listing 2.14. Using overloaded constructors.

```
// put this in the class declaration
Counter(Counter&);

// definition of copy-initializer constructor
Counter::Counter(Counter& reference)
{
        count = reference. count;
}

void main()
{
        Counter object(5);          // use int constructor
        Counter object1 = object;   // use copy-initializer
}
```

The notation can be misleading. The equal sign indicates that some kind of copying is going on between `object` and `object1`. This is not necessarily the case. The equal sign is only a trigger that indicates to the compiler to use a copy initializer constructor. What kind of initialization actually occurs is entirely dependent on the constructor you supply.

Copy constructors are important because they are the only means of making a copy of a class object. Without them, the compiler is not capable of performing this copying. Copying objects is done when objects are passed by value to and from a function. Consider the code in Listing 2.15.

Listing 2.15. Passing objects by value.

```
#include <stdio.h>
// include the header file for class Counter

// take a class variable by value
void report_count(Counter object)
{
        printf("\nThe object count is %ld",
               object.GetValue() );
}

void main()
{
        Counter object(10);
        report_count(object);
}
```

Here the function `report_count()` is passed an entire class object by value. In Borland C++, this is what happens. Function `main()` declares one `auto` variable, but the compiler looks ahead and sees that an object is passed by value into a function. The compiler then reserves room in the stack frame for *two* objects, the `auto` and the function argument. When the function `report_count()` is called, the compiler uses the copy initializer constructor to put a copy of the objects on the stack as an argument. Passing by value does *not* mean that the function necessarily gets a byte-by-byte copy of an object. What the function gets is whatever the copy initializer prepares.

Returning a class object by value is different from returning a structure. In Chapter 1 you saw how functions return structures by value by performing a byte copy of the structure. Class objects are returned using the copy-initializer constructor. Consider the code in Listing 2.16.

Listing 2.16. Returning objects by value.

```
// include the header file for class Counter

Counter get_an_object()
{
        static Counter object(30);
        return object;
}


void main()
{
        Counter object = get_an_object();
}
```

The function `get_an_object()` is declared to return a complete object by value. When the return statement is encountered, the copy-initializer constructor is invoked to copy the object into a destination. When `main()` invokes `get_an_object()`, it passes an invisible pointer to a stack frame area into which `get_an_object()` is expected to copy the return value. As in the case of passing objects as arguments, returning objects by value yields whatever results the copy initializer gives. This may not necessarily be a byte-by-byte copy operation. For example, if a class contains pointers, the copy initializer may choose to initialize them independently rather than simply copy the pointer values from another object.

You cannot return an object from a function without explicitly creating the object. Assume that the following function, which creates and returns an object of class `Counter`, exists:

```
Counter get_another_object()
{
        return Counter(2);
}
```

This function might be invoked like this:

```
void main()
{
        Counter object = get_another_object();
}
```

In the preceding code, function `get_another_object()` uses the class name `Counter` almost like a variable. The function `get_another_object()` creates a temporary object using the copy initializer, then copies the object out of the function using the same constructor again. In Borland C++, the temporary object and the final returned object are the same object. When `main()` invokes `get_another_object()`, the usual invisible pointer is passed that references an empty object in `main()`'s stack frame. This empty object is used in `get_an_object()`, both for the temporary object and for the return object. Other compilers may handle these details differently.

Destructors

Destructors are in the same category as constructors. They are used to carry out certain operations that are necessary when an object is no longer used. Normally destructors carry out the reverse operation of the constructor. If you made a file class, the destructor would probably contain code to close files. If a class's constructor allocates dynamic storage for the class's members, the destructor relinquishes this storage. There are a few important differences between constructors and destructors:

1. Destructors can be `virtual`; constructors can't.
2. Destructors can't be passed arguments.
3. Only one destructor can be declared for a given class.

As for constructors, C++ reserves a special name for a destructor—the name of the class, preceded by a tilde (~). The tilde is supposedly a mnemonic device for deletion, because it is normally used in unary expressions to indicate one's complement, which inverts ones into zeroes and vice versa. The destructor is the inverse of the constructor.

public Destructors

Normally destructors are declared `public` so that they can be used by generic class users. Declaring `private` or `protected` destructors is a practice used only on certain occasions, and is illustrated shortly. Destructors have no return type; it is an error to declare even a `void` return type. Here's an example of a destructor:

```
// this goes in the class declaration
~Counter();

// definition
Counter::~Counter()
{
        printf("\nAnother Counter object being destroyed !");
}
```

Constructors and destructors are elegant ways of wrapping the actions of a class between well-defined functions. These functions—the constructor and the destructor—act like braces enclosing a series of operations, much like a compound expression in C++ syntax. I refer to this enclosing as a *functional closure* and describe it in more detail in later chapters. A class could be written to handle all graphics output in a program. Such a class might be declared like this:

```
class Graphics {

public:

        Graphics();
        void DrawCircle(int x, int y, int radius);
        void DrawDot(int x, int y);
        // other graphics functions
        ~Graphics();
};
```

The constructor is called automatically by the compiler whenever a `Graphics` object is created. This constructor then initializes the graphics system, sets up the hardware as necessary, initializes the display, and so on. The destructor is called when the graphics system is no longer used, perhaps at the end of the program. The nice part is that the destructor is called automatically so that there is no chance of you forgetting to call it. The destructor is used to close the graphics device, restore the display to its previous state, and relinquish any memory allocated to the object. There are many kinds of objects that utilize functional closures, as is shown in the section on Microsoft Windows programming in Chapter 8.

private Destructors

As with just about any part of C++, you can get exotic with destructors. Most of the time, objects are designed for the benefit of the generic user, requiring constructors and destructors to be `public`. In some cases, once objects are created, they should not be allowed to be destroyed by the user. This is when you need `private` destructors. Note that declaring a class with `private` destructors entails that no `auto`, `static`, or `global` objects of that class can be created, since they could not be destroyed later.

Note that in Borland C++, any objects allocated dynamically in your program also should be destroyed before exiting to DOS. Although exiting with objects still in existence does

not cause an error, it is not recommended and probably indicates a bug in your program. Objects allocated dynamically can be created, but they can't be destroyed explicitly through the use of the `delete` operator. To destroy such objects, you need to do one of the following:

1. Declare a `public` member function that destroys the object.
2. Declare a `friend` class to the class, and have one of its member functions destroy the object.

Because `friend` classes haven't been discussed yet, Listing 2.17 provides an example for only the first case.

Listing 2.17. A class with a `private` destructor.

```
class PrivateExample {

private:
        int* value;
        ~PrivateExample() {delete value;}
public:
        PrivateExample() {value = new int [10];}
        void Delete() {delete this;}
};


static PrivateExample object1;            // can't do
PrivateExample object2;                   // can't do

void main()
{
        PrivateExample object3;           // can't do
        static PrivateExample object4;    // can't do

        // this is ok
        PrivateExample* object5 = new PrivateExample;
        delete object5;                   // can't do

        object5->Delete();                // this is ok
}
```

The *friend* Keyword

Sometimes you need two classes that are so close conceptually that you would like one to have unrestricted access to the members of the other. Consider, for example, a linked list implementation: you need a class to represent individual nodes and one to handle the list itself. The list members are accessed via the list manager, but the manager must have complete access to the members of the node class.

A `friend` class solves problems of this type. A `friend` has access to the `private`, `protected`, and `public` members of a class. A `friend` can be another class or a function. A class that hasn't been declared yet can be referenced as a `friend` like this:

```
class Node {
        friend class ObjectList;   // introduces the class
                                   // ObjectList into
                                   // the same scope as the
                                   // class Node
        int value;                 // declare private members
        Node* predecessor;
        Node* successor;
public:
        void Value(int i) {value = i;} // declare a public
};

class ObjectList {              // finally the declaration
                                // of the class, which is
                                // already in scope
private:
        Node* head;             // this class just
                                // handles Node objects

        Node* tail;
        Node* current;
public:
        void InsertNode(Node*) {};
        void DeleteNode(Node*) {};
        int CurrentObject(Node* node) {return node->value;}
};
```

The following statement demonstrates how a `friend` declaration is also equivalent to the incomplete class declaration

```
class ObjectList;
```

as far as the scope of identifier `ObjectList` is concerned. Incomplete declarations are used as a method of *forward referencing,* or introducing an identifier into scope before a complete declaration. The same class or function can be declared `friend` in more than one class.

You also can declare a nonmember function as a `friend` before the function identifier is in scope. For example,

```
class Node {
        friend int GetObject(Node*);
        int value;
        Node* predecessor;
        Node* successor;
```

```
public:
        void Value(int i) {value = i;}
};

int GetObject(Node* n)
{
        return n->value;
}
```

Properties of *friends*

Functions and classes declared `friend` to other classes enjoy special privileges. The concept of having a `friend` is new in C++, and programs sometimes depend on certain properties of friendship to work. Consider the following scenario. If function `foo()` is a `friend` of class `B`, and class `B` is derived from class `A`, does `foo()` also have access to the data members of class `A`? The answer is yes, because the data of class `A` is an integral part of class `B`.

Note that the `friend` relationship is not inherited. Assume `A` is a `friend` of `B`, and `C` is derived from `A`. It doesn't follow that `C` is a `friend` of `B`. Inheritance is described in Chapter 3.

The `friend` property is not transitive. If class `A` is a `friend` of class `B`, and `B` is a `friend` of `C`, `A` is not automatically a `friend` of `C`. Of course, `A` can be *declared* a `friend` to `C`.

Friendship in C++ is not necessarily mutual. In more mathematical terms, the `friend` property is not commutative. If `A` is a `friend` of `B`, it doesn't follow that `B` is a `friend` of `A`. To make two classes mutual `friends`, each must be declared a `friend` of the other.

A function declared `friend` to a class has access to all the data of the class, regardless of whether the declaration appears in the `private`, `protected`, or `public` sections. In the following examples, class `Friend` always has access to all the data members in classes `A`, `B`, and `C`:

```
// class Friend can access all A's data members
class A {
private:
        friend class Friend;
        int a1;
protected:
        int a2;
public:
        int a3;
};

// class Friend can also access all B's data members
class B {
private:
        int b1;
```

```
protected:
        friend class Friend;
        int b2;
public:
        int b3;
};

// class friend can also access all C's data members
class C {
private:
        int a1;
protected:
        int a2;
public:
        friend class Friend;
        int a3;
};
```

So it doesn't matter which section you put a `friend` declaration in. Often the `friend` declaration is put in the first section (regardless of whether it is `private`, `protected`, or `public`) to make it more obvious. When declaring `friend` functions, the declaration is usually put where an equivalent member function would have occurred. For example, consider overloading the stream insertion operator for a class `A`.

```
class A {
public:
        A();
        void Display();
        friend ostream& operator<<(ostream&, A&);
        // other member functions
};
```

Here the `friend` function was declared between other member functions because that is probably where you would look for it. The only restriction on `friend` declarations is that they occur somewhere inside the class declaration.

Advanced Section

This section covers techniques used by expert programmers to solve special kinds of problems. If you are new to C++, I suggest you skip this part of the chapter and go directly to Chapter 3.

Pointers to Member Functions

Member functions of class objects can sometimes be handled the same way as regular ANSI C functions. Just as it is possible to declare a generic pointer to an object's data member, it also is possible to declare a pointer to an object's member function and then invoke the function indirectly through the pointer. Consider the code in Listing 2.18.

Listing 2.18. Using pointers to member functions.

```
class Example {
          long value;
          int time;
public:
          long get_value() {return value;}
          long get_time() {return time + value;}
};

void main()
{
          long (Example::*fp)() = &Example::get_value;
          Example e;

          // invoke Example::get_value() indirectly
          long v = (e.*fp)();

          // invoke Example::get_time() indirectly
          fp = &Example::get_time;
          long t = (e.*fp)();
}
```

The notation is a bit awkward. Maybe that's why some programmers avoid it. The pointer `fp` is used to invoke two separate functions of class `Example`. The same pointer can be used as long as it is used with member functions accepting the same number and type of arguments and returning the same type of arguments. If the pointer is used with member functions requiring arguments, it needs to be declared differently, as shown in Listing 2.19.

Listing 2.19. Pointers to member functions with arguments.

```
#include <string.h>


class Example {
          long value;
          char name [10];
public:
          long set_value(long);
          char* set_name(char*);
};

long Example::set_value(long v)
{
          value = v;
          return value;
}
```

continues

Listing 2.19. continued

```
char* Example::set_name(char* string)
{
         if (strlen(string) < 10)
           strcpy(name, string);
         return name;
}

void main()
{
         long (Example::*fp)(long) = &Example::set_value;
         Example e;

         // invoke Example::set_value() indirectly
         long new_value = 5;
         long v = (e.*fp)(new_value);

         // invoke Example::set_name() indirectly
         char* (Example::*fp1)(char*) = &Example::set_name;
         char* id = "Borland C++";
         char* new_name = (e.*fp1)(id);
         new_name = (e.*fp1)("Borland");
}
```

The preceding code shows three different function calls through pointers. A further variation exists. The function call also can be used with pointers to objects. Here's an example with class `Example`:

```
void main()
{
         // declare an object
         Example example;

         // declare a pointer to it
         Example* e = &example;

         // use a pointer to object
         long (Example::*fp)(long) = &Example::set_value;
         long v = (e->*fp)(103);
}
```

It is illegal to invoke non-`static` member functions without referencing a specific object, whether by value or by pointer. `static` members are different, and pointers to `static` member functions must be declared differently. In fact, `static` members *cannot* be invoked in reference to an object or a pointer to an object. Listing 2.20 is an example.

Listing 2.20. Pointers to `static` member functions.

```
class StaticExample {
public:
          static int foo();
          static int woo();
};

int value;                     // define a global

int StaticExample::foo() {
  return value;          // remember: static functions can't
                         // access data members because they
                         // have no this pointer.
}

int StaticExample::woo() {
  return 3;
}

void main()
{
          int (*fp)() = &StaticExample::foo;
          (*fp)();

          fp = StaticExample::woo;
          (*fp)();
}
```

Arrays and Classes

All the array types declarable in ANSI C also can be declared in C++; however, the introduction of the class type makes a whole new series of arrays possible. The ones that are probably most unusual and interesting are these:

- Arrays of class objects
- Arrays of pointers to class objects
- Arrays of object data members
- Arrays of pointers to class data members
- Arrays of pointers to class member functions
- Arrays of pointers to `static` data members

Of course, other variations and permutations are possible, but the ones I list can be considered the point of departure for more exotic declarations. Each type is described separately.

Arrays of Class Objects

If you can declare an object of a class type, it follows that you must be able to declare an array of objects. The syntax is just like declaring arrays of structures, as shown in Listing 2.21.

Listing 2.21. Using arrays of class objects.

```
#include <stdio.h>

class Value {
          int value;
public:
          Value() {value = 0;}
          Value(int v) {value = v;}
          int GetValue() {return value;}
          void SetValue(int v) {value = v;}
};

Value bills [10];

Value coins [10] = {
  0, 1, 2, 3, 4, 5, 6, 7, 8, 9
};

void main()
{
  for (int i = 0; i < 10; i++)
    printf("\nbills [%d] = %d", i, bills [i]. GetValue() );
  for (i = 0; i < 10; i++)
    printf("\ncoins [%d] = %d", i, coins [i]. GetValue() );
}
```

For each member of an array that is created, the compiler invokes an appropriate class constructor. If such a constructor is not found, an error is generated.

The array `bill` is not initialized in Listing 2.21. This causes the compiler to invoke the default constructor for class `Value` for each member in the array. The array `coins` is initialized in the definition. The compiler invokes the constructor

```
Value::Value(int v);
```

for each member of the array. The member functions (and data members) of the array elements are accessed using the same notation as arrays of structures.

```
printf("\nbills [%d] = %d", i, bills [i]. GetValue() );
```

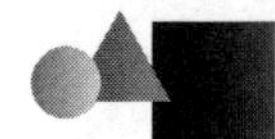

Arrays of Pointers to Class Objects

Arrays of this type are slightly more complicated than arrays of class objects, but the declaration syntax is very similar. Listing 2.22 is an example with class `Value`.

Listing 2.22. Arrays of pointers to class objects.

```
#include <stdio.h>
// include the header file for class Value

Value* bills [3] = {
  new Value(0),
  new Value(1),
  new Value(2)
};
Value* coins [3];

void main()
{
  for (int i = 0; i < 3; i++)
    printf("\nbills [%d] = %d", i, bills [i]->GetValue() );

  for (i = 0; i < 3; i++) {

    // initialize the pointers
    coins [i] = new Value;

     // use the array elements
     printf("\ncoins [%d] = %d", i, coins [i]->GetValue() );
          delete coins [i];
  }
}
```

Notice how the array `bills` is initialized directly with objects allocated from dynamic storage. The compiler automatically invokes the constructor

```
Value::Value(int)
```

for each member of `bills`. Array `coins` is not initialized in the declaration, so no constructors are invoked for it. Function `main()` shows how to use the pointers to access the member functions. The notation is similar to that used with arrays of pointers to structures.

Arrays of Object Data Members

It is perfectly legitimate to declare a pointer to a class object's member variable, which implies that you also can make an array out of such pointers. Arrays of object data members are similar to traditional ANSI C arrays. Listing 2.23 is an example.

Listing 2.23. Arrays of object data members.

```
class SomeData {
public:
          int data;
          SomeData() {data = 0;}
          SomeData(int d) {data = d;}
};

SomeData d1(15), d2;

int Stuff [3] = {
  d1.data,
  d2.data,
  12
};
```

Array `Stuff` just contains integers. Two objects of class `SomeData` are created and initialized. Then they are used in the initialization of array `Stuff`, along with an ordinary integer constant. At this point the array `Stuff` contains the values `{15, 0, 12}`, and can be handled like any array of integers.

Arrays of Pointers to Class Data Members

Pointers to class data members can really be handy, because they give you the potential to reference a whole range of variables in a class. Arrays of pointers merely extend this power. Of special interest here is the declaration of such an array, with possible initialization. Listing 2.24 is an example.

Listing 2.24. Arrays of pointers to class data members.

```
// declare a class with some public data members
class X {
public:
          int value;
          int total;
          int count;
          X(int i) {value = i; total = count = 0;}
          X() {value = total = count = 0;}
};

// define and initialize an array of pointers to
// class data members
int X::*variable [] = {
  &X::value,
  &X::total,
  &X::count
};
```

```
// create some initialized global objects
X a(1), b(304);

// use a pointer to class data member
void IncrementMember(X* object, int X::*member)
{
        object->*member = 3;
}

void main()
{
        // use the array of pointers with global objects
        IncrementMember(&a, variable [0]);
        IncrementMember(&b, variable [1]);

        // create an auto variable
        X* c = new X(-13);

        // use the array of pointers with an auto object
        IncrementMember(c, variable [2]);
}
```

Arrays of Pointers to Class Member Functions

A pointer to a class member function is similar in nature to a pointer to a class data member. Listing 2.25 is an example of an array of such pointers.

Listing 2.25. Arrays of pointers to class member functions.

```
// declare a class with some public member function
class X {
public:
        int value;
        int total;
        int count;
        void SetValue(int v) {value = v;}
        void SetTotal(int t) {total = t;}
        void SetCount(int c) {count = c;}
};

// define and initialize an array of pointers to
// class function members
typedef void (X::*FP)(int);
FP function [] = {
  &X::SetValue,
```

continues

Listing 2.25. continued

```
  &X::SetTotal,
  &X::SetCount
};

// create a global object
X a;

// use a pointer to class member function
void SetMember(void (X::*foo)(int), int v )
{
        (a.*foo)(v);
}

void main()
{
        // use the array of pointers with global objects
        SetMember(&X::SetValue, 5);
        SetMember(&X::SetTotal, -13);
        int start = 10;
        SetMember(&X::SetCount, start);
}
```

You can declare the array `f` pointers without the `typedef` like this:

```
// define array without typedef
void (X::*table[])(int) = {
  &X::SetValue,
  &X::SetTotal,
  &X::SetCount
};
```

Notice how the same function `SetMember()` is used to indirectly invoke different member functions of class `X`. The function receives as an argument an integer value, representing the offset of a function in a table of function pointers in class `X`. All `SetMember()` knows about this function is that it requires an `int` argument and returns nothing.

Arrays of Pointers to *static* Data Members

`static` data members are similar to standard ANSI C `static` variables, as far as pointers go. Listing 2.26 is an example that uses an array of pointers to `static` members.

Listing 2.26. Arrays of pointers to `static` data members.

```
class S {
public:
        static int count;
};

class T {
public:
        static int value;
};

class U {
public:
        static int total;
};

// define the static variables after declaring them
int S::count= 1;
int T::value = 2;
int U::total = 3;

int* static_integers [] = {
  &S::count,
  &T::value,
  &U::total
};


void SetVariable(int* data, int value)
{
        *data= value;
}

void main()
{
     SetVariable(&S::count, 18);
     SetVariable(static_integers [0], 54);
     SetVariable(static_integers [1], 0);
     SetVariable(static_integers [2], -113);
}
```

The function `SetVariable()` is invoked with a pointer to a `static` data member. But as you can see, the function is declared to accept a simple pointer to an integer. Thus the same function could be used to modify any `int` variable defined outside a class. Note that the three `static` data members are defined before being used in the array initialization.

The Anatomy of a Member Function Call

C++ was designed with efficiency as a primary concern. Given the frequency of function calls in typical programs, it was important to reduce the overhead of a call as much as possible. `inline` functions provide an excellent (although not necessarily perfect) solution, at the expense of code size. Regular member functions require some overhead, but little.

This section describes how both kinds of member functions are called at the assembly language level in Borland C++ in the medium memory model.

> **NOTE**
>
> To make the compiler use `inline` functions, you have to disable the option `Out-of-line inline functions` in the Options ¦ Project ¦ +Compiler ¦ Debugging menu.

Listing 2.27 is a short C++ program that uses both `inline` and regular member function calls.

Listing 2.27. A short program illustrating `inline` and not-`inline` member function calls.

```
class FunctionCalls {
          int value;
public:
          void Inline(int v) {value = v;}
          void NotInline(int v);
};

void FunctionCalls::NotInline(int v)
{
          value = v;
}

void main()
{
          // create an auto object
          FunctionCalls f;

          // invoke the inline member
          f.Inline(3);

          // invoke the out-of-line member
          f.NotInline(5);
}
```

Inspecting the code with Turbo Debugger, the following assembly language is generated for function `main()`:

```
_main: void main() {
  push      bp                         ; save previous frame
  mov       bp, sp                     ; start a new frame
  dec       sp                         ; allocate space for
  dec       sp                         ; auto variable

#T#19: f.Inline(3);

  mov       word ptr [bp - 02], 0003   ; inline function
                                       ; call is replaced
                                       ; by its expansion

#T#22: f.NotInline(5);

  mov       ax, 0005
  push      ax                         ; push argument
  lea       ax, [bp - 02]
  push      ax                         ; push this pointer
  push      cs                         ; push cs register
                                       ; (for medium memory
                                       ; model)

  call      FunctionCalls::NotInline

  pop       cx                         ; re-balance the stack
  pop       cx

#T#23: }

  mov       sp, bp                     ; restore stack pointer
  pop       bp                         ; and prior frame pointer
  retf
```

The code produced would have been slightly different if compiled in different memory models. There are basically two interesting things to observe in the assembly language output:

1. The `inline` member function call requires 0 bytes of overhead and is expanded directly into an assignment statement using `private` variable `FunctionCalls::value`.
2. When calling a regular member function, the `this` pointer is passed as if it was the first explicit argument in the function call. Consequently, because arguments are pushed in the right-to-left order of appearance, the `this` pointer is pushed as the last argument. If the invisible `this` was visible in the function call, the C++ code would look something like the following:

```
f.NotInline(&f, 5);
```

The `cs register` is pushed in the preceding code only because I used the medium memory model.

Class Templates

A C++ class is usually designed to handle some kind of data type. Often the functionality of a class also makes sense conceptually with other data types. If you consider a class being a framework around a data type, supporting various operations on that type, then it could make sense to isolate the data type altogether from the class, allowing a single class to deal with a generic data type `T`. Such a class is not really a class, but a description of a class, and is called a *class template.* A class template is used by the compiler to create a real class at compilation time, using a specific data type.

Consider building a class to handle linked lists. The operations on linked lists are not dependent on the type of data handled by the linked list. A single class template can be used to support generic linked lists, integers, structures, or any other defined data type. To declare a class template for a linked list class, you would use the notation in Listing 2.28.

Listing 2.28. Declaring a template class.

```
template<class T> class List {

public:

     List();
     void add(T&);
     void remove(T&);
     void detach(T& t) {remove(t);}
     ~List();
};

template<class T> List<T>::List()
{
     //...
}

template<class T> void List<T>::add(T&)
{
     //...
}

template<class T> void List<T>::remove(T&)
{
     //...
```

```
}

template<class T> List<T>::~List()
{
     //...
}
```

The class declaration begins with the keyword `template`, and then has the expression

```
<class T>
```

to declare a generic data type `T` that will be used inside the class. If you declare a class template and then fail to use any generic `T` data types, Borland C++ 4.5 doesn't complain. A warning message might be appropriate, similar to the warning

```
Parameter 'xyz' is never used
```

that occurs in a function if you declare but don't use a function argument. Apart from the small change in declaration syntax, using a class template is not much different from other classes. When you instantiate a class template, passing a specific data type, you create a *template class*. Don't confuse a class template with template class. The notation is a bit confusing, particularly for people whose mother tongue is not English, but that's the way it is, folks. When you use a template class, the compiler automatically builds all the member functions to deal with the data type you specify. Consider the code in Listing 2.29, which uses the `List` class template.

Listing 2.29. Using template classes.

```
// include the header file for class List

void main()
{
     List<long> phone_numbers;
     List<char*> club_members;

     static long number = 5551000;
     phone_numbers.add(number);

     static char* name = "Michael";
     club_members.add(name);
}
```

The compiler generates code to deal with both `int` and `char*` data types, and generates a complete class for each data type. If a class template declares `static` data members or `virtual` functions, the template classes generated each have their own copies of `static` data members and their own `virtual` functions.

Member functions of a class template require special notation to declare their return type. If a function returns an `int`, it is declared something like this:

```
template<class T> int MyClass<T>::remove(T&)
{
     //...
}
```

where the return type is declared after the `template<class T>` expression.

To declare a class template with more than one argument, you use a syntax similar to that in Listing 2.30.

Listing 2.30. Declaring a class template with multiple arguments.

```
#include <stdlib.h>

template<class T, int i, long L>
class MyClass {

     T* object;
     long offset;
     int size, length;

public:

     MyClass();
     MyClass(int);
     int Foo(long);
};

template<class T, int i, long L>
MyClass<T, i, L>::MyClass()
{
     // use a variable declared with the class template
     offset = L;

     // use a variable declared with the member function
     size = i;

     // use a variable declared both with the class template
     // and with the member function
     object = new T();
}

template<class T, int i, long L>
MyClass<T, i, L>::MyClass(int x)
{
     // assign class template arguments to
     // a private variable
```

```
        length = i;
        offset = L;

        // use a function argument
        size = x;

        // use another class template argument
        object = new T();
}

template<class T, int a, long L>
int MyClass<T, a, L>::Foo(long value)
{
        return (value & 0xFF);
}
```

The class template `MyClass` is declared to take the arguments of type `class T`, `int`, and `char*`. These are arguments to the class as a whole, not arguments to any of the class's member functions. You can use these class arguments only inside the member functions for the class template. To use the `MyClass` class template, you would write code like Listing 2.31.

Listing 2.31. Using template classes with multiple arguments.

```
// include the header file for the class template MyClass

class List {};

void main()
{
        MyClass<int, 5, 100> x(2);
        MyClass<float, 100, 200> y(3);
        MyClass<List, 100, 300> z();
}
```

You also can declare default arguments for a class template.

Nested Template Classes

Is it possible to use a template class in the declaration of another template class? Yes, and sometimes such nested class templates are a perfect solution, especially when dealing with so-called container classes. A container class is a class having the purpose of managing groups of other classes. Consider implementing a generic linked list. First a class template needs to be defined to handle each node in the list. Here is a possible approach:

```
// create a class template for the nodes in a
// linked list
template<class R> class Node {

     Node<R>* previous;
     Node<R>* next;
     R* data;

public:

     Node(Node<R>*, Node<R>*, R*);
     ~Node();
};

template<class R>
Node<R>::Node(Node<R>* p, Node<R>* n, R* d)
{
     previous = p;
     next = n;
     data = d;
}

template<class R>
Node<R>::~Node()
{
     delete data;
}
```

Now the generic `Node<R>` class can be used by a container class to implement the actual linked list, using code like this:

```
// use the previous class template in another
// class template
template<class R> class List {

     Node<R>* head;
     Node<R>* current;

public:

     List();
     void add(R*);
     void remove();
     ~List();
};

template<class R>
List<R>::List()
{
     head = current = 0;
}
```

```
template<class R>
void List<R>::add(R* object)
{
     if (!head) {
       // create the first node of the list
       head = current = new Node<R>(0, 0, object);
     }

     else {
       // splice a new node into the list
       // ...
     }
}

template<class R>
void List<R>::remove()
{
     // unsplice the current node from the list
     // ...

     // delete the node
     delete current;
}

template<class R>
void List<R>::~List()
{
     // delete all the elements in the list
     current = head;
     while (current)
       remove();
}
```

When you create a `List<R>` class, the compiler also automatically creates a `Node<R>` class. The generic class `List<R>` manages both `List<R>` objects and `<R>` objects, even though the declaration for the class mentions only an argument of type `<class R>`.

Class Templates with Multiple Generic Arguments

So far, all the class templates shown have dealt with a single generic argument. It is possible, and sometimes perfectly reasonable, to use multiple generic arguments with a class template. Consider modifying the previous `Node<R>` and `List<R>` classes to support three different objects at each node. Listing 2.32 shows how the code would need to be modified.

Listing 2.32. Using multiple generic arguments in a class template.

```
// create a class template to store three different
// data types at each node
template<class R, class S, class T> class Node {

     Node<R, S, T>* previous;
     Node<R, S, T>* next;
     R* r_data;
     S* s_data;
     T* t_data;

public:

     Node(Node<R, S, T>*,
          Node<R, S, T>*,
          R*, S*, T*);
     ~Node();
};

template<class R, class S, class T>
Node<R, S, T>::Node(Node<R, S, T>* p,
              Node<R, S, T>* n,
              R* r, S* s, T* t)
{
     previous = p;
     next = n;
     r_data = r;
     s_data = s;
     t_data = t;
}

template<class R, class S, class T>
Node<R, S, T>::~Node()
{
     delete r_data;
     delete s_data;
     delete t_data;
}


// use the previous class template in another
// class template
template<class R, class S, class T> class List {

     Node<R, S, T>* head;
     Node<R, S, T>* current;

public:
```

```
    List();
    void add(R*);
    void remove();
    ~List();
};

template<class R, class S, class T>
List<R, S, T>::List()
{
    head = current = 0;
}

template<class R, class S, class T>
void List<R, S, T>::add(R* object)
{
    if (!head) {
      // create the first node of the list
      head = current =
        new Node<R, S, T>(0, 0, object);
    }

    else {
      // splice a new node into the list
      // ...
    }
}

template<class R, class S, class T>
void List<R, S, T>::remove()
{
    // unsplice the current node from the list
    // ...

    // delete the node
    delete current;
}

template<class R, class S, class T>
void List<R, S, T>::~List()
{
    // delete all the elements in the list
    current = head;
    while (current)
      remove();
}
```

The notation with multiple generic arguments is essentially the same as with one generic argument. You can declare as many generic arguments as you want. You can declare both generic and typed arguments for the same class, like this:

```
template<class FIRST, int i, class SECOND, char* name>
class A {

public:

     A();
     // ...
};
```

Class Templates as *friends*

It is possible to declare a class template as a `friend` to another class. The implication is that any subsequent function generated from that class template also will be a `friend` to the class. Consider the code in Listing 2.33.

Listing 2.33. A class template as a `friend`.

```
// declare a complete class template a friend
template<class A>
class Small {

     friend class Large<B>;

public:

     Small();
     // ...
};

template<class A>
class Large {

public:

     Large();
     // ...
};
```

Now any template class of type `Large<A>` will be a `friend` to `Small<A>`. The notation is quite powerful, because it determines a `friend` relationship not for one class, but for a whole class of classes.

Function Templates

Templates can be used not only with classes but also with functions. Sometimes you encounter a situation in which the same function would be useful, but with different

argument types. C programmers typically solved this problem using macros, but the solution is not ideal. Consider needing to determine the greater of two entities. The following macro handles all data types:

```
#define max(a, b) ( (x > y) ? x : y)
```

Such a macro has been used in C programs for years, but it does have its own problems. The macro works, but it prevents the compiler from checking the types involved in the comparison. You could invoke the macro with an integer and a `char` pointer, and no warnings or error messages would be generated.

You could write a function to compare two values, using code like this

```
int max(int a, int b)
{
     return a > b ? a : b;
}
```

but the function would handle only integer types, or data types that can be promoted to integer types. The function is not able to handle other data types, such as `float` or `char*`. If you're interested in dealing only with scalar numbers, you might write a function like this:

```
double max(double a, double b)
{
     return a > b ? a : b;
}
```

This function would handle all data types from `char` up to `double`, by having the compiler perform integer promotions on the arguments. There are at least two significant limitations to the latter function.

1. The return value is always of type `double`, regardless of the argument types passed to `max(...)`. Using such a `max(...)` function in an expression may cause problems. Consider the code

   ```
   void main()
   {
     cout << "Max('3', '5') is "
          << max('3', '5')
          << endl;
   }
   ```

   The code would display the following:

   ```
   Max('3', '5') is 53
   ```

   The problem is that the stream inserter operator assumed it was dealing with a `double` and printed a numeric *53* instead of the character *5*. An explicit typecast would fix this particular problem, but I hardly consider a typecast a general solution.

2. Only data types that can be promoted to `double` are handled. The function `max(double, double)` would not be capable of dealing with pointers, structures, or class objects.

C++ uses a new kind of declaration to implement functions like `max(...)`. The new declaration is called a *function template.* Using the function template, a generalized `max(...)` function would be declared like this:

```
template<class T> T max(T a, T b)
{
     return a > b ? a : b;
}
```

The declaration starts out with the word `template`, which is a new reserved C++ keyword. Next comes the expression `<class T>`, which indicates that some variable of generic name `T` (you can use any identifier you want in place of `T`) will be used in the function. Function `max(...)` is thus declared to take two generic `T` objects, and to return a `T` object. A template function is not restricted to handling class variables: any data type can be used, such as structures, pointers, integers, and so on.

When you use a function template with a specific data type, you create a *template function.* As with class templates, the notation is confusing, so be careful to distinguish a function template from a template function. The code in Listing 2.34 makes use of a template function.

Listing 2.34. A simple program with a template function.

```
#include <iostream.h>

template<class whatever>
whatever max(whatever a, whatever b)
{
     return a > b ? a : b;
}

void main()
{
     cout << "Max(3, 5) is "
          << max(3, 5)
          << endl;

     cout << "Max('3', '5') is "
          << max('3', '5')
          << endl;
}
```

When the compiler sees a template function call, it generates a function to handle the data types used in the call statement. No implicit conversions are attempted, such as integer promotions. If the first argument is an integer, the second argument also must be an integer. If the first argument is a double, the second also must be a double.

Using a template function frees you from having to write a different function for each possible set of arguments that you might need in a program, and also allows the compiler to keep track of argument types. You can overload a template function just like any other function, with the advantage that implicit conversions can be applied to the overloading function, as shown in Listing 2.35.

Listing 2.35. Overloading a template function.

```
#include <stdlib.h>
int max(char* a, char* b)
{
     int x, y;
     x = atoi(a);
     y = atoi(b);
     return x > y ? x : y;
}
```

When the function `max(char*, char*)` is called in your program, the compiler will not attempt to generate a template function for it, but will use your explicit `max(char*, char*)` function. Although template functions are very useful in general, templates are especially useful with class objects.

Inheritance

One of the most extraordinary aspects about living things is their ability to generate offspring with characteristics similar to their progenitors. Nature took billions of years to generate life as we know it, and the summation of that effort is passed on to every descendant of every species. This is the result of inheritance. No life, with its infinite complexity, would be possible without inheritance.

If inheritance led to such astounding results in nature, it should also be useful in computer software as a way of both propagating code for future use and reducing the complexity of code. This thought occurred to researchers back in the 60s and 70s, which led to the development of programming languages that use various forms of inheritance. Inheritance is probably the single feature in C++ that provides the most power to the class concept. In C++, the term *inheritance* applies only to classes and their features. Variables cannot inherit from other variables, and functions cannot inherit from other functions.

Inheritance allows you to continually build and extend classes developed by you or anyone else, with essentially no limit. Starting from the simplest class, you can derive increasingly complex classes that are not only easy to debug, but also simple in themselves.

The main thrust in a C++ project is toward developing classes that solve a given problem. These classes are generally built incrementally starting from basic, simple classes, using inheritance. Each time you derive a new class starting from a previous one, you can inherit some or all of the parent's features, adding new ones as needed. A complete project can have scores or hundreds of classes, but these classes are often derived from just a few basic ones. C++ is different from some object-oriented languages, because it allows not just single inheritance, but also multiple inheritance, which allows a class to be derived from more than one class at the same time, inheriting behaviors from all its ancestors.

Reusability

Reusability is a word you hear often in the object-oriented programming world. Reusability refers to taking a class and either instantiating it directly in your programs or using it as the basis for a new class that inherits some or all of its features. By deriving a class from a base class, you effectively reuse the code in the base class for your own needs. The concept parallels the work of nature: DNA might be considered a basic material, out of which any creature can be made. Every organism reuses DNA, utilizing its own variety of it. Reusability in C++ is amplified through inheritance.

Inheritance

All the previous descriptions may be interesting, but only the details offered through an actual program show what inheritance is and how it works. Here I provide a short example of two classes, the second of which inherits properties from the first.

```
class Box {
public:
      int width, height;
      void SetWidth(int w) {width = w;}
      void SetHeight(int h) {height = h;}

};
class ColoredBox: public Box {
public:
      int color;
      void SetColor(int c) {color = c;}
};
```

Using C++ terminology, class `Box` is called the *base class* for class `ColoredBox`, which in turn is called a *derived class*. Base classes are also sometimes called *parent classes*. Class `ColoredBox` is declared with only one function, but it also inherits two functions and two variables from its base class. Thus, the following code is possible:

```
//make an instance of ColoredBox
ColoredBox cb;
```

```
void main()
{
        // use member functions in ColoredBox
        cb.SetColor(5);             // noninherited
        cb.SetWidth(3);             // inherited
        cb.SetHeight(50);           // inherited
}
```

Notice how the inherited functions are used exactly like noninherited ones. Class `ColoredBox` didn't even have to mention the fact that functions `Box::SetWidth()` and `Box::SetHeight()` were inherited. This uniformity of expression is a great feature in C++. Using a class feature does not require you to know whether it was inherited or not, because the notation is invariant. In many classes there can be a whole string of base classes derived from other base classes. A class derived from such an inheritance tree would inherit characteristics from many different parents. In C++, however, you don't need to worry about where or when a feature was introduced in a class tree.

Power Through Inheritance

Deriving one class from another gives you a lot of flexibility at a low cost—in coding terms. Once you have a solid base class, you know that only the changes you make in the derived classes need debugging. But exactly how do you use a base class, and what kind of changes can you make to it? Again, many similarities exist between C++ and nature. Every new generation of a species varies from its predecessor; some generations are an improvement and some are not. Some of the offspring have better characteristics than their parents, some the same, some worse. Natural selection then takes over.

In a derived C++ class, you can do pretty much the same thing. When inheriting features from a parent, you can make the derived class extend them, restrict them, change them, eliminate them, or use them without any changes. All these variations can be grouped into two basic object-oriented techniques. The first is called *feature restriction*, which limits or eliminates a feature of the parent. The second is called *feature expansion*, which adds something to a parent feature. Both feature expansion and feature restriction are described in detail later in this chapter.

Limitations of C++ Inheritance

Whether and when one class is derived from another is purely a programmer's decision. This may seem obvious, but it is a limitation. The designer of a program must decide at compile time who inherits what from whom, and how and when the inheritance takes place. It's like families prearranging the wedding of their children just after birth: it may work, but it's inflexible.

Conceptually it is possible to have a system in which objects are completely dynamic, in the sense that they not only come and go according to runtime requirements, but they also spawn new derivatives of classes as well. Classes cross-inheriting from other classes would give rise to entirely new class libraries, unforeseen by the programmer. You might call this new type of inheritance *late inheritance*, given its relationship to late binding. Obviously dealing with this kind of situation is entirely beyond the scope of this book and C++. Late inheritance is really in the domain of artificial intelligence. Nevertheless, it illustrates the potential of inheritance in general.

A Different Perspective on Inheritance

Top-down structured programming has been used for years to develop software projects. Using this methodology, a problem is subdivided into increasingly smaller subproblems, until the subtasks are easily manageable. Essentially this subdivision leads to a top-level function that calls a plethora of lower-level functions, each of which use functions from even lower levels. In a sense, the higher-level functions *embody* features implemented in other functions. This notion is not too different from inheritance. Figure 3.1 shows a top-down program.

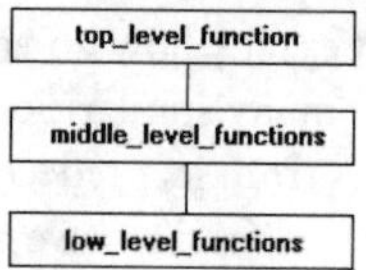

Figure 3.1. The basic architecture of a program developed using structured programming techniques.

The tree for a top-down program bears a striking similarity to the tree for class inheritance as shown in Figure 3.2.

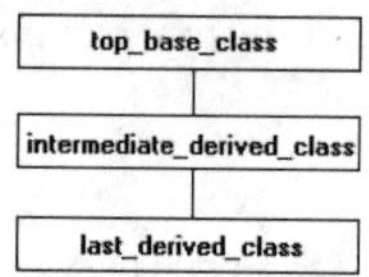

Figure 3.2. The basic architecture of a class hierarchy.

Considering only the graphs by themselves, the main difference between the two is in perspective. In the structured programming world, you look at the tree from the top. Functions at any given level in the tree invoke functions lower down. Lower-level functions have a narrower scope and have a more specialized behavior. In class inheritance, you normally have a class that inherits features from its parents. Thus, you look at the tree from the bottom to see what features it has.

Of course, there are lots of other differences between the two methods, but it is at least worth mentioning that their concepts are not completely disjointed.

Single Inheritance

If a class inherits characteristics from somewhere, it can have one or more parent classes. I start my description of inheritance with the simpler case, referred to as *single inheritance.* Most of the rules for single inheritance can be applied to multiple inheritance, but there are also some important differences.

When to Inherit

Anytime you build a new class, you should determine whether you can use a preexisting class as a base class. Often you find classes that provide *almost* the right behavior. These are good candidates to use, because you can inherit all the desired features and disable the unwanted ones. To disable a function in the parent class, you use a technique called *function overloading*, which is described in detail in Chapter 4, "Overloading." Try to inherit as many features as possible from preexisting classes, because this both reduces the size of your code and the time required for debugging.

What Can't Be Inherited

As in real life, in C++ not everything can be passed on through inheritance. This may initially be considered a drawback or an artificial limitation, but actually a few special cases are inconsistent by definition with inheritance:

1. Constructors.
2. Destructors.
3. User-defined new operators. These are described in Chapter 4.
4. User-defined assignment operators. These are described in Chapter 4.
5. `friend` relationships.

Derived classes automatically invoke the constructor of the base class when they are instantiated, but after they are constructed, the base class constructor is off-limits. Although base class constructors are inherited, they can only be invoked automatically by the compiler when a derived object is constructed. A base class constructor cannot be invoked explicitly in a derived class like other inherited functions. Consider the following code:

```
class Parent {
        int value;
```

```
public:
        Parent() {value = 0;}
        Parent(int v) {value = v;}
};

class Child: public Parent {
        int total;
public:
        Child(int t) {total = t;}
        void SetTotal(int t);
};

void Child::SetTotal(int t)
{
        Parent::Parent(i);     // you can't do this because
                               // the base class constructor
                               // is not inherited like other
                               // functions.
        total = t;
}
```

Similarly, destructors are meant to be invoked automatically when an object goes out of scope. Explicit invocation of a destructor is not allowed in a program.

The `friend` relationship is not inherited. This is similar to real life: Friends of your parents are not automatically friends of yours. Any `friend` relationships declared in classes of an inheritance tree do not propagate up or down in the tree.

Access Specifiers for Base Classes

When a class is derived from a base class, all the names in the base class automatically become `private` in the derived class. For example, consider the following code:

```
class First {
        int value;
public:
        void SetValue(int v) {value = v;}
};

class Second: First {
        int total;
public:
        void SetTotal(int t) {total = t;}
};
```

All the data and functions in class `First` become `private` members for class `Second`. This is the default behavior in C++, but it can easily be changed using base class access specifiers. These are the possible ones:

1. `private`. `private` is the default specifier if none is specified when a class is declared. All the inheritable (that is, `protected` and `public`) names in the base class are `private` in the derived class.
2. `public`. All the `public` names in the base class are `public` in the derived class, and all the `protected` names in the base class are `protected` in the derived class.

Base class access specifiers have no `protected` keyword, so you can't derive a class like this:

```
// can't do this !
class Second: protected First {...}
```

As it turns out, most of the time you'll be declaring derived classes with `public` base classes. It's too bad this isn't the default behavior, but the language implementors wanted to make sure that the base class names would be `public` only through explicit declaration.

Classes Designed to Be Inherited

Given the emphasis on reusability and inheritance in C++, most of the time you make classes that are used subsequently as base classes for other classes. The `private` and `public` access privileges that were defined in the first releases of C++ were deemed insufficient for use with inheritance, so the new access privilege `protected` was introduced. Any identifiers appearing in the `protected` section of a class declaration can be used inside the class implementation, but not by users of the class. `protected` names can be used by all classes derived from the class. This characteristic can be propagated indefinitely down an inheritance tree. Consider the inheritance tree in Figure 3.3 and the C++ code in Listing 3.1.

Listing 3.1. Propagation of `protected` access privileges.

```
class First {
          int value;
protected:
          void SetValue(int v) {value = v;}
};

class Second: public First {
          int total;
public:
          void SetTotal(int t);
};

void Second::SetTotal(int t)
{
          total = t;
```

continues

Listing 3.1. continued

```
        // use a protected member of the base class
        SetValue(t);
}

class Third: public Second {
        int count;
public:
        void SetCount(int c);
};

void Third::SetCount(int c)
{
        count = c;
        // use protected member of base class
        SetValue(c);
}
```

Both classes `Second` and `Third` have access to the protected names in class `First`.

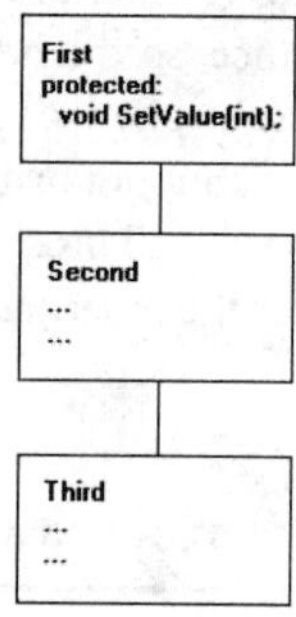

Figure 3.3. A simple inheritance tree with `protected` *members.*

Arguments Passed to a Base Class

When a derived class is instantiated, you often need to make use of a base class constructor that requires parameters. You can pass parameters to a base class constructor using a special notation. The code in Listing 3.2 illustrates this operation for both `inline` and non-`inline` constructors.

Listing 3.2. Passing parameters to a base class constructor.

```
class First {
        int a, b, c;
public:
        First(int x, int y, int z) {a = x; b = y; c = z;}
};

class Second: public First {
        int value;
public:
        Second(int d) : First(d, d+1, d+5) {value = d;}
        Second(int d, int e);
};

Second::Second(int d, int e) : First(d, e, 13)
{
        value = d + e;
}
```

The constructor `Second::Second(int)` is declared `inline`, and thus indicates the base class arguments right inside the class declaration. For non-`inline` constructors, `Second::Second(int, int)` shows the syntax. Any parameters passed to a base class should be valid *before* the body of the constructor is executed, because they are passed to the base class's constructor before the derived class's constructor is executed. I said *shouldn't* and not *can't*. If you really have to pass uninitialized variables to the base class, just be sure the base doesn't use them before you get a chance to initialize them yourself. For example, consider the code in Listing 3.3.

Listing 3.3. Passing uninitialized parameters to a base class.

```
#include <stdio.h>

class Next {
public:
        char* string;
        Next(char* cp) {string = cp;}
};
class Last: public Next {
        int value;
        char name [30];
public:
        Last(int d);
};
```

continues

Listing 3.3. continued

```
// call base class with a null pointer
Last::Last(int d) : Next( (char*) 0)
{
        sprintf(name, "%d", d);

        // initialize the base class variable now
        string = name;

        // save the integer value
        value = d;
}
```

The constructor `Last::Last(int)` is expected to pass a character pointer to its base class, but the pointer isn't known yet. `Last::Last(int)` is forced to pass a *null* pointer, just to make the constructor call work correctly. Inside the body of the derived class's constructor, the proper pointer is computed and used to initialize the base class. The technique works, but has its limitations.

1. If the argument expected by the base class is used to initialize other members, or must be passed to other base classes, you have a problem.
2. You can only defer initialization of members declared `protected` or `public` in the base class. When the base class constructor is called, it can access any data it wants in its class, including `private` data, but derived classes can't.

Order of Invocation of Constructors

When a class is instantiated, its constructor is invoked. If the class was a derived one, the base class constructor also must be called. The order of invocation is fixed in C++. First the base class is built. Then the derived class is built. If the base class is in turn derived, the process repeats recursively until a nonderived base class is reached. The inheritance tree in Figure 3.4 and the following code illustrate the point:

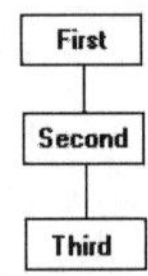

Figure 3.4. A simple inheritance tree.

```
class First { ... };
class Second: public First { ... };
class Third: public Second { ... }
```

When class `Third` is instantiated, the constructors are called like this:

```
First::First()
Second::Second()
Third::Third()
```

The preceding order makes sense, because a derived class is a specialization of a more general class. The specialized part is meant to be added on top of the more general one. This means the constructor for a derived class can use inherited features.

Order of Invocation of Destructors

Destructors for derived classes are called in the reverse order of the way the constructors are called. The same reasoning stands. First, the more specialized features are destroyed, then the more general ones. Thus, the order of destructor calls generated when an instantiation of class `Third` goes out of scope is

```
Third::~Third()
Second::~Second()
First::~First()
```

Seed Classes

In C++ you design classes to fulfill certain goals. Usually you start with a sketchy idea of class requirements, filling in more and more details as the project matures. Often you wind up with two classes that have certain similarities. To avoid duplicating code in these classes, you should split up the classes at this point, relegating the common features to a parent, and making separate derived classes for the different parts. Classes that are made only for the purpose of sharing code in derived classes are called *seed classes*. Seed classes are not necessarily abstract, but generally are not useful by themselves. Consider the example in Listing 3.4.

Listing 3.4. Two derived classes with common features.

```
class BookShelf {
        int      color;
        int      width, height;
        int      shelves;
public:
```

continues

Listing 3.4. continued

```
        BookShelf(int, int, int, int);
        int GetColor() {return color;}
        int GetWidth() {return width;}
        int GetHeight() {return height;}
        int GetShelves() {return shelves;}
};
class Desk {
        int     color;
        int     width, height;
        int     drawers;
        int     material;
public:
        Desk(int, int, int, int, int);
        int GetColor() {return color;}
        int GetWidth() {return width;}
        int GetHeight() {return height;}
        int GetDrawers() {return drawers;}
        int GetMaterial() {return material;}
};

BookShelf::BookShelf(int c, int w, int h, int s)
{
        color = c;
        width = w;
        height = h;
        shelves = s;
}

Desk::Desk(int w, int h, int c, int d, int m)
{
        width = w;
        height = h;
        color = c;
        drawers = d;
        material = m;
}
```

Here there are two classes: `BookShelf` and `Desk`. They have a few features in common, but they are also a little different. The constructor for `BookShelf` has four arguments, whereas the constructor for `Desk` has five. Moreover, the order of the arguments is different. Clearly the common features should be extracted and placed in a parent class. Listing 3.5 shows a possible solution.

Listing 3.5. Splitting up two classes and adding a seed class.

```
// create a common parent class
class Furniture {
          int       color;
          int       width, height;
public:
          Furniture(int, int, int);
          int GetColor() {return color;}
          int GetWidth() {return width;}
          int GetHeight() {return height;}
};

Furniture::Furniture(int c, int w, int h)
{
          color = c;
          width = w;
          height = h;
}

// use parent to simplify this class
class BookShelf: public Furniture {
          int       shelves;
public:
          BookShelf(int, int, int, int);
          int GetShelves() {return shelves;}
};


// use parent to simplify this class
class Desk: public Furniture {
          int       drawers;
          int       material;
public:
          Desk(int, int, int, int, int);
          int GetDrawers() {return drawers;}
          int GetMaterial() {return material;}
};


BookShelf::BookShelf(int c, int w, int h, int s) :
          // pass arguments to base class constructor
          Furniture(c, w, h)
{
          shelves = s;
}

Desk::Desk(int w, int h, int c, int d, int m) :
          // pass arguments to base class constructor
          Furniture(c, w, h)
```

continues

Listing 3.5. continued

```
{
        drawers = d;
        material = m;
}

void main()
{
        // use the two derived classes
        Desk d(1, 2, 3, 4, 5);
        BookShelf b(10, 11, 12, 13);
}
```

Sometimes you realize early that two classes will have common features, but you don't quite know where. You can nevertheless derive them from a provisional class, left empty until more details are learned (see Listing 3.6).

Listing 3.6. Using an empty class as a placeholder in an inheritance tree.

```
// tentative parent class
class Agglomerate { /* ... no info yet !... */ };

// assume this will inherit from Agglomerate
class String: public Agglomerate { /* ... */ };

// assume this will inherit from Agglomerate
class Directory: public Agglomerate { /* ... */ };
```

When a better understanding is reached for `String` and `Directory` classes, the common features can then be moved into `Agglomerate`, which for the moment acts as a holding place in the inheritance tree.

Type Conversions with Derived Classes

In C++ you normally deal not with single disparate classes, but with hierarchies of interrelated ones. This entails that at times you perform certain conversions between classes at different levels in the tree. Consider the following two classes:

```
class A {};
class B: public A {};
```

Because class B is derived from A, it follows that the inheritable members of A are available also to B. Thus, B is somewhat of a superset of A. It is thus possible to convert a B object into an A one, but not conversely. Listing 3.7 is an example.

Listing 3.7. Implicit type conversions between classes.

```
void main()
{
        A a;
        B b;

        A* ap = new A;
        B* bp = new B;

        a = b;                  // this is allowed
        ap = bp;                // and so is this

        b = a;                  // but you can't do this
        bp = ap;                // or this

}
```

Conversions also occur implicitly during function calls where necessary, as shown in Listing 3.8.

Listing 3.8. Implicit type conversions during function calls.

```
void foo(A* object) {}

void main()
{
        A* ap = new A;
        B* bp = new B;

        foo(ap);
        foo(bp);
}
```

This capability of supporting class conversions is an outstanding feature in C++, because the compiler effectively provides compile-time determination and tracking of objects. *Polymorphism* is an extension of this concept, allowing the objects to behave in a completely autonomous manner determined at runtime. Chapter 5 is dedicated to the discussion of polymorphism.

Scope Resolution

By deriving one class from another you can wind up with several classes that use the same name for a function or variable. You need to have a way of telling the compiler exactly which copy of a variable or function to use. Listing 3.9 is an example of two classes using the same member function identifier.

Listing 3.9. Two classes using the same member function identifier.

```
class A {
public:
        int foo() {return 1;}
};

class B: public A {
public:
        int foo() {return 2;}
};


void main()
{
        A a;
        B b;

        int i = a.foo();
        int j = b.foo();
}
```

Novice C++ programmers sometimes get confused about what value the integer `j` has. Class `B` has two `foo()` functions. One was inherited from `A` and the other is native to `B`. Essentially the compiler uses the version of `foo()` that is "closest" to class `B` in a search path starting from `B` and proceeding upward in the inheritance tree. With multiple inheritance, this path is somewhat more complicated.

Getting back to the example, `j` has the value 2, and `i` has the value 1. The compiler called the right member functions, even though `B` had two functions with the same name. The scope rules of C++ allowed this to happen. If a name in a base class is redeclared in a derived class, the name in the derived class obscures the corresponding name in the base class. It's just like declaring the same variable in nested compound statement blocks: Each block has a separate version of variables, with inner names obscuring outer ones.

But there is a difference. In C++ you can force the compiler to "see" outside its current normal scope, and access names that are otherwise obscured. This is done with the *scope resolution operator*, and the process is obviously called *scope resolution*. The general form of the scope resolution operator is

```
<class name> :: <class identifier>
```

where `<class name>` can be the name of any base class or derived class, and `<class identifier>` is the name of any variable or function declared in that class.

To use scope resolution, consider modifying class `B` like this:

```
class B: public A {
public:
        int foo() {return 2;}
        int f()   {return A::foo();}
};
```

Now invoking the function `B::f()` would call the `foo()` function of class `A`. Not only can you use scope resolution inside the functions of a class, but you can also use it at the time of a function call. Listing 3.10 shows two examples.

Listing 3.10. Using the scope resolution operator.

```
void main()
{
        B b;
        B* b1 = new B;

        int x = b.A::foo();     // resolution with an object
        int y = b1->A::foo();   // resolution with a pointer
}
```

If you have several levels of inheritance involved, scope resolution allows you to access the members of any base class to which you have proper access privileges. Consider a class `D` needing to access functions with the same name, but which are declared at different levels in the hierarchy. Figure 3.5 shows a possible class hierarchy in which class `D` has three base classes. Listing 3.11 is a short example illustrating the use of the scope resolution operator with class `D` to access functions at different levels of the hierarchy.

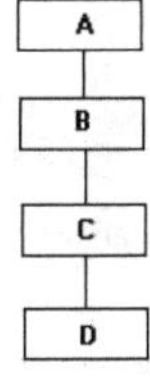

Figure 3.5. Four related classes using the same identifier for a member function.

Listing 3.11. Using scope resolution with different base classes.

```
class A {
public:
        int foo() {return 1;}
};

class B: public A {
public:
        int foo() {return 2;}
};

class C: public B {
public:
        int foo() {return 3;}
};

class D: public C {
public:
        int foo() {return 4;}
        int f1() {return A::foo();}
        int f2() {return B::foo();}
        int f3() {return C::foo();}
        int f4() {return D::foo();}  // redundant, but correct
};
```

The member functions in class `D` show scope resolution for all levels of the hierarchy. Note that scope resolution is necessary only when a derived class uses an identifier that is used in a base class. Consider the code in Listing 3.12.

Listing 3.12. Using scope resolution after the dot operator.

```
class A {
public:
        int value;
};

class B: public A {
public:
        int count;
};


void main()
{
        B b;
```

```
        int i = b.count;
        int j = b. B::count;   // redundant, but correct
        int k = b.value;
        int l = b. A::value;   // also redundant, but correct
}
```

The preceding code shows an unusual syntax with the scope resolution operator. The same syntax can be used also with object pointers and references. It is unnecessary, however, if the identifier you indicate appears only once in an inheritance tree, or is in the current scope by default.

Feature Expansion

Now all of the groundwork has been laid to illustrate a practical use for inheritance. One of the main reasons for deriving one class from another is that the base class provides part of the features needed in the derived one. Often the base class is *almost* like the class you need, but not quite. The base class may have a function that just needs to be extended slightly. It would be a waste of time to write the whole function over again in the derived class. Instead, C++ lets you reuse the code in the base class, expanding it as necessary. All you need to do is redefine in the derived class a function that makes use of the parent class's function. Consider designing a general-purpose pushbutton icon for use in a graphical user interface. This interface might use the inheritance tree in Figure 3.6.

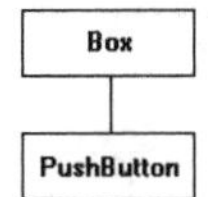

Figure 3.6. A specialized pushbutton class.

Listing 3.13 is a possible implementation.

Listing 3.13. Deriving a pushbutton object for feature expansion.

```
class Box {
public:
        Box(int x, int y, int width, int height) {}
        void Display() {}
};

class PushButton {
        int state;
```

continues

Listing 3.13. continued

```
        Box* outline;
        Box* button;
public:
        PushButton(int px, int py);
        void Display();
        ~PushButton() {}
};

PushButton::PushButton(int x, int y)
{
        const int OUTLINE_WIDTH  = 36;
        const int OUTLINE_HEIGHT = 20;
        const int BUTTON_WIDTH   = 20;
        const int BUTTON_HEIGHT  = 10;

        outline = new Box(x, y, OUTLINE_WIDTH, OUTLINE_HEIGHT);
        int bx = x + (OUTLINE_WIDTH - BUTTON_WIDTH) / 2;
        int by = y + (OUTLINE_HEIGHT - BUTTON_HEIGHT) / 2;
        button  = new Box(bx, by, BUTTON_WIDTH,  BUTTON_HEIGHT);
}

void PushButton::Display()
{
        outline->Display();     // display the button's border
        button->Display();      // display the button's interior
}
```

Class `PushButton` displays a rectangular box on the screen, with a smaller one inside, which serves as a pushbutton, as shown in Figure 3.7.

Figure 3.7. A simple pushbutton icon.

Now suppose you need to make a pushbutton that also displays a legend that identifies the pushbutton's action. It would be nice to use class `PushButton`, adding a function to display a string in it. It's straightforward to derive a class from `PushButton`, to expand the `Display()` function. This new class, which I call `PushButtonWithTitle`, uses `PushButton::Display()` to show the icon. Then `PushButtonWithTitle` provides code for overlaying a legend on top of the icon. The resulting inheritance tree is shown in Figure 3.8.

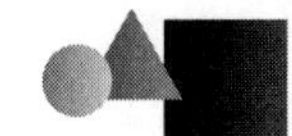

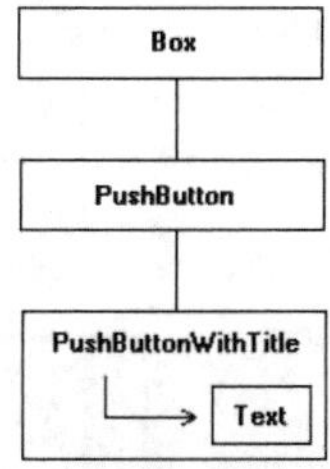

Figure 3.8. A class to display a title on pushbutton objects.

The `Text` class is not derived from `PushButtonWithTitle`, but is incorporated in it. An object of class `Text` is created and managed from within `PushButtonWithTitle`. Listing 3.14 shows how the code might look.

Listing 3.14. Expanding the features of a base class.

```
// include the header file for class PushButton

class Text {
public:
          Text(int x, int y, char* string) {}
          void Display() {}
};


class PushButtonWithTitle: public PushButton {
          Text* title;
public:
          PushButtonWithTitle(int x, int y, char* title);
          void Display();
          ~PushButtonWithTitle() {}
};

PushButtonWithTitle::PushButtonWithTitle(int x, int y, char* legend) :
          PushButton(x, y)
{
          title = new Text(x, y, legend);
}

void PushButtonWithTitle::Display()
{
          PushButton::Display();

          title->Display();
}
```

The expanded feature of `PushButton` is its `Display()` function. The new class has a function with the same name, which not only displays a plain `PushButton`, but also adds code on top of that. In this case a text string is displayed somewhere on the pushbutton, possibly looking like Figure 3.9.

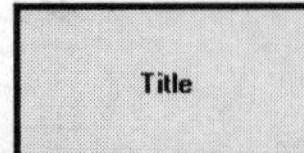

Figure 3.9. A simple pushbutton with a legend.

Function `PushButtonWithTitle::Display()` uses the scope resolution operator to access its parent function, because both classes have a function with the same name. The derived class doesn't really have to define a function with the same name as the base class, but consistency in function names across classes is recommended for clarity and homogeneity.

Feature Restriction

You can derive classes that limit or restrict the actions of the base class. Often you find a class that almost fits your requirements, but does something you don't want. For example, the class may have functions that aren't applicable to your case, or functions that do too much. Consider the preceding example of a pushbutton. Say you need a new pushbutton that displays just a box, rather than a button inside a box. Obviously the function `PushButton::Display()` would have to be changed to eliminate the part that shows the button. Listing 3.15 shows an example of how to define a new class derived from `PushButton`, which I call `SimplePushButton`, that fits this need.

Listing 3.15. Using feature restriction in a class derived from `PushButton`.

```
class PushButton {
protected:                          // variables no longer private
                                    // but protected
          int state;
          Box* outline;
          Box* button;
public:
          PushButton(int px, int py);
          void Display();
          ~PushButton() {}
};


class SimplePushButton: public PushButton {
public:
```

```
        SimplePushButton(int x, int y);
        void Display();
        ~SimplePushButton() {}
};

SimplePushButton::SimplePushButton(int x, int y) :
                PushButton(x, y)
{}

void SimplePushButton::Display()
{
        outline->Display();
}
```

The resulting button looks something like Figure 3.10.

Figure 3.10. A pushbutton without a border.

The only change necessary to class `PushButton` was in the access privileges for its variables. When using classes you or anyone else has written, you must always have access to the header file in which the class is declared. If the class was not designed to be inherited, it might make use of `private` variables or member functions to which you need to gain access. A possible option, not to be abused, is to change the access privileges of important members, so that they can be accessed from derived classes. Changing access privileges doesn't change the binary code of a class; it only affects how the compiler lets you use that class. I don't recommend modifying access privileges in header files, because this violates the structure of predeveloped classes and goes against the grain of object-oriented programming. If a class doesn't fully meet your requirements as a base class, it's better to look for another class or to develop a new one.

The constructor for `SimplePushButton` is really only a shell, because its only function is to invoke its base class with some parameters. The function `SimplePushButton::Display()` is where the interesting (but short) code is. This function prevents objects of class `SimplePushButton` from displaying a box inside a box, like in the base class. Essentially, the function uses the code written for `PushButton::Display()`, with some changes. Changing code in a base class is best done by studying the base class's source code. If you have access to this source code, you don't have a problem. If the base class is a precompiled proprietary class, you have to write your code from scratch. At least the overall task is greatly reduced in complexity.

An Example Using Single Inheritance

To bring some of the topics discussed into focus, I'll show a complete example of inheritance. Consider a topic most people seem to be familiar with: money. Money is always expressed as some kind of number, but the various currencies in use throughout the world are different enough to justify developing different classes for each of them. Money is well-implemented as a class, because it can be applied to operators, it can be converted to and from different currencies, and it has special requirements for dealing with precision and rounding. My example uses the Borland C++ class `bcd` as a base class and creates derived classes to handle the currency of Italy and the United States of America. Italy's unit of currency is called the *lira* (the plural is *lire*), which is abbreviated *Lit.* for *Lire Italiane.* Listing 3.16 is the implementation of class `Lire`.

Listing 3.16. A class for handling Italian currency.

```
#include <bcd.h>
#include <iomanip.h>

class Lire: public bcd {

public:

  Lire() : bcd() {}
  Lire(bcd& l) : bcd(l) {}
  Lire(unsigned long l) : bcd(l) {}
  friend ostream& operator<<(ostream& os, Lire&);
};

ostream& operator<<(ostream& os, Lire& amount)
{
  bcd rounded_amount( real(amount), 0);

  return os << "Lit. " << rounded_amount;
}
```

Handling dollars is a little different, because you have to deal with fractional parts of dollars rather than just integers as with lire. Listing 3.17 is the implementation of class `Dollars`.

Listing 3.17. A class to handle American currency.

```
#include <bcd.h>
#include <iomanip.h>
```

```
class Dollars: public bcd {

public:

  Dollars() : bcd() {}
  Dollars(bcd& d) : bcd(d) {}
  Dollars(int d) : bcd(d) {}
  Dollars(unsigned long d) : bcd(d) {}
  Dollars(double d) : bcd(d) {}
  friend ostream& operator<<(ostream& os, Dollars&);
};

ostream& operator<<(ostream& os, Dollars& amount)
{
  float f = real(amount);
  return os << "$ "
            << setiosflags(ios::showpoint)
            << setprecision(2) << f;
}
```

One lira is worth about 0.1 cents, so most of the time fractional lire are ignored. To ensure that no decimals appear when a `Lire` variable is displayed, the stream insertion operator is overloaded, starting with the declaration

```
friend ostream& operator<<(ostream& os, Lire&);
```

The preceding operator displays the string "`Lit.` ", followed by an integer value. The `Dollars` class also overrides the stream insertion operator, so that dollars are always displayed with two decimals and the $ symbol. Notice that the `include` file *<iomanip.h>* is used. The file is necessary to support the manipulator functions `setiosflags(long)` and `setprecision(int)` that are used in the stream inserter. These manipulators force dollar amounts to be displayed with a decimal point followed by two digits. These and all other manipulators are fully described in Chapter 7, "Streams." Listing 3.18 is a short program that utilizes the two classes.

Listing 3.18. Using the currency classes.

```
#include <lire.h>
#include <dollars.h>
void main()
{
          Lire income(5000), expenses(1000);
          Lire interest, balance;

          balance = income - expenses;
          interest = balance * 0.060311;
```

continues

Listing 3.18. continued

```
        cout << "\nComputations with Italian lire:"
             << "\nIncome:      " << income
             << "\nExpenses:    " << expenses
             << "\nBalance:     " << balance
             << "\nInterest:    " << interest;

        Dollars new_income(50.23), new_expenses(10);
        Dollars new_interest, new_balance;

        new_balance = new_income - new_expenses;
        new_interest = new_balance * 0.060311;
        cout << "\n\nComputations with US dollars:"
             << "\nIncome:      " << new_income
             << "\nExpenses:    " << new_expenses
             << "\nBalance:     " << new_balance
             << "\nInterest:    " << new_interest;
}
```

The program tests both classes. It is relatively easy to add member functions that allow you to mix dollars and lire in an expression. The member functions would convert from one currency to the other, using predefined conversion rates. Dollars know they are dollars, and convert themselves automatically into other currencies. This kind of elegance is exactly what makes object-oriented programming so exciting.

Functional Closures

A closure is a mathematical domain. It has an abstract boundary that encloses an area, which contains elements that are considered to be the domain of the closure. Closures have been used in programming languages for years. Common LISP uses two kinds of closures, called *lexical* and *dynamic*, to establish a context of bindings between symbols and values during function calls.

In this section, I introduce a new type of closure, required to handle some common programming problems. I call this new closure a *functional closure*, and the easiest way to describe it is with examples. Many times in programming projects the need arises to do something like this:

```
Operation preamble
  Operation...
Operation postamble
```

This indicates a sequence of events that must take place in sequence. Because the various events are not valid when separated and executed in isolation from the others, they constitute an *atomic* (undivisible) sequence. For example, to write text to a window in Microsoft

Windows programming you need to utilize an object called a *device context*, or *DC* for short. You obtain a handle to a DC via a Windows call, use the handle to display data, then release the DC handle. This is the sequence:

```
hDC = GetDC(hwnd);                      // preamble: get DC
  TextOut(hdc, x, y, string, size);     // operation: use DC
ReleaseDC(hwnd, hdc);                   // postamble: release DC
```

This type of atomic sequence is extremely common in Windows, and is also common when you are deriving classes in a hierarchy. Consider for example the process of displaying a pop-up window.

```
Save coordinates of window covered   // preamble
  Display popup window               // operation: display
Restore covered image                // postamble
```

The previous two examples illustrate the meaning of a functional closure: a domain of code, whose boundary is constituted by a preamble and a postamble. Functional closures are domains that have meaning only at runtime. With a functional closure, having a preamble function without a corresponding postamble is a runtime error. The preamble and postamble are operations that bracket a section of executable code, like the `{}` characters used in C++ source code.

Implementing a Functional Closure

In many situations you have an operation that must be preceded and followed by a specific set of operations. In this section I show some examples to prove my point. Given the recurrence of functional closures in computing, I show two different C++ techniques for dealing with them. The idea is to put the burden of remembering when to use preambles and postambles on the compiler, thus exploiting characteristics of C++. An extremely common problem in Windows programming is forgetting to close a closure, such as releasing a device context, calling an `EndPaint()` function, and so on. When you write a long sequence of operations, you tend to get lost in the details, making it easy to forget postamble operations. The chapters on Windows programming go into the details of developing closures for most common Windows problems.

Developing Closures Through Inheritance

A functional closure can be implemented in several ways, exploiting the characteristics of C++. The first method I show uses inheritance. The idea is to have a base class that "knows about" functional closures, and a derived class where the actual work is performed inside the closure. Consider implementing the pop-up window code discussed in the preceding paragraph. Making an abstract base class is a good starting point (see Listing 3.19).

Listing 3.19. A base class for a functional closure.

```
class Popup {
public:
        Popup(int x1, int y1, int x2, int y2)
        { // save the coordinate and extent of the popup
          // window to open
        }

        // force class to be abstract
        virtual void Display() = 0;

        virtual ~Popup()
        { // restore the covered area
        }
};
```

Now if you derive a class from `Popup` to display an actual pop-up window, the compiler automatically invokes the base class constructor and destructor, allowing the two functions to behave as the preamble and postamble of a closure (see Listing 3.20).

Listing 3.20. A derived class that implements a functional closure.

```
class SetupPopupWindow: public Popup {
public:
        SetupPopupWindow() : Popup(10, 10, 100, 100)
        { /* build the setup window contents */ }

        void Display()
        {
          /* put the actual display code here */
        }

        ~SetupPopupWindow()
        { /* destroy the setup window contents */ }
};

// use the popup window
main()
{
        SetupPopupWindow help;
        help.Display();
        // ...
}
```

Any time you create an object of class `SetupPopupWindow`, the details of saving and restoring the screen are handled by the compiler. This procedure works well when the functional closure is required in a specialized class obtained through class derivation. Not all situations can be solved through inherited functional closures, but many are. Consider the device context problem shown earlier. This problem also can be handled through inheritance, as shown in Listing 3.21.

Listing 3.21. A device context operation as a functional closure.

```
#include <windows.h>
#include <string.h>

class DeviceContext {
protected:
          HWND hwindow;
          HDC hdc;
public:
          DeviceContext(HWND hwnd) {
            hwindow = hwnd;           // save the current window
            hdc = GetDC(hwnd);        // get a device context
          }

          ~DeviceContext() {
            ReleaseDC(hwindow, hdc); // release device context
          }
};


class Text: public DeviceContext {
public:
          Text(HWND hwnd, int x, int y, char* string) :
              DeviceContext(hwnd)
          {
            TextOut(hdc, x, y, (LPSTR) string, strlen(string) );
          }
};
```

The base class `DeviceContext` hides the details of obtaining and releasing a Windows device context. To display text using the base class, you derive the class `Text` from `DeviceContext`. The base class constructor implements the preamble, thus obtaining the device context. The constructor also displays the text, although this feature could have been relegated to a separate member function. Once the `Text` object goes out of scope, the base class destructor releases the device context, so you can use the `Text` class like this:

```
void SomeWindowsFunction(HWND hwnd)
{
          Text message(hwnd, 3, 5, "Invalid filename.");
}
```

The function `SomeWindowsFunction(HWND)` uses a window handle. The process of getting and releasing window handles constitutes another set of preambles and postambles, indicating that the function `SomeWindowsFunction(HWND)` uses a closure inside a closure. There is nothing magical about nesting closures, as with nesting parentheses in a mathematical expression. Indeed, functional closures can be nested indefinitely.

The implementation of the closure in class `Text` may not be satisfactory if you need to display many different strings inside the same function, because each string would get a new device context, resulting in significant overhead.

Developing Closures Through Instantiation

Exploiting the dynamics of runtime object instantiation is an alternative way of developing functional closures. It is simpler than utilizing inheritance, but is also more limited. The technique relies on the automatic invocation of constructors and destructors like the inheritance technique, but makes no use of inheritance. When you instantiate a class, the class constructor is invoked by the compiler. When the object instantiated goes out of scope, the class destructor is also invoked by the compiler. The constructor and destructor can be used again as preamble and postamble functions.

Bjarne Stroustrup uses the expression *Resource Acquisition is Initialization* to refer to the technique of using class objects to functionally close access to resources. The constructor allocates the resource, the member functions manipulate the resource, and the destructor releases the resource. Because the compiler guarantees that the destructor will be called when the object goes out of scope, there is no chance of the resource being left *dangling* by mistake.

Consider implementing the pop-up window example, as in Listing 3.22.

Listing 3.22. A functional closure using class instantiation.

```
class Popup {
public:
          Popup(int x1, int y1, int x2, int y2)
          { // save the coordinate and extent of the popup
            // window to open
          }

          ~Popup() { /* restore the covered area */ }
};
```

```
class SetupPopupWindow {
public:
        SetupPopupWindow()
        {
          Popup object(10, 10,100, 100);
          // build the setup window contents
          // display the window
          // destroy the setup window contents
        }
};


// use the popup window
main()
{
        SetupPopupWindow help;
        // ...
}
```

Using the preceding implementation of `SetupPopupWindow` is just as easy as with the derived version; in fact, it's easier. The problem with closures-through-instantiation is that instantiated objects can use only the member functions defined in the base class. Object `help` has no `Display()` function to call, so the constructor has to display the object.

For the Windows device context example, I make a new `DeviceContext` class that has a couple of useful member functions (see Listing 3.23).

Listing 3.23. A Windows device context functional closure realized through object instantiation.

```
#include <windows.h>
#include <string.h>

class DeviceContext {
protected:
        HWND hwindow;
        HDC hdc;
public:
        DeviceContext(HWND hwnd) {
          hwindow = hwnd;           // save the current window
          hdc = GetDC(hwnd);        // get a device context
        }

        void TextOut(int x, int y, char* cp)
        {
          ::TextOut(hdc, x, y, (LPSTR) cp, strlen(cp) );
        }
```

continues

Listing 3.23. continued

```
          void GetTextMetrics(LPTEXTMETRIC tm) {
            ::GetTextMetrics(hdc, tm);
          }

          ~DeviceContext() {
            ReleaseDC(hwindow, hdc); // release device context
          }
};


void SomeWindowsFunction(HWND hwnd)
{
          DeviceContext hdc(hwnd);

          hdc.TextOut(3, 5, "Invalid filename.");
          TEXTMETRIC tm;
          hdc.GetTextMetrics(&tm);
}
```

The device context is obtained by instantiating the variable `hdc`. The member functions for `DeviceContext` have the same names as Windows functions. To make them easier to remember, Class `DeviceContext` invokes the global Windows functions using the scope resolution operator. After calling member functions of `DeviceContext`, it is impossible to forget to call `ReleaseDC(...)` because the compiler does it for you. It is also impossible to forget to pass the `hdc` and `hwnd` parameters to Windows, because these details are handled inside class `DeviceContext`. The advantage of using a class instantiation to support functional closures is that the same variable can support multiple operations, without the overhead of creating new closures every time.

Functional closures become very important in systems employing C++ exception handling, which is described in detail in Chapter 6. When an exception is thrown at runtime, a program in effect performs a non-local jump. The system automatically calls the destructors for objects that go out of scope as a result of the jump, but it is very easy for bugs to creep into your program if you don't use functional closures properly. Consider the following code, which uses an OWL 2.5 `TDib` object:

```
void f()
{
  // Create a Device Independent Bitmap object
  TDib* dib = new TDib;

  // use the DIB object

  // free the DIB object
  delete dib;
```

```
}
```

The code looks okay until you consider what happens when an exception is thrown after creating the `TDib` object but before freeing it. The code will perform a non-local jump to the closest suitable exception handler, bypassing the `delete dib` statement and leaving a memory leak. Of course, using a local object would ensure proper compiler-controlled invocation of destructors for objects that go out of scope, so you could rewrite function `f()` as follows:

```
void f()
{
  // Create a Device Independent Bitmap object
  TDib dib;

  // use the DIB object
}
```

No explicit destructor call is needed, so throwing an exception will not result in any leaks. Unfortunately, local objects may not always be usable in a program. For example, OWL uses (and requires you to use) dynamically allocated objects extensively. A functionally closed version of the code above provides a combination of resilience to leaks and brevity of code, yielding something like this:

```
#include <owl\gdiobjec.h>

class SafeDIB {

public:

  TDib* dib;
  SafeDIB(const char* name) {dib = new TDib(name);}
  ~SafeDIB() {delete dib;}
};

void f()
{
  // Create a Device Independent Bitmap object
  SafeDIB dib("BITMAP_SAILBOAT");

  // access the DIB object using SafeDIB::dib
  // ...
}
```

Class `SafeDIB` functionally closes access to the `TDib` resource, guaranteeing `TDib`'s destruction in the event of exceptions. See Chapter 6 for a complete discussion of exception handling.

Multiple Inheritance

In nature, living beings usually have two parents. This arrangement allows greater variety in the offspring, with the potential for greater adaptability and survivability. Similarly in C++, a class is not limited to one parent. In fact, a class can have many parents, inheriting properties from each of its base classes. This kind of inheritance naturally introduces a certain amount of complexity in the language and the compiler, but the benefits are substantial. Consider creating a class `RoundTable`, having not only the properties of tables, but also the geometric characteristic of being round. The tree in Figure 3.11 shows the relationships.

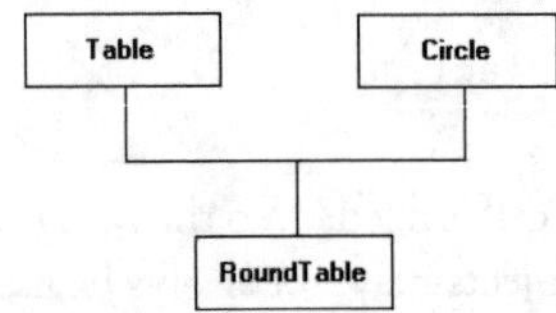

Figure 3.11. Creating a round table through multiple inheritance.

Listing 3.24 is a possible implementation and sample program.

Listing 3.24. A `RoundTable` class built through multiple inheritance.

```
#include <stdio.h>

class Circle {
      float radius;
public:
      Circle(float r) {radius = r;}
      float Area() {return radius * radius * 3.14;}
};


class Table {
      float height;
public:
      Table(float h) {height = h;}
      float Height() {return height;}
};


class RoundTable: public Table, public Circle {
      int color;
public:
      RoundTable(float h, float r, int c);
```

```
      int Color() {return color;}
};


RoundTable::RoundTable(float h, float r, int c) :
      Circle(r), Table(h)
{
      color = c;
}


void main()
{
      RoundTable table(15.0, 3.0, 5);

      printf("\nThe table properties are:");
      printf("\nHeight = %f", table. Height() );
      printf("\nArea = %f", table. Area() );
      printf("\nColor = %d", table. Color() );
}
```

Having inherited most of its properties from its base classes, class `RoundTable` is reduced to a rather trivial implementation. In the declaration of a class derived from multiple parents, you need to declare not only the various base classes, but also the access specifiers for each of the base classes. These specifiers are used just as in simple inheritance. The access specifiers for the base classes do not all have to be the same.

Function `main()` in Listing 3.24 invokes the three member functions `RoundTable::Height()`, `RoundTable::Area()`, and `RoundTable::Color()`, all without indicating which are inherited functions and which are not. This way of referring to inherited members is a natural extension to single inheritance, and the consistent notation is extremely convenient.

Declaring a Class with Multiple Base Classes

The declaration of `RoundTable` introduces the general syntax used: the list of base classes is declared, each with its own access specifier. These bases are called *direct base classes*, as opposed to indirect ones, which are base classes of a base class (grandparents, so to speak). `Table` and `Circle` are direct base classes of `RoundTable`, but any base classes of `Table` or `Circle` would be called indirect base classes of `RoundTable`. The distinction between direct and indirect base classes is important because the compiler applies different rules to each type.

A class can have as many base classes as you want, but the complexity increases rapidly. Just keeping track of things can become a problem. In most C++ libraries, multiple inheritance is used with two base classes, but whether to use two base classes rather than three or more is dictated by programmers rather than C++.

Invoking the Base Class Constructors

Just as in simple inheritance, the constructors in multiple base classes are invoked before the constructor for the derived class. The order of declaration prescribes the order of invocation. Consider the case for `RoundTable`.

```
class RoundTable: public Table, public Circle {
      int color;
public:
      RoundTable(float h, float r, int c);
      int Color() {return color;}
};
```

When an instantiation is made of the preceding class, the constructor invocation order is

```
     Table::Table(float);
     Circle::Circle(float);
     RoundTable::RoundTable(float);
```

In the previous definition of the constructor `RoundTable::RoundTable()`, the following two parameters were passed to base classes:

```
RoundTable::RoundTable(float h, float r, int c) :
      Circle(r), Table(h) {}
```

The order of these constructor calls can cause confusion, because the actual order of invocation is given in the class declaration, not in the constructor definition. `virtual` base class constructors are invoked before any non-`virtual` ones. For `virtual` base classes with `virtual` bases, the constructors are called in the order of declaration. Only then are the non-`virtual` base classes invoked. At this point a description of `virtual` base classes is in order.

Using *virtual* Base Classes

`virtual` base classes are used only in the context of multiple inheritance. Given the complexity of relationships that can arise in an inheritance tree built around multiple inheritance, there are situations in which the programmer needs to have a certain level of control over the way in which base classes are inherited. Consider the inheritance tree in Figure 3.12.

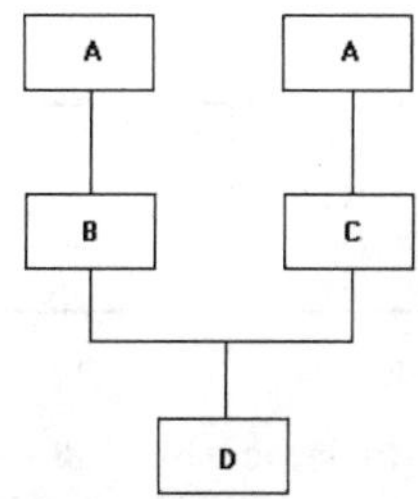

Figure 3.12. An inheritance tree with the same class appearing twice.

The class `D` has `A` as a base class. The problem is that there are *two* distinct A classes that appear as base classes of D, each with its own data. In real life, this situation would be equivalent to having two grandfathers who were not only twins, but even had the same name! How do you deal with this situation? Consider the following code:

```
class A {
public:
      int value;
};

class B: public A {};
class C: public A {};
class D: public B, public C {
public:
      int Value() {return value;}
};
```

The statement-accessing member value in `D` is ambiguous. Borland C++ generates the error

```
"Field 'value' is ambiguous in 'D' in function D::Value()"
```

The compiler doesn't know which copy of `value` is being referred to. The scope resolution operator must be applied to function `D::Value()`.

```
int Value() {return C::value;}
```

A function outside class `D` could also access each of the value members by using scope resolution combined with an object identifier, as shown in Listing 3.25.

Listing 3.25. Using the scope resolution operator in a class with multiple base classes.

```
void main()
{
       D d;
       int v = d.B::value;         // with an object
```

continues

Listing 3.25. continued

```
      D* object = new D;
      int w = object->B::value;   // with an object pointer
};
```

Having multiple copies of the same base class in an inheritance tree is not only confusing, but it may be a waste of storage. Declaring a base class `virtual` solves this problem. It forces the compiler to allow only one copy of a given base class in the declaration of a derived class. Class `D` could be redefined like this:

```
class B: public virtual A {};
class C: public virtual A {};
class D: public B, public C {
public:
     int Value() {return value;}
};
```

The keywords `public` and `virtual` can also be reversed in order without causing compilation errors. The inheritance tree now looks like Figure 3.13.

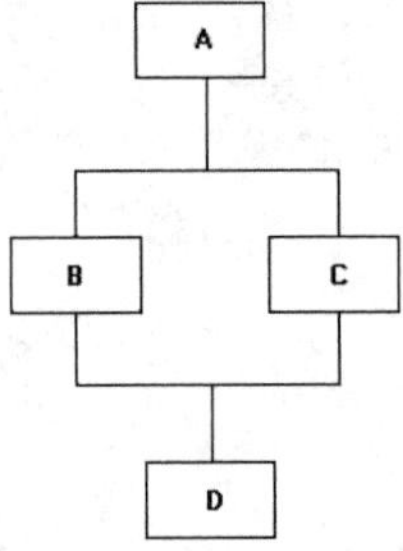

Figure 3.13. An inheritance tree using a `virtual` *base class for A.*

The code in function `D::Value()` no longer needs scope resolution, although using it is not an error.

Using *virtual* and Non-*virtual* Bases Together

A class can have both `virtual` and non-`virtual` base classes, in any order and combination. Here is an example:

```
class A {};
class B: public virtual A {};
```

```
class C: public virtual A {};
class D: public A {};
class E: public B, public C, public D {};
```

It's more intuitive to see the relationship in tree form, as in Figure 3.14.

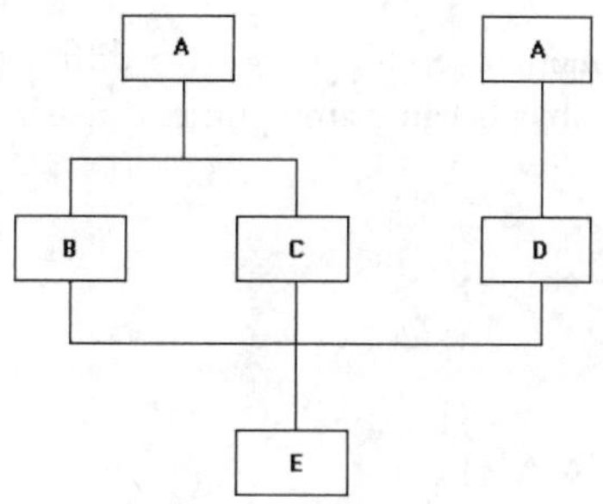

Figure 3.14. An inheritance tree with `virtual` *and non-*`virtual` *base classes together.*

Class `E` winds up with two different copies of `A`. This isn't an error in C++, but it may cause confusion for users. The order of constructor calls for class `E` is `A`, `B`, `C`, `D`, `E`. First the `virtual` bases are built, followed by the remaining bases. The order in which the `virtual` base classes are built corresponds to their order of appearance in the class declaration. After all the `virtual` base class constructors have been invoked, the non-`virtual` constructors are called. Again, the order is based on order of appearance.

Invoking the Destructors

You can invoke a destructor only indirectly, using the `delete` operator. The sequence followed when calling the base class destructors is the reverse of that used in calling the constructors. More specialized destructors are called before more general ones. As usual, no arguments can be passed to destructors, nor can any return types be declared.

Using Type Conversions

With single inheritance you can always convert a pointer to a derived class into a pointer to its base class. The opposite is not true. The following code fragment shows some examples that apply to single inheritance:

```
class A {};
class B: public A {};
```

```
void main()
{
        B* b1 = new B;      // regular declaration
        B* b2 = new A;      // wrong
        A* a1 = new B;      // implicit conversion
};
```

With multiple inheritance, things are more difficult. Converting pointers and references is not always possible, because ambiguities can arise. Consider the following code:

```
class A {
public:
        int value;
};

class B: public A {};
class C: public A {};
class D: public B, public C {};

void main()
{
        A* a1 = new D;      // can't do this
        A* a2 = new B;
        A* a3 = new C;
}
```

The class hierarchy defined by this code is shown graphically in Figure 3.15.

When the compiler sees the statement

```
A* a1 = new D;
```

the compiler finds that class `D` has two different versions of class `A` in it, and doesn't know which one to use in the conversion. You need to provide the following necessary information:

```
A* a1 = (C*) new D;
```

Now the compiler knows to use the `C` version of class `A`. Declaring class `D` with `virtual` base classes would prevent the problem from happening, because only one copy of `A` would be included in `D`. Changing the declaration for classes B and C as follows

```
class B: public virtual A: {};
class C: public virtual A: {};
```

changes the inheritance tree into the one shown in Figure 3.16.

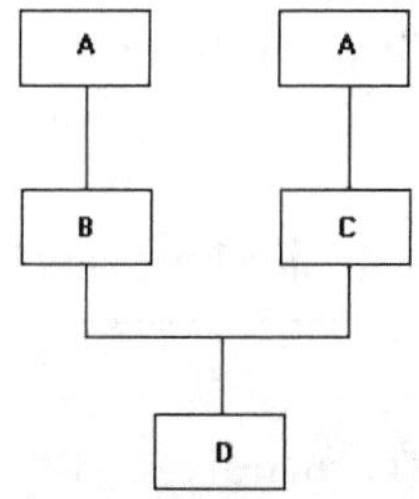

Figure 3.15. An inheritance tree that may cause problems with type conversions from D *to* A.

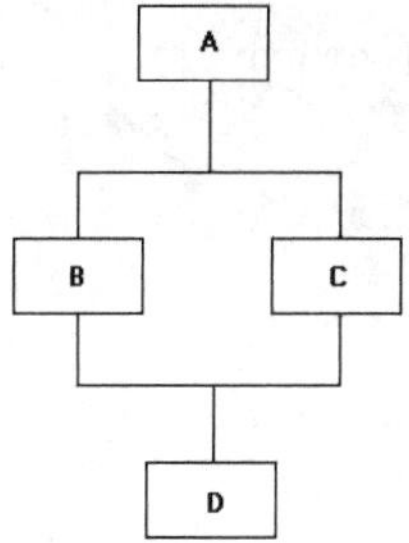

Figure 3.16. The inheritance tree after the declaration for class D *is changed.*

Keeping Base Class Functions Straight

When you invoke a function in a derived class, the compiler goes looking for it using the classes in the inheritance tree that are accessible, following specific rules. If the function is not found in the class it is invoked from, the compiler starts searching for the function through the inheritance tree. This search occurs, therefore, at compile time, not runtime. If several base classes have the same function name, the C++ search rules determine which function gets called. Consider the inheritance tree in Figure 3.17.

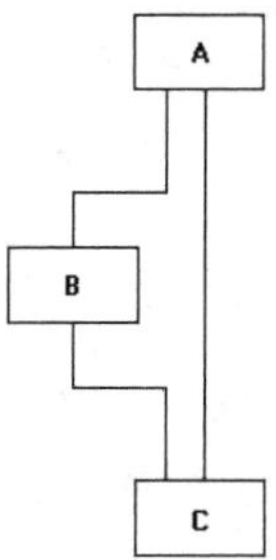

Figure 3.17. An inheritance tree to illustrate how the compiler searches for a member function called inside class C.

This inheritance tree is implemented in the code shown in Listing 3.26. Consider both A and B to have a function by the name foo().

Listing 3.26. Three classes to illustrate function searching.

```
class A {
public:
        int foo() {return 1;}
};

class B: virtual public A {
public:
        int foo() {return 2;}
};

class C: virtual public A, public B {};

void main()
{
        C c;
        int i = c.foo();                // call B::foo()
}
```

Why does the function B::foo() get called? Because of something called the *dominance rule*. The compiler found that both class A and class B had suitable functions. The dominance rule states that if two classes contain the function searched for, and if one class is derived from the other, the derived class dominates. In the preceding example, B satisfied this criterion. If no function dominates, you get a compiler error regarding ambiguous references. The inheritance tree in Figure 3.18, along with the short listing that follows, shows a situation in which the dominance rule cannot be applied, leading to a compiler error.

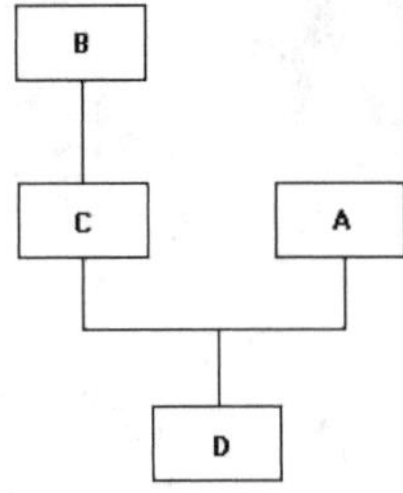

Figure 3.18. An example that the dominance rule cannot handle.

```
class A {
public:
        int foo() {return 1;}
};

class B {
public:
        int foo() {return 2;}
};

class C: virtual public B {};
class D: public C, public A {};

void main()
{
        D d;
        int i = d.foo();                // error: ambiguous function
}
```

Using Scope Resolution with Multiple Inheritance

What if you have a class with the same identifier in more than one base class? Consider, for example, the inheritance tree shown in Figure 3.19, implemented using the code in the following listing:

```
class A {
public:
        int foo() {return 1;}
};

class B: public A {};

class C {};

class D: public C {
public:
        int foo() {return 2;}
};

class E: public B, public D {
public:
        void f();
};

void E::f() {
        int i = foo();     // error: ambiguous function
}
```

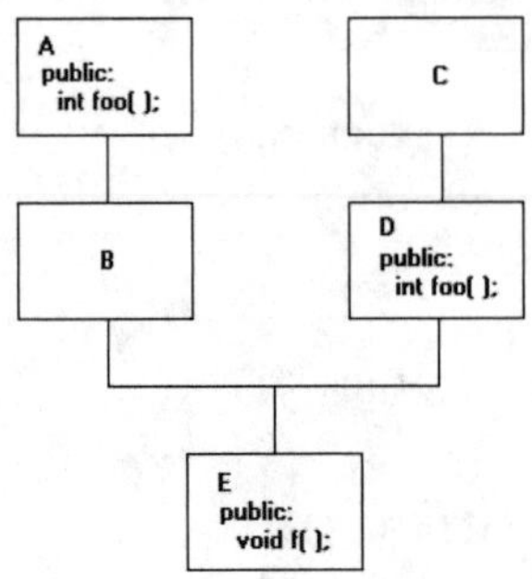

Figure 3.19. An inheritance tree in which the same function identifier appears more than once.

The function call in `E::f()` is ambiguous, because both `A::foo()` and `D::foo()` exist, even if they were declared at different levels of the inheritance tree. Scope resolution resolves the problem.

```
void E::f() {
        int i = A::foo();   // A's foo()
        int j = B::foo();   // still A's foo()
        int k = D::foo();   // D's foo()
}
```

Note that indicating `B::foo()` still gets `A::foo()`, because there is no `B::foo()`. Class `B` uses `A::foo()` as a function of its own. When resolving scope, you only need to provide enough information to reach the correct identifier, in other words, the path you want the compiler to follow to find the right identifier.

Declaring multiple base classes with the same `public` identifiers does not cause a compiler error. Should it? No. Just because identifiers are declared doesn't mean the compiler needs to figure out whether they are accessible. Identifier accessibility is determined only when executable code needs to be generated, because that is the one time an identifier is actually used. Suppose that an identifier is declared that might be ambiguous in an inheritance tree. In such cases, errors are detected only if you write code that attempts to access the ambiguous identifier without using proper scope resolution.

Keeping Track of Memory

One of the beautiful features of using multiple inheritance is that you can funnel considerable power into a single class with little effort. To make things even better, objects that utilize multiple inheritance often have no memory overhead. I say *often* because there is one exception: base classes with `virtual` functions.

For each base class that uses `virtual` functions, Borland C++ allocates a separate `virtual` table pointer in derived classes. These pointers are described in more detail in Chapter 5. Consider the tree in Figure 3.20.

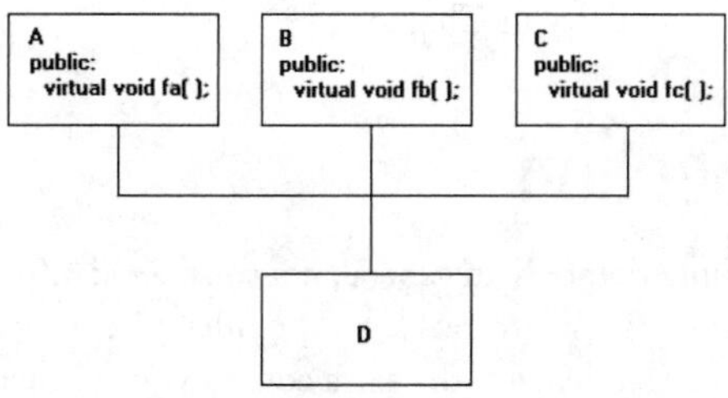

Figure 3.20. An inheritance tree with `virtual` *functions in the base classes.*

This tree could be implemented with the following code:

```
class A {
public:
          virtual void fa() {}

class B {
public:
          virtual void fb() {}
};

class C {
public:
          virtual void fc() {}
};

class D: public A, public B, public C {};
```

Instantiating each of the classes, you wind up with objects with the following number of pointers to `virtual` tables:

Class	*Pointers*
A	1
B	1
C	1
D	3

This table shows that the base classes `A`, `B`, and `C` have no overhead that derives from their use as base classes, but class `D` has three `virtual` table pointers rather than just one. The additional pointers represent a modest amount of overhead for most applications, but they are nevertheless overhead. The topic of `virtual` functions and `virtual` table pointers is discussed in its entirety in Chapter 5.

Advanced Section

The topic of inheritance is, in general, not considered difficult by newcomers to C++, mostly due to the similarities with real life. The rules regarding access privileges sometimes need some additional study, with the extra complexity of inherited member functions and data members, but with a little experience, all these topics are mastered. What is less obvious to programmers, but equally important in order to understand the C++ language, is what code and data the compiler generates in certain situations and how inheritance affects the use of memory. I deal with these and other issues in this section, so beginners may want to skip to the next chapter if they find the material too difficult.

Runtime Considerations

When you invoke a non-`static`, non-`virtual` member function of a class, the only runtime overhead you incur is the invisible passing of the `this` pointer. `static` member functions are even better to call, and have no overhead at all. When dealing with derived classes, C++ is still efficient: invoking an inherited function takes the same number of instructions as invoking a member function. Runtime performance is not degraded, because the compiler itself is smart. At compile time, when an inherited function is invoked, the compiler determines what function is actually to be referenced, what class's member to use, and whether the function is normal, `inline`, `static`, `virtual`, and so on. The compiler then generates the call to the computed function.

`virtual` functions take longer to invoke than normal member functions, whereas `static` functions take less time. For normal and `static` member functions, the efficiency of a call is not dependent on whether a function is inherited or not. `virtual` functions are handled differently, which is an argument Chapter 5 treats in detail.

Inside an Object

To see how efficient the compiler is in making calls to inherited functions, I show the assembly language generated by Borland C++ when calling member functions at different levels in a hierarchy. Consider the inheritance tree in Figure 3.21.

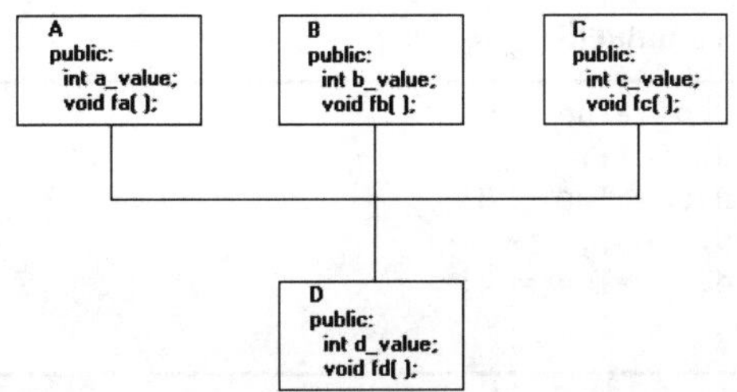

Figure 3.21. A multiple-inheritance tree used to illustrate member function call details.

The tree in Figure 3.21 could be implemented with the code in Listing 3.27.

Listing 3.27. Invoking member functions at various levels in an inheritance tree.

```
class A {
public:
        int a_value;
        void fa() {}
};

class B {
public:
        int b_value;
        void fb() {}
};

class C {
public:
        int c_value;
        void fc() {}
};

class D: public A, public B, public C {
public:
        int d_value;
        void fd() {}
};

void main()
{
        D d;

        d. fa();
        d.a_value = 1;
        d. fb();
```

continues

Listing 3.27. continued

```
        d.b_value = 2;
        d. fc();
        d.c_value = 3;
        d. fd();
        d.d_value = 4;
}
```

To see the assembly language produced, I saved the preceding code in a file named *t.cpp*, then compiled it after setting the `Options ¦ Project ¦ +Compiler ¦ Debugging` switch. Loading the executable file with Turbo Debugger, you obtain the following assembly language (after some editing):

```
_main:    void main()
            push      bp          ; setup stack frame
            mov       bp,sp
            sub       sp,0008
#T#29:    d.fa();
            lea       ax,[bp-08] ; this pointer for A
            push      ax
            call      A::fa
                    pop       cx
#T#30:    d.a_value = 1;
            mov       word ptr [bp-08], 0001   ; A::a_value
#T#31:    d.fb();
            lea       ax,[bp-06] ; this pointer for B
            push      ax
            call      A::fb
            pop       cx
#T#32:    d.b_value = 1;
            mov       word ptr [bp-06], 0002   ; B::b_balue
#T#33:    d.fc();
            lea       ax,[bp-04] ; this pointer for C
            push      ax
            call      A::fc
            pop       cx
#T#34:    d.c_value = 1;
            mov       word ptr [bp-04], 0003   ; C::c_value
#T#35:    d.fd();
            lea       ax,[bp-08] ; this pointer for D
            push      ax
            call      A::fd
            pop       cx
#T#36:    d.d_value = 1;
            mov       word ptr [bp-02], 0004   ; D::d_value
```

```
#T#37:      }
              mov       sp,bp
              pop       bp
              ret
```

The function calls to the four member functions are all implemented with the same number of instructions. The only difference is in the value of the `this` pointer passed. Notice how each member function is called with a `this` pointer pointing to the correct class. Thus, function `A::fa()` is called with a pointer to the `A` part of `D`, `B::fb()` with a pointer to the `B` part, and so on. Each of these member functions is unaware of being used inside a class `D` object. The preceding code is also interesting because it allows you to see the layout of an object in memory with Borland C++. The four `this` pointers and member variables accessed have the values outlined in Table 3.1.

Table 3.1. The `this` pointer used at different levels in an inheritance tree.

Class	*Value of the* `this` *Pointer*
A	[bp - 08]
B	[bp - 06]
C	[bp - 04]
D	[bp - 08]

Variable	*Address*
a_value	[bp - 08]
b_value	[bp - 06]
c_value	[bp - 04]
d_value	[bp - 02]

This table indicates the layout for objects of class `D` that is shown in Figure 3.22.

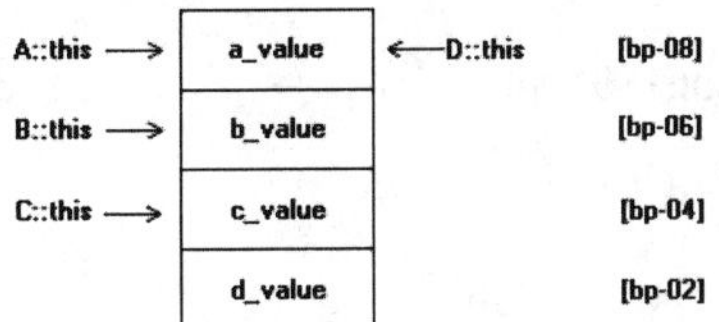

Figure 3.22. The layout of an object of class `D`.

Notice how the this pointer for D is *not* pointing at D::d_value, because class D has all four variables in it, which were acquired through inheritance. You can't infer that a D object was derived from other classes solely by looking at the object's memory layout. You must also realize that member functions are not stored together with the data in an object. All instantiations of a class share the same non-static member functions, but have separate copies of the data members.

An Inherited Debugger

Most of the time in a project you work within the framework of class hierarchies, in which all classes are derived from one or two root classes. For example, the Borland C++ container class library has a class called Object as a root class. Almost all the other classes in the library derive from Object. This means that all the classes inherit the functions of Object, which suggests a way to modify all the classes with little effort.

Suppose you need to browse around the memory used by class objects. One way to do this is by adding a special function, perhaps called MemoryDump() to each class. A better way is to add the MemoryDump() function to class Object, automatically endowing all derived classes with the browse feature. Listing 3.28 is an example using some of the PushButton code described earlier. Some of the functions have not been completely coded, because they have already been shown.

Listing 3.28. Adding a simple browser to a class hierarchy.

```
#include <stdio.h>
#include <string.h>

class Debugger {
public:
          void MemoryDump(int);
};

void Debugger::MemoryDump(int size)
{
          for (int i = 0; i < size; i++)
            printf("\nobject byte [%d] = %02X", i,
                    *( (unsigned char*) (this+i) ) & 0xFF);
}

class Object: public Debugger {/*.. Object code here*/};

class Box: public Object {

          int x, y, width, height;

public:
```

```
        Box(int x, int y, int width, int height) {}
        void Display() {/* ... add code here ...*/}
};

class Text: public Object {

        int x, y;
        char text [40];

public:

        Text(int x, int y, char* string)
        {
          strncpy(text, string, 39);
        }
        void Display() {/* ... add code here...*/}
};
class PushButton: public Object {
protected:
        int state;
        Box* outline;
        Box* button;
public:
        PushButton(int px, int py) {}
        void Display() {/*...add code here...*/}
        ~PushButton() {}
};

void main()
{
        Debugger d;
        d.MemoryDump(sizeof(d) );
        Box b(5, 10, 15, 20);
        b. MemoryDump(sizeof(b) );
        Text t(50, 100, "Sample Text");
        t. MemoryDump(sizeof(t) );
        PushButton p(30, 60);
        p.MemoryDump(sizeof(p) );
}
```

The example above is incomplete. To make it work, you need to add the necessary code to the various `Display()` member functions described earlier in the chapter. I omitted these details to concentrate on the higher-level details of modifying a class hierarchy.

The `Debugger` class is designed as a base class of `Object`. The function `Debugger::MemoryDump()` requires an integer argument indicating how big the object referenced is. The function merely prints the hexadecimal value for each byte in an object. A problem with the code in Listing 3.28 is that now every object created in the `Object` hierarchy has the extra overhead of class `Debugger`. Any local variables declared inside `Debugger` take up storage in every instantiation. This is obviously an intolerable situation for a finished program. A possible solution could be to use a compile-time switch to include or exclude `Debugger` in the class hierarchy.

```
#define DEBUG

// this goes in the header file for class Object

#ifdef DEBUG
class Object: public Debugger {
#else
class Object {
#endif
```

Now a simple change (plus a complete project recompilation) adds the debugger feature to the class library, or eliminates it when everything is fixed. Other features could be added to the overall system in a similar manner. One could easily make a pseudo-single-stepping mechanism, useful in debugging programs. With such a tool, for example, the program could display a message every time an object was created or deleted. Listing 3.29 is an implementation.

Listing 3.29. Adding a pseudo-single-stepping mechanism to a class hierarchy.

```
#include <stdio.h>
#include <string.h>

class Debugger {
          unsigned char* address;
public:
          Debugger();
          ~Debugger();
};

Debugger::Debugger()
{
          address = (unsigned char*) this;
          printf("\ncreating object at address %06X", address);
}

Debugger::~Debugger()
{
          printf("\ndestroying object at address %06X",
                 address);
}

class Object: public Debugger {};

class Box: public Object {
```

```
        int x, y, width, height;
public:
        Box(int x, int y, int width, int height) {}
        void Display() {}
};

class Text: public Object {
        int x, y;
        char text [40];
public:
        Text(int x, int y, char* string)
          {strncpy(text, string, 39);}
        void Display() {}
};

class PushButton: public Object {
protected:
        int state;
        Box* outline;
        Box* button;
public:
        PushButton(int px, int py);
        void Display();
        ~PushButton()
          {delete outline; delete button;}
};

PushButton::PushButton(int x, int y)
{
        const int OUTLINE_WIDTH = 36;
        const int OUTLINE_HEIGHT = 20;
        const int BUTTON_WIDTH = 20;
        const int BUTTON_HEIGHT = 10;
        outline = new Box(x, y, OUTLINE_WIDTH,
                          OUTLINE_HEIGHT);
        button = new Box(x, y, BUTTON_WIDTH,
                         BUTTON_HEIGHT);
}

void PushButton::Display()
{
        outline->Display();
        button->Display();
}

void main()
{
```

continues

Listing 3.29. continued

```
        Debugger d;
        Box b(5, 10, 15, 20);
        Text t(50, 100, "Sample Text");
        PushButton p(30, 60);
}
```

When you execute `main()`, you get a message printed on the display every time an object goes in or out of scope, which also tells you the address of the object. To make a program pause before objects are created or deleted, you could wait for a keystroke after each message is printed.

The preceding examples are rather crude, but they show how inheritance can be put to good use in all kinds of situations. Polymorphic functions also could have been used, achieving even more power. I avoided using them, however, because they are described in Chapter 5. Adding a base class is not the only way to introduce breakpoints in a hierarchy. Because all objects derive from a common root, the root's constructor and destructor are called for every object that is created and deleted. Changing the code for the root class constructor and destructor is a way of adding features to an entire class hierarchy, but because hierarchies are often delivered as libraries, users often don't have access to the source code for the hierarchy.

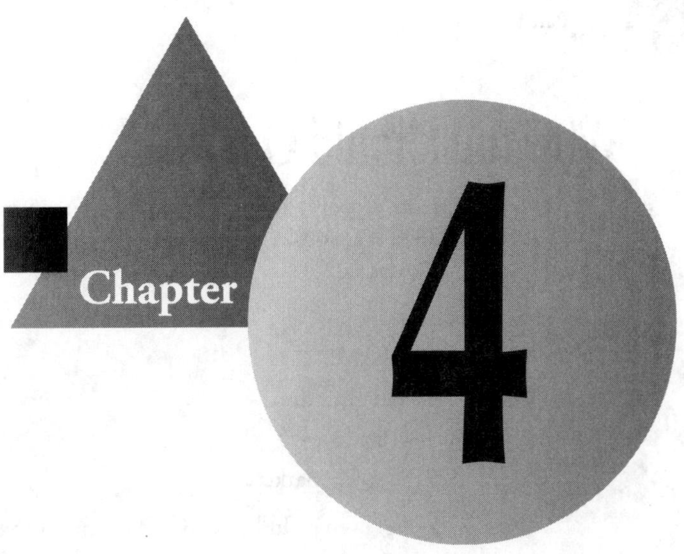

Overloading

Now *there's* a word that sounds out of place. A novice would probably expect a book to show how to *avoid* overloading, rather than encourage it. The term is really a misnomer. Perhaps it's not a good choice, given the confusion it creates for newcomers to C++. In the real world, overloading is commonly associated with electrical circuits, and is a condition in which something is wrong. Overloads of this kind are usually the cause of short circuits or fires. Electrical overloads are caused by a failure to adhere to safe procedures.

The opposite is true in C++. Overloading is not bad. Overloading is good; in fact, it's encouraged and recommended. Overloading refers to the practice of *loading* a function with more than one meaning. Basically, the term expresses that one or more function identifiers are *loaded over* a previous identifier. Having more than one function with the same identifier entails that overloaded functions are no longer distinguishable by their identifier alone. This in turn leads to problems with symbol tables, which are solved by using name mangling (name mangling is described in Chapter 1, "Basics").

Why You Should Overload

In English, as probably in most languages, some verbs are used in different contexts to express different actions. Consider the verb *play*. It can be used in all kinds of situations. You can

Play the piano.

Play basketball.

Play a compact disc.

Play with a toy.

Play the stock market.

This list doesn't even include uses of the word *play* as a noun, such as "a Shakespeare *play*" or "the *play* in a mechanical gearbox," the "best *play* in basketball history," and so on.

In C++ terms, the word *play*, when used as a verb, is said to be overloaded. Each context is associated with a different meaning, but all the uses of the verb are somehow related conceptually. The reuse of the same verb in different but similar situations not only creates an important cue for our thought process, but it also reduces the number of words required in the English language.

When dealing with OOP, simplicity is important. The less you need to know about a system to use it, the better. The same goes for the code. The fewer details needed to call a function, the better. This suggests a need for the compiler to allow variations in function calls and object manipulations. Consider a `Display` function, which takes an argument and prints it on the screen. It would be nice if the function could be used with all kinds of arguments, letting the compiler figure out the details. For example, it would be great to be able to write

```
Display("\nPrint this, please");
Display(123456789);
Display(3.14159);
```

After all, the compiler has complete visibility of the types used in each parameter list, and should be able to use this information somehow. With overloading in C++, three functions could be implemented in such a way as to allow the preceding code to work. Each function is defined separately from the others, and can be distinguished from them by the number and types of parameters the function takes. The function `Display()` is said to be overloaded, because its identifier is associated with more than one function.

Overloading isn't a new concept for programming languages. For example, the = operator is overloaded in many high-level languages, and is used both in assignment statements and conditional expressions, such as

```
a = b
if a = b ...
```

Overloading grants flexibility to C++. Overloading lets people use code with less effort,

because it extends operations that are conceptually similar in nature. The compiler may not think a character string is similar to a floating-point number, but a programmer certainly thinks of the `Display` operation for `strings` and `floats` in similar terms. The emphasis is thus on user friendliness, where the user is a programmer.

The advantage obtained by overloading is not free, because with this advantage comes added complexity for the compiler, which now has to figure everything out. The problem with overloaded words, even in a natural language like English, is that semantics are context dependent. In other words, the exact meaning of an overloaded identifier can only be understood by considering some neighboring words. In C++, the neighboring words are the number and type of the arguments used in the function calls. Thus, overloading is available to functions, but not to variables, classes, or types.

Function Overloading

Having established that overloading is good, it's probably time to get into some details. As mentioned previously, overloaded functions all use the same identifier, and are distinguished by the number and types of their arguments. The return type is *not* used in distinguishing overloaded functions. Thus, the two functions

```
void Display(int);
```

and

```
long Display(int);
```

are not distinguishable and produce a compiler error. Overloaded functions are not required to be members of a class. Both member and nonmember functions can be overloaded.

Overloaded Nonmember Functions

Any function name can be overloaded in C++, but overloading works only within a given scope. One scope worth mentioning is *file scope*. Any function defined outside all classes, and without the `static` keyword, has file scope. Function `main()` is probably the most common such function in C and C++ programs. The following is an example of code using overloaded `Display()` functions, all contained within the same file, and all having file scope:

```
#include <stdio.h>

void Display(char* string) { puts(string); }
void Display(long value) { printf("%ld", value); }
void Display(double value) { printf("%lf", value); }

void main()
```

```
{
        Display("\nPrint this, please");
        Display(123456789);
        Display(3.14159);
}
```

When the compiler sees the various function calls to `Display()`, it looks around for the correct function to use. The result of this search is then saved in the compiled code. The fact that all this work is performed at compile-time is important, because function overloading has no runtime penalty or overhead. Once C++ code is compiled, a call to an overloaded function is indistinguishable from an ordinary function call, so you get all the benefits of uniformity of expression and no disadvantages in code size or execution time. Actually this isn't entirely true. One drawback is an increase in complexity resulting if an overloaded function is called with arguments that don't quite match any of the functions available. In this case you need to be careful, because you may wind up with compiler errors or accidentally invoke the wrong function. Here is an example with the overloaded `Display()`) functions:

```
void main()
{
        Display(333);   // what, a compiler error?
}
```

Yes, this innocuous piece of code causes a compilation error. But what's wrong with it? The problem is that `Display()` is passed an `int` argument, but no such function exists. Two functions can be used after integer promotion to `long` or `double`, thus preventing the compiler from choosing one or the other. The next example instead shows how you might inadvertently call an unexpected function.

```
#include <stdio.h>

void Display(char* string) { puts(string); }
void Display(long value) { printf("%ld", value); }
void Display(float value) { printf("%f", value); }
void Display(double value) { printf("%lf", value); }

void main()
{
        Display(3.14159);
}
```

Everything looks right, and you might expect function `Display(float)` to be called. Actually, the constant value 3.14159 is considered a `double` by the compiler because the value wasn't explicitly declared `float`. Therefore, the function `Display(double)` is invoked. All kinds of similar problems can arise, especially when user conversions and implicit conversions exist. If conversions are required, if default arguments exist, or if variable length argument lists are used, you can expect other problems.

Overloaded Member Functions

Given the emphasis on the class concept, it follows that the primary use of overloading is with class member functions. When more than one member function with the same name is declared in a class, the function name is said to be overloaded in that class. Note that the function name is not overloaded in general, just in that class. In other words, the scope of the overloaded name is just that one class. Other classes might use the same name again, overloading it differently or even not overloading it at all. These classes are entirely separate scopes, and the compiler keeps them separated. Consider the following code:

```
class Example {
        int value;
public:
        void Value(int v) {value = v;}
        int Value() {return value;}
};

void main()
{
        Example e;
        e.Value(3);
        int i = e.Value();
}
```

This code shows that the class `Example` has two overloaded functions, one function to write, and one function to read a variable. This is common use of overloaded functions. In ANSI C, two separate function names have to be used, such as `putValue()` and `getValue()`, but C++ allows you to simplify things. Overloaded functions don't have to be defined `inline`, as I have shown them in my examples. However, typical functions to read and write variables are defined `inline`. Overloaded functions need to differ in either or both of the following ways:

1. The functions must contain a different number of arguments.
2. At least one of the arguments must be different.

As I said earlier, the return type of a function is *not* a factor in distinguishing overloaded functions. Sometimes newcomers to C++ have trouble remembering this fact.

Overloaded Functions in a Class Hierarchy

Things always get harder when multiple classes are used at the same time. Consider using overloaded functions with classes that are part of a hierarchy. You can have classes at different levels that use the same function identifier for different purposes. Consider the inheritance tree in Figure 4.1.

The hierarchy in Figure 4.1 is implemented through the following code:

```
class A {
public:
        int foo(int i) {return i + 1;}
};

class B: public A {
public:
        int foo(float f) {return f + 10;}
};
```

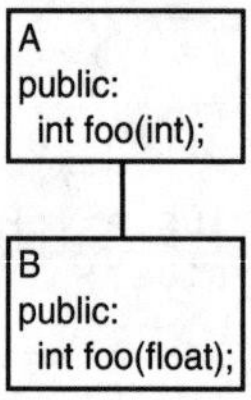

A
public:
int foo(int);

B
public:
int foo(float);

Figure 4.1. An inheritance tree with function identifiers repeated at different levels.

Is function `foo()` overloaded in the hierarchy? One way to find out is to see what the compiler does. The following code shows some interesting facts:

```
void main()
{
       B b;
       int i = b.foo(2);        // A::foo or B::foo called?
}
```

Class `B` has two functions called `foo()`: one function that is inherited and one that is not. So, what value does the variable `i` have at the end of `main()`? The answer is 12. The compiler used function `B::foo(float)`, which required an implicit conversion from `int` to `float`, even though the base class had a function requiring no conversions. Is this a bug? No, overloading is valid only within the same scope. Thus, the functions defined in class `B` are in a different scope from those defined in class `A`, just as nested blocks define different scopes, as shown here:

```
{
  int a;
  {                  // new scope
    int a;           // new variable a
  }
}
```

Any redefinition of functions in a derived class obscures all functions with the same name in all base classes. You must realize that this occurs even if the base class functions use totally different arguments. Once the function name is redefined in a derived class, the same function name is invisible in base classes, unless the scope resolution operator is used.

Functions declared in a derived class *disable* overloading of the same function name in base classes, in the absence of scope resolution.

To illustrate the point even further, consider a function taking a pointer to a class A, which was shown in Figure 4.1.

```
int f(A& a)
{
        return a.foo(3.14159F);
}

void main()
{
        B b;
        int i = f(b);
}
```

The function called by `f(A&)` is `A::foo()`—even though an implicit type conversion is required—because the function thinks it is passed an `A` object. The fact that this `A` object is also part of a `B` object is irrelevant. The compiler cannot defer to runtime the process of making a decision, so it blindly chooses `A::foo(int)` in function `f(A&)`. However, if the function had been declared `virtual`, things would have been different. I discuss this type of situation in Chapter 5, "Polymorphism."

Overloading Is Not Overriding

As it turned out, function `foo()` was really not overloaded at all in the previous example. The behavior of the code was determined by the compiler at compile time. Note that using `virtual` functions in a hierarchy can result in runtime determinations of function calls, which entails an entirely different mechanism from that used by overloading. `virtual` functions are used to *override* base class functions, not *overload* them. Don't confuse the terms. Overriding and overloading are two different things. See Chapter 5 for details on function overriding.

Scope Resolution

Is it possible to access function names redefined in a base class, like function `foo()` in the previous example? No problem; just use the scope resolution operator. Just keep in mind that functions defined in different classes are not considered overloaded, so sometimes explicit scope resolution is not required. However, if you're in doubt, use scope resolution. You can use the scope resolution operator either inside the member functions of any derived class, or at the time of a function call. The following code shows both cases:

```
class A {
public:
        int foo(int i) {return i + 1;}
```

```
};

class B: public A {
public:
        int foo(float f) {return f + 10;}
        int foo(int i) {return A::foo(i);}
};

void main()
{
        B b;
        int i = b.foo(2);       // use B::foo(int)
        int j = b.A::foo(2);    // use A::foo(int)
        float z = 3.14;
        int k = b.foo(z);       // use B::foo(float)
}
```

Class `A` contains two overloaded `foo(...)` functions, and `main()` invokes member functions of both class `B` and class `A` through an instantiation of `B`, using scope resolution. Function `B::foo(int)` uses the operator to invoke `A::foo(int)`.

Argument Matching

The topic of argument matching is both an important and a complicated one. Nevertheless, in C++, argument matching needs to be understood to successfully utilize function overloading. When the compiler finds a function call for an overloaded function, it must decide just which function is supposed to be called. If the compiler finds a function whose arguments match exactly, no problem. Otherwise it looks for an alternative function. In doing so, the compiler attempts to match the arguments with those of the overloaded functions. This procedure is referred to as *argument matching*. Consider the following example:

```
void some_function(int value)
{
     value = value + 1;
}

void some_function(float value)
{
     value = value - 1;
}

void main()
{
     // invoke a function with a char parameter
     some_function('A');
}
```

Here, two functions with the name `some_function()` take different parameters. In `main()`, a call is made to a function that takes a char parameter, but such a function is not defined. The compiler doesn't generate an error, because it sees that there is an acceptable function taking type int. The compiler produces code to convert the char parameter to int, then calls the function some_function(int). Had the function some_function(char) been declared, it would have represented a better match and would have been used instead.

This short example gives you a glimpse at the kind of decisions the compiler must make, but often things may be a bit more complicated. When the compiler looks for the function to invoke, it may find several possible candidates. However, if more than one of them is acceptable, an ambiguity arises and the compiler is forced to give up and generate an error message. These are the argument-matching rules for overloaded function selection within the same scope:

1. No conversions are necessary. Functions requiring no argument conversions are the best candidates.
2. Argument promotions are necessary. One or more arguments are promoted along the path char->int->long->float->double->long->double.
3. Argument conversions are necessary. One or more arguments are converted according to standard or user-defined conversions.

Overloaded Constructors

One of the most common uses of function overloading is with constructors. The reason is that when you are instantiating a class, you should keep things as flexible as possible so that users can make different kinds of instances. Consider a class for a pop-up window in a graphical user interface package. You might want to instantiate windows like this:

```
// create a window with all default parameters
PopupWindow window;

// create a window at specified coordinates
PopupWindow window_1(x, y);

// create a window with controlled dimensions
PopupWindow window_2(x, y, width, height);

// make a window just like another one
PopupWindow window_3 = window_2;
```

The implementation for such a class might look something like Listing 4.1.

Listing 4.1. Overloaded constructors for a pop-up window class.

```
class PopupWindow {
          int x, y, width, height;
public:
          PopupWindow();
          PopupWindow(int, int);
          PopupWindow(int, int, int, int);
          PopupWindow(PopupWindow&);
};

// set all values to default
PopupWindow::PopupWindow()
{
          x = y = 100;
          width = height = 100;
}

// set width and height to default
PopupWindow::PopupWindow(int px, int py)
{
          x = px;
          y = py;
          width = height = 100;
}


// initialize all variables
PopupWindow::PopupWindow(int px, int py, int w, int h)
{
          x = px;
          y = py;
          width = w;
          height = h;
}


// make an object just like another one
PopupWindow::PopupWindow(PopupWindow& pw)
{
          x = pw.x;
          y = pw.y;
          width = pw.width;
          height = pw.height;
}
```

The class uses four overloaded constructors to do the job. The less the user has to know about instantiating a class, the better the class is. Overloading gives tremendous flexibility. With overloaded constructors, you can let the user specify which variables are to be explicitly initialized, and which are to assume their default values. In Microsoft Windows programming, there are lots of cases in which you need to supply lists of arguments, even if you only want the default values to be assumed. C++ overloading lets you program without always having to use a rigid set of arguments.

Overloaded copy constructors sometimes provide a shorthand for setting up new instances. You can specify which parameters to change with respect to the object copied. For example,

```
PopupWindow::PopupWindow(PopupWindow& pw, int px, int py)
{
        x = px;
        y = py;
        width = pw.width;
        height = pw.height;
}
```

This code copies some or all of the variables of a reference object, but initializes some of its own variables differently. You can define as many copy initializers as you need, as long as they are all distinguishable by their arguments.

Some Special Cases

Can `static` member functions be overloaded? Yes they can, with the usual proviso that each overloaded function be distinguishable by the number and type of its arguments.

Destructors cannot be overloaded. Because they don't take arguments, there is only one way to call, and hence define, a destructor.

`virtual` functions can also be overloaded. To be able to access the overloaded `virtual` functions in a derived class using a reference to a base class object, all the base classes must have identically declared functions that are also `virtual`. For example, consider deriving a class `Dialog` from class `PopupWindow`, both with overloaded `virtual` functions, such as in the inheritance tree in Figure 4.2. This tree is implemented with the code in Listing 4.2.

Listing 4.2. A class hierarchy that overloads `virtual` functions.

```
class PopupWindow {
        int x, y;
public:
        virtual void Set(int, int);
        virtual void Set(int, int, int, int);
};
```

continues

Listing 4.2. continued

```
class Dialog: public PopupWindow {
        int a, b;
public:
        virtual void Set(int, int);
        virtual void Set(int, int, int, int);
};

void PopupWindow::Set(int px, int py)
{
        int x = px;
        int y = py;
}

void PopupWindow::Set(int px, int py, int w, int h)
{
        int x = px;
        int y = py;
        int width = w;
        int height = h;
}

void Dialog::Set(int px, int py)
{
        int x = px;
        int y = py;
}

void Dialog::Set(int px, int py, int w, int h)
{
        int x = px;
        int y = py;
        int width = w;
        int height = h;
}

void f(PopupWindow& pw)
{
        pw.Set(1, 1, 1, 1);
}

void main()
{
        Dialog d;
        f(d);
}
```

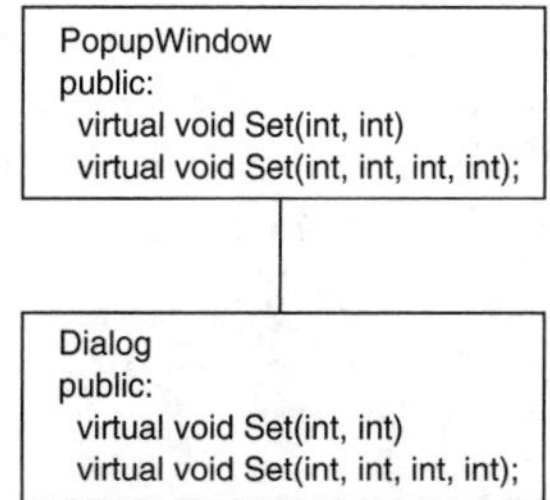

Figure 4.2. Overloading `virtual` *functions.*

Invoking function `f(PopupWindow&)` with a reference to a `Dialog` object results in the correct overloaded `virtual` function being called for object `d`. If the `virtual` functions in the base classes are not declared identically, things change. Consider modifying class `Dialog` as follows:

```
class Dialog: public PopupWindow {
          int a, b;
public:
          virtual void Set(int, int);
          virtual void Set(int, int, short, short);
};
```

With the preceding declaration, function `Dialog::Set(int, int, short, short)` no longer overrides its base class function `PopupWindow::Set(int, int, int, int)`, so the latter function is called.

User Conversions Through Overloading

C++ has rules for converting built-in types. For example, a `char` may be promoted to `int`, and `int` may be promoted to `long`, `float`, or `double`, depending on the circumstances. What kind of rules apply to user classes? None, unless you define them. Conversion rules for user classes can be defined with overloaded class constructors or with special conversion functions.

Using Overloaded Constructors

Conversions using overloaded constructors are the most commonly used conversions in C++. They allow you to convert anything into anything, as long as the conversion makes sense to you. The keyword here is *you*, because only you as the programmer know what conversions make sense, and how a conversion is to be performed. Consider having a function that takes an argument of class `Counter`, like the following:

```
void foo(Counter& c) {/*.. do something here ..*/}
```

Any attempts to invoke function `foo(Counter&)` without an explicit `Counter` object reference cause a compiler error, because the compiler doesn't know how to obtain `Counter` objects from other objects. To define a user-conversion rule from a generic type `T` to class `Counter`, all you need is to define a constructor for `Counter` that takes a single argument of type `T`. The compiler uses this constructor whenever it needs to convert a `T` object into a `Counter` object. The code in Listing 4.3 shows several user-defined conversions for class `Counter`.

Listing 4.3. Performing conversions between built-in types and user classes.

```
class Counter {
        int value;
public:
        Counter();            // default constructor
        Counter(int);         // conversion from int
        Counter(long);        // conversion from long
        Counter(double);      // conversion from double
};

Counter::Counter() {value = 0;}
Counter::Counter(int i) {value = i;}
Counter::Counter(long l) {value = l;}
Counter::Counter(double d) {value = d;}

void foo(Counter& c) { /* .. do something .. */ }

void main()
{
        Counter c;
        foo(1);               // convert from int to Counter
        foo(2L);              // convert from long to Counter
        foo(3.14);            // convert from double to Counter
        foo(c);               // no conversions necessary
}
```

You can also specify a user conversion from one class to another. The code in Listing 4.4 shows a user-defined rule for converting class `Example` into class `Counter`.

Listing 4.4. Performing conversions from one class to another.

```
class Example {
public:
        int word;
        Example() {word = 0;}
};
```

```
class Counter {
        int value;
public:
        Counter() {value = 0;}    // default constructor
        Counter(Example);         // conversion from Example
};

// define the conversion rule
Counter::Counter(Example e) {value = e.word;}

void foo(Counter c) { /* .. do something .. */ }

void main()
{
        Example e;
        foo(e);         // invoke the conversion rule from
                        // Example into Counter
}
```

Whenever the compiler automatically invokes a constructor for the purpose of converting one type of object into another, an implicit conversion is said to have taken place. The conversion is implicit because the original source code doesn't invoke a conversion constructor explicitly. The use of implicit conversions by the compiler becomes more reasonable if you consider that the function call

```
foo(e);
```

is equivalent to the call

```
foo(Counter(e) );
```

User-defined implicit conversions are performed in many different situations by the compiler. The most common of these are

1. With object initializers.
2. With function calls.
3. With function return values.

Of course, user-defined conversions are used also in explicit conversions, such as in

```
void main()
{
        Example e;
        Counter c = (Counter) e;    // explicit conversion
}
```

The choice of whether to provide user-defined conversions between two classes is dependent on the relationship between the classes. In many cases, conversions wouldn't make sense, such as when attempting a conversion from a `char` pointer to class `Counter`. In any case, it's your decision. Conversions are nice because they not only make your classes more forgiving, but they also make them more general-purpose and easy to use.

Using Special Conversion Functions

The previous section dealt with declaring constructors for a user class, enabling conversions from built-in user class types. The conversion from `int` to `Counter` is one such conversion. The use of constructors also permits the conversion between user classes. It is also possible, with some restrictions, to convert a user class into a generic type. Here is an example showing the conversion from a pointer to user object to a pointer to `int`:

```
class Counter {
        int value;
public:
        Counter() {value = 0;}  // default constructor
        operator int*() {return &value;}
};

void main()
{
        int* ip;
        Counter* c = new Counter;
        ip = (int*) c;         // convert (Counter*) to (int*)
}
```

To convert a user class into a built-in type, you need to declare a *typecasting operator*. The typecasting operator is a special kind of operator, for which you don't declare a return type. The compiler automatically uses the operator's typed name as the return type. You can similarly define other casting operators for the built-in C++ types, such as `char`, `int`, `unsigned long`, `void*`, `float*`, and so on. What you *can't* do with these special conversion functions is attempt to convert a class into another class, into an enumeration, or into user types declared with a `typedef`. The constructor conversion method works in these cases. Converting a user class into a built-in type is an operation that makes sense only for certain classes and built-in types. It would be absurd to define a typecast operator to convert class `Counter` into a `char`, for example. Only the class implementor knows what makes sense and what doesn't.

Overloading *static* Member Functions

Does it make sense to overload a `static` member function of a class? Conceptually, yes, although the actual need for such functions depends on the class. Keep in mind that `static` member functions don't have a `this` pointer passed to them when they are invoked, so they don't have access to the data of any object, unless a pointer is passed explicitly. Moreover, a `static` member function is not invoked in reference to any class instantiations. Listing 4.5 contains some examples.

Listing 4.5. Using overloaded `static` member functions.

```
class Counter {
public:
        static void Set(int);
        static void Set(double);
};

int v;

void Counter::Set(int i) {v = i;}
void Counter::Set(double d) {v = d;}

void main()
{
        // you don't need a Counter object to make these
        // calls to static member functions

        Counter::Set(1);
        Counter::Set(3.14159);
}
```

Operator Overloading

Object-oriented programming is a methodology that achieves much of its power by having objects keep track of themselves at runtime. Using overloaded functions allows not only uniformity of expression in function calls for different objects, but also greater intuitiveness in function names.

Operator overloading is not as new a concept as you might think: it's been part of natural languages for thousands of years. Consider the generic *addition* operation. You can

Add two numbers together.

Add oranges together.

Add oranges to apples.

Add sugar to water.

or, a little more abstractly:

Add wood to the fire.

Add suspense to a story.

Addition can be applied indifferently to objects that are countable, like apples and oranges, and to abstract things, such as suspense. Thus, the concept of addition is intuitive, in the sense that it is used to convey an action of increasing a number, intensifying an attribute, and so on. The important thing here is that the concept of addition is rather vague, unless it is associated with a context.

C++ operators are much the same. They are built into the C++ language, and are defined to perform certain operations on the C++ built-in types. Although operators are typically associated with mathematical or logical functions, they are simply an alternative notation for a function call. The dualism between operators and function calls suggests the possibility of overloading operators, enabling different object types to use operators, as appropriate. Using operators in a manner similar to natural languages is desirable, so it would be convenient to be able to use the following expressions:

```
Orange my_oranges, his_oranges;
my_oranges = my_oranges + his_oranges

Apple my_apples;
Fruit my_fruit;
my_fruit = my_oranges + my_apples;

CakeIngredient sugar, water, batch;
batch = sugar + water;
```

and also the more abstract expressions like

```
Fuel wood;
Combustion fire;
fire += wood;

Attribute suspense;
Drama story;
story += suspense;
```

Allowing all of the preceding notations is exactly what operator overloading is about. Again, the goals are simplicity in notation and uniformity of expression. The burden of applying an operator in an expression is on the objects acted upon, rather than the programmer. Overloaded operators are even more powerful because they can be inherited (with some exceptions) throughout a class hierarchy. Operator overloading is used in other programming languages, but without a special name. In some languages, such as Pascal, it is possible to do the following:

```
structure_a := structure_b + structure_b;
```

which causes a bytewise addition of structures b and c to be copied into structure a. This syntax implies that the addition operator is overloaded for structures, albeit with certain rules on type conformance. The preceding example also used an overloaded assignment operator, because a structure copy operation was triggered by the statement rather than a default scalar assignment.

What is really new in C++ is not so much the concept of operator overloading as much as the extension of function overloading to include operators, which are equivalent to function calls.

Operators as Function Calls

There are two ways operators can be implemented for class objects: as member functions and as friends. A unary operator applied to an object is equivalent to a function call. Given an object `W` and a unary operator `@`, the expression

```
@W
```

is equivalent to the function calls

```
W.operator@()          // using a member operator
operator@(W)           // using a friend operator
```

A binary operator applied to two objects is also equivalent to a function call. Given the objects `X` and `Y`, and an operator `@`, the expression

```
X @ Y
```

is equivalent to the function calls

```
X.operator@(Y);        // using a member operator
operator@(X,Y);        // using a friend operator
```

The preceding code shows that operators can invoke two different functions, one function that is a member, and one that is a `friend`. This fact is important, and the two types of functions have different behaviors at times. If both types of functions are available to the compiler (because you declared them), argument-matching determines which type to use. If both are usable in an expression, the compiler generates an error message regarding the ambiguous overloaded functions.

Note that the member function `Y::operator@(X)` is never considered by the compiler to resolve the expression `X@Y`, because this would assume that the `@` operator enjoyed the commutative property. Similarly, the `friend operator@(Y,X)` is not considered when the compiler attempts to satisfy the function call `Y.operator@(X)`.

Overloaded Operators as Member Functions

Overloaded member functions have already been described in detail, but functions implementing operators are slightly unusual. To begin with, their names must begin with the string `operator`, followed by the characters representing the operator being implemented. For example, the member function to implement the addition operator would have to be named `operator+`. The second restriction is in the number of arguments these functions can take. Member functions implementing unary operators must take no arguments, whereas those implementing binary operators can take only one argument. The reason for this is clear if you study the type of function call generated when an operator is encountered by the compiler. For an instantiation w of class W with overloaded operators, the operator member functions are invoked like this:

```
w.operator@()          // unary operator @w
w.operator@(y);        // binary operator w@y
```

Attempting to declare more than one argument in an operator member function causes a compiler error. The return type for a member operator function can be anything you want; however, operators are generally designed to be used in expressions, such as

```
a + b + c + d + e
```

Statements such as these require that the result of a + b yield a type that allows the compiler to continue the evaluation of the expression. This in turn requires an operator for a class W to return a reference to class W. Listing 4.6 is a short example with overloaded operators implemented as member functions.

Listing 4.6. Overloaded operators as member functions.

```
class Counter {
public:
        int value;
        Counter(int i) {value = i;}
        Counter operator!();             // unary operator
        Counter operator+(Counter& c); // binary operator
};

Counter Counter::operator!()
{
        return Counter(!value);
}

Counter Counter::operator+(Counter& c)
{
        return Counter(value + c.value);
}


void main()
{
        Counter c1(3), c2(5);     // declare two objects
        c1 = !c1;                 // apply unary operator
        c1 = c1 + c2;             // apply binary operator
}
```

The use of the operators in `main()` is completely intuitive, and doesn't require you to have knowledge of class implementation details to guess the outcome of the operations. This is the way operators are designed to be overloaded. It would have been just as easy to make the overloaded + operator perform a subtraction between objects, but this would be unacceptable (unless you were participating in an Obfuscated C Contest). Notice how the operator return types are `Counter`, allowing the operator to be concatenated in `long` expressions as described earlier.

You can declare multiple overloaded operator functions for the same operator, as long as the compiler is able to distinguish them through the number and type of arguments. The restriction on the number of arguments (one at most) limits the possibilities, but that is imposed by the way operators are used, not by C++ itself. The example in Listing 4.7 overloads the same operator three times.

Listing 4.7. Using multiple overloaded operators, implemented as member functions.

```
class M {

public:
        int value;
        M(int i) {value = i;}
        M operator+(M& m);
        M operator+(int i);
        M operator+(double d);
};

M M::operator+(M& m)
{
        return M(value + m.value);
}

M M::operator+(int i)
{
        return M(value + i);
}
M M::operator+(double d)
{
        return M(value + d);
}

void main()
{
        M m1(3), m2(10);     // define some objects
        m1 = m1 + m2;        // use M::operator+(M&)
        m1 = m2 + 200;       // use M::operator+(int)
        m1 = m2 + 3.14159;   // use M::operator+(double)
}
```

When the compiler encounters an overloaded operator for a class X in an expression, it searches for a member operator function of class X using the ordinary argument-matching rules for overloaded functions. However, no user-defined conversions are attempted on class X if the search fails. Consider modifying class M somewhat.

```
class M {
public:
      int value;
      M(int i) {value = i;}
      M(char* cp) {value = 0;}
      M operator+(M);
};

M M::operator+(M m)
{
      return M(value + m.value);
}

void main()
{
      M m1(3), m2(10);
      m1 = m2 + "ABC";       // uses M::operator+(M)
      m1 = "ABC" + m2;       // error: no operator defined
}
```

The first addition in `main()` causes the compiler to use the constructor `M(char*)` to convert `"ABC"` into an `M` object. Then the function `M::operator+(M)` is used to evaluate the expression.

The second addition causes a compilation error because the string `"ABC"` is of a type for which the operator + has not been overloaded.

Notes on Operator Member Functions

It is possible to declare an operator member function to be `virtual`, because the mechanics of invoking a member operator function and a regular member function are the same. An example of `virtual` operators is given in Chapter 5.

You are not allowed, however, to declare an operator member function to be `static`. Why? The function needs to operate on a specific object; however, `static` functions are not automatically invoked with a `this` pointer, and can be invoked without reference to any object in particular. You aren't even allowed to declare a `static` operator member function that takes an explicit `this` pointer as an argument.

Overloaded Operators as *friend* Functions

Operators can be overloaded outside all classes. In this case, they are overloaded over the built-in C++ operators themselves and are like global operators. Consider the following examples:

```
int a, b, c;
a = b + c;            // built-in operator+(int, int) used

long d, e, f;
d = e + f;            // built-in operator+(long, long) used

class X {};
X g, h, i;
g = h + i;            // which '=' and '+' operators are used?
```

The last expression doesn't have assignment or addition operators defined for it. Class `X` is not built in. To use class `X` as shown in the preceding code, you need to tell the compiler what to do. You can obviously add the appropriate member operator functions to class `X`, but you can also overload the global operators, and then declare the overloaded functions `friends` of class `X`, like in Listing 4.8.

Listing 4.8. Using `friend` overloaded operators.

```
class X {
        friend X operator+(X&, X&);
public:
        int value;
        X(int i) {value = i;}
        X& operator=(X&);
};

X& X::operator=(X& b)
{
        value = b.value;
        return *this;
}

X operator+(X& a, X& b)
{
        return X(a.value + b.value);
}

void main()
{
       X g(2), h(5), i(3);
       g = h + h + i;
}
```

The preceding example declares the + operator to be a `friend` and the = operator to be a member function for class `X`. It was done this way because the = operator is allowed to be overloaded only as a member function, not as a `friend` function, which implies that the global = operator cannot be overloaded. The language implementors decided that to allow `friend` functions to change the meaning of the assignment operator would cause more problems than it would solve.

The global + operator is overloaded by class `X`'s `friend` function `operator+(X&, X&)`. The function returns an object of class `X`, to yield correct results when invoked repeatedly during the evaluation of long expressions.

In general, `friend` overloaded operators behave pretty much the same as member functions, with one exception: function calls requiring user conversions. In this regard, `friend` operator functions are more versatile than member functions. Consider the statement from the previous section, which caused a compiler error.

```
// operator functions are not commutative !
m1 = "ABC" + m2;     // error: no operator defined
```

The error occurred because there was no + operator defined for character strings, and because the compiler made no attempt (and shouldn't have) to convert a string to an `M` object. Changing the `operator+()` function in class `M` to a `friend` function fixes this problem. With a `friend` operator function, the compiler sees a function declared with two arguments, and thus can attempt user conversions on both of them. Changing class `M` as shown in Listing 4.9 makes function `main()` work for both assignment statements. This increased flexibility for `friend` operators often makes them easier to use than member functions, requiring less knowledge of implementation details by the class user. Listing 4.9 shows the modified implementation of class `M` using a `friend` operator.

Listing 4.9. `friend` operators and user conversions.

```
class M {
public:
       int value;
       M(int i) {value = i;}
       M(char* cp) {value = 0;}
       friend M operator+(M, M);
};

M operator+(M a, M b)
{
       return M(a.value + b.value);
}

void main()
```

```
{
        M m1(3), m2(10);
        m1 = m2 + "ABC";     // uses operator+(M, M)
        m1 = "ABC" + m2;     // uses operator+(M, M)
}
```

The Assignment Operator

The assignment operator is one of the most fundamental operators a class has. The assignment operator can be declared only as a member function, never as a `friend`. The reason? An assignment operation is considered to be tightly bound to a class, much like the class constructor and destructor. Consider the following two statements:

```
M m3 = m2;              // use the copy constructor
m1 = m2;                // use the assignment operator
```

The statements are similar in notation, except that the first statement both declares and defines a variable. The second statement only gives a value (within the context of class `M`) to a variable. The copy constructor can only be called once for a given variable, but you can make assignments to it all day. Given the similarity in the copy operation that takes place in the copy constructor and the assignment operator, one operation is probably best defined in terms of the other. In effect, an assignment operation is implicitly used in a copy constructor. There may, however, be cases in which the initialization in the copy constructor is slightly different from that in the assignment operator. Listing 4.10 is a possible implementation for class `M`, in which the copy constructor uses the assignment operator.

Listing 4.10. Using a copy constructor and an assignment operator in the same class.

```
class M {
public:
          int value;
          M(M& m);                  // copy constructor
          M(int i) {value = i;}    // initializer constructor
          M& operator=(M&);        // assignment operator
};

// copy constructor
M::M(M& m)
{
          // perform necessary object initialization
          // ...
```

continues

Listing 4.10. continued

```
        // copy values into object using the
        // assignment operator
        *this = m;
}

// assignment operator
M& M::operator=(M& b)
{
        value = b.value;
        return *this;
}


void main()
{
        M m1(3), m2(10);
        M m3 = m2;
        m1 = m2;
}
```

If an assignment operator is not explicitly defined for a class and is required by the compiler to resolve a statement, a default operator is generated automatically to perform a member-by-member copy operation. An overloaded assignment operator is not inherited by derived classes. Consider the code in Listing 4.11.

Listing 4.11. An example showing the use of default assignment operators.

```
class M {
public:
        int value;
        M(M& m);                // copy constructor
        M(int i) {value = i;}   // initializer constructor
        M& operator=(M&);       // assignment operator
};

class N: public M {
public:
        N(N& n) : M(n) {}       // copy constructor
        N(int i) : M(i) {}      // initializer constructor
};


M::M(M& m)
{
        // perform necessary object initialization
        // ...
```

```
        // copy values into object
        *this = m;
}

M& M::operator=(M& b)
{
        value = b.value;
        return *this;
}


void main()
{
        M m1(3), m2(10);
        m1 = m2;                    // use M::operator=(M&)

        N n1(3), n2(10);
        N n3 = n2;
        n1 = n2;                    // use default N::operator=(N&)
}
```

The last assignment might be expected to generate an error, because no such operator was defined for class `N` and the base class's assignment operator cannot be inherited. In practice, the assignment is performed by the default assignment operator that is generated by the compiler, resulting in each of the members of `n2` being copied into `n1`.

The Function Call *operator()*

Contrary to the assignment operator, the function call `operator()` is not frequently overloaded, and does not have a default operator. In fact, the operator itself is rather unusual. Consider a generic binary operator `@`. The expression

```
a @ b
```

translates into the function call

```
a.operator@(b)
```

So, every operator really turns into a function call. The function call operator also turns into a function call. Is this just? Classes are not all the same. It is conceivable to have a class in which a function call represents the most intuitive way of performing some operation. The most distinguishing feature of the function call operator is that it is not a binary operator, but an "n-ary" operator: it can be applied to multiple arguments. The function call operator is the only kind of operator that can have more than one argument. Consider a class in which a function is used as an `lvalue` in expressions like this:

```
a(x, y, z) = a(x+1, y, z) + a(x, y+1, z);
```

The preceding expression might be used in multidimensional matrices. In this usage, the function call is being used conceptually as a subscripting operator taking multiple arguments. As it turns out, the overloaded function call operator is often used in situations where the subscripting operator was indicated, but couldn't be used because of the need for multiple arguments. The function call is more flexible because it can take as many arguments as you want (including none), whereas the subscripting operator can have only one argument. The code to implement statements like the one preceding this paragraph is shown in Listing 4.12.

Listing 4.12. Using the overloaded function call operator to support multidimensional matrices.

```
class A {
          int value [10] [10];
public:
          int& operator()(int, int);
};

int& A::operator()(int x, int y)
{
          return value [x] [y];
};

void main()
{
          A a;
          int x = 3;
          int y = 4;

          // use the function call also as an lvalue
          a(x, y) = a(x+1, y) + a(x, y+1);
}
```

During the evaluation of the last statement, the function call operator is called three times, with the following arguments:

```
a(4, 4)
a(3, 5)
a(3, 4)
```

The + operator is not defined for class `A`, but because the function call operators for class `A` return a reference to `int`, the compiler uses the built-in addition operator for `int` types.

The function operator is syntactically grouped with binary operators, even though it may be declared to accept any number of operands, such as in the call

```
p(3, 5, "Fred", 12000);
```

which would be interpreted as

```
p.operator()(3, 5, "Fred", 12000);
```

The function call operator is restricted to being declared as a non-`static` member function. `friend` function call operators are not allowed.

A bit of confusion may arise in classes using both an initializer constructor and an overloaded function call operator. Consider adding an initializer constructor to class `A`, which allows statements like

```
A a(i, j);
```

This kind of initialization might be perfectly legitimate in declaring a bidimensional matrix, dynamically allocated, of dimensions `i` and `j`. Modifying class `A` to accommodate an initializer constructor taking two arguments, you have the following:

```
class A {
        int* value;
public:
        A(int, int);
        int& operator()(int, int);
};

A::A(int i, int j)
{
     // dynamically allocate the required matrix
     value = new int [i * j];
}

int& A::operator()(int x, int y)
{
        return value [x + y];
};
```

Now consider carefully the statement

```
A a(20, 10);
```

How is the compiler going to handle this code? Is the compiler going to invoke the class constructor or the function call operator? The compiler is fortunately smart enough to realize that the statement declares and initializes a variable, thus only the initializer constructor is called. Expressions like

```
a(20, 10) = 3;
```

would on the contrary invoke the function call operator. The compiler has no trouble keeping the two cases distinct (and neither should programmers).

The Subscripting Operator

Subscripting is indicated with a set of square brackets `[]`, not to be confused with curly braces `{}`. Brackets are considered an operator. Braces (even when used to enclose an initialization list) aren't considered an operator, and therefore can't be overloaded. The subscripting operator is intuitively associated with arrays. That doesn't mean that its use is restricted to arrays only; however, users expect an array operation to take place when using the subscripting operator. The subscripting operator is considered a binary operator. It can take only one argument, such as in the expression

```
a = b [20];
```

So expressions like

```
a = b [20] [10];
```

are not possible with overloaded subscripting operators. If you need this kind of notation for a class, use the function call operator instead, which yields notation like

```
a = b(20, 10);
```

The subscripting operator is restricted to being declared as a non-`static` member function. `friend` subscripting operators are not allowed. You can make the subscripting operator return a reference to a value, permitting the operator to be used on the left side of an assignment operator.

```
a [20] = b [30];
```

Also, the type used as a subscript can be anything you want, which allows some associative array accessing, like

```
phone_number = Directory ["John Smith"];
```

The following example shows these types of features:

```
#include <string.h>

typedef struct {
          char* name;
          long number;
} DIRECTORY_ENTRY;

class PhoneDirectory {
          int length;
          DIRECTORY_ENTRY* listing;
public:
          PhoneDirectory(int);
          long operator[] (char*);
          char* operator[] (long);
};
```

```
PhoneDirectory::PhoneDirectory(int size)
{
          // create a phone directory of specified size
          listing = new DIRECTORY_ENTRY [size];
          length = size;
}

// look up a person's telephone number
long PhoneDirectory::operator[](char* name)
{
          // search the directory for the name
          for (int i = 0; i < length; i++)
            if (strcmp(name, listing [i]. name) == 0)
              return listing [i]. number;
          return 0;
}

          // find the person who has a given telephone number
          char* PhoneDirectory::operator[](long number)
{
          // search the directory for the number
          for (int i = 0; i < length; i++)
            if (number == listing [i]. number)
              return listing [i]. name;
          return 0;
}

void main()
{
          PhoneDirectory directory(100);
          // assume the directory is initialized with names
          // and telephone numbers

          // find the number of a person
          long number = directory ["John Smith"];

          // find who a number belongs to
          char* name = directory [5551111];
}
```

Operator Overloading Limitations

Overloading operators is one of those object-oriented features that users learn to expect (and rightly so) for the classes they use. But as for all things, what can be done with overloaded operators has limits. Not all operators can be overloaded, which is intended to prevent undesirable interactions with the C++ language itself. The following operators *cannot* be overloaded:

.   Structure component selector

.* member pointer dereferencer

:: Scope resolution operator

?: Conditional ternary operator

Scope Resolution with Operators

Overloaded operators are no different from ordinary overloaded functions in regards to inheritance, with the exception of the assignment operator. In derived classes, the overloaded operators of base classes are always accessible if declared `protected` or `public`. If an overloaded operator in a derived class obscures the operator of a base class, the scope resolution operator is there to help. Consider the inheritance tree in Figure 4.3.

The code in Listing 4.13 shows the scope resolution operator applied to an overloaded operator.

Listing 4.13. The scope resolution operator with overloaded operators.

```
class M {
public:
        int value;
        M(int i) {value = i;}
        int operator+(int);
};

class N:public M {
public:
        N(int i) : M(i) {}
        int operator+(int);
};


int M::operator+(int v)
{
        return value + v;
}

int N::operator+(int v)
{
        return M::operator+(v);
}

void main()
{
```

```
        M m1(3);
        m1 = m1 + 3;     // use M::operator(int)
        N n1(5);
        n1 = n1 + 10;    // use N::operator(int)
}
```

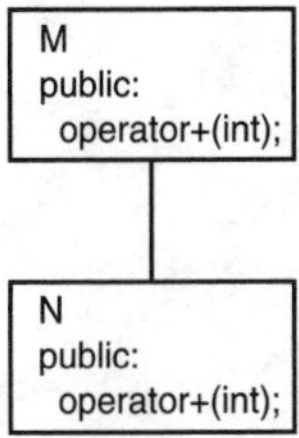

Figure 4.3. An inheritance tree showing scope resolution with overloaded operators.

Advanced Section

This section covers techniques used by expert programmers to solve special kinds of problems. If you are new to C++, I suggest you skip this part of the chapter and go directly to Chapter 5.

Rules for Name Mangling

> **NOTE**
>
> The name-mangling rules shown in this section are valid only when the Options Data Calling option is disabled (which is the default condition). This option is accessed via the menu command `Options ¦ Project.`

Because any number of overloaded functions can use the same name, C++ uses name mangling to keep track of each function individually. As described in Chapter 1, the function name is modified to encode the number and type of arguments. Note that a function's return type is not used in name mangling. Name mangling occurs at the compiler level, not at the linker level. The linker resolves external references to overloaded functions easily, because as far as it can tell, each function has an unambiguous name.

The rules used for name mangling in Borland C++ are relatively simple. The following class shows several overloaded function declarations with their corresponding mangled names for a general class name:

```
class Klass {
public:
  void Set();                                  // @Klass@Set$qv
  void Set(int);                               // @Klass@Set$qi
  void Set(int, int, int);                     // @Klass@Set$qiii
  long Set(long);                              // @Klass@Set$ql
  long Set(long, long, long);                  // @Klass@Set$qlll
  void Set(float);                             // @Klass@Set$qf
  void Set(float, float);                      // @Klass@Set$qff
  void Set(double);                            // @Klass@Set$qd
  void Set(double, double);                    // @Klass@Set$qdd
  void Set(int, long);                         // @Klass@Set$qil
  void Set(long, int);                         // @Klass@Set$qli
  long Set(long, float);                       // @Klass@Set$qlf
  long Set(float, long, int);                  // @Klass@Set$qfli
  void Set(float, double, int, long);          // @Klass@Set$qfdil
  void Set(unsigned int);                      // @Klass@Set$qui
  void Set(unsigned int, unsigned long);       // @Klass@Set$quiul
  void Set(unsigned long);                     // @Klass@Set$qul
  void Set(unsigned char);                     // @Klass@Set$quc
  void Set(unsigned char, signed char);        // @Klass@Set$quczc
  void Set(signed char);                       // @Klass@Set$qzc
};
```

From the preceding code you easily can see the basic rules: the class name is used first, preceded by the `@` character. Next comes the function name, preceded by the `@` character. If a function is not part of a class, the mangled name starts with the `@` followed by the function name. Case is significant for all identifiers. The function name is followed by a `$q` sequence, after which lowercase letters designate each argument type that is declared. Table 4.1 is a list of the letters appearing with the built-in C++ types:

Table 4.1. The argument encoding in mangled names.

Argument Type	*Letters*
`void`	`v`
`void*`	`pv`
`unsigned char`	`uc`
`unsigned char*`	`puc`
`unsigned char&`	`ruc`

Argument Type	*Letters*
`signed char`	`zc`
`signed char*`	`pzc`
`signed char&`	`rzc`
`int`	`i`
`int*`	`pi`
`int&`	`ri`
`unsigned int`	`ui`
`unsigned int*`	`pui`
`unsigned int&`	`rui`
`long`	`l`
`long*`	`pl`
`long&`	`rl`
`unsigned long`	`ul`
`unsigned long*`	`pul`
`unsigned long&`	`rul`
`float`	`f`
`float*`	`pf`
`float&`	`rf`
`double`	`d`
`double*`	`pd`
`double&`	`rd`

Using the information in Table 4.1, you can easily predict the mangled names for many functions. Here are some examples:

Function Declaration	*Mangled Name*
`int My::resize(long, unsigned int*);`	`@My@resize$qlpui`
`void Display(char*);`	`@Display$qpzc`
`long A::PhoneNumber(unsigned int&);`	`@A@PhoneNumber$qrui`

Using class names in an argument list complicates the mangling process somewhat, but here are a few examples:

Function Declaration	*Mangled Name*
`void Klass::Set(Toy);`	`@Klass@Set$q3Toy`
`void Klass::Set(Toy*);`	`@Klass@Set$qp3Toy`
`void Klass::Set(Klass&);`	`@Klass@Set$qr5Klass`

Judging from the mangled names, the rules for mangling class identifiers appear to be straightforward: the complete class identifier is included, preceded by an integer indicating the identifier string length. The usual `p` or `r` characters are added to indicate pointers or references.

The examples shown are generic. You will encounter cases that aren't illustrated here, such as the mangled names of constructors, destructors, names qualified through scope resolution, and so on. The simplest way to sort things out for special cases is to use the compiler itself to tell you how it mangles a function name. Create a file and write some null functions in it with the required declarations, like this:

```
class XYZ {
public:
          XYZ(int*);
          ~XYZ();
};

XYZ::XYZ(int*) {}
XYZ::~XYZ() {}
```

Name the file *test.cpp*. At the DOS command level, invoke the command-line version of the Borland C++ compiler with the `-S` option.

```
bcc -S test.cpp
```

This action produces the assembly language file called *test.asm*, in which you find the mangled names. In this case the names are

`@XYZ@$bctr$qpi`	For the constructor.
`@XYZ@$bdtr$qv`	For the destructor.

Note that name mangling is compiler dependent, so these rules may not be applicable to non-Borland C++ compilers.

Overloading *new* and *delete*

In the first releases of C++ by AT&T, you weren't allowed to overload the **`new`** and **`delete`** operators. To take control over dynamic storage, you had to go through a delicate process of assigning a value to the `this` pointer. Fortunately this is no longer true. You can gain full control over memory allocation and deallocation by using your own **`new`** and **`delete`** operators for a class. Why overload these functions? The first reason for overloading **`new`** is efficiency in memory allocation. Consider an overloaded **`new`** operator that allocates memory in big chunks, rather than bytes. This operator would use up memory faster, but would also make frequent calls to the allocator unnecessary.

Consider a graphics package that allocates objects out of VGA memory on the video card, or that uses RAM disk memory that is unsupported by the compiler. These cases require the use of your own overloaded **`new`** and **`delete`** operators, as shown in Listing 4.14.

Listing 4.14. Overloading `new` and `delete` with fixed allocation sizes.

```
#include <stddef.h>
const int BYTES_PER_BITMAP = 100 * 100;

class BitMap {
          unsigned char* bit_map;
public:
          BitMap();
          void ClearBitMap() {}
          void* operator new(size_t);
          void operator delete(void*);
};

BitMap::BitMap()
{
          // clear bitmap to zero: the memory for the object
          // has already been allocated !
          ClearBitMap();

          // do whatever else the constructor requires...
}
```

continues

Listing 4.14. continued

```
void* BitMap::operator new(size_t s)
{
        // use the global new operator to
        // simulate getting memory from RAM disk
        // reserve space for the bitmap
        return new unsigned char* [BYTES_PER_BITMAP];
}

void BitMap::operator delete(void* a)
{
        // simulate relinquishing memory from a RAM disk,
        //  using the global delete operator
        delete a;
}

void main()
{
        BitMap* image = new BitMap();
        // manipulate image...
        delete image;
}
```

The program uses memory allocated from a RAM disk to store bitmaps, which are bidimensional arrays of pixels. The class uses its own **new** and **delete** operators to effect nonstandard memory management. I won't go into the actual details of managing a RAM disk, because the focus here is on overloaded operators. The argument declared for the overloaded **new** operator is supplied automatically by the compiler at invocation time. This argument is declared of type `size_t`, and indicates the size (in `unsigned chars`) of an `unsigned int` and is used for portability across C++ compilers. Borland C++ uses 16 bits (2 `unsigned chars`) to store unsigned integers, but other compilers may vary, depending on the characteristics of the machine they are designed to run on.

An overloaded **new** operator is considered `static` by the compiler, even without an explicit declaration. This entails that the operator is invoked *before* the constructor is. Likewise, the **delete** operator is `static`, ensuring it is invoked *after* the destructor. The reason for this is that an object can be constructed in memory only after memory has been allocated, and must be destructed before its memory is relinquished.

The preceding class has an inherent limitation: the size of a bitmap is fixed at compile time. It might be convenient to have bitmaps that are of variable size to accommodate images of all sizes. This requires changing the class somewhat, as shown in Listing 4.15.

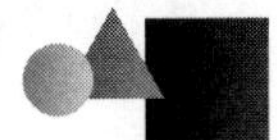

Listing 4.15. Overloading new and `delete` with variable allocation sizes.

```
#include <stddef.h>

class BitMap {
          int width, height;
          unsigned char* bit_map;
public:
          BitMap(int, int, int);
          void ClearBitMap(int color) {}
          void* operator new(size_t s)
            {return ::operator new(s);}
          void* operator new(size_t, int, int);
          void operator delete(void*);
};

BitMap::BitMap(int x, int y, int color)
{
          // save the size of the bitmap
          width = x; height = y;
          // clear bitmap to zero: the memory for
          // the object has already been allocated !
          ClearBitMap(color);

          // do whatever else the constructor requires...
}


void* BitMap::operator new(size_t s, int x, int y)
{
          // use the global new operator to
          // simulate getting memory from RAM disk
          // reserve space for the bitmap
          return new unsigned char* [x * y];
}

void BitMap::operator delete(void* a)
{
          // simulate relinquishing memory from a RAM disk,
          //  using the global delete operator
          delete a;
}

const int BLACK = 0;

void main()
{
```

continues

Listing 4.15. continued

```
        BitMap* image = new(200, 300) BitMap(200, 300, BLACK);
        // manipulate image...
        delete image;
}
```

The preceding example has lots of interesting points. First, notice the notation of the first statement in `main()`. It is really unusual, and allows no deviations. The operator `BitMap::operator new()` is called with the `width` and `height` arguments required to allocate the amount of storage needed. The class constructor is called with additional arguments. The arguments for **`new`** and the constructor are independent from each other. Because `BitMap::operator new` is `static`, it doesn't have a `this` pointer, and it can't access member variables of object `image`. To save the `width` and `height` inside the object, the arguments must also be passed to the constructor. For generality, I also passed an additional argument, which the constructor uses to initialize the bitmap.

There are two overloaded **`new`** operators, one with a single argument and one with three arguments. The first operator is declared and defined solely for the benefit of the Borland C++ compiler. The function is not used, but the compiler issues the error message

```
"Too few parameters in call to 'BitMap::operator new(unsigned int,
int)' in function BitMap::BitMap(int, int, int)"
```

if you leave the function out. Note how the first argument declared for operator **`new`** is passed automatically. Attempting to pass it explicitly is an error. This means that the call

```
BitMap* image = new(200, 300) BitMap(200, 300, BLACK);
```

really turns into the call

```
BitMap* image = new(2, 200, 300) BitMap(200, 300, BLACK);
```

because Borland C++ uses two bytes to store an `unsigned int`. The **`new`** operator can be overloaded as many times as you want, as long as each operator is distinguishable from the others by the number and type of its arguments. The **`delete`** operator is not as flexible: it can be declared only with a single argument of type `void*`, and must return a `void` type. This implies that only one overloaded **`delete`** operator can exist for a given class.

Prefix and Postfix Operators

If there is a topic in the C++ language that gives a sense of incompleteness, the topic of *`prefix`* and *`postfix`* operators is it. In fact, the problems encountered in prefix and postfix operators expose a problem with all C++ overloaded unary operators. Any computer language is bound to have its soft spots, including C++. The evolving nature of the language makes certain variations possible in the future, but the more people involved in the decision-making process, the more difficult it is to obtain a consensus. But first things first. A prefix operator is of the type shown in the following statements:

```
a = ++b;
a = --b;
```

The operator is applied *before* the expression is evaluated. A postfix operator is of the type shown in the next two statements:

```
a = b++;
a = b--;
```

Here the operator is applied *after* the expression is evaluated. In C++, all unary operators are prefix operators (except obviously the postfix ++ and -- operators). The C++ language originally allowed you to overload only prefix operators. Popular demand forced the language implementors at AT&T to come up with a method to solve this problem. The solution they provided is rather crude compared to the rest of the language. Perhaps a solution may be to endow all unary operators with the ability to be declared prefix or postfix, although unary operators are typically prefix. With a postfix operator, you could do something like this:

```
a = b!    // this is not valid C++ code
```

which would read the value of `b` into `a`, then perform the `!` operation on `b`.

Regarding the matter of overloaded postfix operators, Borland C++ version 2.0 differs from versions 3 and 4. Version 2.0 didn't support postfix operators, but 3 and 4 do. The following discussion of postfix operators, therefore, pertains only to Borland C++ 3 and 4. Declaring an overloaded `operator++` with no arguments makes it prefix (the usual default type). To get a postfix operator, you declare the operator function with a single `int` argument, just to make it distinguishable from the prefix operator. The argument is really not used at all by the compiler. In fact, the argument is set to zero during invocation at runtime. Listing 4.16 is an example of using prefix and postfix operators.

Listing 4.16. Using prefix and postfix operators.

```
// NOTE: Borland DOESN'T support postfix overloaded
// operators in Borland C++ 2.0, but does support
// them in versions 3 and 4
class X {
public:
          int value;
          X& operator++();      // prefix operator
          X& operator++(int);  // postfix operator
};
```

continues

Listing 4.16. continued

```
X& X::operator++()
{
        value += 1;
        return *this;
}

X& X::operator++(int)
{
        value += 1;
        return *this;
}

void main()
{
        X x;
        ++x;                    // use X::operator++()
        x++;                    // use X::operator(int)
}
```

The argument that is passed to postfix operators should not be used inside the operator's function body. Its value is always zero in Borland C++, but the argument is meant to be used only as a signal by the compiler. Given the roughness in this implementation of postfix operators, I wouldn't be too surprised if the people at AT&T decided to make some changes, relegating the current method to the list of C++ anachronisms.

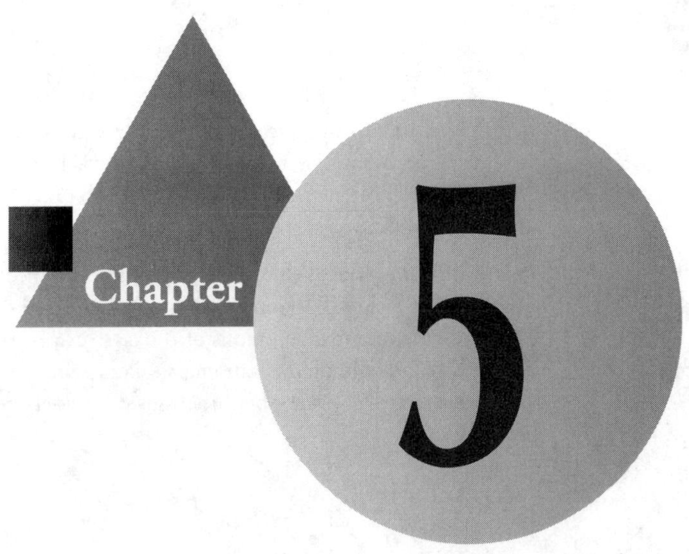

Polymorphism

One of the most obscure features of C++ for newcomers is *polymorphism*. The word *polymorphism* is rather exotic, which is probably why the term stuck despite the fact that the same characteristic can be described in other ways. Programmers are a bunch of strange folks. They thrive on obscure ways of doing things and sometimes make things difficult just for fun. There is even an annual contest for C programmers, which gives first prize to the most difficult program to understand. Programming languages generate support for themselves through books, magazine articles, conference papers, and so on. The more people take interest in a language, the better. Terms that sound bizarre are more likely to generate curiosity, which in turn stimulates people to study the new features of a language. If enough people do this, the language acquires critical mass and becomes a success. Such is what happened to C++, and the term *polymorphism* may have attracted more than one curious reader while building up mass.

The origin of the word *polymorphism* is simple: It comes from the two Greek words *poly* (many), and *morphos* (form)—multiform. Polymorphism describes the capability of C++ code of behaving differently depending on runtime situations. This behavior is often beyond the direct control of the programmer, who must rely on C++ objects to keep track of themselves. In real programs, the possible ways in which objects can interact with one another is combinatorial, reaching astronomical numbers with even small class hierarchies. As a result, you often are compelled to rely on object polymorphism to develop medium and large projects.

Polymorphism is not as much a characteristic of objects as it is a characteristic of member functions for a class. Polymorphism is implemented through the class architecture; however, only the member functions of the class can be polymorphic, rather than the entire class. This kind of implementation is similar to the use of verbs in natural languages, which are equivalent to C++ member functions. Consider the ways an object can be used in real life. You can

Clean it

Move it

Disassemble it

Repair it

Paint it

to mention only a few. These verbs denote only generic actions, because you don't know what kind of object is being acted on. For example, moving a pencil requires completely different actions from those required to move a house, even though the two concepts are similar. The verb *move* can be associated with a particular set of actions only once the object acted on is made known.

Early and Late Binding

In C++, a polymorphic function can become associated with one of many possible functions only when an actual object is passed to the polymorphic function. In other words, the source code itself doesn't always tell you how a section of code is going to execute, indicating that the function-calling mechanism is different from that of ANSI C. In C++, a function call is only *indicated* in the source code, without specifying the exact function to call. This is known as *late binding*. In most traditional programming languages, such as C and Pascal, the compiler calls fixed function identifiers, based on the source code. The linker then takes these identifiers and replaces them with a physical address. This process is known as *early binding*, because function identifiers are associated with physical addresses before runtime, during the process of compilation and linkage.

The problem with early binding is that the programmer must predict what objects will be used in all function calls in every situation. This is not only limiting, but it's sometimes impossible. Moving the binding process further downstream forces the runtime code to sort out the binding of identifiers and addresses. The best thing about early binding is that it's fast. The only runtime overhead incurred is in passing arguments, performing a function call, and cleaning up the stack. However, early binding is tremendously limiting.

The problem with late binding is obviously its runtime efficiency. The code itself must deduce at runtime which function to invoke, and then invoke it. Some languages, such as Smalltalk, use late binding exclusively. Exclusive use of late binding results in an extremely powerful language, but one that suffers from certain speed penalties. On the other hand, ANSI C uses early binding exclusively, resulting in high speed but a lack of flexibility.

C++ Is a Hybrid Language

C++ is not a traditional procedural language like Pascal, but it isn't a pure object-oriented language either. C++ is a hybrid language. It uses both early binding and late binding and gives you the best features of each of the two methods. Everything is under the programmer's direct control. For code that is deterministic in its runtime behavior, you can force C++ to use early binding. For more complicated situations, you can resort to late binding. You can achieve both high speed and high flexibility. However, with these two attributes comes greater complexity in the C++ language and the code it generates. The burden is on the programmer to figure out when to use early binding and when to use late binding. The compiler, however, still handles most of the work.

virtual Functions

In C++, you specify late binding for a function by declaring it `virtual`. Late binding makes sense in C++ only for objects that are part of a class hierarchy. Declaring a function `virtual` for a class that is not used as a base class is syntactically correct, but results in unnecessary runtime overhead. Listing 5.1 shows `virtual` functions for the simple inheritance tree shown in Figure 5.1.

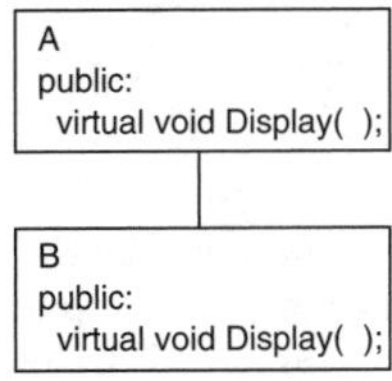

Figure 5.1. `virtual` *functions in a simple hierarchy.*

Listing 5.1. Using `virtual` functions.

```
#include <stdio.h>

class A {
public:
      virtual void Display() {puts("\nClass A");}
};

class B: public A {
public:
      virtual void Display() {puts("\nClass B");}
};

void Show(A* a)
{
      a->Display();    // find out at runtime which
                       // function to use
}

void main()
{
      A* a = new A;
      B* b = new B;
      a->Display();     // use A::Display()
      b->Display();     // use B::Display()
      Show(a);          // use A::Display()
      Show(b);          // use B::Display()
}
```

The polymorphic behavior of the member function `Display()` in classes `A` and `B` is not obvious when you look solely at function `main()`. The polymorphic behavior does show up in function `Show()`, in which it is impossible to predict—by solely examining its source code—whether function `A::Display()` or `B::Display()` will be invoked. If the `virtual` keyword were dropped in the two class declarations, the following behavior would arise:

```
void main()
{
      // behavior with non-virtual functions

      Show(a);    // use A::Display()
      Show(b);    // use A::Display()
}
```

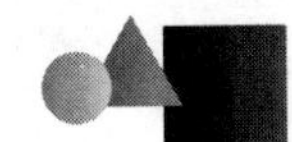

The second function call causes `A::Display()` to be called, because the argument `B*` is converted to `A*`, and then passed to the function `Show(A*)`. The call `a->Display()` is bound early to the function `A::Display()`, resulting in the fixed behavior.

Declaring a function `virtual` doesn't mean that it is overridden in a derived class, merely that it *can* be. To propagate the polymorphic behavior of a function down an inheritance tree, each derived class must declare the same function to be `virtual`.

Function Overriding

In the previous example, `virtual` function `B::Display()` is selected dynamically at runtime inside function `::Show()`. Function `B::Display()` is therefore said to *virtually override* function `A::Display()`. A function declared in a derived class overrides a `virtual` base class function only if it has the same name and uses the same number and type of arguments as the `virtual` base class function. If even one argument is different, it is considered an entirely new function, and no overriding occurs. Consider the inheritance tree in Figure 5.2.

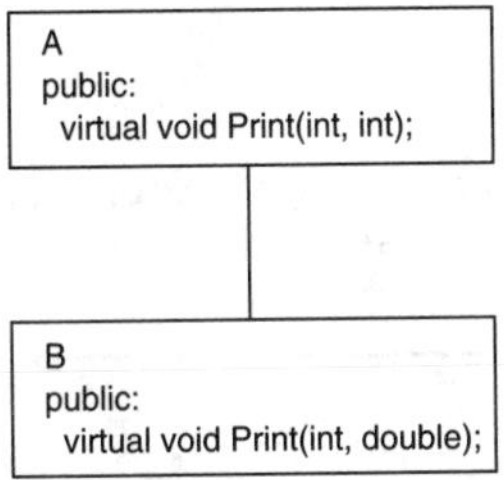

Figure 5.2. A class hierarchy containing no overriding.

The inheritance tree in Figure 5.2 is implemented with the code in Listing 5.2.

Listing 5.2. An example showing how `virtual` functions override only identically declared functions in base classes.

```
#include <stdio.h>

class A {
public:
      virtual void Print(int, int);
};

class B: public A {
public:
```

continues

Listing 5.2. continued

```
        virtual void Print(int, double);
};

void A::Print(int a, int b)
{
        printf("\na = %d, b = %d", a, b);
}

void B::Print(int a, double d)
{
        printf("\na = %d, d = %lf", a, d);
}

void Show(A* a)
{
        a->Print(3, 5);    // always invoke A::Print(int, int)
}

void main()
{
        A* a = new A;
        B* b = new B;
        Show(a);      // use A::Print(int, int)
        Show(b);      // use A::Print(int, int)
}
```

The function `Show(A*)` always invokes the same function, because the function `B::Print(int, double)` is declared differently from `A::Print(int, int)`, thus the former doesn't override the latter. A function in a derived class does not have to be declared `virtual` to override a `virtual` base class function. Declaring a function `virtual` allows it to be overridden in subsequent derived classes, but doesn't guarantee that this will occur.

Improved User Interfaces for Classes

`virtual` functions are used with class hierarchies. Unless you arrange classes in some kind of inheritance hierarchy, `virtual` functions don't really make much sense. Often, you have many classes to which a conceptually similar function can be applied. This implies that many classes have a `virtual` function in common. Consider the inheritance tree in Figure 5.3.

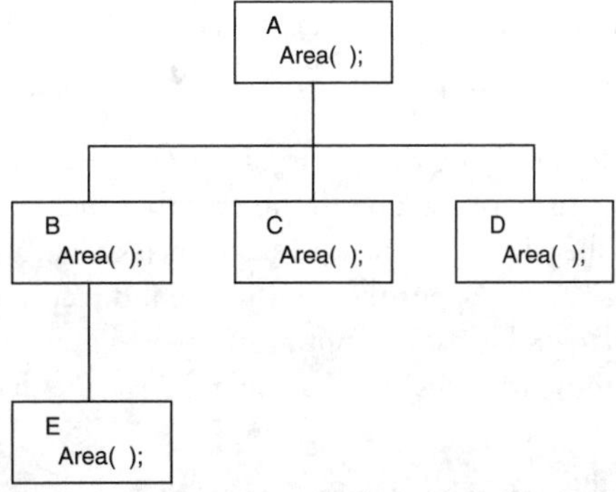

Figure 5.3. Multiple null `virtual` *functions in a class hierarchy.*

In the tree in Figure 5.3, not all the classes need an `Area()` function. To access function `E::Area()` through a reference to class `A`, both classes `A` and `B` must declare the function `Area()` to be `virtual`. Because these classes presumably don't have the need for such a function, the functions are implemented as null `virtual` functions. In practical class hierarchies, members at the top tend to have many (possibly nothing but) null `virtual` functions, or even pure `virtual` functions, for the sole purpose of providing a clean interface to classes that are lower in the tree. Pure `virtual` functions are discussed in the next section.

Abstract Classes

Classes appearing at or near the top of a hierarchy often have one or more null `virtual` functions. These functions make for a more consistent user interface when dealing with the hierarchy. In turn, the consistent interface allows the late binding process to be used extensively and relieves the programmer from keeping track of objects at runtime. Classes at the top have all the common functions declared in them, allowing C++ polymorphism to distinguish individual class functions through the `virtual` function mechanism.

Consider a class that has only null `virtual` functions. Would it make sense to instantiate the class? Probably not, because the class doesn't do anything, but the compiler still allows you to do so. The problem is that you would wind up with a useless object that takes up storage without providing any service.

C++ makes it possible to restrict the use of such classes by declaring them abstract. Attempts to instantiate an abstract class are then trapped by the compiler as an error. Before a class can be made abstract, it must have at least one `virtual` function. To declare an abstract class, at least one of its `virtual` functions must be declared to be *pure* `virtual`, which requires the special C++ notation

```
virtual void printOn() = 0;   // a pure virtual function
```

which is not to be confused with the declaration of a null `virtual` function

```
virtual void printOn() {}    // a null virtual function
```

The notation for declaring a pure `virtual` function is easier to remember if you consider the assignment-to-zero notation to indicate that there is no definition for the function. Although it is illegal to instantiate an abstract class, you are allowed to declare a pointer to an abstract class. This opens the door to the indirect manipulation of an abstract class, which can lead to problems. Attempting to invoke a pure `virtual` function causes a runtime error. Just to show what *not* to do, Listing 5.3 is code that causes this kind of error.

Listing 5.3. Deliberately invoking a pure `virtual` function.

```
class A {
public:
      virtual void printOn() = 0;  // a pure virtual function
};

void f()
{
      A* a;
      a->printOn();        // big trouble here...
}
```

The function call in `f()` is trapped by the system at runtime, producing a runtime error message.

In effect, invoking a pure `virtual` function is an attempt to use an uninitialized pointer to indirectly invoke a function. The internal implementation of the `virtual` function mechanism in Borland C++ is illustrated later in this chapter.

Abstract classes are set up for the benefit of derived classes. This suggests that abstract classes occur at or near the root of a hierarchy. There can be several abstract classes in the same hierarchy. Figure 5.4 and Listing 5.4 are a complete example of the proper usage of an abstract class.

Listing 5.4. Using a class hierarchy that has an abstract class.

```
#include <stdio.h>

class A {
public:
      virtual void printOn() = 0;  // a pure virtual function,
                                   // making class A abstract
```

```
};

class B: public A {
public:
      virtual void printOn() {puts("\nClass B");}
};

class C: public B {
public:
      virtual void printOn() {puts("\nClass C");}
};

void Show(A* a)
{
      a->printOn();
}

void main()
{
      B* b = new B;
      C* c = new C;
      Show(b);            // use B::printOn()
      Show(c);            // use C::printOn()
}
```

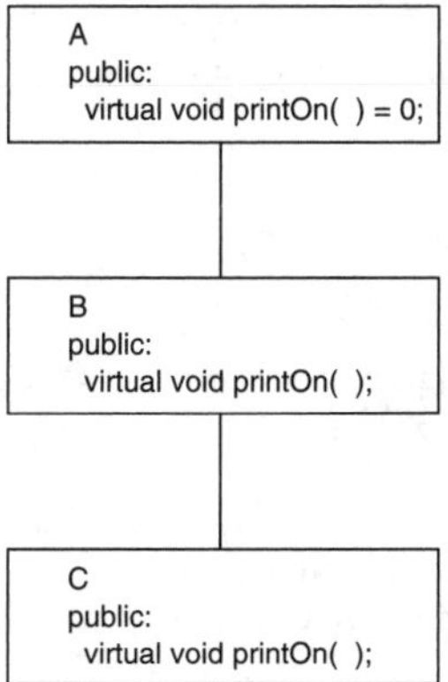

Figure 5.4. The use of an abstract class in a hierarchy.

Class `A` is used exclusively as the base class for other classes. The function `::Show(A*)` determines at runtime the function to be used, based on the type of object passed to `::Show(A*)`.

Deriving a class from an abstract class doesn't necessarily yield a class that can be instantiated. If a class overrides any of the `virtual` functions in its base class with new pure `virtuals`, the new class is also abstract. By the way, C++ requires you to override all pure `virtual` functions in derived classes. Failure to do so necessarily causes a compiler error, because if you were able to *not* override a pure `virtual` function, the `virtual` mechanism would not be propagated to further derived classes. If a class derived from an abstract one is itself abstract, one or more of its `virtual` functions must be pure. This implies that you can override a pure `virtual` with a new pure `virtual`.

Failure to override a pure `virtual` function leads to compiler errors. The next code fragment illustrates some of the problems that could arise if a derived class were allowed to not override all the pure `virtual` functions in its base class. Consider the simple tree in Figure 5.5.

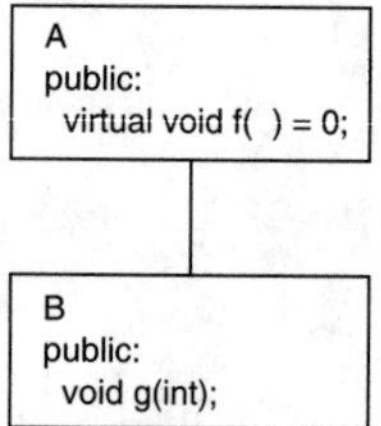

Figure 5.5. A derived class that fails to override a pure `virtual` *function of its base class.*

The tree shows a class `B` derived from `A` without overriding the pure `virtual` function `A::f()`. Here's how the code would look:

```
class A {
public:
      virtual void f() = 0;
};

class B: public A {
      // add a variable
      int value;
public:
      // add a member function
      void g(int i) {value = i;}
};
```

If pure `virtuals` behaved like regular `virtual` functions, class `B` would inherit `A::f()`, because `B` doesn't override `A::f()`. Assume a new class, called `C`, is derived from `B`. If `C` declared a `virtual` function `f()`, this function would not be accessible through an `A*` or `B*` pointer, because the chain of `virtual` functions is interrupted in class `B`. Invoking `C::f()` through an `A*` pointer would cause the pure `virtual` function `A::f()` to be invoked, triggering a runtime error. Pure `virtual` functions must be overridden in derived classes (even if they are redeclared pure) to avoid this problem.

Limitations of *virtual* Functions

You can't use `virtual` functions like typical ANSI C functions, because `virtual` functions apply only to class objects. Global functions cannot be declared `virtual`; only the member functions of a class can be declared `virtual`. Moreover, `virtual` functions can't be declared `static`, because `static` functions can be invoked without referencing a specific class instantiation. The `virtual` function invocation mechanism utilizes a special `vptr` pointer to locate the correct `virtual` function for an object at runtime. Without a `this` pointer, `static` functions don't provide an invocation path for `virtual` function calls.

virtual friends

The idea of a `virtual` function being a `friend` to another class may sound a bit perplexing. So far I have illustrated `virtual` functions applied to the class in which they were defined or to a derived class. Is it possible for functions that are external to a class, such as a `friend`, to be `virtual`? Yes, but with one proviso: A `virtual friend` is required to be a member function of some class, because the `virtual friend` requires the use of a `vptr` and a `vtab` to be invoked. Figure 5.6 and Listing 5.5 are a collection of classes that utilize `virtual friends`.

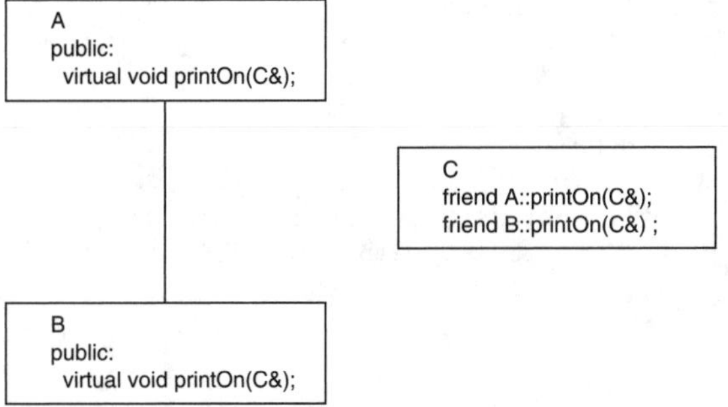

Figure 5.6. `virtual` *functions as* `friend`*s.*

Listing 5.5. Using `virtual` functions as `friends`.

```
#include <stdio.h>

class C;            // introduce into scope

class A {
public:
```

continues

Listing 5.5. continued

```
    int a;
    A(int i) {a = i;}
    virtual void printOn(C&);
};

class B: public A {
public:
    int b;
    B(int i, int j) : A(i) {b = j;}
    virtual void printOn(C&);
};

class C {
    friend void A::printOn(C&);
    friend void B::printOn(C&);
    int a, b, c;
public:
    C(int i, int j, int k) {a = i; b = j; c = k;}
};

void A::printOn(C& t)
{
    printf("\nClass A member a = %d", a);
    printf("\nClass C member c = %d", t.c);
}

void B::printOn(C& t)
{
    printf("\nClass B member b = %d", b);
    printf("\nClass C member c = %d", t.c);
}

void main()
{
    A a(10);
    B b(10, 20);
    C c(10, 20, 30);
    a.printOn(c);
    b.printOn(c);
}
```

In effect, the `friend` relationship is a compile-time attribute, whereas the `virtual` function mechanism is a runtime sequence. Although the same function can be declared both `virtual` and `friend`, the two attributes trigger completely different processing by the compiler. In particular, the `friend` attribute causes absolutely no runtime overhead.

virtual Operators

Because operators can be implemented as member functions, they can also be declared `virtual`. Although possible, `virtual` operators are not easy to implement in all situations. Consider the simple inheritance tree shown in Figure 5.7, in which there is a `virtual operator+=`.

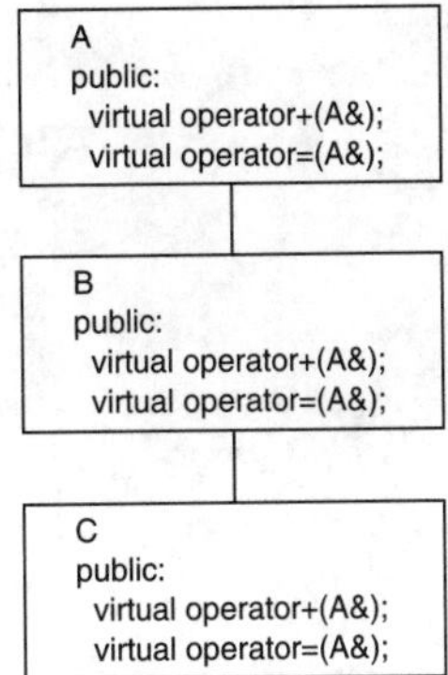

Figure 5.7. `virtual` *operators in a class hierarchy.*

Each class in the inheritance tree uses a `virtual` operator, as shown in Listing 5.6.

Listing 5.6. Using `virtual` operators.

```
class A {
public:
  int value_a;
  A(int i) {value_a = i;}
  virtual A& operator+=(A&);
  virtual int a() {return value_a;}
  virtual int b() {return 0;};
};

class B: public A {
public:
  int value_b;7
  B(int i, int j) : A(i) {value_b = j;}
  virtual A& operator+=(A&);
  virtual int b() {return value_b;}
};

A& A::operator+=(A& t)
{
```

continues

Listing 5.6. continued

```
  value_a += t.a();
  return *this;
}

A& B::operator+=(A& t)
{
  value_a += t.a();
  value_b += t.b();
  return *this;
}

void f()
{
      A a(10);
      B b(10, 20);

      a += b;
      b += a;
}
```

The code in Listing 5.6 works, but has its limitations. For example, it has no `operator+` or `operator-` functions. The problem with these kinds of functions is that they need to return a new object whose value is computed from two other objects. You might want to implement an `operator+` function like this:

```
class A {
public:
  // ...
  virtual A operator+(A&); {return A(value_a += t.a() );}
};

class B: public A {
public:
  // ...
  virtual A operator+(A&); {return B(value_a += t.a(), value_b +=
t.b() ); }
};
```

Unfortunately, this won't work. The function `A::operator+()` takes an `A&` parameter and returns an `A` object, which is okay because the returned object really is an `A` object. The problem is in `B::operator+()`, because this function is declared (like the function it is overriding) to return an `A` object, but in reality it needs to return a `B` object. The `B` object is implicitly converted by the compiler to an `A` object upon return, so the `B` part of the object is lost.

The solution appears to be the use of references. If the `operator+` functions returned an `A&` object rather than an `A` object, then `A::operator+()` could return a reference to an `A` object, and `B::operator+()` could return a reference to a `B` object. From a C++ language perspective, this is correct, but there is a problem in memory allocation. If `A::operator+()` were implemented like this:

```
class A {
  // ...
  virtual A& operator+(A& t) {return A(value_a += t.a()); }
};
```

The compiler would issue the warning

```
attempting to return a reference to a local object
```

The warning tells you that the temporary object `A` in the return statement is allocated on the stack, and that you are attempting to return a reference to this stack object. As soon as the function returns, the stack object disappears, so the reference will be invalid. To properly return a reference, you need to have an object that hangs around after the function returns. A `static` object would serve the purpose, like this:

```
class A {
  // ...
  virtual A& operator+(A& t) {
    static A a(value_a += t.a());
    return a;
  }
};
```

This approach does work, but has other problems. Operators are often used repeatedly in expressions, such as

```
 a = b + c + d
```

Using a single `static` variable to hold intermediate results would not work in expressions using the operator multiple times, because each invocation of the operator function would overwrite the previously held value. To return a real reference, you would unfortunately have to dynamically allocate an object, initialize the reference variable, return the reference, and later remember to delete the allocated variable when you were done with it. That's an awful lot of work, and that's also why you'll almost never see virtual operators used for things like `+` and `-` operators.

An Example of Polymorphism

To get the most out of C++, you should exploit polymorphism as much as possible. Not only does polymorphism make your program simpler, but it also makes it much more flexible and robust. In this section, I give a short example of a program using `virtual` functions to illustrate the great power of polymorphism.

Consider a series of classes used to implement a database that keeps track of fine arts masterpieces. The classes are organized into a hierarchy, with the intention of allowing the programmer to access any object in the database without knowing what kind of object it is. Figure 5.8 is the inheritance tree for this series of classes.

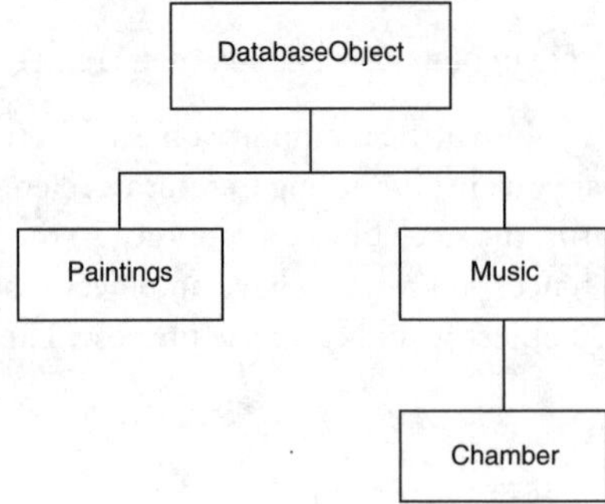

Figure 5.8. A simple database class hierarchy.

Any common features across the database belong in the highest node possible in the tree. Every opus in the database has an author and a date. Other information may vary among the classes, such as the method used to display information about an object. This display function is a good candidate for polymorphism and is implemented with the `virtual` function mechanism. Listing 5.7 shows the class implementations.

Listing 5.7. Using polymorphism in a class hierarchy.

```
#include <stdio.h>
#include <string.h>

class DatabaseObject {
      char author [50];
      char title  [50];
      char date   [50];
public:
      DatabaseObject(char*, char*, char*);
```

```
     virtual void Display();
};


class Painting: public DatabaseObject {
     int width, height;
public:
     Painting(char*, char*, char*, int, int);
     virtual void Display();
};

class Music: public DatabaseObject {
     char key [40];
public:
     Music(char*, char*, char*, char*);
     virtual void Display();
};

class Chamber: public Music {
     int number_of_musicians;
public:
     Chamber(char*, char*, char*, char*, int);
     virtual void Display();
};


DatabaseObject::DatabaseObject(char* who,
                               char* what,
                               char* when)
{
     strcpy(author, who);
     strcpy(title,  what);
     strcpy(date,   when);
}

void DatabaseObject::Display()
{
     printf("\n\nAuthor: %s", author);
     printf("\nTitle : %s", title);
     printf("\nDate  : %s", date);
}

Painting::Painting(char* author, char* title,
                   char* date, int w, int h)
     : DatabaseObject(author, title, date)
{
     width = w;
     height = h;
```

continues

Listing 5.7. continued

```
}

void Painting::Display()
{
      DatabaseObject::Display();
      printf("\nType  : Painting");
      printf("\nSize  : width = %d, height = %d",
            width, height);
}

Music::Music(char* author, char* title, char* date,
           char* k)
     : DatabaseObject(author, title, date)
{
      strcpy(key, k);
}

void Music::Display()
{
      DatabaseObject::Display();
      printf("\nType  : Music");
      printf("\nKey   : %s", key);
}


Chamber::Chamber(char* author, char* title, char* date,
           char* key, int size)
        : Music(author, title, date, key)
{
      number_of_musicians = size;
}

void Chamber::Display()
{
      Music::Display();
      printf("\nOther : Chamber music, %d musicians",
            number_of_musicians);
}

void PrintData(DatabaseObject& d)
{
      d.Display();
}

void main()
{
      Music symphony("Beethoven, Ludwig van",
                  "Symphony no. 9",
```

```
                "1824",
                "D minor");
    Painting painting("da Vinci, Leonardo",
                "Mona Lisa",
                "1503",
                24, 36);

    Chamber opus("Mozart, Wolfgang Amadeus",
                "Hoffmeister",
                "1786",
                "D major",
                4);

    PrintData(symphony);
    PrintData(painting);
    PrintData(opus);
}
```

The following output is generated when the program is run:

```
Author : Beethoven, Ludwig van
Title  : Symphony no. 9
Date   : 1824
Type   : Music
Key    : D minor

Author : da Vinci, Leonardo
Title  : Mona Lisa
Date   : 1503
Type   : Painting
Size   : width = 24, height = 36

Author : Mozart, Wolfgang Amadeus
Title  : Hoffmeister
Date   : 1786
Type   : Music
Key    : D major
Other  : Chamber music, 4 musicians
```

Stream operators were not used in the example to print information on the screen, because they are described in Chapter 7. Polymorphism allows generic `Database` object references to be passed around in the program, such as in calling function `PrintData(Database&)`. As long as the objects derive from `Database` and utilize `virtual` functions to carry out the requested task, this method works eminently. In fact, it is highly recommended as a way to let C++ handle the details to simplify your code.

Scope Resolution Disables Polymorphism

There is considerable freedom in calling a `virtual` function. A `virtual` function can be invoked by practically any function that has proper access privileges. A `virtual` function in a derived class is even allowed to invoke a `virtual` function in its base class with the same name, without causing infinite loops or crashing the system. To invoke a `virtual` function in the base class of a derived class, you have to use the scope resolution operator to indicate explicitly which base class to use. This operator tells the compiler that you wish to bypass deliberately the `virtual` function mechanism. Consider the code taken from Listing 5.7:

```
void PrintData(DatabaseObject& d)
{
      d.Display();
}
```

in which `d` references a `Music` object. The function `Music::Display()` overrides the base class function `DatabaseObject::Display()`, so the `virtual` function table translates the function call `DatabaseObject::Display()` into the function call `Music::Display()`. What happens inside the latter function when the statement

```
DatabaseObject::Display();
```

is executed? Is it a vicious circle, causing `Music::Display()` to be called again? No, using explicit scope resolution forces the compiler to generate a compile-time function call that skips the `virtual` function vectoring. Thus, no overhead is incurred, and no infinite looping is caused. Scope resolution defeats polymorphism.

virtual Functions with Non-*virtual* Functions

Using `virtual` and non-`virtual` functions together in a class hierarchy initially might cause confusion for the novice. Consider the inheritance tree in Figure 5.9.

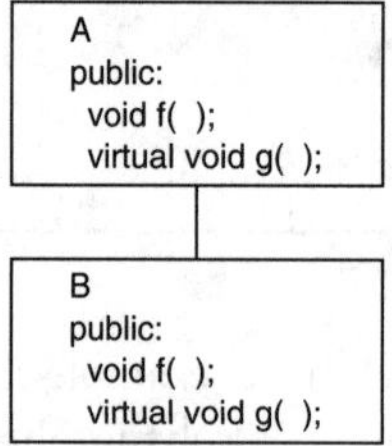

Figure 5.9. A class hierarchy using both `virtual` *and non-*`virtual` *functions together.*

The tree in Figure 5.9 is implemented in Listing 5.8.

Listing 5.8. Using `virtual` and non-`virtual` functions together.

```
#include <stdio.h>

class A {
      int a;
public:
      void f()          {puts("Function A::f()");}
      virtual void g() {puts("Function A::g()");}
};

class B: public A {
      int b;
public:
      void f()          {puts("Function B::f()");}
      void g()          {puts("Function B::g()");}
};

void Do(A& a)
{
      a.f();
      a.g();
}

void main()
{
      A a;
      B b;

      Do(a);
      Do(b);
}
```

The following output is obtained:

```
Function A::f()
Function A::g()
Function A::f()
Function B::g()
```

Memory Layout of *vptr* and *vtab* Structures

It is easier to understand how the compiler locates `virtual` functions at runtime by considering the data structures involved and the memory layout used with class objects using `virtual` functions.

In the previous example, calling `Do(A&)` with a `B` object results in the functions `A::f()` and `B::g()` being called. This happens because in the function call

```
Do(b);
```

the `B&` reference is implicitly converted to an `A&` reference. The compiler sees that `A::f()` is not a `virtual` function, so code is generated to call `A::f()` directly. The function call `a.g()` in `Do(A&)` is handled differently, because the compiler sees that `g()` is declared `virtual` in class `A`. This provokes the generation of code to use the `virtual` function mechanism. The two classes are laid out in memory as shown in Figure 5.10.

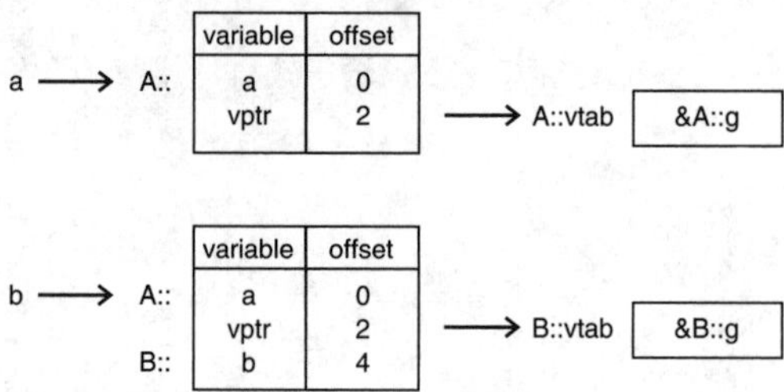

Figure 5.10. The layout of two objects in memory.

At runtime, the code vectors through class `B`'s `vptr` to find which function to call for `g()` and finds `B::g()`. The `vptr` of class `B` is stored in the same offset as the `vptr` in class `A`, so `Do(A&)` can access the correct function no matter which type of object is passed to `Do(A&)`. Note, however, that the `vptr`s for `A` and `B` objects reference different `vtab` tables.

virtual Functions Don't Have to Be Overridden

Declaring a function `virtual` forces the compiler to generate runtime vectoring through a `vptr` pointer to invoke functions. The `virtual` keyword tells the compiler that the function *may* be overridden in a base class. What happens if it isn't? In fact, what happens if there are no derived classes at all? Fortunately, nothing unexpected happens. A `virtual` function doesn't necessarily have to be overridden.

In the class hierarchy of Figure 5.9, class `B` was laid out in memory so that class `B` included a complete `A` object in it. The `vptr` for the two classes was different. In any case, class `A` was completely "oblivious" to the fact that it was used as a base class for other classes. A `virtual` function does not have to be overridden in a derived class. In fact, a `virtual` function declared in a class doesn't even have to be defined, in which case, it is a pure `virtual` function. Of course, pure `virtual` functions can't be invoked directly, unless you want to force a runtime error.

The classes in commercial class libraries often have many of their member functions declared `virtual` in order to allow users the option of overriding them. This improves the flexibility of classes at the expense of runtime performance. Languages such as Objective-C are less flexible, forcing the use of late binding for all function calls, even when it's not necessary.

Consider a derived class that overrides only some of the `virtual` functions in its base class. How does the compiler handle its `virtual` functions? Consider the inheritance tree in Figure 5.11.

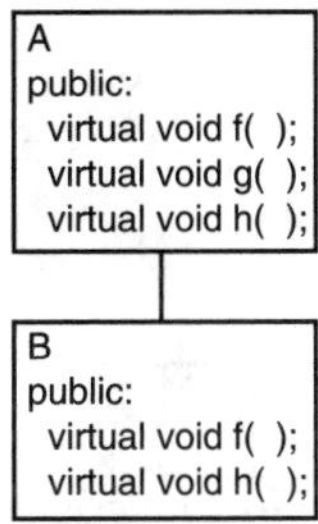

Figure 5.11. A class hierarchy in which not all base class `virtual` *functions are overridden.*

The inheritance tree in Figure 5.11 is implemented with the code in Listing 5.9.

Listing 5.9. Using classes that override only some of the `virtual` functions in their base classes.

```
#include <stdio.h>

class A {
      int a;

public:
      virtual void f() {puts("Function A::f()");}
      virtual void g() {puts("Function A::g()");}
      virtual void h() {puts("Function A::h()");}
};
```

continues

Listing 5.9. continued

```
class B: public A {
      int b;
public:
      virtual void f() {puts("Function B::f()");}
      virtual void h() {puts("Function B::h()");}
};

void Do(A& a)
{
      a.f();
      a.g();
      a.h();
}

void main()
{
      A a;
      B b;

      Do(a);
      Do(b);
}
```

Class `B` does not override all its base class `virtuals`, which causes the compiler to create an unusual `vtab` for class `B` to guarantee correctness in polymorphic behavior. Figure 5.12 shows how Borland C++ lays out the objects in memory.

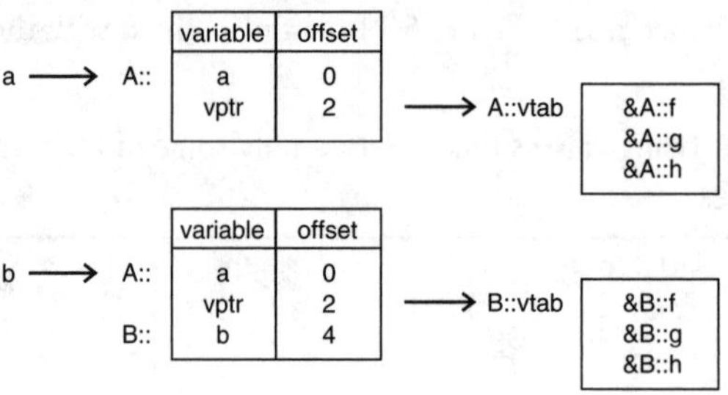

Figure 5.12. The `vptr` *and* `vtab` *structures used with classes when not all base class* `virtual` *functions are overridden.*

Study the pointers in `B::vtab`. You might have expected to see only pointers to `B::f` and `B::h`, because these are the only `virtual` functions declared in class `B`. As you can see, a pointer to function `A::g` is also included, because the pointer wasn't overridden in class `B`. Thus `A::g` becomes the default function for `B` also. In addition, this makes all the entries in `A::vtab` and `B::vtab` occur in the same order and with the same offset, guaranteeing that it calls the correct function when given a reference to `A` or to `B`.

To Be or Not to Be *virtual*

You can declare any member function to be a `virtual` function, with the following restrictions:

1. Constructors
2. `static` member functions

These two restrictions leave the door open to most of the functions in a typical program, but the overhead associated with `virtual` functions (and the late binding mechanism that goes with it) makes it advisable to use `virtuals` only when needed. Whether a polymorphic function is needed is not always immediately obvious. For instance, you can immediately rule out `virtual` functions in classes that aren't designed to be derived from, but how do you know that sometime in the future you or somebody else won't use the class for this purpose? It's really a subjective call. However, a few guidelines ease the choice between `virtual` or non-`virtual` functions. You should consider `virtual` functions at least in these cases:

1. In classes designed to be at the top or near the top of a class hierarchy.
2. For functions that describe class attributes that depend on the structure or type of a class.
3. For functions that implement input or output for a class.
4. For functions that have actions defined only for specific classes.

Consider the class inheritance tree for objects in a fine arts database, such as the one described earlier. Each class in the tree might be augmented with functions to identify an object, to read in the data for an object from a terminal, to return responses to user queries, and so on. Consider endowing the root class `DatabaseObject` with these functions and operators:

```
Display
IsA
AuthoredBy
Date
PrintOn
ReadFrom
ExhibitedAt
TreeAncestors
```

Some of these are candidates for polymorphic behavior and others aren't. Let's look at them one at a time.

`Display`	The `Display` function prints the contents of a class on the user terminal. Each class has a potentially different internal structure from its ancestor. Thus, according to guidelines 1, 2, and 3, this function needs to be polymorphic.
`IsA`	Each class is a new type and thus must return its identifier correctly. Guideline 2 dictates using a `virtual` again.
`AuthoredBy`	The object returned by the `AuthoredBy` function is a string, declared in class `DatabaseObject`. The name of the author is not likely to be a function of the type of object, so polymorphic behavior is probably not required.
`Date`	The date of a piece of art probably is not dependent on the type of object being considered, but here again, you can't be absolutely sure. The function declared here returns an integer year value. But what about objects with creation periods spanning several years? This is another subjective call.
`PrintOn` and `ReadFrom`	Using guideline 3, these functions used for input and output of a class's contents should always be `virtual`.
`ExhibitedAt`	The `ExhibitedAt` function would probably describe the museum or other place in which an object is currently on display. This location is possibly class-dependent, so a `virtual` function could be required.
`TreeAncestors`	The `TreeAncestors` function might be used as a debugging function, illustrating the immediate base classes of a function. This function would then support class hierarchy browsing. This is definitely a polymorphic function.

virtual Functions Can Also Be *private*

The fact that a `virtual` function is normally used to create a consistent and polymorphic interface to the class users doesn't mean that the `virtual` function has to be accessible to users. If you have a class in which a `virtual` function is designed to be invoked exclusively from another member function, the `virtual` function can be declared `private`. The inheritance tree in Figure 5.13 and the code in Listing 5.10 illustrate the details.

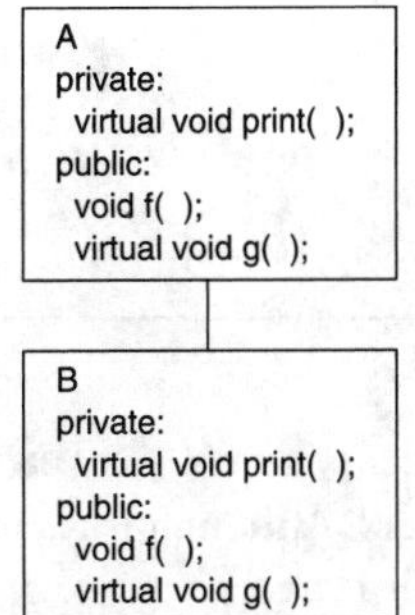

Figure 5.13. A class hierarchy using `private virtual` *functions.*

Listing 5.10. Using `private virtual` functions.

```
#include <stdio.h>

class A {
      int a;
      virtual void print() {puts("Called via A::g()");}

public:
      void f()           {puts("Function A::f()");}
      virtual void g() {print();}
};

class B: public A {
      int b;
      virtual void print() {puts("Called via B::g()");}
public:
      void f()           {puts("Function B::f()");}
      virtual void g() {print();}
};

void Do(A& a)
{
      a.g();
}

void main()
```

continues

Listing 5.10. continued

```
{
        A a;
        B b;

        Do(a);
        Do(b);
}
```

Both classes A and B have a private virtual called print(), which is not meant to be called directly by class users. Although it is rather unusual, nothing is wrong with declaring a virtual function private.

Advanced Section

virtual functions give great flexibility to C++ programs, and hide most of the complexity of late binding from the user. However, for those readers who are interested in what happens behind the scenes, I show in this section exactly what kind of code and data the compiler handles to support virtual functions. As was stated in regard to the previous advanced sections, novice programmers may skip ahead to the next chapter without loss of continuity.

The Mechanics of Polymorphism

The power of polymorphism is considerable, especially because using virtual functions is so easy. virtual functions are different on the inside from ordinary member functions, however. The compiler generates special code to support virtual functions by looking up and vectoring through function pointers at runtime. The code generated depends on whether a virtual function is used in a class with a single base class or with multiple base classes. I discuss each case separately.

Polymorphism with Single Inheritance

Single inheritance carries no memory overhead in objects unless virtual functions are used. Even so, the implementation of virtual functions with single inheritance is straightforward. The best way to study the runtime characteristics of a compiler is to look at the code generated. Consider the inheritance tree in Figure 5.14.

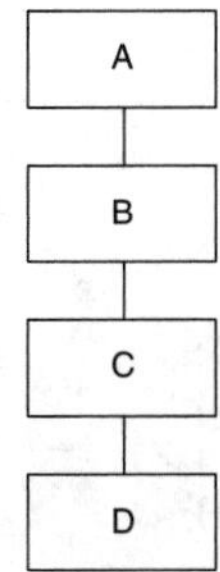

Figure 5.14. A class hierarchy using single inheritance.

Each class has its own identical sets of variables, member functions, and `virtual` member functions. Listing 5.11 is the implementation.

Listing 5.11. Using classes derived by single inheritance.

```
class A {
public:
      int v1, v2, v3, v4;
      void V1() {v1 = 1;}
      void V2() {v2 = 2;}
      void V3() {v3 = 3;}
      void V4() {v4 = 4;}

      virtual void VV1() {v1 = 1;}
      virtual void VV2() {v2 = 2;}
      virtual void VV3() {v3 = 3;}
      virtual void VV4() {v4 = 4;}
};

class B: public A {
public:
      int v1, v2, v3, v4;
      void V1() {v1 = 1;}
      void V2() {v2 = 2;}
      void V3() {v3 = 3;}
      void V4() {v4 = 4;}

      virtual void VV1() {v1 = 1;}
      virtual void VV2() {v2 = 2;}
      virtual void VV3() {v3 = 3;}
      virtual void VV4() {v4 = 4;}
```

continues

Listing 5.11. continued

```
};

class C: public B {
public:
      int v1, v2, v3, v4;
      void V1() {v1 = 1;}
      void V2() {v2 = 2;}
      void V3() {v3 = 3;}
      void V4() {v4 = 4;}

      virtual void VV1() {v1 = 1;}
      virtual void VV2() {v2 = 2;}
      virtual void VV3() {v3 = 3;}
      virtual void VV4() {v4 = 4;}
};

class D: public C {
public:
      int v1, v2, v3, v4;
      void V1() {v1 = 1;}
      void V2() {v2 = 2;}
      void V3() {v3 = 3;}
      void V4() {v4 = 4;}

      virtual void VV1() {v1 = 1;}
      virtual void VV2() {v2 = 2;}
      virtual void VV3() {v3 = 3;}
      virtual void VV4() {v4 = 4;}
};

void Show(A* a)
{
      a->v1 = 1;
      a->v2 = 2;
      a->v3 = 3;
      a->v4 = 4;

      a->VV1();
      a->VV2();
      a->VV3();
      a->VV4();
}

A* a = new A;
B* b = new B;
C* c = new C;
D* d = new D;
```

```
void main()
{
        Show(a);
        Show(b);
        Show(c);
        Show(d);
}
```

By studying the compiled code with Turbo Debugger, you can determine the structure of each class and the invocation sequences for each function call. I won't show the assembly language that is generated because it is quite long. However, Figure 5.15 is the resulting memory layout for a class `A` object pointed at by `a`.

a ⟶ A::

variable	offset
v1	0
v2	2
v3	4
v4	6
vptr	8

Figure 5.15. The memory layout of an object of class `A`.

Everything looks pretty normal, except for the field called `vptr` at offset 8. It is a pointer to a table of pointers through which the compiler vectors the code at runtime when invoking a `virtual` function. The table of pointers referenced by `vptr` is called the `virtual` function table, or `vtab` for short. Figure 5.16 shows what the `vtab` for class `A` looks like.

vptr ⟶ vtab

pointer	offset
&A::VV1	0
&A::VV2	2
&A::VV3	4
&A::VV4	6

Figure 5.16. The `vtab` *for objects of class* `A`.

Any object of a class with `virtual` functions is allocated the necessary extra storage for the `vptr` and the `vtab`. Calling a `virtual` function involves using the offset of a `virtual` table pointer in `vtab`. This offset is added to `vtab` at runtime to determine the address of the `virtual` function to call. The structures for the derived classes `B`, `C`, and `D` follow (see Figures 5.17, 5.18, and 5.19).

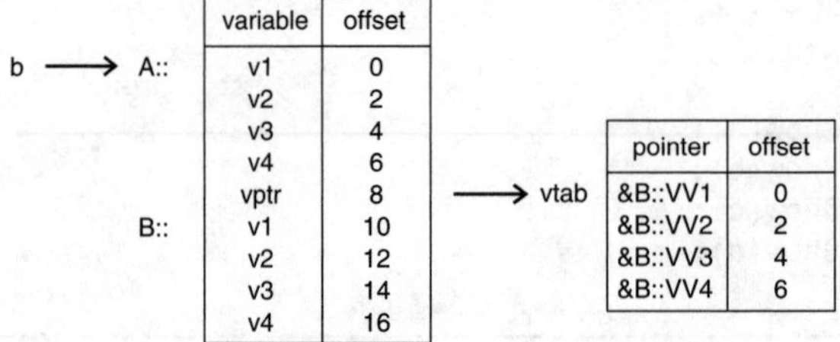

Figure 5.17. The memory layout of an object of class B.

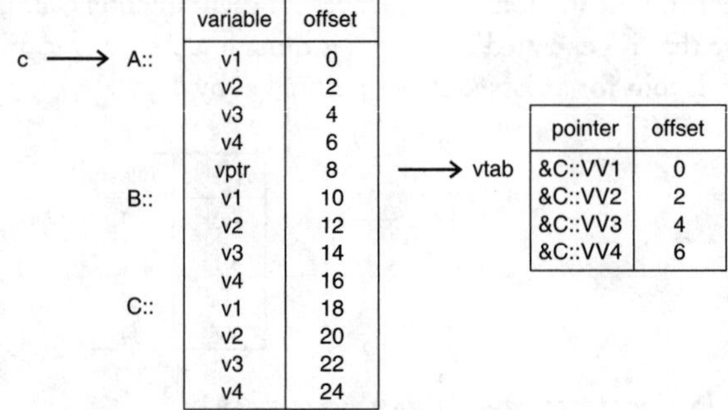

Figure 5.18. The memory layout of an object of class C.

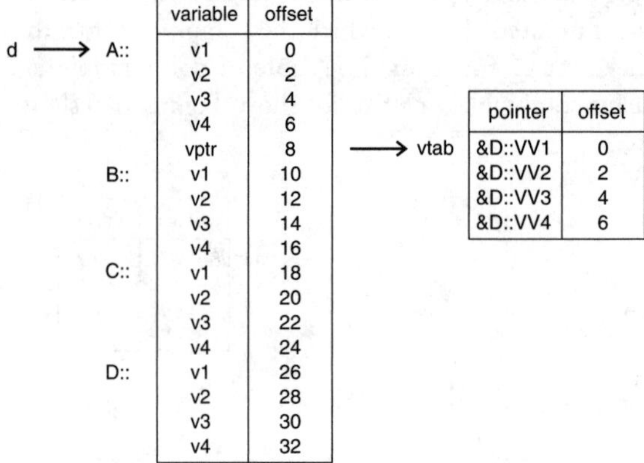

Figure 5.19. The memory layout of an object of class D.

Notice the position of `vptr` in each class: `vptr` is always placed at the end of the variables of the first base class. Each class has a `vptr`, but its value is different for each class. The `vptr` references the `vtab` to use for each class. Thus, by changing only the `vptr`, different `vtab`s are accessible, and different `virtual` functions can be invoked.

The vtab for a derived class is different from the vtab of its base classes. This includes class D, which includes integral A, B, and C objects in itself. If a D object is converted to an A object, the D object continues to have a different vtab from A objects. Understand also that a class such as D, which has three levels of base classes, still has only one vptr. Consider an abbreviated version of Show() and main() in Listing 5.12.

Listing 5.12. A short example showing the use of inherited objects.

```
void Show(A* a)
{
      a->VV4();
}

A* a = new A;
D* d = new D;

void main()
{
      Show(a);
      Show(d);
}
```

The code generated is shown in Listing 5.13 with some editing and name unmangling.

Listing 5.13. The assembly language generated for the simple inheritance example.

```
Show:
      push  bp                          ; save old frame
      mov   bp,sp                       ; setup new frame
      push  si
      mov   si,word ptr [bp+4]          ; get this pointer for
                                        ; the object passed
   ;
   ;  {
         a->VV4();
   ;
      push  si                          ; push this pointer
      mov   bx,word ptr [si+8]          ; get vptr
      call  word ptr [bx+6]             ; call (vptr+6)
      pop   cx
   ;
   ;  }
   ;
```

continues

Listing 5.13. continued

```
        pop   si
        pop   bp
        ret

main:
        push  bp                        ; save old frame
        mov   bp,sp                     ; set up new frame
    ;
    ;   {
            Show(a);
    ;
        push  word ptr DGROUP:_a        ; push argument 'a'
        call  near ptr Show             ; invoke Show(A&)
        pop   cx                        ; clean up stack
    ;
          Show(d);
    ;
        push  word ptr DGROUP:_d        ; push argument 'd'
        call  near ptr Show             ; invoke Show(A&)
        pop   cx                        ; clean up stack
    ;
    ;   }
    ;
        pop   bp                        ; restore old frame
        ret
```

The same function `Show(A&)` invokes different functions when it is passed pointers to different objects, even though it is declared to accept an argument of type `A&`. The difference in `vptr` for each class makes this possible.

Polymorphism with Multiple Inheritance

Multiple inheritance is obviously more involved than single inheritance. This is true both at the programming level and at the compiler level. Classes that have multiple base classes employing `virtual` functions utilize multiple `vptr` pointers and `vtab` tables, so the mechanics of polymorphism are similar to the single inheritance case. Consider the inheritance tree in Figure 5.20.

The inheritance tree in Figure 5.20 is implemented with the code in Listing 5.14.

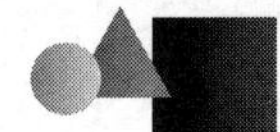

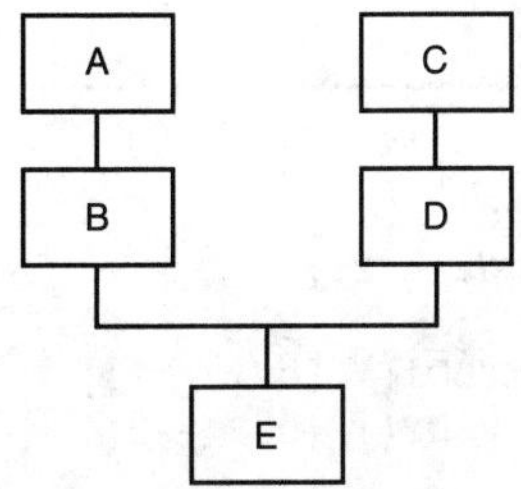

Figure 5.20. A multiple inheritance hierarchy.

Listing 5.14. Using multiple inheritance with classes that have `virtual` functions.

```
class A {
public:
      int ab1, ab2;
      void AB1() {ab1 = 1;}
      void AB2() {ab2 = 2;}

      virtual void VAB1() {ab1 = 1;}
      virtual void VAB2() {ab2 = 2;}
};

class B: public A {
public:
      int ab1, ab2;
      void AB1() {ab1 = 1;}
      void AB2() {ab2 = 2;}

      virtual void VAB1() {ab1 = 1;}
      virtual void VAB2() {ab2 = 2;}
};

class C {
public:
      int cd1, cd2;
      void CD1() {cd1 = 1;}
      void CD2() {cd2 = 2;}

      virtual void VCD1() {cd1 = 1;}
      virtual void VCD2() {cd2 = 2;}
};

class D: public C {
public:
```

continues

Listing 5.14. continued

```
        int cd1, cd2;
        void CD1() {cd1 = 1;}
        void CD2() {cd2 = 2;}

        virtual void VCD1() {cd1 = 1;}
        virtual void VCD2() {cd2 = 2;}
};

class E: public B, public D {
public:
        int ab1, ab2, cd1, cd2;
        virtual void VAB1() {ab1 = 1;}
        virtual void VAB2() {ab2 = 2;}
        virtual void VCD1() {cd1 = 1;}
        virtual void VCD2() {cd2 = 2;}
};

void ABShow(A* a) {a->VAB2();}
void CDShow(C* c) {c->VCD2();}

B* b = new B;
D* d = new D;
E* e = new E;

void main()
{
        ABShow(e);
        CDShow(e);
}
```

By using Turbo Debugger to look at the code that is generated, you can see that the objects are laid out in memory as shown in Figures 5.21, 5.22, and 5.23.

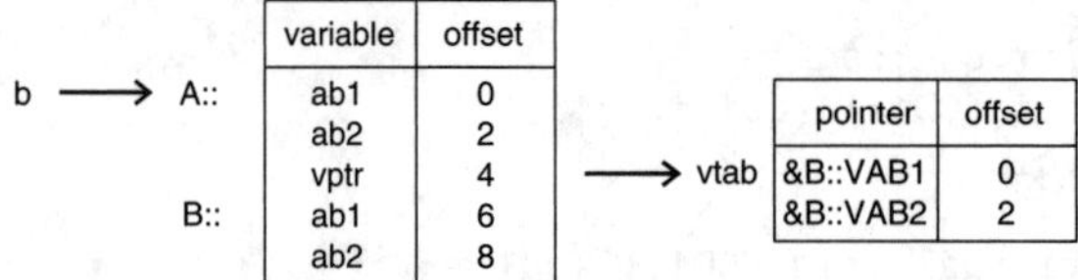

Figure 5.21. The layout of objects of class B.

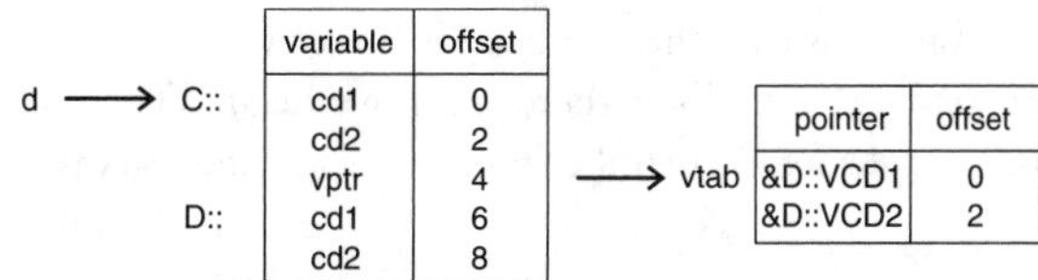

Figure 5.22. The layout of objects of class D.

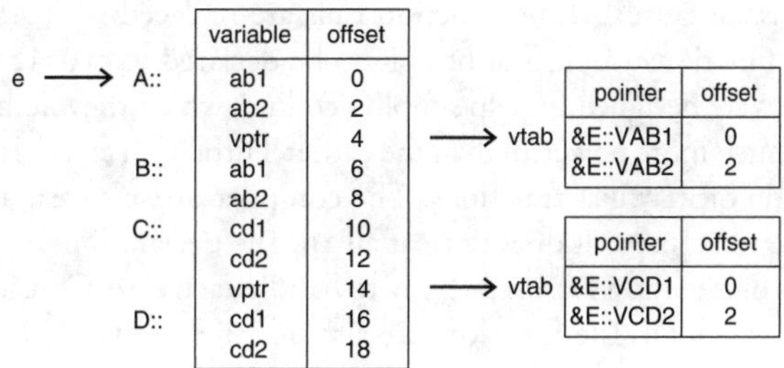

Figure 5.23. The layout of objects of class E*, derived using multiple inheritance.*

Objects of class B and D have their own vptrs. Class E contains two vptrs. The allocation order of the subobjects inside E is determined by the declaration order of the base classes in E. The preceding code shows two essential parts in the polymorphic behavior of class E. Consider the two function calls in main().

```
ABShow(e);
CDShow(e);
```

In both cases, implicit conversions are performed. If the conversions were made explicit, they would look like this:

```
ABShow( (A*) e);
CDShow( (C*) e);
```

The first conversion is trivial, because the beginning of an E object is an A object, so there is no change in the pointer e. The fact that an E object begins with an A subobject entails that the E object passed uses the vptr field defined in the A subobject for virtual function calls. The second conversion is more complicated. To convert a pointer to E into a pointer to C, an offset must be added to the E pointer to get to the C subobject. The Borland C++ compiler takes care of all these details transparently, so that polymorphism is handled seamlessly, even with multiple inheritance.

When a derived class has multiple base classes, it may also have multiple vptrs. For each base class that uses virtual functions, there is one vptr, so a class can have any number of virtual table pointers. Obviously all these vptrs represent memory overhead in objects, but the good news is that the overhead is under your direct control. If none of the base classes has `virtual` functions, there is no overhead. The amount of overhead is a function of the complexity of the inheritance tree and the use of `virtual` functions.

inline virtual Functions

Chapter 2 illustrated the implementation of `inline` functions for regular non-`virtual` functions. Because `inline` function calls are replaced with straight code, it seems that `inline` functions would not be able to be declared `virtual`. This is not the case. C++ compilers are designed to help simplify coding, which they do by being "smart." Borland C++ is much more powerful than the earlier Turbo C, a fact that is evidenced by its implementation of `virtual` functions. The compiler doesn't treat all `virtual` function calls the same way, just as it doesn't treat all `inline` declarations equally. The code generated depends on the most reasonable way to handle each case. Consider the example in Listing 5.15, in which `inline` functions are also declared `virtual`.

Listing 5.15. A class hierarchy using `inline virtual` functions.

```
class A {
      int a, b, c;

public:
      inline virtual int f() {return a;}
      inline virtual int g() {return b;}
      inline virtual int h() {return c;}
};

class B: public A {
      int a, b, c;

public:
      inline virtual int f() {return a;}
      inline virtual int h() {return c;}
};
```

Note that class `B` does not override the base class `virtual` function `A::g()`. To show how the compiler handles calls to these functions depending on the runtime context, I invoke the `virtual` functions in different manners with the code in Listing 5.16.

Listing 5.16. A short program using `inline virtual` functions.

```
void Do(A& a)
{
      a.f();
      a.g();
      a.h();
}

int i;
A a;
B b;

void main()
{
      i = a.f();
      i = a.g();
      i = a.h();

      i = b.f();
      i = b.g();
      i = b.h();
}
```

The objects `a` and `b` are laid out in memory like Figures 5.24 and 5.25.

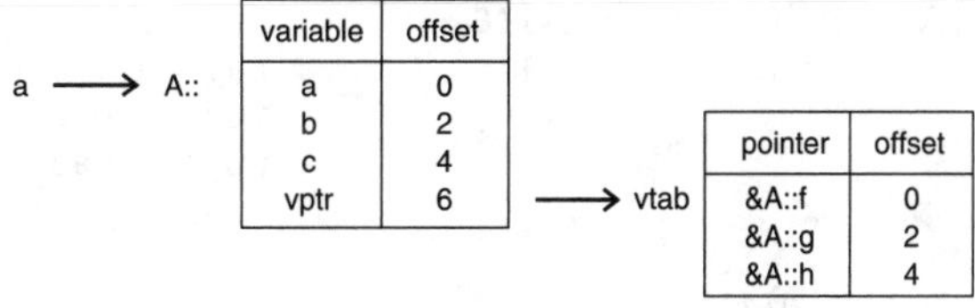

Figure 5.24. The layout of class A *objects.*

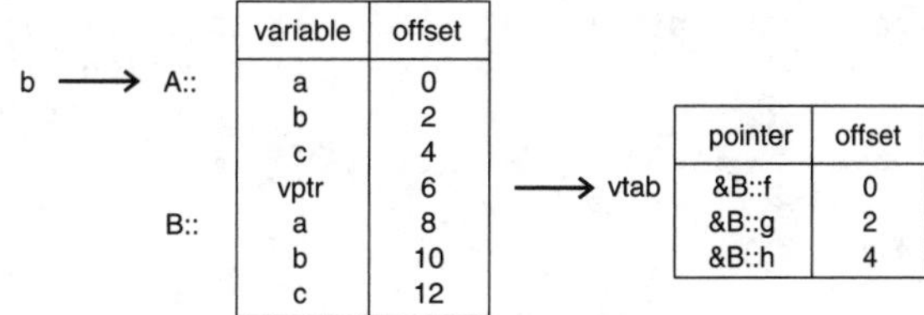

Figure 5.25. The layout of class B *objects.*

Listing 5.17 shows the assembly language generated by Borland C++, with some editing.

Listing 5.17. The code generated when `inline virtual` functions are used.

```
      ;
      ;     void Do(A& a)
      ;
Do:
      push  bp                         ; save old frame
      mov   bp,sp                      ; create new frame
      push  si
      mov   si,word ptr [bp+4]         ; get 'this' pointer
                                       ; of argument a
   ;
   ;  {
   ;        a.f();
   ;
      push  si
      mov   bx,word ptr [si+6]         ; get A::vptr
      call  word ptr [bx]              ; call f() virtual
                                       ; function of whatever
                                       ; object was passed
      pop   cx
   ;
   ;        a.g();
   ;
      push  si
      mov   bx,word ptr [si+6]         ; get A::vptr
      call  word ptr [bx+2]            ; call g() virtual
                                       ; function of whatever
                                       ; object was passed
      pop   cx
   ;
   ;        a.h();
   ;
      push  si
      mov   bx,word ptr [si+6]         ; get A::vptr
      call  word ptr [bx+4]            ; call h() virtual
                                       ; function of whatever
                                       ; object was passed
      pop   cx
   ;
   ;  }
   ;
      pop   si
      pop   bp                         ; restore old frame
      ret
```

```
    ;
    ;  void main()
    ;

_main:
       push  bp
       mov   bp,sp
    ;
    ;  {
    ;
    ;        i = a.f();
    ;
       mov   ax,word ptr _a          ; use inline code, rather
                                     ; than virtual function
       mov   word ptr _i,ax          ; mechanism
    ;
    ;        i = a.g();
    ;
       mov   ax,word ptr _a+2        ; use inline code
       mov   word ptr _i,ax
    ;
    ;        i = a.h();
    ;
       mov   ax,word ptr _a+4        ; use inline code
       mov   word ptr _i,ax
    ;
    ;
    ;        i = b.f();
    ;
       mov   ax,word ptr _b+8        ; use inline code
       mov   word ptr _i,ax
    ;
    ;        i = b.g();
    ;
       mov   ax,offset _b            ; this time the inline
       push  ax                      ; code is ignored, and a
       mov   bx,word ptr _b+6        ; full fledged virtual
       call  word ptr [bx+2]         ; function call is used
       pop   cx
       mov   word ptr _i,ax
    ;
    ;        i = b.h();
    ;
       mov   ax,word ptr _b+12       ; use inline code
       mov   word ptr _i,ax
    ;
    ;
       pop   bp
       ret
```

The compiler is smart enough to know whether it can replace an `inline virtual` function call with the `inline` code. The function calls in function `Do(A&)` use an object reference, and thus, the compiler has no way of knowing whether the function will be invoked later with a reference to an `A` object or a reference to an object derived from `A`. This forces the compiler to use the complete `virtual` function-calling mechanism throughout `Do(A&)`. The function calls in `main()` are different. Here the compiler knows the exact object types that are used in the various function calls and thus exploits `inline` coding. There is one exception, though. The function call

```
i = b.g();
```

is handled as a regular `virtual`, because the function invoked is `A::g()`. Although class `B` does in this case, class `B` may not always know how class `A` accesses its `virtual` function `A::g()`. In the preceding example, the compiler had the full declarations and definitions for both classes `A` and `B`, so it could have used `inline` code even for the `b.g()` function call. For safety, the Borland C++ compiler treats all cases conservatively and safely vectors the `b.g()` call through the `virtual` mechanism.

Invoking Polymorphic Functions in a Base Class

When you have a library of related classes, member functions in one class frequently need to invoke functions higher in the inheritance tree. Invoking `virtual` functions in this manner can provide an elegant object-oriented solution in many cases. The problem with directly invoking a base class function is that you normally use scope resolution to identify at compile time which base class to use. As mentioned earlier, the scope resolution operator disables late binding, so you can't get a polymorphic function call this way. Things have to be done slightly differently to get the desired results. Consider the inheritance tree in Figure 5.26.

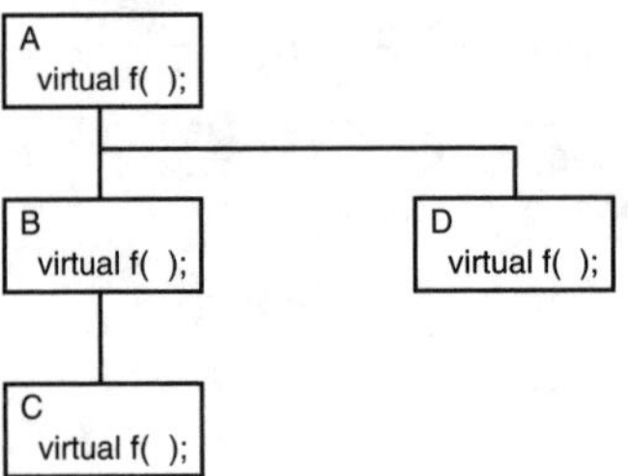

Figure 5.26. An inheritance tree in which a base class `virtual` *function is used.*

What if you need to write a function that takes a generic `A&` parameter as its argument and needs to invoke a `virtual` function in the object referenced and in its parent? Scope resolution obviously won't work, because at compile time, you don't know the type of object that will be passed to your function; therefore, you don't know who the parent will be. A

simple polymorphic interface at the class A level solves the problem immediately. Listing 5.18 is a possible solution.

Listing 5.18. Invoking `virtual` functions in a base class.

```
class A {
public:
      virtual void f() {}
      virtual void g() {f();}
};

class B: public A {
public:
      virtual void f() {}
      virtual void g() {A::f();}
};

class C: public B {
public:
      virtual void f() {}
      virtual void g() {B::f();}
};

class D: public A {
public:
      virtual void f() {}
      virtual void g() {A::f();}
};


void Show(A& a)
{
      // invoke f() for object passed, then f() for object's
      // parent
      a.f();
      a.g();
}

void main()
{
      A a;
      B b;
      C c;
      D d;

      Show(a);
      Show(b);
      Show(c);
      Show(d);
}
```

In Listing 5.18, `Show(A&)` needs to invoke a function `f()` for the object referenced and also the function `f()` in the object's parent. Essentially, what is needed is a way to extend polymorphism in a derived object into the object's base class. This is easily accomplished by adding a new `virtual` function `g()` to each class in the hierarchy. Function `g()` is defined to polymorphically invoke `f()` in its base class. Obviously, any other base class function could be called through `g()`, including functions further up the inheritance tree.

virtual Functions and Classification Hierarchies

Consider another more complicated case: You have an extended hierarchy, characterized by *classification nodes* at random locations along the tree. These special classes are conceptually significant because they identify major branches in the hierarchy. The problem is that not all classes are classification nodes. Consider the classification tree in Figure 5.27.

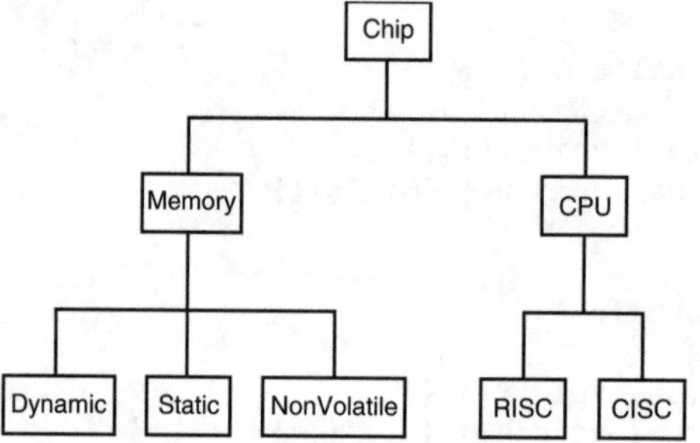

Figure 5.27. A classification class hierarchy used to illustrate polymorphic function calls in a base class.

The classes `Memory` and `CPU` are major classifications for the tree. Assume you need a function that takes a generic `Chip&` argument, invokes a polymorphic function for it, and then prints the classes' major classification. This requires you somehow to obtain a polymorphic behavior in a base class, departing from a class that is unknown at compile time. To solve this problem, you might have each class invoke a classification function in its base class. Closer inspection reveals that this would work only for classes one level down from a classification node. A different approach is required. Listing 5.19 is the implementation.

Listing 5.19. Polymorphic function calls through base classes.

```
#include <stdio.h>

class Chip {
public:
      virtual void Classification();
```

```
        virtual void f() {}
};

class Memory: public Chip {
public:
        virtual void Classification();
        virtual void f() {}
};


class CPU: public Chip {
public:
        virtual void Classification();
        virtual void f() {}
};

class Dynamic: public Memory {
public:
        virtual void f() {}
};

void Chip::Classification() { puts("Unknown classification");}
void Memory::Classification() { puts("Memory chip");}
void CPU::Classification() { puts("CPU chip");}

class Static: public Memory {
public:
        virtual void f() {}
};

class NonVolatile: public Memory {
public:
        virtual void f() {}
};

class RISC: public CPU {
public:
        virtual void f() {}
};

class CISC: public CPU {
public:
        virtual void f() {}
};

class M41256: public Dynamic {
public:
        virtual void f() {}
};
```

continues

Listing 5.19. continued

```
class M6264: public Static {
public:
      virtual void f() {}
};

class M1230: public NonVolatile {
public:
      virtual void f() {}
};

class M88000: public RISC {
public:
      virtual void f() {}
};

class M68000: public CISC {
public:
      virtual void f() {}
};

void Use(Chip& chip)
{
      // invoke f() for the passed object type
      chip.f();

      // print object's classification type
      chip.Classification();
}

void main()
{
      M41256 hitachi;
      M88000 motorola;
      Memory device;
      Chip and_gate;
      CISC microprocessor;
      NonVolatile ram;

      Use(hitachi);
      Use(motorola);
      Use(device);
      Use(and_gate);
      Use(microprocessor);
      Use(ram);
}
```

Invoking the function `Classification()` through the `Chip&` reference compels the compiler to use a polymorphic function call, resulting in late binding. From a different perspective, the `virtual` function mechanism causes the code to search the inheritance tree for a function called `Classification()`, starting at the class `Chip`. The `Classification()` function that is invoked is the one that overrides all the others, that is, the one defined in the lowest class. Consider the call

```
Use(hitachi);
```

The `virtual` table for class `M41256`, for example, is such that the function `Memory::Classification()` is invoked. The correct classification function would similarly be called for a class defined at any other arbitrary level in the hierarchy. All the details are handled transparently by the compiler. In fact, the lower levels in the hierarchy may not even be aware that a `Classification()` function exists above them. That's OOP at its best.

Invoking *virtual* Functions in a Constructor

The `virtual` function mechanism is normally used after an object has been constructed. What happens if you attempt to use a `virtual` function in the body of a constructor? Is it even allowed? Consider the code

```
class A {
public:
      A() {f();}
      virtual void f() {}
};

void main()
{
      A* a = new A;
}
```

The constructor for class `A` invokes a `virtual` function. If you try to compile the preceding code, you'll find that not only does it compile without errors, but it also works (even though it obviously doesn't do much).

The reason it works is that the `vptr` and `vtab` structures are set up for a class just before the body of the constructor executes. This allows you to use `virtual` functions without problems inside the constructor. Things get a little trickier, however when a constructor invokes a base class constructor, which in turn invokes a `virtual` function. This produces different results. Consider the following example:

```
class A {
public:
      A() {f();}
```

```
        virtual void f() {}
};

class B: public A {
public:
        B() : A() {}
        virtual void f() {}
};

void main()
{
        B* b = new B;
}
```

The constructor for class `B` invokes the base class constructor `A::A()`, which in turn invokes a `virtual` function. Whose function `f()` is invoked? This is what happens: The constructor for `B` invokes the constructor for class `A` just before setting up its own `virtual` mechanism. When `A::A()` is called, it establishes its own `virtual` tables, so the call `f()` causes the invocation of `A::f()`. After the `A` constructor is executed, control returns to `B::B()`. Just before the body of the constructor is executed, the class `B` `virtual` mechanism is put into place. If the `virtual` function `f()` were invoked inside the body of `B::B()`, the function `B::f()` would be executed.

Exception Handling

In life, things don't always go as expected. A negative occurrence that goes against our expectations is called a *bummer*. In computer programming, a condition that is unexpected or unusual is called an *exception*. Both bummers and exceptions usually denote problems that someone or something—be it yourself, your parents, your lawyers, or your code—is going to have to deal with. Bounced checks, traffic tickets, and losing your wallet are typical bummers. Resource exhaustion and hardware errors are typical exceptions.

When the first programming languages were developed back in the fifties, bummers were well known—although under a different name. The topic of exceptions and exception handling, however, had not really occurred to anyone yet. Programmers had enough trouble getting a system to do what they wanted under normal circumstances without worrying about the theory of error recovery and exception management. Programs dealt with the unexpected in a plethora of unstructured ways for many years. Computer programming evolved rapidly with the advent of compilers, and larger programs came into being, giving rise to an attempt to deal systematically with errors in structured systems.

Dealing with exceptions in a systematic way is challenging for a number of reasons. Before even looking at those reasons, it is best to get some terminology straight, and to examine what constitutes an exception. When a program detects an exception, it notifies the rest of the system by *throwing* the exception. Somewhere in the program there should

be code that handles (catches) the exception. The following are true statements regarding exceptions:

1. Exceptions normally represent something *bad* that happened. If a low-level function is designed to write data to a disk, an exception could represent a failure of the hardware—not success in writing the data. I don't know if I would want to work on the same project with a programmer who considered it bad to succeed in writing disk data (unless the code was only supposed to *read* data...).
2. Exceptions are unusual or unexpected conditions. A memory allocation routine will normally consider allocation failures to be exceptions, because the calling program expects the memory request to be honored. Although it is perfectly possible to flag an exception when succeeding in getting the requested memory, such an exception would be both misleading and conceptually wrong. It would be like answering a question with "Oh, my God! How could you ask such a thing? By the way, the answer is 4."
3. Exceptions can be caused by environmental or external factors, by something in your program, or both. For example, memory is something the operating system makes available to programs. If a program runs out of memory, it might either be caused by the OS not allocating enough memory, or by a memory leak in the program, or both. Because exceptions can be caused by external factors, a program can't always fix the problem and recover.

A program can encounter many conditions that may or may not be considered exceptions. Rare events may be considered exceptions, but what if these events are expected? Consider an ATM machine that times out if the customer fails to enter the password code within a given amount of time. This is probably a rare but certainly not an unexpected condition. Should it be handled as an exception? Probably not. How about a program that stores objects in containers. Should an exception be thrown if the same object is found in more than one container? That depends on whether it is good or bad (read that right or wrong) for the same object to be in multiple containers. What one program considers good might be bad for another.

Old Ways to Handle Exceptions

Before the development of formal exception handling, C++ programmers (as other programmers) resorted to a variety of ways to handle errors, unexpected conditions, and failures. The following list shows the most common ways that errors and exceptions are handled.

1. The entire program is terminated. This is the technique used by the `ASSERT` macro in C. Program termination should be regarded as the last resort in error handling, when recovery is impossible, difficult, hazardous, or unreliable.

Sometimes, terminating a program in the presence of an error can be more dangerous than continuing the execution. Consider a nuclear reactor control program that experiences a floating-point error. The last thing you want the program to do is terminate! The exception should be handled and the program should be able to continue execution somehow (preferably after warning the operator...).

2. Functions detecting an exception return a status value indicating that something went wrong. A function might return 1 if it succeeded, 0 if an error occurred. A global variable might be used to store the error type between function calls. Future calls to low-level functions could be forced to fail if the global error variable indicated a previous problem. This is the technique used in the C `stdio` library, in which the variable `errno` holds error codes. It is also used in OWL 1.0 and 2.0, in which the variable `TModule::Status` was set to indicate various runtime errors.

   The problem with this technique is that, although it does a fine job at detecting errors, it doesn't do anything to handle them or to recover. The calling functions are relied on to check the function return codes and error variables. This technique handles exceptions as a two-part process: low-level code detects errors, and high-level code handles errors.

   The two-part process opens the door to problems. If the low-level code does its job and correctly detects all errors, there is no guarantee that the system using that code will process the errors correctly (or at all). On the other hand, if all the high-level code checks diligently for low-level errors, there is no guarantee that the checked errors will be detected at the lower level. Moreover, if every function call to a low-level function needs to be checked for errors, programs could become extremely large, devoting more code to the unexpected situations than to the expected ones.

3. Establish an error-handling callback function, to be invoked by low-level functions when an exception occurs. This is the technique used in C++ to handle dynamic memory allocation failures. The function `set_new_handler()` allows application programs to establish a custom handler, which the system calls at runtime when a request for memory allocation can't be satisfied. The technique is often used in combination with method 2, but also allows programs to have handlers that at least attempt to recover from an error.

   Consider a callback installed with `set_new_handler()`. The callback might swap blocks of memory to disk and reattempt the memory allocation. If the second allocation fails, the exception is reported; otherwise the program continues without incident.

4. Perform a non-local jump. C programmers used `setjmp()` and `longjmp()` to allow low-level functions to unwind the stack to return to an execution point marked with a `setjmp()` statement.

5. Raise a signal. A signal is a synchronous interrupt that requests the system to invoke a previously installed signal handler. Signal handlers are similar to installable callbacks, described in method 3, but the implementation and availability of signals is implementation dependent, and more a function of the operating system and system hardware than the programming language.

An OOP Approach for Handling Exceptions

As you can see, exceptions are difficult to define, and even more difficult to handle in a uniform manner. The folks at AT&T thought the same, and decided three things:

1. Exception handling should be made a programming language feature, both to ensure that exception handling is not implementation dependent, and to bring some order to the chaos of exception-handling methodologies.
2. The exception-handling method will have to be OOP-oriented to enable inheritance and `virtual` functions to handle exceptions, without the tedium of `switch` statements to check for exception types. Someone once said (I think it was me), "`switch` statements are to C what `virtual` functions are to C++."
3. Exception handling must be flexible, supporting all the most common types of exceptions and exception handling. As a last resort, the exception-handling mechanism must be overridable by the programmer, and the default handling should not break existing code.

That all sounds like a tall order—a very tall order. But that's why it took several years for exception handling to make its way into the working ANSI draft of C++. It took a lot of help from lots of people, but what they have come up with is not only attractive—it's even useful (!).

Throwing an Exception

The C++ technique for exception handling is based on the concept of the non-local jump. When an exception is detected, the program *throws* an exception. Throwing an exception causes the program to perform a non-local jump before continuing execution. Listing 6.1 shows how an exception is thrown.

Listing 6.1. Throwing an exception.

```
#include <iostream.h>

const int CACHE_ERROR = -1;
```

```
void WriteCacheBlock(unsigned char* data, long size)
{
  if (size > 1000)
    //  can't handle that much data!
    throw CACHE_ERROR;

  // .. write the data to disk
}
```

When the `throw` statement is executed in Listing 6.1, the function `WriteCacheBlock()` is terminated, and execution continues elsewhere. The statements following the `throw` statement are skipped. In that sense a `throw` statement is like a `return` statement, except that execution doesn't continue on the statement following the line that invoked the function. A `throw` statement may or may not indicate an exception variable. It is allowable to have a `throw` statement without an exception variable only when an exception is re-thrown in the handler while processing a previous exception.

Throwing Initialized Objects

The code in Listing 6.1 showed the use of a scalar exception in the `throw` statement. You can also instantiate a regular object, and initialize it before throwing it. By initializing the object, you can pass additional information to the exception handler. The code in Listing 6.1 can be modified to pass the value of the invalid size to the `catch` statement, using the code in Listing 6.2.

Listing 6.2. Using an initialized object with a `throw` statement.

```
#include <iostream.h>

class SizeError {

  int size;

public:

  SizeError(int value) {size = value;}
  char* ErrorMessage() {return "Size Error";}
  int Size() {return size;}
};

void WriteCacheBlock(unsigned char* data, long size)
{
  if (size > 1000) {
```

continues

Listing 6.2. continued

```
    SizeError error(size);
    throw error;
  }

  // .. write the data to disk
}

void WriteCache(unsigned char* cache)
{
  try {
    WriteCacheBlock(cache, 100);
  }

  catch(SizeError error) {
    cout << error.ErrorMessage()
      << ": "
      << error.Size()
      << endl;
  }
}
```

Now the handler has access to the size of the cache request that caused the exception to be thrown. You might use the technique to pass the name and line number of the file where an exception was detected, as the `ASSERT` macro does. Listing 6.3 shows an example.

Listing 6.3. Initializing an exception before throwing it.

```
#include <strstrea.h>
#include <string.h>

class SizeError {

  char filename [80];
  int line;

public:

  SizeError(char* f, int l);
  char* ErrorMessage();
};

SizeError::SizeError(char* f, int l)
{
  strcpy(filename, f);
  line = l;
}
```

```
char* SizeError::ErrorMessage()
{
  char buffer [100];
  ostrstream message(buffer, sizeof buffer);
  message << "Cache size error in file "
       << filename
       << "on line "
       << line
       << endl;
  return buffer;
}

void WriteCacheBlock(unsigned char* data, long size)
{
  if (size > 1000)
    throw SizeError(__FILE__, __LINE__);

  // .. write the data to disk
}

void WriteCache(unsigned char* cache)
{
  try {
    WriteCacheBlock(cache, 100);
  }

  catch(SizeError error) {
    cout << error.ErrorMessage() << endl;
  }
}
```

The exception handler would print an error message such as the following:

```
Cache size error in file TEST.CPP on line 11
```

Catching an Exception

After a `throw` is executed at runtime, execution is transferred to the closest `catch` statement that can handle the exception type thrown. A function that wants to handle exceptions must use a C++ construct: `try` blocks. What is a `try` block? When you write code that could cause an exception, you must enclose the code in a `try` block, and follow it with a `catch` statement, as follows:

```
try {
  // the code in this block may cause an exception
  // ...
}
```

```
catch (some_type) {
  // handle exceptions thrown with a
  // parameter of type some_type
}
```

Any exceptions thrown before execution reaches the end of the `try` block can (but aren't guaranteed to) be caught by the associated `catch` statement. If the code in the `try` block invokes a function that also has a `try` block, exceptions could be handled in the latter function, and would never be seen by the calling function. `catch` statements resemble function definitions. They are defined to accept a single typed parameter, and are followed by a pair of curly braces enclosing a block of zero or more statements. Listing 6.4 shows a function with a `try` block for the function in Listing 6.1.

Listing 6.4. Catching an exception.

```
void WriteCache(unsigned char* cache)
{
  try {
    WriteCacheBlock(cache, 100);
  }

  catch(int CACHE_ERROR) {
    cout << "Cache couldn't be written to disk." << endl;
  }
}
```

A `catch` statement handles typed exceptions. In the preceding example, the `throw` statement passes an `int` parameter. When executing the `throw`, the system will search for the nearest `catch` statement that handles `int` arguments. `catch` statements are searched in order, from nearest to farthest. The nearest is the one associated with the last `try` block executed. The nearest `catch` statement is the one following the nearest `try` block. The nearest `try` block is the last one executed.

A `catch` statement handles exceptions of a given type. An exception type may be used to represent a whole class of exceptions. Consider changing the code of Listings 6.1 and 6.2 to handle two kinds of exceptions, using the code shown in Listing 6.5.

Listing 6.5. Handling two exceptions with the same type.

```
#include <iostream.h>

const int
  CACHE_ERROR  = -1,
  RANGE_ERROR = -2;
```

```
void WriteCacheBlock(unsigned char* data, long size)
{
  if (size < 0)
    throw RANGE_ERROR;
  if (size > 1000)
    throw CACHE_ERROR;

  // .. write the data to disk
}

void WriteCache(unsigned char* cache)
{
  try {
    WriteCacheBlock(cache, 100);
  }

  catch(int error_type) {
    if (error_type == RANGE_ERROR)
      cout << "Range error." << endl;
    else
      cout << "Cache error." << endl;
  }
}
```

There is essentially no limit to the number of exceptions you can handle with a type, but using a single type to catch more than one exception type leads to the use of `if` or `switch` statements. A better approach is to use different types (classes, to be precise) for each exception, and let inheritance and `virtual` functions sort out the details. See the sections "Using Multiple Catch Blocks" and "Hierarchies of Exception Types" in this chapter for details.

Catching Untyped Exceptions

What if you want to write a function that catches all possible exceptions, regardless of the type? Because a `catch` statement resembles a function definition, C++ uses the ellipsis notation, used in function parameter lists, to designate universal `catch` statements. The rationale of the notation is that the ellipsis is used with functions taking any type of parameters. The generic `catch` statement can be written like this:

```
try {
  // whatever
}

catch(...) {
  // trap ALL exceptions
}
```

Catching exceptions with the ellipsis notation is something you should do with caution. The problem is that you don't know the exact type of exception that was thrown. You can't reference an exception argument, because you have no way to declare it in the parameter list for the `catch` statement. Still, if you know *a priori* all the types of exceptions that can occur in a `try` block, or if you really don't care which specific exception was thrown, the ellipsis notation can be handy.

Using Multiple Catch Blocks

Often, a `try` block can have code that detects different types of exceptions. Using a single exception type to indicate more than one exception can get cumbersome because you wind up with a very un-object-oriented `switch` or `if..else` construct statement to sort out each exception, as shown in Listing 6.5. A better approach is to use a separate type for each exception. This approach is particularly elegant when using class variables for exceptions, which are covered in the next section.

For the moment, I'll limit the discussion to scalar exception types, just to introduce a few basic ideas. Consider the function `WriteCacheBlock()`, shown in Listing 6.5. Using separate types for the exceptions allows you to use a separate `catch` statement for each exception type. I'll change the code in Listing 6.5 to use an `int` for `CACHE_ERROR` and a signed char for `RANGE_ERROR`. The code now looks like that shown in Listing 6.6.

Listing 6.6. Handling two exceptions with separate `catch` statements.

```
#include <iostream.h>

const int         CACHE_ERROR = -1;
const signed char RANGE_ERROR = -2;

void WriteCacheBlock(unsigned char* data, long size)
{
  if (size < 0)
    throw RANGE_ERROR;
  if (size > 1000)
    throw CACHE_ERROR;

  // .. write the data to disk
}

void WriteCache(unsigned char* cache)
{
  try {
    WriteCacheBlock(cache, 100);
  }

  catch(int) {
```

```
    cout << "Range error." << endl;
  }

  catch(signed char) {
    cout << "Cache error." << endl;
  }
}
```

The `catch` statements now have no `if` or `switch` statements. The compiler produces code that executes the `catch` statement associated with the actual exception type thrown at runtime. Letting the compiler take care of calling the right `catch` statement based on a parameter type is reminiscent of overloaded functions. You might think of the separate `catch` blocks as a form of `catch` overloading. The more work you let the compiler do for you (in the way of determining the right exception handler), the more you are exploiting the built-in features of C++, and the less likely you are to add bugs of your own.

Using *catch/throw* versus *setjmp/longjmp*

A `throw` statement causes a non-local jump. C programmers had the option of causing non-local jumps using the function `longjmp()`. Although both `throw` and `longjmp()` cause non-local jumps, there is a fundamental difference between them.

With `longjmp()`, you don't specify an exception to be handled, but rather a place to jump to. To effect the jump, you specify a task state. The task state is a struct that contains things like the stack pointer and the program counter of a non-local point in your program. Task states are created using `setjmp()`. Specifying a task state in a `longjmp()` call forces the programmer to keep track of the various task states that a program must use. Basically the programmer is responsible for knowing where the `longjmp()` will make the program jump to.

Using `longjmp()` is also potentially unsafe, because calling the function with a task state that wasn't initialized by a call to `setjmp()` will crash the program. In C++ programs, `longjmp()` is not only unsafe but potentially catastrophic. As the program effects its non-local jump, local class objects whose stack frames disappear are destroyed without having their destructors called. Both `setjmp()` and `longjmp()` are therefore completely incompatible with class objects and should be considered obsolete in C++.

Finding the Right Exception Handler

`throw` statements are much more sophisticated and safe than `longjmp()`. With a `throw` statement, you don't specify a destination to jump to, only the kind of exception that occurred. It is up to the compiler to determine where the program will go. When the compiler finds a `throw` statement, it generates code that, at runtime, will search the call chain for the first function containing a `catch` statement able to handle the exception type thrown. If no suitable `catch` statement is found, a default one is used that causes termination of your program.

Unwinding the Stack

To find the right exception handler for an exception, the compiler calls a runtime piece of code to figure out what function in the call chain has a suitable `catch` statement. While climbing the stack in search of this `catch` statement, the compiler calls destructors for all local objects whose stack frames are unwound. The compiler ensures that destructors for derived classes are called before the destructors for base classes, duplicating the normal destructor call sequence that occurs when an object goes out of scope. For objects containing subobjects, the compiler ensures also that destructors are called only for objects whose constructors have been completely executed.

Consider the following call chain of functions:

```
#include <iostream.h>
#include <cstring.h>
#include <except.h>

void g();
void h();

void f()
{
  try {
    g();
  }
  catch(xalloc) {
    cerr << "caught in f()";
  }
}

void g()
{
  string a("string a");
  try {
    h();
  }
  catch(xmsg) {
    cerr << "caught in g()";
  }
}
```

```
void h()
{
  string b("string b");

  new char [10000];
  throw(xmsg(string("we're dead") ) );
}
```

When the program reaches function `h()`, the situation will be roughly that shown in Figure 6.1.

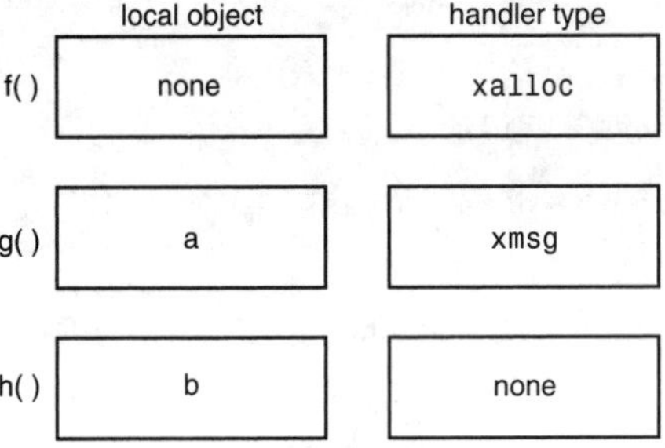

Figure 6.1. The local objects and exception handlers accessible through the stack from function `h()`.

Function `h()` can throw two kinds of exceptions: if the `new` operator fails due to insufficient memory, an `xalloc` exception will be thrown. The runtime handling code sees that the nearest handler that takes `xalloc` exceptions is in `f()`. Performing a non-local jump to `f`'s exception handler causes the unwinding of the stack frame of functions `h()` and `g()`, so the destructors for local objects `a` and `b` are called.

If function `h()` throws an `xmsg`, the runtime handling code sees that the nearest handler is in function `g()`. The destructor for object `b` is called, and execution continues in the exception handler of function `g()`.

If the runtime handling code can't find a suitable exception handler for the exception thrown, the stack is completely unwound, and the function `terminate()` is called. By default, `terminate()` calls abort(), but you can install your own handler to be called by `terminate()`. See the section "The `terminate()` Function" at the end of this chapter for more details.

Exceptions as Class Objects

The real power of C++ exception handling is realized if class objects are thrown and caught. A `throw` statement can throw an exception of any type you want—scalars, structs, classes. Consider the cache-writing function in Listing 6.1. Using a class for the exception the code might look as shown in Listing 6.7.

Listing 6.7. Using a class exception object.

```
#include <iostream.h>

class SizeError {

public:

  char* ErrorMessage() {return "Size Error";}
};

void WriteCacheBlock(unsigned char* data, long size)
{
  if (size > 1000)
    throw SizeError();

  // .. write the data to disk
}

void WriteCache(unsigned char* cache)
{
  try {
    WriteCacheBlock(cache, 100);
  }

  catch(SizeError error) {
    cout << error.ErrorMessage() << endl;
  }
}
```

An unnamed object of class `SizeError` is instantiated and thrown. The `catch` statement is declared to accept exceptions of type `SizeError`. If an exception was derived from class `SizeError`, it will be "cut down" to a `SizeError` inside the handler block, and the derived portions of the exception will not be accessible.

Handling Exceptions by Reference

Exception handlers can be defined also to accept references and pointers, allowing you to use base class references or pointers to handle generic exceptions derived from a single class. Using a reference in the code of Listing 6.7, the `throw` statement would remain the same, and the `catch` statement would become:

```
catch(SizeError& error) {
  cout << error.ErrorMessage() << endl;
}
```

Using a reference allows you to use `virtual` functions to call `member` functions of the exception thrown. If `ErrorMessage` was declared `virtual`, then classes derived from `SizeError` could override the function. Calling `ErrorMessage()` in the exception handler would result in polymorphic behavior.

Using a pointer to pass exceptions is similar to using references, except that the `throw` and `catch` statements must use the address of the exception. The `throw` statement for `SizeError` would look something like this:

```
throw &SizeError(__FILE__, __LINE__);
```

and the `catch` statement would look like this:

```
catch(SizeError* error) {
  cout << error.ErrorMessage() << endl;
}
```

Hierarchies of Exception Types

The advantage of using classes for exceptions becomes significant when you have many types of exceptions that can be put into a hierarchy because you can use `virtual` functions in the exception handlers. The only requirement for the `catch` statement is that you catch exceptions by reference or pointer rather than by value.

Consider a library function that writes data to a removable media (for example, floppy) disk. Lots of different kinds of errors can occur, such as an open diskette door, an unformatted diskette, no diskette present, a write-protected diskette, and so on. It makes sense to organize disk errors into a hierarchy, as shown in Figure 6.2.

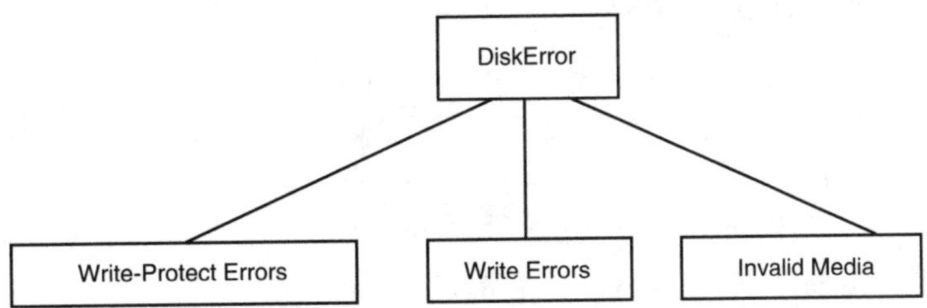

Figure 6.2. A hierarchy of disk-related errors.

The hierarchy can be easily implemented as a class hierarchy. Listing 6.8 shows a partial implementation.

Listing 6.8. A hierarchy of exceptions.

```
#include <strstrea.h>
#include <string.h>

class DiskError {

public:

  char* ErrorMessage() {
    return "Unknown disk error";
  }
};

class DiskWriteError {

public:

  char* ErrorMessage() {
    return "Disk write error";
  }
};

class DiskWriteProtectedError {

public:

  char* ErrorMessage() {
    return "Disk error: disk is write-protected";
  }
};

void WriteDiskData()
{
  // call OS to see if disk is write-protected
  // ...

  if (diskIsWriteProtected)
    throw DiskWriteProtectedError();

  // call OS to write the data
  // ...

  if (couldntWriteData)
    throw DiskWriteError();

  // .. write the data to disk
}
```

Using the exception hierarchy, it becomes very simple to deal polymorphically with any disk error. The caller of `WriteDiskData()` could handle the exception using code like this:

```
void WriteDisk()
{
  try {
    WriteDiskData();
  }

  catch(DiskError& error) {
    cout << error.ErrorMessage() << endl;
  }
}
```

The function call

```
error.ErrorMessage()
```

will be bound at runtime to the correct `member` function, based on the exception type thrown. The caller of `WriteDiskData()` does not need to know what kind of exception was thrown, other than the fact it was derived from `DiskError`.

Handling Common Errors with Exceptions

Several recurring scenarios are known to cause problems (errors) in C++ programs. Most non-trivial programs have ways of dealing with these errors, but often inconsistently. With the advent of exception handling, C++ permits the development of consistent, standard, and robust ways to overcome typical problems. I'll discuss a few common errors in the following sections.

Exceptions and Resource Acquisition

Programs often deal with resources—be they memory, disks, bitmaps, or other. When dealing with resources, you normally follow three steps:

1. Obtain the resource.
2. Use the resource.
3. Release the resource.

Resources are often required to be locked, to avoid simultaneous use by multiple processes. Locks are used in these cases. The problem with the simplistic 1-2-3 approach is that it doesn't take into account the possibility of exceptions being thrown. If the code for steps 1 through 3 is contained in a single function, an exception thrown while obtaining the resource would cause the function to be exited. The remaining steps 2 and 3 would be bypassed by the error-handling mechanism and the resource would be left dangling.

A first solution could be to add a `try` block to the code, and catch all exceptions that could be thrown while using the resource. Consider writing code that uses Windows device contexts for GDI operations. The code might look like that shown in Listing 6.9.

Listing 6.9. Handling exceptions thrown during GDI operations.

```
#include <windows.h>

void UseDC()
{
  // get DC for the entire screen
  HDC hdc = GetDC(NULL);

  try {
    // perform some GDI operations on the DC
  }
  catch(...) {
    // something happened while using the DC
    ReleaseDC(NULL, hdc);
  }

  // normal termination
  ReleaseDC(NULL, hdc);
}
```

This approach is semantically correct, but ugly and verbose. DCs will be used over and over again, and each time a DC is used, you will need to write a complete function. Not only does this require a lot of coding, but there is the danger that at some point in the future you forget about exceptions in GDI operations, and write code that doesn't handle GDI exceptions.

Using Functional Closures

To remedy the preceding problems, a solution is to create a stand-alone class that creates a functional closure around the resource. Stroustrup refers to this technique with the somewhat obscure expression *resource acquisition is initialization.* To handle device contexts, whether exceptions are thrown or not, you could write a small class:

```
#include <windows.h>

class MyDC {
```

```
  HDC hdc;

public:

  MyDC() {hdc = GetDC(NULL);}
  operator HDC() {return hdc;}
  ~MyDC() {ReleaseDC(NULL, hdc);}
};
```

Using this class, you no longer need to worry about exceptions leaving the device context dangling. A function could use `MyDC` like this:

```
void foo()
{
  MyDC dc;

  // call the GDI functions on the DC
  // ...
}
```

If an exception is thrown while processing GDI operations on the device context, `foo()` will be exited, but the compiler will invoke the destructor for `MyDC` in the process of unwinding the stack to locate an exception handler.

Functional closures become very important in C++ programming when exceptions are expected. All resources should be functionally closed, to prevent memory leaks, deadly embraces, and deadlocked code. Classes that deal with dynamically allocated memory typically do something like this:

```
class A {

  int* array;

public:

  A() { array = new int [100]; do_something(); }
  void do_something();
  ~A() { delete [] array; }
};
```

The code looks all right, until you consider what happens if an exception is thrown inside `A::do_something()`. Because the function is called inside the body of the constructor, the `A` object hasn't been completely constructed yet. The code will jump to the nearest compatible exception, bypassing the destructor for `A`. The code just sprang a memory leak!

One solution could be to place the call to `do_something()` before allocating the memory. Obviously this isn't possible if `do_something()` uses the allocated memory. Moreover, the exact order of the code shouldn't determine whether a memory leak occurs or not. The complete solution, again proposed in Stroustrup 91, is to functionally close the memory resource. This can be done by implementing the following class:

```
class A {

  int* array;

public:

  A(int size) { array = new int [size]; }
  ~A() { delete [] array; }
  operator int*() {return array;}
};
```

Now you can include the class anywhere you want, with the guarantee that the compiler will always deallocate A's memory in the event of an exception. Consider how a user of A would look:

```
void foo()
{
  A table(100);

  // use the table object
  // ...
}
```

There is no exception handling code required to clean up class A. Obviously, you may want to catch exceptions for other purposes, but at least your code is guaranteed by the compiler to have no leaks. You can include functionally closed resources even in other classes, like this:

```
class B {

  A table;

public:

  B() : table(100) {do_something();}
  void do_something() {}
};
```

Exceptions and Constructors

A long-standing problem in C++ has been the handling of errors in constructors, because constructors return no value and therefore have no direct way of communicating failures to the caller. Consider the following class:

```
class SetMemory {

  char* memory;

public:
```

```
  SetMemory();
};

SetMemory::SetMemory()
{
  memory = new char [10000];

  if (memory) {
    // initialize the allocated memory
  }
}
```

If the constructor succeeds in getting the memory, everything is fine. If it doesn't, it must abort. The caller will naturally assume that the `SetMemory` object was constructed, so an additional error-handling facility must be added to the class. Constructors can fail for many reasons. Here are just a few:

- A file couldn't be opened.
- A resource couldn't be located.
- Memory couldn't be allocated.
- A connection couldn't be made to another process.

Functional closures are often the most elegant way to deal with errors in exceptions. In other cases, throwing an exception is the perfect way for a constructor to inform the rest of the system that it failed in some way. When you throw an exception inside a constructor, the system makes a non-local jump to the nearest compatible handler. In the process of unwinding the stack, the destructors are called for all completely constructed local objects that were stored on the portion of the stack that is unwound. The object whose constructor threw the exception in the first place is not destructed because the object had not been completely constructed at the time of the exception. Listing 6.10 shows a constructor throwing an exception.

Listing 6.10. Throwing an exception in a constructor.

```
#include <fstream.h>

class NoConfigFile {};

class TrySomething {

public:

  TrySomething() {
    ifstream file("c:\\config.sys");
    if (!file)
```

continues

Listing 6.10. continued

```
      // big trouble...
      throw NoConfigFile();
    }
};

void foo()
{
  try {
    // see if the constructor succeeds
    TrySomething thing;
  }
  catch(NoConfigFile) {
    cerr << endl << "Couldn't locate CONFIG.SYS file";
    // use defaults instead of the CONFIG.SYS settings
    // ...
  }
}
```

The function `foo()` constructs a `SomeThing` object inside a `try` block. If the constructor fails, the `NoConfigFile` exception is thrown; otherwise, `foo()` continues merrily on with its own defaults.

Exceptions in Objects with Subobjects

When a class includes other class objects as data members, exception handling takes on special rules, because exceptions can theoretically occur in the constructor for any of the subobjects. Consider the following example in Listing 6.11.

Listing 6.11. An object with subobjects.

```
#include <fstream.h>
#include <owl\except.h>

class A {

public:

  A(const char*);
};

A::A(const char* name)
{
  ifstream file(name);
```

```
  if (!file)
    throw TXOwl("Couldn't read file");
}

class B {

  A file;

public:

  B();
};

B::B()
 : file("C:\\CONFIG.SYS")
{
  char* cp = new char [10000];
  // ...
}
```

Class `B` includes a data member of class `A`. If an exception is thrown in the constructor for class `A`, the `B` object won't have been completely constructed. The following code instantiates a local `B` object:

```
void foo()
{
  try {
    // attempt to create a B object
    B b;
  }

  catch(TXOwl) {
    return;
  }

  catch(xalloc) {
    return;
  }
}
```

What happens if an exception is thrown in the constructor for `A`? The code will jump to the exception handler in `foo()`. The destructors for `A` and `B` will not be invoked, because neither object was completely constructed at the time of the exception.

What happens if the constructor for `A` succeeds and the constructor for `B` fails? The constructor for `B` could easily fail if the `new` operator couldn't allocate the `char` array. The code will again make a non-local jump to the exception handler in `foo()`, but this time the destructor for class `A` will be called.

The introduction of exception handling in the C++ language has introduced a certain degree of complexity to the language, but allows you to deal with errors and problematic situations in a consistent manner.

Standard C++ Exceptions

Exceptions can occur in any computing environment, whether Windows, DOS, UNIX, or other. Many types of exceptions are environment dependent, but some are so basic that the ANSI C++ committee decided to define a few standard exceptions. The basic ones are defined in the ANSI X3J16/91 WG21/N0059 draft document.

- `xmsg`
- `xalloc`

Then there are a few exceptions related specifically to the new `string` class:

- `string::outofrange`
- `string::lengtherror`

The ANSI committee may very well define additional exceptions in the future. The following figure shows the relationship between the various standard exception types.

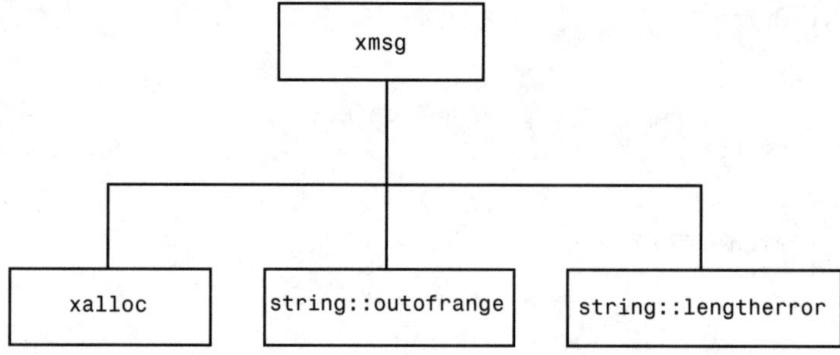

Figure 6.3. The standard C++ exceptions.

The following sections describe each exception.

`xmsg` Exceptions

`xmsg` is the root class of the exception class hierarchy. It is a class declared like this:

```
class xmsg {

    string* str;

public:
```

```
    xmsg(const string& msg);
    xmsg(const xmsg& msg);
    ~xmsg();

    const string& why() const;
    void raise() throw(xmsg);
};
```

`xmsg` is designed to take an error message as a parameter. You can then use the string to report the error to the user. `xmsg` is rarely used directly because it carries no information about exceptions other than the string message. Mostly you'll use `xmsg` as a base class for more specialized exceptions. OWL exceptions are all derived from `xmsg`.

`xalloc` Exceptions

Any time a program allocates memory dynamically, there is the possibility that the memory request can't be honored due to insufficient or fragmented memory. Memory allocation failures are so important that they are handled by a standard C++ exception type called `xalloc`. When you dynamically allocate a C++ object, the global `new` operator is called with a class constructor. If the operator fails to obtain enough memory, it throws an `xalloc` exception—*before* calling the constructor. Because the constructor wasn't called, no new object was created, so there are no new objects to destruct. By default, `xalloc` (like all other exceptions that aren't caught) calls `terminate()`, which by default calls `abort()`, which kills your program. You can easily change the error handling for memory failures by adding your own `xalloc` handler. Listing 6.12 shows how to catch `xalloc` exceptions.

Listing 6.12. Handling `xalloc` exceptions.

```
#include <owl\window.h>
#include <owl\framewin.h>

class TMyApp : public TApplication {
  public:
    TMyApp() : TApplication() {}

    void InitMainWindow() {
      try {
       MainWindow =
          new TFrameWindow(0, "xalloc exceptions");
      }
      catch(xalloc) {
     cerr << endl << "Insufficient memory" << endl;
      }

    }
};

static TMyApp App;
```

Any time you request dynamically allocated memory, it is important that your code be ready to catch `xalloc` exceptions. It may seem like a pain to have to catch `xalloc` exceptions everywhere you create an object or allocate memory. You might be able to minimize the overhead by catching `xalloc` exceptions in the Main Window of your application, or at a small number of strategic points in the application, allowing you to ignore the exceptions at lower levels in your code.

`string::outofrange` Exceptions

This kind of exception is associated with arrays. The only standard C++ class that deals with arrays is `string`, so the `outofrange` exception is declared inside class `string`. An `outofrange` exception will be thrown any time you attempt to access a `string` element that is beyond the end of the character array. Assume that you create a `string` object like this:

```
string message("Hello");
```

The string object internally allocates an array to hold the characters. If you attempt to access beyond the fifth element, a `string::outofrange` error will be thrown. Listing 6.13 presents a short example.

Listing 6.13. Causing and handling a `string::outofrange` exception.

```
#include <cstring.h>

void foo()
{
  string message("Message");
  try {
    char c = message [100];
  }
  catch(string::outofrange) {
    MessageBox(NULL,
            "\nOut of range error\n",
            "String Error",
            MB_OK);
  }
}
```

`string::lengtherror` Exceptions

`string` objects automatically allocate internal memory to handle characters. Class `string` has various operators and member functions that let you add characters to a `string`. For example, `string::operator+=` allows you to append characters. When you append characters to a `string`, an array managed internally by `string` is made to "grow" to hold the

extra data. Growing is accomplished by allocating a new expanded array, copying the characters from the old array into the new array, and deleting the old array. If there is insufficient memory to allocate the new array, `string` will throw a `string::lengtherror` exception.

Error Handling in OWL

OWL 1.0 and 2.5 are different in the way they deal with errors. OWL 1.0 was relatively crude, OWL 2.0 more refined—although not quite ideal. In the following sections I'll discuss how OWL 1.0 and 2.5 handle errors.

OWL 1.0

Before the advent of C++ exception handling, library developers were forced to develop their own technique to deal with errors. In OWL 1.0, basic errors were flagged in the data member `TModule::Status`, checked in the member function `TModule::ValidWindow()`, and reported by the member function `TModule::Error()`. The sequence for creating an OWL window was as follows:

```
TWindow window =
  GetApplication()->MakeWindow(new TWindow(this, "Title");
```

First, the `TWindow` constructor was called, then a pointer to the constructed object was passed to `TApplication::MakeWindow()`, which had the following code:

```
PTWindowsObject TModule::MakeWindow(PTWindowsObject AWindowsObject)
{
  if ( AWindowsObject && ValidWindow(AWindowsObject) )
    if ( (AWindowsObject->Create()) )
      return AWindowsObject;
    else
    {
      Error(AWindowsObject->Status);
      AWindowsObject->ShutDownWindow();
    }
  return NULL;
}
```

NULL `TWindow` pointers would cause `MakeWindow()` to return NULL, which the caller would then assign to a local variable. Making indirect calls to `TWindow` functions through this pointer would make the code RIP. For non-NULL `TWindow` pointers passed to `MakeWindow()`, a call to `TModule::ValidWindow()` would check the value of `TModule::Status`. Non-zero values indicated some kind of error, which would then be reported by a call to `TModule::Error`.

OWL 2.5

The error-handling capability of OWL 1.0 was relatively limited, but did work as long as you knew when to call `TModule::ValidWindow()`, when to check for NULL `TWindow` pointers, and always checked for errors at all possible places. The problem was that error handling was not centralized in the code, and that to really check for all possible errors you almost wound up with more code to deal with the exceptions than the normal situations. OWL 2.5 uses C++ exception handling to deal with errors. Moreover, the only error handling that OWL 1.0 really had was for memory and window creation failures. OWL 2.5 is much more powerful and organized when it comes to error handling. OWL 2.5 has a whole hierarchy of exceptions it can throw, shown in Figure 6.4.

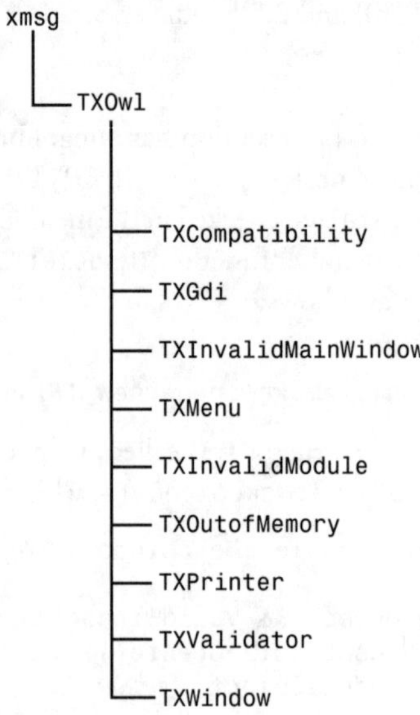

Figure 6.4. The OWL exception class hierarchy.

The following sections describe the OWL exceptions and how a typical application should catch them.

TXOwl Exceptions

Most OWL exceptions thrown are specialized: their type tells you what kind of problem occurred. The exception hierarchy in OWL 2.5 uses `TXOwl` as a base class. This class is rarely used directly when throwing exceptions.

You can use either string IDs or `string` objects with `TXOwl` constructors. `TXOwl` can be convenient to throw your own exceptions, without the hassle of creating your own exception class.

TXCompatibility Exceptions

OWL 1.0 used the data member `TModule::Status` to indicate error conditions. The problem was that `TModule::Status` was an int, and assigning a value to it wouldn't guarantee that the error would be processed. OWL 2.5 uses a class object for `TModule::Status`, of type `TStatus`. The class has an overloaded assignment operator, which takes control when you assign a new value to `TModule::Status`, and throws a `TXCompatibility` exception. You can throw a `TXCompatibility` exception in your own code, but you shouldn't abuse this exception type. It is meant to handle (as its name indicates) basic problems in the OWL code regarding compatibility.

TXGdi Exceptions

OWL 2.5 supports a number of Windows GDI (Graphics Device Interface) objects, such as bitmaps, pens, and brushes. When creating or working with these GDI objects, there may be any number of things that can go wrong. OWL uses the `TXGdi` exception to flag problems that prevent a GDI operation from being carried out. `TXGdi` exceptions (like all other exceptions derived from `xmsg`) contain a string data member, describing the exact type of problem encountered. The strings are as follows in Table 6.1.

Table 6.1. The strings used in `TXGdi` exceptions.

String	*Description*
`GDI allocate failure`	Thrown when a GDI operation could not be carried out by OWL due to insufficient memory. For example, when you create a `TBitmap` object, OWL sets up a couple of `TMemoryDC` objects to handle the bitmap. If there is insufficient memory to create the `TMemoryDCs`, OWL will throw a `TXGdi` exception.
`GDI resource load failure`	Thrown when a GDI object could not find a resource (such as a bitmap) with the given name. For example, when creating a `TDib` object, you can specify the resource name of the bitmap to use. If you specified the resource name "BITMAP_PICTURE", OWL will throw an exception if a bitmap resource by that name is not found in the .EXE or .DLL file associated with your OWL code module.

continues

Table 6.1. continued

String	*Description*
`GDI file read failure`	OWL allows you to create certain GDI objects, passing to them the name of the file that contains the actual resource. For example, with `TDib` objects, you can specify a .bmp file. If OWL can't locate or read that file (maybe because it doesn't have the right BMP format), it will throw this kind of `TXGdi` exception.
`Invalid DIB handle passed`	OWL GDI objects can sometime share a single Windows resource. For example, `TDib` objects can share the same bitmap. You can share resources by creating GDI objects through handles. OWL checks the handle to verify that it refers to data in the correct format. If you try to create a `TDib` object using an invalid handle (one that doesn't refer to a BITMAPINFO struct), OWL will throw a `TXGdi` exception with the string `Invalid DIB handle passed`.
`GDI failure`	This string is defined but not used.

> **CAUTION**
>
> If a `TXGdi` exception is thrown while constructing an OWL GDI object, you need to delete that object while handling the exception. Failure to do so will guarantee a memory leak.

TXInvalidMainWindow Exceptions

OWL requires every application program to have a main window. This window is usually constructed in the `InitMainWindow` member function of your `TApplication` object, using code like this:

```
void TMyApp::InitMainWindow()
{
  MainWindow = new TMyWindow("Test");

  // setup the window before exiting
  // ...
}
```

OWL later uses the data member MainWindow to create the main window on the screen. If MainWindow is NULL, OWL will throw a TXInvalidMainWindow exception, and abort.

TXInvalidModule Exceptions

OWL creates a TModule object to handle both application programs and DLLs. OWL cannot run if it doesn't have a valid TModule, so it throws an exception if it detects something invalid in its TModule. There are two basic points at which OWL can throw a TXInvalidModule exception:

1. When creating a TModule object
2. When creating a TWindow in a DLL

The former can be thrown both in an application program or a DLL. The latter can occur only in a DLL that was statically linked to OWL. When you create such a DLL, OWL maintains a list of the applications that use the DLL. If the application that calls your DLL to create a new window isn't on the list, OWL throws the TXInvalidModule exception.

TXMenu Exceptions

If you attempt to use a TMenu object, a TXMenu exception will be thrown if TMenu cannot load a menu resource properly. The most common cause of this type of exception is an incorrect resource string or resource ID. For example, if your resource file has the string "MENU_MAIN" and you try to load the menu "MAIN_MENU", OWL will throw a TXMenu exception. TMenu objects are handled internally by class TFrameWindow, to support a menu-merging mechanism that is similar to the one used in OLE 2.0.

TXOutOfMemory Exceptions

This exception is somewhat of an extension to the standard xalloc exception. Whereas xalloc is related to ::operator new, TXOutOfMemory is related to GlobalAlloc(). TXOutOfMemory is thrown by OWL when a GlobalAlloc() request fails, usually in the constructor for an OWL object. OWL uses GlobalAlloc() calls internally to get memory for various kinds of resources, such as DIBs. You might want to catch TXOutOfMemory exceptions in the same place you catch xalloc exceptions.

A TXOutOfMemory exception may be problematic to handle sometimes because the exception can be thrown both during the construction of OWL objects and later. When handling the exception, you don't know if you're dealing with a completely or partially constructed object. The normal way to handle TXOutOfMemory exceptions is to just assume that the OWL object is unusable, and delete it. A TXOutOfMemory exception indicates that an OWL object was at least partially constructed, but that an internal memory pointer or reference could not be initialized due to a `GlobalAlloc()` failure. OWL objects that throw `TXOutOfMemory` exceptions must not be referenced. When catching a `TXOutOfMemory` exception, you need to delete the related OWL object, as shown in Listing 6.14.

Listing 6.14. Handling `TXOutOfMemory` exceptions.

```
#include <owl\applicat.h>
#include <owl\framewin.h>
#include <owl\dc.h>
#include <except.h>

class TMyWindow : public TWindow {

  TDib* MyDib;

public:

  TMyWindow();
  ~TMyWindow() {delete MyDib;}
};

TMyWindow::TMyWindow()
      : TWindow(0, 0, 0), MyDib(0)
{
  try {
    MyDib = new TDib("newton.bmp");
  }
  catch(TXOutOfMemory) {

    // kill the partially constructed Dib
    delete MyDib;

    // and let the standard xalloc handler take over
    throw xalloc("Dib allocation error", -1);
  }
}
```

If there is insufficient memory for a `TDib` object, an `xalloc` exception will be thrown. The code in Listing 6.14 doesn't handle `xalloc` exceptions. If there was enough memory to hold the `TDib` object, but not enough to store the associated bitmap, a `TXOutOfMemory` exception will be thrown. The `TMyWindow` constructor handles this exception by deleting the `TDib` object. You have to delete this object yourself, because the compiler will delete only local objects that were completely constructed. The code in Listing 6.14 handles the `TXOutOfMemory` exception by throwing an `xalloc` exception.

The destructor for `TMyWindow` deletes the `TDib` object. This is necessary and doesn't cause any problems, although it may initially seem like the class deletes `MyDib` twice. In reality, if the constructor handles the `TXOutOfMemory` exception, a new exception is thrown. The constructor for `TMyWindow` hasn't completed execution, so the compiler will never invoke the class's destructor automatically. If the destructor is invoked, it is because `TMyWindow` went out of scope—not because of exceptions.

TXPrinter Exceptions

In order to print, you normally create an object derived from class `TPrintout`. The constructor for this object will instantiate an object of type `TPrinter`, which handles the actual GDI operations required for printer output. The code might look something like this:

```
class TWindowPrintout : public TPrintout {
protected:
    TWindow* Window;
public:
 // ...
 TWindowPrintout(const char* title, TWindow* window)
    : TPrintout(title) {Window = window;}
  void PrintPage(int page, TRect& rect, unsigned flags);
};

class TMyWindow: public TFrameWindow {
  TPrinter* Printer;
public:
  TMyWindow(TWindow* parent, const char* title)
    : TFrameWindow(parent, title),
      TWindow(parent, title)
  { Printer = new TPrinter;
    // ...
  }
// assume the following function has an entry in the
// event response table
void CmFilePrint()
  { TWindowPrintout printout("Printout", this);
    printout.SetBanding(TRUE);
    Printer->Print(this, printout, TRUE);
  }
  // ...
};
```

The printing actually occurs with the statement:

```
Printer->Print(this, printout, TRUE);
```

Inside this function, OWL attempts to get a DC to use with the printer. If a DC can't be obtained, OWL throws the `TXPrinter` exception. If this exception is thrown, there really isn't too much you can do in your application. You might display an error message, indicating that, due to a temporary load, Windows lacks sufficient resources to carry out printing and the user should try again at a later time. Of course, it is also possible that a DC couldn't be obtained because of an ill-behaved application that forgot to release a DC after using it. If that is the case, that application will probably crash the system sooner or later (and probably sooner!).

TXValidator Exceptions

OWL 2.5 allows you to attach validator objects to edit fields, to support data validation. When you attach a picture validator, using a `TPXPictureValidator` object, you must pass the validator a picture string in the constructor call, using code looking something like this:

```
// assume we're in the constructor for a TDialog-derived object

// create an edit control
TEdit* edit = new TEdit(this, 103, 10);
edit->SetValidator(new TPXPictureValidator("###-####");
```

If you pass a picture string that is invalid, OWL will throw a `TXValidator` exception. How can a picture string be invalid? Lots of ways—especially when you use brackets or braces. The following string is an example:

```
"*3{#&"
```

The `*3` characters tell OWL to repeat three times the pattern that follows. The pattern is either a single character or a group of characters enclosed in curly braces (`{}`). In the preceding string, the trailing `}` character is missing.

TXWindow Exceptions

The machinery for error detecting and handling in OWL 1.0 was concentrated in class `TModule`, from which `TApplication` is derived. Calls to `MakeWindow()` and `ValidWindow()` took care of window creation problems, such as using a nonexistent Windows resource name, or running out of memory.

In OWL 2.5, there is no longer a need to call `MakeWindow()` or `ValidWindow()`, because errors are handled by throwing C++ exceptions. After constructing a new `TWindow` object, its `Create()` member function is called to create the window element to be displayed on the screen. Typically, two kinds of exceptions can be thrown when you create a new OWL window: `xalloc` exceptions and `TXWindow` exceptions. The former are thrown when there is not enough memory to create the object; the latter are thrown when OWL runs into some other kind of problem when attempting to create the window element to be displayed on the screen.

The following code fragment shows a typical way of dealing with errors occurring when constructing or creating a window:

```
#include <owl\window.h>

class TMyWindow: public TWindow
{
  void foo();
};

void TMyWindow::foo()
{
  try {
    TWindow* myWindow = new TWindow(this, "Title");
    myWindow->Create();
  }

  catch(xalloc) {
    // no memory for the TWindow
    // ...
  }

  catch(TWindow::TXWindow& e) {
    // memory was allocated to the TWindow,
    // but a subsequent error occurred
    // ...

    // clean up
    delete e.Window;
  }
}
```

If `::operator` **`new`** fails due to insufficient memory, it will throw the standard C++ exception `xalloc`. By default, `xalloc` exceptions will cause your program to terminate. The exception `TXWindow`, declared inside class `TWindow`, carries with it a pointer to the `TWindow` that threw the exception. After a `TXWindow`, it is necessary to delete the failed `TWindow`. A `TXWindow` exception will be thrown if OWL is unsuccessful in registering the window element associated to the OWL window object. The following conditions will cause a `TXWindow` exception to be thrown.

Table 6.2. The conditions that will cause a `TXWindow` exception to be thrown by OWL.

Condition	*Description*
Failure to register window class	A call to the Windows API function `RegisterClass()` failed.
Failure to register child window class	A child window of a window could not be created. This exception can be thrown only if the child window that failed is a user-written class whose `Create()` function failed to properly throw an exception upon creation failure. For OWL windows, if a child window fails to be created, that child window will throw a *Failure to register window class* `TXWindow` exception.
Failure to create a window	This condition will occur if, after attempting to register a window, the window handle (`TWindow::HWindow`) is null. A null window handle can be the result of various errors: an invalid resource name for a dialog box, an invalid resource ID for a child window, an invalid module pointer in the constructor call for `TWindow`, and so on. If you get this error while creating a dialog box, check the resource IDs of its child controls. You probably used an ID that wasn't defined in the .RC or .RES file.
Failure to execute a window	This will occur if you try to run modally a dialog box that wasn't created correctly. A dialog box may fail to be created properly if it has an invalid resource ID, if errors occur while creating its child controls, and so on.

Caveats in Windows Programming

Handling exceptions in a Windows program requires special considerations. Windows is basically a message-driven system, and your application code is generally written to handle calls from Windows, via callback functions. Callback functions represent something of a world in themselves, from the point of view of exception handling. Add the complications of multithreaded and multiprocessing code under Windows NT, and you have a lot to watch out for.

Exception Handling and Callback Functions

Each message handler you write is essentially a callback function and has a life of its own with regards to exception handling. The exception handling built into C++ is stack directed: the runtime exception handling code uses the stack to guide the search for a suitable handler. Each callback function is invoked separately by Windows and receives its stack from Windows. Exceptions thrown in one callback function cannot be handled by other callback functions, because other callbacks are not part of the calling stack at the time of the exceptions.

For example, assume that you have a `Paint()` callback that uses a `TMemoryDC` object. If the `Paint()` function throws exceptions like this:

```
void TMyWindow::Paint(TDC& dc, BOOL, TRect&)
{
  TMemoryDC memDC(dc);
  if (!memDC)
    throw TXGdi(IDS_GDIALLOCFAIL);

  // ...
}
```

then the exception can only be caught by OWL, because no other user functions are on the stack: Windows called OWL, and OWL—after several levels of function calls—called `Paint()`. Setting up an exception handler in a window's constructor or `SetupWindow()` member function will not enable you to catch exceptions thrown in callback functions like `Paint()`.

Exception Handling in Multithreaded Code

With Win32, you can write code that has multiple threads of execution. Exception handling is compatible with multithreaded code, as long as you understand how it works and what to expect. When a thread is executing, it has its own stack. When an exception is thrown, the runtime handling code searches only the functions on the thread's stack for a suitable handler. This means that an exception can be handled only in the same thread that threw it.

An additional problem is how to ensure that an exception thrown in one thread will not leave other related threads in an unstable condition. Consider having two threads in a scientific computation program that evaluates fractional expressions. You might have one thread that evaluates the numerator and one that evaluates the denominator. If the denominator thread detects a null value, it might throw a divide-by-zero exception. Because this exception can be handled only by the denominator thread, you will need to develop a way for the numerator thread and the main application thread to be notified of the problem. C++ has no built-in mechanism for dealing with exceptions in multithreaded applications.

In multiple-threaded code, you must also be extremely careful with the order of construction and destruction of local objects in the various threads. The constructors for these objects will be called based on the order of execution of the threads. The destructors will be called when the objects go out of scope. With exception handling, an object might go out of scope prematurely in one thread. If your threads rely on a given order of destruction for their local objects, the code will RIP. If you add the possibility of multiprocessing, where threads execute in a purely asynchronous manner, you can see how difficult things can get. The solution is to never write code in which threads rely on the order of destruction of local objects shared between them.

Exception Interface Specifications

When you use a class library, you often don't have access to its source code. All you have is the library's interface specification, in the form of one or more header files. Theoretically, by studying the header files, you should be able to use the library without any knowledge of how the library is actually implemented. My personal experience has shown that things aren't really that simple. I have yet to come across a header file or a library user manual that was so well documented that I didn't need access to the source code to answer certain questions. In any event, the idea of a header file telling *everything* about a library is extended to include exception handling.

Users of a function may be interested in knowing whether a function—or any function called directly or indirectly by that function—can throw an exception. A function can indicate this by declaring the exceptions that could be thrown. Assume that you have a function declared like this:

```
void foo(int size);
```

If the function `foo()`—or any function called directly or indirectly by `foo()`—can throw a `Problem` exception or any exception derived from `Problem`, then you could place this information in the function declaration like this:

```
void foo(int size)   throw(Problem);
```

In the definition of a function, the `throw` specification must appear after the function's parameter list and before the function body. I prefer to place the throw portion on a separate line, like this:

```
void foo(int size)
     throw(Problem)
{
  // ...
}
```

The declaration and definition for a function must match, in terms of exception specifiers. If a function can throw more than one exception, you must declare all the exceptions in the same `throw` specification. For example:

```
class P1 {};
class P2 {};
class P3 {};

void foo(int size) throw(P1, P2, P3);

void foo(int)
     throw(P1, P2, P3)
{
  // ...
}
```

You can also declare exceptions declared inside other classes, as long as they are declared publicly. Consider the exception `B` declared inside class `A`, like this:

```
class A {

public:

  class B {};
};
```

A function that throws exceptions of class `A::B` would be declared and defined like this:

```
void foo(int size) throw(A::B);

void foo(int)
     throw(A::B)
{
  // ...
}
```

The use of nested exception classes can be seen in the standard C++ `string` class, declared like this:

```
class string {

public:

  class outofrange : public xmsg {

  public:

    outofrange();
  };

  // ... other exception classes

  // ... remainder of declaration of string
};
```

A function wishing to throw `string::outofrange` exceptions would be declared and defined like this:

```
#include <cstring.h>

void foo(int size) throw(string::outofrange);

void foo(int)
     throw(string::outofrange)
{
  // ...
}
```

If a function declares an exception, the function isn't required to actually throw that exception. The compiler makes no check to ensure that a function does what it declares it will do. Because a declaration may not necessarily be truthful, exception declarations in real-life projects—where code changes constantly during the evolution of a project—may not always be reliable. I treat exception specifications in programs like comments: they are handy and usually helpful, but only the code tells it the way it is. On the contrary, where exception specifications are important and credible is in standard classes and libraries. You should expect such specifications to be correct, although there are no guarantees.

Exception specifications are designed to be backward compatible. If a function does not have an exception specification, then it is assumed that it can throw any exception. The function

```
void foo(int);   // this function can throw anything
```

can throw any exception. Conversely, you can declare a function that throws no exceptions by using the notation

```
void foo() throw();   // this function can't throw anything

void foo()
     throw()
{
  // ...
}
```

What a function declares and what it actually does may be two different things, and that's where the `unexpected()` function comes into play.

The *unexpected()* Function

When you make an exception specification, you are essentially telling the compiler and the world which exceptions to expect. If you then throw an exception that isn't in the exception specification, you are violating a statement you made, and the compiler will

automatically make a call to the standard C++ function `unexpected()`. By default, `unexpected()` calls `terminate()`, which calls `abort()`.

The function `unexpected()` will be called only from a function that has an exception specifier. Adding an exception specification implicitly adds a `try` block to a function. The function

```
void foo()
     throw(Problem)
{
// ...
}
```

actually generates code that behaves like this:

```
void foo()
     throw(Problem)
{
  try {
    // ... whatever
  }
  catch(Problem) {
    throw;  // let the caller handle the exception
  }
  catch(...) {
    unexpected();  // this shouldn't have happened!
  }
}
```

You can change what `unexpected()` does. By default it calls `terminate()`, but using the function `set_unexpected()`, you can install your own handler.

`set_unexpected()` is declared basically like this:

```
typedef void (*unexpected_function)();
unexpected_function set_unexpected(unexpected_function);
```

It is a function taking and returning a pointer to a function. Calling `set_unexpected()` installs a new handler and returns a pointer to the previously installed handler, allowing you to set up a chain of handlers. The following example shows how to install a new handler:

```
#include <except.h>
#include <windows.h>

void DisplayError()
{
  MessageBox(NULL, "Unexpected exception",
                   "Error", MB_OK);
}
```

```
void foo()
{
  // install a new hander for unexpected exceptions
  unexpected_function old_handler;
  old_handler = set_unexpected(DisplayError);

  // ... do something that might cause an
  // unexpected exception ...

  // reinstall the old handler
  set_unexpected(old_handler);
}
```

Calls to `unexpected()` generally occur during development of a project, while exceptions are frequent and not yet well defined. A call to `unexpected()` in a released program is to be considered a sign of incomplete development or testing of your code. The easy way out—which undoubtedly will be a temptation in rushed projects—is to simply eliminate the exception specifications from problematic areas of code. This will eliminate calls to `unexpected()`, but may result in calls to `terminate()` due to uncaught exceptions.

The best way out is to determine what exception was thrown and fix the problem at the source. Finding out the type of exception is not easy, because by the time `unexpected()` is called, there is no information left regarding the exception.

The *terminate()* Function

When a function throws an exception, it doesn't necessarily know whether or where the exception will be handled. Consider the standard class string. If you attempt to reference a string element that is beyond the end of the string, a `string::outofrange` exception will be thrown. Class string has no idea regarding the code that invoked it, or whether there is a handler for the exceptions it throws.

Because the process of throwing an exception is entirely separate from that of handling the exception, there is always the possibility that an exception has no handler for it. In such cases, the compiler generates code to invoke a default handler. This handler is a function called `terminate()`.

By default, `terminate()` kills your program by calling `abort()`. With Windows, `abort()` displays an error message with the caption `Program aborted`, and exits with the error value 3.

You can change what `terminate()` does by using the function `set_terminate()`.

`set_terminate()` is declared basically like this:

```
typedef void (*terminate_function)();
terminate_function set_terminate(terminate_function);
```

 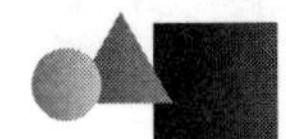

It is a function taking and returning a pointer to a function. Calling `set_terminate()` installs a new handler and returns a pointer to the previously installed handler, allowing you to set up a chain of handlers. The following example shows how to install a new handler:

```
#include <except.h>
#include <windows.h>

void DisplayError()
{
  MessageBox(NULL, "Uncaught exception",
                   "Error", MB_OK);
}

void foo()
{
  // install a new hander for uncaught exceptions
  terminate_function old_handler;
  old_handler = set_terminate(DisplayError);

  // ... do something that might cause an
  // uncaught exception ...

  // reinstall the old handler
  set_terminate(old_handler);
}
```

Debugging Calls to *terminate()*

If you have a program that aborts unexpectedly, it may be due to uncaught exceptions. It isn't too difficult to determine which exception is not being caught. Assume that you have a function `f()` that calls code in which an uncaught exception is thrown. If your code uses exceptions that are all derived from the common base class `xmsg` (and it should!), then you could catch a typed exception like this:

```
void f()
{
  try {
    // execute the code the causes the
    // uncaught exception
  }
  catch(xmsg& error) {
    MessageBox(NULL,
              error.why().c_str(),
              "Uncaught Exception caught in f()",
              MB_OK);
  }
}
```

In an OWL program, you don't have to add any special code of your own, because the implicit `WinMain()` function handles `xmsg` exceptions for you, using code that looks like this:

```
int PASCAL WinMain(/* ... */)
{
  try {
    // try to create and run the application
  }
  catch (xmsg& e) {
    HandleGlobalException(e);
  }
  return 0;
}
```

In OWL, as long as all your exceptions are derived from `xmsg`, you will never get a call to `terminate()`, because the `xmsg` handler in `WinMain` will take over. This handler calls `HandleGlobalException()`, which will display an error message like this:

```
void HandleGlobalException(xmsg& e)
{
  ::MessageBox(0, e.why().c_str(),
               "ObjectWindows Exception", MB_OK);
}
```

which would look something like Figure 6.5.

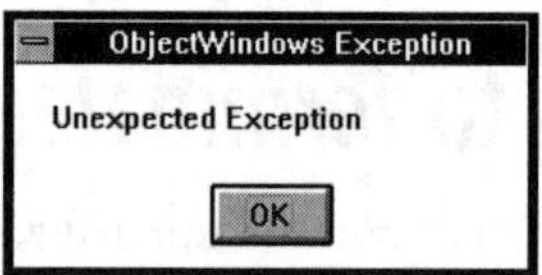

Figure 6.5. How OWL displays unexpected or uncaught exceptions.

The message displayed in the message box comes from the `string` parameter passed in the `xmsg` exception.

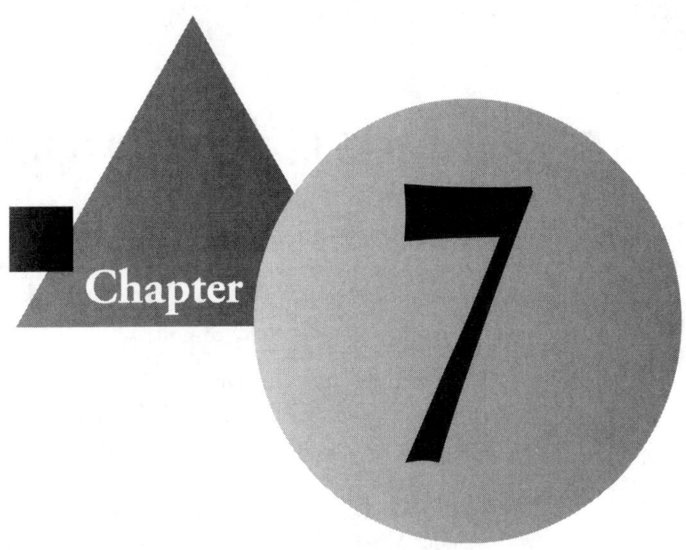

Streams

The topic of streams is one of the least understood in C++, mainly because the technical literature lacks good descriptions of streams. Streams are a new C++ technique for handling I/O. In most cases, the stream technique is quite a bit different from (and better than) ANSI C functions. Old ANSI C used a method based on files, file pointers, and file handles. Why did the language implementors change the I/O part of C++? The main reason was to give input and output operations a more object-oriented flavor by merging them into the rest of the language. Now I/O is done largely through the use of overloaded operators, rather than through functions.

NOTE

If you're new to C++, you can set aside this chapter's "Advanced Section" for now. There are a lot of new concepts for you to digest in the first part of this chapter.

The Drawbacks of the *stdio* Approach

The original C language was somewhat peculiar for its time. It had no built-in keywords for many of the operations that are common in most programs, such as I/O, string handling, and so on. The language implementors at AT&T decided to relegate these operations to a runtime library. The resulting compiler was both smaller and more portable than most other contemporary compilers.

I/O is a particularly sticky area in any language, because it is closely connected to both the operating systems and hardware. ANSI C solved many of the problems of I/O portability by implementing a particular runtime library, which allows a C program to use any I/O device uniformly—be it a disk, a tape, a terminal, or a printer—as if it were a file. You have to provide the compiler with a name that tells what kind of device you wish to deal with. Under MS-DOS, devices use the reserved names in Table 7.1.

Table 7.1. The device names used with Borland C under MS-DOS.

Device Name	*Device Type*
`COMx`	Serial port
`LPTx`	Printer port
`PRN`	Printer port
`AUX`	Auxiliary port
`CON`	Console device

The ANSI C I/O system is good, but it's not perfect. The use of "standard" I/O files for input, output, and errors makes possible some valuable features, such as I/O redirection and pipes. The problem is that although the method is elegant, it fails to take into account the sometimes vast differences in device handling from the programmer's perspective. For one thing, devices can be divided into two categories: block devices and character devices. For example, disks and tapes are block devices, whereas terminals are character devices. Block devices require buffering to be read and written efficiently, whereas character devices don't.

Hardware I/O devices obviously have many more differences than that. Several exceptions were introduced into the library to handle special devices. Treating hardware devices like files was innovative in the late sixties, but it has a lot of drawbacks. It's nice to have uniformity in function calls for I/O; however, most of the time you don't handle hardware devices the way you would handle a file.

This problem led to the addition of new functions in C, because programmers sometimes had to know whether they were dealing with a disk file or a hardware device. For example, in Borland C++ the ANSI compatible function `isatty()` tells whether a file pointer references a real file or a hardware device. The function `ioctl()` gives the programmer control over various aspects of device I/O. The problem is that it requires you to know the device that is being handled in order to get correct results. Many other examples of I/O functions behave differently (sometimes incorrectly) if used with hardware devices rather than regular files. The following six functions may not work correctly if they are applied to hardware devices:

The functions

```
ftell(...), fseek(...), fsetpos(...), fgetpos(...)
```

deal with the file pointer for a file. It makes no sense to request the file pointer for many I/O devices, such as a printer, a terminal, or a serial port.

The functions

```
gftime(...), setftime(...)
```

deal with a file's time stamp. I/O ports and hardware devices obviously don't have time stamps.

The C++ Stream

The concept of a stream is not new to C++. In fact, ANSI C utilizes so-called *streams* to indicate a kind of abstract port through which unstructured raw data can flow uni- or bidirectionally. An ANSI C stream is considered a low-level I/O construct, on top of which the more structured file system is overlaid. C++ was developed for classes, but the language itself uses classes rarely, and even then through libraries. Using classes through libraries keeps the compiler smaller and more portable. C++ streams are different from most other parts of the language, because they are implemented exclusively through classes. In fact, streams are implemented through an entire class hierarchy, which is the only major hierarchy delivered with the AT&T release 3.0. Versions of AT&T C++ up through release 1.2 came with something called the *stream class library*, now considered obsolete. Borland C++ will no longer support these anachronistic streams in future releases. Instead, it will use the newer *iostream class library*, which was introduced with AT&T C++ release 2.0. Because the old streams are being phased out, I concentrate on describing the newer ones. Unless otherwise specified, all descriptions apply to the new iostreams. In the rest of the book, I will use the terms *stream* and *iostream* interchangeably to indicate the iostream class library.

Streams are implemented separately from the `stdio` functions. Because of this, using both streams and `stdio` in a program may lead to problems. If you output a character with a stream operation and then output a character with `stdio` function `putc(...)`, the characters may not be issued in the correct order, depending on the internal buffering and automatic buffer flushing.

Streams as Generalized Filters

Streams constitute a protective shell that endows I/O operations with polymorphism and other object-oriented features. Although streams are often associated with I/O, they are really an abstraction for the generic transfer of data from one object to another, generally using a buffering mechanism. This means that any function used to move data from one memory location to another, with or without changing the data, can be considered a stream operation. For example, the old ANSI C functions

```
memmove(...), sprintf(...), strcpy(...)
```

can be implemented as stream operations, because they involve memory-to-memory data transfers: data flows as if it is in a stream. A well-structured OOP design "prefers" to adopt the stream notation over these older functions.

The stream library has many classes, but all of them fit into one of three categories. Table 7.2 shows the new stream categories, with a list of some of the old ANSI functions that they replace.

Table 7.2. New stream categories and examples of the ANSI functions they replace.

Stream Category	*Examples of ANSI Functions Replaced*
Standard I/O	`scanf(...), printf(...)`
File I/O	`fopen(...), fread(...), fclose(...)`
In-memory formatting	`sscanf(...), sprintf(...)`

Each of these categories is discussed separately and in detail. Although it is possible to use both stream I/O and ANSI I/O functions together in a program, it is not recommended because of problems of synchronization with buffer flushing between the two. For example,

```
#include <iostream.h>
#include <stdio.h>

void main()
{
     int value = 3.0;
     cout << "\nThere";
     printf(" are %d ", value);
```

```
     cout << "bicycles left";
}
```

might be intended to produce the output

```
There are 3 bicycles left
```

On my system with Borland C++, this is indeed the case. But the order in which the `printf(...)` output occurs is not guaranteed with respect to stream output, based on buffering requirements that may differ from compiler to compiler. It is possible to force synchronization between stream and ANSI I/O, but at a substantial runtime penalty. There really is no need to use the old ANSI functions with C++ programs unless you have older C programs that were partially upgraded to C++.

Standard Stream I/O with Built-In Data Types

Streams bring many of the elegant features of operator overloading and object orientation to I/O. The goal of streams is to allow uniform notation across disparate types for input/output, with the compiler figuring out the details. A stream statement uses the following notation:

```
input_stream >> typed_variable;
output_stream << typed_variable;
```

The stream object is always placed on the left side of the expression. The >> and << operators are used to indicate the flow of data from one object to the other. Any built-in C++ type can be used with stream I/O. User classes can also use stream I/O if the classes were implemented to support such I/O, as shown later in this chapter. The examples in Listing 7.1 are all valid in C++.

Listing 7.1. A simple stream I/O example.

```
#include <iostream.h>

void main()
{
     int a;
     char c;
     float f;
     double d;

     cin >> a;
     cin >> c;
     cin >> f;
     cin >> d;
```

continues

Listing 7.1. continued

```
        cout << a;
        cout << c;
        cout << f;
        cout << d;
        cout << "\nThis is a short string";

        cout << "\nAnd this is a three"
             << "\nline message that"
             << "\nis a little longer";
}
```

C++ maintains the definition of standard data paths for input and output, but uses streams rather than files. The stream `cin` is the standard input stream. `cin` is a character input stream that usually is connected to the operator keyboard. It replaces `stdin`, which is used for the same purpose in ANSI C. The stream `cout` is the counterpart of `stdout`, and is normally connected to a character output device, such as the PC display. Two other standard streams are defined in Borland C++: `cerr` (which replaces `stderr` as the standard output path), and `clog` (which has no counterpart in ANSI C). `clog` is similar to `cerr`. `clog` provides buffering, however, whereas `cin`, `cout`, and `cerr` do not. Each of these four streams is discussed separately.

The four standard streams `cin`, `cout`, `cerr`, and `clog` are automatically opened *before* function `main()` is executed; they are closed *after* `main()` has completed. Therefore, you don't have to worry about declaring, opening, and closing the streams. Stream flushing may be necessary sometimes, based on your program requirements.

To use any of these streams, you need to `#include` the standard header file *iostream.h* in your file. A stream object must appear on the left side of the >> or << operators; however, multiple stream operations can be concatenated on a single line, even when they refer to objects of different types. The >> sequence is called the *extraction operator* because it is used to get characters from a stream. The << sequence is called the *insertion operator* because it is used to put characters into a stream. Listing 7.1 can be rewritten more concisely like this:

```
void main()
{
        int a;
        char c;
        float f;
        double d;

        cin  >> a >> c >> f >> d;      // input all data
        cout << a << c << f << d;      // output all data
}
```

The compiler keeps track of type conversions and formats for you automatically. In the first statement, the compiler generates four separate input operations, one for each variable. The >> operator is associative from left to right, so variable a is read before variable c. In the second statement, four output operations are performed. The << operator is also associative from left to right, so a is output before c. All I/O formatting is provided automatically by the streams themselves, which reduces the level of detail to a minimum. Formatting can be controlled in various ways, using special stream manipulator functions, as shown later in this chapter.

On the contrary, ANSI C input functions require the programmer to provide several arguments, a requirement that increases the chance of errors. A common pitfall for C programmers using the old `scanf(...)` and `printf(...)` functions is to do something like this:

```
int i;
float f;
scanf("%d", i);    /* oops: passed parameter by value! */
printf("%d", f)    /* wrong formatting character! */
```

instead of the correct notation:

```
int i;
float f;
scanf("%d", &i);   /* this is correct */
printf("%f", f);   /* and so is this */
```

All kinds of other errors can be introduced if you're not careful, however, such as not matching the number of parameters with the number expected in the formatting string. The stream notation is so simple that bugs are much less likely to creep in, with respect to old ANSI C. The burden of checking for the proper type matching and argument number is shifted from the programmer to the compiler.

I/O with *char* and *char** Types

Character operations on streams are extremely simple because no formatting is involved. When you are reading in characters from a stream, keep in mind that everything qualifies as a valid character, including the so-called *white space characters.* A white space character is a space, a tab, a line feed, or a similar character that is normally used to separate data items. If the characters you want to read in are separated from each other by white space characters, you need to skip over the space yourself, or use a manipulator to explicitly tell the system to do so. Listing 7.2 is a short example that extracts characters from a stream.

Listing 7.2. A short program to extract characters from a stream.

```
#include <iostream.h>

void main()
{
        char c;
        cout << "\nHit a key ";

        cin >> c;
        cout << "\nThe key typed was: " << c;
}
```

The program displays a message on the screen, and then waits for the user to hit a key followed by a carriage return. The `cin` stream is then read with a character extractor and the value is used in an output statement. To enter data into the program, the user must end with a carriage return or a line feed. Reading input characters before a carriage return is typed can be accomplished by resorting to a nonstream function that supports raw input, such as `getch()` or `getche()`, like this:

```
char c = getch();
```

If your application requires this kind of modification to the `cin` stream, you should consider deriving a new class from it and giving it the necessary behavior. For example, you may need to turn off echoing when characters are typed, or restrict typed keys to certain values, and so on. A derived class is perfect for this kind of specialization.

When sending characters to `cout`, escape sequences are recognized, as in the `stdio` library. The allowed sequences are in Table 7.3.

Table 7.3. Escape sequences for `stdio` and `iostream` classes.

Sequence	*Meaning*
`\a`	Make a beep
`\b`	Backspace
`\f`	Form feed
`\n`	New-line character
`\r`	Carriage return
`\t`	Horizontal tab
`\v`	Vertical tab
`\\`	Backslash character

Sequence	*Meaning*
`\'`	Single quotation mark
`\"`	Double quotation mark
`\O`	Octal base
`\x`	Hexadecimal base
`\X`	Hexadecimal base
`\0`	Null terminator

I/O with *int* and *long* Types

Reading and writing integers or `long`s is simple because the built-in stream insertors and extractors do all the work. When extracting `int`s and `long`s, the system automatically skips over white space characters. The following code is an example:

```
#include <iostream.h>

void main()
{
      cout << "\nType a number ";
      int i;
      cin >> i;

      cout << "\nType another number ";
      long l;
      cin >> l;

      cout << "\nThe two numbers were "
           << i << " and " << l;
}
```

You can control how numbers are read and written by changing the following attributes:

Number base (decimal, octal, hex)

Field width

Field alignment

Field padding

The presence of the + sign

The use of uppercase (for hexadecimal numbers)

Changing the attributes is accomplished with special stream manipulators, which are described later. During output, the default is to print only the digits in a number, with no padding. During input, anytime a character is encountered that is not a digit, a plus sign, or a minus sign, the extraction operation terminates and the value returned is the number of characters read up to that point. For example, typing

```
12b 333
```

with the preceding program results in the assignment of the values 12 and 0 to the variables `i` and `l`, respectively. This occurs because the `b` character is invalid, so the first extraction terminates without taking it. The second extraction terminates immediately due to the `b`, and gives a value of 0. In this regard, `cin` behaves like `scanf(...)`, which often is unacceptable for real programs. Again, the best solution is to derive a custom I/O class from `cin` to deal with special requirements.

I/O with *float* and *double* Types

`floats` and `doubles` are just as easy to read and write as integers and `longs`. When extracting numbers, white space characters are skipped first, and the extraction stops at the first character that is incompatible with floating-point numbers. The built-in stream insertors and extractors provide default behaviors that can be used directly. Consider the following program:

```
#include <iostream.h>

void main()
{
      cout << "\nType a number ";
      float f;
      cin >> f;

      cout << "\nType another number ";
      double d;
      cin >> d;

      cout << "\nThe two numbers were "
           << f << " and " << d;
}
```

Typing the numbers 1.234 and 5.67890 results in the output

```
The two numbers were 1.234 and 5.6789
```

The format used to display `floats` and `doubles` (and `long doubles`) can be changed using stream manipulators. In particular, you can control the following attributes:

Number of decimals

Use of scientific notation

Printing of the + sign

Padding

Field width

Field alignment

The reading of `floats`, `doubles`, and `long doubles` stops anytime an invalid character is encountered. This invalid character is not removed from the stream.

I/O with User Classes

You can use the elegance of streams not only with the built-in C++ data types, but also with your own classes. All you need to do is overload the stream insertion and extraction operators. Listing 7.3 is an example with a class called `Point`.

Listing 7.3. Stream I/O with a user class.

```
#include <iostream.h>

class Point {

      float x, y, z;

public:

      Point(float i, float j, float k) {
        x = i; y = j; z = k;
      }

      friend ostream& operator<< (ostream& os, Point& p);
      friend istream& operator>> (istream& os, Point& p);
};

ostream& operator<< (ostream& os, Point& p)
{
      return os << '('
              << p.x << " "
              << p.y << " "
              << p.z << ")";
}

istream& operator>> (istream& is, Point& p)
{
      return is >> p.x >> p.y >> p.z;
}
```

continues

Listing 7.3. continued

```
void main()
{
      Point p(2, 3, 5);
      cout << "\n\nCoordinates of p are " << p;

      // get new coordinates
      cout << "\nNew coordinates ? ";
      cin >> p;

      // display the new coordinates
      cout << "\nCoordinates of p are " << p;
}
```

Putting the knowledge of how to perform I/O inside a class gives a great deal of consistency to C++ programs. In ANSI C, programmers seldom used the `scanf(...)` function because it didn't handle any special cases. What if your class needs to read only certain characters in the input stream and ignore others? Listing 7.4 shows a variation of the last example that skips over characters which aren't digits. This variation lets the user input data in a more flexible format. For example, all the formats shown in the following code are acceptable as input for class `Point`.

```
10 20 30

(10, 20, 30)

(10
 20
 30)
```

Listing 7.4 shows the changes that support this.

Listing 7.4. A user class that skips nondigits when extracting characters from a stream.

```
#include <ctype.h>
#include <iostream.h>

class Point {

      float x, y, z;

public:

      Point(float i, float j, float k) {
        x = i; y = j; z = k;
      }
```

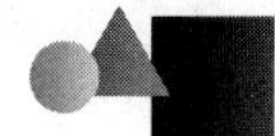

```
        friend ostream& operator<< (ostream& os, Point& p);
        friend istream& operator>> (istream& os, Point& p);
};

ostream& operator<< (ostream& os, Point& p)
{
        return os << '('
             << p.x << " "
             << p.y << " "
             << p.z << ")";
}

void SkipNonDigits(istream& is)
{
        char c;
        while (1) {
       is >> c;
       if (isdigit(c) ) {
         is.putback(c);
         return;
       }
        }
}

istream& operator>> (istream& is, Point& p)
{
        SkipNonDigits(is);
        is >> p.x;
        SkipNonDigits(is);
        is >> p.y;
        SkipNonDigits(is);
        is >> p.z;
        return is;
}
```

Manipulators

With the ANSI I/O library comes a considerable flexibility in the way data can be formatted. Both file and in-memory formatting are possible via the functions `printf(...)` and `sprintf(...)`. Conversely, formatted data can be read into variables with `scanf(...)` and `sscanf(...)`. In C++ the ANSI I/O library is meant to be avoided by using streams. It follows that there must be an equivalent method of formatting that works with streams. Actually, this was not true in early releases of AT&T C++, a fact that forced programmers to revert to the ANSI library at the drop of a hat. This in turn caused problems of synchronization between the streams and the standard I/O functions, because the act of interleaving streams and ANSI I/O function calls would sometimes produce unexpected results.

The solution to the problem came in the form of *manipulators,* which are special functions that are specifically designed to modify how a stream works. The `iostream` library comes with a number of built-in manipulators, but new ones can be added easily. Most of the time, manipulators are used to indicate formatting, such as the width of a field, the precision to use in floating points, and so on. But manipulators are not restricted to formatting alone; you can design a manipulator to do all kinds of things. Peculiarly, manipulators are used in the middle of a stream insertion or extraction sequence. Most manipulators take no arguments and are designed to make formatting as simple as possible.

Because the iostream library supports formatted I/O through class `ios`, the built-in manipulators can be used only on classes that are derived from class `ios`. This is not as limiting as it might sound, because all three categories of streams are supported: standard I/O, file I/O, and in-memory formatting.

The best way to describe manipulators is through an example. Consider the built-in `hex` manipulator, used in the following code to print a value in hex format on the screen:

```
#include <iostream.h>
#include <iomanip.h>

void main()
{
     cout << hex << 20;
}
```

The resulting value printed is 14 because that is the value of 20 expressed in base 16. To use one of the built-in manipulators, you must include the standard header file *iomanip.h.* The action of most manipulators is permanent on a stream, meaning that any changes in stream formatting remain in effect until they are changed. Here is a list of the built-in manipulators:

`dec`	Sets the conversion base to decimal. Integers and `longs` will be affected. Streams use base 10 by default.
`hex`	Sets the conversion base to 16.
`oct`	Sets the conversion base to 8.
`ws`	Extracts whitespace characters from an input stream. The stream will be read until a non-whitespace character is found or a stream error occurs.
`endl`	Inserts a new-line character into an output stream and then flushes the stream.
`ends`	Inserts a `'\0'` into an output stream.

`flush`	Flushes output streams.
`setbase(int)`	Sets the conversion base to any of the following four values: `0`: Default base. Decimal is used for output. During input, numbers beginning with the digit `'0'` are considered octal, and numbers beginning with `'0x'` are considered hexadecimal. Otherwise, decimal is assumed to be the base. `8`: Use octal for I/O. `10`: Use decimal for I/O. `16`: Use hexadecimal for I/O. All other values are ignored. The `iostream` library doesn't support arbitrary bases like 3, 12, and so on. If you need to represent values in bases other than 8, 10, or 16, you must perform the conversions explicitly.
`resetiosflags(long)`	Clears one or more of the formatting flags in `ios::x_flags`.
`setiosflags(long)`	Sets one or more of the formatting flags in `ios::x_flags`.
`setfill(int)`	Sets the fill character. The fill character is used to pad fields when the width of a variable is less than the width specified by the user. Padding will not occur unless the user specifies a minimum field width using the `setw(int)` manipulator or the function `ios::width(int)`. The default fill character is the space character. Padding will occur on the left, right, or other, based on the value of the `ios::adjustfield` bits set by a call to `ios::setf(long)`.
`setprecision(int)`	Establishes the number of digits used on the right side of the decimal point with floating-point numbers. This manipulator affects only output streams.
`setw(int width)`	Sets the width of the next variable that is inserted into an output stream to a particular number. If the value of the next variable requires fewer than `width` characters to be expressed, padding will occur automatically with the character specified by the `setfill(int)` manipulator.

> **NOTE**
>
> The width is automatically reset back to 0 after each stream insertion.

Using Number-Base Manipulators

Lists of names and descriptions are useful as a reference, but you can learn more easily from examples. I show a number of short examples for each category of manipulators. Let's play with the conversion base first, starting with the default case (see Listing 7.5).

Listing 7.5. Stream operations with the default number base.

```
#include <iostream.h>
#include <strstrea.h>
#include <iomanip.h>

void main()
{
      // create a string
      char numbers [] = "\n  10 010 0x10";

      // associate the string with a string stream
      istrstream is(numbers, sizeof(numbers) );

      // extract from stream using different bases
      int v1, v2, v3;
      is >> v1 >> v2 >> v3;

      // display the results
      cout << "\n" << v1 << " " << v2 << " " << v3;
}
```

First, an input string stream is created and initialized to contain three numbers in decimal, octal, and hex formats. Then the stream is read into three variables and the variables are displayed. The screen output is

```
10 8 16
```

because the library correctly recognized the base of each number in the input stream. Changing the base to decimal during the stream extraction, like this:

```
is >> dec >> v1 >> v2 >> v3;
```

results in the output

```
10 10 0
```

The last value is 0 because the extraction stopped when the `x` character was encountered, because it isn't a decimal digit. Changing the conversion base to hex, like this:

```
is >> hex >> v1 >> v2 >> v3;
```

produces the (perhaps surprising) output

```
16 16 0
```

The reason for this output is that when you specify an explicit base, only characters valid for that base are recognized. The `x` character is not in the set of valid hex characters. Hex characters are those in the set {0..9, A..F, a..f}. The program in Listing 7.6 shows the base manipulators used during output.

Listing 7.6. Using different number bases with streams.

```
#include <strstrea.h>
#include <iomanip.h>

void main()
{
      const int v = 100;

      // display the results in different bases
      cout << "\n" << v << " "
           << oct << v << " "
           << hex << v << endl;
}
```

The output on the screen is

```
100 144 64
```

Setting and Clearing the Formatting Flags

The built-in formatting flags available for streams are implemented in class `ios`, which is a base class for the iostream library. Each of these flags can be set or reset using a built-in manipulator. The manipulators `setiosflags(long)` and `resetioflags(long)` let you set or reset one or more formatting flags. For example, in Listing 7.6 you can force the compiler to indicate the base that is used with each number by turning on the `ios::showbase` flag. Changing the code to

```
// display the results in different bases
cout << setiosflags(ios::showbase)
     << "\n" << v << " "
     << oct << v << " "
     << hex << v << endl;
```

results in the output

```
100 0144 0x64
```

Changing Field Widths and Padding

Most programs need to format output data in various ways. A common requirement is to reserve an area of a printed page for a field, without knowing exactly how many characters the data of that field will occupy. To keep the data neatly lined up, the field must be aligned to the left or right of the field, and padded with some character. Consider printing checks for a payroll. Assume that you have the following three money values: $1300.23, $320.99, and $54,430.00. The program in Listing 7.7 handles the formatting correctly.

Listing 7.7. Using formatting commands to format money values.

```
#include <iostream.h>
#include <iomanip.h>

void main()
{
      float v1 = 1300.23;
      float v2 = 320.99;
      float v3 = 54430.00;

      cout << setiosflags(ios::showpoint | ios::fixed)
           << setprecision(2)
           << setfill('*')
           << setiosflags(ios::right);
      cout << "\nCheck Value: $" << setw(10) << v1;
      cout << "\nCheck Value: $" << setw(10) << v2;
      cout << "\nCheck Value: $" << setw(10) << v3;
}
```

The following output is produced:

```
Check Value: $***1300.23
Check Value: $****320.99
Check Value: $**54430.00
```

The flag `ios::showpoint` forces the stream to print a decimal point even if there are 0 cents. The flag `ios::fixed` selects fixed-decimal format rather than scientific notation.

The call `setprecision(2)` tells the output stream to print only two digits after the decimal, and `setfill('*')` makes the stream use the `'*'` character for padding. The `ios::right` flag tells the stream to align data on the right side of a field. The width of the money fields has to be set just before inserting the check value, because the width is set back to 0 after each insertion.

Using the Formatting Manipulators

The manipulator `setiosflags(long)` allows you to set any formatting flag in the `ios` you're using. To turn off the `showbase` option, you can use the manipulator `resetiosflags(ios::showbase)`. The following is a list of the parameters than can be supplied to `setiosflags(long)` and `resetiosflags(long)`:

```
skipws
left
right
internal
dec
oct
hex
showbase
showpoint
uppercase
showpos
scientific
fixed
unitbuf
stdio
```

Each flag is fully described in the `ios` class. The flags `skipws`, `dec`, `oct`, and `hex` also can be set and cleared using the direct manipulators `ws`, `dec`, `oct`, and `hex`. The program in Listing 7.8 shows several manipulators in action.

Listing 7.8. Using the manipulator `setiosflags` with more than one formatting flag.

```
#include <iostream.h>
#include <iomanip.h>

void main()
{
      const float f = 3.14159;

      // display float using lots of manipulators
      cout << setiosflags(ios::showpos ¦ ios::scientific)
           << "\nThe value of PI is "
```

continues

Listing 7.8. continued

```
            << setprecision(3)
            << setw(15) << setfill('_')
            << setiosflags(ios::right)
            << f;
}
```

The output of the program is

```
The value of PI is _____+3.142e+00
```

The preceding listing shows the use of the manipulator `iossetflags(long)` with the two flags `ios::showpos` and `is::scientific`. All flags must be bitwise-`OR`ed together before being passed to `setiosflags(long)`. The manipulators don't have to be in any special order, as long as they appear somewhere *before* the variable they are meant to affect.

There is nothing magic about the standard streams `cin` and `cout`, in terms of manipulators. You can use the built-in manipulators with string streams for in-memory formatting, with file streams, or even with user streams that are derived from the `iostream` classes. Listing 7.9 shows a trivial Windows program that uses in-memory formatting to display a message using the function `MessageBox()`.

Listing 7.9. Using manipulators for in-memory formatting.

```
#include <windows.h>
#include <strstrea.h>
#include <iomanip.h>

int PASCAL WinMain(HINSTANCE, HINSTANCE, LPSTR, int)
{
  const float f = 3.14159;
  char message [100];
  ostrstream buffer(message, sizeof message);

  // do in-memory formatting with manipulators
  buffer << setiosflags(ios::showpos | ios::scientific)
      << "\nThe value of PI is "
      << setprecision(3)
      << setw(15) << setfill('_')
      << setiosflags(ios::right)
      << f << ends;

  MessageBox(NULL, message, "In memory formatting", MB_OK);
}
```

The program's output is shown in Figure 7.1.

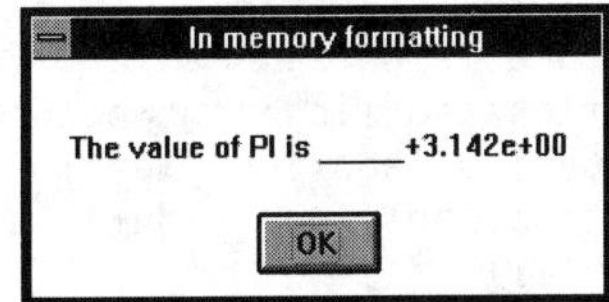

Figure 7.1. Formatting a string using in-memory streams.

The array `message` is managed by an `ostrstream` object. I used the same formatting commands as in Listing 7.8, except for the `ends` manipulator that puts a null terminator in the stream. Unless you specifically insert a null terminator yourself, the buffer managed by `ostrstream` objects will not be terminated and will not be usable as a regular string.

User-Defined Manipulators

An important feature of C++ streams is that they can work as well with built-in manipulators as they can with the ones you write. User manipulators can be written to work with any kind of stream, including user-derived streams. In this section, I show two examples of user manipulators. The first acts on a built-in stream, whereas the second acts on a user-defined stream.

Why would you want to define a manipulator for a built-in stream? All the formatting flags are essentially already supported one way or another, so it may not be obvious why a new manipulator could be needed. Consider a situation in which you need to specify the same formatting commands repeatedly. A user manipulator provides a simple shorthand notation, somewhat like a macro. Consider the program in Listing 7.10.

Listing 7.10. A program that uses the same formatting instructions repeatedly.

```
#include <iostream.h>
#include <iomanip.h>


void main()
{
      float deductible, already_paid;
      int dependents;

      deductible = 100;
      already_paid = 13.75;
      dependents = 3;
```

continues

Listing 7.10. continued

```
        cout << "\nTotal Deductible      = "
             << setprecision(2)
             << setiosflags(ios::showpoint)
             << resetiosflags(ios::left)
             << setiosflags(ios::right)
             << setfill('*')
             << setw(10)
             << deductible;

        cout << "\nNumber of dependents = "
             << setfill(' ')
             << setiosflags(ios::left)
             << setw(1)
             << dependents;

        cout << "\nDeductible paid      = "
             << setprecision(2)
             << setiosflags(ios::showpoint)
             << resetiosflags(ios::left)
             << setiosflags(ios::right)
             << setfill('*')
             << setw(10)
             << already_paid;
}
```

The program produces the output

```
Total Deductible     = ***1.0e+02
Number of dependents = 3
Deductible paid      = *******14
```

Two kinds of formatting are used—one for integers and one for money values. Because the same formats might be used several times throughout the program, you can make two custom manipulators to do all the work. A manipulator is a function that takes and also returns a reference to a stream. The manipulators to do the preceding work are in Listing 7.11.

Listing 7.11. Two manipulators to provide a shorthand notation for custom user formatting.

```
#include <iostream.h>
#include <iomanip.h>

ostream& money(ostream& os)
{
      return os << setprecision(2)
```

```
                << setiosflags(ios::showpoint)
                << resetiosflags(ios::left)
                << setiosflags(ios::right)
                << setfill('*')
                << setw(10);
}

ostream& people(ostream& os)
{
        return os << setfill(' ')
                << setiosflags(ios::left)
                << setw(1);
}
```

Now you can use these manipulators just like the other ones, which allows you to shorten output expressions considerably, as shown in Listing 7.12.

Listing 7.12. A user program that uses custom manipulators.

```
#include <iostream.h>
#include <iomanip.h>

ostream& money(ostream& os)
{
        return os << setprecision(2)
                << setiosflags(ios::showpoint)
                << resetiosflags(ios::left)
                << setiosflags(ios::right)
                << setfill('*')
                << setw(10);
}

ostream& people(ostream& os)
{
        return os << setfill(' ')
                << setiosflags(ios::left)
                << setw(1);
}

void main()
{
        float deductible, already_paid;
        int dependents;

        deductible = 100;
        already_paid = 13.75;
        dependents = 3;
```

continues

Listing 7.12. continued

```
        cout << "\nTotal Deductible     = "
             << money
             << deductible;

        cout << "\nNumber of dependents = "
             << people
             << dependents;

        cout << "\nDeductible paid      = "
             << money
             << already_paid;
}
```

You might regard these custom manipulators as the equivalent of the style sheets used in many word processing programs. They encapsulate entire sequences of formatting commands in a single identifier, thus producing more consistent data formatting throughout a program.

Manipulators with Parameters

Most manipulators take no parameters and are simple to use. Sometimes you need to pass data to the manipulator, however, as with the built-in manipulator `setw(int)`. To make your own manipulators like this is unfortunately different than before, and requires special macros that are contained in *iomanip.h*. In this section I show how to make manipulators with one and two parameters. The technique is always essentially the same, so you could easily create your own manipulators with even more parameters. Assume that you want to create screen manipulators to enable you to do something like this:

```
cout << clear_screen(RED)
     << xy(10, 10) << "Display one line"
     << xy(20, 15) << "and then another";
```

This operation requires two manipulators: `clearscreen(int)` and `xy(int, int)`. The first one takes only one parameter and is defined in Listing 7.13.

Listing 7.13. Defining a user manipulator that takes one argument.

```
// a user-manipulator with one parameter
#include <iostream.h>
#include <iomanip.h>
#include <conio.h>

ostream& clear_screen(ostream& os, int color)
{
```

```
        textcolor(color);
        clrscr();
        return os;
}

OMANIP(int) clear_screen(int c)
{
        return OMANIP(int) (clear_screen, c);
}
```

Two functions are called `clear_screen`, the second of which seems to be unnecessary. `OMANIP(int)` is a macro defined in *iomanip.h* that allows you to declare manipulators that take parameters. You can use `OMANIP`, `IMANIP`, or `IOMANIP` for creating output, input, and input/output manipulators. When the compiler sees the `clearscreen(int)` manipulator in a stream insertion expression, it uses the second function to call the first. You need to use this double-function method anytime you define a manipulator that requires one or more parameters. This procedure is more complicated than one might expect. Maybe a future release of the stream library will solve this problem.

The second manipulator needed is `xy(int x, int y)`, which requires some additional work to be created. The problem is that the macros used previously accept only a single parameter, so you need to use a structure or a class to pass multiple parameters. I assume that (x, y) positions are defined by user class `Point`. Before using `Point` in a manipulator, a call to `IOMANIPdeclare(type)` is required.

```
class Point {
public:
        int x;
        int y;
};

IOMANIPdeclare(Point);
```

Once this is done, the rest is easy. `IOMANIPdeclare(type)` accepts only a simple identifier, so passing pointers or references requires the use of a temporary `typedef`. As Listings 7.14 and 7.15 show, the two overloaded manipulator functions follow the preceding technique.

Listing 7.14. Defining a user manipulator that takes two arguments.

```
#include <conio.h>
#include <iostream.h>
#include <iomanip.h>

class Point {
```

continues

Listing 7.14. continued

```
public:

      int x;
      int y;
};

IOMANIPdeclare(Point);

ostream& xy(ostream& os, Point p)
{
      gotoxy(p.x, p.y);
      return os;
}

OMANIP(Point) xy(int x, int y)
{
      Point p;
      p.x = x; p.y = y;
      return OMANIP(Point)(xy, p);
}
```

With the manipulators defined, Listing 7.15 is a complete program that defines and uses them.

Listing 7.15. A program using custom manipulators that take multiple parameters.

```
#include <iostream.h>
#include <iomanip.h>
#include <conio.h>

ostream& clear_screen(ostream& os, int c)
{
      textcolor(c);
      clrscr();
      return os;
}

OMANIP(int) clear_screen(int c)
{
      return OMANIP(int) (clear_screen, c);
}

class Point {
public:
```

```
        int x;
        int y;
};

IOMANIPdeclare(Point);

ostream& xy(ostream& os, Point p)
{
        gotoxy(p.x, p.y);
        return os;
}

OMANIP(Point) xy(int x, int y)
{
        Point p;
        p.x = x; p.y = y;
        return OMANIP(Point)(xy, p);
}

void main()
{
        cout << clear_screen(RED)
             << xy(10, 10) << "Display one line"
             << xy(20, 15) << "and then another";
}
```

The program clears the screen and then displays the two strings in red. With Borland C++, the standard output stream doesn't support color changes on a character basis; however, clearing the entire screen to a given text color makes the stream functions utilize the selected color.

Manipulators with User Stream Classes

Consider a user-defined stream called `ioCircularFIFOstream`, which handles a circular first-in, first-out buffer by means of a streambuf class called `CircularFIFO`. Assume that during the process of extracting characters from the circular FIFO, you want to skip over a few characters. You can do this by adding a custom manipulator called `skipover(int)` to class `ioCircularFIFOstream`, as shown in Listing 7.16. The manipulator `skipover(int)` takes a parameter indicating how many characters to skip.

Listing 7.16. A user class with a custom manipulator.

```
#include <iostream.h>
#include <iomanip.h>
```

continues

Listing 7.16. continued

```
class CircularFIFO: public streambuf {

      char* buffer;      // fifo ring buffer
      int size;          // size of buffer

      int overflow(int);
      int underflow();

public:

      CircularFIFO(int size);
      ~CircularFIFO() {delete buffer;}
      IsEmpty();
      IsFull();
};

CircularFIFO::CircularFIFO(int s) : streambuf()
{
      // allocate a buffer of the requested size, and
      // attach it to the strstream
      buffer = new char [size];
      setbuf(buffer, s);
      size = s;

      // initialize put and get areas: no putback area
      // in get area
      setp(buffer, &buffer [size] );
      setg(buffer, buffer, &buffer [size] );
}

// this function is called when the put pointer hits the
// end of the buffer
int CircularFIFO::overflow(int c)
{
      // report error if FIFO is full
      if (IsFull() ) return EOF;

      // wrap the put pointer back to the beginning
      setp(base(), ebuf() );

      // and store the character and advance the put
      return sputc(c);
}

// this function is called when the get pointer hits the
// end of the buffer
int CircularFIFO::underflow()
{
```

```
        // report error if FIFO is empty
        if (IsEmpty() ) return EOF;

        // wrap the get pointer back to the beginning,
        // leaving no putback area
        setg(base(), base(), ebuf() );

        // retrieve the next character and advance the get
        // pointer
        return sgetc();
}

// see if the FIFO is empty
int CircularFIFO::IsEmpty()
{
        return (gptr() == pptr() ) ? 1 : 0;
}

// see if the FIFO is full
CircularFIFO::IsFull()
{
        if (gptr() == base() )
       return (pptr() == ebuf() ) ? 1 : 0;
        else
       return (pptr() == gptr() - 1) ? 1 : 0;
}
class ioCircularFIFOstream: public iostream {

public:

        ioCircularFIFOstream(CircularFIFO* cf)
           : iostream(cf) {}
        int IsFull()  {
           return ( (CircularFIFO*)rdbuf() )->IsFull();}
        int IsEmpty()
           {return ( (CircularFIFO*)rdbuf() )->IsEmpty();}
        friend istream& skipover(istream&, int);
};

istream& skipover(istream& is, int n)
{

        ioCircularFIFOstream& ios =
       (ioCircularFIFOstream&) is;
        while (n) {
       if (!ios.IsEmpty() ) {
         // consume the next character
         char c;
```

continues

Listing 7.16. continued

```
         ios >> c;
          }
        }
        return is;
}

IMANIP(int) skipover(int n)
{
        return IMANIP(int)(skipover, n);
}
```

To use your own manipulators with your own stream classes, you need to define a `friend` function that operates on an `istream` object, because the manipulator `skipover(int)` can be used only on input streams, even though `ioCircularFIFOstream` supports both input and output.

Then you have to declare a second function using the special macros. The built-in macros for generating custom manipulators support only the generic stream classes `istream`, `ostream`, and `iostream`. This forces the `friend` function to use an `istream` object rather than an `ioCircularFIFOstream` object; however, a simple typecast fixes that. Invoking the custom manipulator for a stream class other than `ioCircularFIFOstream` will most likely result in a system crash, because the function call `ioCircularFIFOstream::IsEmpty()` would vector off into nowhere. Listing 7.17 is a short program that utilizes the new class.

Listing 7.17. A short program using a user class with a custom manipulator.

```
void main()
{
        // create a circular FIFO
        CircularFIFO fifo(10);

        // associate the FIFO with a stream
        ioCircularFIFOstream rendez_vous(&fifo);

        char c = '0';
        char d;

        // cycle through the FIFO stream
        for (int i = 0; i < 40; i++, c++) {

          // insert data into the FIFO
          if (!rendez_vous.IsFull() )
            rendez_vous << c++;
```

```
        if (!rendez_vous.IsFull() )
          rendez_vous << c++;

        if (!rendez_vous.IsFull() )
          rendez_vous << c;

        // extract data from the FIFO
        if (!rendez_vous.IsEmpty() ) {
          int j;
          rendez_vous >> skipover(2) >> d;
        }

        // display the results
        cout << "\n Value " << i << " = " << d;
      }
}
```

Listing 7.17 inserts three characters into the stream, then skips over the first two to read the third. The process is repeated several times to cycle through the entire FIFO.

File I/O with Streams

The elegance and simplicity of streams are available also to user files, both in text mode and binary mode. Several classes in the library deal with files, but the classes used most are `ifstream` and `ofstream`. `ifstream` supports files opened for reading, whereas `ofstream` supports files opened for writing. All the file classes are described in detail in the "Advanced Section" later in this chapter, but I show the basics of file usage in this section as an introduction.

Using Text Files for Input

A text file is considered to be a sequence of ASCII characters divided into lines. Each line ends with a new-line character. The file stream classes have functions for opening and closing files, reading and writing lines of text, and miscellaneous other uses. Listing 7.18 shows how to open a text file, test it for errors, and copy it to the display.

Listing 7.18. Reading a file and testing it for errors.

```
#include <iostream.h>
#include <fstream.h>

void main()
{
```

continues

Listing 7.18. continued

```
      // open a pre-existing file
      ifstream help_file("\\BC45\\README.TXT   ");

      // check for errors when opening file
      if (!help_file) {
        cout << "\nCouldn't open file \\BC45\\README";
        return;
      }

      // display the file
      while (help_file) {
        char buffer [100];
        help_file.getline(buffer, sizeof(buffer) );
        cout << "\n" << buffer;
      }
}
```

When using file streams, you need to include the standard file *fstream.h*. To open a file for reading, all you need to do is define an `ifstream` object, which indicates the name of the file. A full path name can be used; however, it is not necessary if the file is in the current directory. Two consecutive backslash characters are required to separate directories in the path name, because the backslash is used as an escape character inside strings, and gives special significance to the next character. To force a backslash character into a string, you need to use two backslashes in a row. With the statement

```
ifstream help_file(FILENAME);
```

you define an input file object with a given filename. The object attempts to open the named file in input mode; however, because there is no return value, you don't know immediately whether the operation succeeded or not. There are several ways to handle characters in a text file. You can use a statement like

```
help_file.getline(buffer, sizeof(buffer) );
```

which gets the next string of characters up to the new-line terminator (which is not extracted from the file). You can also handle single characters or other built-in data types like this:

```
char c;
char* cp;
int i;
long l;
float f;
double d;

help_file >> c >> cp >> i >> l >> l >> f >> d;
```

The character extractor treats new-line characters like any other characters. The character extractor is much less efficient than `getline(...)`; however, it can be handy if you're processing the characters before using them. The extraction for a non-`char` type terminates when a character is found that is a white space character or is incompatible with the data type.

One of the nice features of C++ is that objects tend to take care of themselves. If you open a file with a local `ifstream` variable, the file is automatically closed for you when the function terminates, so you often don't need to close files using explicit C++ code. In general, any file is closed when the stream object associated with it goes out of scope.

Most of the built-in file inserters and extractors operate in the text mode, which doesn't support binary operations. In text mode, input streams are considered to be a sequence of character strings, with each string being terminated by a new-line character. Extracting from a text file stream into a variable causes an automatic conversion of the data into the proper format. In text mode, certain characters in the ASCII range (0..0x1F) assume special meaning. The sequence `'\r' '\n'` is converted into `'\n'` during insertion, and the character `'\n'` is converted into the sequence `'\r' '\n'` during extraction.

Testing a Stream for Errors

Errors can occur during the course of stream operations. You might attempt to open a nonexistent file, read past the end-of-file, insert data with an invalid format, and so on. All these conditions cause errors, which must be detected and dealt with. There are several methods to test a stream for errors. The simplest is to use expressions like these:

```
// test stream for errors
if (!stream)
  // errors occurred


if (stream)
  // no errors occurred
```

These two methods are possible because both `operator!` and `operator void*` are overloaded for streams. Special functions in class `ios` can be used to investigate the cause of errors, and can be read with the function `ios::rdstate()`. An alternative way of testing for stream errors is more ANSI C in flavor.

```
if (stream.bad() )
  // errors occurred

if (stream.eof() )
  // end of file

if (stream.good() )
  // no errors occurred
```

Because the name of a stream can be used to test for errors, the expression

```
// display the file
while (help_file) {
  // copy file to cout
}
```

is possible. The loop executes until an error of some kind occurs, which is typically an end-of-file condition. Because the loop is dealing with two streams (`help_file` and `cout`), it is advisable to abort if errors occur in either stream. The following code shows how you can test more than one stream at a time for errors.

```
// better to test all streams involved in the loop
while (help_file && cout) {
  // copy file to cout
}
```

When an error occurs during a stream operation, one or more of the error flags in Table 7.4 is set.

Table 7.4. The error flags in a stream.

Error Bit	*Bit Value*
`ios::eofbit`	1
`ios::failbit`	2
`ios::badbit`	4

You can read the error bits using the function `ios::rdstate()`. Once an error bit is set, all further insertions or extractions from that stream fail until the error bit is explicitly cleared by you. Stream error bits are cleared using the function `ios::clear(int)`. Unfortunately, the name of this function is quite confusing, because `ios::clear(int)` can be used not only to clear error flags, but also to set them. In effect, `ios::clear(int)` sets the error flags to a given value. The default value is 0, which clears all errors like this:

```
// clear all error bits for a stream
file.clear();
```

If you write your own stream inserter or extractor, you may need to set an error bit yourself. Here is an example:

```
// set the error state to ios::failbit
// Reset all other flags
file.clear(ios::failbit);
```

If you want only to clear a specific bit without disturbing the others, you could do this:

```
// set one error bit without clearing the others
file.clear(file.rdstate() ¦ ios::failbit);
```

Conversely, to clear only one error bit, this works:

```
// clear only one stream error bit
//  without affecting the others
file.clear(file.rdstate() & ~ios::failbit);
```

A common use of `ios::clear()` is to clear the end-of-file flag. Once this flag is set, to continue using the file, you need to rewind its `get` pointer and clear the `ios::eofbit` flag, like this:

```
file.clear();        // clear all error flags
file.seekg(0);       // rewind the file's get pointer
```

Rewinding the `get` pointer doesn't automatically clear the `ios::eofbit` flag or any other error flags. Also, make sure to rewind the `get` pointer *before* trying to clear the `ios::eofbit` flag!

Using Text Files for Output

Writing to a file is almost as easy as reading a file. There is a slight complication in that when you open a file in the output mode you need to be aware of *how* the file will be written to. The default is to truncate existing files to a length of 0 at open time, but the default can be changed with optional parameters. Listing 7.19 opens the Borland *README* file and copies its first four lines into a new file called *COPY*.

Listing 7.19. A simple program to write to a text file stream.

```
#include <iostream.h>
#include <fstream.h>
void main()
{
      // open a pre-existing file
      ifstream help_file("\\BC45\\README.TXT    ");

      // open a file and truncate it
      ofstream copy_file("COPY");

      // check for errors when opening file
      if (!help_file) {
        cout << "\nCouldn't open file \\BC45\\README";
        return;
      }
```

continues

Listing 7.19. continued

```
      if (!copy_file) {
        cout << "\nCouldn't open file COPY";
        return;
      }

      // copy the first 4 lines of the README file
      int line_count = 0;
      while (help_file && copy_file) {
        char buffer [80];
        help_file.getline(buffer, sizeof(buffer) );
        copy_file << buffer << "\n";
        if (++line_count == 4) break;
      }
}
```

The statement

```
copy_file << buffer << "\n";
```

writes a null-terminated string to the file, then adds the new-line character so that the file can later be read back with the standard character extractors. You can also write single characters or other built-in data types like this:

```
char c;
char* cp;
int i;
long l;
float f;
double d;

copy_file << c << cp << << i << l << f << d;
```

To open a file for writing without losing the text it already has, you can use the append mode.

```
// open an output file in the append mode
ofstream copy_file("COPY", ios::app);
```

With the change, running the previous program adds a copy of the first four lines of *README* to *COPY* each time it is executed. You may need to impose other conditions when opening an output file, such as making sure that the file *doesn't* already exist, or making sure that the file *does* already exist. Both conditions are handled through flags when a file stream object is created.

```
// make sure the file doesn't already exist
ofstream copy_file("COPY", ios::noreplace);
```

```
//make sure the file already exists
ofstream copy_file("COPY", ios::nocreate);
```

To detect errors that occur as a result of a file-open condition you have set, you can use the error-processing techniques shown in the previous section. As an example, let's say that you have an application that needs to open a configuration file to access initialization data. Obviously, you need to make sure that the configuration file already exists before you start using it. The following code shows how to do this.

```
// open the config file, making sure the file exists
ofstream config_file("config.cfg", ios::nocreate);
if (!config_file)
  // ... the config file doesn't exist
```

Besides reading or writing data sequentially to a file, you can also perform random access using the functions `seekg(...)` and `seekp(...)`. See the "Advanced Section" later in this chapter for a complete discussion.

Using Binary Files for Input

With binary files, data is not considered to have delimiters of any kind, and no characters have special meaning. This includes the `'\0'` character, meaning that strings are not assumed to be null-terminated in a binary file. In fact, strings themselves have no particular meaning in binary format. Binary files need to be treated differently from text files because they don't contain white space characters, the data isn't organized into lines with new-line terminators, and essentially any eight-bit value can occur in them. Even so, the handling of binary files is straightforward. Opening and closing binary files is the same as for text files, except for the `ios::binary` flag passed to the open function. It is perfectly possible to open a text file in binary mode, as shown in Listing 7.20.

Listing 7.20. Reading a text file in binary mode.

```
#include <iostream.h>
#include <fstream.h>
void main()
{
      // open a pre-existing file
      ifstream help_file("\\BC45\\README.TXT    ",
                             ios::binary);

      // check for errors when opening file
      if (!help_file) {
        cout << "\nCouldn't open file \\BC45\\README";
        return;
      }
```

continues

Listing 7.20. continued

```
      // display the readme file
      while (help_file) {
        char c;
        help_file.get(c);
        cout << c;
      }
}
```

The main difference is in the extraction operators that you can use. Because the binary data is considered to be unformatted, only the character extractors are guaranteed to work. If you extract into a character buffer, the size of the buffer must be indicated.

```
char buffer [100];
help_file.read(buffer, sizeof(buffer) );
```

If errors occur while reading, the state of the stream is set to an appropriate error code. Errors can be detected by testing the stream, just as for text files.

```
if (help_file)
  // no errors

if (!help_file)
  //errors occurred
```

After a binary read, you can assume that the buffer has been filled with the requested number of characters. If errors are flagged after the read operation, you can find out how many characters (if any) were read before the error with the function `gcount()`. Listing 7.21 is a short program that illustrates the point.

Listing 7.21. Reading a binary file.

```
#include <iostream.h>
#include <fstream.h>
void main()
{
  // open a pre-existing file
  ifstream help_file("\\BC45\\README.TXT   ", ios::binary);

  // check for errors when opening file
  if (!help_file) {
    cout << "\nCouldn't open file \\BC45\\README";
    return;
  }
```

```
  struct {
    char name [10];
    char surname [20];
    int age;
    float salary;
  } data;

  while (help_file) {
    help_file.read( (char*) &data, sizeof(data) );
  }

  cout << "\nThe last read operation yielded only "
       << help_file.gcount() << " characters instead of "
       << sizeof(data);
}
```

You also can read in the binary values for an entire class using the same format, as shown with the following simple class:

```
class Data {
  char name [10];
  char surname [20];
  int age;
  float salary;
public:
  Data() {age = 0;}
  int Age() {return age;}
  ~Data() {}
};

Data employee;

while (help_file)
  help_file.read( (char*) &employee, sizeof(employee) );
```

When you are reading data into a class, only the data members are affected, not the member functions. The access privileges for the data members are irrelevant during binary reading or writing, so even `private` members can be transferred.

Using Binary Files for Output

There are two basic methods to writing binary data to a file: writing one character at a time, and writing blocks of data. The first method uses the function `put(char)`, whereas the second method uses `write(char*, int)`. Listing 7.22 shows both.

Listing 7.22. Writing binary data to a file using two methods.

```
#include <iostream.h>
#include <fstream.h>

  class Data {
    char name [10];
    char surname [20];
    int age;
    float salary;
  public:
    Data() {age = 0;}
    int Age() {return age;}
    ~Data() {}
  };

void main()
{
  // open a pre-existing file
  ofstream company_records("RECORDS.DAT", ios::binary);

  // check for errors when opening file
  if (!company_records) {
    cout << "\nCouldn't open file RECORDS.DAT";
    return;
  }

  Data employee;

  int number = 0;
  while (number < 10 && company_records) {
   company_records.put( (char) number++);
   company_records.write( (char*) &employee,
                            sizeof(employee) );
  }
}
```

Listing 7.22 writes 10 employee records from a class object to a binary file. As always, you need to check for stream errors during loops that read or write streams. Using the `write(...)` function with classes that have `virtual` functions or other complex constructs may lead to writing data that can't be read back correctly with `read(...)`. When in doubt, use structures rather than classes for complex data to be written.

Binary files are more difficult to use than text files because of the unstructured nature of their data. When you insert a binary object into a file, you need to tell the compiler *exactly* how many bytes long the object is, because there is no longer a string delimiter to indicate this length. The same rule applies during extractions. Listing 7.23 demonstrates the use of

a binary file that is used to store a user object consisting of text and integer data. The program sets a `Symbol` class object to a default state, then attempts to read a file containing previously written data. If the read succeeds, the old data is used. Otherwise, the default data is kept. After performing this simple processing, the `Symbol` is written out to disk. The program is short, but it has most of the ingredients necessary to save and load class objects from disk. Objects that are capable of loading and saving themselves automatically are said to be *persistent.*

Listing 7.23. A program using persistent objects.

```
#include <iomanip.h>
#include <mem.h>
#include <string.h>
#include <fstream.h>

const int NAME_SIZE = 32;

class Symbol {

      char name [NAME_SIZE];
      int flags;
      long value;

public:

      Symbol(char* n, long v, int f) {Reset(n, v, f);}
      void Reset(char* n, long v, int f) {
        // clear out the char array first
        memset(name, 0, NAME_SIZE);
        strcpy(name, n);
        value = v;
        flags = f;
      }
      char* Name() {return name;}
      long& Value() {return value;}
      friend ofstream& operator<< (ofstream&, Symbol&);
      friend ifstream& operator>> (ifstream&, Symbol&);
};

// insert a Symbol object into a file stream
ofstream& operator<< (ofstream& stream, Symbol& sym)
{
      stream.write(sym.name, sizeof(sym.name) );
      stream.write( (unsigned char*) &sym.value,
                     sizeof(sym.value) );
      stream.write( (unsigned char*) &sym.flags,
                     sizeof(sym.flags) );
```

continues

Listing 7.23. continued

```
        return stream;
}

// extract a Symbol object from a file stream
ifstream& operator>> (ifstream& stream, Symbol& sym)
{
        stream.read(sym.name, sizeof(sym.name) );
        stream.read( (unsigned char*) &sym.value,
                        sizeof(sym.value) );
        stream.read( (unsigned char*) &sym.flags,
                        sizeof(sym.flags) );
        return stream;
}


// demonstrate binary file operations with a user class
void main()
{
        const char DATABASE_FILE [] = "database.dat";

        // setup a default symbol
        Symbol symbol("InitialValue", 0, 0);

        // attempt to read in objects from disk
        ifstream in_file(DATABASE_FILE, ios::binary);
        if (in_file.good() )
          // read in values from disk, otherwise use the
          // default values previously established.
          in_file >> symbol;

        // change a value...
        symbol.Value()++;

        // create a new data file if necessary
        ofstream out_file(DATABASE_FILE, ios::binary);
        if (!out_file) {
          cerr << "\nDatabase file couldn't be created.";
          return;
        }

        // save the objects on disk in binary format
        out_file << symbol;
}
```

Notice how the file streams are opened explicitly in binary mode with the calls

```
ifstream  in_file(DATABASE_FILE, ios::binary);
ofstream out_file(DATABASE_FILE, ios::binary);
```

These calls are necessary because the default for file streams is text mode. The streams `in_file` and `out_file` are not closed explicitly, because the class destructors for `ifstream` and `ofstream` are closed automatically when the program terminates. The overloaded `operator!` is used as a shorthand to check a file stream for errors. Although the example saves only a few short items on disk, it could just as easily save a large array of objects, such as an entire database.

In many cases, you need objects like the one handled in Listing 7.23. Such objects are said to possess the property of *persistence* because they survive the program that created them. Persistent objects must be able to read themselves back from disk. Their constructors have code to read in values from a file, and their destructors store values in a file. Both the constructor and the destructor are called automatically by the compiler, so the user of a persistent class doesn't need to be aware of the disk details, nor does the user need to give special instructions to persistent objects. From a user perspective, a persistent object is no different from any other object, except that its initial state is not random, and depends on the values stored somewhere, such as in non-`volatile` memory or in a file.

Copying Files

Progams often read one file, do something with the data, and then copy it to another file. File copying can be accomplished with the `iostream` classes in a number of ways, some of which are very handy. In this section I'll show some of the most common methods used. The simplest conceptual way to copy a file is to read and write one character at a time until the end-of-file is reached. The following code shows how.

```
#include <fstream.h>

void f()
{
  ifstream input("c:\\t.bat");
  ofstream output("c:\\u.bat");
  char c;
  while (input.get(c) )
    output.put(c);
}
```

The function `istream::get()` returns a NULL when the end-of-file is detected, in which case the character `c` is set to 0xFF. Because `istream::get()` returns a nonzero value until the end-of-file is reached, the function can be used as the `while` loop condition. Character reading and writing using `istream::get()` and `ostream::put()` can be applied both to text and nontext files.

Copying one character at a time is very slow and inefficient, although the `iostream` classes provide automatic buffering (blocking/unblocking) of disk data. A much better way to copy data is to transfer it in *chunks*. How a chunk is defined depends on the kind of file you are copying. For text files, a good definition of chunk might be a single line of text. The function `istream::getline()` can be used to read text files by lines, like this:

```
#include <fstream.h>
#include <windows.h>

int PASCAL WinMain(HINSTANCE, HINSTANCE, LPSTR, int)
{
  ifstream input("c:\\t.bat");
  ofstream output("c:\\u.bat");
  char buffer [200];
  while (input && output) {
    input.getline(buffer, sizeof buffer);
    output << buffer << endl;
  }
}
```

For binary files, chunks can't be defined so easily. You might copy data using a buffer, reading and writing the entire buffer until end-of-file occurs on the input file. If the binary file is organized into fixed-sized records, you might want to copy the data one record at a time. The following simple Windows program copies a file 512 bytes at a time.

```
#include <fstream.h>
#include <windows.h>

int PASCAL WinMain(HINSTANCE, HINSTANCE, LPSTR, int)
{
  ifstream input("c:\\t.bat", ios::binary);
  ofstream output("c:\\u.bat", ios::binary);
  char buffer [512];
  while (input && output) {
    input.read(buffer, sizeof buffer);
    output.write(buffer, input.gcount() );;
  }
}
```

The output file writes data using the binary function `ostream::write()`. When the last block of data is read from the input file, the buffer may not be completely filled. To avoid writing the entire buffer to the output file, with the trailing garbage, the function `istream::gcount()` is used. This function returns the number of `chars` read by the last `istream::read()` call.

There is an even better way to copy files with the `iostream` library: using `filebuf` objects. Given an input stream called `input`, the statement

```
  streambuf* sb = input.rdbuf();
```

gets a pointer to the low-level `filebuf` object that actually manages a file's data. You can insert a `filebuf` directly into an output stream, allowing a file to be copied in two lines of code, like this:

```
  streambuf* sb = input.rdbuf();
  output << sb;
```

You can even combine the two lines together, to achieve file copying with a single line. The following is a complete example:

```
#include <fstream.h>
#include <windows.h>

int PASCAL WinMain(HINSTANCE, HINSTANCE, LPSTR, int)
{
  ifstream input("c:\\t.bat");
  ofstream output("c:\\u.bat");
  output << input.rdbuf();          // copy an entire file
}
```

You can use symmetrical operations with `filebufs`: you can either insert a `filebuf` into an output stream, or you can insert an input stream into the `filebuf` of an output stream, like this:

```
  input >> output.rdbuf();          // copy an entire file
```

The two methods are entirely equivalent. What you can't do is insert an input stream directly into an output stream, like this:

```
// you can't do this
input >> output      // won't work correctly
output << input      // won't work correctly
```

When you are done copying a file, the input stream has its end-of-file flag on. If you want to use the same input stream for subsequent operations, you'll need to rewind the `istream`'s `get` pointer, and clear the EOF flag, using code like this:

```
  input.seekg(0);      // rewind the file pointer to the beginning of
                          the file
  input.clear();       // clear all error flags, including ios::eofbit
  input >> output2.rdbuf();
```

The act of rewinding an input stream's `get` pointer does not clear the end-of-file flag automatically. You need to call `ios::clear()` to clear the `ios::eofbit` flag. The following code copies the same file twice, showing how to use a stream after the EOF flag is set.

```
#include <fstream.h>
#include <windows.h>
```

```
int PASCAL WinMain(HINSTANCE, HINSTANCE, LPSTR, int)
{
  ifstream input("c:\\t.bat");
  ofstream output1("c:\\u.bat");
  ofstream output2("c:\\v.bat");
  input >> output1.rdbuf();
  input.seekg(0);      // rewind the file pointer
  input.clear();      // clear all error flags
  input >> output2.rdbuf();
}
```

In-Memory Formatting

Many times you need to format data without displaying it. ANSI C programs use the `sprintf(...)` function for this purpose. The formatted data is saved in a memory buffer for subsequent use. The stream library comes with the in-memory formatting class called `strstream`, which can be used for insertions and extractions. Listing 7.24 is a complete example that shows how an `strstream` can be used just like an `fstream`, with inserters, manipulators, and dynamic buffering.

Listing 7.24. Using `strstream` for formatted in-memory insertions.

```
#include <iostream.h>
#include <strstrea.h>
#include <iomanip.h>
#include <fstream.h>
#include <stdlib.h>

void main()
{
      // create an empty strstream. Memory will be
      // allocated dynamically to it as needed.
      strstream buffer;

      // make some variables
      int number = 30;
      char* color = "RED";
      float weight = 135.96;

     // build a formatted string in the strstream
      buffer << "\nThere are " << number;
      buffer << " chairs that are " << color;
      buffer << ", with a total weight of ";
      buffer << setprecision(2) << weight << " kilos.";

      // open a log file
      ofstream report("report.doc");
```

```
        if (!report) {
          cerr << "Can't open the report file.";
          exit(1);
        }

        // save the data in the file
        report << buffer.rdbuf();
}
```

Listing 7.24 shows an `strstream` object used to build a formatted string, which is then saved in a text file. File *REPORT.DOC* contains the string

```
There are 30 chairs that are RED, with a total weight of 135.96 kilos.
```

If you need to extract formatted data from an in-memory stream, you can use the class `istrstream`. First, you create an `istrstream` object and associate it with a buffer that contains the data you wish to extract. Then you extract the data using the normal extractor functions. Listing 7.25 is a short but complete example.

Listing 7.25. Using `istrstream` for formatted in-memory extractions.

```
#include <iostream.h>
#include <strstrea.h>

void main(int argc, char** argv)
{
        istrstream argument(argv [0]);

        cout << "\nThere are " << argc
             << " arguments. The first was "
             << argument.rdbuf();
}
```

Listing 7.25 uses `argv [0]`, the first command-line argument, to initialize an `istrstream` object. Streams are often more convenient to use than simple character arrays because they have more flexibility, built-in pointer handling, dynamic buffering, and so on. If your programs make extensive use of strings, you may want to consider switching over to `strstreams` or the standard C++ class *`string`* to get away from the old ANSI string manipulation functions.

In many situations, you need to perform several formatting operations in the same function. For example, if you're using Microsoft Windows or another graphical user interface, you have to format data in-memory, then call an interface function to display the formatted data. To format data in-memory, you can use the class `ostrstream`, which supports insertion operations for all the built-in C++ types. If you create a single output string stream, you can use it over and over again to format data, but with the proviso that you "rewind" it before each reuse. Listing 7.26 is a short example.

Listing 7.26. Using a single stream to support multiple in-memory formatting operations.

```
#include <strstrea.h>
#include <iomanip.h>

void main()
{
      char buffer [80];
      ostrstream text(buffer, sizeof(buffer) );
      int i = 10;
      char* code = "Unknown";

      text << "\nThere are "
           << i
           << " objects"
           << ends;

      cout << buffer;

      // rewind the stream put pointer
      // before using it again
      text.seekp(0);
      text << "\nThe error code is: "
           << code
           << ends;
      cout << buffer;
}
```

Always remember to end insertions with the `ends` manipulator, otherwise the characters inserted will not be null-terminated. Streams themselves don't need null-terminators; however, any time you use their contents as a string, a null-terminator is required. The function call `seekp(0)` rewinds the `put` pointer back to 0, preparing the stream for subsequent use. This allows you to use a stream repeatedly.

Using the Printer as a Stream

It is common for programs to require printing. The ANSI I/O library uses `fopen(...)`, `fprintf(...)`, and `fclose(...)` to support printing, using the reserved file names *PRN*, *LPT1*, or *LPT2* for the printer. The device *PRN* is connected by default to *LPT1*. Listing 7.27 uses ANSI C I/O functions to write to a printer.

Listing 7.27. Using ANSI C I/O functions to write to a printer.

```
#include <stdio.h>

void main()
{
      FILE *fp;
      fp = fopen("LPT1", "w");
      if (!fp) {
        printf("\nCan't access printer");
        return;
      }

      // print something...
      fprintf(fp, "Testing\n");
      fclose(fp);
}
```

An equivalent program using streams looks like Listing 7.28.

Listing 7.28. Using streams to write to a printer.

```
#include <iostream.h>
#include <strstrea.h>
#include <fstream.h>
#include <stdlib.h>

void main(int argc, char** argv)
{
      strstream record;

      // make some formatted data to print
      record << "\nThere were " << argc
             << " arguments, and the first was "
             << argv [0] << endl << ends;

      ofstream printer("PRN");
      if (!printer) {
        cerr << "\nCouldn't access the printer.";
        exit(1);
      }

      // print some data
      printer << "This is a command-line summary:"
            << record.rdbuf();
}
```

Using streams, the notation is simpler than with ANSI functions. You can use the names *PRN*, *LPT1*, or *LPT2* to open a printer stream, as with ANSI I/O. Sending data to a printer stream follows the rules applied to any `ofstream`, so you can insert characters to it, check it for errors, and so on. Random-access operations on a printer stream have no meaning and will probably get you in trouble. Because an `ofstream` is used, the usual data formatting is supported with manipulators.

Windows programs treat the printer in a completely different manner from DOS programs. Printers are considered graphical output devices rather than character-oriented streams. OWL 2.5 does not use streams for printing, but instead uses a variety of ad hoc classes, such as `TPrinter`, `TPrintout`, `TPrintDC`, and `TPrintDialog`.

Advanced Section

This section describes in detail the classes used to implement the streams that are available in the `iostream` library. This new version of the library was introduced with AT&T release 2.0, and renders obsolete certain classes that were part of the older stream library. I do not discuss the obsolete classes in detail, and I recommend that new programs avoid using the anachronistic features of the library. Examples of usage are shown for most of the classes in the `iostream` library.

The `iostream` hierarchy is rather complex. The stream classes can be used as a point of departure for your own specialized classes, so I show several instances of classes derived from the stream library.

> **NOTE**
>
> In this chapter and in Chapter 8, I use a special style to describe classes that are included in Borland C++ 4.5. Because class descriptions often cover several pages, it is easy to lose track of where a class starts, where it ends, and which access section an identifier appears in. To facilitate reading, here is how a generic class will be laid out:

```
class Sample {
private:
  // private members
protected:
  // protected members
public:
  // public data members
};
```

The access specifiers `private`, `public`, and `protected` (if used) will be printed in boldface to make them stand out. When looking up a member of a class, it is particularly easy to lose track of which access section the member appears in, but the highlighting should help solve this problem. Members in each access section will be separated from each other by a line, and will appear like this:

```
// constructor for class streambuf
streambuf(char* buffer, int size);
```

The *streambuf* Hierarchy

The lowest-level details of I/O are handled in class `streambuf` and its derived classes. All movement of data from a source to a destination requires the basic mechanisms of buffering that are supported by the `streambuf` hierarchy. All stream classes are either derived from `streambuf`, or manipulate objects derived from `streambuf`. Polymorphism is used to adapt the class to different kinds of operations, such as handling files, handling hardware devices, and so on. Class `streambuf` handles unformatted buffering, and can also be used to derive your own classes. Figure 7.2 is the entire `streambuf` inheritance tree with Borland C++.

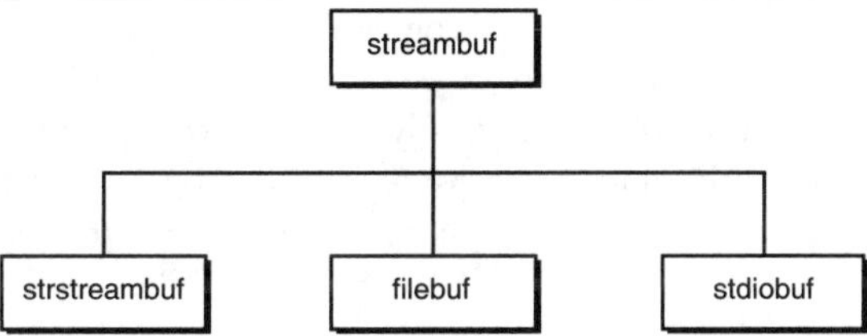

Figure 7.2. The `streambuf` *inheritance tree.*

Class `streambuf` handles most of the details of buffer housekeeping, but it doesn't know how its buffer is associated with the outside world. It doesn't know how to fill an input buffer, or how to empty an output buffer. These operations are possible only once you know what kind of object the buffer is attached to: a file, a memory buffer, a hardware I/O device, and so on. Thus, it doesn't make sense to instantiate `streambuf` directly, a fact that suggests that `streambuf` should be an abstract class. Unfortunately, this is not how it is implemented. In any case, `streambuf` is designed to be used exclusively as a base class for other classes.

Classes `strstreambuf` and `filebuf` are discussed in this chapter. The former is designed to handle in-memory string buffers, whereas the latter supports file operations. Class `filebuf` uses low-level file descriptors as opposed to high-level file pointers, to avoid using the ANSI C I/O library functions. Class `stdiobuf` applies to standard I/O. It is considered obsolete in AT&T release 3.0, which uses `fstream` and related classes instead, so I won't be describing `stdiobuf` in this book.

The *ios* Hierarchy

The `ios` hierarchy is the core hierarchy for streams that are compatible with AT&T 3.0. The `ios` hierarchy uses multiple inheritance for some of its members, unlike release 1.2 streams. Using multiple inheritance is not only a more elegant approach, but it is also efficient in code utilization. The basic stream classes are `istream` and `ostream`. The former supports input, whereas the latter supports output. Both classes have a great deal in common, such as a stream state, a stream access mode, formatting flags, numeric conversion bases, and so on. All these were extracted from the two classes and assigned to the base class `ios`. The `ios` hierarchy provides for basic buffered or unbuffered I/O, such as for display output, keyboard input, string formatting, and so on.

Class `ios` is a simple (albeit rather large) class. `ios` provides all the commands for handling the lower-level class `streambuf`. One `streambuf` object is associated with each `ios` object. A `streambuf` is simply a buffer manager class that allows read and write operations to a buffer, filling and flushing, and so on. A `streambuf` has no formatting capability by itself, which is where `ios` comes into play. Class `streambuf` can be used as a base class for your own classes any time you need to deal with buffers. The nice thing about `streambuf` is that its code is already in your program (if you use stream I/O at all), so there is no additional memory cost to reuse it. Also, `streambuf` has quite a few member functions, so most of the common buffer operations are already implemented.

Class *filebuf*

Class `filebuf` uses the buffer support functions of `streambuf` for basic file operations. Low-level ANSI C functions such as `::open(...)`, `::read(...)`, and `::write(...)` are used to implement the file interface. This results in a portable class. The use of these functions also results in a stream architecture that is not built around or on top of the ANSI C high-level file functions such as `::fopen(...)`, `::fwrite(...)`, and `::fread(...)`. The most common file handle used among the `fstream` member functions is the low-level file descriptor. The low-level file descriptor is an index to a table of file structures, and is used also by the low-level ANSI I/O library.

Class `filebuf` is different from classes like `streambuf` because it can be instantiated to produce a usable object. It has built-in methods for opening a file, closing a file, reading data, writing data, and so on. The class manipulates a buffer through its base class `streambuf`, adding only a few extra file-related functions. The `virtual` functions `streambuf::overflow(int)` and `streambuf::underflow()` are overridden to support file reading and writing. Here is a simplified and edited version of the declaration of class `filebuf`:

`class filebuf : public streambuf {`

`protected:`

`int xfd;`

This declaration indicates the file descriptor for the file that is attached to the `filebuf` object. File descriptors used in the C++ streams are the same as those used in the low-level ANSI C file functions. If no file is attached to a `filebuf`, the value of `xfd` is EOF.

`int mode;`

This `protected` variable shows which mode was used to open the attached file. The possible values are

`ios::in`	Read only.
`ios::out`	Write only.
`ios::ate`	Go to the end of the file when a file is opened.
`ios::app`	Append data to the end of the file when writing.
`ios::trunc`	Clear old contents if the file exists.
`ios::nocreate`	Open a file that must already exist.
`ios::noreplace`	Open a file that must *not* already exist.
`ios::binary`	Open a file for binary data. If this flag isn't used, files will be opened in the text mode.

Each of these values is defined in the standard header file *iostream.h*. Multiple flags can be `OR`ed together.

`short opened;`

This function is nonzero if a file has been opened, and 0 otherwise.

`long last_seek;`

This member variable is used to keep track of the last place to which a seek operation went.

```
char* in_start;
int last_op();
```

These variables are declared for compatibility with AT&T C++, but are not documented.

```
char lahead [2];
```

This array is a small buffer for unbuffered inputs (sometimes called a *look-ahead* buffer).

public:

```
static const int openprot;
```

Because this variable is a `static` member variable, there is only one copy of it in the entire system, regardless of how many `filebuf` objects are created. The member variable `filebuf::openprot` indicates the type of access protection given to the file. DOS systems offer limited protection mechanisms, so the default file protection is set to `(S_IREAD | S_IWRITE)`, which allows reading and writing to the file. UNIX systems can use the protection mode to grant read, write, and execute privileges to specific owner categories. The constant variable `filebuf::openprot` is initialized outside all functions, and therefore is set up before any user code is executed.

```
filebuf();
```

This constructor creates a `filebuf` and allocates a `dynamic` buffer to it, but does not open any files.

```
filebuf(int fd);
```

This constructor takes a file descriptor as an argument, assuming it refers to a file that is already open. A `dynamic` buffer is allocated, and the file is attached to it. The access mode (read, write, and so on) is unknown; therefore, it is set to 0. A 0 mode is therefore an indicator of a file that does not belong to the `filebuf`, preventing the file from being deleted in the destructor.

```
filebuf(int fd, char* buffer, int s);
```

This constructor is like the previous one, except a buffer of size `s` is passed and attached to the file having its descriptor in the parameter `fd`. No `dynamic` buffer is allocated.

```
~filebuf();
```

This destructor does one of two things. If the `mode` variable is 0, which is an indication that no file was opened or that it doesn't belong to `filebuf`, the buffer is flushed to the file. If the mode is nonzero, the buffer is flushed to the file, and the file is closed.

```
int is_open();
```

The access function returns nonzero if a file has been opened. The function returns nonzero even when `filebuf` didn't actually open a file itself, but received a file descriptor as an argument in a constructor.

```
int fd();
```

This access function returns the value of the file descriptor in use. If no file is open, the function returns an EOF.

```
filebuf* open(const char* n,
              int m,
              int p = filebuf::openprot );
```

This function opens the file `n`, in the mode `m`. See the description of the `private` variable `filebuf::mode` for the possible values. If a file is not successfully opened, a 0 is returned. The low-level function `::open(...)` is used to actually open the file. The access protection level `p` is defaulted. See `filebuf::openprot` for details.

```
filebuf* close();
```

This function flushes the file buffer to the file attached to a `filebuf` (if any) and closes the file. If any errors occur, a 0 is returned.

```
filebuf* attach(int fd);
```

This function takes a file descriptor and attaches the `filebuf` object to it. If the `filebuf` has no buffer connected to it, a `dynamic` buffer is allocated and initialized. If the `filebuf` is already connected to a file, this function does nothing and returns a value of 0. If `filebuf::attach(int)` succeeds in attaching a `filebuf` object to a file, a pointer to the `filebuf` object is returned.

```
virtual int overflow(int c = EOF);
```

This `virtual` function flushes the data in the `filebuf` buffer to a file. If errors occur, an EOF is returned. Otherwise, the integer 1 is returned. The low-level function `::write(...)`

is used to actually write data to a file. The parameter `c` is used to write an additional byte into the `filebuf` buffer after the flushing. If its value is EOF, nothing is written after the buffer flush.

```
virtual int underflow();
```

This `virtual` function reads a block of data into the `filebuf` buffer from the file currently associated with a `filebuf` object. If any errors occur, an EOF is returned. Otherwise, the first character that was read is returned. The low-level function `::read(...)` is called to do the actual file reading.

```
virtual int sync();
```

This function empties out both the `put` and `get` areas of the `filebuf` buffer. The `put` area is flushed to the file, and the pointers for the `put` and `get` areas are reinitialized to reflect an empty status. The file seek index `last_seek` is backed up to allow any characters lost in the `get` area to be read again. This function returns 0 if no errors occur. Otherwise, it returns an EOF.

```
virtual long seekoff(long offset, seek_dir dir, int mode);
```

This function moves the file seek index `last_seek` to the given location, dependent on the seek direction: from the beginning of the file, from the current seek index, or from the end of the file. The value returned from this function is the new seek position, if no errors occur. A return value of EOF indicates that an error occurred during the seek operation. Before seeking, this function flushes the `put` area of the `filebuf` to the file, using the low-level function `::write(...)` rather than the usual `filebuf::overflow(int)`. The file-seeking is performed via the low-level function `::lseek(...)`.

```
virtual streambuf* setbuf(char*, int);
```

This `virtual` function can be used to attach a `filebuf` to a buffer. If the `filebuf` already has a buffer with an opened file connected to it, the function aborts and returns 0. If no file is opened, the new buffer replaces the old one (if one exists), then the `put` and `get` pointers are initialized. If an old buffer existed, it is also deleted.

```
};
```

Deriving a Class from *filebuf*

Now that class `filebuf` has been described in detail, an example is in order to demonstrate its reusability and power. I'll derive a class from `filebuf` and call it `HexFile`. `HexFile` stores its data on disk differently from typical files. Rather than store binary data that can't

be inspected with a text editor, `HexFile` converts all data to a special hexadecimal ASCII format. Thus, the binary byte 00 is stored as 0x30 0x30, so typing it out shows `00` on the screen. The value CF is stored on disk as 0x43 0x46, so it is displayed as `CF` on the screen. The full range of hex values is handled, so a buffer with arbitrary binary data is saved as a printable ASCII file.

Only two functions actually are involved in all this: a `private` function `Ascii(char)` that takes a nibble (a binary value in the range 0..F), and returns the ASCII value for it, and a `public` function to write data to disk using the hex ASCII format. The function `streambuf::overflow(int)` is overridden and provides both the data conversion and disk writing. To make data look nicer on the display, `HexFile::overflow(int)` inserts a new-line character every 16 bytes. The low-level function `::write(...)` is used to store data on a disk.

The overall program opens a file named *test.hex* and stores 200 bytes of data into it in hex ASCII format. The file is then closed. For simplicity I didn't provide functions for reading the file back into memory or for converting it from hex ASCII into binary. This is a straightforward procedure that I leave as an exercise for the reader. Listing 7.29 is the code.

Listing 7.29. `HexFile` is a simple class derived from `filebuf`.

```
#include <io.h>
#include <fstream.h>

// set up a suitable buffer size
const int BUFFER_SIZE = 200;

// store all data in printable ASCII hex format
class HexFile: public filebuf {

      char Ascii(char);

public:
      HexFile() : filebuf() {}
      virtual int overflow(int);
};

char HexFile::Ascii(char c)
{
      static char character [] = {"0123456789ABCDEF"};
      return character [c & 0x0F];
}

int HexFile::overflow(int c)
{
      // buffer for hex ASCII data
      char hex_buffer [3 * BUFFER_SIZE];
```

continues

Listing 7.29. continued

```
        if(!opened)
          // oops: no file opened yet !
          return EOF;

        // see how many characters there are to write
        int count = out_waiting();
        if (count) {

          // convert all chars to printable hex ascii
          for (int i = 0, j = 0; i < count; i++, j += 2) {
            if ( (i % 0x10) == 0)
              // start a new line every 16 bytes
              hex_buffer [j++] = '\n';
            hex_buffer [j]     = Ascii( *(base() + i) >> 4);
            hex_buffer [j + 1] = Ascii( *(base() + i) );
          }

          // there are 2 ascii characters for each byte
         count = j;

          // invoke low-level I/O to write a block of data
          if(::write(xfd, hex_buffer, count) != count )
            // something went wrong...
            return EOF;

        }

        // reset get and put areas
        setp( base(), ebuf() );
        setg( base(), base(), ebuf() );
        return c;
}

void main()
{
        char* filename = {"test.hex"};
        HexFile file;
        char buffer [BUFFER_SIZE];

        // open the file
        file. open(filename, ios::out);

        // fill a buffer with a succession of integers
        for (int i = 0; i < BUFFER_SIZE; i++)
          buffer [i] = i;

        // copy the buffer into the file's buffer
        file. sputn(buffer, sizeof(buffer) );
```

```
    // close the file and flush buffer if necessary
    file. close();
}
```

Class *fstream*

The `fstream` class is a combination of `ifstream` and `ofstream`, and therefore supports input and output operations on files. Here is a succinct, edited version of the class:

```
class fstream : public fstreambase, public iostream {
```

```
public:
```

```
fstream();
```

This constructor does nothing except invoke the default constructors for its two base classes, to set up a `filebuf` for subsequent file operations. No files are opened, and a call must be made to `fstream::open(...)` to open a file.

```
fstream(const char* name,
        int mode,
        int p = filebuf::openprot);
```

This constructor is different from the corresponding one in `ifstream` and `ofstream` because there is no default value for the file-open `mode` parameter. You can use an `fstream` to open a file for input, output, or both. See the data member `filebuf::mode` for a description of the file open modes.

```
fstream(int file_descriptor);
```

This constructor associates an `fstream` object to a file, which is assumed to already be open.

```
fstream(int file_descriptor, char* buffer, int size);
```

This constructor takes a buffer of length `size` and uses it to build an internal `filebuf` object. The `filebuf` object is to be used in accessing a file having the low-level descriptor `file_descriptor`. This file is assumed to be open.

```
~fstream();
```

This destructor does nothing, because the base class destructors do all the work. The base classes deallocate any storage allocated dynamically for `filebuf` buffers. If a buffer was passed to the `fstream` using the constructor `fstream(int, char*, int)`, the `filebuf` does *not* deallocate the buffer.

```
filebuf* rdbuf();
```

This function returns a pointer to the `filebuf` object being used to buffer file reading and writing operations inside class `fstream`.

```
void open(const char* name,
          int mode,
          int p = filebuf::openprot);
```

This function is different from the corresponding one in `ifstream` and `ofstream` because there is no default value for the file-open `mode` parameter. See `filebuf::mode` for a description of the file open modes.

```
};
```

Most of the member functions correspond to the functions that are described in classes `ifstream` or `ofstream`. When you open a file for output, using mode `ios::out` will truncate any existing file of the same name to zero. To prevent this truncation, use the mode flag `ios::ate`, which positions the file pointer to the end of the file after opening it. Then you can use `seekp(...)` to jump around in the file if you need to. If the open mode uses the flag `ios::app`, all data written is appended to the end of the file *regardless* of any `seekp(...)` commands issued; however, `seekg(...)` commands continue to have an effect on read operations.

Using Class *fstream*

If you use I/O files in your programs, you will need to use class `fstream`. I show a small program that highlights some of the behaviors of `fstream` objects. Listing 7.30 is the code.

Listing 7.30. Using `fstream` for I/O operations on files.

```
#include <fstream.h>
#include <dir.h>

// open a file for input/output and access it
void main()
{
```

```
    cout << "\nOpening file 'output.txt' for I/O.\n";

    // open an I/O file for output and truncate it if
    // already exists
    fstream file("output.txt", ios::in | ios::out | ios::trunc);

    if (file. bad() ) {
      cout << "\n\t**************************************"
           << "\n\t* Error: couldn't open 'output.txt'. *"
           << "\n\t**************************************\n";
      return;
    }

    // display the initial file size: it must be zero !
    file. seekp(0, ios::end);
    long size = file. tellp();
    cout << "\nThe initial size of 'output.txt' is "
         << size << " bytes.\n";

      // save the current directory in the file
     struct ffblk file_block;
      if (findfirst("*.*", &file_block, 0) ) {
        file << "Error accessing directory...";
        return;
      }
      do
        file << file_block. ff_name << "\n";
      while (!findnext(&file_block) );

    // use the file in input mode
    file. seekg(0, ios::beg);
    char buffer [80];
   for (int i = 0; i < 10; i++)
      file. getline(buffer, sizeof(buffer) );
   cout << "\nThe 10th line of the file is:\n\t'"
         << buffer << "'\n";

    // insert data in the middle of the file
    file. seekp(0, ios::end);
    long middle = file. tellp() / 2;
    file. seekp(middle);
    file << "\n\nThis was added right in the middle of "
         << "the file\n\n";

    // read another line of text: file's GET pointer was
    // modified by the last seekp() operation, so it is
    // beyond the middle of the file
    file. getline(buffer, sizeof(buffer) );
    cout << "\nThe line after the file insertion at the middle"
         << " of the file is:\n\t'" << buffer << "'\n";
}
```

Listing 7.30 shows the use of a file for interleaved input and output operations. Note that changing a file's `get` pointer also affects the `put` pointer, and vice versa. The two are always kept together to simplify the stream classes.

Keep in mind the affect of the `ios::app` bit when you are opening a file. The `put` pointer is always set to the end of file before write operations, irrespective of `seekp(...)` commands.

Class *fstreambase*

`fstreambase` is an intermediate class in the stream hierarchy that embodies the common features used in lower classes. As such, it can be considered a *seed* class. It supports a number of file operations, including opening, closing, and flushing. Here is an edited version of its declaration:

`class fstreambase : virtual public ios {`

`private:`

```
filebuf buf;
```

The preceding statement declares the `filebuf` object utilized for all file I/O operations.

`protected:`

```
void verify(int);
```

This is declared but not defined. It is included in the class for compatibility with AT&T C++ release 3.0.

`public:`

```
fstreambase();
```

This constructor sets up a `filebuf` object to be used in subsequent file operations. No files are opened.

```
fstreambase(const char* f,
            int m,
            int p = filebuf::openprot);
```

This constructor opens the file `f` in the mode `m`. The mode can be a combination of the bits described in variable `filebuf::mode`, and indicates whether a file is opened for input, output, or both. The file access protection level `p` is defaulted. See `filebuf::openprot` for details.

```
fstreambase(int fd);
```

This constructor takes a file descriptor and connects a `filebuf` to the corresponding file. The file is assumed to be open already.

```
fstreambase(int fd, char* buffer, int size);
```

This constructor takes a file descriptor and a buffer of a given size. The buffer is used for the `filebuf` object inside `fstreambase`. The file referenced by the file descriptor is assumed to have been opened already.

```
~fstreambase();
```

This destructor does nothing.

```
void open(const char* n,
          int m mode,
          int p = filebuf::openprot);
```

This function opens a file `n` in the mode `m`. The file access protection level `p` is defaulted. See `filebuf::openprot` for details.

```
void attach(int fd);
```

This function takes a file descriptor and attaches the `fstreambase` object to the corresponding file. If the `fstreambase` already is connected to a file, an error flag is set in `ios::state`.

```
void close();
```

This function flushes the stream buffer and closes the associated file.

```
void setbuf(char* buffer, int s);
```

This function connects the `fstreambase filebuf` to the given buffer of size `s`. If the `fstreambase` object already has both a buffer and an open file, no action is taken. If no file is open, the new buffer is connected and the old one is deleted.

```
filebuf* rdbuf();
```

This function returns the address of the `filebuf` buffer being used by an `fstreambase` object.

```
};
```

The only thing of particular interest in the declaration of class `fstreambase` is the first member variable, `fstreambase::buf`. This is the first stream class encountered that includes a class object inside itself. All of the previous stream classes utilized pointers to class objects. With this new architecture, constructors for `fstreambase` need to initialize the `filebuf` object somehow. In practice this is performed using the member object initialization syntax. Here is how one of the constructors looks:

```
// initializing of a member object in fstreambase
fstreambase::fstreambase(int fd, char* buffer, int size)
            : buf(fd, buffer, size)
{
   // ... initialize the rest of the object
}
```

The initializer `buf(fd, buffer, size)` is executed before the body of the constructor so that a completely constructed object can be dealt with immediately in the constructor.

Using Class *fstreambase*

Although the `fstreambase` class wasn't designed to be used directly, it is possible to instantiate it directly. I show a short example of how it might be used. Listing 7.31 is a program that opens a text file named *dir.txt* and displays it on the screen. I left out error checking to avoid cluttering up the code with details. Most errors that can occur are reported through status bits in `ios::state`.

Listing 7.31. A short program that dumps an entire file to the display.

```
#include <fstream.h>

void main()
{
      fstreambase file("dir.txt", ios::in);
      cout << file. rdbuf();
}
```

This short program opens a file and displays its contents on the user display. That's not bad for two statements. As usual, the file is not required to be closed explicitly, because the destructor for object `file` takes care of it for you. The `fstreambase` function `rdbuf()` is inherited from class `ios`, and returns a pointer to the `streambuf` associated with the `fstreambase` object. The output stream `cout` defines an insertion operator that takes a pointer to `streambuf`. Using this pointer, the operator inserts all the data stored in the `streambuf` buffer into the output stream.

Deriving a Class from *fstreambase*

The class `fstreambase` is a good point of departure for new file handling classes. However, it lacks a feature that would make its use even simpler than in the previous example: the ability to use an `fstreambase` object directly on the right side of an extraction or insertion operator. To copy a file, it would be most elegant to be able to write

```
cout << file;
```

It is a simple matter to derive a class from `fstreambase` and endow it with the power to be used directly in insertion and extraction statements. Listing 7.32 is an example.

Listing 7.32. A class derived from `fstreambase` to facilitate file dumping.

```
#include <fstream.h>

class SimpleInputFile: public fstreambase {

public:
      SimpleInputFile(char* s)
             : fstreambase(s, ios::in) {}
      friend ostream& operator<<(ostream& o,
                                 SimpleInputFile&);
};

// define an overloaded operator for class SimpleInputFile
ostream& operator<<(ostream& o, SimpleInputFile& s)
{
      o << s.rdbuf();     // copy file to output stream
      return o;           // return ostream&
}


void main()
{
      // open the file and display it on the console
      SimpleInputFile file("dir.txt");
      cout << file;
}
```

Given the size of class `SimpleInputFile`, it is obvious that most of the work is done in the base class. In fact, the only thing the class really does is declare a `friend` operator to allow the desirable notation with `cout`. Another feature is provided by the constructor, which requires only a file name to open a file for input. The access mode is passed automatically as `ios::in` to the base class. It's hard to imagine a simpler notation for displaying a file than that in Listing 7.32.

Class *ifstream*

`ifstream` is the most important class in the stream hierarchy for handling files for input. It embodies all the functions for opening, reading, and closing a file. It also supports random and sequential access to files. Files are handled in `ifstream` through a `filebuf` object, which is inherited from the base class `fstreambase`. This `filebuf` object assumes the responsibilities of pointer management and buffering for the file. Here is an edited version of the declaration of `ifstream`:

```
class ifstream : public fstreambase, public istream {
```

```
public:
```

```
ifstream();
```

This constructor builds an input file stream with no file connected to it.

```
ifstream(const char* n,
         int m = ios::in,
         int f = filebuf::openprot);
```

This opens a file `n` and sets it for input mode with the file protection level `f`, which is defaulted. The file name `n` can be a full path name with a drive number and multiple subdirectories, such as the string `c:\\borlandc\\classlib\\include\\bag.h`. See `filebuf::openprot` for more details. The `ifstream` then attaches the file to itself.

```
ifstream(int fd);
```

This constructor takes a file descriptor `fd`, which is assumed to refer to a file that has already been opened. The file is connected to the `ifstream` object. The file descriptors used in the stream functions are the same as those used in the low-level ANSI C I/O functions.

```
ifstream(int fd, char* buffer, int size);
```

This constructor takes the file descriptor `fd` of an opened file and connects the file to the `ifstream` object. As with the previous constructor, the file name can be a fully qualified path name. A buffer of a given size is also used in building a member object of class `filebuf`.

```
~ifstream();
```

This function invokes the base destructors to deallocate the storage (if any) that is assigned to the `filebuf` member object.

```
filebuf* rdbuf();
```

This returns the address of the `filebuf` that is used by the `ifstream`.

```
void open(const char* n,
          int m = ios::in,
          int p = filebuf::openprot);
```

This opens a file `n` for input and gives it file access protection level `p`, which is the default. The name of the file can be a fully qualified path name, as described in the constructor `ifstream::ifstream(const char*, int, int)`. See `filebuf::openprot` for more details on the protection modes for files.

};

The class doesn't add a single line of code to its base classes: The only purpose served by the various member functions is to funnel parameters through to the base classes.

Using the default open mode, the file pointer is set to the beginning of the file. Using the mode `ios::ate`, the file pointer is positioned to the end of the file.

Using Class *ifstream*

As stated earlier, `ifstream` is an essential class for handling operations on files that are used for input. Listing 7.33 is an example of `ifstream` usage. The program opens a file named *dir.txt*, which must be a text file, and performs miscellaneous operations on it. Both random and sequential access operations are shown. Stream error bits are both tested and cleared.

Listing 7.33. Using `ifstream` to open and use a file.

```
#include <fstream.h>

// open a file for input and access it in various ways
void main()
{
      ifstream file("dir.txt");
      if (file. bad() ) {
        cout << "\n\t**********************************************"
             << "\n\t* Error: couldn't open file 'dir.txt'. Please *"
             << "\n\t* create the file using the DOS command:      *"
             << "\n\t*                                              *"
             << "\n\t*             dir > dir.txt                    *"
             << "\n\t*                                              *"
```

continues

Listing 7.33. continued

```
        << "\n\t* and try again.                                        *"
        << "\n\t*******************************************
           *********\n";
    return;
  }

  // display the whole file
  cout << file. rdbuf();
  file. seekg(0, ios::end);
  long size = file. tellg();
  cout << "\nThe size of the file is "
       << size << " bytes.\n";

  // step over a few initial entries
  char buffer [80];
  file. seekg(0, ios::beg);
  for (int i = 0; i < 5; i++)
    file. getline(buffer, sizeof(buffer) );

  char word1 [80];
  char word2 [80];
  file >> word1 >> word2;
  cout << "\nThe fifth entry is: '" << buffer << "'";
  cout << "\nThe next two words in the file are: "
       << "\n1:\t'" << word1 << "'"
       << "\n2:\t'" << word2 << "'\n";

  // count the number of entries in the file
  file. seekg(0);
  int line_count = 0;
  while (!file. eof() ) {
    file. getline(buffer, sizeof(buffer) );
   line_count++;
  }
  cout << "\nThe file has " << line_count
       << " lines of text\n";

  // random access the file: display the first entry
  // after the middle of the file

 // go to middle of file
  long middle = size / 2;
  file. seekg(middle, ios::beg);

  // clear the eof flag (and all other flags) now
  file. clear();

 // discard the first line
 file. getline(buffer, sizeof(buffer) );
```

```
        // read the next line
        file. getline(buffer, sizeof(buffer) );

         // display the line of text
        cout << "\nThe first line of text after the middle"
             << " of the file is:\n\t'"
             << buffer << "'\n";
}
```

The function `ifstream::getline(char*, int)` fetches an entire line of text from a file, replacing the new-line character with a null terminator. The stream pointer is advanced with each call, so that successive lines of text are fetched. In the loop that counts the number of lines in the file, the `eof` flag is set when the end-of-file is reached. This flag remains set until it is reset explicitly, even if a successful seek to the beginning of the file is performed. This seems a bit awkward to me, but that's how it is. To clear the `eof` flag, I used the call

```
// clear all status flags
file. clear();
```

This clears all the bits in `ios::state` except for the `hardfail` bit. To move around in the file, I used `ifstream::seekg(long, seek_dir)`. This function allows complete freedom of movement. Its counterpart `ifstream::tellg()` reports the current position of the stream pointer.

Class *ios*

The `ios` class is the point of departure for the entire stream hierarchy. Actually, the stream library contains two class hierarchies: a small one based on `streambuf`, and a big one based on `ios`. Figures 7.3 and 7.4 split the `ios` hierarchy into two parts for clarity.

Class `ios` doesn't do much by itself, but it maintains all the flags used in processing normal stream I/O. These flags indicate the following types of information:

- File errors
- Status conditions
- Formatting flags

Class `ios` is not really operational until it is associated with an object derived from class `streambuf`. To build an `ios` object to manage files, you associate an `ios` with a `filebuf` object, which has the methods for handling file reading, writing, opening, and closing. A `filebuf` is a specialized type of `streambuf` that is passed around within the `ios` class functions using a pointer to `streambuf`. The polymorphic `streambuf` functions (which are overridden by `filebuf`) do all the work.

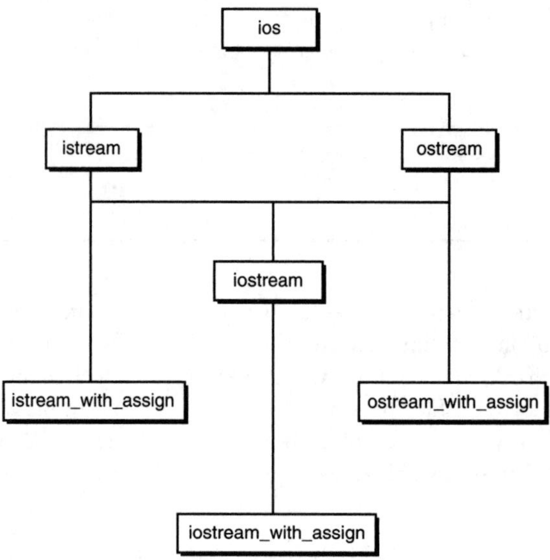

Figure 7.3. The upper part of the `ios` *hierarchy.*

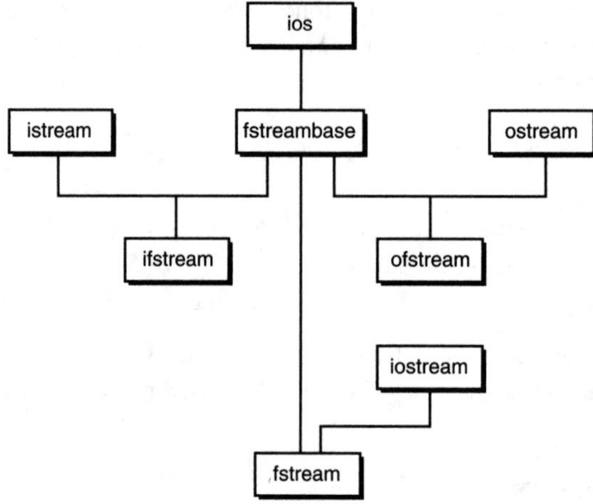

Figure 7.4. The lower part of the `ios` *hierarchy.*

An important feature of class `ios` is that it recognizes that the flags it supports are not always sufficient to represent every possible stream. For this reason, it provides a mechanism for declaring special user flags, which are then manipulated by `ios` class users directly. These flags are stored in a dynamically allocated array, so the number of flags you can define is practically unlimited. Here is an edited version of the entire declaration of class `ios`:

class ios {

private:

```
static long nextbit;
```

This `static` member variable indicates the value of the last allocated flag bit.

```
static int usercount;
```

This `static` member variable indicates how many words have been allocated to the array `userwords`. Each new user word is assigned a unique index, starting from 0. This index is then used to access a user word in the array `userwords`. Indices are in the range 0..0x7FFF. Class `ios` starts out with a `usercount` value of 0. Each time you request the class to allocate a new word, the count is incremented. User words are allocated inside class `ios` for the purpose of storing user information that supposedly is related to class `ios`. Later, I show an example of the employment of user words in an actual program.

```
union ios_user_union *userwords;
```

This `private` variable is the pointer to the base of the dynamic array that is allocated for the storage of user words. The following is the declaration for `union`:

`ios_user_union`:

```
union ios_user_union {
  long lword;
  void *pword;
};
```

Each entry in the array can therefore be used to store a `long` integer or a generic pointer.

```
int nwords;
```

This variable indicates the size of the dynamic array allocated for the storage of user words. If you don't explicitly create any user words, this value is 0.

```
void usersize(int size);
```

This function allocates storage for user words. The `size` argument indicates the size of the dynamic array to be allocated. If an array already exists and is expanded through a call to this function, the contents of the old array are copied into the new array.

```
ios(ios&);
```

This `private` constructor is declared but not defined anywhere. Its purpose is to prevent your code from using a copy constructor with class `ios`. Declaring a function without defining it is a common trick used in the `iostream` library to restrict the way users can manipulate the library classes.

```
void operator= (ios&);
```

This `private` operator is defined and not declared, so that your code can't use the assignment operator with class `ios`.

public:

The following bits show the status of the last operation attempted on a stream. These bits are used with `ios::state`, `ios::ispecial`, and `ios::ospecial`.

```
enum io_state   {
  goodbit  = 0x00,  // everything is okay
  eofbit   = 0x01,  // end of file reached
  failbit  = 0x02,  // last operation failed somehow
  badbit   = 0x04,  // illegal operation was attempted
  hardfail = 0x80   // some kind of fatal stream error
};
```

These bits indicate how a stream was opened. The bits are stored in the `protected` variable `filebuf::mode`. The `filebuf` is referenced through `ios::bp`.

```
enum open_mode  {
```

`in    = 0x01,`	Stream for input only.
`out   = 0x02,`	Stream for output only.
`ate   = 0x04,`	The stream seek pointer is set to the end of the stream (at end). No more input is available, and outputting results in appending to the stream.
`app   = 0x08,`	The stream is opened for appending. All writing appends data at the end of the stream.
`trunc= 0x10,`	This flag causes the stream to be truncated to a length of 0 if it already exists.
`nocreate = 0x20,`	The stream open command must fail if the file indicated doesn't exist.
`noreplace= 0x40,`	The stream open command must fail if the file indicated already exists.

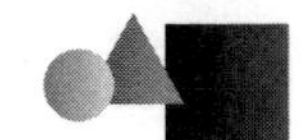

`binary = 0x80`	The stream is opened in binary mode. In this mode, the stream is assumed to contain data other than text information. If this flag is not set, the stream is assumed to contain text data, which is typically organized by lines. Most functions reading text files expect each line to be terminated by a new-line character.

```
};
```

The following bits determine the direction of a stream seek. The bits are not stored anywhere in class `ios`.

```
enum seek_dir {
  beg = 0,        seek from the beginning of the stream.

  cur = 1,        seek from the current stream position.

  end = 2         seek from the end of the stream.
};
```

The following flags control stream I/O formatting. The flags are stored in `ios::x_flags`.

```
enum {
```

`skipws = 0x0001,`	Indicates to skip over white space during input operations. White space is the set of characters that causes the ANSI C function `isspace(int)` to return a nonzero value. This set includes spaces, tabs, carriage returns, line feeds, and form feeds.
`left = 0x0002,`	Causes stream output to be left-aligned.
`right = 0x0004,`	Causes output to be right-aligned.
`internal = 0x0008,`	This formatting flag affects only the way floating-point numbers are handled. The flag causes padding characters to be inserted after a sign or base indicator and before the value itself.
`dec = 0x0010,`	Indicates that input data will be in decimal. Output is also expected to be in decimal.
`oct = 0x0020,`	Indicates that input and output data will be in octal.

`hex = 0x0040,`	Indicates that input and output data will be in hexadecimal.
`showbase = 0x0080,`	Forces a base indicator to be inserted on output, when numeric values are being handled.
`showpoint = 0x0100,`	Forces a decimal point always to be shown for the output of floating-point numbers.
`uppercase = 0x0200,`	Forces any nonnumeric characters that appear in numbers to be inserted as uppercase. This includes the *x* character when it is used as a hexadecimal base indicator, the *e* used for floating-point exponents, and the characters *a..f* in the hex character set.
`showpos = 0x0400,`	Forces the + sign to be used with positive numbers. Normally a sign is used only with negative numbers.
`scientific = 0x0800,`	Forces the use of scientific notation when handling floating-point numbers. Thus, the number *1234.5* would be inserted into an output stream as *1.2345E3*. The *E* character will be inserted in uppercase if the uppercase flag is set.
`fixed = 0x1000,`	Forces the use of fixed-point format when handling floating-point numbers.
`unitbuf = 0x2000,`	Causes the stream to use a "unit-sized" buffer, meaning that the stream is flushed after every insertion.
`stdio = 0x4000`	Forces the flushing of `cout`, `cerr`, and `clog` after insertions.

```
};
```

```
static  const long basefield;    dec ¦ oct ¦ hex
static  const long adjustfield;  left ¦ right ¦ internal
static  const long floatfield;   scientific ¦ fixed
```

These constants indicate bit fields for flags stored in the variable `ios::x_flags`. The constants are used as the second argument in calls to `setf(long, long)`. The description for this function appears later in the header file for class `ios`. The following values `OR`ed together refer to the value of the constants.

```
ios(streambuf*);
```

This constructor takes a pointer to an object derived from `streambuf`. Usually this object will be either an `strstreambuf` or a `filebuf`. The stream is initialized and attached to the given `streambuf` derivative.

```
virtual ~ios();
```

This `virtual` destructor does nothing except delete the `dynamic` storage allocated to user flags (if any were set up) and clear out `static` data members.

```
long flags();
```

This function returns the value of the variable `ios::x_flags`.

```
long flags(long f);
```

This function sets `ios::x_flags` to a new value `f`, and returns the previous value of `x_flags`.

```
long setf(long s, long f);
```

This function uses a parameter `f`, interpreted as a bit field. It sets to 1 those bits in `ios::x_flags` that are set in parameter `s` and are contained in the bit field `f`. All bits in parameter `s` that are zero but are contained in the bit field `f` are cleared. For example

```
s = 0x0080
f = 0x0FF0
```

causes bit 7 to be set in `ios::x_flags`, because it is set in parameter `s` and in the bit field `f`. Bits 4..6 and bits 8..11 are cleared because they are cleared in parameter `s`, but are set in bit field `f`. Here is the equivalent code that updates `ios::x_flags` inside `ios::setf(long, long)`:

```
x_flags &= ~f;          // clear all bits in the field f
x_flags |= (s & f);     // set the required bits on
```

Function `ios::setf(long, long)` returns the previous value of `ios::x_flags`, ANDed with the field `f`. The parameter `f` is typically one of the following bit fields:

`basefield`	For setting the base to use decimal, octal, and hexadecimal.
`adjustfield`	For setting the alignment of a value inside a field to left-aligned, right-aligned, or padded internally.
`floatfield`	For setting the way floating-point values are represented: either in scientific notation or with a fixed decimal point.

The value returned by `ios::setf(long, long)` is the old value of `ios::x_flags` ANDed with the parameter `f`.

```
long setf(long s);
```

Sets bits in `ios::x_flags`. The bits set are those set to 1 in parameter `s`. Bits that are 0 in `s` leave the corresponding bits in `ios::x_flags` unchanged. The value returned is the old value of `ios::x_flags` ANDed with `s`.

```
long unsetf(long s);
```

Clears bits in `ios::x_flags`. The bits cleared are those set to 1 in parameter `s`. Bits that are 0 in `s` leave the corresponding bits in `ios::x_flags` unchanged. The value returned is the old value of `ios::x_flags` ANDed with `s`.

```
int width();
```

Returns the value currently stored in `ios::xwidth`.

```
int width(int);
```

Sets `ios::xwidth` to a new value and returns the old value. The default width is 0, meaning that no padding occurs.

```
char fill();
```

Returns the current character to be used in padding. Padding is used whenever the width of a variable to be inserted into a stream is less than the field width. The default field width is 0, which disables padding.

```
char fill(char);
```

Sets `ios::x_fill` to a given character and returns the previous fill character. The specified character will be used any time it becomes necessary to pad a data value during stream insertion.

```
int precision();
```

Returns the number of digits used when inserting floating point numbers into an output stream. The value is kept in `ios::x_precision`.

```
int precision(int);
```

Sets `ios::x_precision` to a given value and returns the previous value. Changing `ios::x_precision` allows you to set the desired number of decimal digits to use with floating-point numbers.

```
ostream* tie(ostream*);
```

Ties the `ios` object to an output stream. A pointer to the previous tied output stream is returned. A tied output stream is flushed when the `ios`'s `streambuf` needs characters (that is, when it underflows), or when the `streambuf` is flushed.

```
ostream* tie();
```

This function returns the current output stream tied to the `ios` object.

```
int rdstate();
```

This returns the value of `ios::state`.

```
int eof();
```

This returns nonzero if the `eofbit` bit is set in `ios::state`, allowing expressions like

```
if (some_stream.eof() )
  // end of file detected
```

```
int fail();
```

This function returns nonzero if one or more of the following bits in `ios::state` are set:

```
failbit
badbit
hardfail
```

```
int bad();
```

This function returns nonzero if the `badbit` or `hardfail` bits are set in `ios::state`, which allows expressions such as

```
if (some_stream.bad() )
  // errors occurred
```

```
int good();
```

This returns nonzero if no `state` bits are set, allowing expressions such as

```
if (some_stream. good() )
  // no errors on stream
```

```
void clear(int s = 0);
```

This function sets the flags in `ios::state` to a given value `s`, without changing the `hardfail` bit. The name of this function is something of a misnomer, because the function sets flags as well as clears them.

```
operator void* ();
```

This operator returns 0 if `ios::fail()` returns nonzero. Otherwise, the `this` pointer for the `ios` object is returned. This operator makes it possible to use a stream name directly in an expression such as

```
if (some_stream)
  // no errors on some_stream
```

```
int operator! ();
```

This overloaded operator returns the value returned by `ios::fail()`, allowing you to use the name of a stream in expressions such as

```
if (!some_stream)
  // errors pending on some_stream
```

```
streambuf* rdbuf();
```

This function returns the pointer to the `streambuf` that is connected to the `ios` object. This `streambuf` pointer is stored in `ios::bp`.

```
static long bitalloc();
```

This function determines the value of the next available bit for a user flag. The highest bit number allowed is 31. If no more bits are available, a 0 is returned. Otherwise, the bit number (in the range 15..31) is returned. The first 16 bits (0..15) are reserved by the `ios` class. All flag bits (those for the user and those reserved by class `ios`) are allocated in the variable `ios::x_flags`.

```
static int xalloc();
```

This function allocates a new index for a user word. You need to call this function every time you need a new user word. The index returned can then be used to index into the `ios::userwords` array, where the user word is actually stored.

```
long& iword(int i);
```

This function returns a reference to the `i`th user word, considering the word to contain a long integer. If the index `i` is beyond the end of the currently allocated array of user words, a new array is allocated and the old array is copied into it. The value for the index `i` must have been obtained through a call to the function `ios::xalloc()`. Attempting to access an index that hasn't been allocated yet by `ios::xalloc()` results in an error, which is indicated by a null return value.

```
void*& pword(int);
```

This function is like the previous one, except a user word is returned, which is considered to be a pointer instead of a long integer.

```
static void sync_with_stdio();
```

This function empties the standard streams. The operation can be performed only once. Additional attempts are ignored. The purpose is to synchronize the ANSI C `stdio` streams with the `iostream` streams in programs that use both simultaneously.

```
int skip(int);
```

This function is obsolete. It was used in the old 1.2 stream implementation. Its main purpose was to set or reset the `ios::skipws` flag in `ios::x_flags` and the `ios::skipping` flag in `ios::ispecial`.

`protected:`

```
streambuf* bp;
```

This member variable points to the `filebuf` or `strstreambuf` (if any) that is associated with the `ios` object. No useful operations are possible with an `ios` that doesn't have some kind of `streambuf` derivative associated to it.

```
ostream* x_tie;
```

This points to an output stream that is "tied" to the `ios` object. If a stream is tied to an `ios`, the stream is flushed when the `ios`'s `streambuf` underflows or is flushed.

```
int state;
```

This variable contains the flags that indicate the outcome of the last access to an `ios` object. The flags are defined in the `enum ios::io_state`, and are

```
goodbit
eofbit
failbit
badbit
hardfail
```

See the preceding definition of `ios::io_state` for a description of each flag.

```
  int ispecial;
obsolete status bits for 1.2 streams.

  int ospecial;
more obsolete bits from 1.2 streams.
  long x_flags;
```

These are the basic formatting flags for I/O. They are defined in the untagged `enum` described previously, which has the following flags:

```
skipws
left
right
internal
dec
oct
hex
showbase
showpoint
uppercase
showpos
scientific
fixed
unitbuf
stdio
```

```
int x_precision;
```

This indicates the number of digits to use when outputting floating-point numbers.

```
int x_width;
```

This indicates the width of a field that is used to output a variable (such as a floating-point number).

```
int x_fill;
```

This is the character to use for padding. Padding is used when the width of a variable is less than the field set for it.

```
ios();
```

This constructor builds an `ios` object; however, the object has no associated `filebuf` or other `streambuf` derivative. Without some kind of `streambuf` to handle, you can't really do anything with an `ios`. Even the `ios` data members are left uninitialized by this constructor.

```
void init(streambuf*);
```

This function attaches a `filebuf` or `strstreambuf` (passed through a pointer to `streambuf`) to an `ios` object, then initializes the non-`static` data members of the class.

```
void setstate(int s);
```

This function assigns the value `s` to the variable `ios::state`. This function differs from `ios::clear(int)` because it also affects the `hardfail` bit in `ios::state`.

```
static void (*stdioflush)();
```

This function is presumably a pointer to the function that is to be used for flushing the standard streams, which is something that is done in `ios::sync_with_stdio()`. I say *presumably* because I haven't been able to document any actual use for this pointer.

```
};
```

Using Class *ios*

There is little need to instantiate class `ios`. The operation of its user flags is rather obscure, however. To illustrate some of the ways you can manipulate the user words and user flags in class `ios`, in this section I'll derive a class from `ios` and set up two extra user features in it. The class, which I call `CharacterStream`, could be extended to support file operations for reading and writing. The class is capable of automatically converting its text data to uppercase or lowercase. In addition, it has the ability to filter out specific characters in the text stream. The characters to be removed are stored in a character string, which is referenced in the `ios` user area. The user of a `CharacterStream` object indicates the flag values by passing appropriate parameters to the class constructor. Listing 7.34 is the implementation for class `CharacterStream`.

Listing 7.34. `CharacterStream` is a class derived from `ios`.

```
#include <fstream.h>
#include <string.h>

class CharacterStream: public ios {

  int character_index;      // index into user flags
  int filter_index;         // index into user flags
  long special_stream_flag; // one bit only is used

public:
   enum cs_case {
     any_case,
     upper_case,
     lower_case,
     filter
   };
   CharacterStream(filebuf*,
                   cs_case = any_case,
                   char* = 0);
};

CharacterStream::CharacterStream(filebuf* fb,
                                 cs_case mode,
                                 char* filter_string)
                 : ios(fb)
{
      // find index for user flags
      character_index = xalloc();

      // extend the user flag area, and set a user flag
      iword(character_index) = mode;

      // allocate a bit for a user flag
      special_stream_flag = bitalloc();

      // set the user flag to the proper state
      if (special_stream_flag) {
        if (mode != any_case)
          setf(special_stream_flag);
        else
```

```
            // this isn't really necessary, but I show it
            // for completeness
            unsetf(special_stream_flag);
        }

        // setup filter characters if requested
        if (mode == filter) {

          // find index for user flags
          filter_index = xalloc();

          // extend the user flags and save string pointer
          pword(filter_index) = filter_string;
        }
}
```

The function `ios::xalloc()` returns the index of the next available user word, and the value is used in the call to `ios::iword(int)` to create storage for the user flag. The word is then set to a specific value. User words can be of two kinds in Borland C++: long integers and pointers to void. Listing 7.34 uses both kinds, via the functions `ios::iword(int)` and `ios::pword(int)`. Note that a reference is returned by these two functions. *Never* store the value of these references to use them later. The storage referenced is dynamically allocated, and can be moved around at any time by class `ios` if additional storage is needed for user words. If you build a class in which large amounts of storage are required for user words, it would be best to allocate this storage dynamically inside your class, and to save only a pointer to it in the user word area. The largest index into a user word area is limited to 0x7FFF, because a signed `int` is used for this purpose.

Class `ios` uses a number of built-in flags for formatting, file control, and error reporting. These flags are assigned to a `static` long integer, which in Borland C++ equates to a 32-bit value. Having a `static` store the flag information indicates that all `ios` objects share the same flags. Class `ios` uses only the first 16 of these bits, so 16 bits are left over for user flags. There is also a built-in procedure for allocating these leftover bits for your own flags, in a way that allows all `ios` objects to set up their own user flags without interfering with each other. The only limitation is that a total of 16 user flag bits are available. To get the number of the next available user flag bit, you call the function `ios::bitalloc()`. If a nonzero value is returned, that's the value of the user flag you can use. In Listing 7.34, I didn't really need a user flag, because all the information about the stream conversions is stored in the user words. I added the user flag for completeness. To set or clear a user flag, you use the same procedure as you do for the built-in flags: You use the functions `ios::setf(long)` and `ios::unsetf(long)`.

Class *iostream*

Class `iostream` is a general I/O stream that is capable of supporting formatted and unformatted operations on objects that are derived from `streambuf`. The class is simply the combination of `istream` and `ostream`. It really provides no additional features besides those already supported by its base classes. Here is an edited version of its declaration:

```
class iostream : public istream, public ostream {
```

```
protected:
```

```
iostream();
```

This constructor builds an `iostream` that has limited use until it is associated with some kind of `streambuf` object. It is designed for use with standard stream classes that are derived from `iostream`.

```
public:
```

```
iostream(streambuf* s);
```

This builds an `iostream` object and attaches it to a `streambuf` for immediate use. The pointer `s` typically references a `filebuf` (for file operations) or an `strstreambuf` (for inmemory operations).

```
virtual ~iostream();
```

This destructor doesn't do anything by itself. It is designed to be overridden in derived classes.

```
};
```

Deriving a Circular FIFO from *iostream*

Because the class has so many features built into it, it makes sense to use it as a base class. Lots of power can be obtained with minimal code. Consider using the `CircularFIFO` class described in Listing 7.35 to build a stream. Such a stream is attractive because it has FIFO architecture and the insertion and extraction operators.

Listing 7.35. Deriving a circular FIFO stream class from `iostream`.

```
#include <iostream.h>

class CircularFIFO: public streambuf {

      char* buffer;      // fifo ring buffer
      int size;          // size of buffer

      int overflow(int);
      int underflow();

public:

      CircularFIFO(int size);
      ~CircularFIFO() {delete buffer;}
      IsEmpty();
      IsFull();
};

CircularFIFO::CircularFIFO(int s) : streambuf()
{
      // allocate a buffer of the requested size, and
      // attach it to the strstream
      buffer = new char [size];
      setbuf(buffer, s);
      size = s;

      // initialize put and get areas: no putback area
      // in get area
      setp(buffer, &buffer [size] );
      setg(buffer, buffer, &buffer [size] );
}

// this function is called when the put pointer hits the
// end of the buffer
int CircularFIFO::overflow(int c)
{
      // report error if FIFO is full
      if (IsFull() ) return EOF;

      // wrap the put pointer back to the beginning
      setp(base(), ebuf() );

      // and store the character and advance the put
      return sputc(c);
}

// this function is called when the get pointer hits the
// end of the buffer
```

continues

Listing 7.35. continued

```
int CircularFIFO::underflow()
{
      // report error if FIFO is empty
      if (IsEmpty() ) return EOF;

      // wrap the get pointer back to the beginning,
      // leaving no putback area
      setg(base(), base(), ebuf() );

      // retrieve the next character and advance the get
      // pointer
      return sgetc();
}

// see if the FIFO is empty
int CircularFIFO::IsEmpty()
{
      return (gptr() == pptr() ) ? 1 : 0;
}

// see if the FIFO is full
CircularFIFO::IsFull()
{
      if (gptr() == base() )
        return (pptr() == ebuf() ) ? 1 : 0;
      else
        return (pptr() == gptr() - 1) ? 1 : 0;
}

class ioCircularFIFOstream: public iostream {

public:

      ioCircularFIFOstream(CircularFIFO* cf)
      : iostream(cf) {}
      int IsFull()  {
        return ( (CircularFIFO*)rdbuf() )->IsFull();}
      int IsEmpty() {
        return ( (CircularFIFO*)rdbuf() )->IsEmpty();}
};
```

The functions are all coded `inline`, insulating the user from FIFO details without incurring runtime penalties. The constructor merely passes a pointer to a FIFO to the base class. An additional constructor might be designed to take no parameters, thus using a dynamically allocated FIFO. The last two functions in class `ioCircularFIFOstream` give back the status of the FIFO. Using the stream class is straightforward. Listing 7.36 is an example.

Listing 7.36. A short program that uses the circular FIFO I/O stream.

```
void main()
{
      // create a circular FIFO
      CircularFIFO fifo(10);

      // associate the FIFO with a stream
      ioCircularFIFOstream rendez_vous(&fifo);

      char c = '0';
      char d;

      // cycle through the FIFO stream
      for (int i = 0; i < 40; i++, c++) {

        // insert data into the FIFO
        if (rendez_vous.IsFull() ) return;
        rendez_vous << c;

        // extract data from the FIFO
        if (rendez_vous.IsEmpty() ) return;
        int j;
        rendez_vous >> d;

        // display the results
        cout << "\n Value " << i << " = " << d;
      }
}
```

Characters are put into the stream, fetched, and displayed. The `for` loop cycles enough times to run the FIFO `get` and `put` pointers through the buffer several times, which proves that the wrap-around behavior of class `CircularFIFO` is working correctly. I tested the class only with the character inserter and extractor, so I can't guarantee that it works correctly with all other inserters and extractors.

Class *iostream_withassign*

The `iostream_withassign` class is similar in nature to a combination of `istream_withassign` and `ostream_withassign`, but it is not derived from either of them. Class `iostream_withassign` is derived from `iostream`, and adds a couple of overloaded operators to its base class. There is no use for `iostream_withassign` in the stream hierarchy, but it was defined nonetheless for completeness. Here is an edited version of `iostream_withassign`'s declaration:

```
class iostream_withassign : public iostream {
```

```
public:
```

```
iostream_withassign();
```

This constructor does nothing except call its base class constructor.

```
virtual ~iostream_withassign();
```

This `virtual` destructor does nothing, and is designed to be overridden in derived classes.

```
iostream_withassign& operator= (ios&);
```

This associates an `iostream_withassign` object with the `streambuf` used by an `ios` object. This leads to more than one object handling the same `streambuf`, a situation that could be dangerous if one of the objects destroys the `streambuf` without the others knowing about it.

```
iostream_withassign& operator= (streambuf*);
```

This operator associates an `iostream_withassign` object directly with a `streambuf` object, which is typically a `filebuf` or an `strstreambuf`.

```
};
```

Class *istream*

The `istream` class supports the basic operations for stream input. Streams typically are connected to a file (through a `filebuf` pointer) or a memory buffer (through an `strstreambuf` pointer). Class `istream` was part of the original stream package; however, AT&T release 2.0 significantly changed the class. Borland C++ version 4 provides both the old and the new parts for `istream`. I won't discuss the obsolete functions left over from release 1.2. Borland states that these may no longer be supported in future releases of Borland C++.

The greatest change in the implementation of `istream` was brought about by the introduction of multiple inheritance. Multiple inheritance made it possible to separate completely the input classes from the output classes. Class `istream` is near the root of the stream class hierarchy, and for this reason is declared `virtual`. The main function of `istream` is to extract data from a stream. The overloaded >> operator serves this purpose, providing for characters, `long`s, `double`s, and all the other built-in types. You can use class `istream` directly to implement a read-only file object, as is shown later. The following shows an edited version of the declaration for class `istream`, with the obsolete stream features deleted. In the following comments, and for C++ streams in general, an extraction operation is not necessarily the same as a `get` operation.

`class istream : virtual public ios {`

`private:`

```
int gcount_;
```

This indicates the number of characters read during the last unformatted extraction operation.

```
signed char do_get();
```

This function obtains the next character from the input stream. It is a low-level function that is used by other extractor functions and operators.

`protected:`

```
istream();
```

This constructor sets up an input stream with no `streambuf` object attached to it. The `istream` object is essentially useless until it is associated with an object derived from a `streambuf`, typically either a `filebuf` or an `strstreambuf`.

```
void eatwhite();
```

This function consumes white space characters from the `istream`. (White space is the set of characters that includes tabs, new-line characters, form feeds, and so on.)

`public:`

```
istream(streambuf* s);
```

This function creates an `istream` and attaches a `streambuf` object to it. The pointer to `streambuf` actually either points to a `filebuf` or an `strstreambuf` object. A `filebuf` is used for files, and an `strstreambuf` is used for in-memory streams.

```
virtual ~istream();
```

This destructor does nothing because no `dynamic` storage was allocated inside class `istream`. At runtime, the `virtual` mechanism locates the destructor for classes that are derived from `istream`.

```
int ipfx(int count = 0);
```

This is known as the `input prefix` function. It is called every time something needs to be extracted from the stream. The function provides for flushing of any output stream that has been tied to the `istream` object. What occurs when you flush a stream depends on what type of `streambuf` is attached to the stream. For file streams, flushing causes all buffered characters to be written to the file. If the parameter `count` is 0, flushing occurs unconditionally. If `count` is nonzero, flushing occurs only if the `get` area of the `istream`'s `streambuf` contains less than `count` characters. The function is called `prefix` because the flushing occurs *before* characters are extracted from the `istream`.

```
int ipfx0();
```

This invokes `istream::ipfx(int)` with a 0 argument; thus, a tied output stream always will be flushed.

```
int ipfx1();
```

This invokes `istream::ipfx(int)` with the argument set to 1. Thus, a tied output stream will be flushed only if no characters are in `istream`'s `streambuf` buffer.

```
void isfx();
```

This is known as the `input suffix` function, and it is currently unused. Presumably the function will be used to support operations that are required *after* data is extracted from an `istream`. I say *presumably* because I have not been able to document any uses for the `input suffix` function.

```
istream& seekg(long p);
```

This function positions the stream's `get` pointer to the offset `p` from the beginning of the stream. If the `istream` is connected to a `filebuf`, the operation entails performing a file seek. If the `istream` is connected to an `strstreambuf`, a memory pointer is adjusted. Input streams are not equipped with `put` pointers.

```
istream& seekg(long p, seek_dir point);
```

This function is similar to the previous one, except that the stream seek destination is relative to a point `p`, which can be one of the following: `ios::beg`, `ios::cur`, or `ios::end`. This arrangement allows the seek to start from the beginning, the current place, or the end of the stream. Positive values for `p` advance the `get` pointer toward the end of the stream. Negative values move it toward the beginning.

```
long tellg();
```

This returns the current value of the `istream` `get` pointer.

```
int sync();
```

This function's purpose depends on the type of `streambuf` object associated with an `istream`. For `filebufs`, function `istream::sync()` flushes the `put` area of the buffer to disk and throws away any characters waiting in the `get` area. The value returned is 0 if no errors occur when flushing data to disk, and EOF if errors do occur. When the `streambuf` attached to an `istream` is an `strstreambuf`, function `istream::sync()` only checks the state of the buffer. The function returns 0 if no characters are present either in the `get` or the `put` areas, and EOF otherwise.

```
istream& get(signed char* buffer,
             int size,
             char delimiter = '\n');
```

This function extracts (reads) characters from an `istream` and copies them into a buffer. No formatting is done during the copying. The operation stops when the end of the file is reached, when `size` characters have been copied, or when the delimiter character that is indicated is found. This delimiter is *not* copied, and is left in the `istream` `streambuf`. The buffer is always null terminated.

```
istream& get(unsigned char* buffer,
             int size,
             char delimiter = '\n');
```

Same as the previous function, except that it uses a buffer of unsigned `chars` to store the characters that are read.

```
istream& read(signed char* buffer, int size);
```

Similar to the previous function, except no delimiter is provided and the buffer is *not* null terminated. The function is used to read blocks of binary data. The number of characters read is stored in `istream::gcount_`.

```
istream& read(unsigned char*, int);
```

Same as the previous function, but with unsigned `chars`.

```
istream& getline(signed char* buffer,
                 int size,
                 char delimiter = '\n');
```

This function is essentially the same as `istream::get(signed char*, int, char)`, except that the delimiter is extracted from the `istream` (but it is not copied into the buffer). The buffer is null terminated. This is the primary function for extracting lines of text from an input stream.

```
istream& getline(unsigned char* buffer,
                 int size,
                 char  delimiter = '\n');
```

This function is the same as the previous function, except for the fact that this function uses unsigned `char`s.

```
istream& get(streambuf& s, char delimiter = '\n');
```

This function copies data from an `istream` into a `streambuf`, stopping on the EOF or when a delimiter is encountered. The delimiter is not copied, and is left in the `istream` `streambuf`. No null terminating is performed on the `streambuf s`.

```
istream& get(unsigned char& c);
```

This reads a single character from an `istream` into a character variable. If errors occur, `c` is set to the value 0xFF.

```
istream& get(signed char&);
```

Same as the previous function, except for the fact that this one uses signed `char`s.

```
int get();
```

This function extracts the next available character from the `istream` or EOF if the end of the file is encountered.

```
int peek();
```

This function returns the next character that is available in the `istream` without removing that character from the `istream`. This allows you to check the next character without taking it. EOF is returned on end-of-file.

```
int gcount();
```

This returns the number of characters read during the last unformatted extraction. All the extractors that were listed previously (such as `istream::get()`, `istream::getline(signed char*, int, char)`, and so on) are unformatted.

```
istream& putback(char c);
```

The character `c` is put back into the `get` area of `istream`'s `streambuf`, if there is room.

```
istream& ignore(int count = 1, int target = EOF);
```

This function extracts characters from an `istream` and throws them away until one of the following conditions occurs:

- The function has extracted `count` characters.
- The character `target` has been found.
- End-of-file is encountered.

```
istream& operator>> (istream& (*_f)(istream&));
```

This is a general-purpose operator. It is provided to support the use of stream manipulators that act on `istream` settings.

```
istream& operator>> (ios& (*_f)(ios&) );
```

This operator is similar to the previous one, except that it handles manipulators that deal with `ios` settings.

```
istream& operator>> (streambuf* s);
```

This operator copies characters from an `istream` into a designated `streambuf s`, starting from the current position in the stream. The operator stops copying when either the `istream` or the `streambuf` reaches the end-of-file.

The following operators extract a single type of object from an `istream`. Formatting is performed as is appropriate, and as is indicated by the various flags in `ios::x_flags`.

```
istream& operator>> (signed char*);
istream& operator>> (unsigned char*);
istream& operator>> (unsigned char&);
istream& operator>> (signed char&);
```

```
istream& operator>> (short&);
istream& operator>> (int&);
istream& operator>> (long&);
istream& operator>> (unsigned short&);
istream& operator>> (unsigned int&);
istream& operator>> (unsigned long&);
istream& operator>> (float&);
istream& operator>> (double&);
istream& operator>> (long double&);
```

```
};
```

Using Class *istream*

As for the other stream classes, I provide a short example of the usage of `istream`. Listing 7.37 creates a `filebuf`, attaches it to a file, and then attaches the `filebuf` to an `istream`. It would be rare to see this done in a real-world program because class `ifstream` supports all these steps transparently. What is important in the example is the procedure of connecting a `filebuf` to an `istream`. If you create your own class that is derived from `streambuf`, `filebuf`, or `strstreambuf`, you can set up a formatted stream class for it through `istream`. You can't do that with `ifstream`, which is designed for `filebuf` objects.

Listing 7.37. Using an `istream` directly with a `filebuf`.

```
#include <fstream.h>

// demonstrate use of class istream
void main()
{
  char buffer [80];
  filebuf directory_file;

  // attach a file to the filebuf object
  if (!directory_file. open("dir.txt", ios::in) ) {
    cout << "\n************************************************"
         << "\n* ERROR...Please create a file called 'DIR.TXT'*"
         << "\n* using the DOS command 'dir > DIR.TXT' and    *"
         << "\n* then try again.                              *"
         << "\n************************************************\n";

    return;
  }

  // create an input stream with an attached file
  istream directory_stream(&directory_file);

  cout << "\n\t************************************************"
```

```
      << "\n\t* This program reads a file called DIR.TXT and *"
      << "\n\t* displays it one line at a time on the screen *"
      << "\n\t***********************************************\n";

  while (1) {
    // read the next line of text with istream::getline()
    directory_stream. getline(buffer, sizeof(buffer) );
    if (directory_stream. eof() )
      // end of file reached
      break;

    // print the line of text on the screen
    cout << "\n" << buffer;
  }

  // no need to close the file explicitly: the destructor
  // for directory_file will handle that automatically.
}
```

The program in Listing 7.37 uses most of its code to print messages on the user display. The part that actually manipulates `filebufs` and `istreams` is short. In fact, the stream-reading operation is performed with the single statement

```
directory_stream. getline(buffer, sizeof(buffer) );
```

which reads a line of text into a buffer. The new-line character at the end of the line is replaced by a `'\0'` character. The input stream also can be read with an extractor operator, such as with the statement

```
directory_stream >> buffer;
```

This statement reads a single string into the buffer and stops when a white space character is found. The function `istream::get(signed char*, int, int)` also can be used, but the new-line character must be consumed separately. For example,

```
// read the next line of text, leaving '\n' in istream
directory_stream. get(buffer, sizeof(buffer) );

// consume the line delimiter
directory_stream. ignore(1, '\n');
```

There is an even quicker way of copying an entire file. It involves the use of `istream::operator>>(streambuf*)`. This function does everything without the need for loops, end-of-file checking, or the insertion of a new-line character. The `while` loop in Listing 7.37 shown previously can be replaced by one line of code.

```
// copy the whole file
directory_stream >> cout.rdbuf();
```

The expression `cout.rdbuf()` returns a pointer to the `streambuf` used by the standard output stream. The function `istream::operator>>(streambuf*)` is then called, and executes until `directory_stream` reaches an end-of-file or until errors of some kind occur.

Class *istream_withassign*

The `istream_withassign` class was designed specifically to declare the standard input stream `cin`. The class is derived from `istream` and differs from it only in its use of two overloaded assignment operators. Here is an edited version of its declaration:

```
class istream_withassign : public istream {
```

```
public:
```

```
istream_withassign();
```

This constructor does nothing except call its base class constructor.

```
virtual ~istream_withassign();
```

This destructor does nothing. It is designed to be overridden in derived classes.

```
istream_withassign& operator= (istream&);
```

This operator associates the `istream_withassign` object with the `streambuf` used by an `istream` object, which leads to more than one object handling the same `streambuf`. This situation could be dangerous if one of the objects destroys the `streambuf` without the other knowing about it. This is not a problem with the standard streams, because all of them are destroyed together after the user program has terminated.

```
istream_withassign& operator= (streambuf* sb);
```

This operator is similar to the previous one, except that it directly associates the `istream_withassign` with a `streambuf`.

```
};
```

Class `istream_withassign` was set up to make defining the standard input stream `cin` more compact and elegant. To bring class `istream_withassign` more into perspective, I'll discuss briefly its use in the definition of the standard input stream `cin`. Here is how `cin` is initially defined:

```
istream_withassign cin;
```

This sets up an `istream_withassign` object with no `filebuf` connected to it. To build a complete `istream_withassign`, you have to define a `filebuf` object like this:

```
static filebuf *stdin_filebuf;
```

This declares a `filebuf` pointer to be used later when constructing `cin`. It must be `static` so that it has internal linkage, and so that it has storage permanently assigned to it (as opposed to an `auto` variable). Using a `static` is important because all the parts that make up `cin` are required *before* the `main()` program is executed. `static` objects guarantee this. Note that the keyword `static` in the declaration of the `filebuf` pointer refers to the pointer, not to the `filebuf`. Before the pointer can be used in constructing a `cin` object, the pointer must be initialized, using a statement like this:

```
stdin_filebuf = new filebuf(F_stdin);
```

This initializes the pointer so that it references a constructed `filebuf`, allocated dynamically from the heap. The value of `F_stdin` alludes to the number of the file descriptor to be used for standard input. The value 0 is used. To complete the declaration of `cin`, a `filebuf` is connected to it using the assignment operator, and `cout` is tied to `cin`. Here are the statements used:

```
cin = stdin_filebuf;
cin.tie(&cout);
```

The last statement ties `cin` with `cout`, so that `cout` is flushed every time a new character is extracted from `cin`. This is important because if your code displays a prompt for the user to input code, you want to be sure the user is shown the message *before* the program waits for a response.

Part of the preceding code is external to any function, whereas part of it is inside the runtime library function `Iostream_init()`. `Iostream_init()` is guaranteed to be invoked before `main()`.

Class *istrstream*

`istrstream` is designed to be instantiated directly by user code. It provides for buffered operations to extract characters from an in-memory string, which makes it similar to the ANSI function `sscanf(...)`. However, class `istrstream` provides considerably more power than `sscanf(...)`. Here are some of the class's features:

- It allows the buffer's `get` pointer to be repositioned.
- An extraction delimiter can be specified.
- An entire line of text can be extracted at once.
- The entire buffer can be made accessible for direct use.

All the preceding operations are provided through the base classes of `istrstream`, so the implementation of the class is almost trivial. Here is an edited version of the header file:

```
class istrstream : public strstreambase, public istream {
```

```
public:
```

```
istrstream(char* string);
```

This constructor takes a pointer to a null-terminated string. The class determines the length of the string and sets up internal `streambuf` buffer pointers accordingly.

```
istrstream(char* buffer, int length);
```

This constructor takes a pointer to a buffer that is not required to be null terminated. The length of the buffer is indicated by `length`. The constructor sets up all the `streambuf` buffer pointers based on this length. This constructor can be used to associate an `istrstream` with a fixed-sized buffer, regardless of whether the buffer is used with binary data or text data.

```
~istrstream();
```

This destructor doesn't do anything directly because the destructors for the base classes take care of all the necessary details.

```
};
```

Notice the absence of a default constructor for class `istrstream`. When an `istrstream` object is constructed, it is meant to allow data to be extracted from a buffer. There are no provisions in the class for putting data into this buffer, so you have to pass a buffer to the class when constructing an `istrstream`.

Using Class *istrstream*

As stated earlier, class `istrstream` is convenient for handling the parsing of in-memory strings or binary data. Listing 7.38 shows an `istrstream` object that is used to parse out the individual words contained in a text string.

Listing 7.38. Using an `istrstream` object to parse the contents of a buffer.

```
#include <strstrea.h>

// use an istrstream for character formatting
void main()
```

```
{
     const int LENGTH = 10;
     const int SIZE = 20;
     char array [LENGTH] [SIZE];

     // initialize an istrstream object
     istrstream text("A new programming language");

     // extract each word into a separate array entry
     for (int i = 0; i < LENGTH; i++) {
       text. get(&array [i] [0], SIZE, ' ');
       text. get();
     }

     // display the parsed words on separate lines
     cout << "\nThe words extracted from the string \""
          << text.rdbuf()->str() << "\"\nare";

     // unfreeze the stream buffer, so it won't be left
     // around in the system when the program terminates
     text.rdbuf()->freeze(0);

     // display the individual words in the stream
     for (int j = 0; j < LENGTH; j++) {
       if (array [j] [0] == '\0') break;
       cout << "\n\t" << &array [j] [0];
     }
}
```

The output produced by this program is the following:

```
The words extracted from the string "A new programming language"

are

A
new

programming
language
```

Note that, in the process of extracting words from the string, the following function call might look redundant:

```
text.get();
```

On the contrary, this function call is important because the previous `text.get(&array [i] [0], SIZE, ' ')` call extracts characters from the `istrstream` only up to the delimiter character (in this case, a space character). The delimiter itself is left in the `istrstream`, so the call `text.get()` is used to remove the delimiter. As an alternative to using `text.get()`, it is possible (and preferable) to use an input stream manipulator. This is how the parsing loop looks with the manipulator:

```
// extract each word into a separate array entry
for (int i = 0; i < LENGTH; i++) {
  text. get(&array [i] [0], SIZE, ' ');
  text >> ws;      // consume the white space
}
```

The last line in the loop uses the manipulator `ws`, applied to an `istrstream`. The use of manipulators makes for a more natural notation when combining operations on streams because manipulators can be put right in the middle of an extraction expression. Manipulators are discussed separately at the end of this chapter.

One of the drawbacks of an `istrstream` object is that it is rather limited in the way it can be written to. But that's pretty much to be expected because the class is defined as an *input* stream. To achieve freedom for both reading and writing, class `strstream` comes to the rescue. I describe it a little bit later in this chapter. The preceding example contains a slightly unusual notation, namely the expression

```
text.rdbuf()->str(),
```

which occurs inside the standard output stream insertion expression. This expression invokes `text.rdbuf()`, which returns a pointer to an `strstreambuf` object. The pointer is then used to invoke `strstreambuf::str()`, which has the side effect of freezing the buffer. It is necessary to unfreeze the buffer explicitly, unless you wish to take over the responsibility for deleting the buffer when you're done using it.

Class *ofstream*

`ofstream` is the cornerstone class for controlling files that are used for output. The class has all the member functions required for manipulating files that are used for writing. You can open, flush, and close a file. Like `ifstream`, `ofstream` handles files through a `filebuf` object that is inherited from the base class `fstreambase`. You can access files both randomly and sequentially. The `ofstream` has overloaded insertion operators for all of the built-in types. Here is an edited version of `ofstream`'s declaration:

`class ofstream : public fstreambase, public ostream {`

`public:`

```
ofstream();
```

This constructor sets up a `filebuf` in preparation to associate it with a file to be opened by a subsequent call to `ofstream::open(...)`.

```
ofstream(const char* n,
         int m = ios::out,
         int p = filebuf::openprot);
```

This constructor builds an `ofstream` object, opens the file `n` for output, and connects a `filebuf` to it. The file name `n` can be a full path name with a drive number and multiple subdirectories, such as the string `c:\\borlandc\\classlib\\include\\bag.h`. The default open mode `m` is `ios::out`. If the file already exists, it is truncated to length 0. Other values can be used for `m`, but they must be a bitwise `OR` combination of the flags that are described under `filebuf::mode`. The access protection level `p` is defaulted. See `filebuf::openprot` for further details.

```
ofstream(int fd);
```

This constructor takes a file descriptor, which is assumed to refer to a file that is already open. The file is then connected to the `ofstream` object.

```
ofstream(int fd, char* buffer, int size);
```

This constructor takes a file descriptor and a buffer of a given size. The file is assumed to be open already. The `ofstream` uses the buffer for its `filebuf`.

```
~ofstream();
```

This destructor does nothing except call the base class destructors.

```
filebuf* rdbuf();
```

This access function returns a pointer to the internal `filebuf` object.

```
void open(const char* n,
          int m = ios::out,
          int p = filebuf::openprot);
```

This function opens a file `n` for output. The file name `n` can be a fully qualified path name, as described in the constructor `ofstream::ofstream(const char*, int, int)`. The default mode for `m` is `ios::out`. If the file already exists, it is truncated to length 0. The access protection level `p` is defaulted. See `filebuf::openprot` for details regarding the protection level.

```
};
```

As for class `ifstream`, `ofstream` doesn't add any code of its own to that of its base classes. All the member functions of `ofstream` pass along arguments to the base classes, adding nothing of their own. Using the default open mode, you get the following results:

1. If the file already exists, it is truncated to length 0. To prevent this from happening, use the open mode bit `ios::ate`, which causes output to the file to occur at the end of the existing file. Using the bit `ios::app` also causes data that is written to be appended at the end of the file. However, there is a difference between `ios::ate` and `ios::app`. If the open mode uses the flag `ios::app`, all data written is appended to the end of the file *regardless* of the `seekp(...)` commands issued. No matter where you try to position the file pointer, data is always appended to the end of the file. With `ios::ate`, the file pointer is initially positioned at the end of the file; however, `seekp(...)` commands can be used to affect where data is subsequently written.
2. The open command succeeds whether the file already exists or not. To prevent the command from opening a pre-existing file, use the open mode bit `ios::noreplace`. To force an error if the file *doesn't* already exist, use the mode bit `ios::nocreate`.

Using Class *ofstream*

Class `ofstream` can be used directly in a program to support writing to files. I show an example that opens a file called *output.txt* for output and writes to it both sequentially and randomly. Data is inserted both in the middle of the file and at the end. I used text only because you can easily display the file or print the results. Listing 7.39 is the code.

Listing 7.39. Using `ofstream` to open a file and write to it.

```
#include <fstream.h>

// open a file for output and access it in various ways
void main()
{
      // open a file for output and truncate it if
      // already exists
      ofstream file("output.txt");
      if (file. bad() ) {
     cout << "\n\t*********************************************"
          << "\n\t* Error: couldn't open file 'output.txt'. *"
          << "\n\t*********************************************\n";
        return;
      }

      // display the initial file size
```

```
        file. seekp(0, ios::end);
        long size = file. tellp();
        cout << "\nThe initial size of file 'output.txt' is "
             << size << " bytes.\n";

        // write some data to the file
        file << "\nFile 'output.txt': \n";

        // copy an entire file into it
        ifstream directory("dir.txt");
        file << directory. rdbuf();

        // extend the file and add text to it
        file. seekp(0, ios::end);
        file << "\nThis was added after the end of the file";

        // insert data in the middle of the file
        file. seekp(0, ios::end);
        long middle = file. tellp() / 2;
        file. seekp(middle);
        file << "\n\nThis was added right in the middle of "
             << "the file\n\n";

        // display the new file size
        file. seekp(0, ios::end);
        size = file. tellp();
        cout << "\nThe ending size of file 'output.txt' is "
             << size << " bytes.\n";
}
```

To see the results of the program, print the file *output.txt*. The program uses `ofstream::seekp(long, seek_dir)` and `ofstream::tellp()` to manipulate the stream pointer. The character `p` in the function names indicates that the `put` pointers are involved. Using random accessing, you can jump around a file at will, which allows you to add data at the end of a file or anywhere else. Note that if you position the `put` pointer of an `ofstream` to any position other than the end of the stream, writing operations overwrite old data in the stream, rather than "pushing it aside." An analogy with a word processor is typing text in the overtype mode rather than in the insert mode.

Class *ostream*

The `ostream` class specializes `ios` to handle output streams. As usual, the `ios` base class is used only to manipulate the stream flags for formatting, errors, and so on. Class `ostream` handles output only. Data flows into a buffer that is referenced through a pointer to `streambuf`. In practice, this pointer references either a `filebuf` object (for files) or an `strstreambuf` object (for in-memory buffers).

The main purpose of ostream is to provide a uniform set of insertion operators for outputting data to a stream. Insertion operators are provided for all the built-in data types to support formatted output. Binary (raw and unformatted) output is also supported. Here is an edited version of the declaration of class ostream:

class ostream : virtual public ios {

private:

```
void outstr(const signed char* data,
            const signed char* prefix);
```

This private function is used by other ostream member functions to output text to the stream. The data argument is output *after* the prefix string. Padding is performed using the fill character that is defined in ios::x_fill. The string is aligned according to ios::x_flags.

protected:

```
int do_opfx();
```

This function is normally called by ostream::opfx() just before outputting data to an output stream. It flushes any stream that is tied to the ostream object. The function's name is an abbreviation of *output prefix.*

```
void do_osfx();
```

This function is normally called by ostream::osfx() after data has been output to a stream. It flushes the ostream buffer (if the buffer is unit buffered) and flushes the standard streams if the ios flags indicate to do so. The function's name is an abbreviation of *output suffix*, before it is called after inserting data into a stream.

```
ostream();
```

This constructor does nothing.

public:

```
ostream(streambuf* s);
```

This constructor takes a streambuf and connects the ostream object to it. The pointer s typically references a filebuf or strstreambuf object.

```
virtual ~ostream();
```

This destructor does nothing except flush the `streambuf` that is attached to the `ostream` object.

```
int opfx();
```

This function is referred to as the `output prefix` function. It normally calls `ostream::do_opfx()` to handle those operations that need to be performed before writing data to the `ostream` object.

```
void osfx();
```

This function is referred to as the `output suffix` function. It normally calls `ostream::do_osfx()` to perform operations that must take place right after writing data to the `ostream` object.

```
ostream& flush();
```

This function flushes the `streambuf` buffer that is associated with the stream object. The flush is performed by calling the member function `sync()` for the `streambuf` object associated with the `ostream`. If any errors occur during the `sync()`, the bit `ios::badbit` is set in the variable `ios::state`.

```
ostream& seekp(long p);
```

This function acts on the `put` area pointer of the `ostream streambuf`. The function performs a seek to the position `p`, which is computed from the beginning of the `streambuf` buffer.

```
ostream& seekp(long displacement, seek_dir s);
```

This performs an operation that is similar to the previous function, except that the `put` pointer is displaced by a certain amount `p` from the reference point `s`. The values for `s` are `ios::beg`, `ios::cur`, and `ios::end` to indicate the beginning, current location, or end of the `streambuf` buffer.

```
long tellp();
```

This function returns the offset of an `ostream`'s `put` pointer from the beginning of the `put` area.

```
ostream& put(char c);
```

This function writes a character `c` to the `ostream`. It is the lowest-level inserter function, it can deal with text or binary data, and it never performs formatting.

```
ostream& write(const signed char* buffer, int size);
```

This function writes the contents of a buffer to the `ostream`. Characters are copied until an error occurs, or `size` characters are transferred. The buffer is copied without formatting. Null characters are not handled differently from others. This function handles block transfers of raw data (binary or text) to an `ostream`.

```
ostream& write(const unsigned char* buffer, int size);
```

This function is similar to the previous one, except that it deals with a buffer of `unsigned` characters.

The following operators support formatting stream insertions for all the built-in data types.

```
ostream& operator<< (signed char c);
ostream& operator<< (unsigned char c);
ostream& operator<< (short);
ostream& operator<< (unsigned short);
ostream& operator<< (int);
ostream& operator<< (unsigned int);
ostream& operator<< (long);
ostream& operator<< (unsigned long);
ostream& operator<< (float);
ostream& operator<< (double);
ostream& operator<< (long double);
ostream& operator<< (const   signed char*);
ostream& operator<< (const unsigned char*);
```

The last two functions write a null-terminated string to an output stream. The null terminator is *not* copied.

```
ostream& operator<< (void*);
```

This is used to write the value of a generic pointer to an `ostream`. A string of the form `0x8f9affa4` is written.

```
ostream& operator<< (streambuf*);
```

This operator inserts data into an `ostream` after extracting it from a `streambuf`. You can use this operator to copy entire files.

```
ostream& operator<< (ostream& (*_f)(ostream&));
```

This is a generic operator that is designed to support stream manipulator functions that act on `ostream` settings.

```
ostream& operator<< (ios& (*_f)(ios&));
```

This is similar to the previous function, except that it handles manipulators that deal with `ios` settings.

```
};
```

Class `istream` declares its base class `ios` to be `virtual`. The reason is that several classes lower in the stream hierarchy support both input and output operations, and thus are derived from both `istream` and `ostream`. The `virtual` keyword ensures that only one copy of the base class `ios` is used in these derived classes.

Using Class *ostream*

Class `ostream` is normally not instantiated directly. It provides a solid base class for `ofstream` and `ostrstream`, supporting many formatted and unformatted writing functions. To illustrate how an `ostream` object could be used to handle file output, I wrote a small program that associates a `filebuf` to an `ostream`, using a file called *dir.txt* to store the current directory. I could have used the Borland class `Directory` rather than the old functions `findfirst(...)` and `findnext(...)` to build the file directory. Listing 7.40 is the program.

Listing 7.40. Using class `ostream` in a user program.

```
#include <fstream.h>
#include <dir.h>

// demonstrate use of class ostream
void main()
{
      char buffer [80];
      filebuf directory_file;

      // attach a file to the filebuf object
      if (!directory_file. open("dir.txt", ios::out) ) {
        cout << "\n Fatal error while creating 'dir.txt'...";
        return;
      }
```

continues

Listing 7.40. continued

```
        // create an output stream with an attached file
        ostream directory_stream(&directory_file);

        cout << "\n\t*************************************************"
             << "\n\t* This program saves the current directory in  *"
             << "\n\t* a file named 'dir.txt'.                       *"
             << "\n\t*************************************************\n";

          // find the pathname of the current directory
          if (getcwd(buffer, sizeof(buffer) ) == 0) {
            cout <<
               "\nFatal error while reading directory...\n";
            return;
          }

          // save the directory path name
          directory_stream << "\n Directory of  "
                           << buffer << "\n\n";

          // save the directory in the file
          struct ffblk file_block;
          if (findfirst("*.*", &file_block, 0) ) {
            directory_stream << "Error accessing directory...";
            return;
          }
          do
            directory_stream << file_block. ff_name << "\n";
          while (!findnext(&file_block) );

        // no need to close the file explicitly: the destructor
        // for directory_file will handle that automatically.
}
```

The program is fairly straightforward. It opens a file, scans the current directory, and saves the file names in the file. If any errors occur, the program terminates with a brief error message. As with the example given with class `istream`, here again it isn't necessary to explicitly close the file *dir.txt* because the destructor for `directory_file` handles that for you.

Class *ostream_withassign*

The `ostream_withassign` class is the exact counterpart for `istream_withassign`. It is designed to make the process of setting up the standard output streams `cout`, `cerr`, and `clog` as straightforward and elegant as possible. Here is an edited version of its declaration:

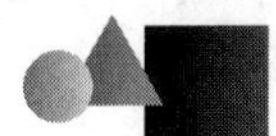

```
class ostream_withassign : public ostream {
```

```
public:
```

```
ostream_withassign();
```

This constructor does nothing except call its base class constructor.

```
virtual ~ostream_withassign();
```

This `virtual` destructor does nothing, and is designed to be overridden in derived classes.

```
ostream_withassign& operator= (ostream&);
```

This associates an `ostream_withassign` object with the `streambuf` used by an `ostream` object. This leads to more than one object handling the same `streambuf`, a situation that could be dangerous if one of the objects destroys the `streambuf` without the other objects knowing about it. In practice, all the standard output streams are destructed together after the `main()` program has terminated.

```
ostream_withassign& operator= (streambuf*);
```

This operator associates an `ostream_withassign` object directly with a `streambuf` object, which is typically a `filebuf`.

```
};
```

Just as I showed the use of `istream_withassign` in setting up the standard input stream `cin`, here I'll show how `ostream_withassign` is used to build the three standard output streams `cout`, `cerr`, and `clog`. Here is how the output streams are initially defined:

```
ostream_withassign cout;
ostream_withassign cerr;
ostream_withassign clog;
```

The three preceding statements set up output streams without connecting them to a `filebuf`. Now some `filebuf` pointers need to be defined so that they can subsequently be used to associate the output streams with `filebuf` objects. Here is how the pointers are defined:

```
static filebuf *stdout_filebuf;
static filebuf *stderr_filebuf;
```

Two `static filebuf` pointers are declared rather than three because `cerr` and `clog` share the same `filebuf`. Before using the pointers, they are initialized with the following statements:

```
stdout_filebuf = new filebuf(F_stdout);
stderr_filebuf = new filebuf(F_stderr);
```

Two filebuf objects are allocated for subsequent use with cout, cerr, and clog. F_stdout is the value that is used as a file descriptor for cout, and its value is 1. The value of F_stderr is 2. Now the filebufs created can be associated with their respective output streams, with the following statements:

```
cout = stdout_filebuf;
clog = stderr_filebuf;
cerr = stderr_filebuf;
```

The overloaded assignment operator is used to elegantly connect a filebuf to each of the standard output streams. Note how cerr and clog share the same filebuf object. The standard streams clog and cerr are required to be in synchronization with cout. The following two statements guarantee this:

```
clog.tie(&cout);
cerr.tie(&cout);
```

The output streams are tied to cout, so that flushing cerr or clog results in cout also being flushed. One last matter of business must be taken care of. It is desirable to have cerr and cout be unit-buffered to force the two streams to be flushed every time a character is written to them. This facilitates synchronization between user prompts and user input. If cerr or cout buffered characters up, an error message or a user prompt may not be displayed immediately on the user display. Here are the statements that turn off buffering for cerr and cout:

```
cerr.setf(ios::unitbuf);
cout.setf(ios::unitbuf);
```

clog is not unit-buffered, which means it behaves as if it were unbuffered.

Class *ostrstream*

Class ostrstream is generally used more often than istrstream because it supports in-memory string formatting, much like the old ANSI sprintf(...) function. In-memory formatting is extremely useful, especially when you are writing user interface code and you can't use stream I/O functions, but instead have to utilize reserved functions. For example, consider writing a message to the screen in a Windows program. With class ostrstream, you can first set up a formatted string in memory, then call the appropriate Windows function to display it.

Class ostrstream inherits all the insertion operators from its base class ostream, so not only can you insert any of the built-in types, but you also can overload the insertion operator to support your own classes. This capability alone makes ostrstream vastly superior to sprintf(...). As for many of the other classes in the stream library that use multiple inheritance, ostrstream is so short that it is trivial. Virtually all of its power is inherited from its base classes `strstreambase` and `ostream`. Here is an edited version of `ostrstream`'s declaration:

```
class ostrstream : public strstreambase, public ostream {
```

```
public:
```

```
ostrstream(char* buffer, int s, int mode = ios::out);
```

This constructor takes a pointer to a buffer of size `s` and connects it to a new `ostrstream` object. Handing a buffer over to the constructor this way is convenient when you are dealing with a pre-existing buffer, and it's also fast. There are drawbacks, however, because this "wires" the `ostrstream` to a buffer of a fixed size, and prevents the `ostrstream` from owning the buffer.

```
ostrstream();
```

This appears to be an almost useless constructor, whereas in fact it is extremely powerful. This constructor sets up an `ostrstream` object with a dynamically allocated buffer. The `ostrstream` is said to *own* the buffer, which can be expanded automatically at runtime if more space is needed.

```
~ostrstream();
```

This destructor deallocates the stream buffer only if the `ostrstream` object owns it.

```
char* str();
```

This returns a pointer to the beginning of the `ostrstream` buffer. Invoking this function automatically freezes the stream buffer, which transfers ownership of the buffer to you. Only if you explicitly unfreeze the buffer with the function `strstreambuf::freeze(0)` will the buffer be deleted when the `ostrstream` object goes out of scope.

```
int pcount();
```

This returns the number of characters inserted into the stream since the buffer was created, or since the last `seekp(...)` operation. Performing a `seekp(...)` on an `ostrstream` buffer that contains characters can lead to unexpected results in the return value of `ostrstream::pcount()`. You can use `ostrstream::pcount()` pretty much as the ANSI function `strlen(char*)` is used with strings, with the proviso that `ostrstream` buffers are not automatically null terminated.

```
};
```

Using Class *ostrstream*

You can use an `ostrstream` object to replace ANSI `sprintf(...)` function calls, with the important advantage that user classes can also be supported. Listing 7.41 shows some in-memory formatting with `sprintf(...)` and `ostrstream`. I pass a buffer to the `ostrstream` constructor to show how you can associate a new `ostrstream` with a pre-existing buffer, even one that has valid data. The constructor does not modify the buffer contents in any way. The class does not destroy the buffer when the `ostrstream` object goes out of scope.

Listing 7.41. Using an `ostrstream` object for in-memory formatting operations.

```
#include <strstrea.h>
#include <stdio.h>

// use an ostrstream for in-memory string formatting
void main()
{
      const int LENGTH = 100;
      char buffer [LENGTH];

      // use the ANSI sprintf(...) function first
      char* cp = "buffer";
      sprintf(buffer, "\nThis %s is %d words long", cp, LENGTH);
      cout << buffer;

      // now go and do the same thing with an ostrstream

      // initialize an istrstream object
      ostrstream text(buffer, LENGTH);

      // format the string in memory, then display it
      text << "\nThis " << cp << " is still "
           << LENGTH
           << " words long" << '\0';
      cout << text.str();
}
```

This program produces the following output:

```
This buffer is 100 words long
This buffer is still 100 words long
```

Notice the explicit insertion of the null terminator into the `ostrstream` object, without which the system would "run off the end of the buffer" when you attempted to display the contents of the buffer. The technique shown previously for inserting the terminator may not work if other data is subsequently added to the buffer, or if the buffer's put pointer is moved around before insertions, as shown in the next listing (Listing 7.42). As an alternative for the insertion expression

```
text << '\0';
```

you can use the special manipulator ends:

```
text << ends;
```

The notation isn't too different, but it seems to flow better. Using the manipulator to format the string in the preceding example, you would write

```
// format the string in memory, and use an I/O manipulator
text << "\nThis " << cp << " is still "
     << LENGTH
     << " words long" << ends;
cout << text.str();
```

Other manipulators can be applied to ostrstreams, and these are shown in detail later in this chapter. Two member functions in ostrstream have no correspondence in istrstream: oststream::str() and ostrstream::pcount(). The first function is a handy shorthand for getting a pointer to the stream buffer without the ugly notation that is used in istrstream.

```
// these two function calls are equivalent
char* cp = text.rdbuf()->str();
char* cp = text.str();
```

Obviously, the simpler notation is more convenient. Both functions have the effect of freezing the ostrstream buffer. The function ostrstream::pcount() tells you how many characters are present in the put area of the stream buffer. Actually, the returned value may be different from the number of characters you inserted into the stream. As described in the declaration for ostrstream, the number of characters in the buffer is computed using the value for the put pointer. If you reposition the pointer using seekp(...), ostrstream::pcount() may return a value that you didn't expect.

There is an important difference between sprintf(...) and ostrstream when you are creating a formatted string in memory: sprintf(...) always null terminates the string, whereas ostrstream doesn't. This means you have to remember to append the terminator to the buffer yourself.

Listing 7.42 shows an ostrstream with a dynamically allocated buffer, the details of which, fortunately, are hidden inside the class.

Listing 7.42. Using an `ostrstream` with a dynamically allocated buffer.

```
#include <strstrea.h>

// use an ostrstream for in-memory string formatting
void main()
{
  // create a ostrstream without passing a buffer to it
  ostrstream empty;

  // insert characters into it
  empty << "\nThese characters were added to an empty "
        << "ostrstream" << ends;
  cout << empty.str();

  // The stream owns its internal buffer. We must
  // unfreeze this buffer to let the ostrstream
  // destructor destroy it
  empty.rdbuf()->freeze(0);
}
```

The object `empty` starts out with no internal buffer. When the characters are inserted into it, a buffer is dynamically allocated and used. This buffer is allocated in chunks, so the memory allocator doesn't have to be called every time you add a character to the buffer.

Listing 7.43 demonstrates the use of random access in an `ostrstream`. Inserting characters in different places at different times can lead you to overwrite the null terminator because you lose track of where the end of the data is. The function `ostrstream::pcount()` solves this problem.

Listing 7.43. Performing random accesses on an `ostrstream` object.

```
#include <strstrea.h>

// use an ostrstream for in-memory string formatting
void main()
{
      const int LENGTH = 100;
      char buffer [LENGTH];

      // demonstrate random access during stream insertion
      char array [LENGTH];
      ostrstream random(array, LENGTH);
      random << "\n1111111111";
      random.seekp(0, ios::beg);
      random << "\n22222";
      random.seekp(0, ios::beg);
```

```
        random << "\n33";
        random.seekp(11, ios::beg);
        random << "\t44444" << '\0';

        cout << random.str();

        // calling str() takes ownership of the internal
        // buffer away from ostrstream. Call freeze(0)
        // to return ownership to the stream, so the
        // destructor for ostrsteam can destroy the
        // buffer
        random.rdbuf()->freeze(0);
}
```

Listing 7.43 produces the following output:

```
3322211111      44444
```

This output is actually the result of successively overlaying the following strings over the same `ostrstream` buffer:

```
1111111111
22222
33
                44444
```

You have to be careful about where you put the null terminator because subsequent stream insertions may overwrite it. I put the terminator after the `"44444"` string because I knew that was going to be the end of the buffer. An alternative method is to use `ostrstream::pcount()`, as shown in Listing 7.44.

Listing 7.44. Using `ostrstream::pcount()` to find the end of an `ostrstream` buffer.

```
#include <strstrea.h>

// use an ostrstream for in-memory string formatting
void main()
{
        const int LENGTH = 100;
        char buffer [LENGTH];

        // demonstrate random access during stream insertion
        char array [LENGTH];
        ostrstream random(array, LENGTH);
        random << "\n1111111111";
        random.seekp(11, ios::beg);
```

continues

Listing 7.44. continued

```
    random << "44444";

    // insert null-terminator at the end of the buffer
    random. seekp( random.pcount(), ios::beg);
    random << '\0';
    cout << random.str();
    random.rdbuf()->freeze(0);
}
```

This results in the (possibly unexpected) output

```
1111
```

The first `seekp(...)` operation moves the pointer `pbase_` forward by 11, then sets the pointer `pptr_` to reference the same location. This makes the buffer look empty, as far as `ostrstream::pcount()` is concerned. After the first `seekp(...)` operation, five characters are inserted into the buffer; therefore, `ostrstream::pcount()` returns a value of `5`. Displaying the first five characters in the buffer causes the string `"\n1111"` to be output. The `"44444"` string is still in the buffer, but is beyond the null terminator and out of reach.

Class *streambuf*

Class `streambuf` handles the lowest-level functions for streams, supporting buffered and unbuffered operations. Class `streambuf` is essentially a first-in, first-out (FIFO) buffer controller, allowing characters to be put into or taken out of the buffer. Buffers handle data that moves between two points. The data is moved into the buffer from a source (a producer), and is removed from the buffer into a destination (a consumer). This is the general behavior of `streambuf` objects: for output buffers, characters are usually put in one at a time and flushed out all at once when the buffer fills up and overflows. For buffers that are used for input, characters are usually read one at a time, with the buffer being filled all at once when it becomes empty and underflows.

Class `streambuf` probably would have been best implemented as an abstract class, because it can't support overflow or underflow operations; however, the library implementors decided against implementing it as an abstract class for some reason. Conceptually, all `streambuf`s must support the operations of underflow and overflow, but it isn't possible to be specific until the type of object connected to a `streambuf` is known. Class `streambuf` uses a series of pointers and other variables to control a buffer that is laid out in memory like Figures 7.5 and 7.6.

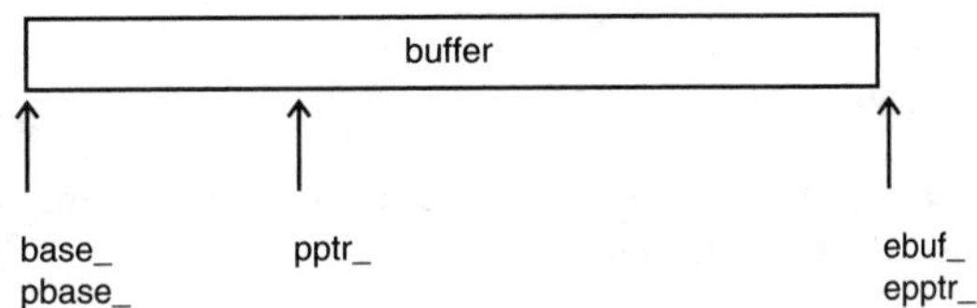

Figure 7.5. A `streambuf` *buffer used for output.*

The pointers that start with a `p` are used for putting characters into the buffer. The pointers `gptr_` and `eback_` are used for getting characters out of the buffer. The pointers are used as follows:

- `base_` Points to the beginning of the buffer, that is, its first byte.
- `pbase_` Points to the beginning of the `put` area.
- `pptr_` Points to the next location at which a character will be put into the buffer.
- `ebuf_` Points to one location past the end of the buffer, thus a valid buffer pointer always must be *less* than `ebuf_`.
- `epptr_` Points to one location past the end of the `put` area of the buffer.
- `gptr_` Points to the next character that will be read out of the buffer. When a character is read, it is removed from the buffer.
- `eback_` After a character is read from the buffer, it is sometimes possible to put it back into the buffer. Putback operations move the `gptr_` backward. Pointer `eback_` shows how far back `gptr_` can be moved.

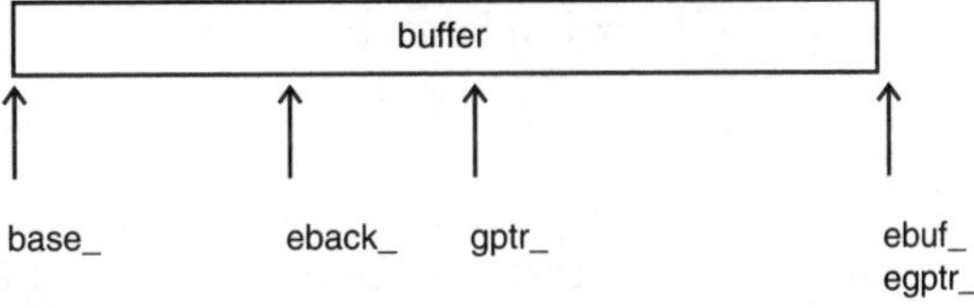

Figure 7.6. A `streambuf` *buffer used for input.*

Here is an edited version of class `streambuf`:

`class streambuf {`

`public:`

`streambuf();`

This default constructor builds a `streambuf` with no buffer. All pointers are set to 0.

```
streambuf(char*, int);
```

This constructor is passed a buffer pointer and a buffer length. It builds a `streambuf` object and associates the buffer with it.

```
virtual ~streambuf();
```

This `virtual` destructor allows proper disposal of objects derived from `streambuf`. Many member functions in the stream hierarchy make use of pointers to `streambufs`. When a pointer or reference to a `streambuf` is passed around but actually refers to a `filebuf` or an `strstreambuf`, a `virtual` destructor is necessary to guarantee proper object destruction.

```
streambuf*  setbuf(unsigned char*, int)
```

This is the basic function for setting up the buffer pointers for a `streambuf`. This function is required for proper operation of a `streambuf`, and shouldn't be overloaded. All this function does is invoke the `virtual` function `streambuf::setbuf(signed char*, int)`.

```
virtual streambuf* setbuf(signed char*, int);
```

This `virtual` function is declared for the benefit of derived classes. Note the use of a `signed` parameter rather than an `unsigned` parameter. The signed parameter is used to distinguish the `virtual` function from the non-`virtual` version. This `virtual` function is passed the address and length of a buffer to attach to a `streambuf`. If the `streambuf` already has a buffer, the old one is deleted and the new one is used.

```
int sgetc();
```

This returns the next character from the `get` area without updating the buffer pointers unless a buffer underflow occurs. In such a case, the `virtual` function `streambuf::underflow()` is called, resulting in a possible updating of pointers. If errors occur, `streambuf::sgetc()` returns an EOF.

```
int snextc();
```

This function is the same as `streambuf::sgetc()`, except that the `get` pointer is advanced before a character is read from the `streambuf` buffer.

```
int sbumpc();
```

This function is similar to `streambuf::sgetc()`, except that the `get` pointer is advanced after the character is fetched.

```
void stossc();
```

This function advances the `get` pointer by one character, which has the effect of *tossing out,* or ignoring, the next character in the `get` area.

```
int sgetn(char* s, int n);
```

This function reads the next `n` characters into the buffer `s`. Buffer underflows are handled if necessary. This function calls `streambuf::do_sgetn()` to do the work if less than `n` characters are in the buffer. The return value indicates the number of characters the function has read.

```
virtual int do_sgetn(char* s, int n);
```

This is a `virtual` function to implement `streambuf::sgetn(...)` in derived classes. This function handles buffer underflows, copying the next `n` characters from the `streambuf`'s `get` area into the destination array `s`. The return value indicates how many characters the function copied.

```
virtual int underflow();
```

This function is called when a character needs to be fetched from the `get` area of a `streambuf` buffer, but the buffer is empty. The default function `streambuf::underflow()` doesn't really do anything except return an EOF because the details of how an underflow should be handled are known only in derived classes. Thus, `streambuf::underflow()` is required to be overridden in order for a `streambuf` to work.

```
int sputbackc(char);
```

This function puts a character into the `get` area if there is room. You can put any character back into the buffer, not only those that were just read from it. The consequences of such an action, however, depend on your code. If the putback operation succeeds, the value returned by `streambuf::sputback(int)` is the character that was put back. If there is no more room to put back characters in the buffer, the virtual function `streambuf::pbackfail(int)` is called with the character to be put back. The value returned from `streambuf::sputback(int)` is then the value returned by `streambuf::sputback(int)`, which is EOF by default.

```
virtual int pbackfail(int);
```

This `virtual` function is provided for the benefit of derived classes. This function is called by `streambuf::sputback(char)` when a putback operation fails due to insufficient room in the putback area of the `get` buffer. Function `streambuf::pbackfail(int)` is the default error handler and returns EOF. Classes derived from `streambuf` can modify the way putback errors are handled by overriding function `streambuf::pbackfail(int)`.

```
int in_avail();
```

This function returns the number of available characters in the `get` buffer.

```
int sputc(int);
```

This function puts a character into the buffer using the `pptr_` pointer, then updates the pointer. The function returns the character that is written, or it returns an EOF if errors occur.

```
int sputn(const char*, int);
```

This function takes a pointer to a string and copies the first `n` characters of the string into the buffer. The `pptr_` pointer is then updated accordingly. The return value indicates the number of characters written.

```
virtual int do_sputn(const char* s, int n);
```

This `virtual` function is provided for the benefit of derived classes. It is called by `streambuf::sputn(...)` if the `put` area is too small to handle all the characters. The function handles buffer overflows, and must return the number of characters written.

```
virtual int overflow(int = EOF);
```

This function needs to be overridden in a derived class for a `streambuf` to work. This function is called when the buffer fills up, and should copy all buffer contents to the device or destination buffer associated with the `streambuf` object. When this function returns, the buffer must have room for additional data. The parameter passed is the character that causes the buffer overflow condition. The character is expected to be returned by the function. An EOF is returned if errors occur.

```
int out_waiting();
```

This function indicates how many characters are available in the `put` area.

```
virtual streampos seekoff(streamoff,
                          seek_dir,
                          int = (ios::in ¦ ios::out) );
```

This `virtual` function displaces `streambuf` buffer pointers by the number of characters given by the first parameter. The default function `streambuf::seekoff(...)` does nothing but return an EOF because the way in which pointers are to be handled depends on the implementation of derived classes. The second parameter indicates the direction of displacement, and is an enumerated type defined in class `ios` like this:

```
enum seek_dir { beg=0, cur=1, end=2 };
```

The value `beg` indicates an offset from the beginning of the buffer. The value `cur` indicates an offset from the current buffer position. The value `end` indicates an offset from the end of the buffer. The last parameter indicates whether the `put` or the `get` pointers are to be changed, or both. The default is to change both the `put` and the `get` pointers.

```
virtual streampos seekpos(streampos,
                          int = (ios::in ¦ ios::out));
```

This `virtual` function is similar to the previous one, except that a displacement direction is not used. The first parameter is the absolute buffer position to seek. The last parameter indicates whether the `get` or `put` pointers are affected. Again, the default is both the `get` and `put` pointers.

```
virtual int sync();
```

This function returns nonzero if data is available in the `get` or `put` areas, otherwise it returns 0.

---

protected:

The following functions access `private` `streambuf` variables:

```
char* base();       // Return base_
char* ebuf();       // Return ebuf_
int   blen();       // Return (ebuf_ - base_)
char* pbase();      // Return pbase_
char* pptr();       // Return pptr_
char* epptr();      // Return epptr_
char* eback();      // Return eback_
char* gptr();       // Return gptr_
char* egptr();      // Return egptr_
```

```
void  setp(char*, char*);
```

This function sets up the put pointers for the buffer. The first parameter initializes pptr_ and pbase_, whereas the second parameter initializes eptr_. The two parameters should point to different locations.

```
void setg(char* , char*, char*);
```

This function initializes the pointers for the get area. The first parameter is the value for eback_. The second parameter is the value for gptr_. The third parameter is the value for egptr_.

```
void pbump(int amount);
```

This function moves pptr_ forward or backward by a given amount. Positive values for parameter amount move the pointer forward.

```
void gbump(int amount);
```

This function moves gptr_ forward or backward by a given amount. As for the previous function, positive values of amount move the pointer forward.

```
void setb(char*, char*, int = 0 );
```

This function sets up the basic buffer pointers for a streambuf object. If the streambuf already has a buffer allocated to it when this function is called, the old buffer is deleted and replaced with the new one. Otherwise, the new buffer is used. The first parameter is the value for base_, whereas the second is the value for ebuf_. The last parameter indicates whether or not the buffer already contains data, and how many chars of data it contains. The default indicates that the buffer has no data.

```
void unbuffered(int);
```

A streambuf is associated with a buffer, and allows operations that read and write single bytes to the buffer to proceed efficiently, even when the ultimate device is capable of only block transfers (as is the case with disks). It is also possible to use a streambuf buffer in the *unbuffered* mode, which might sound like a contradiction of terms. Each time a character is written to a streambuf in the unbuffered mode, the buffer is also flushed to the ultimate consumer (for example, a disk file). A streambuf has a private variable called unbuf_, which indicates whether the buffered or unbuffered mode is active. Calling the function streambuf::unbuffered(int) with a nonzero argument causes unbuf_ to be

set, which then disables buffering. Each time a byte is written to the `streambuf`, an overflow occurs and the buffer is flushed to the ultimate consumer. Any time a byte is read from the `streambuf`, an underflow occurs and the ultimate producer is requested for data. To enable buffering, you call `streambuf::unbuffered(int)` with a 0 as an argument.

```
int unbuffered();
```

This function returns nonzero if the buffer is operating in the unbuffered mode.

```
int allocate();
```

This function uses the pointers `base_` and `ebuf_` to allocate storage for a new buffer. The function returns 0 if a buffer already was allocated or if its mode is set to `unbuffered`. Otherwise, it returns the value returned by `streambuf::doallocate()`.

```
virtual int doallocate();
```

This `virtual` function is for the benefit of derived classes. It is called from `streambuf::allocate()`, which should not be overloaded. The function returns an EOF if allocation errors occur. Otherwise, it returns 1.

```
private:
```

```
int do_snextc();
```

This function is used to get a character from a `streambuf`. The function is called by `streambuf::snextc()` when the `streambuf` has an uninitialized `get` pointer, or when the `get` buffer has no more characters available. Function `streambuf::snextc()` is expected to set up a `get` area and read characters into it from the ultimate producer.

```
streambuf(streambuf&);
```

This function is declared but not defined, which prevents the user from copy-initializing a `streambuf`.

```
void operator= (streambuf&);
```

This overloaded assignment function is similar to the previous function, because it is declared but not defined, preventing users from copying `streambuf` objects.

```
};
```

Using *put* and *get* Pointers

When using only put pointers, it is easy to determine when a buffer is full and needs flushing: If the put pointer reaches the end of the buffer, the buffer is full. Conversely for input-only buffers, if the get pointer reaches the end of the buffer (or the last available character in the buffer, whichever comes first), the buffer needs to be filled.

In many cases, buffers are bidirectional, thus involving the simultaneous use of both put and get pointers. In these cases, the rules for underflow and overflow checking are different. The buffer is used as a circular FIFO (first-in, first-out), with the put and get pointers chasing each other. For an empty buffer, the put and get pointers refer to the same location, which is not necessarily the beginning location in the buffer, as shown in Figure 7.7.

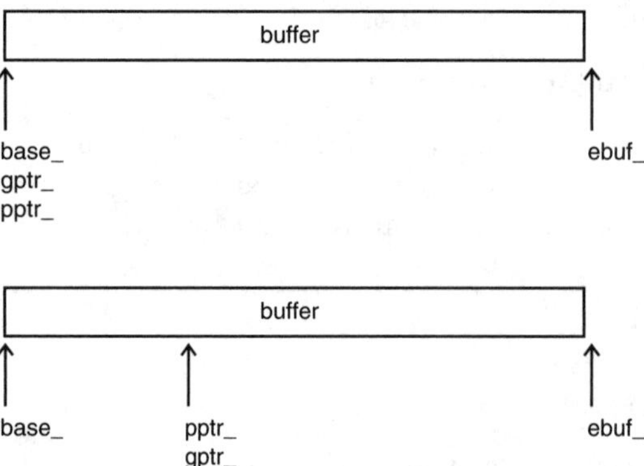

Figure 7.7. Two examples of empty buffers.

When a character is put into the buffer, the put pointer is updated. When a character is taken out of the buffer, the get pointer is updated. If the get pointer catches up with the put pointer, the buffer is considered empty. If the put pointer catches up with the get pointer, the buffer is considered full. Figure 7.8 shows a full buffer that uses four pointers.

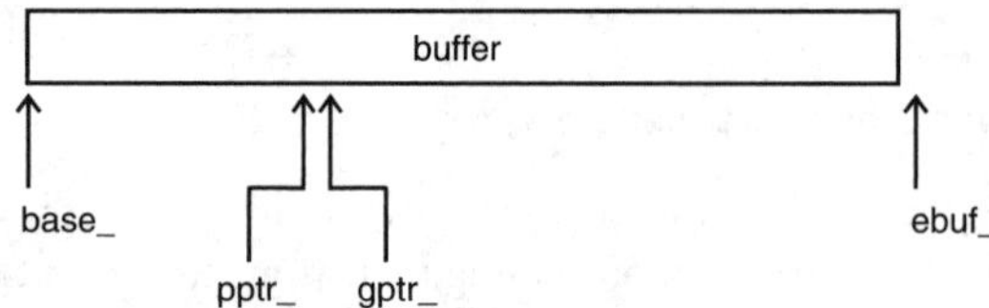

Figure 7.8. A full buffer utilizing four pointers.

In a complete buffer implementation, even more pointers are used than shown in Figure 7.8. The buffer function `streambuf::sputback(char)` allows characters to be returned to the buffer. This complicates the pointer dynamics somewhat, requiring two additional pointers: `epptr_` and `eback_`. The pointer `epptr_` determines the end of the `put` area, and is not necessarily aligned with the `gptr_`. The pointer `eback_` indicates how far you can go when putting characters back into the buffer. To make the `put` and `get` areas completely independent, the end pointer `egptr_` is also required for the `get` area. The built-in stream classes make use of all the pointers; however, classes you derive from `streambuf` don't necessarily have to make use of all the pointers if you need a unidirectional buffer.

Deriving a Class from *streambuf*

To demonstrate the use of `streambuf` as a base class for a user class, consider implementing a type of buffered I/O driver for a local area network. I call the class `LANBuffer`, and provide it with a few methods to illustrate the general use of `streambuf`. The most interesting new member function is called `LANBuffer::SendTestPacket(char)`. This function fills the buffer with a given character and flushes the buffer to the output device, which in Listing 7.45 is redirected to `cout`.

Listing 7.45. A class derived from `streambuf`.

```
#include <iostream.h>

// make the buffer the size of a LAN packet
int const LAN_BUFFER_SIZE = 200;

class LANBuffer: public streambuf {
  int port_address;
  char buffer [LAN_BUFFER_SIZE];

public:

  LANBuffer()
    : streambuf(buffer, LAN_BUFFER_SIZE) {}

  void SendTestPacket(char);  // fill and flush buffer

  void Address(int a)         // assign station address
    { port_address = a; }

  int overflow(int);          // flush buffer to LAN
};

void LANBuffer::SendTestPacket(char c)
{
```

continues

Listing 7.45. continued

```
        for (int i = 0; i <= blen(); i++)
       sputc(c);
}

// this function overrides streambuf::overflow(int)
int LANBuffer::overflow(int i)
{
        // ignore EOFs
        if (i == EOF) return EOF;
        if (!out_waiting() ) {
       // pointers not initialized yet
       setp(base(), ebuf() );

       // go back and put the character into the buffer
          return sputc(i);
        }

        // send char to cout for simplicity
        char* cp = pbase();
        for (int j = 0; j < blen(); j++, cp++)
          cout << *cp;

        // show the buffer as empty
        setp(base(), ebuf() );
        return (unsigned char) i;
}

void main()
{
        LANBuffer port;
        port.Address(10);          // establish station ID
        port.SendTestPacket('a');  // broadcast a test packet
}
```

The techniques shown in `LANBuffer::overflow(int)` are basically the same as those used in built-in classes derived from `streambuf`, such as `filebuf`. Important points are the use of the following `protected streambuf` member functions to manipulate and access `private streambuf` variables:

`out_waiting()`	To test the empty or full state of the `put` buffer.
`setp()`	To set up `put` area pointers.
`blen()`	To determine the size of the `put` buffer.
`base()`, `ebuf()`, and `pbase()`	To access `private streambuf` pointers.

Typical classes derived from `streambuf` differ from the code in Listing 7.45 because they need to manipulate both the `get` and the `put` pointers; however, the procedure remains the same.

Making a Ring Buffer

In many computing projects, data flows from one place to another, such as from a user keyboard into your program. A problem arises when the rate of data production is not exactly the same as the rate of data consumption. This problem is solved with a circular FIFO, which uses a buffer with `get` and `put` pointers that chase each other around in a circle.

The advantage of a circular FIFO is that when the rates of production and consumption are not too different, the size of the buffer is small. Unused slots in the buffer are used repeatedly. The production and consumption processes are not only asynchronous, but sometimes they are under the control of different processes or even different computers. Using a circular FIFO to manage keyboard data, you could write an interrupt routine to store data into the FIFO and have your program periodically check the FIFO for data. As long as you check the FIFO before the user fills it up, you won't lose any keystrokes.

A few rules must be spelled out before you can use such a circular FIFO. When the FIFO is created, the `get` and `put` pointers are both set to point at the first character in the buffer. When a character is put into the buffer, the `put` pointer is used and then advanced. When a character is fetched from the buffer, the `get` pointer is used and then advanced. When either pointer reaches the end of the buffer, it wraps around to the beginning again. You must check for two exceptions: fetching characters from an empty buffer and putting characters into a full buffer. A FIFO is full any time the `get` and `put` pointers reference the same location. The FIFO is empty when the `put` pointer is one character behind the `get` pointer, taking into account pointer wrap-around. Listing 7.46 is a circular FIFO that uses `streambuf` as a base class.

Listing 7.46. A circular FIFO derived from `streambuf`.

```
#include <iostream.h>

class CircularFIFO: public streambuf {

      char* buffer;        // fifo ring buffer
      int size;            // size of buffer

      int overflow(int);
      int underflow();

public:
```

continues

Listing 7.46. continued

```
        CircularFIFO(int size);
        ~CircularFIFO() {delete buffer;}
        IsEmpty();
        IsFull();
};

CircularFIFO::CircularFIFO(int s) : streambuf()
{
        // allocate a buffer of the requested size, and
        // attach it to the strstream
        buffer = new char [size];
        setbuf(buffer, s);
        size = s;

        // initialize put and get areas: no putback area
        // in get area
        setp(buffer, &buffer [size] );
        setg(buffer, buffer, &buffer [size] );
}

// this function is called when the put pointer hits the
// end of the buffer
int CircularFIFO::overflow(int c)
{
        // report error if FIFO is full
        if (IsFull() ) return EOF;

        // wrap the put pointer back to the beginning
        setp(base(), ebuf() );

        // and store the character and advance the put
        return sputc(c);
}

// this function is called when the get pointer hits the
// end of the buffer
int CircularFIFO::underflow()
{
        // report error if FIFO is empty
        if (IsEmpty() ) return EOF;

        // wrap the get pointer back to the beginning,
        // leaving no putback area
        setg(base(), base(), ebuf() );

        // retrieve the next character and advance the get
        // pointer
        return sgetc();
}
```

```
// see if the FIFO is empty
int CircularFIFO::IsEmpty()
{
        return (gptr() == pptr() ) ? 1 : 0;
}

// see if the FIFO is full
CircularFIFO::IsFull()
{
        if (gptr() == base() )
          return (pptr() == ebuf() ) ? 1 : 0;
        else
          return (pptr() == gptr() - 1) ? 1 : 0;
}
```

Listing 7.47 is a simple program to test class `CircularFIFO`. It sets up a small 10-byte buffer, then stores and fetches characters using the buffer. The example shows that one character is extracted for each character that is inserted into the FIFO, making the rates of production and consumption equal. In general, this doesn't have to be the case, but it made for a simpler test program, which is shown in Listing 7.47.

Listing 7.47. Testing the `CircularFIFO` class.

```
void main()
{
        // create a 20 byte FIFO ring buffer
        CircularFIFO fifo(10);

        int j;

        // write data
        for (int i = '0'; i < '0' + 120; i++) {

          // insert data into the FIFO
          if (fifo.IsFull() ) return;
          fifo. sputc(i);

          // extract data from the FIFO
          if (fifo.IsEmpty() ) return;
          j = fifo. sbumpc();

          // display the results
          cout << "\n " << j;
        }
}
```

Class *strstream*

This class combines the functionality of both `istrstream` and `ostrstream`, although it isn't derived from either, and supports insertions and extractions on string streams. Most of the time you'll be interested in either reading or writing an in-memory string, but not both simultaneously. Using an `strstream`, you can create a single object to use for operations that in ANSI C would have utilized `sscanf(...)` and `sprintf(...)`. The following is an edited version of the declaration for `strstream`. As usual, multiple inheritance allows the class to be extremely short.

`class strstream : public strstreambase, public iostream {`

`public:`

```
strstream();
```

This constructor takes no arguments and is used whenever you want the `strstream` object to create and manage its own dynamically allocated buffer. The buffer is automatically enlarged if it isn't sufficient to hold all the characters you insert.

```
strstream(char* buffer, int s, int mode);
```

This constructor takes a pointer to a buffer of size `s` and associates the `strstream` to it. The parameter `mode` is used to indicate how the `put` pointer is to be positioned initially. The `get` pointer is not affected by the `mode` flag, which can assume the values

```
ios::out
ios::ate
ios::app
```

The first value indicates normal operation: The `put` pointer is initialized to the beginning of the buffer. The values `ios::ate` and `ios::app` cause the pointer to be set to the end of the buffer, which in this case must contain a null-terminated string. If the buffer has binary data, the function does not function correctly with the `ios::ate` or `ios::app` flags because it is not able to determine where the data ends.

```
~strstream();
```

This constructor does nothing by itself because the base classes do all the work. If the class owns the stream buffer (because no buffer was passed to the constructor), then the buffer is destroyed. Otherwise, no action is performed.

```
char* str();
```

This function returns a pointer to the beginning of the stream buffer, which is then tagged `frozen`. This transfers ownership of the buffer to the user, who must either unfreeze the buffer after using it or delete it explicitly.

```
};
```

Using Class *strstream*

Sometimes it is convenient to be able to use memory as a temporary scratch pad for formatted string operations that include writing and reading. Consider a simple program that parses the words written into a string stream. Listing 7.48 shows some of the possible operations.

Listing 7.48. Using an `strstream` object for formatted in-memory input and output.

```
#include <strstrea.h>

// use an strstream for in-memory string I/O formatting
void main()
{
  const int LENGTH = 200;
  char buffer [LENGTH];

  strstream text;
  const float pi = 3.14159;
  const char* cp = "PI";

  // load a formatted string into the buffer
  text << "\n\tThe value of " << cp << " is " << pi;
  text << "\n\tThe result of 121 * 321 is "
       << (121L * 321L) << '\0';

  // print the entire stream buffer
  cout << "\nThe entire stream buffer is"
       << "\n\t**********************************"
       << text.str()
       << "\n\t**********************************";
  // release the buffer (frozen by calling text.str() )
  text.rdbuf()->freeze(0);

  // print the second word in the formatted string
  char array [LENGTH];
  text.ignore(LENGTH, ' ');
```

continues

Listing 7.48. continued

```
    text. get(array, LENGTH, ' ');
    cout << "\n\n\tThe second word in the string is ["
         << array << "]";

    // get the word int the middle of the buffer
    int middle = text.rdbuf()->out_waiting() / 2;
    text.seekg(middle, ios::beg);
    text. get(array, LENGTH, ' ');
    cout << "\n\tThe word in the middle of the string is ["
         << array << "]";

    // get the next full word
    text.ignore(LENGTH, ' ');
    text. get(array, LENGTH, ' ');
    cout
      << "\n\tThe word after the middle of the string is ["
      << array << "]";
}
```

Listing 7.48 produces the following output:

```
The entire stream buffer is
        ********************************
        The value of PI is 3.14159
        The result of 121 * 321 is 38841
        ********************************

        The second word in the string is [value]
        The word in the middle of the string is [he]
        The word after the middle of the string is [result]
```

You can jump around in the stream both in the `get` area and the `put` area independently. Class `strstream` does not have a function corresponding to `ostrstream::pcount()` to return the number of characters in the `put` area. Instead it uses the more indirect notation

```
int middle = text.rdbuf()->out_waiting() / 2;
```

to compute the offset to the middle of the `put` area. As for the function `ostrstream::pcount()`, moving the `put` pointers with `seekp(...)` causes the preceding expression to return values that may not correspond with the actual number of characters inserted into the stream. The function call

```
text.ignore(LENGTH, ' ');
```

is used to advance the `get` pointer from its current location by as many as `LENGTH` characters, or until a space is encountered. This allows the program to skip from one word to the next. As for ostrstream objects, don't forget the null terminator when you are inserting data, even when you are using only strings as data. The following program, which seems harmless, is wrong:

```
// oops: no null-terminator inserted
strstream text;
text << "\n\tThe value of PI is 3.14159";
cout << text.str();
```

The cout stream insertion would display the characters inserted, but then would run off the end of the text buffer, displaying garbage characters until a null was found. The reason a null isn't inserted automatically during a string insertion is to allow operations to be concatenated at will. Using the ANSI C function strcpy(...) is different because it does null terminate the destination string after copying. Its limitation lies in the clumsiness of concatenating multiple copy operations.

Class *strstreambase*

The strstreambase class embodies the common features used by several other classes in the stream hierarchy. It has limited power by itself; however, it is used extensively in the hierarchy as a base class for classes that manipulate in-memory objects, such as strings and buffers. Because strstreambase is the base class for both input and output streams, its base class ios is declared virtual to prevent multiple occurrences of ios in I/O stream classes. Here is an edited version of its declaration:

class strstreambase : public virtual ios {

private:

```
strstreambuf buf;
```

This statement declares the object that contains the memory buffer and put and get pointers. This is one of the few classes in the iostream library to contain a complete object. Most classes manipulate others through pointers.

protected:

```
strstreambase(char* b, int s, char* p);
```

This initializer sets up a memory buffer b of size s by calling the function strstreambuf::init(b, s, p). See the description of this function for more details.

```
strstreambase();
```

This sets up an object with no buffer associated with it.

```
~strstreambase();
```

This destructor does nothing.

```
public:
```

```
strstreambuf* rdbuf();
```

This function returns the address of the `private` `buf` object.

```
};
```

The member object `buf` is initialized the same way as in class `fstreambase`: by using the member initializer syntax in the class constructors. The following code shows how:

```
strstreambase::strstreambase(char* b, int s, char* p)
             : buf(b, s, p)
{
  // initialize the object...
}
```

Deriving a Class from *strstreambase*

Class `strstreambase` is not designed to be instantiated directly. To prevent instantiations, all the class constructors are declared `protected`. I'm not sure why the class wasn't simply made `abstract`. I derive a simple class from `strstreambase` to illustrate some of its potential. In general, you probably won't use `strstreambase` to derive classes because most of the functionality needed is already available in classes further down in the stream hierarchy. Nevertheless, Listing 7.49 is an example. The class `SimpleString` allows you to create an initialized object that contains a string. The class uses an overloaded `operator<<` to write (insert) its characters to an output stream.

Listing 7.49. A small class derived from `strstreambase` to handle strings.

```
#include <strstream.h>

class SimpleString: public strstreambase {

public:
```

```
        SimpleString(char*);
        friend ostream& operator<<(ostream&, SimpleString&);
};

SimpleString::SimpleString(char* string)
        : strstreambase(string, 0, string) {}

ostream& operator<<(ostream& o, SimpleString& s)
{
        o << "\n" << s.rdbuf()->str() << "\n";
        s.rdbuf()->freeze(0);
        return o;
}

void main()
{
        // create an initialized object
        SimpleString buffer("SimpleString buffer contents");

        // display the string on a line by itself
        cout << buffer;
}
```

In `operator<<(ostream&, SimpleString&)`, the expression

`s.rdbuf()`

returns a pointer to the `strstreambuf` that is used to store the string characters. Using this pointer in the expression

`s. rdbuf()->str()`

returns a pointer to the string that is manipulated by class `SimpleString`. Better ways to handle string objects exist, but I used this example to show some of the features of `strstreambase`. Note that the function `strstreambuf::str()` also freezes the `strstreambuf` buffer. Because of this, it is necessary to explicitly unfreeze the buffer, using the function `strstreambuf::freeze(0)`. If you don't unfreeze the buffer, the `strstreambuf` object will not deallocate it automatically. The buffer will linger in memory until you reboot your system.

Class *strstreambuf*

A `streambuf` object has no specific methods for handling buffer underflow or overflow. A `streambuf` is just a buffer handler. A buffer doesn't *have* to be connected to an I/O device. A good use for streams is to transfer data from one place to another in memory, much like the ANSI `memcpy()` function.

Class `strstreambuf` (an abbreviation of `string streambuf`) is a specialized `streambuf` for dealing with memory buffers. In contrast to `streambuf`, it does have underflow and overflow functions that work reasonably well with memory buffers. `strstreambuf` can be useful as a base class for making your own memory-filling, copying, and formatting operations. It is derived from `streambuf`, and uses many of the member functions of its base class.

Here is a simplified and edited version of the declaration of class `strstreambuf`:

`class strstreambuf: public streambuf {`

`private:`

```
void* (*allocf)(long);
```

This is a pointer to a function. If defined, it indicates the function to use in allocating memory for the buffer. The default is a *null* pointer, which causes `::operator new` to be used. Any functions used to allocate memory must also take care of setting up the buffer pointers correctly.

```
void  (*freef)(void*);
```

This is the counterpart for the previous variable. It points to the memory deallocator to be used when you are disposing of a buffer. The default for this variable is a null pointer, which causes `::operator delete` to be used. If you implement your own memory deallocator, make sure it sets all buffer pointers to NULL, so that the `strstreambuf` object doesn't try to use them.

```
short ssbflags;
```

This variable contains various mode settings for the buffer, using the untagged `enum`:

```
enum {dynamic = 1, frozen = 2, unlimited = 4};
```

If the `dynamic` flag is set, the buffer can be manipulated in certain ways. A buffer flagged as `dynamic` can be expanded by class `strstreambuf` if it is too small. The buffer is also deleted when the `strstreambuf` object goes out of scope. If you don't pass a buffer pointer to an `strstreambuf` constructor, a buffer is allocated automatically, and it is labeled `dynamic`. On the contrary, if you use one of the `strstreambuf` constructors that take a pointer to a buffer, the buffer will *not* be labeled `dynamic`, and you will have to delete the buffer yourself when the `strstreambuf` object goes out of scope.

If the `frozen` flag is set, the buffer will not be allowed to be expanded should it overflow. The `frozen` flag can be manipulated directly with the function `strstreambuf::freeze(int)`. Only `dynamic` buffers can be set to the `frozen` state. The logic is that if the `strstreambuf` object doesn't "own" the buffer, it certainly doesn't have the authority to freeze it from use by others.

If you indicate a negative size for an `strstreambuf` buffer, the flag is set to `unlimited`, and the buffer size is set to 0x7FFF. When an `unlimited` buffer is set up, you can't use function `streambuf::streamoff(...)` to index into it starting from the end because it conceptually doesn't have an end (although physically it does). An `unlimited` buffer cannot be expanded in size. The function `strstreambuf::overflow(int)` attempts to expand the buffer if it runs out of space, but only for buffers that are not `unlimited`.

```
int next_alloc;
```

This integer is the size of the memory block that will be allocated the next time `strstreambuf::do_allocate()` is called.

```
void init(signed char* start,
            int size,
            signed char* offset);
```

This `private` function is called by those constructors that take a pointer to a buffer, that is, `strstreambuf(signed char*, int, signed char*)` and `strstreambuf(unsigned char*, int, unsigned char*)`. The buffer's `dynamic` flag is not set in this case, because the buffer was not allocated by `strstreambuf`, and thus doesn't belong to it. The buffer pointers are initialized like this:

```
base_ = start
ebuf_ = start + size
pbase_ = offset
pptr_ = offset
epptr_ = start + size
eback_ = start
gptr_ = start
egptr_ start + size
```

Pictorially, this code sets the buffer up like Figure 7.9.

If you call `strstreambuf::init(...)` with the third parameter set to 0, no `put` area is created, and the entire buffer is a `get` area. In this case, the `put` pointers are set to 0, and `egptr_` has the same value as `ebuf_`.

The value of the parameter `size` doesn't have to be greater than 0. If its value is 0, the buffer is assumed to contain a null-terminated string. The size of the buffer is then determined dynamically by the length of the null-terminated string. If the `size` argument passed is less than 0, the buffer is considered to be an `unlimited` buffer. Its size is set to 0x7FFF, and the buffer flag is set to `unlimited`.

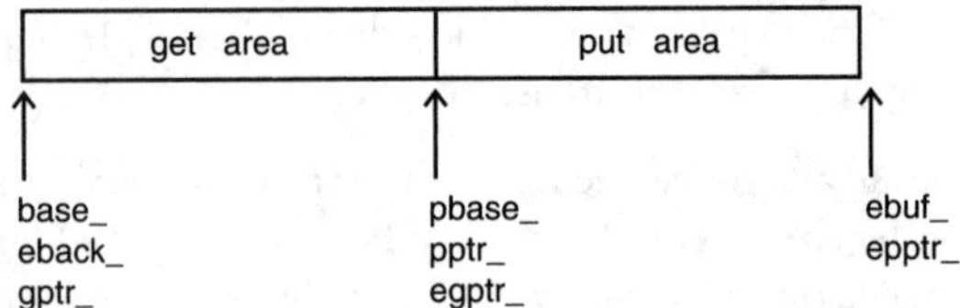

Figure 7.9. A buffer set up by `strstreambuf::init(...)`.

---

public:

```
strstreambuf();
```

This is the default constructor. No buffer is actually allocated, and all pointers are set to null.

```
strstreambuf(int n);
```

This constructor allocates a buffer of size `n`, marking it `dynamic` in the flag variable `strstreambuf::sbbflags`. The buffer pointers are all null, except for `base_` and `ebuf_`, which are set to indicate the starting and ending of the buffer that is allocated.

```
strstreambuf(void* (*allocate)(long),
             void (*deallocate)(void*) );
```

This constructor doesn't allocate any buffer, but instead sets up an allocator function and a deallocator function for the buffer.

```
strstreambuf(  signed char* s,int i,  signed char* t = 0);
strstreambuf(unsigned char* s,int i,unsigned char* t = 0);
```

These constructors are used when a buffer is already allocated somewhere, and you wish to set up an `strstreambuf` object to use this buffer. Both constructors call `strstreambuf::init(char*, int, char*)` to do all the work.

```
~strstreambuf();
```

This destructor deallocates the buffer only if the buffer is `dynamic` and not `frozen`. If a deallocator was set up previously, it is called; otherwise, `::operator delete` is used.

```
void freeze(int = 1);
```

The function allows you to set or clear the `frozen` flag in `strstreambuf::ssbflags`. The default is to set the `frozen` flag. A buffer in the `frozen` state will be prevented from being expanded or deleted inside class `strstreambuf`. If a buffer is in the `frozen` state when an `strstreambuf` object goes out of scope, the user must assume the responsibility for deleting this buffer.

```
char* str();
```

This function gives you access to the buffer that is handled by an `strstreambuf` object. The function returns a pointer to the beginning of the buffer and freezes the buffer so it won't be modified or deleted until it is explicitly `unfrozen`. If an `strstreambuf` object is deleted while its buffer is `frozen`, the buffer is considered to be owned by the user, who therefore must assume the responsibility for deleting the buffer.

```
virtual int doallocate();
```

This `virtual` function overrides the one declared in the base class `streambuf`. Function `strstreambuf::doallocate()` attempts to allocate a buffer for the `strstreambuf`, and returns an EOF if allocation errors occur. Otherwise, it returns 1. If a special allocator function was set up, it is invoked. Otherwise, `::operator new` is used. The buffer pointers are set up like Figure 7.10.

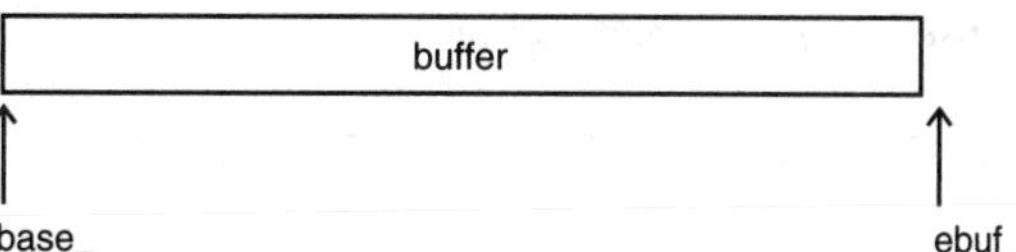

Figure 7.10. The buffer pointers that are set up by `strstreambuf::doallocate()`.

All other pointers are left unmodified. The first character in the buffer is set to 0.

```
virtual int overflow(int);
```

This `virtual` function is called when the base class function `streambuf::sputc(int)` needs to store a character in the buffer and no more room is left. If the buffer is `dynamic` and not `frozen`, it is expanded by a certain minimum size to accommodate extra characters. A buffer created as `unlimited` cannot be expanded. A buffer is expanded by creating an entirely new (and larger) buffer, copying all the buffer characters into it, and changing the buffer pointers to reflect the change.

```
virtual int underflow();
```

This `virtual` function is called by the base class function `streambuf::sgetc()` when no more characters are left in the `get` area of the buffer. The `get` area is then modified to coincide with the put area. If no put area exists, an EOF is returned. Otherwise, the next character available in the get area is returned.

```
virtual streambuf* setbuf(char* s, int i);
```

This function sets the value of the private variable next_alloc_ to i. The character pointer s is not used, and must be null. If a nonzero pointer is passed, the function returns null. Otherwise, it returns a pointer to the strstreambuf object.

```
virtual long seekoff(long offset, seek_dir dir, int mode);
```

This function moves some of the buffer pointers around, according to the arguments passed. The mode can be ios::in (affecting the get pointers), ios::out (affecting the put pointers), or both. The seek_dir argument indicates from which point in the buffer to compute the offset. Its value is in the enum ios::seek_dir, and can be ios::beg (from the beginning of the buffer), ios::cur (from the current point in the buffer), or ios::end (from the end of the buffer). It is illegal to seek from the end of a buffer that was set to unlimited. The offset indicates the distance to compute from the beginning point, current point, or end point. Positive values move pointer values toward the end, whereas negative values move pointer values toward the beginning. Thus, it is illegal to specify a negative offset value with mode set to ios::beg.

```
};
```

Deriving a Class from *strstreambuf*

Class strstreambuf is not as useful by itself as it is as a base class for your own buffer-handling classes. Listing 7.50 shows the implementation of a general-purpose buffer that allows you to perform operations such as setting all contents to a given character, copying strings, and copying binary data. I call the class CharacterBuffer. Most of the work is done in the base class, a fact that really makes the implementation of CharacterBuffer simple. Listing 7.50 is the code.

Listing 7.50. A buffer-handling class derived from `strstreambuf`.

```
#include <strstrea.h>

// define a suitable buffer size
int const CHARACTER_BUFFER_SIZE = 50;

class CharacterBuffer: public strstreambuf {
      int caps_lock;     // add a private variable just
                 // for the heck of it
public:
      CharacterBuffer() :
```

```
        strstreambuf(CHARACTER_BUFFER_SIZE) {}
      void Set(char);
      void Copy(char*);
      void StringCopy(char*);
      char* Contents() {return base(); }
};

// set all the buffer characters to a given value
void CharacterBuffer::Set(char c)
{
      // initialize put pointers
      setp(base(), ebuf() );

      // insert characters one by one
      for (int i = 0; i < blen(); i++)
        sputc(c);
}

// perform a binary copy: stop when the entire buffer
// has been copied over.
void CharacterBuffer::Copy(char* cp)
{
      // initialize put pointers
      setp(base(), ebuf() );

      // copy characters one at a time
      for (int i = 0; i < blen() - 1; i++)
        sputc(*cp++);

      // guarantee a string terminator, in case the buffer
      // contents are handled like a string
      sputc(0);
}

// perform a string copy: stop when a null is reached,
// or when the entire buffer has been filled
void CharacterBuffer::StringCopy(char* cp)
{
      setp(base(), ebuf() );
      for (int i = 0; i < blen(); i++) {
        sputc(*cp++);
        if (*cp == 0) return;
      }
}

void main()
{
  char* string  = {"abcdefghijk"};
  char stuff [] = {'1', '2', '3', '4'};

  CharacterBuffer buffer;     // create an empty buffer
```

continues

Listing 7.50. continued

```
  buffer. Set('a');            // emulate memset()
  buffer. Copy(stuff);         // emulate memcpy()
  cout << buffer.Contents();   // use with stream I/O
  buffer. StringCopy(string);  // emulate strcpy()
  cout << buffer.Contents();   // use with stream I/O
}
```

Listing 7.50 shows how easy it is to set up your own class to completely do away with the old ANSI memory operations. Not only are the new functions simpler, but they also can be set up to be polymorphic.

The Object-Based Container Library

One of the most common problems in real applications is the handling of groups of items. C programmers deal primarily with arrays and lists, but there are more complex ones, like symbol tables and trees, that often wind up taking lots of time to write and debug. Programmers have to solve the same problems repeatedly with each application. With C++, one of the goals is to provide programmers with a solid collection of reusable container classes, so that people can concentrate more on the application and less on implementation details. Containers are one of the most useful concepts of object-oriented programming.

Borland C++ has two separate container classes. The first is based on the class `Object`, and has been around since Borland C++ 2.0. The second is a template-based container class, and was introduced in Borland C++ 3.0. The `Object`-based containers are being gradually phased out, but are still being shipped with 4.5. Future versions of the compiler will probably drop the `Object`-based containers altogether, so I don't recommend starting any new projects using them.

The idea of reusable and generic classes is not new. Smalltalk, which is probably the most mature OOP language around, has had an extensive library of classes for more than 10 years. To capitalize on the power and stability of the Smalltalk library, K. E. Gorlen of the National Institutes of Health in Maryland decided to implement parts of the Smalltalk library in C++. That was in 1985. Today his work is referred to as the *NIH classes.* For years the NIH classes represented one of the major sources of C++ code available in the public domain. C++ compiler vendors used the NIH classes to test their own compilers. Borland decided to include a variation of the NIH classes starting with Borland C++ 2.0. These container classes are known as the `Object`*-based container classes.*

NOTE

The programs listed in this chapter will not run unless you build the necessary TCLASSL Library File. Instructions for making this library file can be found in \BC45\DOC\COMPAT.TXT, under the heading, "Using the Object-Based Class Library with Borland C++ 4.5." Once you have built your class library, you must implement the following change in order to run the programs in this chapter:

- Change the global include directory by issuing the command `OPTIONS|PROJECTS|DIRECTORIES`, to add C:\B45\INCLUDE\CLASSLIB\OBSOLETE to the end of the existing line.

Class Categories

The C++ language has no standard classes or hierarchies other than those used with streams. Any code you write that makes use of Borland C++ container classes may not be portable to other C++ compilers, unless the compiler supports templates, multiple inheritance, and some of the other standard C++ features that the Borland container classes use. The classes included in the library are designed to be as generic as possible. The library contains classes that are organized into two logical groups:

- Container classes
- Iterator classes

Each container class has an associated iterator class. Most containers can be traversed using two different methods: internal iterators, based on member functions of the container; and external iteration, using iterator objects. The containers are organized into groups, with each group managing its contents using a different paradigm. The `Object`-based containers have the following groups:

- Arrays
- Associations
- Bags
- Binary trees
- Deques
- Dictionaries
- Double lists
- Hash tables
- Lists
- Queues
- Sets
- Stacks
- `TShouldDelete`
- Vectors

Container classes can contain a whole series of other objects, which may in turn be containers themselves. Examples of containers are classes `Collection`, `Stack`, and `Bag`. The combination of classes makes for enormous power with little or no extra code. I show some complete examples of container class usage later in this chapter. Figure 8.1 shows the complete inheritance trees for the `Object`-based container classes.

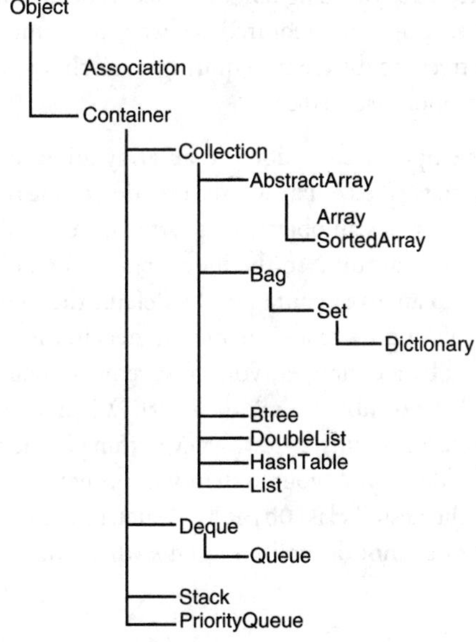

Figure 8.1. The inheritance tree for the Borland C++ `Object`*-based container classes.*

There is also a class hierarchy of iterators for the `Object`-based containers. The iterators are independent of class `Object`, and are declared `friends` in the classes over which they iterate. The following are the available iterators:

```
ArrayIterator
BtreeIterator
DoubleListIterator
HashTableIterator
ListIterator
```

These iterators all derive from the common base class `ContainerIterator`. Iterators are needed to visit, or traverse, the elements in a container and to considerably simplify the use of container classes. The following sections cover each of the `Object`-based container classes in detail, and with coding examples.

Class *AbstractArray*

Arrays are among the most common data structures used in C++. Built-in ANSI C array types support fixed-size arrays. Borland C++ has a special `array` class hierarchy that supports memory, which is allocated dynamically from the heap. The two instantiable classes of this hierarchy are `Array` and `SortedArray`. All the features that these two classes have in common were migrated to the seed class `AbstractArray`. A *seed class* is simply a class designed to incorporate the common features of its descendents. Seed classes are therefore rather incomplete and often abstract classes.

Arrays are characterized by being randomly accessible in constant time; regardless of which element you access, the time required is always the same. Other data structures, such as linked lists and trees are different, requiring a search operation of varying duration in order to access a random element.

Arrays start out empty. Items added to an array are inserted and maintained at specific spots inside the array. Class `Array` lets the user determine the array index explicitly, whereas class `SortedArray` keeps all objects in a sorted order. `SortedArray` arrays have the freedom to move objects around, so the index in which an object is stored may vary. When you add an item to an array container, by default the item is considered to be owned by the array. This rule applies to all other containers in the class library. If you delete an object that is owned by a container, you must remove the item from the container, or else you're going to have trouble (to say the least). When a container goes out of scope while owning the objects it contains, it destroys everything in the container. If one of these objects had already been destroyed, your system will probably crash. Ownership, which is controlled through the nested class `Object::TShouldDelete`, allows you to specify whether a container can or cannot delete its contents when going out of scope.

Arrays allocated from the heap have the added advantage of variable runtime size. This means you can allocate a small amount of initial memory to an array, and the array will automatically grow at runtime if it needs more storage. A class implementation allows all the data-management details to be hidden from users, giving way to a powerful abstraction that is useful in a variety of situations.

Here is an edited version of the header file for `AbstractArray`, as declared when you are *not* using template classes:

`class AbstractArray:  public Collection {`

`public:`

```
AbstractArray(int upper, int lower = 0, sizeType s = 0);
```

This function creates an array of (`lower`..`upper`) elements, where `lower` may be greater than 0. If parameter `s` is nonzero, the array is enabled to grow at runtime in increments of `s` entries. Otherwise the array is restricted to a fixed size. In this case, attempts to access elements outside the array, or to add more objects than the container can handle, result in a runtime error message.

```
virtual ~AbstractArray();
```

This function checks to see whether the contained objects are owned. If they are, the function iterates through the elements in the array and deletes them.

```
Object& operator [] (int i) const;
```

This function returns a reference to the item at index `i`. You can use this operator in classes derived from `AbstractArray` both to read and write values, using expressions such as the following:

```
Array array(50);
Object& obj1 = array [12];
array [13] = obj1;
```

```
int lowerBound() const;
```

This returns the lowest usable index for the array. The value is the one passed to the class constructor. It cannot be changed. If you add more elements than will fit into an array, the array is dynamically enlarged at runtime (if the array's `delta` value is greater than 0) by allocating more slots and increasing the upper bound.

```
int upperBound() const;
```

This is the highest index currently assigned to the array. Contrary to the lower bound, the upper bound can vary as the array is expanded. Its value is allowed only to increase because arrays never are shrunk at runtime.

```
sizeType arraySize() const;
```

This function returns the size of the allocated array. The value is computed as (`upperbound - lowerbound + 1`), using the class's private data members.

```
virtual void detach(Object&, DeleteType = NoDelete);
```

This function searches through an array (starting at the lowest index) for a given object. If it finds the object, it detaches and optionally deletes it by calling member function `AbstractArray::detach(int, DeleteType)`. If the object is not found, no action takes place and no error messages are issued if `DEBUG` has the value 0. If `DEBUG` is 1 or greater, an error message is displayed and the program is aborted. If the same object occurs more than once in the array, only the object at the lowest index is detached. You have to be extremely careful about inserting the same object more than once into a container because the object can't be deleted until all its occurrences in a container have been removed.

```
virtual void detach(int i, DeleteType = NoDelete);
```

This function removes the object in slot `i` and replaces it with `theErrorObject`. If slot `i` is outside the bounds of the array, a runtime error occurs. The array's item count is updated to reflect the removed item. If you detach something without having it deleted, you assume responsibility for deleting the object yourself.

```
void destroy(int i);
```

This function removes and deletes the object at slot `i` in the array, using member function `AbstractArray::detach(int, DeleteType)`.

```
virtual void flush(DeleteType = DefDelete);
```

This function iterates through all the objects in an `AbstractArray`, removes them, and optionally deletes them.

```
virtual int isEqual(const Object&) const;
```

This function returns nonzero if two arrays are equal. Two arrays are considered to be equal

if they have the same upper and lower bounds, and if they contain the same elements at the same indices.

```
virtual void printContentsOn(ostream&) const;
```

This function uses the function `printOn(ostream&)`, which must be defined in a derived class, to insert a printable representation of all the objects of an `AbstractArray` into an output stream. Empty array slots are skipped over.

```
virtual ContainerIterator& initIterator() const;
```

This function returns a reference to an `ArrayIterator` object, which can then be used to iterate through the objects in an array. The iterator object returned is allocated from the heap, so after using it you must remember to delete it. For example:

```
Array array(100);
ContainerIterator& next = array.initIterator();
while (next)
  cout << "\n" << (Object&) next++;
delete &next;
```

Failure to delete the iterator object may result in runtime memory allocation failures and mysterious system crashes. It is easy to forget to delete iterators because the compiler does not "say a word" if you do; it has no idea of exactly what is going on.

`protected:`

```
Object& objectAt(int i) const;
```

This returns a reference to the object that is at a given slot in an array. If no object is there, `NOOBJECT` is returned. Slots and array indices will be different if the lower bound of an array is not 0. For example, if you have an array with bounds (5..10), the element at index 5 will occupy slot 0.

```
Object* ptrAt(int i) const;
```

This returns a pointer to the object that is at a given slot in an array. If no object is there, a pointer to `theErrorObject` is returned. See the previous member function for the difference between a slot and an index with `AbstractArray` objects.

```
int find(const Object&);
```

This function searches through an `AbstractArray` for a given object. If the object is found, its slot number is returned. Otherwise, the value `INT_MIN` is returned.

```
void reallocate(sizeType);
```

This function is called inside classes `SortedArray` and `Array` when an array needs to be expanded. It allocates a new array of appropriate size, then copies all the old array items into it while maintaining the same object indices. Unused entries in the new array are filled with pointers to `theErrorObject`. Attempts to access these entries through `AbstractArray::objectAt(int)` yield the return value `NOOBJECT`.

```
void setData(int s, Object*);
```

This function sets slot `s` of an `AbstractArray` (where 0 is always the first slot, regardless of the value of the lower array bound), to point to a given `Object`. The previous pointer in slot `s` is overwritten.

```
void insertEntry(int s);
```

This function makes room for a new entry at slot `s`. It moves all entries at and above slot `s` up one slot. The value in the new slot `s` is left at its previous value.

```
void removeEntry(int s);
```

This function removes slot `s` by recompacting an array and copying all the items at and above `s` down one slot.

```
void squeezeEntry(int);
```

This function serves the same purpose as the previous function.

```
sizeType delta;
```

This value is used when an array needs to be expanded. When this happens, `delta` new slots are added to the array. The value of `delta` is fixed for each `AbstractArray`, and is established by the parameter that is used in the constructor call. The default is 0, in which case arrays are not enabled to grow under any circumstance.

```
int lowerbound;
int upperbound;
```

These are the values that define the bounds that constrain index values. The lower bound is fixed in the constructor; however, the upper bound may increase if the array is expandable.

```
int lastElementIndex;
```

This is the index that will be used the next time an object is inserted without using an explicit array index. The value starts out at `lowerbound` and is incremented each time an object is inserted. This enables you to insert objects in consecutive slots without worrying about array indices.

`private:`

```
Object** theArray;
```

This is a pointer to the actual array used to store array items. Each entry of the array referenced is a generic pointer to `Object`, and can reference anything derived from class `Object`.

```
int zeroBase(int loc) const;
```

This function converts an index into a slot number. If the lower bound of an array is 0, slot and index values will match.

```
int boundBase(unsigned loc) const;
```

This function converts a slot number into an index. If the lower bound of an array is 0, slot and index values will match.

```
friend class ArrayIterator;
```

This declaration grants full class access privileges to class `Chapter ArrayIterator`. All container classes must be declared with an iterator class declared as a `friend` to it, in order to enable the iterator full freedom in accessing the class.

`};`

Because class `AbstractArray` is abstract, there can be no direct uses for it other than as a base class.

Class *Array*

Class `Array` is the object-oriented extension of the arrays you use in ordinary C programs. The storage space for the array items is allocated from the heap, and each array entry contains a pointer to an object. Arrays are enabled to grow at runtime if they need more space, but only if they are designated as expandable when they are constructed. Normally, you insert objects into an array using an index; however, class `Array` gives you the option of using a default index. Any time you add an object without giving an index (using function `Array::add(Object&)`), `Array` determines the index of an unused array slot. Adding objects this way yields an array with the objects stored at consecutive indices.

Here is an edited version of the header file for `Array`, as declared when you are *not* using template classes:

```
class Array: public AbstractArray {
```

```
public:
```

```
Array(int upper, int lower = 0, sizeType s = 0);
```

This constructor builds an array with the requested upper and lower bounds for its indices. For example, building an array with bounds 13 and 19 yields an array with seven (rather than six) elements. This size is correct because it leaves room for the boundary elements at indices 13 and 19. If the parameter `s` is nonzero, the array is expandable and is expanded by `s` elements each time more space is required. The constructor for class `Array` doesn't actually do anything itself because it invokes the constructor of base class `AbstractArray` to do all the work.

```
virtual void add(Object&);
```

This function adds an object at the next default array index. To determine this index, the class scans the array entries, looking for the first available entry. If it doesn't find one, the array is expanded (if possible). The next scan starts where the previous scan finished. If the last default index was 10 and you delete the element at index 8, the default index is still searched starting from 10. Freed array entries are not necessarily reused.

```
void addAt(Object&, int);
```

This adds an item at a given index in the array. If the index is beyond the end of the array, the array is expanded, if possible. Otherwise an error message is issued.

```
virtual classType isA() const
virtual char _FAR *nameOf() const
```

These two functions aid in identifying `Array` objects at runtime. The first function returns a value that is unique to class `Array`. The second returns a pointer to the constant string `"Array"`.

```
};
```

The main advantage of arrays is their ability to access any item in the same amount of time. To access an object at a specified index, you use `operator[](int)`. You have two

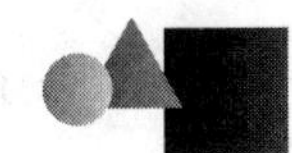

options for storing objects: member function `Array::addAt(Object&, int)` or member function `Array::add(Object&)`.

Using Class *Array*

To better illustrate the features of the class, I show a few short programs that create `Array` objects, fill them with `String` objects, and manipulate the array items.

Listing 8.1. Using an `Array` container.

```
#include <strng.h>
#include <array.h>

void main()
{
       String& one   = *new String("1");
       String& two   = *new String("2");
       String& three = *new String("3");
       String& four  = *new String("4");

       Array array(5, 0, 9);
       array.addAt(one, 5);
       array.addAt(two, 4);
       array.add(three);
       array.add(four);

       cout << array;
}
```

The output produced is

```
Array {
    3,
    4,
    2,
    1 }
```

The `Array` container is created with indices in the range 0..5. It uses a `delta` value of 9, meaning that the array is expandable and grows in increments of nine. The function `Array::add(Object&)` uses the first available slot to store its argument in the array.

The array is displayed through the insertion operator, which is overloaded to invoke `AbstratArray::printContentsOn(ostream&)`. The latter function skips over empty array slots. Note that in the previous example, slots 2 and 3 of the array are empty and therefore contain a pointer to `theErrorObject`.

continues

Reusing Slots

When you use `Array::addAt(Object&, it)` to add an object to an array slot that already has an object, the old object is deleted to make room for the new one. You also can delete and detach array objects explicitly, as shown in Listing 8.2.

Listing 8.2. Reusing slots in an `Array` container.

```
#include <strng.h>
#include <array.h>

void main()
{
      String& one   = *new String("1");
      String& two   = *new String("2");
      String& three = *new String("3");
      String& four  = *new String("4");
      String& five  = *new String("5");

      Array array(3, 0, 9);

      array.add(one);
      array.add(two);
      array.add(three);

      cout << "\nBefore making changes:\n"
           << array;
      Object& obj = array [2];
      array.detach(obj);
      array.addAt(four, 1);
      array.add(five);

      cout << "\nAfter making changes:\n"
           << array;

      // remember to destroy obj !
      delete &obj;
}
```

The output produced is

```
Before making changes:
Array {
      1,
      2,
      3}
```

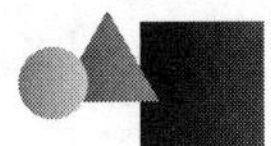

```
After making changes:
Array {
    1,
    4,
    5 }
```

When an object is detached or destroyed in an `Array`, the slot it occupied becomes available for subsequent `Array::addAt(Object&, int)` calls. The preceding code shows the following sequence:

3 is detached (from slot 2)

4 replaces 2 (in slot 1)

5 goes into slot 2

Class *Association*

An association is a relationship that exists between two entities. In the Borland container library, the entities are items derived from class `Object`. What the relationship between the objects means is entirely up to you; in fact, the class doesn't even have a way of handling the concept of a relationship. The first entity in an `Association` is called the *key,* whereas the second is called the *value.* `Association` objects are useful in all kinds of programming situations, but most of the time you use entire groups of them, such as in symbol tables and databases. In a symbol table, you would normally use a symbol as the association key and the symbol's meaning as the association value. Here is an edited version of the class `Association` declaration:

```
class Association : public Object, public virtual
                    Object::TShouldDelete {
```

`public:`

```
Association(Object& key, Object& value);
```

This constructor takes two `Object` references and uses them to initialize the two private data members `aKey` and `aValue`.

```
Association(const Association&);
```

This copy constructor takes a reference to another `Association`, initializing itself with the same key and value.

```
virtual ~Association();
```

The destructor is declared `virtual` for the purpose of providing derived classes with a way to clean out memory when they are destructed through a generic `Object` reference. The destructor for `Association` doesn't do anything by itself. However, the compiler automatically invokes the destructors for the two objects used in the association. This is important because it implies that any objects used in an association must be allocated dynamically rather than from global memory or from the stack.

```
Object& key() const;
Object& value() const;
```

These functions retrieve the values of the private objects stored in the `Association`.

```
virtual classType isA() const;
```

This returns a unique unsigned `int` to identify the `Association` class at runtime.

```
virtual char* nameOf() const;
```

This returns the string `"Association"`. This string better identifies the class at runtime, in case the value returned by `is A()` is insufficient.

```
virtual hashValueType hashValue() const;
```

This function returns a hash value computed using the key object of an association. The hash value is computed polymorphically by the key object itself.

```
virtual int isEqual(const Object&) const;
```

This can be a misleading function, due to the different ways in which "equality" can be tested. This function returns nonzero (true) if the two associations have the same value for member `aKey`. The `aValue` data members are not tested.

```
virtual int isAssociation() const;
```

This function merely returns a nonzero value so that you can check objects referenced through an `Object&` to see if they are `Associations`.

```
virtual void printOn(ostream&) const;
```

This is the polymorphic function called by the output stream inserter `::operator<<(ostream&, Object&)`. It produces a string description of the entire association, which can be inserted into any output stream. The following program:

```
#include <iostream.h>
#include <strng.h>
#include <assoc.h>

void main()
{
      // create a couple of string
      // objects from the heap
      String* charles = new String("Charles");
      String* karen = new String("Karen");

      // use them to create an association
      Association a(*charles, *karen);

      // display the association
      cout << "\n" << a;
}
```

produces the screen output:

```
Association { Charles, Karen }
```

The printed string starts with a space character, and ends with a new-line character.

```
private:
```

```
Object& aKey;
Object& aValue;
```

These private objects can reference any object derived from class `Object`. The key is usually the starting point for an association, but you can also search through associations for a value rather than a key. The class itself imposes no restrictions or rules on how an association is to be used. Both the key and the value of an association are free format. Whether they contain `Strings` or other nontrivial types derived from `Object` is solely up to you. The destructors for `aKey` and `aValue` are automatically invoked when an `Association` object is destructed.

```
};
```

Defining Objects to Be Used with *Associations*

When you use two objects to form an `Association`, you need to pass the objects to class `Association` by reference. From this point on, the objects are considered to belong to `Association`. When the `Association` object goes out of scope, it automatically invokes the destructors for the objects it owns. This means that only objects allocated from the heap can be passed to `Association`. Attempts to use auto, static, or global objects in an `Association` result in random system crashes. The following example shows code that might appear to work, but is incorrect:

```
// THIS WILL COMPILE, BUT WON'T WORK
// create two auto objects
String charles("Charles");
String karen("Karen");
Association a(*charles, *karen);
```

The correct way to create objects for `Associations` is through the heap, like this:

```
// THIS IS OKAY
// create two heap objects
String& charles = *(new String("Charles") );
String& karen   = *(new String("Karen") );
Association a(charles, karen);
```

If you prefer to use pointers to heap objects, try this:

```
// ANOTHER CORRECT EXAMPLE
// create two heap objects
String* charles = new String("Charles");
String* karen   = new String("Karen");

// associate them together
Association a(*charles, *karen);
```

Using Class *Association*

A single `Association` is rather limited in power. `Associations` really make sense only when there are lots of them to deal with.

The container library uses `Association` objects in class `Dictionary` to organize information. I show only a few simple examples here, to avoid getting involved with `Dictionary` objects, which are described elsewhere.

Listing 8.3. Using `Association` containers.

```
#include <iostream.h>
#include <strng.h>
#include <assoc.h>

void main()
{
      String* key [] = {
        new String("Alpha"),
        new String("Bravo"),
        new String("Charlie")
      };

      String* translation [] = {
        new String("A"),
        new String("B"),
        new String("C")
```

```
    };

    Association* lookup_table [3] = {
      new Association(*key [0], *translation [0]),
      new Association(*key [1], *translation [1]),
      new Association(*key [2], *translation [2])
    };

    cout << "\nHere is the result of the translations:";
    for (int i = 0; i < 3; i++) {
      cout << "\n"
           << lookup_table [i]->key()
           << " translates into "
           << lookup_table [i]->value();
    }
}
```

The output produced is

```
Here is the result of the translations:
Alpha translates into A
Bravo translates into B
Charlie translates into C
```

The program initializes three arrays of pointers to objects, using a notation that is slightly unusual. An array of `Association` objects is created and initialized with strings, which are then printed out. Notice the use of `::operator<<(ostream&, Object&)` to display the key and value of each association. Instead of using class `Array`, I used an array of `Association` objects that use standard C arrays to avoid unnecessary details.

It is unusual to create and initialize `Association` objects simultaneously. Most of the time you build `Associations` from data that is read from the operator or from a file. Listing 8.4 shows some examples.

Listing 8.4. Building `Associations` from user responses.

```
#include <iostream.h>
#include <strstrea.h>
#include <strng.h>
#include <assoc.h>

void main()
{
     const int SIZE = 4;
     const int BUFFER_SIZE = 100;
     Association* directory [SIZE];
```

continues

Listing 8.4. continued

```
        char* name = new char [BUFFER_SIZE];
        char* number = new char [BUFFER_SIZE];

        for (int i = 0; i < SIZE; i++) {

          // get some data
          cout << "\nName ? ";
          cin >> name;
          String* name_string = new String(name);

          cout << "\nNumber ? ";
          cin >> number;
          String* number_string = new String(number);

          // save it as an association
          directory [i] =
              new Association(*name_string, *number_string);
        }

        delete name;
        delete number;

        // print out the results
        cout << "\nHere is your phone directory:";
        for (i = 0; i < SIZE; i++) {
          cout << "\nEntry [" << i << "] = "
               << directory [i]->key()
               << ": "
               << directory [i]->value();
        }
}
```

The program displays results that are something like this:

```
Here is your phone directory:
Entry [0] = Ted: 555-1000
Entry [1] = Katie: 555-2000
Entry [2] = Michelle: 555-3000
Entry [3] = Larry: 555-4000
```

Deriving a Class from *Association*

The human mind forms an association between different things based on certain relationships. To model such a behavior with class `Association` requires modifying the class somehow to support a way of storing and handling the concept of *relationship*. Rather than modify the class itself, the correct procedure is to derive a class from `Association` and

add the necessary features. For example, consider building a class to store the names of a person's family members. Obviously there is an association between people; however, the same person is associated in different ways to many others. The relationships can be complex, but in the example shown in Listing 8.5, I limited them to the simple cases *has father, has sister,* and *has child.*

Listing 8.5. A derived `Association` class that stores relationships.

```
#include <iostream.h>
#include <strng.h>
#include <assoc.h>

static char* how_related [] = {
            " has father ",
            " has sister ",
            " has child "
            };

class Relative: public Association {

public:

  enum relation {has_father, has_sister, has_child};

private:

  relation  person;

public:

  Relative::Relative(Object& p1, relation r, Object& p2)
         : Association(p1, p2) {person = r;}
  char* relationship() {return how_related [person];}
};
```

The relation is implemented as an `enum`, but it also could have been stored as a character array or another type. Using the class `String` or some other class derived from `Object` would allow the relationship to be handled more elegantly than through the use of an array of strings with a lookup index. Listing 8.6 is a short program that uses the class.

Listing 8.6. A program that uses relationships in an `Association`.

```
void main()
{
      // make some String objects, but
      // remember to use heap variables !
      String& wendy   = *(new String("Wendy") );
      String& brad    = *(new String("Brad") );
      String& cheryl  = *(new String("Cheryl") );
      String& michael = *(new String("Michael") );

      Relative* family [] = {
        new Relative(wendy, Relative::has_father, brad),
        new Relative(wendy, Relative::has_sister, cheryl),
        new Relative(wendy, Relative::has_child, michael)
      };

      cout << "\nHere are some family relations:\n";
      for (int i = 0;
           i < sizeof(family) / sizeof(void*);
           i++) {

             cout << "\n"
                << family [i]->key()
                << family [i]->relationship()
                << family [i]->value();
      }
}
```

The output produced is

```
Here are some family relations:

Wendy has father Brad
Wendy has sister Cheryl
Wendy has child Michael
```

Class *Bag*

A `Bag` is a "plain vanilla" type of unordered container. It can hold multiple occurrences of the same object. Once an object is put into such a container, however, you can't make any assumptions about where the object is stored, or in what order. Borland chose to implement `Bag`s as hashed tables, but this is an internal implementation decision that doesn't affect the way a `Bag` is used. Here is an edited version of the header file for `Bag`, as declared when you are *not* using template classes:

```
class Bag: public Collection {
```

```
public:
```

```
Bag(sizeType bagSize = DEFAULT_BAG_SIZE);
```

This constructor initializes the private `hashTable` data member with 29 elements, which is a pretty good compromise value for many situations. You can change this default value by assigning a value to the parameter `bagSize` when you call the `Bag` class constructor. Once the size of a `Bag`'s hash table has been set, it can't be changed. This doesn't mean the `Bag` will overflow because the underlying hash table resorts to an additional internal data structure to store its data. If you anticipate storing thousands of objects in a `Bag`, you'll probably want to use a `bagSize` in the hundreds, such as 311, 517, and so on. You don't have to use a prime number, but hash table entries are usually more evenly distributed if the number of entries is prime.

```
virtual void add(Object&);
```

This function adds a new entry to the `hashTable` container used to support `Bag` objects. See class `HashTable` for a description of object insertions.

```
virtual void detach(Object& o, DeleteType dt = NoDelete);
```

This function removes and optionally deletes an object from a `Bag`. If multiple occurrences of the same object are present in a `Bag`, only the most recently inserted instance will be removed.

```
virtual void flush(DeleteType dt = DefDelete);
```

This function removes and optionally deletes all the items in a `Bag`.

```
virtual int isEmpty() const;
```

This function returns a nonzero value if there are no items in a `Bag`.

```
virtual countType getItemsInContainer() const;
```

This function returns the number of items (whether distinct or not) inserted into a `Bag`.

```
void forEach(void (*f)(Object&, void*),
                    void* args);
```

This is an internal iterator function. The function `f(...)` is invoked for each element present in a `Bag`.

```
Object& firstThat(int (*f)(const Object&, void*),
                  void* args) const;
```

This is another internal iterator function, which is used to traverse the items in a `Bag` to locate the first item that returns a nonzero value for the function `f(...)`. If multiple occurrences of the same object are present in a `Bag`, the instance most recently inserted will be returned by `firstThat(...)`. If no object is found, `NOOBJECT` is returned.

```
Object& lastThat(int (*f)(const Object&, void*),
                 void* args) const;
```

This is similar to the previous function, except that the object returned is the last item in a `Bag` to return a nonzero value for the function `f(...)`. If multiple occurrences of the same object are present in a `Bag`, the first instance inserted will be returned by `lastThat(...)`. `NOOBJECT` is returned if no item is located.

```
virtual int hasMember(Object& obj) const;
```

This function returns a nonzero value if the target object `obj` is found in a `Bag`.

```
virtual Object& findMember(Object& obj) const;
```

This function searches a `Bag` for a target element `obj`. If the element is found, it is returned without being removed from the `Bag`. If the object is not found, `NOOBJECT` is returned. If multiple occurrences of the same object are present, the last item inserted is the one returned.

```
virtual ContainerIterator& initIterator() const;
```

This function returns an external iterator object to be used to iterate over the elements in a `Bag`. The iterator is allocated dynamically from the heap and *must* be deleted after being used.

```
virtual classType isA() const;
virtual char* nameOf() const;
```

These two functions aid in identifying objects at runtime. The first function returns a unique value for class `Bag`. The second returns a pointer to the constant string `"Bag"`.

```
int ownsElements();
```

This function returns a nonzero value if a `Bag` container owns its contents.

```
void ownsElements(int del)
```

This function is used to give ownership to or remove ownership from a `Bag`. When a `Bag` owns its contents, it owns *all* the objects it contains. When the `Bag` goes out of scope, it will delete all the items it contains.

`private:`

```
HashTable table;
```

This private data member is the hash table used to store the data contained in a `Bag`.

`};`

Because the items in a `Bag` are stored in a `HashTable`, iteration through a `Bag` will not return objects in any specific order. Listing 8.7 is a short example that uses local objects with a `Bag`.

Listing 8.7. Using local objects in a `Bag`.

```
#include <iostream.h>
#include <strng.h>
#include <bag.h>

void main()
{
      Bag family;

      // remove object ownership from the Bag,
      // since local objects will be used !!
      family.ownsElements(0);

      // create some local objects
      String father("William");
      String mother("Laura");
      String son("Kevin");
      String daughter("Martha");

      family.add(father);
      family.add(mother);
      family.add(son);
      family.add(daughter);

      // print out the family
      ContainerIterator& next = family.initIterator();
      cout << "\nThe family members are:\n";
      while (next)
        cout << (next++) << " ";
      delete &next;
}
```

The output produced is

```
The family members are:
Martha William Kevin Laura
```

Note the apparent randomness of the order in which the family members were printed. The hashing function for the items in a `Bag` determines the order of storage of each object. Because the hashing function is virtual, it depends on the type of object stored. Care must be taken to remove element ownership from the `Bag` object when you are using non-heap objects, otherwise the `Bag` will attempt to delete its contents when it is going out of scope. Listing 8.8 is a short example that uses a dynamically allocated object with a `Bag`.

Listing 8.8. Using heap objects in a `Bag`.

```
#include <iostream.h>
#include <strng.h>
#include <bag.h>

void show(Object& obj, void*)
{
        cout << obj << " ";
}

void main()
{
      Bag family;

      // create some heap objects
      String& father   = *new String("William");
      String& mother   = *new String("Laura");
      String& son      = *new String("Kevin");
      String& daughter = *new String("Martha");

      family.add(father);
      family.add(mother);
      family.add(son);
      family.add(daughter);

      // print out the family, using an internal
      // iterator function
      cout << "\nThe family members are:\n";
      family.forEach(show, 0);
}
```

The output produced is

```
The family members are:
Martha William Kevin Laura
```

Because heap objects were used in `Bag`, ownership was left with the `Bag`. As an extra twist, I used the internal iterator function `forEach(...)` to iterate through the objects in the `Bag`. As you can see, the output is the same as the previous example, shown in Listing 8.7, that used an external iterator.

Class *BaseDate*

Calendar dates are used frequently in computer programs. With ANSI C, you were compelled to use a variety of functions to do something as simple as displaying the current date on the screen. With a class implementation for handling calendar dates, you can handle a complete date as a scalar data type. Displaying a date is as simple as this:

```
// display today's date
cout << Date();
```

The preceding statement uses a temporary variable, initializes it to today's date, and sends a printable representation of it to the standard output stream. It couldn't be easier. The problem with calendar dates is that there is no universal way of representing a date. Some countries base their year on events other than the birth of Christ. Some use a lunar calendar rather than one based on 12 variable-length months. Possibly because of these differences, Borland implemented the calendar dates with two classes. One stores dates in Western civilization format, which uses years, months, and days. The class is defined abstract, however, to force you to use another class to actually handle the way a date is converted to printable format, which is accomplished by class `Date`. Here is an edited version of class `BaseDate`:

`class BaseDate: public Sortable {`

`public:`

```
unsigned Month() const;
```

This function returns an unsigned integer value in the range 1..12, representing the months January through December.

```
unsigned Day() const;
```

This returns the day of the month in the range 1..31.

```
unsigned Year() const;
```

This returns the complete year in the range 0..65535.

```
void SetMonth( unsigned char );
```

This takes a value in the range 1..12 and stores it in the private variable MM. To set the month to April, you pass a value of 4.

```
void SetDay( unsigned char );
```

This function stores a value into the private variable DD. There are a few problems with this member function. Although calendar months have days in the range 1..31, passing a 0 causes no errors. Moreover, the function doesn't check to see whether the day value is consistent with the month stored in MM, which allows you to set the date to something like February 31.

```
void SetYear( unsigned );
```

This function sets the YY member variable to a certain value in the range 0..65535.

```
virtual hashValueType hashValue() const;
```

This function returns a hash value computed using the day, month, and year in a `BaseDate` object. It returns the following value:

```
//compute a hash value for a date
return hashValueType(YY + MM + DD);
```

```
virtual int isEqual(const Object&) const;
virtual int isLessThan(const Object&) const;
```

These virtual functions establish a way of ordering date objects. Because they are called polymorphically by the global operators `::operator==(Object&, Object&)` and `::operator<(Object&, Object&)`, you rarely need to invoke these functions directly. Function `BaseDate::isEqual(const Object&)` performs equality checking, returning nonzero if two dates are the same.

```
virtual void printOn(ostream&) const = 0;
```

This pure virtual function forces any derived classes to provide their own functions for inserting a date into an output stream. This function is then called polymorphically by the global operator `::operator<<(ostream&, Object&)`. The function `Object::printOn(ostream&)` in a derived class should insert a printable character representation of a date into a stream.

```
protected:
```

```
BaseDate();
```

This default constructor builds an object using the current date, by calling `SetMonth(...)`, `SetDay(...)`, and `SetYear(...)` for each of its arguments. If the date were June 17, 1993, this constructor would cause the following values to be stored:

```
// The data stored for June 17, 1993
MM    6
DD    17
YY    1993
```

```
BaseDate(unsigned char, unsigned char, unsigned);
```

This constructor lets you set the date explicitly. Unfortunately, it doesn't check that the day is consistent with the month, enabling you to set the date to something like February 30 or September 31. Also, the format used for the year is user-dependent. Some people use only two digits for the year. You can do so with this constructor too, but I don't recommend it. The default constructor `BaseDate()` builds a date, which includes the century (for example, *1992*). The ordering member functions `isEqual(...)` and `isLessThan(...)` would return incorrect results comparing dates with different formats. For all the class knows, the date *92* is different from *1992.*

```
BaseDate(const BaseDate&);
```

This copy constructor builds a new `BaseDate` object using the values stored in another BaseDate object.

`private:`

```
unsigned char MM;
```

This private data member stores the month as a value in the range 1..12. January is represented by a 1, February by a 2, and so on.

```
unsigned char DD;
```

This private data member stores the day as a value in the range 1..31. When you set the day value by using the class constructor or the function `BaseDate::SetDay(unsigned char)`, the class fails to check the month, allowing you to set the date to something like June 31.

```
unsigned int YY;
```

This private data member stores the year as a non-negative value. The value stored includes the century, so that *1991* is stored as *1991*. If you use *91* to represent *1991*, you will have problems when comparing dates set this way to dates set through the default constructor `BaseDate()`.

```
};
```

Class `BaseDate` is abstract, so no objects can be instantiated from it. See class `Date` for details on the use of class `BaseDate` as a base class.

Class *BaseTime*

Keeping track of time is an essential process. Programs use time variables to tag files and records in databases. Time functions are used to compute program delays, differences between times, time zone variations, and so on. Time is used so often that Borland decided to make a class to handle it. The problem with times is in format. Europeans and Asians often use a 24-hour clock, whereas Americans use a 12-hour clock. Another important consideration is the precision (not to be confused with accuracy) of a time value. If you're clocking a downhill ski competition, you'll probably need to display milliseconds. If you just need to display the time of day on your computer screen, you probably need only hours, minutes, and maybe seconds. The variations in formatting time are significant enough to justify a multiclass approach. An abstract class `BaseTime` is used to store the basic time parameters, including hours, minutes, and seconds, whereas the specifics for displaying the time and handling different formats are deferred to derived classes.

Borland supplies the derived class `Time` to handle time formats that are commonly used in the United States; however, it is easy to derive classes that support any format, which is shown in the section dealing with class `Time`. Here is an edited version of the header file for class `BaseTime`:

```
class BaseTime: public Sortable {
```

```
public:
```

```
unsigned hour() const;
unsigned minute() const;
unsigned second() const;
unsigned hundredths() const;
```

These access functions return the values stored in the private variables HH, MM, SS, or HD.

```
void setHour(unsigned char);
void setMinute(unsigned char);
void setSecond(unsigned char);
void setHundredths(unsigned char);
```

These functions allow you to set the private member variables HH, MM, SS, or HD to specific values. If you pass arguments that are invalid, your program is aborted and an

error message is displayed. Function `BaseTime::setHour(unsigned char)` expects its argument to be a value in the range 0..23. If you want to set a morning time, use 0..11. For afternoon and evening times, use 12..23. There is no a.m./p.m. variable in class `BaseTime` because the hour itself indicates a.m. or p.m. unambiguously.

```
virtual classType isA() const = 0;
```

This pure virtual forces classes derived from `BaseTime` to provide their own functions that return a unique value, which is used to identify classes at runtime.

```
virtual char* nameOf() const = 0;
```

This pure virtual forces classes derived from `BaseTime` to provide their own functions that return a printable representation of a class, which is used in identifying classes at runtime.

```
virtual hashValueType hashValue() const;
```

This function computes a hash value from the time. It computes the value by adding the values of the four variables HH, MM, SS, and HD. Note that a `BaseTime` object does not keep track of time by itself. Once you set the variables in a `BaseTime` to certain values, they stay that way until you change them. This implies that the hash value returned from a `BaseTime` object does not change automatically with the passing of time.

```
virtual int isEqual(const Object&) const;
```

This function tests to see whether two times are equal. Function `isEqual(Object&)` is called polymorphically by the global `::operator==(Object&, Object&)`.

```
virtual int isLessThan(const Object&) const;
```

This compares the values of two times. The function is called polymorphically by the global `::operator<(Object&, Object&)`.

```
virtual void printOn(ostream&) const = 0;
```

This pure virtual forces classes derived from `BaseTime` to provide their own functions to insert a printable representation of a `BaseTime` into an output stream. This function is called polymorphically by the global `::operator<<(ostream&, Object&)`.

`protected:`

```
BaseTime();
```

This default constructor builds a `BaseTime` object using the current system time. Once the object is built, its time variables remain constant unless you explicitly change them.

```
BaseTime(const BaseTime&);
```

This copy constructor builds one `BaseTime` object using the time values of another.

```
BaseTime(unsigned char,
         unsigned char = 0,
         unsigned char = 0,
         unsigned char = 0);
```

This function lets you build a `BaseTime` object with a precise time value. You use this constructor rather than the default constructor if you want to use a time other than the system time.

```
private:
```

```
unsigned char HH;
```

This private data member stores the hour in 24-hour format, with values in the range 0..23. A 0 indicates midnight, whereas a 12 indicates noon.

```
unsigned char MM;
```

This private data member stores the minutes as a value in the range 0..59.

```
unsigned char SS;
```

This private data member stores the seconds as a value in the range 0..59.

```
unsigned char HD;
```

This data member stores hundredths of a second, using values in the range 0..99. Because the time is updated 18.2 times a second (about every 0.05494 seconds) in PCs and compatibles, there isn't enough resolution to provide exact hundredths of a second. Because of this, the hundredths field varies in increments of 5.494. Sometimes the difference between near-equal times can be 5 hundredths, and sometimes it can be 6 hundredths.

```
};
```

`BaseTime` is an abstract class, as you can tell by its pure virtual functions. It provides only a minimal framework for dealing with time variables, but does not support arithmetic operations between `BaseTime` objects. Support for arithmetic operations is provided by a class I derive later from `Time`.

Class *Btree*

A rather conspicuous absence in the Borland C++ 2.0 container class library is a class to support trees. Trees are used extensively in computer science, and have advantages over linked lists and arrays because they support sorted collections of objects with little memory overhead.

A Tree Primer

Some readers may be unfamiliar with b-trees, so I'll provide a short, informal introduction to trees in general and b-trees in particular. Tree structures have been used in computer science for many years. A tree can be considered the logical extension of a linked list, and is used primarily to facilitate the searching of sorted data. Data is referenced by nodes, and nodes are organized into a tree structure. Lists have a unidimensional structure, whereas trees have a bidimensional one. Figure 8.2 shows a generic tree.

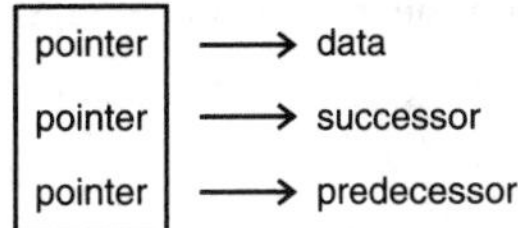

Figure 8.2. A tree data structure.

The number of descendents that a node can have is called the *order* of a tree. In a binary tree, nodes have two descendents. In a ternary tree, nodes have three descendents. In an *m*-ary tree, nodes have *m* descendents. The various forms of trees vary significantly, not only in the layout in memory, but also in the difficulties of searching, adding, and removing items. All trees use the concept of comparison to locate items. Comparison requires a way to determine whether items are *equal to*, *less than*, or *greater than* each other. For scalar data types, such as integers and characters, there is no problem. To use class objects in a tree, there must be proper ordering operators available. In the following sections, the comparison operators are assumed to be those defined for the type of objects used.

Binary Trees

Binary trees are among the simplest forms of trees. Each node stores an item (or a pointer to an item), plus two pointers to descendents: a left descendent and a right descendent. When a node has no descendent, the corresponding pointer is null. A node with no descendents is called a *terminal node.*

Item Additions

When you add an item to a binary tree, the item is compared to the item in the root node. If the value is *equal* to the item at the root, the item is already contained in the tree. Binary trees often disallow multiple insertions of the same item, but it is possible to use a counter variable in each node to count the number of insertions of a given item. If the item is *less than* the item at the root, the left descendent pointer is chosen; otherwise, the right descendent pointer is chosen. The process of going from a node to its descendent repeats until a node is found that has no descendent, or the item is located. If the item is not located, it is inserted into the tree as a descendent of the last node visited.

Item Searches

The processes of adding and searching for items are mutually dependent. You can't search for items unless there is a tree with elements already in it, and you can't add items unless you can search a tree. Searching is accomplished by traveling from the one node to one of its descendents, until either the item or the end of the tree is found. If the target item is *less than* the item at a given node, the left descendent is selected. Otherwise, the right descendent is used.

Item Deletions

In binary trees, deleting items can be, in general, much more complicated than adding items. There are three types of nodes, each of which affects a binary tree differently.

- Terminal nodes (no descendents): You just set the node's pointer in the parent to null.
- Inner nodes (one descendent): You set the pointer in the parent node to point at the node's only descendent.
- Inner nodes (two descendents): This is where things get complicated. You have to arrange the left and right descendents of the node into the remaining tree. If the descendents are terminal nodes, the process is simple. If the descendents are the roots of sub-trees, you have to combine the two sub-trees into a single sub-tree, then replace the deleted inner node with the combined sub-tree. The details aren't too complicated, but are beyond the scope of this book.

Performance

The performance of a binary tree depends on how balanced the tree is, which in turn depends on the order of insertion of items. If items are inserted in random order, the tree tends to be well balanced. To locate an item in a balanced tree with *N* items requires an amount of processing proportional to $\log_2(N)$. If the tree is degenerately unbalanced, which reduces it to essentially a unidimensional linked list, the amount of average processing is

proportional to N/2. Consider, for example, a balanced binary tree with 1 million elements. The maximum number of nodes to visit will be about 10. If the tree is completely unbalanced, the maximum number of nodes to visit will be 1 million. In practice, binary trees are somewhere in the middle, and often are closer to being perfectly balanced than completely unbalanced.

B-Trees

B-trees are specialized balanced trees. B-trees are not binary trees, and were developed as a solution to the inefficiencies of unbalanced trees. Although it is possible to balance a binary tree after any insertion, in practice there is too much overhead if items are inserted frequently. B-trees are used when the amount of data to be managed is unknown and is expected to be quite large. It isn't uncommon to come across commercial programs that use b-trees to manage hundreds of thousands or even millions of objects. B-trees are *multiway* trees, meaning that each node can have not just two, but many descendents. The number of descendents of a node defines the order of a b-tree. Speaking of order, the Borland documentation defines the order of a b-tree differently from the computer science literature. Knuth defines the order to be the maximum number of descendents a node can have, whereas Borland defines the order as the number of descendents minus one. Because I describe Borland's implementation of b-trees, I use Borland's notation throughout this book.

NOTE

In this section, the order of a b-tree is defined as a node's maximum number of descendents minus one. This is the Borland definition, and it is different from the definition commonly found in computer science literature (for example, see Donald E. Knuth's *The Art of Computer Programming*, volume 3).

The Structure of B-Trees

With b-trees, performance is guaranteed because the structure of the tree is guaranteed to remain balanced. What makes b-trees so superior to binary trees and other kinds of trees is a set of rules used to expand and shrink the tree. I describe these rules in the next section, but first let's take a look at a typical b-tree containing some data. Consider a b-tree of order 5. Such a b-tree will have nodes containing five keys (data elements) and six pointers to descendents. Terminal nodes can contain 2*(5+1) keys. Figure 8.3 shows a small fifth-order b-tree used to manage names in a short telephone directory.

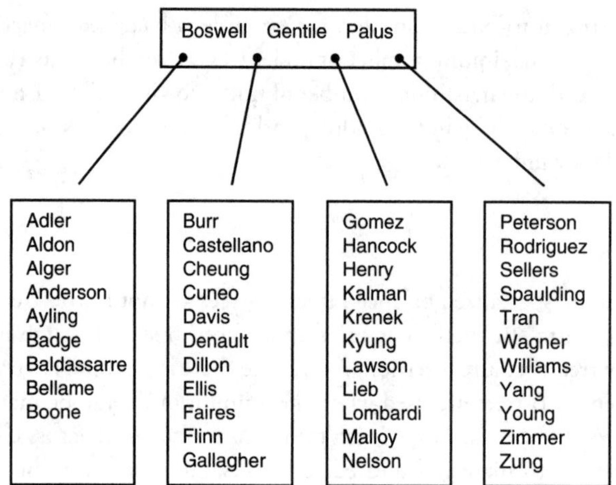

Figure 8.3. A small fifth-order b-tree containing strings.

Each leaf can contain up to 12 keys. Each inner node can contain up to five keys. If adding a key to a leaf node results in more than 12 keys, the node overflows and its keys are rearranged in a manner that is described in the next section. The minimum number of keys allowed in a leaf node is given by the variable `LeafLowWaterMark`. If, after deleting a key from a leaf node, there are less than `LeafLowWaterMark` keys, the leaf is merged with another node or keys are taken from a brother node. The minimum number of keys for an inner node is given by the variable `InnerLowWaterMark`. Adding two entries to the node containing the names (Burr..Gallagher) results in a leaf node overflow, as shown in Figure 8.4.

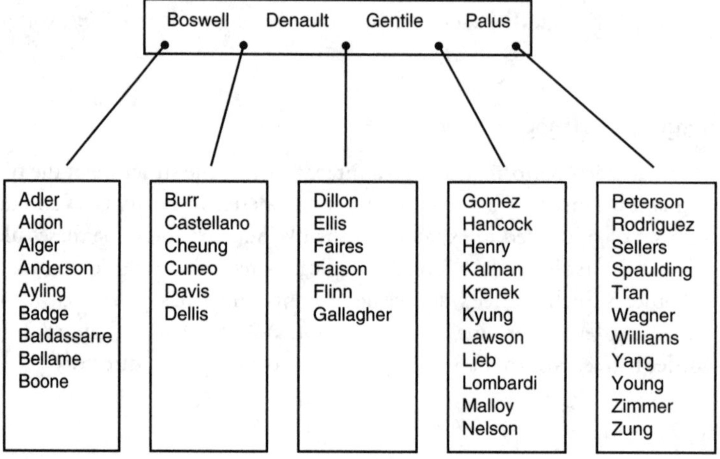

Figure 8.4. Adding items to a b-tree, resulting in the overflow of a node.

Adding the names *Dellis* and *Faison* results in a leaf node overflow. The center key, *Denault,* is moved up one level and the leaf is split into two. Deleting a key is just as simple as inserting one. If the deletion of a key causes an underflow at a node, a key is taken from the parent node. If the parent node also underflows, the process repeats.

Node Overflows

When adding a key to a node produces an overflow condition, the keys in the node must be rearranged in the b-tree. Listing 8.9 fills a third-order b-tree with `String` objects, forcing overflows. You can see how the tree keys are rearranged by studying the output of the program.

Listing 8.9. A program to force node overflows.

```
#include <btree.h>
#include <strng.h>
#include <iostream.h>
#include <fstream.h>

void main()
{
      String& a = *new String("a");
      String& b = *new String("b");
      String& c = *new String("c");
      String& d = *new String("d");
      String& e = *new String("e");
      String& f = *new String("f");
      String& g = *new String("g");
      String& h = *new String("h");
      String& i = *new String("i");
      String& j = *new String("j");
      String& k = *new String("k");
      String& l = *new String("l");
      String& m = *new String("m");
      String& n = *new String("n");

      // create a local b-tree of default
      // order 3
      Btree tree;

      tree.add(a);
      tree.add(b);
      tree.add(c);
      tree.add(d);
      tree.add(e);
      tree.add(f);
```

continues

Listing 8.9. continued

```
        ofstream output("output.log");
        output << "\n" << tree;

        tree.add(g);
        output << "\n" << tree;
        tree.add(h);
        output << "\n" << tree;
        tree.add(i);
        output << "\n" << tree;
        tree.add(j);
        output << "\n" << tree;
        tree.add(k);
        output << "\n" << tree;
        tree.add(l);
        output << "\n" << tree;
        tree.add(m);
        output << "\n" << tree;
        tree.add(n);
        output << "\n" << tree;
}
```

The output produced in file *output.log* is

```
 < a b c d e f >
 < a b c d e f g >
 [ /4 < a b c d > e/3 < f g h >  ]
 [ /4 < a b c d > e/4 < f g h i >  ]
 [ /4 < a b c d > e/5 < f g h i j >  ]
 [ /4 < a b c d > e/6 < f g h i j k >  ]
 [ /4 < a b c d > e/7 < f g h i j k l >  ]
 [ /6 < a b c d e f > g/6 < h i j k l m >  ]
 [ /6 < a b c d e f > g/7 < h i j k l m n >  ]
```

Nodes are delimited by the <> characters. The number appearing after the slash indicates the number of keys in the following node. The last tree produced has the following structure:

```
a
b
c
d
e
          f
g
h
i
j
          k
```

```
l
m
n
o
p
```

The keys *f* and *k* are contained in the root node, whereas the other keys are in terminal nodes. When an overflow occurs in a node, the keys are distributed into a brother node, if possible; otherwise, the node is split into two parts and the middle key is moved up to the parent node. The distribution of keys in brother nodes is known as *node balancing*. For high-order b-trees, the difference in processing time between balancing a node and splitting a node may be substantial. Borland b-tree containers automatically select whether to balance or split a node on overflow, based on the instantaneous contents of the tree.

When an overflow occurs at a node and the node is split into two nodes, the center key is moved to the parent node. If the parent node also overflows and is split, the process repeats. If the root node overflows and splits, a new root node is created, causing the height of the tree to increase by one level. Whereas binary trees grow from the root downward, b-trees grow from the leaves upward.

The Borland B-Tree Rules

Class `Btree`, as implemented in the Borland C++ container class library, is a variant on the b-tree data structure described by D.E. Knuth. Because of the differences, it is suitable at this point to list the rules of Borland b-trees explicitly. Here are the basic rules for an arbitrary Borland b-tree of order *M*:

- Nonterminal nodes can have at most *M* keys and *M*+1 descendents.
- Terminal nodes can have at most 2*(*M*+1) keys. Terminal nodes by definition have no descendents.
- All nodes (except the root node) must have a minimum number of keys, determined by the variables `InnerLowWaterMark` and `LeafLowWaterMark`.
- All leaf nodes are the same distance from the root.
- The order of a b-tree is greater than or equal to 3.
- Only objects derived from class `Sortable` may be handled as keys.

Each inner node in a Borland b-tree of order M has at most M keys ($K_1..K_m$) and M+1 pointers ($P_0..P_m$) to descendents. Pointer P_0 points to the descendent having keys that are all less than K_0. Pointer P_1 points to the descendent having keys that are between K_0 and K_1. Pointer P_m points to the descendent having keys that are greater than K_m. Figure 8.5 is a graphical representation, using a b-tree of order 3, having keys that are integers.

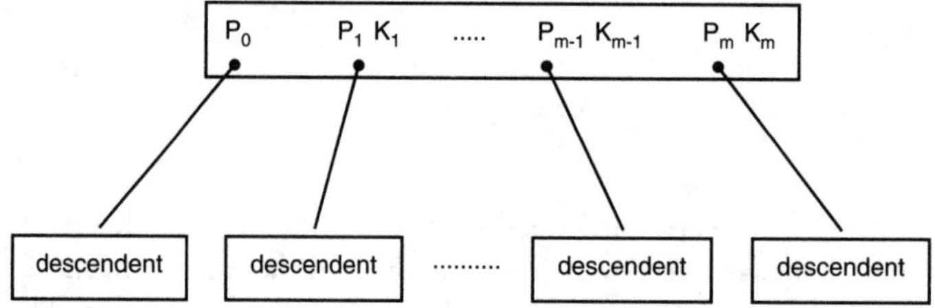

Figure 8.5. The keys and pointers used by an inner node of a Borland b-tree.

Each node has one more pointer than it has keys. Figure 8.6 is a small b-tree of order 3 that has keys that are integers.

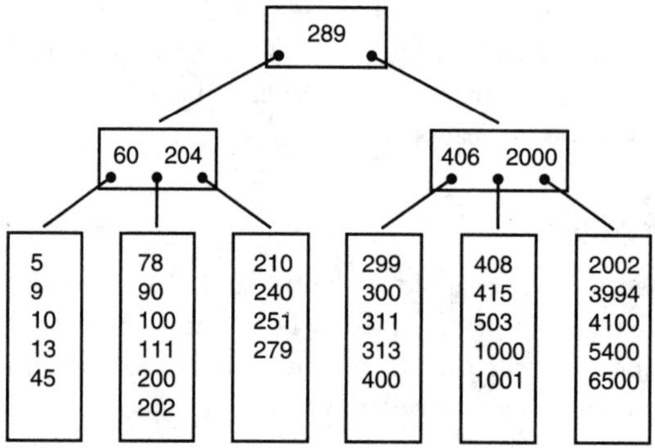

Figure 8.6. An example of a Borland b-tree of order 3.

Borland b-trees use a class object called Node to handle both a key and a pointer in each node. For inner nodes, the key K_0 is left unused. For terminal nodes, the pointers are used to hold keys. It follows that inner nodes can hold M keys, and terminal nodes can hold 2*(M+1) keys.

Although b-trees were originally designed for data structures that could be used with file data structures, Borland b-trees are implemented only for primary memory (RAM) data structures. If you wish to handle data structures that are larger than available RAM, you need to derive your own class from `Btree` and incorporate the necessary features.

B-Trees Are Not Binary Trees

Don't confuse a binary tree with a b-tree. The two kinds of data structures are both trees, but are also quite different. A binary tree is made up of nodes, each having two possible successors. Inserting data into a binary tree results in a tree structure that is a function of the order of data insertions. If data is inserted in random order, a balanced tree tends to

develop. If data is inserted in sorted order, a degenerate tree results, which looks more like a linked list than a tree.

A b-tree is quite different. B-trees are much more efficient when you deal with a large amount of data, and are self-balancing trees. B-trees are typically used with orders greater than 3. B-trees with orders over 100 are not unusual for large databases.

The Declaration of Class *Btree*

Class `Btree` goes a long way toward hiding the inner complexities of b-trees, to the point that you can use a `Btree` container pretty much the same way as the other containers in the `Object`-based class library. `Btree` uses a few ancillary classes to implement internal details; however, because the user doesn't deal with these classes directly, I will not describe them. Here is an edited version of the header file for class `Btree`:

```
class Btree : public Collection {
```

```
public:
```

```
Btree(int ordern = 3);
```

This constructor creates a b-tree with a default order of 3.

```
~Btree();
```

This destructor deletes all the nodes and objects handled by a b-tree.

```
void add(Object&);
```

This function adds an object to a b-tree. Only objects derived from class `Sortable` are allowed to be placed into a b-tree. Multiple occurrences of the same object are allowed.

```
void detach(Object&, DeleteType = NoDelete);
```

The function removes a selected item from a b-tree. By default, the removed object is not deleted, but you can force it to be deleted by giving the value `DeleteType::Delete` for the second argument. The first argument returns a reference to the object removed (if it is found in the b-tree); otherwise, it will refer to NOOBJECT.

```
void flush(DeleteType = DefDelete);
```

This function removes all the objects from a b-tree. By default, the function also deletes all the objects.

```
virtual int hasMember(Object&) const;
```

This function returns a nonzero value if a given object is found to be present in a b-tree.

```
virtual Object& findMember(Object&) const;
```

This function returns a reference to a given object—if that object is present in a b-tree. If the object is not found, a reference to NOOBJECT is returned.

```
virtual int isEmpty() const;
```

This function returns a nonzero value if there are no items in a `Btree`.

```
virtual countType getItemsInContainer() const;
```

This function returns the number of objects in a container. Multiple occurrences of the same object are counted separately.

```
virtual classType isA() const;
```

This function returns a unique value to indicate `Btree` objects.

```
virtual char* nameOf() const;
```

This function returns a pointer to the static string `"Btree"`.

```
virtual int isEqual(const Object&) const;
```

This function determines whether two b-trees are *equal.* Equality is based on whether two trees contain the same elements, regardless of the internal structure of the trees.

```
virtual void printOn(ostream&) const;
```

The function inserts all the items of a `Btree` into an output stream. Here is a sample output:

```
[ /4 < a b c d > e/5 < f g h i j >  ]
```

The tree is delimited by [] characters. Nodes are delimited by <> characters. The values appearing after a slash tell how many items are contained in the following node. The previous sample output corresponds to the b-tree structure in Figure 8.7.

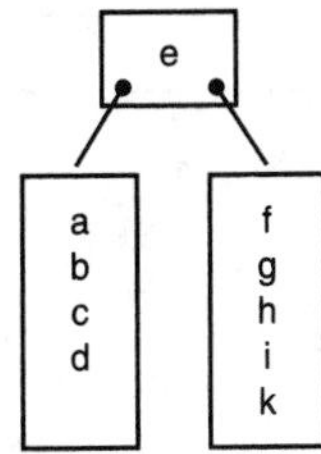

Figure 8.7. The structure of a simple `Btree` *object.*

```
virtual ContainerIterator& initIterator() const;
```

This function returns a reference to a dynamically allocated b-tree iterator. After using this iterator, you must delete it yourself.

```
int order();
```

This function returns the order of a b-tree. Borland b-trees have a default order of 3, meaning that each inner node can contain at most three objects and four pointers to descendents. Terminal nodes can have at most eight objects.

```
Object& operator[](long i) const;
```

This returns the *i*th largest value in a `Btree`. If you want the smallest object, use a value of 0. For the largest object, use the value returned by `Btree::getItemsInContainer()` minus 1.

```
long rank(const Object&) const;
```

This determines the rank of a given object. If a b-tree does not contain multiple occurrences of the same object, the smallest object in a b-tree has rank 0, the next smallest has rank 1, and so on. The largest object's rank is the same as the value returned by `Btree::getItemsInContainer()` minus 1. If an object occurs multiple times, the rank of the first occurrence is returned. Consider the b-tree with the structure shown in Figure 8.8.

Here are the ranks of a few selected keys:

Key	*Rank*
a	0
f	7
g	8
m	14

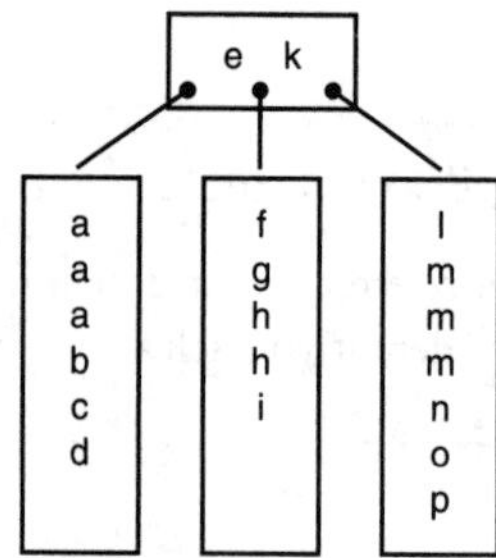

Figure 8.8. A simple b-tree with multiple occurrences of items.

protected:

```
void incrNofKeys() { itemsInContainer++; }
void decrNofKeys() { itemsInContainer--; }
```

The two previous functions are designed for use in derived classes, when objects are added or removed from a b-tree.

```
long i_add(const Object&);
```

This function inserts an object into a b-tree and returns the rank of the inserted object.

private:

```
int Order;
```

This private variable stores the order of a b-tree.

```
int Order2;
```

This variable stores the value 2*(order + 1), the maximum number of items allowed in a terminal node. This value is computed once to improve the runtime speed of `Btrees`.

```
int Inner_LowWaterMark;
int Leaf_LowWaterMark;
int Inner_MaxIndex;
int Leaf_MaxIndex;
```

The previous four private variables store the values representing the lower and upper limit on the number of keys that can be stored in a node.

```
Node* root;
```

This points to the root node of a b-tree.

```
void finishInit(int);
void rootIsFull();
void rootIsEmpty();
```

The previous three functions implement internal processing functions, the details of which are beyond the scope of this book.

```
unsigned itemsInContainer;
```

This variable stores the number of objects stored in a b-tree. Multiple occurrences of the same object are counted separately.

```
};
```

A Complete *Btree* Example

`Btree`s are by far the most complicated container in the class library, but the implementation is such that using them is very straightforward. I present a short program here that catalogs the phone numbers from the list of names shown in Figure 8.3. The program in Listing 8.10 makes use of both an internal iterator and an external iterator, and demonstrates the use of most of the `Btree` public member functions.

Listing 8.10. A program using a `Btree` object.

```
#include <btree.h>
#include <strng.h>
#include <assoc.h>
#include <math.h>
#include <fstream.h>

class PhoneEntry: public Sortable {
```

continues

Listing 8.10. continued

```
        String& aKey;
        String& aValue;

public:

    enum {phoneEntryClass = __firstUserClass};

    PhoneEntry(char* name, char* value)
    : aKey(*new String(name) ),
      aValue(*new String(value) ) {}
    PhoneEntry()
    : aKey(*new String("") ),
      aValue(*new String("") ) {}

    virtual classType isA() const
      { return phoneEntryClass; }

    virtual char _FAR *nameOf() const
      { return "PhoneEntry"; }

    virtual int isEqual(const Object&) const;
    virtual int isLessThan(const Object&) const;

    virtual hashValueType hashValue() const
      { return aKey.hashValue(); }
    virtual void printOn(ostream& os) const
      { os << aKey << ":" << aValue; }

    String& key() const {return aKey;}
    String& value() {return aValue;}

    ~PhoneEntry() {delete &aKey; delete &aValue;}
};


int PhoneEntry::isEqual(const Object& e) const
{
        return key() ==
            ((PhoneEntry&)(Association&)e).key();
}

int PhoneEntry::isLessThan(const Object& e) const
{
        return key() <
            ((PhoneEntry&)(Association&)e).key();
}

void main()
{
```

 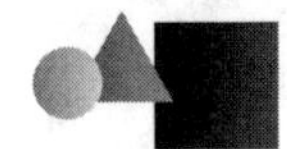

```
// open a log file
ofstream output("output.log");

// create a fifth order b-tree
Btree p(5);

p.add( *(Association*) new PhoneEntry("Yang", "555-1039") );
p.add( *(Association*) new PhoneEntry("Castellano", "555-1010") );
p.add( *(Association*) new PhoneEntry("Ayling", "555-1004") );
p.add( *(Association*) new PhoneEntry("Badge", "555-1005") );
p.add( *(Association*) new PhoneEntry("Baldasarre", "555-1006") );
p.add( *(Association*) new PhoneEntry("Bellame", "555-1007") );
p.add( *(Association*) new PhoneEntry("Henry", "555-1023") );
p.add( *(Association*) new PhoneEntry("Kalman", "555-1024") );
p.add( *(Association*) new PhoneEntry("Boone", "555-1008") );
p.add( *(Association*) new PhoneEntry("Alger", "555-1002") );
p.add( *(Association*) new PhoneEntry("Williams", "555-1038") );
p.add( *(Association*) new PhoneEntry("Boswell", "555-1008") );
p.add( *(Association*) new PhoneEntry("Cheung", "555-1011") );
p.add( *(Association*) new PhoneEntry("Cuneo", "555-1012") );
p.add( *(Association*) new PhoneEntry("Dillon", "555-1015") );
p.add( *(Association*) new PhoneEntry("Ellis", "555-1016") );
p.add( *(Association*) new PhoneEntry("Adler", "555-1000") );
p.add( *(Association*) new PhoneEntry("Wagner", "555-1037") );
p.add( *(Association*) new PhoneEntry("Toung", "555-1040") );
p.add( *(Association*) new PhoneEntry("Aldon", "555-1001") );
p.add( *(Association*) new PhoneEntry("Faires", "555-1017") );
p.add( *(Association*) new PhoneEntry("Kyung", "555-1026") );
p.add( *(Association*) new PhoneEntry("Lawson", "555-1027") );
p.add( *(Association*) new PhoneEntry("Flinn", "555-1018") );
p.add( *(Association*) new PhoneEntry("Gallagher", "555-1019") );
p.add( *(Association*) new PhoneEntry("Gentile", "555-1020") );
p.add( *(Association*) new PhoneEntry("Gomez", "555-1021") );
p.add( *(Association*) new PhoneEntry("Hancock", "555-1022") );
p.add( *(Association*) new PhoneEntry("Krenek", "555-1025") );
p.add( *(Association*) new PhoneEntry("Lieb", "555-1028") );
p.add( *(Association*) new PhoneEntry("Lombardi", "555-1029") );
p.add( *(Association*) new PhoneEntry("Malloy", "555-1030") );
p.add( *(Association*) new PhoneEntry("Nelson", "555-1031") );
p.add( *(Association*) new PhoneEntry("Palus", "555-1032") );
p.add( *(Association*) new PhoneEntry("Peterson", "555-1033") );
p.add( *(Association*) new PhoneEntry("Rodriguez", "555-1034") );
p.add( *(Association*) new PhoneEntry("Sellers", "555-1035") );
p.add( *(Association*) new PhoneEntry("Anderson", "555-1003") );
p.add( *(Association*) new PhoneEntry("Burr", "555-1009") );
p.add( *(Association*) new PhoneEntry("Spaulding", "555-1035") );
p.add( *(Association*) new PhoneEntry("Tran", "555-1036") );
p.add( *(Association*) new PhoneEntry("Zimmer", "555-1041") );
p.add( *(Association*) new PhoneEntry("Davis", "555-1013") );
```

continues

Listing 8.10. continued

```
p.add( *(Association*) new PhoneEntry("Denault", "555-1014") );
p.add( *(Association*) new PhoneEntry("Zung", "555-1042") );

output << "\n" << p << endl;

int items = p.getItemsInContainer();

output << "\nThere are "
     << items
     << " entries in the directory";

output << "\nThe first entry is "
     << (PhoneEntry&) (p [0]);

output << "\nThe sixth entry is "
     << (PhoneEntry&) (p [5]);

output << "\nThe third last entry is "
     << (PhoneEntry&) (p [items - 3]);

output << "\nThe last entry is "
     << (PhoneEntry&) (p [items - 1]);

// create objects to search for
PhoneEntry kalman("Kalman", "");
PhoneEntry burr("Burr", "");
PhoneEntry myers("Myers", "");

output << "\n" << kalman.key()
     << " is entry number "
     << p.rank(kalman)
     << " in the directory.\n"
     << kalman.key() << "'s phone number is"
     << ((PhoneEntry&)(p.findMember(kalman))).value();

output << "\nThere are "
     << labs(p.rank(kalman) - p.rank(burr) )
     << " entries between "
     << kalman.key()
     << " and "
     << burr.key();

int member = p.hasMember(myers);
if (member) {
  output << "\n" << myers.key()
       << " is entry number "
       << p.rank(myers)
       << " in the phone directory";
}
```

```
  else {
    output << "\n" << myers.key()
           << " is not in the directory, "
           << "but it would have been entry number "
           << p.rank(myers);
  }
}
```

The output produced in file *output.log* is the following (the b-tree entries are actually all on one line, but are shown here in a more readable format):

```
[ /9 < Adler:555-1000 Aldon:555-1001 Alger:555-1002
       Anderson:555-1003 Ayling:555-1004 Badge:555-1005
       Baldasarre:555-1006 Bellame:555-1007 Boone:555-1008
     >

       Boswell:555-1008/11

     < Burr:555-1009 Castellano:555-1010 Cheung:555-1011
       Cuneo:555-1012 Davis:555-1013 Denault:555-1014
       Dillon:555-1015 Ellis:555-1016 Faires:555-1017
       Flinn:555-1018 Gallagher:555-1019
     >

       Gentile:555-1020/11

     < Gomez:555-1021 Hancock:555-1022 Henry:555-1023
       Kalman:555-1024 Krenek:555-1025 Kyung:555-1026
       Lawson:555-1027 Lieb:555-1028 Lombardi:555-1029
       Malloy:555-1030 Nelson:555-1031
     >

       Palus:555-1032/11

     < Peterson:555-1033 Rodriguez:555-1034 Sellers:555-1035
       Spaulding:555-1035 Toung:555-1040 Tran:555-1036
       Wagner:555-1037 Williams:555-1038 Yang:555-1039
       Zimmer:555-1041 Zung:555-1042
     >
 ]
There are 45 entries in the directory
The first entry is Adler:555-1000
The sixth entry is Badge:555-1005
The third last entry is Yang:555-1039
The last entry is Zung:555-1042
Kalman is entry number 25 in the directory
Kalman's phone number is 555-1024
There are 15 entries between Kalman and Burr
Myers is not in the directory, but it would have been entry number 21
```

The internal structure of a b-tree depends on the order of insertion of its keys, but the end result is always a sorted tree, if traversed from the top (or left-most) terminal node to the bottom (or right-most) terminal node. You can tell by studying the output that the keys {Boswell, Gentile, Palus} are stored in the root node—given the order of insertion shown. The 45 entries I used in the previous example are not enough to cause a fifth-order b-tree to grow beyond a height of 2, so the b-tree has no inner nodes besides the root. All keys not stored in the root node are therefore stored in terminal nodes.

As you can see from the example, b-trees are not only easy to use, but they are also efficient and convenient—particularly with large amounts of data. I create a custom association class to deal with sortable associations. I could have derived class `PhoneEntry` multiply from `Association` and `Sortable`, but because `Object` is not declared a virtual base class in either class, it would have been cumbersome to convert `PhoneEntry` references to `Object` references as required during the implementation and use of `PhoneEntry`. Each conversion would have looked like this:

```
Object& obj = (Object&)(Association)(name);
```

The double typecast would have been necessary to tell the compiler into which copy of the base `Object` you wished to convert the phone association. The implementation of class `PhoneEntry` in the previous example lets you look up the phone number from a name but doesn't let you find the name associated with a given phone number. It is a simple matter to change `PhoneEntry` to support such reverse associations and others.

Class *Collection*

A `Collection` class is a specialized form of container, which can be used as a base class to keep track of *groups* of objects. The objects in this group don't have to be of the same type. The only requirement is that they all derive somehow from class `Object`.

Class `Collection` is abstract, because the ways in which objects are managed and accessed are known only in derived classes. Here is an edited version of the header file for class `Collection`:

`class Collection: public Container {`

`public:`

```
virtual void add(Object&) = 0;
```

This pure virtual function forces classes derived from `Collection` to provide their own functions to add an object. This operation can't be supported by class `Collection`, because the way in which an object is added depends on the type of `Collection` being used. Linked lists insert objects between others and require appropriate list pointers, whereas

arrays don't. HashTables are even more different. Attempts to add an object that is already in a collection are handled differently by the derived classes. Sometimes the attempt might be ignored, as with class Set, whereas other times the attempt is honored, as with class HashTable.

```
virtual void detach(Object&, DeleteType = NoDelete) = 0;
```

This function is declared pure virtual because detaching an object from a collection has consequences that are unknown in class Collection. The second parameter controls whether a detached object is also deleted. If you choose not to have the object deleted, you assume responsibility for doing so. Note that if a container has more than one occurrence of the same object, only *the first occurrence* will be detached. See member function Container::findMember(...) for a description of *the first occurrence.*

```
void destroy(Object&);
```

This function invokes Container::detach(...) to remove and delete a given object from a container.

```
virtual int hasMember(Object& obj) const;
```

This function returns nonzero if a given object occurs at least once in a collection. Otherwise it returns 0.

```
virtual Object& findMember(Object& obj) const;
```

This virtual function finds *the first occurrence* of a given object obj in a collection. What *the first occurrence* means depends on the type of container being used. With arrays, the first occurrence is the object at the lowest array index. With bags, hash tables, and linked lists, the first occurrence is the last instance added to the container. If findMember(...) fails in locating the target object, it returns NOOBJECT.

```
};
```

When an object is added to a collection, it becomes the property of that collection by default. If you delete an object that was placed into a collection, the system will crash when the collection attempts to reference that item. If you need to delete an object after it is put into a collection, you have two alternatives:

- You can remove it from the collection by using the function Collection::detach(Object&), then delete the object yourself. This is convenient when you need to process the object before deleting it.

- You can use function `Collection::destroy(Object&)` to detach and delete the object for you.

Watch out when you are detaching and deleting objects, because certain `Collection` classes (such as linked lists) allow multiple occurrences of the same object to be in the collection. If you only remove one of the occurrences of an object and then delete it, you'll probably cause a system crash.

Class *Container*

Class `Container` is possibly the most powerful abstraction in the entire library. A container is simply an object into which you can put other objects, without particular regard for order. The power of class `Container` stems from its ability to act collectively on all of the objects it contains, performing a requested operation. Container objects have two ways of iterating: using internal iterators and using external iterators. Internal iterators are provided by the member functions `forEach(...)`, `firstThat(..)`, and `lastThat(...)`. External iteration is supported by the iterator class `ContainerIterator`.

Class `Container` is an abstract class, because it defines the kinds of actions that can be applied to groups of objects, but not how those actions are to be carried out. For example, to iterate through the objects in a container, you need to know how the objects are organized: as arrays, linked lists, stacks, and so on.

When you create a container object, it contains no objects. You must put objects into it yourself, using functions defined in classes derived from class `Container`. Because the class is abstract, just about the only thing it can do that applies to any type of derived container is to keep a count of the number of objects it contains. Here is an edited version of the declaration of `Container`:

```
class Container : public Object,
                  public virtual Object::TShouldDelete {
```

```
public:
```

```
Container();
```

This constructor merely initializes the item count to 0. Note that there is no dynamically allocated memory used in a container other than that of the objects put into it.

```
virtual void flush(DeleteType = DefDelete) = 0;
```

This pure virtual function must be overridden in derived classes. The purpose of a flush operation is to remove all the objects from a container, optionally deleting them.

```
virtual int isEmpty() const;
```

This virtual function returns a nonzero value if there are no objects in a container.

```
virtual countType getItemsInContainer() const;
```

This virtual function returns the number of objects in a container. The way objects are counted depends on the type of container. Certain containers may wish to count multiple occurrences of the same object as a single object; others may wish to count each occurrence separately. By default, the latter method is used.

```
virtual void forEach(iterFuncType f, void*);
```

This function allows you to apply a function to each of the objects in a container by iterating through all the contained objects and calling function `f(...)` with them. If containers contain objects that are themselves containers, `forEach(...)` is applied recursively. Here is how the function is implemented:

```
Container::forEach(iterFuncType actionPtr,
                        void *paramListPtr)
{
    PRECONDITION(actionPtr != 0);
    ContainerIterator& containerIterator = initIterator();
    while(containerIterator != 0)
      containerIterator++.forEach(actionPtr, paramListPtr);
    delete &containerIterator;
}
```

The `actionPtr` argument is a pointer to a user-supplied function. The pointer is declared like this:

```
typedef void (*iterFuncType)(class Object&, void*);
```

This first argument is the object to which the function is to be applied. The second argument points to an argument list that may or may not be required by the action function. The argument list pointer can be null if no arguments are required. You can implement this argument list however you prefer, but often arrays, pointers to scalars, or pointers to structures are used. The following example shows an action function requiring an array of pointers to characters:

```
#include <iostream.h>
#include <clstypes.h>
#include <object.h>

// display an object, followed by a series of words
void Display(Object& o, char** args)
```

```
{
        cout << o;
        while (*args) {
          cout << *args;
          (*args)++;
        }
}
```

As an example, assume that aContainer is some kind of container that has objects in it. To apply Display(...) to all the objects in aContainer, you do something like this:

```
// set up an array of parameters for Display(...)
char* words [] = {
  "first",
  "second",
  0           // add a mark to terminate the array
};
// apply Display to all the objects in the Container
aContainer. forEach(Display, words);
```

When you pass parameters to the action function, you can either send a fixed number of parameters or a variable number of parameters. If you send a variable number of parameters, you need a method to convey how many parameters you passed. In the preceding example, I added a null pointer at the end of the array to act as a parameter list terminator. Passing fixed parameters is obviously much simpler, but it's also less flexible.

```
virtual Object& firstThat(condFuncType, void*) const;
virtual Object& lastThat(condFuncType, void*) const;
```

These two functions allow you to search through the objects in a container for the first or last object that satisfies some condition. The condition is tested by a user-supplied function that is of type condFuncType. Here is how the condFuncType typedef looks:

```
typedef int (*condFuncType)(const class Object&, void*);
```

If a container variable contains objects that are themselves containers, the search proceeds recursively along a depth-first path. To illustrate a depth-first search, consider the following container:

```
Container A
      Object B
      Container C
            Object D
            Object E
            Object F
      Object G
      Container H
            Object I
            Object J
```

In this case a depth-first search would explore the objects in container A in the following order:

```
A B C D E F G H I J
```

This search order entails that the objects *D*, *E*, and *F* are found before G, even though they are "deeper" inside container A. The same search path is used for both `firstThat(...)` and `lastThat(...)`. The action function must be provided by the user and must return 0 if the target condition is not met. A nonzero return value indicates success. If no objects are found that satisfy the user condition, the functions `Container::firstThat(...)` and `Container::lastThat(...)` return NOOBJECT.

```
virtual classType isA() const = 0;
```

This pure virtual forces any classes derived from `Container` to provide an `isA()` function, which should return a unique value that can serve to identify derived classes at runtime.

```
virtual char* nameOf() const = 0;
```

This pure virtual forces classes derived from `Container` to provide a `nameOf()` function, which should return a pointer to a string that identifies the class.

```
virtual hashValueType hashValue() const;
```

This pure virtual function forces derived classes to provide their own functions for returning a hash value, computed in a class-dependent manner. The containers in the class library return the value 0 as a hash value.

```
virtual int isEqual(const Object&) const;
```

This virtual function is a little tricky. It does not determine whether two containers are the same container, but whether the two containers contain the same objects in the same order. The function is declared virtual to allow derived container classes to modify the way "equality" is tested.

The function `Container::isEqual(...)` applies the overloaded operator `Object::operator==(Object&, Object&)` to each object in the two containers. If containers contain objects that are containers themselves, `Object: :operator==(Object&, Object&)` is applied recursively along a depth-first path.

```
virtual void printOn(ostream&) const;
```

This function inserts a suitable string representation for a container and all the objects in it. This function is called from the overloaded stream inserter `operator<<(ostream&,`

`Object&)`. The result essentially is a list of objects in a container, separated by a comma. Consider the following code:

```
#include <iostream.h>
#include <strng.h>
#include <stack.h>

void main()
{
      String& hello = *(new String("hello") );
      String& world = *(new String("world!") );
      Stack stack;

      stack.push(hello);
      stack.push(world);
      cout << stack;
}
```

The preceding code produces the following output:

```
List        {
            world!,
            hello }
```

First, an iteration header is inserted, then the names of the objects, then an iteration trailer. The header and trailer are printed via virtual functions, so derived classes can change them if necessary. The objects are printed as they appear following a depth-first search path. The name for each object is separated from the others by a class-dependent separator field, which in the preceding case defaults to the string `",\n      "`.

```
virtual void printHeader(ostream&) const;
```

This inserts a class-dependent iteration header used by the function `Container::printOn(ostream&)`. The default header is a string with the name of the container followed by " { ". You can override this function to change its behavior. For example, you might want to have a header that looks like this:

```
<class_name>: [
```

This is easily accomplished by supplying your class derived from `Container` with the function

```
void DerivedContainer::printHeader(ostream& os) const
{
    os << "\t\t\t" << nameOf() << ": [";
}
```

```
virtual void printSeparator(ostream&) const;
```

This inserts a separator string into a stream. The separator is used while printing the list of objects that are in a container, via the function `Container::printOn(ostream&)`. The default separator is the string `",\n     "`, but the default can be changed easily in classes derived from `Container` by overriding `Container::printSeparator(ostream&)`.

```
virtual void printTrailer(ostream&) const;
```

This inserts an iteration trailer string into a stream. This function is called by `Container::printOn(ostream&)` after all the objects in the container have been inserted. The default trailer string is `" }\n"`, but the default can be changed by an overriding function.

```
virtual ContainerIterator& initIterator() const = 0;
```

This pure virtual function forces classes derived from `Container` to provide their own version of `initIterator()`. Here is how the function is implemented in class `Btree`:

```
ContainerIterator& Btree::initIterator() const
{
  return *((ContainerIterator*) new BtreeIterator(*this));
}
```

The `initIterator()` function allocates an iterator object from the heap and returns a reference to it. This implies that after calling `initIterator()`, the caller assumes responsibility for deleting the iterator object. Function `initIterator()` is designed to be used with `friend` iterator classes in expressions like this:

```
// initialize an iterator for accessing the objects
// inside a container
ContainerIterator& next = container.initIterator();

// iterate through the container objects
while(next) {

  // test an object in a container, then go to
  // the next object
  Object& listObject = next++;
  // ...
}

// delete the iterator object
delete &next;
```

```
friend class ContainerIterator;
```

`ContainerIterator`s must be declared `friend` to `Container`s so that they have unrestricted access to `Container` internals.

```
protected:
```

```
unsigned itemsInContainer;
```

This protected variable stores the number of items in a container.

```
};
```

Class *Deque*

A `Deque` (pronounced *deck*) is simply an enhanced `Queue`. It allows you to insert and remove objects at both ends of the queue, thus blurring the meaning of front and back. Still, `Deque`s don't allow complete freedom because they don't allow you to insert or delete objects in the middle of the queue. If you need this kind of functionality, you probably need something like an array. `Deque`s in the Borland container class library use an internal, doubly-linked list to actually store their data. The list handles most of the details of inserting and deleting objects and list traversal. Here is an edited version of the header file for `Deque`, as declared when you are *not* using template classes:

```
class Deque : public Container {
```

```
public:
```

```
~Deque();
```

This destructor deletes all the items in `Deque`—if the `Deque` owns the items.

```
Object& peekLeft() const;
Object& peekRight() const;
```

These two functions return references to the objects at each end of a `Deque` without removing the objects from the `Deque`. Once you obtain an object reference this way, you must be careful not to delete the object, because it is still considered to be owned by the `Deque`. NOOBJECT is returned by these two functions if a `Deque` is empty.

```
Object& getLeft();
Object& getRight();
```

These two functions remove the left or right object from a Deque.

NOOBJECT is returned for empty Deques.

```
void putLeft(Object&);
void putRight(Object&);
```

These functions insert an object into a Deque. Once an object is inserted, it is owned by the Deque. If you explicitly delete such an object before removing it from the Deque, you'll probably crash the system.

```
virtual void flush(DeleteType dt = DefDelete);
```

This function removes and optionally deletes all the objects in a Deque.

```
virtual int isEmpty() const;
```

This function returns a nonzero value if there are no objects in a Deque.

```
virtual countType getItemsInContainer() const;
```

This function returns the number of objects in a Deque. Multiple occurrences of the same object are counted separately.

```
virtual ContainerIterator& initIterator() const;
```

This function initializes an external iterator for stepping through the members of a Deque. What is returned is a reference to a DoubleListIterator object allocated from the heap. It is your responsibility to delete this object when you're finished with it.

```
virtual classType isA() const;
virtual char* nameOf() const;
```

These two functions aid in identifying Deque objects at runtime.

The function isA() returns a unique value for Deque objects. Function nameOf() returns the string "Deque".

---

private:

```
DoubleList theDeque;
```

This private data member is the doubly-linked list used to store all the data in a Deque. All the objects in this data member are destroyed when a Deque object goes out of scope.

```
};
```

Deque objects are used in the same contexts as Queue objects. You can rely on the function Container::printOn(ostream&) to display the contents of a Deque, but this function doesn't let you modify the display order of the dequeued objects. Listing 8.11 shows how to iterate through a Deque, starting at either end.

Listing 8.11. Using class Deque.

```
#include <iostream.h>
#include <strstrea.h>
#include <strng.h>
#include <deque.h>

void main()
{
      Deque deque;
      const int COUNT = 5;

      for (int i = 0; i < COUNT; i++) {
        char buffer [80];
        ostrstream text(buffer, sizeof(buffer) );
        text << "This is item " << i << ends;
        deque.putLeft( *new String(buffer) );
      }

      cout << "\nDeque objects from front:";
      ContainerIterator& k = deque.initIterator();
      while (k)
        cout << "\n  " << ( (Object&) k++);

      cout << "\nDeque objects from back:";
      while (!deque.isEmpty() )
        cout << "\n  " << deque.getRight();
}
```

The output produced is the following:

```
Deque objects from front:
  This is item 4
  This is item 3
  This is item 2
  This is item 1
  This is item 0
Deque objects from back:
  This is item 0
  This is item 1
  This is item 2
```

```
  This is item 3
  This is item 4
```

To display a Deque using the overloaded stream insertion operator <<, just do this:

```
// display a deque polymorphically
cout << deque;
```

which results in the output

```
Double List {
    This is item 4,
    This is item 3,
    This is item 2,
    This is item 1,
    This is item 0 }
```

As you can see, the Deque objects are displayed from back to front (or from left to right, if you prefer).

Class *Dictionary*

A Dictionary object is used to manage collections of objects. Class Dictionary, as implemented in the container class library, is quite a bit different from a dictionary used in everyday life. Probably the most significant difference is that class Dictionary is not ordered. It is internally implemented with a hash table. As a result, the order of its objects depends on hash values computed at runtime. Class Dictionary is derived from Set, which implies that multiple occurrences of the same Association object are not allowed. If you try to insert one that is already present, the operation is ignored.

If you browse through a dictionary using an iterator, you see that the object ordering is fairly unpredictable. Neither alphanumeric nor chronological order is used. Such a dictionary would be useless as a book, but as a class it has many applications. The main advantage of the class is that it allows you to directly look up the value associated with a key object. You don't have to do any iterating yourself, because that's hidden away inside the class. Because objects are stored in a hash table, typical lookup times are reasonable. Here is an edited version of the header file of class Dictionary:

class Dictionary: public Set {

public:

```
Dictionary(unsigned sz = DEFAULT_HASH_TABLE_SIZE);
```

This constructor uses the base class constructor to set up an initially empty Dictionary. All Dictionary containers start out empty and grow as Associations are added to them. By default, the size of the HashTable used in a Dictionary is 111. You can change this value if you want, but always use a prime number to maximize the efficiency of `HashTable` storage.

```
virtual void add(Object&);
```

This function takes a reference to `Object`, which is assumed to refer to an `Association`, and puts the `Association` into a `Dictionary`. If you try to insert an object other than an `Association`, an error message is displayed at runtime and your program is terminated. Attempts to add more than one occurrence of the same `Association` into the dictionary are ignored. If an `Association` is already in the `Dictionary`, nothing is added and no errors are reported. It is not considered an error to attempt to insert the same `Association` more than once. If you have `Associations` for which the same key is associated to different values, you need to use a different type of container than `Dictionary`.

```
Association& lookup(const Object&) const;
```

This function takes a reference to an `Object`, which is considered to be the key to look for in a `Dictionary`. If an `Association` is found that has the key requested, the `Association` is returned. Otherwise NOOBJECT is returned.

```
virtual classType isA() const
virtual char _FAR *nameOf() const
```

These two functions aid in identifying `Dictionary` objects at runtime. The first returns a unique value. The second returns a pointer to the constant string `"Dictionary"`.

```
};
```

A *Dictionary* Example

To illustrate some of the details of `Dictionary`, I show a short program that uses a `Dictionary` container. The following program reads all the file names in the root directory, storing them in a `Dictionary` with their sizes. It displays the directory as a list of `Associations`, then looks up the size of file *\CONFIG.SYS* and displays it. Listing 8.12 is the code.

Listing 8.12. A program that reads the files in the root directory and stores them in a `Dictionary`.

```
#include <strng.h>
#include <iostream.h>
#include <strstrea.h>
#include <dir.h>
```

```
#include <assoc.h>
#include <dict.h>

void main()
{
      // read all the files in the current directory
      // into a dictionary

      Dictionary dictionary;
      char buffer [100];
      char* mask = "\\*.*";
      struct ffblk fileBlock;

      int fileName = !findfirst(mask, &fileBlock, 0);

      while(fileName) {
        String& name = *new String(fileBlock.ff_name);
        ostrstream text(buffer, sizeof(buffer) );
        text << fileBlock.ff_fsize << ends;
        String& size = *new String(buffer);
        Association& entry = *new Association(name, size);
        dictionary.add(entry);
        fileName = !findnext(&fileBlock);
      }

      // print the directory
      cout << "\nHere is the entire ROOT directory:\n"
           << dictionary;

      // lookup the size of \CONFIG.SYS
      String config("CONFIG.SYS");
      String& filesize =
             (String&) dictionary.lookup(config).value();
      cout << "\nThe size of \\CONFIG.SYS is "
           << filesize
           << " bytes"
           << endl;
}
```

The output produced depends on the contents of your root directory, but will be something like this:

```
Here is the entire ROOT directory:
Dictionary {
     Association { CONFIG.BAK, 205 }
,
     Association { T.OBJ, 25921 }
,
     Association { HIMEM.SYS, 11304 }
```

```
,
     Association { MOUSE.SYS, 34581 }
......
......
 }
The size of \CONFIG.SYS is 137 bytes
```

If you want to display the contents of a directory without all the `Association` stuff showing up, you have to provide your own function to do so. Actually, it is a simple task, because you can use the virtual function `Object::forEach(...)` to iterate through the `Dictionary` and invoke your own display function. Listing 8.13 is an example.

Listing 8.13. Displaying the members of a `Dictionary` with a custom function.

```
#include <strng.h>
#include <iostream.h>
#include <strstrea.h>
#include <dir.h>
#include <assoc.h>
#include <dict.h>

void ShowFileData(Object& obj, void* os)
{
      *(ostream*) os << "\n"
          << ( (Association&) obj). key()
          << "  "
          << ( (Association&) obj). value();
}

void main()
{
      // read all the files in the current directory
      // into a dictionary

      // ...

      // print the directory
      dictionary.forEach(ShowFileData, &cout);
}
```

The output produced is similar to this:

```
CONFIG.SYS  137
MOUSE.SYS  34581
HIMEM.SYS  11304
AUTOEXEC.BAT  2170
```

Function `ShowFileData(...)` is invoked for each `Association` in the `Dictionary`. It is not a member function of any class, and therefore has no `this` pointer. It requires a

reference to an `Object`, which it uses to display the key and value of an `Association`. `ShowFileData(...)` is declared to take a second argument of type `void*`. This is consistent with the way the function is declared in class `Object`. Of particular interest is the way the standard output stream is passed to `ShowFileData(...)`. Its address is passed and then typecast into an `ostream` pointer. Note that the insertion operations occur after dereferencing this pointer.

External Iteration with *Dictionary* Containers

As with all containers in the Borland classlib, you can use either an external or internal iterator to traverse the items in a `Dictionary`. Listing 8.13 showed the use of the internal iterator `forEach(...)` to display the contents of a `Dictionary`. Listing 8.14 shows the use of an external iterator to accomplish the same task.

Listing 8.14. Displaying the members of a `Dictionary` with an external iterator.

```
ContainerIterator& next = dictionary.initIterator();

while (next) {
  Association& entry = (Association&) (Object&) next++;
  cout << "\n"
       << entry.key()
       << " "
       << entry.value();
  }
delete &next;
```

Note the double typecast in the statement:

```
Association& entry = (Association&) (Object&) next++;
```

The `(Object&)` typecast returns the item currently being iterated over, and the second `(Association&)` typecast is required to correctly assign the reference returned from the iterator to the variable `entry`. After using the external iterator `next`, the iterator is deleted.

Class *DoubleList*

A list is just a sequence of memory elements tied together through pointers. In a singly-linked list, each element has only a pointer to the successor. In a doubly-linked list, each element has two pointers: one to the predecessor and one to the successor. Figure 8.9 is the layout of a `DoubleList` object in memory.

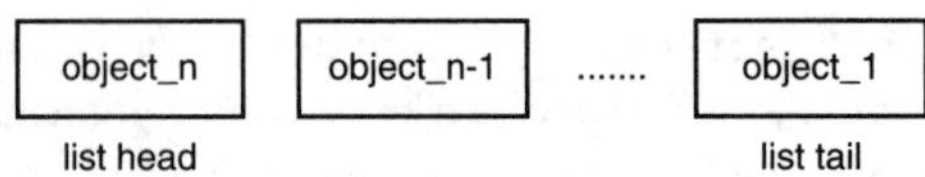

Figure 8.9. The layout of a doubly-linked list.

A doubly-linked list has a head and a tail. By default, adding elements to a list in the Borland C++ library causes the list to "grow backward." The first element inserted is at the tail, whereas the last is at the head. New elements can be added either at the head or the tail using specific insertion functions, but not in the middle. Some implementations of linked lists are circular, with the tail element pointing back to the head. The Borland list classes are not circular: The head's predecessor pointer and the tail's successor pointer are both null.

Because it has double pointers, a doubly-linked list can be traversed both forward and backward. Adding objects at the head of a list causes them to be stored in reverse order: The last object added is stored at the beginning of the list. Deleting the object at the head of a list causes the next element to become the new head. Each element in such a linked list is of class `DoubleList::ListElement`, which is a private nested class of `DoubleList`. The structure of a class `DoubleList::ListElement` is shown in Figure 8.10.

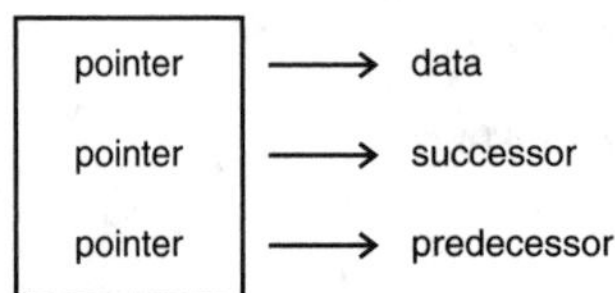

Figure 8.10. The layout of a `ListElement` *object used in class* `DoubleList`.

Doubly-linked lists are powerful because they combine the advantages of runtime flexibility and low memory overhead. When you create a doubly-linked list, its size is initially 0. As you add and delete items from it, it grows and shrinks dynamically. This is handy, because there are situations in which you don't know how many objects are going to be dealt with at runtime. Of course, you can use dynamic arrays or hash tables in some cases, but lists are still a commonly used data structure. Here is an edited version of the header file for class `DoubleList`:

```
class DoubleList : public Collection,
                   private DoubleListBlockInitializer {
```

```
public:
```

```
DoubleList();
```

This constructor creates an initially empty list.

```
~DoubleList()
```

This destructor removes all the objects in the list. If `DoubleList` also owns these objects, they are deleted as well. If there are no objects in the list, no action takes place.

```
Object& peekAtHead() const;
Object& peekAtTail() const;
```

These two functions return a reference to the objects at the head and tail of a list. Be careful not to delete these objects, because they are still owned by the list.

```
virtual void add(Object& toAdd);
```

This adds an object at the head of a linked list. The object that was previously at the head of the list is now in second place.

```
virtual void detach(Object&, DeleteType = NoDelete);
```

This searches for an object, starting at the head of a list. If the object is found, it is removed from the list and optionally deleted.

```
virtual void flush(DeleteType = DefDelete);
```

This function removes and optionally deletes all the objects in a list.

```
void addAtHead(Object&);
void addAtTail(Object&);
```

These functions add an object to the head or tail of a list. The newly added object becomes the new head or tail. Class `DoubleList` allows multiple occurrences of an object to appear in a list, but each instance is treated as an individual object.

```
void destroyFromHead(Object&);
void destroyFromTail(Object&);
```

These two functions detach and delete the object at the head or tail of a list. If the same object appears more than once in the list, you should use function `DoubleList::detach(Object&, DeleteType)`. If you delete an object that is still owned by the list, the system will probably crash.

```
void detachFromHead(Object&, DeleteType = NoDelete);
void detachFromTail(Object&, DeleteType = NoDelete);
```

These are safer functions than the previous ones, unless you request detached objects to also be deleted. Before deleting an object detached from a list, you must be sure the object doesn't occur multiple times in the list. You can determine this with the function `Collection::hasMember(Object&)` if you're not sure.

```
int isEmpty() const;
```

This function returns a nonzero value if there are no elements in a list.

```
countType getItemsInContainer() const;
```

This function returns the number of elements in a list. If multiple occurrences of the same object are present, they are each counted separately.

```
virtual ContainerIterator& initIterator() const;
ContainerIterator& initReverseIterator() const;
```

These two functions return references to iterator objects allocated from the heap. After using these iterators, you must delete them. The two iterators can be used completely independently from each other, even simultaneously.

```
virtual classType isA() const;
virtual char* nameOf() const;
```

These functions aid in identifying `DoubleList` objects at runtime.

The first one returns a unique value for class `DoubleList`. The second returns a pointer to the string `"DoubleList"`.

`private:`

```
class ListElement {...};
```

This nested class is used by class `DoubleList` to manage the individual nodes in a list. Being a private nested class, it is usable only inside class `DoubleList`.

```
ListElement* head;
ListElement* tail;
```

These private data members are pointers to the first and last nodes in a list.

```
ListElement headEntry, tailEntry;
```

These are the nodes that correspond to the first and last elements in a list. All the other nodes in a list are allocated from the heap.

```
unsigned itemsInContainer;
```

This private data member stores the number of objects stored in a doubly-linked list.

```
};
```

I give a simple example for class `DoubleList`, showing the effect of adding elements at the head and tail ends of the list.

Listing 8.15. Using class `DoubleList` to insert elements at the head and the tail of the list.

```
#include <strng.h>
#include <dbllist.h>

void main()
{
      DoubleList list;

      String& one = *new String("1");
      String& two = *new String("2");
      String& three = *new String("3");
      String& four = *new String("4");
      String& five = *new String("5");
      String& six = *new String("6");
      String& seven = *new String("7");

      list.add(one);
      list.add(two);
      list.add(three);

      // display the entire list
      cout << list;

      list.destroy(two);

      list.addAtHead(four);
      list.addAtTail(five);
      list.addAtHead(six);
      list.addAtTail(seven);
```

continues

Listing 8.15. continued

```
        cout << "\nThere are "
             << list.getItemsInContainer()
             << " objects in the list: \n";

        // use an external iterator to display
        // the list contents in one direction
        ContainerIterator& next = list.initIterator();
        cout << "\nForward iteration: ";
        while (next)
          cout << " " << next++;

        // use an external iterator to display
        // the list contents in the opposite direction
        DoubleListIterator& previous =
          (DoubleListIterator&) list.initReverseIterator();
        cout << "\nReverse iteration: ";
        while (previous)
          cout << " " << previous—;

        // delete the iterators
        delete &next;
        delete &previous;
}
```

The output produced is

```
DoubleList {
    3,
    2,
    1 }

There are 6 objects in the list:

Forward iteration:  6 4 3 1 5 7
Reverse iteration:  7 5 1 3 4 6
```

Note that with forward iteration, elements that were inserted at the head are displayed in the reverse order of their insertion. If you insert from the tail, the list elements are displayed in the correct order. For example, see Listing 8.16.

Listing 8.16. Inserting elements at the tail of a `DoubleList`.

```
#include <strng.h>
#include <dbllist.h>
```

```
void main()
{
      DoubleList list;

      String& one = *new String("1");
      String& two = *new String("2");
      String& three = *new String("3");
      String& four = *new String("4");

      list.addAtTail(one);
      list.addAtTail(two);
      list.addAtTail(three);
      list.addAtTail(four);

      cout << "\n" << list;
}
```

Listing 8.16 produces the following output:

```
DoubleList { 1,
             2,
             3,
             4 }
```

You can delete elements with more flexibility than you can insert them. Although insertions are allowed only at the head or tail of the list, deletions can occur anywhere in a list. When you delete an element with the function `DoubleList::destroyFromHead(Object&)` or `DoubleList::destroyFromTail(Object&)`, the list searches for the given item starting at the head or tail. The list deletes the first occurrence that is found.

Class *Error*

Class `Error` is not used like the other classes in the container library. It is declared to facilitate error handling during dynamic allocation of objects in the library, and to identify situations in which functions returning a reference to `Object` failed. The class is instantiated once, in the file *object.cpp*, like this:

```
Error theErrorObject;
```

After setting up an `Error` variable, the following establishes a permanent reference to it:

```
Object *Object::ZERO = &theErrorObject;
```

You shouldn't instantiate class `Error` yourself. The data member `Object::ZERO` is declared static, thus there is only one instance of it in the entire container library. When you dynamically allocate an item derived from `Object`, the pointer returned is invalid if there is insufficient memory to honor the request. The returned pointer in this case is set to point at `theErrorObject`. To make things a little easier on you, there is a macro called NOOBJECT to simplify the notation somewhat. NOOBJECT is defined like this:

```
#define NOOBJECT  (*(Object::ZERO))
```

NOOBJECT is used with functions that are designed to return a reference to an `Object`, such as the object `Object::firstThat(...)` and the object `Collection::findMember(...)`. If no object is found that satisfies some condition, NOOBJECT is returned. If you add classes of your own to the container library, be sure to follow this convention. Here is an edited version of the declaration of `Error`:

class Error: public Object {

public:

```
virtual classType isA() const;
```

This virtual function simply returns a unique value to allow runtime identification of objects of class `Error`.

```
virtual char* nameOf() const;
```

This virtual function returns a printable name for the class.

This function is provided with the previous one for runtime object identification, and returns a pointer to the constant string `"Error"`.

```
virtual hashValueType hashValue() const;
```

This virtual function returns the value 0, for use with hashed arrays.

```
virtual int isEqual(const Object&) const;
```

This function always returns the value 1. When you compare two objects using `::operator==(Object&, Object&)` like this:

```
void foo(Object& obj1, Object& obj2)
{
        if (obj1 == obj2)
          ...
}
```

the operator first tests the objects to see whether they are of the same class, like this:

```
int operator== (const Object& test1, const Object& test2)
{
    return (test1.isA() == test2.isA())   &&
            test1.isEqual(test2);
}
```

If you compare two `Error` objects to one another, the member function `Error::isEqual(...)` is called. Because there is only one `Error` object defined for the

entire container class library, two `Error` objects are always considered to be the same object.

```
virtual void printOn(ostream&) const;
```

This virtual function is called during stream insertion operations. It copies the string `"Error\n"` to the stream.

```
void operator delete(void*);
```

It is not allowable to delete objects of class `Error`. If you try to do so, this function will be invoked and will terminate your program after displaying an error message.

```
};
```

You should never use class `Error` directly in your code, although references to `theErrorObject` can be used at will, via the macro NOOBJECT. Listing 8.17 is a complete example.

Listing 8.17. Using `theErrorObject` through the macro NOOBJECT.

```
#include <btree.h>
#include <strng.h>
#include <stdlib.h>

void main()
{
        // create a 10th order b-tree
        Btree tree(10);

        // add items to the b-tree
        for (int i = 0; i < 100; i++) {
           char string [20];
           ltoa(i, string, 10);
           tree.add(*new String(string) );
        }

        // search for an item
        String word("1022");
        if (tree.findMember(word) == NOOBJECT) {
          cout << "\nThe string "
               << word
               << " was not found in the b-tree"
               << endl;
        }
}
```

The output produced is

```
The string 1022 was not found in the b-tree
```

If you really want to handle `theErrorObject` directly, there is little you can do. Listing 8.18 contains some examples.

Listing 8.18. Using `theErrorObject` directly.

```
#include <object.h>

void main()
{
      // get a reference to the error object
      Object* error = Object::ZERO;

      // invoke member functions of theErrorObject
      cout << "\nThis is class "
           << error->nameOf()
           << " whose hash value is "
           << error->hashValue()
           << "\nand whose isA() value is "
           << error->isA();
}
```

The program produces the following output:

```
This is class Error whose hash value is 0 and whose isA() value is 1
```

Of interest is the way you obtain a reference to `theErrorObject` through `Object::ZERO`. Because this variable is declared static in `Object`, you don't need any specific instance of `Object` with it.

Class *HashTable*

Class `HashTable` is one of the most generic types of usable collection in the container class library. You can use `HashTable` containers any time you need to handle unordered groups of objects. `HashTable`, as implemented in the Borland class library, is a combination of arrays and linked lists. The array feature permits random access to an array element, the index of which is computed—or hashed—directly from the data being used. This array element then points to a linked list where data is actually stored. Figure 8.11 is a graphic representation of a hash table that contains two linked lists.

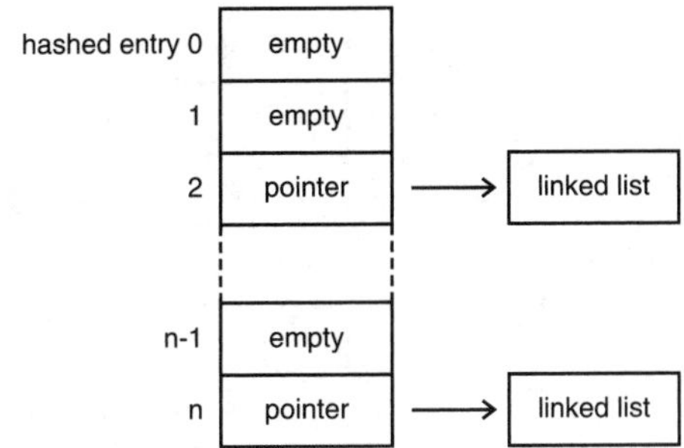

Figure 8.11. A `HashTable` *with two used entries.*

The empty entries contain null pointers. When you add an object `Obj` to a hash table, class `HashTable` computes a hash value for `Obj`. Using this value as an array index, `HashTable` looks in the table to see whether there is already an object at the computed index. If there isn't, a linked list is created and initialized with the single object `Obj`, and a pointer to the list is inserted in the table. If a list already exists, `Obj` is inserted at the head of it.

A default `HashTable` object starts out with an array with 111 entries. This isn't a particularly magic number, but it is a prime. A hash table is always more efficient if its length is a prime number, because the table length is used to map the set of all possible hash values into array indices, using the expression

```
// compute array index for a hash table entry
int table_index = anObject.hashValue() % table_size;
```

Using a prime number for `table_size` makes it more likely that the distribution of computed `table_index` values will be more uniform. It is possible for a hash table to become "clustered" if the objects it contains have hash values that are concentrated around a certain set of values. Consider 111 different objects with hash values that all have the same value. Taking the modulus of this value, your hash table array winds up with a single entry, and all the inserted objects are in a single linked list. The other table entries are empty. Accessing items in this hash table is slower than accessing them in a linked list, because of the hashing and array indexing. This kind of clustering is considered a pathological degeneration.

On the other hand, it is possible to have 111 objects that all have different hash values. Now you would wind up with a hash table with a single object (a linked list containing only one object) at each entry. With such a hash table, object accesses would be almost as efficient as with an array. This kind of object distribution is an ideal case. Normally, hash tables turn out to be somewhere between the extremes. In any event, using prime numbers for table lengths reduces the probability of clustering. Figure 8.12 shows a well-utilized hash table.

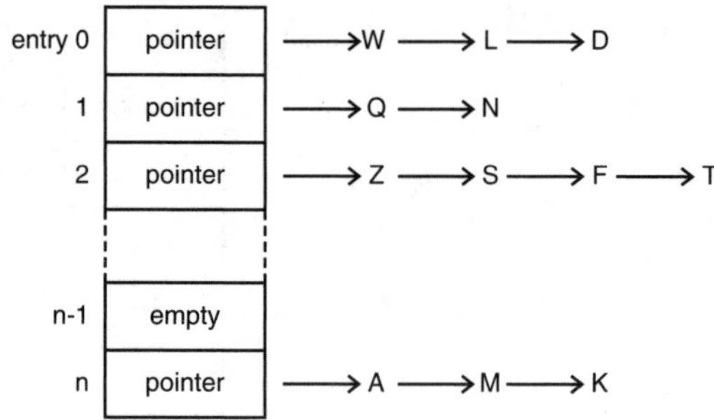

Figure 8.12. A `HashTable` *with good distribution.*

Most of the table entries are utilized, and most lists are about the same length. The linked lists in class `HashTable` behave somewhat like LIFO (last-in, first-out) queues, or stacks, when the same object appears more than once. If you put two identical objects into a hash table, the two will have the same hash values, and thus will wind up on the same linked list.

Figure 8.13 shows a hash table after adding objects A and B, which are identical and have the same hash value.

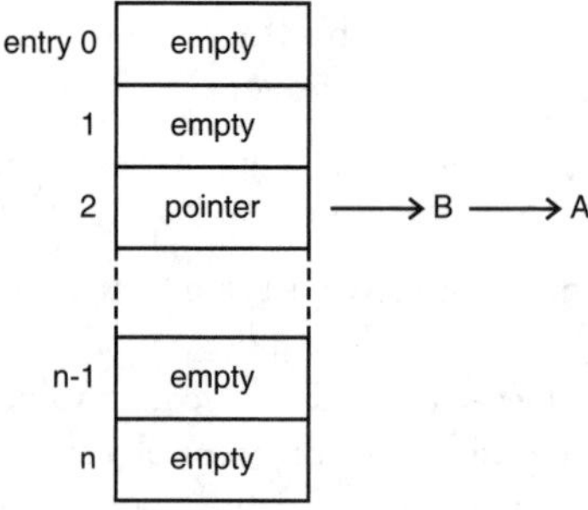

Figure 8.13. A `HashTable` *after inserting two objects with the same hash value. Object A was inserted first.*

When deleting an object from a linked list, the object is searched by traversing the list starting at the head. This means that B will be deleted before A. Here is an edited version of the header file for class `HashTable`:

```
class HashTable: public Collection {
```

```
public:
```

```
friend class HashTableIterator;
```

All containers are declared to have an iterator class as a `friend`. Such iterators are called *external iterators,* and allow the user to control the manner in which the objects in a container are traversed.

```
HashTable(sizeType = DEFAULT_HASH_TABLE_SIZE);
```

This constructor allows you to build a hash table of a certain length, with a default of 111 entries. Each entry is subsequently used as a pointer to the head of a linked list. Data inserted in a `HashTable` object is actually stored in these linked lists.

```
virtual ~HashTable();
```

This destructor removes all the elements from a `HashTable`. If the elements are owned by the container, they are also deleted.

```
virtual void add(Object&);
```

This adds a generic object to the table. Multiple occurrences of the same object are freely allowed with hash tables. Once an object is added to a hash table, by default it is owned by the table. If you delete objects while they are still in the hash table, you'll probably crash the system.

```
virtual void detach(Object&, DeleteType = NoDelete);
```

This removes an object from a hash table. If the object is not found in the table, no action is taken and no errors are generated. The second argument allows you to remove, or to remove and delete an object.

```
virtual void flush(DeleteType = DefDelete);
```

This function removes and optionally deletes all the objects in a `HashTable`.

```
virtual int isEmpty() const
```

This function returns a nonzero value if there are no objects in a `HashTable`.

```
virtual countType getItemsInContainer() const
```

This function returns the number of objects in a `HashTable`. Multiple occurrences of the same object are counted separately.

```
virtual Object& findMember(Object&) const;
```

This function searches for a given object in a `HashTable`. If the object is found, a reference to it is returned. Otherwise, NOOBJECT is returned. If multiple occurrences of the same object are present in the table, the last one inserted is returned.

```
virtual ContainerIterator& initIterator() const;
```

This function returns a reference to a dynamically allocated object `HashTableIterator`. You can use this iterator to traverse the items contained in a `HashTable` object. Once you obtain such an iterator object, you become responsible for deleting it.

```
virtual classType isA() const
virtual char* nameOf() const
```

These functions aid in identifying `HashTable` objects at runtime.

Function `isA()` returns a unique value for class `HashTable`. Function `nameOf()` returns a pointer to the string `"HashTable"`.

`private:`

```
hashValueType getHashValue(Object&) const;
```

This function computes the final hash value for an object in a manner that distributes the hash objects over the hash table.

```
sizeType size;
```

This private data member stores the size of the hash table. Once a hash table has been constructed, its size cannot be changed.

```
BI_IVectorImp<Object> table;
```

This data member is the hash table itself. It is an array allocated dynamically from the heap. The hash table may not be expanded or shrunk after it is initially constructed. Each entry in the array is used as a pointer to a separate linked list, where the `HashTable` items are stored. See a description of the template-based container classes for a description of `BI_IVectorImp<Object>`.

```
unsigned itemsInContainer;
```

This private data member stores the number of objects in a `HashTable`.

`DeleteType delItem( DeleteType dt )`

This function indicates whether a `HashTable` owns its elements. A return value of `DeleteType::Delete` indicates ownership.

};

`HashTable`s are used frequently in programming, because they offer a combination of the advantages of arrays and linked lists. A hash table doesn't allow you to order the objects contained in it. The ordering is computed at runtime by using hash values that depend on specific object contents. Listing 8.19 inserts 10 `String` objects into a `HashTable`, then prints the container's contents.

Listing 8.19. Inserting `String`s into a `HashTable`.

```
#include <iostream.h>
#include <strstrea.h>
#include <strng.h>
#include <hashtbl.h>

void main()
{
      HashTable bunch;
      char buffer [100];

      for (int i = 0; i < 10; i++) {
        ostrstream text(buffer, sizeof(buffer) );
        text << "The next string is " << i << ends;
        String& string = *(new String(buffer) );
        bunch.add(string);
      }

      cout << bunch;
}
```

The output produced is

```
HashTable {
    The next string is 2,
    The next string is 3,
    The next string is 4,
    The next string is 5,
    The next string is 6,
    The next string is 7,
    The next string is 8,
```

```
The next string is 9,
The next string is 0,
The next string is 1 }
```

Notice how the hash table objects are not printed in any particular order. The actual order is computed at runtime. Your program should never rely on a specific `HashTable` ordering to work. If object ordering is important to you, use one of the ordered collection classes, such as `Btree` or `SortedArray`. In the preceding code, an output string stream was used to format a string in-memory, before inserting it into the `HashTable`. The expression

```
cout << bunch;
```

causes the compiler to invoke the virtual function `Container::printOn()`, which then iterates through the `HashTable` and displays its contents. Listing 8.20 inserts random numbers into a `HashTable` after converting them to `String` objects. The contents of the table are then displayed in ascending order.

Listing 8.20. Printing the members of a `HashTable` in numerical order.

```
#include <stdlib.h>
#include <iostream.h>
#include <strstrea.h>
#include <strng.h>
#include <hashtbl.h>

void main()
{
      HashTable bunch;
      char buffer [100];
      const int MAX_VALUE = 1000;

      // initialize the random number generator
      randomize();

      for (int i = 0; i < 10; i++) {
        ostrstream text(buffer, sizeof(buffer) );
        text << random(MAX_VALUE) << ends;
        String& string = *(new String(buffer) );
        bunch.add(string);
      }

      cout << "\nHere are the hash table values:";

      for (i = 0; i < MAX_VALUE; i++) {
        ostrstream text(buffer, sizeof(buffer) );
        text << i << ends;
        String& string = *(new String(buffer) );
```

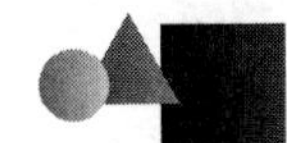

```
        if (bunch.hasMember(string) )
          cout << "\n\t" << bunch.findMember(string);
      }
}
```

The output produced is random, but will be similar to the following:

```
Here are the hash table values:
      93
      213
      319
      332
      385
      531
      548
      902
      945
      976
```

Of course, you can insert objects other than `Strings` into a `HashTable`, as long as they derive from class `Object`. One commonly used object is the `Association`, which is used often to build a symbol table. Listing 8.21 builds a symbol table containing all the file names in the current directory. It stores them as ordered pairs (file name, size) and uses a `HashTable` to hold them.

Listing 8.21. Storing a file directory, using `Associations` in a `HashTable`.

```
#include <strstrea.h>
#include <strng.h>
#include <assoc.h>
#include <hashtbl.h>
#include <iomanip.h>
#include <dir.h>

void main()
{
      HashTable bunch;
      char buffer [100];
      char* mask = "*.*";
      struct ffblk fileBlock;

      int fileName = !findfirst(mask, &fileBlock, 0);

      while(fileName) {
        String& name = *new String(fileBlock.ff_name);
        ostrstream text(buffer, sizeof(buffer) );
        text << fileBlock.ff_fsize << ends;
```

continues

Listing 8.21. continued

```
        String& size = *new String(buffer);
        Association& entry = *new Association(name, size);
        bunch.add(entry);
        fileName = !findnext(&fileBlock);
      }

      cout << "\nDirectory of files:";
      ContainerIterator& i= bunch.initIterator();
      int count = 0;
      while(i) {
        Object& obj = i++;
      cout << "\n"
             << setw(16)
             << setiosflags(ios::left)
             << ( (Association&) obj).key()
             << "    "
             << ( (Association&) obj).value();
        if (++count == 5) break;
      }
      delete &i;
}
```

The entire directory is stored in the HashTable, but only the first few members are displayed. The output will depend on the contents of your current directory, but will be something like this:

```
Directory of files:
TLINK.CFG   19
TRANCOPY.EXE   17620
WRT.HLP   171520
BCCX.OVY   502692
TD286.EXE   509677
```

Remember that objects used in HashTable objects must not be allocated from the stack, unless ownership is removed from HashTable before the container goes out of scope. Listing 8.22 uses local objects of different types with a HashTable:

Listing 8.22. Storing local objects in a heterogeneous HashTable.

```
#include <strstrea.h>
#include <strng.h>
#include <hashtbl.h>
#include <ldate.h>
#include <ltime.h>
```

```
void main()
{
      HashTable stuff;

      // remove ownership from the HashTable
      stuff.ownsElements(0);

      char buffer [100];
      ostrstream text(buffer, sizeof(buffer) );

      text << "The time is " << Time() << ends;
      String time(buffer);
      stuff.add(time);

      text.seekp(0);
      text << "The date is " << Date() << ends;
      String date(buffer);
      stuff.add(date);

      String salute("Ave Caesar, morituri te salutant!");
      stuff.add(salute);

      cout << "\nHeterogeneous contents:";
      ContainerIterator& next = stuff.initIterator();
      while (next)
        cout << "\n" << next++;

      delete &next;
}
```

The output produced obviously depends on the system date and time, but is something like this:

```
Heterogeneous contents:
The time is 11:06:20.26 am
The date is December 28, 1991
Ave Caesar, morituri te salutant!
```

You don't necessarily have to remove ownership from a container before you add local objects to it, but ownership must be removed before the container goes out of scope.

Class *List*

A linked list is a chain of elements, linked together by pointers. Class `List` implements singly-linked lists, meaning that each element has only one pointer, which points to the element's successor. In a singly-linked list, you can travel in only one direction, because pointers from an element to its predecessor are not available. Graphically, a linked list looks something like Figure 8.14.

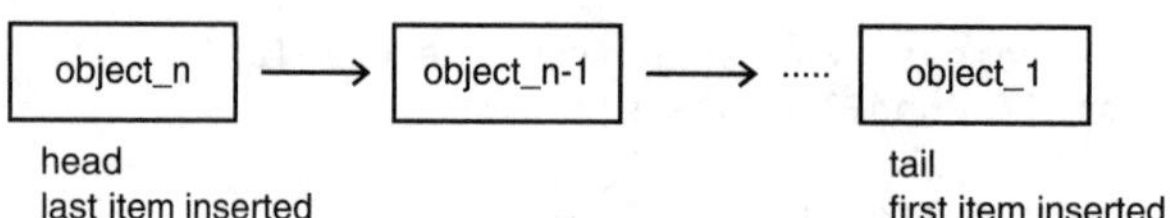

Figure 8.14. The layout of a linked list.

A list has a head and a tail. The head is where objects are inserted. Adding objects to a list causes them to be stored in reverse order: the last object added is stored at the beginning of the list. Deleting the node at the head of a list causes the next node to become the new head. Each node in such a linked list is of class `List::ListElement`, which is a private nested class. The structure of a `List::ListElement` is shown in Figure 8.15.

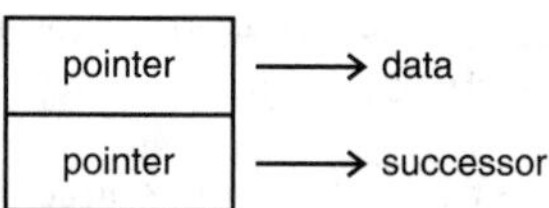

Figure 8.15. The layout of a `List::ListElement` *object.*

Linked lists are used often in computing. The size of a linked list starts out as 0. As nodes are added to it at runtime, it grows. Linked lists are convenient when you don't know how many objects a program will be dealing with in a collection. The memory overhead associated with lists is the storage for one pointer for each node. A drawback of lists is that they aren't randomly accessible. To access element *p*, you have to traverse all the predecessors of *p*. If a list is long, there may be a noticeable delay in accessing members at the end of the list. In these cases, it might be preferable to use hash tables or arrays rather than lists.

A linked list can contain multiple occurrences of the same object. When you ask the list to delete an object, only the last instance added is affected. The other copies of the object remain in the list. Here is an edited version of the header file for class `List`:

```
class List: public Collection, private ListBlockInitializer {
```

```
public:
```

```
List();
```

This constructor creates an empty list. Elements can be added to the list only through the member function `List::add(Object&)`.

```
virtual ~List();
```

This virtual destructor removes and optionally deletes all the items in a `List` container. Objects are deleted only if the `List` owns the items it contains.

```
Object& peekHead() const;
```

This function returns a reference to the first element in a `List` container. Note that the first element is the last one that was inserted.

```
void add(Object&);
```

This function adds an object to a list. The object is added at the head of the list, and the previous head object becomes the second item in the list.

```
virtual void detach(Object&, DeleteType = NoDelete);
```

This function searches through a linked list for a given object.

The search starts at the head and ends at the tail. If the object is found, it is removed from the list. The second argument controls whether the removed item is also deleted. No errors occur if the object is not located. If multiple occurrences of the same object appear in a `List`, the last instance inserted is detached.

```
virtual void flush(DeleteType = DefDelete);
```

This function removes and optionally deletes all the objects in a `List` container.

```
virtual int isEmpty() const;
```

This function returns a nonzero value if there are no items in the `List`.

```
virtual countType getItemsInContainer() const;
```

This function returns the number of objects in a `List`. If multiple occurrences of the same object appear, they are counted separately.

```
virtual ContainerIterator& initIterator() const;
```

Every specialized container class needs to have this function, which returns a reference to an iterator that is allocated from the heap. Once you obtain an iterator this way, you must remember to delete it when you're through with it.

```
virtual classType isA() const;
virtual char* nameOf() const;
```

These two functions aid in identifying `List` objects at runtime. The first function returns a value that uniquely identifies a `List` container. The second one returns a pointer to the constant string `"List"`.

`private:`

```
class ListElement {/*...*/};
```

This nested class is used by class to manage the individual nodes in a list. Being a private nested class, it is usable only inside class `List`. Note that the nested class `DoubleList::ListElement` is an entirely different class.

```
ListElement* head;
ListElement* tail;
```

These private data members are pointers to the first and last nodes in a list.

```
ListElement headEntry, tailEntry;
```

These are the nodes that correspond to the first and last elements in a list. All the other nodes in a list are allocated from the heap.

```
unsigned itemsInContainer;
```

This private data member stores the number of objects stored in a singly-linked list.

```
ListElement* findPred(const Object& obj);
```

This function finds the list node that immediately precedes a given `Object obj`. If `obj` is not found, the tail node is returned.

`};`

The nicest thing about lists is that you never have to make any compromising decisions regarding how much space to allocate to them: they grow and shrink automatically as needed at runtime, as shown in Listing 8.23.

Listing 8.23. Using class `List` to store `String`s.

```
#include <list.h>
#include <strng.h>
#include <iostream.h>

void main()
{
      List agenda;

      String* wake_up = new String("wake up");
      String* go_work = new String("go to work");
      String* go_home = new String("go home");
      String* sleep   = new String("go to bed");

      agenda.add(*sleep);
      agenda.add(*go_home);
      agenda.add(*go_work);
      agenda.add(*wake_up);

      cout << "\n" << agenda;
      cout << "\nThere are "
           << agenda.getItemsInContainer()
           << " things on the agenda";

      Object& last_item = agenda.peekHead();
      agenda.detach(last_item);

      if (!agenda.hasMember(*wake_up) )
        cout << "\nWhat a day...!";

      cout << "\nThe first thing on the agenda is: "
           << agenda.peekHead();

      // delete this object, because it was removed from
      // the list. The other list objects will be destructed
      // by the list itself.
      delete &last_item;
}
```

The output produced is

```
List {
    wake up,
    go to work,
    go home,
    go to bed }

There are 4 things on the agenda
What a day...!
The first thing on the agenda is: go to work
```

Notice how the items placed in the linked list are printed in reverse order. With class `List`, this is the only way the list can be traversed. Class `DoubleList` supports forward or backward traversing of lists. The preceding code also uses a few member functions inherited from `Container` and `Collection`, such as `Container::getItemsInContainer()` and `Collection::hasMember(Object&)`.

Class *Object*

Class `Object` is where it all starts. In Smalltalk, everything derives from a class called `Object`, including integers, floating-point numbers, and strings. In Borland C++, `Object` is only the root (along with its nested class `Object::TShouldDelete`) of the container class library.

`Object` is an abstract class, and is structured to force derived classes to provide certain functions. This guarantees a certain consistency throughout the library and makes library objects easier to use. The root class `Object` is designed to provide an interface for single objects and groups of objects. To support groups, it provides functions for iterating through sequences of objects and for accessing the first or last object that satisfies a certain relationship. Here is an edited version of the `Object` header file:

`class Object {`

`public:`

```
virtual ~Object()
```

This destructor doesn't do anything, but is virtual to allow classes derived from `Object` to be destructed correctly at runtime. The function is also a good place for breakpoints during debugging.

```
virtual classType isA() const = 0;
```

This pure virtual member function forces all classes derived from `Object` to supply `isA()` functions of their own, which must return a unique value of type `classType`. The list of assigned `classTypes` exists in the header file *\BC4\INCLUDE\CLASSLIB\OBSOLETE\CLSTYPES.H.* User classes derived from `Object` must also be sure to use unique `classType` values of their own. This function attempts to solve a basic C++ problem: classes cannot be treated as objects. If you want an object to identify itself at runtime, you need to supply it with a proper virtual function, such as something like function `isA()`.

```
virtual char* nameOf() const = 0;
```

This pure virtual forces all classes derived from `Object` to supply a `nameOf()` function, which must return a pointer to a string of characters that identify an object's class. This function, with `isA()`, allows you to keep track of the identity of class objects at runtime.

```
virtual hashValueType hashValue() const = 0;
```

A `hashValueType` is a value that a class object must supply through the `hashValue()` function. The returned value should be unique (or *reasonably* unique) for each class. Hash keys are used as a lookup index in hashed collections, which are of type `HashTable`, `Bag`, `Set`, and `Dictionary`. See class `HashTable` for a description of how hashed collections work. Because function `hashValue()` is a pure virtual, all classes derived from `Object` are required to supply a `hashValue()` function of their own.

```
virtual int isEqual(const Object&) const = 0;
```

This pure virtual is used to test whether any two objects derived from `Object` are "equal."

The way equality between objects is tested depends on the types of objects. For example, `Btrees` are considered to be equal if they contain the same keys, regardless of internal structural differences among the trees. `Association` objects are considered equal if they have the same key.

```
virtual int isSortable() const;
```

This virtual function is used in derived classes to indicate whether a class can be sorted or not, and returns 0 by default. Any classes derived from `Object` that are sortable must override this function and return a nonzero value. Actually, this is done for you in class `Sortable`, so if you're developing a sortable class, it should be derived from `Sortable`.

```
virtual int isAssociation() const;
```

This virtual member function indicates whether or not a derived class is an `Association`. An `Association` is an ordered pair of items derived from class `Object`. The default return value is 0. Class `Association` overrides this function and returns a nonzero value.

```
void* operator new(size_t);
```

This is an important member function. It allocates storage for objects derived from class `Object`, using the global `::operator new`. If there is insufficient heap memory to satisfy a request, the function returns ZERO, which is a pointer to a statically allocated object. A possible problem with `Object::operator new` is that every time you allocate an object, you need to check the returned pointer to make sure the operation succeeded. This checking is not only tedious, but can also represent an undesirable amount of overhead. To alleviate the problem somewhat, you can install a custom handler for memory allocator faults and have it handle any allocation problems automatically.

```
virtual void forEach(iterFuncType, void*);
```

The container class library is populated by classes that contain multiple objects, hence it is convenient to have a single virtual function to iterate through them while calling a function. The first argument is a `typedef` declared like this:

```
typedef void (*iterFuncType)(Object&, void*);
```

Therefore, the argument is a pointer to a function. This is the function that is applied to each member in a container. The second argument for `Object::forEach(...)` is a `void*`, which points to an opportune parameter list to pass on to the `iterFuncType` function. When invoking function `forEach(...)` through a generic `Object` reference, you don't know whether you are using a single object or a container object. Container objects override `forEach(...)`, calling the `iterFuncType` function for each of the objects contained in them. If `Containers` contain objects that are themselves containers, `forEach(...)` is applied recursively, following a depth-first path.

```
virtual Object& firstThat(condFuncType, void*) const;
virtual Object& lastThat(condFuncType, void*) const;
```

When dealing with entire groups of objects, you often need to find the first or last object that satisfies some condition. The order of iteration through the members of a group is class-dependent, so the definition of "first" and "last" is not absolute. The first parameter is a `typedef` declared like this:

```
typedef int (*condFuncType)(const class Object&, void*);
```

Therefore, the parameter is a pointer to a function that performs a test, returning nonzero if the test succeeds and returning zero otherwise. This function is invoked for each object in a container. The iteration stops when either the first or last object is found that causes the `condFuncType` function to return a nonzero value.

```
virtual void printOn(ostream&) const = 0;
```

This pure `virtual` function is a stream inserter. It is necessary to allow polymorphic insertions, which couldn't be handled directly by overloading the friend `::operator<<(ostream&, const Object&)`. Stream insertions in the container class library are meant to be performed with the notation:

```
stream << object_a << object_b << object_c;
```

With a type of statement such as the preceding, the member function `Object::printOn(ostream&)` is invoked by `::operator<<(ostream&, const Object&)`, thus supporting polymorphic insertions.

```
static Object* ZERO;
```

This is a static data member that points to a statically allocated object called `theErrorObject`. There is only one object called `theErrorObject` in the entire system. When you dynamically allocate storage for an object in the container class library, a return value of ZERO indicates a memory failure.

```
static Object& ptrToRef(Object* p)
```

This function converts a point-to-`Object` into a reference-to-`Object`. If *p* is a null pointer, a reference to `theErrorObject`, also called NOOBJECT, is returned.

```
friend ostream& operator<< (ostream&, const Object&);
```

The friend function `::operator<<(ostream&, const Object&)` invokes the polymorphic `Object::printOn(ostream&)` function for a given object, allowing the stream insertion operator to be used with any object in the container class.

```
class TShouldDelete {
```

Class `TShouldDelete` is nested inside class `Object`. `TShouldDelete` is used in the `Object`-based class library to control ownership of objects inside containers. For more information, see the description of class `TShouldDelete` in the next chapter.

`public:`

```
enum DeleteType {NoDelete, DefDelete, Delete};
```

This enum specifies the deletion attributes of contained objects.

A `DeleteType` value affects all the items in an indirect container.

```
TShouldDelete(DeleteType dt = Delete);
```

This constructor creates a `TShouldDelete` object using a given deletion type. By default, a `TShouldObject` owns the items it contains and deletes them when the container goes out of scope.

```
int ownsElements()
```

This function returns a nonzero value if a `TShouldDelete` object owns the items it contains.

```
void ownsElements( int del )
```

This function can be used to set or remove object ownership from an indirect container. A nonzero value for `del` gives ownership to the container, whereas a 0 removes it. Ownership can be given or removed from a container at will. If a container has ownership when it goes out of scope, it will delete all the objects it contains.

`protected:`

```
int delObj( DeleteType dt )
```

This function returns a nonzero value if an indirect container will delete its contained objects when it goes out of scope.

`private:`

```
TShouldDelete shouldDelete;
```

This private data member specifies the current ownership state for an indirect container.

`};`

`};`

The global `::operator<<(ostream&, const Object&)` supports polymorphic stream insertions by invoking `Object::printOn(ostream&)` for an object. There are two other global operators that are overloaded for use with class `Object`. They are `::operator==(const Object&, const Object&)` and `::operator!=(const Object&, const Object&)`.

The global `::operator==(const Object&, const Object&)` performs equality testing between objects, using the first object's member function `isEqual(...)`. It also checks whether the two objects are of the same class, using the polymorphic `Object::isA()` function.

This operator provides safe equality checking for objects.

The global `::operator!=(const Object&, const Object&)` tests two objects for inequality, using the previous operator. It is a good practice to use the global operators ==

and != with objects instead of calling `Object::isEqual(...)`. Equality testing performed this way is more conclusive, and the use of overloaded operators is more in line with the object-oriented style.

Class *PriorityQueue*

`Queue`s and `Deque`s implement buffering based on the order of insertion. There are times when you want to deal with collections of items based not on insertion order, but on some notion of *priority.* Consider, for example, a queueing mechanism that stores commands to activate a large milling machine. A command to stop everything would probably be the highest priority command, commands to request machine status would be intermediate-level commands, and commands to initiate motion would be low-level commands. Although commands could be inserted into the queue in any order, they would need to be removed only according to message priority.

Class `PriorityQueue` implements exactly such a buffering mechanism. The way priority is determined is dependent on the < operator defined for the queued items. Here is an edited version of the header file for `PriorityQueue`:

```
class PriorityQueue : public Container,
                      public virtual TShouldDelete {
```

```
public:
```

```
int isEmpty() const;
```

This member function returns a nonzero value if there are no objects in `PriorityQueue`.

```
countType getItemsInContainer() const;
```

This function returns the number of items in the queue. Multiple occurrences of the same object are counted separately.

```
void put(Object&);
```

This adds an item to the queue. `PriorityQueue`s are allowed to contain multiple references to the same object, in which case they will be read back in the order of insertion. If all the objects inserted are of the same priority, `PriorityQueue` will behave like a regular `Queue`, as far as the removal order of objects is concerned.

```
Object& get();
```

This function returns the item that has either the lowest or the highest priority in the queue, depending on the way the member function `isLessThan(...)` is implemented for the items inserted in the queue. NOOBJECT is returned if the `PriorityQueue` is empty.

```
Object& peekLeft();
```

This function returns the object with the lowest or highest priority, depending on the implementation of the function `isLessThan(...)` for the items in the `PriorityQueue`. If there are no items in the queue, NOOBJECT is returned.

```
void detachLeft(DeleteType dt = NoDelete);
```

This function removes and optionally deletes the item that would be returned by `PriorityQueue::peekLeft()`. The item is deleted only if the `PriorityQueue` owns the items it contains.

```
void flush(DeleteType dt = DefDelete);
```

This function removes and optionally deletes all the items in a `PriorityQueue`.

```
int hasMember(Object& obj) const;
```

This function searches a `PriorityQueue` for a given target `Object obj`. A nonzero value is returned if `obj` is found.

```
int ownsElements();
```

This function returns a nonzero value if a `PriorityQueue` owns the elements it contains.

```
void ownsElements(int);
```

This function allows you to give or remove ownership from a `PriorityQueue`. When a container owns its contents, it owns all the objects. You can't specify ownership for only some of the objects in a container.

```
virtual classType isA() const;
virtual char _FAR *nameOf() const;
```

These two functions aid in identifying `PriorityQueue` objects at runtime. The first function returns a value unique to class `PriorityQueue`. The second returns a pointer to the constant string `"PriorityQueue"`.

```
virtual ContainerIterator& initIterator() const;
```

This function initializes an external iterator for stepping through the members of a `PriorityQueue`. What is returned is a reference to a `BtreeIterator` object allocated from the heap. It is your responsibility to delete this object when you're finished with it.

```
private:
```

```
Btree tree;
```

This private data member is the container that actually stores the objects of a `PriorityQueue`. See class `Btree` for a description of b-trees.

```
};
```

Using Class *PriorityQueue*

Consider implementing a priority-based message system to handle the commands described earlier to control a milling machine. Assume that the following three commands are in the command set: *stop, status request,* and *move.* These commands are given the priority levels shown in Figure 8.16.

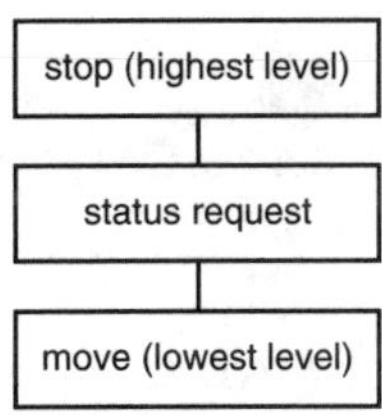

Figure 8.16. The command priority levels.

To implement these three messages, I use a small class hierarchy that looks like Figure 8.17.

Because `Message` is derived from `Sortable`, the class must override all the pure virtual functions in its base class in order to be an instantiable class. The most important of these functions is

```
virtual int isLessThan(const Object _FAR& m) const
  {return priority < ( (Message&) m).priority;}
```

which determines the priority order of items stored in a priority queue. As class `PriorityQueue` is implemented in the container class library, objects are read out of the queue in SIFO (smallest-in, first-out) order. Later I show how to make class `PriorityQueue` work as a GIFO (greatest-in, first-out) queue. Listing 8.24 is a short program to illustrate the use of the `Message` objects with a `PriorityQueue`.

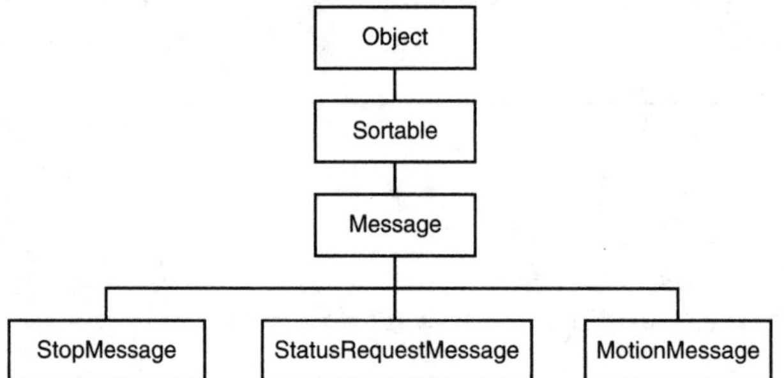

Figure 8.17. The `Message` *class hierarchy.*

Listing 8.24. A smallest-in, first-out priority queue with user objects.

```
#include <sortable.h>
#include <priortyq.h>
#include <iostream.h>
#include <string.h>
#include <clstypes.h>

class Message: public Sortable {

protected:

     enum PRIORITY {LOW_PRIORITY,
                    MEDIUM_PRIORITY,
                    HIGH_PRIORITY};

     enum {messageClass = __firstUserClass + 1};
     enum {MESSAGE_LENGTH = 20};

private:

     char message [MESSAGE_LENGTH];
     PRIORITY priority;

public:
     Message();
     Message(const char*, PRIORITY);
     virtual classType isA() const
       {return messageClass;}
```

 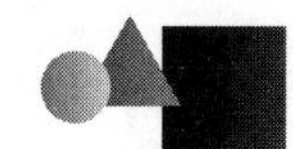

```
     virtual char _FAR *nameOf() const
       {return "Message";}
     virtual hashValueType hashValue() const
       {return 0;}
     virtual int isEqual(const Object _FAR& m) const
       {return priority == ( (Message&) m).priority;}
     virtual int isLessThan(const Object _FAR& m) const
       {return priority < ( (Message&) m).priority;}
     virtual void printOn(ostream _FAR& os) const
       {os << message;}
};

Message::Message()
{
     message [0] = '\0';
     priority = LOW_PRIORITY;
};

Message::Message(const char* cp, PRIORITY p)
{
     strncpy(message, cp, MESSAGE_LENGTH - 1);
     priority = p;
}

class StopMessage: public Message {

public:

     StopMessage()
       : Message("STOP", HIGH_PRIORITY) {}
};

class StatusRequestMessage: public Message {

public:

     StatusRequestMessage()
       : Message("STRQ", MEDIUM_PRIORITY) {}
};

class MotionMessage: public Message {

     int x, y;

public:

     MotionMessage(int a, int b)
       : Message("MOVE", LOW_PRIORITY)
         {x = a; y = b;}
```

continues

Listing 8.24. continued

```
     virtual void printOn(ostream _FAR& os) const
       {Message::printOn(os);
        os << " " << x << " " << y;}
};


void main()
{
     PriorityQueue q;

     q.put(*new MotionMessage(4, -2) );
     q.put(*new StatusRequestMessage() );
     q.put(*new MotionMessage(1, 3) );
     q.put(*new StopMessage() );
     q.put(*new MotionMessage(0, 0) );

     // display the queue contents, in order
     // or message priority
     cout << "\nPriorityQueue messages:\n";
     while (!q.isEmpty() ) {
       Message& m = (Message&) q.get();
       cout << m << endl;
     }
}
```

The output produced is

```
PriorityQueue messages:
MOVE 0 0
MOVE 1 3
MOVE 4 -2
STRQ
STOP
```

The lowest priority message is read out of the queue first. Using an external iterator to traverse the priority list provides the same ordering as using `PriorityQueue::get()`. Changing the listing in the previous example as shown in Listing 8.25 produces the same output sequence as before.

Listing 8.25. Using an external iterator with class `PriorityQueue`.

```
void main()
{
     PriorityQueue q;

     q.put(*new MotionMessage(4, -2) );
     q.put(*new StatusRequestMessage() );
```

```
    q.put(*new MotionMessage(1, 3) );
    q.put(*new StopMessage() );
    q.put(*new MotionMessage(0, 0) );

    // display the queue contents, in order
    // or message priority
    ContainerIterator& next = q.initIterator();
    cout << "\nIterated messages:\n";
    while (next) {
      Message& m = (Message&) next++;
      cout << m << endl;
    }
    delete &next;
}
```

The output of Listing 8.25 is

```
Iterated messages:
MOVE 0 0
MOVE 1 3
MOVE 4 -2
STRQ
STOP
```

Converting a *PriorityQueue* into a GIFO

`PriorityQueue` is implemented as a SIFO (smallest-in, first-out) queue. To turn it into a GIFO (greatest-in, first-out) is simple: You need to change only the way the member function `Message::isLessThan(...)` works. Changing the function like this

```
virtual int isLessThan(const Object _FAR& m) const
  {return priority > ( (Message&) m).priority;}
```

and running the program in Listing 8.25, the following output is produced:

```
Iterated messages:
STOP
STRQ
MOVE 0 0
MOVE 1 3
MOVE 4 -2
```

Class *Queue*

A `Queue` is an unordered container object. The word *queue* is used more in British English than in American English. It indicates a succession of items, such as people standing in line or cars backed up on the freeway. The idea of a queue is that the first item in line is serviced first. Programmers often call this a *first-in, first-out* (FIFO) structure. Queues are used frequently in programs because they can act as controlled buffers between a producer process and a consumer process that operate at different rates. For example, if the producer is a keyboard interrupt service routine and the consumer is the keyboard dispatcher, keystrokes can be queued up on one end and unqueued at the other end. If there is a burst of activity at the producer end, the queue fills up a little, but the consumer then has time to come around and service the characters that are stored.

In this section, I use the terms *front* and *back* to refer respectively to what the Borland documentation calls the right and left of a `Queue`. Here is an edited version of the header file for class `Queue`, as declared when you are *not* using template classes:

`class Queue: public Deque {`

`public:`

```
Object& get();
```

This function returns a reference to the object at the front (right) of the queue, removing the object from the container. The second object in line becomes the front of the `Queue`. When you remove an object from a `Queue`, you become responsible for deleting it. If no objects are in a `Queue`, the function `Queue::get()` returns NOOBJECT.

```
void put(Object&);
```

This function adds an object at the back (left) of a `Queue`. As long as the object is in the `Queue`, it is considered by default to be owned by the container. If you want to delete the object, you have to first remove it with `Queue::get()`.

```
virtual classType isA() const;
virtual char* nameOf() const;
```

These functions aid in identifying a `Queue` object at runtime. The first function returns a unique value for class `Queue`. The second returns a pointer to the constant string `"Queue"`.

`private:`

```
Object& getLeft();
Object& getRight();
void putLeft(Object&);
void putRight(Object&);
```

These functions are declared private, but not defined. The purpose is to prevent `Queue` users from accessing the corresponding public member functions defined in the base class `Deque`.

```
};
```

As with all other containers in the library, class `Queue` owns by default any objects put into it. These objects are automatically deleted when the container goes out of scope, unless ownership is removed from the container, using the inherited function `TShouldDelete::ownsElements()`. Objects are inserted at the back of the queue and removed from the front.

Once an object is put in a `Queue`, it can be removed only when it reaches the front, and not before. Figure 8.18 is a graphical representation of a `Queue`.

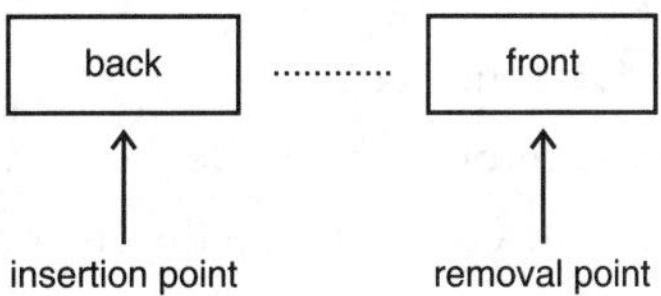

Figure 8.18. A graphical representation of data stored in a `Queue`.

There are two functions inherited from `Deque` for peeking at the front and back objects in a queue without removing them. They are `peekRight()` and `peekLeft()`, respectively. Listing 8.26 shows a simple use of class `Queue`.

Listing 8.26. Adding data to a `Queue`.

```
#include <queue.h>
#include <iostream.h>
#include <strstrea.h>
#include <strng.h>

void main()
{
      Queue fifo;
      const int COUNT = 5;

      for (int i = 0; i < COUNT; i++) {
        char buffer [80];
        ostrstream text(buffer, sizeof(buffer) );
        text << "This is item " << i << ends;
        fifo.put( *new String(buffer) );
      }

      cout << fifo;
}
```

The following output is produced:

```
Double List {
    This is item 4,
    This is item 3,
    This is item 2,
    This is item 1,
    This is item 0 }
```

This output may not be what you expected. In practice, the function `Container::printOn(ostream&)` inserts data into a stream starting from the back of the `Queue`. To display data starting at the front, you have essentially three options:

- You can use class `Deque` rather than `Queue`.
- You must iterate through the `Queue` yourself, using an external iterator.
- You can use a `Stack` object to flip the order of the objects.

The choice is yours, but the first option is generally better. If you use an external iterator to traverse a `Queue`, you have a problem. If you use the `peek(...)` member functions, you have access only to the front or back items in the `Queue`. This forces you to remove objects with `Queue::get()` to "peel away" successive items to gain access to those behind it. This means the queue will be emptied as it is iterated, like this:

```
// display contents of a queue, in the proper order.
// Queue is empty after being displayed.
while (!fifo.isEmpty() )
  cout << "\n  " << fifo.get();
```

If you want to iterate through the objects in a `Queue` and display them in the order of their insertion, you also can read the `Queue` objects into a temporary `Stack`, and then display the `Stack` contents, as in Listing 8.27.

Listing 8.27. Displaying the contents of a `Queue` in proper order without emptying the container.

```
#include <queue.h>
#include <iostream.h>
#include <strstrea.h>
#include <strng.h>
#include <stack.h>

void main()
{
      Queue fifo;
      const int COUNT = 5;

      for (int i = 0; i < COUNT; i++) {
        char buffer [80];
```

```
    ostrstream text(buffer, sizeof(buffer) );
    text << "This is item " << i << ends;
    fifo.put( *new String(buffer) );
  }

  cout << "\nOrdered Queue objects:";
  Stack stack;
  stack.ownsElements(0);
  ContainerIterator& k = fifo.initIterator();
  while (k)
    stack.push( (Object&) k++);

  while (!stack.isEmpty() )
   cout << "\n  " << stack.pop();
}
```

The following output is produced:

```
Ordered Queue objects:
  This is item 0,
  This is item 1,
  This is item 2,
  This is item 3,
  This is item 4
```

There is one caveat in the program: When you copy objects from one container into another, both containers by default own the objects. It is important to remove ownership from at least one of the two containers, using a statement like

```
stack.ownsElements(0);
```

You can also put local or other nonheap objects into a container if you have removed ownership from it, but then you take direct responsibility for the deletion of any objects placed in such containers.

Class *Set*

Class `Set` implements the abstraction of mathematical sets. `Set` is really a bare-bones class, lacking the operators that make sets powerful. There is no union operator and no intersection operator. That's a pity, because they were easy to implement. You can derive your own class from `Set` to add these powerful functions, as I show later. In class `Set`, only one occurrence of an object is allowed, and attempts to insert multiple occurrences of the same object are ignored. Here is an edited version of the header file for class `Set`, as declared when you are *not* using template classes:

```
class Set: public Bag {
```

```
public:
```

```
Set( sizeType setSize = DEFAULT_SET_SIZE );
```

This constructor does nothing itself. It relies on the base class `HashTable` to build a table that defaults to having 29 entries.

This value is adequate for many applications. If you anticipate storing hundreds or even thousands of objects in a `Set`, however, you should use a larger hash table. Remember that a hash table is more efficient when its size is a prime number.

```
virtual void add( Object _FAR & toAdd )
```

This function adds an object to a `Set`, but only if the object is not already in the `Set`. Multiple occurrences of the same objects are not allowed. If you try to add a second copy of an object already in the `Set`, no action takes place and no error messages are generated.

```
virtual classType isA() const
virtual char _FAR *nameOf() const
```

These two functions aid in identifying objects at runtime. The first function returns a unique value for class `Set`. The second returns a pointer to the constant string `"Set"`.

```
};
```

A `Set` allows only one occurrence of the same object to be inserted into it. Class `Set` allows any item derived from `Object` to be used, but allowing this is sometimes too generic. Depending on the types of items you insert into a `Set`, you may have to change some of the features of the class. The next section shows a simple example.

A *Set* Class to Handle *Strings*

I built a special `Set` class used only for handling `String` objects. Its new feature is to disallow storing multiple occurrences of strings containing the same characters, even though they may be distinct objects. Case is not considered when comparing strings. Listing 8.28 is the class, which I call `Words`.

Listing 8.28. `Words`, a class derived from `Set`.

```
#include <set.h>
#include <string.h>
#include <strng.h>
#include <iostream.h>
```

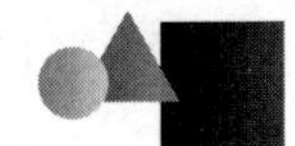

```
class Words: public Set {

public:

      void add(Object&);
};

void Words::add(Object& obj)
{
      // make sure the object is a string
     if (obj.isA() != stringClass) return;

      // get the null-terminated char string to insert
      const char* target = (const char*) ( (String&) obj);

      // make sure the character sequence is not
      ContainerIterator& i = initIterator();
      while ( (int) i) {
        const char* cp = (String&) ( (Object&) i++);
        if (strcmpi(target, cp) == 0) {
         // found a match: can't insert new object
         delete &i;
          return;
        }
      }
      // add the new object
      Set::add(obj);

      // remember to delete the iterator object !!
      delete &i;
}

void main()
{
      Words list;

      String& a = *new String("This is a sentence");
      String& b = *new String("This is a SENTENCE");
      String& c = *new String("This is a another sentence");
      String& d = *new String("This is a ANOTHER sentence");

      list.add(a);
      list.add(b);
      list.add(c);
      list.add(d);

      cout << "\nThe words stored are:\n"
          << list;
```

continues

Listing 8.28. continued

```
        // remove ownership from the Set
        list.ownsElements(0);

        // delete all the items explicitly
        delete &a;
        delete &b;
        delete &c;
        delete &d;
}
```

The output produced is

```
The words stored are:
Set {
    This is a sentence,
    This is another sentence }
```

As you can see, the duplicated character strings were not stored in the container. The various `Strings` are deleted explicitly, because some of them are in the `Set` container and some of them aren't. Rather than check one by one which Strings are in the container, I removed ownership from the `Set` and deleted the objects myself.

A More Mathematical *Set* Class

A set, in the mathematical sense, is quite a powerful abstraction. The standard operators for math sets allow you to do the following:

- Test a set for membership
- Compute the union of two sets
- Compute the intersection of two sets

Testing for membership is already possible for class `Set`, using the member function `hasMember(const Object&)`. Computing the union and intersection of two sets is not supported, so in Listing 8.29 I show the implementation of a simple class derived from `Set` that does support these operations.

Listing 8.29. A `Set` class that supports union and intersection operations.

```
#include <set.h>
#include <string.h>
#include <strng.h>
#include <iostream.h>
```

```
class MathSet: public Set {

public:

      MathSet() : Set() {}
      MathSet(MathSet&);
      MathSet& operator&(MathSet&);
      MathSet& operator¦(MathSet&);
};

MathSet::MathSet(MathSet& m)
{
        ContainerIterator& next = m.initIterator();
        while (next)
          add(next++);
        delete &next;
}

MathSet& MathSet::operator&(MathSet& m)
{
        static MathSet intersection;
        intersection.ownsElements(0);

        ContainerIterator& next = initIterator();
        while (next) {
          Object& obj = next++;
          if (m.hasMember(obj) )
            intersection.add(obj);
        }
        delete &next;
        return intersection;
}

MathSet& MathSet::operator¦(MathSet& m)
{
        static MathSet unionSet = *this;
        unionSet.ownsElements(0);

        ContainerIterator& next = m.initIterator();
        while (next)
          unionSet.add(next++);
        delete &next;

        return unionSet;
}

void main()
{
      MathSet names1, names2;
```

continues

Listing 8.29. continued

```
// create a number of local Strings
String a("Alpha");
String b("Bravo");
String c("Charlie");
String d("Delta");
String e("Echo");
String f("Foxtrot");
String g("Golf");

// add some Strings to the first Set
names1.add(a);
names1.add(b);
names1.add(d);
names1.add(e);

// add some Strings to the second Set
names2.add(a);
names2.add(b);
names2.add(c);
names2.add(f);
names2.add(g);

// compute the union and intersection of
// the two sets
MathSet unionSet = names1 ¦ names2;
MathSet intersection = names1 & names2;

// remove ownership from all containers,
// since we're using local objects with them
names1.ownsElements(0);
names2.ownsElements(0);
unionSet.ownsElements(0);
intersection.ownsElements(0);

cout << "\nSet 1 has the words:\n";
ContainerIterator& next1 = names1.initIterator();
while (next1)
  cout << " " << next1++;

cout << "\nSet 2 has the words:\n";
ContainerIterator& next2 = names2.initIterator();
while (next2)
  cout << " " << next2++;

cout << "\nThe union of the sets is:\n";
ContainerIterator& next3 = unionSet.initIterator();
while (next3)
  cout << " " << next3++;
```

```
    cout << "\nThe intersection of the sets is:\n";
    ContainerIterator& next4 = intersection.initIterator();
    while (next4)
      cout << " " << next4++;

    // delete the iterators
    delete &next1;
    delete &next2;
    delete &next3;
    delete &next4;
}
```

I added a short test program to show the usage of class `MathSet`. The output produced by the program is

```
Set 1 has the words:
 Alpha Echo Delta Bravo
Set 2 has the words:
 Golf Foxtrot Alpha Charlie Bravo
The union of the sets is:
 Golf Foxtrot Alpha Echo Delta Charlie Bravo
The intersection of the sets is:
 Alpha Bravo
```

I used the | and & symbols to indicate respectively union and intersection, given the similarity with Boolean `OR` and `AND` operations. The intersection and union member operators both declare a static `MathSet` object to be returned to the caller. It is important that these internally used containers are prevented from owning the objects they contain, to prevent them from deleting objects that are likely to be contained in other objects.

Class *Sortable*

Class `Sortable` is an abstract class that is the common ancestor for `String`, `BaseDate`, and `BaseTime`. `Sortable` objects are those that have the comparison functions `isEqual(const Object&)` and `isLessThan(const Object&)` defined, allowing containers with `Sortable` objects to be ordered. Here is an edited version of the class:

```
class Sortable: public Object {
```

```
public:
```

```
virtual int isEqual(const Object&) const = 0;
```

This pure `virtual` function forces classes derived from `Sortable` to supply their own implementation of the member function `isEqual(const Object&)`. An overriding

`isEqual(const Object&)` function is expected to return a nonzero value if two objects are considered to be equal, and 0 otherwise. The meaning and depth of equality is class dependent.

```
virtual int isLessThan(const Object& obj) const = 0;
```

This pure `virtual` forces classes derived from `Sortable` to supply their own versions of `isLessThan(const Object&)`. The overriding function is expected to return a nonzero value if an object is less than `obj`, and 0 otherwise.

```
virtual int isSortable() const;
```

This function returns a 1. I'm not sure why the function was declared virtual. I certainly don't recommend overriding it in derived classes. If a class is derived from `Sortable`, it should be sortable always and unconditionally.

```
virtual classType isA() const = 0;
```

This pure `virtual` forces derived classes to supply an `isA()` function of their own, which should return a unique value that identifies the class. See file *\BC45\INCLUDE\CLASSLIB\OBSOLETE\CLSTYPES.H* for a definition of the `classType` values used in the container class library.

```
virtual char* nameOf() const = 0;
```

This pure `virtual` forces classes derived from `Sortable` to supply a `nameOf()` function of their own that returns a string representation of the class name.

```
virtual hashValueType hashValue() const = 0;
```

This pure `virtual` forces classes derived from `Sortable` to supply their own `hashValue()` function, which must return a value to be used as a hash key in hashed containers.

```
virtual void printOn(ostream&) const = 0;
```

This is the polymorphic function to insert a printable representation of a class into a stream. It is called by the global stream inserter `::operator<<(ostream&, const Object&)`.

```
};
```

The class has no explicit constructor, because a `Sortable()` default constructor is supplied automatically by the compiler where necessary. I won't show any uses for class `Sortable` because it is abstract and can't be instantiated. See class `String` for an example of usage of `Sortable` as a base class.

Class *SortedArray*

Class `SortedArray` is an ordered container that stores items in an array that is sorted in ascending order. An array is generally thought of as being randomly accessible when reading data as well as when writing data. A `SortedArray` is a little different, because it doesn't allow elements to be inserted at random locations. Only objects derived from class `Sortable` can be inserted into a `SortedArray`. The class applies `::operator<(const Sortable&, const Sortable&)` to determine the insertion index for new objects. `SortedArrays` don't physically store the objects you insert into them; they store only the pointers to these objects. Here is an edited version of the header file for `SortedArray`, as declared when you are *not* using template classes:

```
class SortedArray: public AbstractArray {
```

```
public:
```

```
SortedArray(int upper, int lower = 0, sizeType aDelta = 0);
```

This constructor allocates storage for an array, using the constructor of base class `AbstractArray` to do all the work. If you want the array to have the capability to grow at runtime should it run out of storage, use a nonzero value for parameter `aDelta` in the constructor call. Using a nonzero value allows the array to grow in increments of `aDelta` slots.

```
virtual void add(Object&);
```

This inserts an object into an array, keeping the array sorted in ascending order. The sort order is determined by the objects stored in the array, using the global `::operator<(const Sortable&, const Sortable&)`. If the object needs to be inserted between two occupied array slots, the array elements are moved to make room for the new element.

```
virtual void detach(Object&, DeleteType = NoDelete);
```

This function removes an object from a sorted array and recompacts the array so that no empty slots are left behind.

```
virtual classType isA() const;
virtual char* nameOf() const;
```

These functions aid in identifying a `SortedArray` object at runtime. The first function returns a unique value for class `SortedArray`. The second returns a pointer to the constant string `"SortedArray"`.

```
};
```

There are several ways to remove objects from a sorted array. In fact, there are too many ways:

- Using `AbstractArray::detach(int, DeleteType = NoDelete)`
- Using `AbstractArray::destroy(int)`
- Using `SortedArray::detach(Object&, DeleteType = NoDelete)`

Do not use the `AbstractArray` functions to remove objects from sorted arrays. If you do, a “hole” containing a pointer to `theErrorObject` will be left behind in the sorted array. Listing 8.30 shows a number of operations with `SortedArray` containers.

Listing 8.30. Using class `SortedArray`.

```
#include <strng.h>
#include <sortarry.h>

void main()
{
      String& one   = *new String("1");
      String& two   = *new String("2");
      String& three = *new String("3");
      String& four  = *new String("4");
      String& five  = *new String("5");

      SortedArray array(5, 0, 9);

      array.add(one);
      array.add(two);
      array.add(three);

      cout << "\nBefore making changes:\n"
           << array;

      // delete object "two"
      array.detach(two, TShouldDelete::Delete);

      cout << "\nAfter deleting the '2':\n"
          << array;

      array.add(five);
      array.add(four);

      cout << "\nAfter adding a '5' and a '4':\n"
           << array;
}
```

 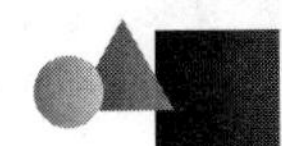

The output produced is

```
Before making changes:
SortedArray {
    1,
    2,
    3 }

After deleting the '2':
SortedArray {
    1,
    3 }

After adding a '5' and a '4':
SortedArray {
    1,
    3,
    4,
    5 }
```

The program uses a `SortedArray` object allocated on the stack, then fills it with objects allocated from the heap. Any time you remove an object using `SortedArray::detach(Object&, NoDelete)`, you assume full responsibility for deleting the object. The array deletes all the objects it contains when it goes out of scope, so you don't have to worry about deleting the objects.

Class *Stack*

`Stack`s are unordered containers. They store objects based on the order of insertion, rather than on the object inserted. Once an object is put on a `Stack`, it obscures objects inserted before it. Removing it makes the object inserted before it visible again. The only object that can be accessed in a `Stack` is the last one inserted. This means that inserting a sequence of objects into a `Stack` and then removing them causes the object sequence to be reversed, like this:

> `Stack` input sequence: A B C D E
>
> `Stack` output sequence: E D C B A

`Stack`s are usually shown graphically as vertical objects. Objects stack in the upward direction, so the top object is the last one inserted. Figure 8.19 is a graphic representation of a stack.

The process of inserting objects into a stack is usually called *pushing,* as if there is some force to overcome in order to succeed. The process of removing the top object from a stack is usually called *popping.*

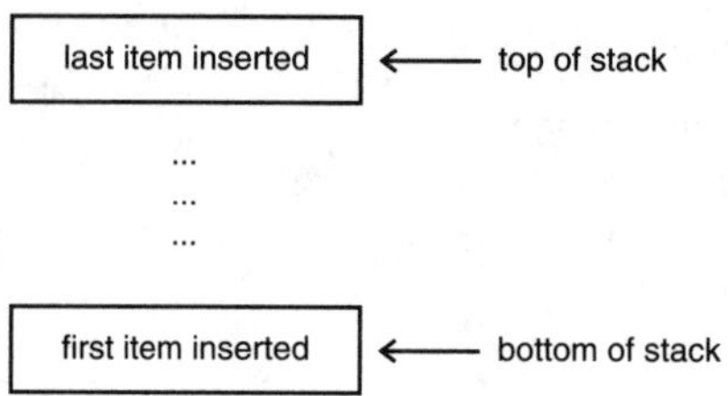

Figure 8.19. A graphic representation of a stack.

Stack objects in the container class library actually use a linked list to manage the objects in a stack, but this fact is completely invisible to users. Here is an edited version of the `Stack` header file, as declared when you are *not* using template classes:

`class Stack: public Container {`

`public:`

`void push(Object&);`

This pushes an object onto the stack. This new object remains on the top of the stack until it is removed or covered by another object.

`Object& pop();`

This function removes the object that is on the top of the stack.

`Object& top() const;`

This function returns the object that is on top of the stack without removing it.

`virtual int isEmpty() const;`

This function returns a nonzero value if there are no items in the container.

`virtual countType getItemsInContainer() const;`

This function returns the number of items in a `Stack`. If multiple occurrences of the same object appear, they are each counted separately.

`virtual void flush(DeleteType dt = DefDelete);`

This function removes and optionally deletes all the items in a `Stack`.

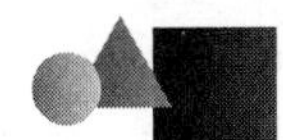

```
virtual ContainerIterator& initIterator() const;
```

This initializes an iterator for stepping through the contents of a `Stack`. The iterator is actually a class object allocated dynamically from the heap. When you are finished using this iterator, you must delete it.

```
virtual classType isA() const;
virtual char* nameOf() const;
```

These functions aid in identifying a `Stack` object at runtime. The first function returns a unique value for class `Stack`. The second returns a pointer to the constant string `"Stack"`.

`private:`

```
List theStack;
```

This private data member is the object that actually stores the items in a `Stack`. Although `Stack` containers internally manage items using a linked list, this fact is completely invisible to users. When a `Stack` goes out of scope, the compiler automatically calls the destructor for this List object, which then causes all the objects on the `Stack` to be deleted, if owned by the `Stack`.

`};`

Stacks are easy to use, primarily because they are rather limited. Still, there are times when a stack is just what you need. Pushing values on a stack is just like putting pieces of paper on a stack of paper: The last piece put on the stack is the one on top of the stack. When a stack is popped, the value on top is returned, like removing a piece of paper from the paper stack.

Listing 8.31 shows the results of pushing and popping items from a stack.

Listing 8.31. Using a `Stack` object.

```
#include <strstrea.h>
#include <strng.h>
#include <stack.h>

void main()
{
      Stack stack;
      int COUNT = 5;
```

continues

Listing 8.31. continued

```
      for (int i = 0; i < COUNT; i++) {
        char buffer [100];
        ostrstream text(buffer, sizeof(buffer) );
        text << "Item " << i << ends;
        stack. push(*new String(buffer) );
      }

      cout << "\n\n" << stack;

      cout << "\nIterated Stack contents:";
      ContainerIterator& next = stack.initIterator();
      while (next)
        cout << "\n " << next++;
      delete &next;

      cout << "\n\nPopped Stack contents:";
      for (i = 0; i < COUNT; i++)
        cout << "\n " << stack.pop();
}
```

The output produced is

```
Stack {
    Item 4,
    Item 3,
    Item 2,
    Item 1,
    Item 0 }

Iterated Stack contents:
 Item 4
 Item 3
 Item 2
 Item 1
 Item 0

Popped Stack contents:
 Item 4
 Item 3
 Item 2
 Item 1
 Item 0
```

You can put any kind of object you want in a `Stack`, as long as it was derived from `Object`. This would allow you to do rather unusual things, such as pushing a stack on a stack. A real world analogy of this comes to mind. If you have papers that represent different chapters of a book, when you stack them you might lay each chapter at a right angle to the one below it, creating a stack of stacks. Although this kind of situation can occur, it

is rare, and you won't see too many stacks of stacks in actual programs. Similarly, you could have a stack of linked lists, or a list of stacks. The combinations are yours for the choosing.

Class *String*

Strings are used so often in programs that Borland wrote a class just for them. In C++, a string is just an array of null-terminated characters. However, class `String` is much more than that in the container library. `String` objects contain and manage their own dynamically allocated memory for storing character arrays. They have functions to test for equality and alphabetical order. Finally, they know how to insert themselves into an output stream.

> **NOTE**
>
> The Borland class `String` has been replaced by a new standard C++ class called **`string`**, recently adopted into the language by the ANSI X3J16 C++ committee. Being a standard part of the C++ language, and not part of the container class library, I won't describe the ANSI class **`string`** in this book.

Here is an edited version of the declaration for the Borland class `String`:

```
class String: public Sortable {
```

```
public:
```

```
String(const char* = "" );
```

This constructor takes a pointer to a null-terminated string and copies the string into a dynamically allocated buffer. When the `String` object is destructed, the buffer is also deallocated. You can pass any kind of null-terminated array to this constructor—static, auto, or global—because it is used only to be copied in the constructor, and not referenced elsewhere in class `String`.

```
String(const String&);
```

This constructor makes a new `String` object, copying the contents of another `String` object into an internally allocated buffer.

```
virtual ~String();
```

This function deallocates the buffer used to store the null-terminated string. The buffer is returned to the heap.

```
String& operator=(const String&);
```

This constructor copies the contents of another `String` object.

The old `String` contents are overwritten.

```
operator const char*() const;
```

This operator returns a pointer to the null-terminated character array managed by a `String` object. The pointer should be used only to read the null-terminated string, but not to write to it.

```
virtual int isEqual(const Object&) const;
virtual int isLessThan(const Object&) const;
```

These functions are called polymorphically through the global ordering operators `::operator==(const Object&, const Object&)`, `::operator!=(const Object&, const Object&)`, and `::operator<(const Object&, const Object&)`.

```
virtual classType isA() const;
```

This `virtual` function returns a value that uniquely identifies `String` objects. The value returned is `stringClass`, and it is defined in the file *\BC45\INCLUDE\CLASSLIB\OBSOLETE\CLSTYPES.H.*

```
virtual char* nameOf() const;
```

This function returns a pointer to the constant string `"String"`, regardless of what characters are stored in a `String` object.

```
virtual hashValueType hashValue() const;
```

This function computes a hash key based on the contents of a `String` object. The key can subsequently be used as an index for the `String` into hashed arrays. The hash value returned is an unsigned integer. The algorithm employed gives a good distribution over the 65,536 possible hash values. The algorithm iteratively performs an `XOR` and a left shift of all the characters in a string, like this:

```
// compute the CRC hash value for a string
unsigned int value = 0;
for(int i = 0; i < len; i++) {
  value ^= theString[i];
  value = _rotl(value, 1);
}
```

This type of algorithm is used extensively in digital communications for error checking, and generates a value called a *CRC-16* (for *Cyclic Redundancy Check—16 bits*). The hash value is initialized to a 0 before starting the computation, making null strings always return a 0 hash key.

```
virtual void printOn(ostream&) const;
```

This function is polymorphically called by the global insertion operator `::operator(ostream&, const Object&)`. It allows a printable representation of a string to be sent to any output stream. The function copies the `String` object's characters to the assigned stream up to, but not including, the null terminator. Watch out for this detail if you're performing in-memory stream operations, because you may need a null terminator to read the string back or to further process the stream.

`private:`

```
sizeType len;
```

This private data member stores the length of the dynamically allocated buffer used to store a null-terminated string. The value is one greater than the number of displayable characters in a string, to include the null terminator.

```
char* theString;
```

This is a pointer to a dynamically allocated buffer in which a null-terminated string is stored. When a `String` object is destructed, this buffer is deleted as well.

`};`

Using Class *String*

Strings know how to handle some of the most common operations, such as displaying themselves and assigning characters to themselves. Although you don't see the operators < , >, ==, and != in class `String`, they are supported through the use of the following global operators

```
::operator==(const Object&, const Object&)
::operator!=(const Object&, const Object&)
::operator<(const Sortable&, const Sortable&)
::operator>(const Sortable&, const Sortable&)
::operator>=(const Sortable&, const Sortable&)
::operator<=(const Sortable&, const Sortable&)
```

which invoke the appropriate virtual function in class `String` to do the actual work. This allows you to write expressions like

```
// test the lexical ordering of strings
void test(String& s1, String& s2, String& s3)
{
      if (s1 < s3)
        cout << "\n" << s1 << " is less than " << s3;

      if (s2 > s1)
        cout << "\n" << s2 << " is greater than " << s1;

      if (s2 == s1)
        cout << "\n" << s2 << " is equal to " << s1;

      if (s2 != s1)
        cout << "\n" << s2 << " is not equal to " << s1;
}
```

You also can create `String` objects in all sorts of ways, as shown in Listing 8.32.

Listing 8.32. Creating `String` objects in different ways.

```
#include <iostream.h>
#include <strng.h>

// define a global String
String global("global!");

void main()
{

      // declare two strings using a reference and
      // a pointer
      String& first  = *(new String(" A first string") );
      String* second =   new String(" A second string");

      // define a string with the same characters as before
      String& third  = *(new String(" A first string") );

      // declare a local variable;
      String fourth(" A fourth string");
```

```
        // declare one string from another
        String& fifth = *(new String(first) );

        cout << "\n\n" << first << *second << third;
        cout << "\n" << fourth << fifth;

        // assign a new string to a String variable
        fifth = " A new fifth string";
        cout << "\n" << fifth;

        cout << "\nDisplaying a string like this:"
             << first
             << "\nis exactly the same as this:   "
             << (const char*) first;

        // you can do this too !
        static String yo("Yo!");
        cout << "\n\t" << yo << "   " << global;

        // delete the heap objects
        delete &first;
        delete second;
        delete &third;
        delete &fifth;
}
```

The output produced is

```
 A first string A second string A first string
 A fourth string A first string
 A new fifth string
Displaying a string like this: A first string
is exactly the same as this:   A first string
        Yo!  global!
```

Notice the different syntax used when declaring a reference to a `String` and a pointer to a `String`. This is standard C++ notation, applicable to all classes and types. You also can declare static and global variables of type `String`. Be careful when inserting a `String` into a stream if you're using a pointer. You must use this notation

```
cout << *pointer_to_string;
```

unless you want to display the address of the string. The typecast `(const char*)` is needed with strings only when you need to revert to the low-level array notation for ANSI functions like `strchr(...)` and `strcat(...)`. The next section shows how to derive a new string class that handles both of these ANSI functions in an object-oriented manner—using overloaded operators.

Deriving a Class from *String*

Class `String` is powerful; however, it may not meet all your requirements. It is often convenient to use strings in arithmetic operations and treat them like scalar types. The operators I miss most in `String` are these:

Operator	*Meaning*
`operator+`	Concatenate two strings
`operator+=`	Concatenate two strings
`operator( )`	Find a substring in a string

With the last operator, you can write expressions like

```
if (some_string("abc") )
  // substring found
```

or

```
if (cp = some_string("abc") )
  // cp points to located substring
```

These operators are small improvements to `String`, but they really turn out to be handy. Listing 8.33 is the implementation of class `MyString` that supports them.

Listing 8.33. Class `MyString` is derived from `String` to handle a few simple operators.

```
#include <iostream.h>
#include <string.h>
#include <strng.h>

class MyString: public String {

public:

  MyString(const String& s) : String(s) {}
  MyString(const char* s) : String(s) {}

  // concatenation operators
  MyString& operator+(MyString& s1);
  void operator+=(MyString& s1);

  // search operators
  char* operator()(String&);
  char* operator()(char*);
  char* operator()(char);
};
```

```
MyString& MyString::operator+(MyString& s1)
{
      static MyString temp("");
      int size = strlen( (const char*) *this);
      size += strlen( (const char*) s1);
      char* buffer = new char [size + 1];
      strcpy(buffer, (const char*) *this);
      strcat(buffer, (const char*) s1);
      temp = buffer;
      return temp;
}

void MyString::operator+=(MyString& s1)
{
      *(this) = *(this) + s1;
}

char* MyString::operator()(String& s1)
{
      return strstr( (const char*) *this,
                     (const char*) s1);
}

char* MyString::operator()(char* s1)
{
      return strstr( (const char*) *this, s1);
}

char* MyString::operator()(char c)
{
      return strchr( (const char*) *this, c);
}
```

Listing 8.34 is a program that uses the new features added to `MyString`.

Listing 8.34. Using class `MyString`.

```
void main()
{
      MyString s1("First ");
      MyString s2("Second ");
      MyString s3("Third ");
      MyString s4("");

      s4 = s1 + s2 + s3;
      cout << "\n\nThe three strings are: " << s4;
```

continues

Listing 8.34. continued

```
      s2 += s1;
      cout << "\n" << s2;

      // search for a substring
      MyString sentence("In the course of humans events");
      if (sentence("of") ) {
       cout << "\nThe phrase starting with the word "
             <<  "'of' is: \n\t" << sentence("of");
      }

      // search for a letter
      char* cp = sentence('s');
     if (cp) {
        cout << "\n's' is the "
             << (int) (cp - (char*) (const char*) sentence)
             << "th character in the sentence";
      }

      // search for a string
      String word("the");
      if (sentence(word) ) {
        cout << "\nThe phrase starting with the word "
             <<  "'the' is: \n\t" << sentence(word);
      }
}
```

The output produced is

```
The three strings are: First Second Third
Second First
The phrase starting with the word 'of' is:
        of human events
's' is the 11th character in the sentence
The phrase starting with the word 'the' is:
        the course of human events
```

Class *Time*

This class is used to read the system time without having to deal with low-level details of system ticks, time formats, and ANSI C standards. The essential variables for storing and setting time are contained in class `BaseTime`, which is a base class for `Time`. Class `Time` adds a method for displaying the time in the format:

```
<hours>:<minutes>:<seconds>.<hundredths> am/pm
```

Class `Time` doesn't have any operators to add or subtract times, but it is still quite useful. Here is an edited version of its header file:

```
class Time: public BaseTime {
```

```
public:
```

```
    Time();
    Time(const Time&);
    Time(unsigned char,
         unsigned char = 0,
         unsigned char = 0,
         unsigned char = 0);
```

These three constructors do nothing but pass parameters to the base class `BaseTime`, where all the work is done. See class `BaseTime` for further details.

```
virtual classType isA() const;
virtual char* nameOf() const;
```

These two functions aid in identifying `Time` objects at runtime. The first returns a value that uniquely identifies a `Time` object. The second returns a pointer to the constant string `"Time"`.

```
virtual void printOn( ostream _FAR & ) const;
```

This function inserts a printable representation of time into an output stream. The function supports only a 12-hour format, so times are given as "*HH*:*MM*:*SS*.*hh* am" or "*HH*:*MM*:*SS*.*hh* pm", in which *HH* is in the range 1..12, *MM* and *SS* are in the range 0..59, and *hh* is in the range 0..99.

```
};
```

Using Class *Time*

Once you create a `Time` object, the values stored inside it for hours, minutes, and so on remain frozen. Users sometimes expect a `Time` object to somehow update itself, so that displaying it at a later time would yield the correct time. This is not the case.

Time objects are easy to use. Because they freeze the values at a particular moment in time, they often are used as temporary objects, like this:

```
cout << "\nthe time is: " << Time();
```

which would display something like:

```
the time is: 12:31:58.98 pm
```

If all you need to display is the current time, it makes sense to use a temporary object, because you won't need the object again in the program. Of course, you also can create variables of class `Time` and use them like any other object. Listing 8.35 is an example.

Listing 8.35. Using a `Time` object.

```
#include <iostream.h>
#include <ltime.h>

void main()
{
      Time time;

      cout << "\nAttributes of class "
           << time.nameOf()
           << ":\n\t isA() value: "
           << time.isA()
           << "\n\t hashValue(): "
           << time.hashValue()
           << "\n\t Time: "
           << time;
}
```

The output produced depends on the system time, but will be something like this:

```
Attributes of class Time:
         iaA() value: 20
         hashValue(): 66
         Time: 5:35:04.10 pm
```

The hash value is computed using the hours, minutes, seconds, and hundredths of a second stored in a `Time` object. You can use time objects allocated from the heap, from the stack, or from global memory. You can copy the time from one `Time` object to another, as shown in Listing 8.36.

Listing 8.36. Using multiple `Time` objects.

```
#include <iostream.h>
#include <ltime.h>

void main()
{
      // initialize a time object
      Time time(15, 01, 30);
```

```
    // create objects on the heap
    Time* time1 = new Time();
    Time* time2 = new Time(time);
    Time* time3 = new Time(*time2);

    // initialize an auto object
    Time time4(10, 20);

    cout << "\ntime : " << time;
    cout << "\ntime1: " << *time1;
    cout << "\ntime2: " << *time2;
    cout << "\ntime3: " << *time3;
    cout << "\ntime4: " << time4;
}
```

The output produced depends on the system time, but will be something like this:

```
time : 3:01:30.00 pm
time2: 3:01:30.00 pm
time3: 3:01:30.00 pm
time4: 10:20:00.00 am
```

The example shows how to use both auto and heap `Time` objects.

When creating a `Time` with a specific time, you can omit the minutes, seconds, and hundredths of a second if necessary.

Deriving a Class from *Time*

Times are often used in arithmetic expressions to compute durations, completion times, and so on. This functionality is missing in class `Time`, and requires the use of operators to add and subtract times. I implement a class called `MyTime`, derived from `Time`, that adds the necessary arithmetic operators and displays the time in a 24-hour European format, without the hundredths-of-a-second field.

Listing 8.37. `MyTime` is an improved time class derived from `Time`.

```
#include <iostream.h>
#include <iomanip.h>
#include <ltime.h>

class MyTime: public Time {
```

continues

Listing 8.37. continued

```
public:

  MyTime() : Time() {}
  MyTime(BaseTime&);
  MyTime(unsigned char, unsigned char,
       unsigned char = 0, unsigned char = 0);
  void setHour(unsigned char);
  void setMinute(unsigned char);
  void setSecond(unsigned char);
  void setHundredths(unsigned char);
  void printOn(ostream&) const;
  BaseTime& operator+(BaseTime&);
  BaseTime& operator-(BaseTime&);
};


MyTime::MyTime(BaseTime& b)
      : Time(0, 0)       // force time to zero until
                         // the parameters have been
                         // bounds-checked
{
      // set the time values, after performing
      // argument bounds checking

      setHour(b.hour() );
      setMinute(b.minute() );
      setSecond(b.second() );
      setHundredths(b.hundredths() );
}

MyTime::MyTime(unsigned char hour,
             unsigned char minute,
             unsigned char second,
             unsigned char hundredths)
      : Time(0, 0)       // force time to zero until
                         // the parameters have been
                         // bounds-checked
{
      // set the time values, after performing
      // argument bounds checking

      setHour(hour);
      setMinute(minute);
      setSecond(second);
      setHundredths(hundredths);
}
```

```
void MyTime::setHour(unsigned char hours)
{
      if (hours < 24)
        BaseTime::setHour(hours);
}

void MyTime::setMinute(unsigned char minutes)
{
      if (minutes < 60)
        BaseTime::setMinute(minutes);
}

void MyTime::setSecond(unsigned char seconds)
{
      if (seconds < 59)
        BaseTime::setSecond(seconds);
}

void MyTime::setHundredths(unsigned char hund)
{
      if (hund < 100)
        BaseTime::setHundredths(hund);
}

void MyTime::printOn(ostream& os) const
{
      os << setfill('0') << hour() << ":" << setw(2)
         << minute() << ":" << setw(2) << second();
}

BaseTime& MyTime::operator+(BaseTime& b)
{
      int carry, hh, mm, ss, hd;

      hd = hundredths() + b.hundredths();
      if (hd > 100) {
        hd -= 100;
        carry = 1;
      }
      else
        carry = 0;

      ss = second() + b.second() + carry;
      if (ss > 60) {
        ss -= 60;
        carry = 1;
      }
      else
        carry = 0;
```

continues

Listing 8.37. continued

```
        mm = minute() + b.minute() + carry;
        if (mm > 60) {
          mm -= 60;
          carry = 1;
        }
        else
          carry = 0;

        hh = hour() + b.hour() + carry;
        if (hh > 24)
          hh -= 24;

        static MyTime result(hh, mm, ss, hd);
        return result;
}

BaseTime& MyTime::operator-(BaseTime& b)
{
        int borrow, hh, mm, ss, hd;

        hd = hundredths() - b.hundredths();
        if (hd < 0) {
          hd += 100;
          borrow = 1;
        }
        else
          borrow = 0;

        ss = second() - b.second() - borrow;
        if (ss < 0) {
          ss += 60;
          borrow = 1;
        }
        else
          borrow = 0;

        mm = minute() - b.minute() - borrow;
        if (mm < 0) {
          mm += 60;
          borrow = 1;
        }
        else
          borrow = 0;

        hh = hour() - b.hour() - borrow;
        if (hh < 0)
          hh += 24;
```

```
        static MyTime result(hh, mm, ss, hd);
        return result;
}

void main()
{
        MyTime now(2, 24, 39);
        MyTime start(17, 55);
        MyTime duration = now - start;

        cout << "\nIt is now: " << now
             << "\nThe test started at: " << start
             << "\nIt took " << duration << " hours."
             << "\nIf the test began now, it would "
             << "end at " << (now + duration);
}
```

The output from the program is

```
It is now: 2:24:39
The test started at: 17:55:00
It took 8:29:39 hours.
If the test began now, it would end at 10:54:18
```

The program uses the stream manipulators `setfill(int)` and `setw(int)` to force the minutes and seconds fields to use two characters, filling them with a 0 if necessary. Using class `MyTime` simplifies the handling of time expressions to a minimum, and also prevents the display of annoying error messages. If an invalid parameter is passed to a `MyTime` object, it is ignored. This behavior may not be suitable for all applications, of course, but it is easy to change `MyTime` or derive a class from it.

Iterators

The container class library has several classes that are capable of storing multiple objects. To handle the objects inside these containers, you need a way to iterate through them. Borland chose to do this with special iterator classes, which allow you to iterate through the objects in a container almost as easily as you can iterate through a simple array. Listing 8.38 is a short example.

Listing 8.38. Iterating through a container class with an external iteration object.

```
#include <array.h>
#include <strng.h>
#include <iostream.h>
```

continues

Listing 8.38. continued

```
void main()
{
      Array list(4, 0, 4);

      String& a = *new String("One");
      String& b = *new String("Two");
      String& c = *new String("Three");
      String& d = *new String("Four");

      list.add(a);
      list.add(b);
      list.add(c);
      list.add(d);

      ContainerIterator& next = list.initIterator();

      while (next) {
        Object& obj = next++;
        if (obj == NOOBJECT) break;
        cout << "\n" << obj;
      }

      delete &next;
}
```

The following output is produced:

```
One
Two
Three
Four
```

This output shows that before you enter an iteration loop, you create an iterator object with a statement like

```
// this creates an iterator on the heap
ContainerIterator& i = list.initIterator();
```

This same statement works with any kind of container, such as class `Array`, class `HashTable`, or class `DoubleList`, because all iterators are derived from class `ContainerIterator`. The class `DoubleList` has additional flexibility, allowing the creation of iterators that proceed backward, from the end to the beginning of a list. If you need a backward iterator for a `DoubleList`, it has to be declared like this:

```
// this creates a backward double list iterator
DoubleListIterator& iterator =
```

```
(DoubleListIterator&) list.initReverseIterator();
```

The typecast is necessary because you must declare the member function `DoubleList::initReverseIterator()` to return a reference to a `ContainerIterator`. When you create an iterator, you obtain a reference to an object that is allocated from the heap. When you're through with the iterator, you must delete it yourself. Once the iterator is created, you can test it as an integer to see when there are no more items to iterate through, like this:

```
// see if iteration is finished
while (iterator)
  // ... more items to iterate over
```

This statement is made possible by the iterator class member function operator `int()`, which returns 0 only when there are no more items left in an iteration. Once you have an iterator, you can use it to access the next item in a container, as shown here:

```
// with any ContainerIterator& iterator
Object& obj = iterator++;

// only with DoubleListIterator& iterator
Object& obj = iterator--;
```

Only double lists are provided with the capability of iterating in reverse order. It would be nice if `Array` objects had this feature as well, because the physical capability exists intrinsically for `Arrays`. All iterators have the member operator `Object()`, which returns a reference to the current object in an iteration. The last note to add about using class iterators is that you must remember to delete them. It's easy to forget, especially because the objects are allocated inside a function call.

The Template-Based Container Library

The `Object`-based container library introduced with Borland C++ 2.0 represented a great step forward for C++, but it was not without problems. The main one was that only items derived from `Object` could be used with a container. If you wanted to do something as simple as create a bag of `float`s, you had to derive some kind of `Float` class from `Object`, override all the pure virtual functions in `Object`, and add a data member to hold the `float` value. That's a lot of work—too much, in fact.

To overcome the limitations of the `Object`-based library, Borland developed a library built around a variety of class templates. The new hierarchy is called *BIDS,* for *Borland International Data Structures.* The BIDS containers come in two basic flavors: direct containers and indirect containers. The former store complete objects, the latter pointers to objects. You can store both scalar and class objects in both types of containers.

FDS and ADT Containers

The *BIDS* containers are divided into two categories, based on the level of abstraction they support: *FDSs* (*Fundamental Data Structures*) and *ADTs* (*Abstract Data Structures*). The low-level containers that implement vectors, linked lists, and doubly-linked lists are FDSs. The high-level containers that implement stacks, deques, queues, bags, and arrays are ADTs. All ADT classes are built using FDS classes with class templates. This arrangement allows you to implement any ADT class with any FDS class, so you can use a stack class built around vectors, linked lists, or doubly-linked lists. The choice of which FDS to use with a particular ADT is yours, and usually will be dependent on trade-offs of runtime efficiency and memory usage.

FDS Containers

An FDS does not equate directly to a class. The BIDS library has only three FDSs, but many classes. An FDS is a collection of classes that together implement some kind of container abstraction. Borland C++ 4.5 defines the following three containers as FDSs:

- Vectors
- Singly-linked lists
- Doubly-linked lists

B-trees were implemented in the `Object`-based hierarchy but not included in the BIDS FDS containers. The name for each FDS container comes from the memory scheme used to implement it. Vectors are made up of adjacent bytes of memory, allowing random access in constant time. Linked lists are built up by connecting a series of nodes with pointers. A list is made up of nodes, each containing only one pointer, making it possible to traverse a list in only one direction. A doubly-linked list uses two pointers for each node—one to the predecessor node and one to the successor node—which allows you to traverse a doubly-linked list either forward or backward.

FDS Storage Paradigms

There are essentially no restrictions on the types of data that can be stored in an FDS container, but there are two ways an item can be stored: directly or indirectly. With direct storage, an FDS internally allocates storage for an item, then copies the item to be stored. The internal copy is then completely independent from the original object. Direct storage FDS containers are homogeneous because only one type of object can be handled by a given container at a given time. Basically, any type of data can be stored in a direct FDS container, but because the object is copied into the container, the data type must be something that can be copied. For scalar data types there is no problem, but for class objects a copy operator must be defined.

With indirect storage, a pointer to an item is stored in the FDS. Any type of item can be referenced with a pointer, so you use indirect storage with any data type. Moreover, an indirect FDS can be heterogeneous because it can contain pointers to disparate data types. Using indirect storage is often more efficient than using direct storage, but it adds another level of difficulty to a program. One problem with indirect storage is that a container doesn't know whether it owns the referenced item. If it isn't clear who owns an object, then it isn't clear whose responsibility it is to delete the object when the container goes out of scope. To solve this problem, the FDS indirect containers inherit class `TShouldDelete`, which addresses some of the issues of ownership.

FDS Containers

Most of the time you won't need to deal with the low-level FDS containers because the ADT containers manage FDS objects and provide more power. To optimize the performance of the ADT containers, however, you will need to understand a few basics about FDSs.

Each FDS container can be used in more than one way. Consider a simple vector. If you add an item, you can specify the index where you want the item stored, but you may wish array entries to be automatically maintained in alphabetical order. Or you may want the vector itself to keep track of the last index used, so you could insert items at ascending indices without having to give an index at all. Each type of FDS is implemented with a separate class template, giving rise to quite a few templates. In the following sections, I list the main ones.

FDS Vector Containers

There are six built-in types of FDS vector containers. The types are as follows: simple, counted, sorted, simple indirect, counted indirect, and sorted indirect. Which type you need depends on the kind of data you are dealing with, how much data you expect, how often you need to access it, and so on. The six FDS vector container types are related to each other in a rather complex hierarchy, in which parameterized types are used as base classes. When a base class is a parameterized type, passed as a template parameter, you don't know what the base class is until a specific data type is used with the template. Consider, for example, the class

```
template <class T, class BASE> class Derived: public BASE {};
```

The base class is not known until the `BASE` parameter is given in a template declaration. Because of this deferral in base class determination, there is tremendous power in the previous template declaration, allowing the same class to appear at different points in a class hierarchy. Figure 9.1 shows the complete class hierarchy for the FDS vector containers.

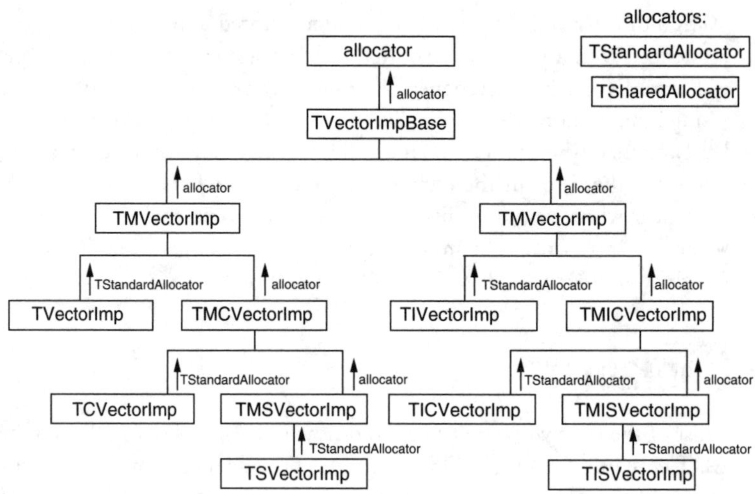

Figure 9.1. The FDS vector container class hierarchy.

The root of the hierarchy is an allocator class: `TStandardAllocator` or `TSharedAllocator`. You can create your own allocator, like `TEnhancedSubAllocator` or `TLocalMemoryAllocator`, for special purposes. To use these allocators, you need to derive a class template from one of the managed containers, and pass the allocator name to the base class.

Simple Direct Vectors

The simplest type of vector FDS is implemented by the class template `TVectorImp<T>`, in which the `<T>` stands for whatever data type you wish to store in the vector. `TVectorImp<T>` requires you to specify the insertion index when you add items, and it doesn't keep track of insertions; that is, if you insert an object at a slot that already contains something, the old object will be overwritten without being destructed or deleted. `TVectorImp<T>` is the lowest-level vector class, and is similar to class `Array` in the `Object`-based class library. To read or write vector elements, you use the subscripting `operator[]`. Listing 9.1 is a short example.

Listing 9.1. Using direct vectors of integers.

```
#include <classlib\vectimp.h>
#include <iostream.h>

void main()
{
```

```
    // create a local vector
    TVectorImp<int> a(50);

    // insert a few items
    a [8]  = 1;
    a [10] = 1000;

    // read some data back
    cout << "\nHere are some vector values:"
         << "\na [0] =  " << a [0]
         << "\na [8] =  " << a [8]
         << "\na [10] = " << a [10]
         << endl;
}
```

The output produced is

```
Here are some vector values:
a [0] =  34
a [8] =  1
a [10] = 1000
```

When a `TVectorImp<T>` container object is created, it contains random data, so the value of `a[0]` is random in the previous example. As you can see, `TVectorImp<T>` can be used with the same syntax as a plain old C array. The nice thing about direct storage is that you never have to worry about ownership. Ownership of an object is never transferred into the container because the container uses a copy of the data you give it. With the `Object`-based container classes, containers own by default any data put into them. You are therefore restricted from using local (or even global) objects with `Object`-based containers. There are no such limitations with BIDS direct-storage FDS containers.

The following listing shows the use of the template class `TVectorImp<T>` with `string` objects. Class `string` was recently added to the preliminary draft by the ANSI X3J16 committee.

```
#include <classlib\vectimp.h>
#include <iostream.h>
#include <cstring.h>

void main()
{
  // create a local vector
  TVectorImp<string> a(50);

  // insert a few items
  a [0] = string("who");
  a [1] = string("are");
  a [2] = string("you?");
```

```
  // iterate over the array using an external
  // iterator object
  TVectorIteratorImp<string> next(a);
  cout << "\nDirect Vector items:\n";
  while (next)
    cout << next++ << " ";
  cout << endl;
}
```

The output produced is:

```
Direct Vector items:
who are you?
```

As you can see, the BIDS containers allow you to manage class objects just as simply as scalar objects.

Counted Direct Vectors

When you don't need to keep track of where something is stored in a vector, you can use a counted vector. This container type is derived from `TVectorImp<T>`, but defines an `Add(T)` member function to allow the insertion of an item into *the next slot* of a vector. If you remove an item using `Detach(...)`, the container is recompacted. Listing 9.2 is a short example that shows how elements can be inserted and read back.

Listing 9.2. Using direct counted vectors.

```
#include <classlib\vectimp.h>
#include <iostream.h>

void main()
{
     // create a local vector
     TCVectorImp<int> a(50);

     // insert a few items
     a [2] = 10;
     a.Add(11);
     a.Add(12);

     // read some items back
     cout << "\nThe first 4 items are "
          << a [0] << ", "
          << a [1] << ", "
          << a [2] << ", "
          << a [3] << endl;
}
```

The output produced is:

```
The first 4 items are 11, 12, 10, 490
```

The last value, stored in `a[3]`, is again random because it was never initialized. Note that counted vectors do not sort data—they just insert elements at the next available slot.

Sorted Direct Vectors

This type of vector attempts to keep its items in sorted order. I said *attempts* because you can directly insert an item anywhere you want into a sorted array, using the subscripting `operator[]`. The normal way to put items into a sorted vector is with the `add(T)` member function, which determines where the item needs to go to keep the rest of the vector sorted. Sorting is carried out by using the `operator<`, applied to the container items, so sorted containers are applicable only to sortable objects. Listing 9.3 is a short example using a scalar data type with sorted vectors.

Listing 9.3. Using direct sorted vectors.

```
#include <classlib\vectimp.h>
#include <iostream.h>

void main()
{
     // create a local vector
     TSVectorImp<int> a(50);

     // insert a few items
     a.Add(17);
     a.Add(3);
     a.Add(-6);

     // read some data back
     cout << "\nHere are some vector values:"
          << "\na [0] = " << a [0]
          << "\na [1] = " << a [1]
          << "\na [2] = " << a [2]
          << endl;
}
```

The output produced is

```
Here are some vector values:
a [0] = -6
a [1] = 3
a [2] = 17
```

If you remove items from a direct sorted vector using `detach(...)`, the container will be automatically recompacted. When you use direct sorted vectors with user class objects, the following member functions must be defined in the user class:

- Default constructor
- `operator<`
- `operator==`

Listing 9.4 shows a short example of direct sorted vectors with user class objects.

Listing 9.4. Using direct sorted vectors with user class objects.

```
#include <classlib\vectimp.h>
#include <iostream.h>
#include <string.h>

class MyString{

  enum {MAXSIZE = 50};
  char string [MAXSIZE];

public:

  MyString() {string [0] = '\0';}
  MyString(char*);
  operator char*() const;
  int operator<(const MyString&) const;
  int operator==(const MyString&) const;
};

MyString::MyString(char* cp)
{
  strncpy(string, cp, MAXSIZE - 1);
}

MyString::operator char*() const
{
  return (char*) string;
}

int MyString::operator<(const MyString& c) const
{
  return stricmp(string, (char*) c) < 0 ? 1 : 0;
}

int MyString::operator==(const MyString& c) const
{
  return stricmp(string, (char*) c) == 0 ? 1 : 0;
}
```

```
void main()
{
  // create a local list of user class objects
  TSVectorImp<MyString> a(5, 6);

  // create a few items
  MyString m("What");
  MyString n("am");
  MyString o("I");
  MyString p("doing?");

  // insert a few items
  a.Add(m); a.Add(n); a.Add(o); a.Add(p);

  // iterate over the array using an external
  // iterator object
  TSVectorIteratorImp<MyString> next(a);
  cout << "\nVector items:\n";
  while (next)
    cout << (char*) next++ << " ";
  cout << endl;

  // display the array contents one at a time
  cout << "\nVector items again:";
  cout << "\na [0] = " << (char*) (a[0])
       << "\na [1] = " << (char*) (a[1])
       << "\na [2] = " << (char*) (a[2])
       << "\na [3] = " << (char*) (a[3])
       << endl;
}
```

The output produced by Listing 9.4 is

```
Vector items:
am doing? I What

Vector items again:
a [0] = am
a [1] = doing?
a [2] = I
a [3] = What
```

I used an external iterator object to traverse the vector container items. Also note how the vector a is created with the statement

```
TSVectorImp<MyString> a(5, 6);
```

which creates an initial vector with five slots, with a growth delta of 6. The growth delta is the number of slots that are added to a vector when the container runs out of slots.

If you don't specify a growth delta, the vector will behave erratically if it runs out of slots at runtime.

In the previous example, the user class `MyString` didn't really do much, except encapsulate a string. `MyString` is convenient to use in examples because it is simple and shows everything you need to create a class that can be used in a BIDS sorted vector. There is actually a better way to handle strings, though, using the standard ANSI class `string`. Unfortunately, class `string` is not directly compatible with BIDS sorted containers, so you have to derive a class from `string`, and change its < and == operators, as shown in Listing 9.5.

Listing 9.5. Using direct sorted vectors with ANSI `string` objects.

```
#include <classlib\vectimp.h>
#include <iostream.h>
#include <cstring.h>

class MyString: public string {

public:

  MyString() : string("") {}
  MyString(MyString& s) {string::assign(s);}
  MyString(char* s) {string::assign(s);}
  int operator<(const MyString&) const;
  int operator==(const MyString&) const;
};

int MyString::operator<(const MyString& c) const
{
  return stricmp(c_str(), c.c_str() ) < 0 ? 1 : 0;
}

int MyString::operator==(const MyString& c) const
{
  return stricmp(c_str(), c.c_str() ) == 0 ? 1 : 0;
}

void main()
{
  // create a local list of user class objects
  TSVectorImp<MyString> a(5, 6);

  // create a few items
  MyString m("What");
  MyString n("am");
  MyString o("I");
  MyString p("doing?");
```

```
  // insert a few items
  a.Add(m); a.Add(n); a.Add(o); a.Add(p);

  // iterate over the array using an external
  // iterator object
  TSVectorIteratorImp<MyString> next(a);
  cout << "\nVector items:\n";
  while (next)
    cout << next++ << " ";
  cout << endl;

  // display the array contents one at a time
  cout << "\nVector items again:";
  cout << "\na [0] = " << (a[0])
       << "\na [1] = " << (a[1])
       << "\na [2] = " << (a[2])
       << "\na [3] = " << (a[3])
       << endl;
}
```

The output produced is the same as for Listing 9.4. Because `string` knows how to insert itself into output streams, you no longer need the `(char*)` typecast with stream insertion operations.

Simple Indirect Vectors

When you need to manage vectors of large objects, such as structures or class objects, the direct storage paradigm may be too slow or require too much memory to be feasible. With large objects or objects that don't have a copy operator defined, you can use indirect vectors. Indirect containers are a little more tricky to manage than direct ones. You need to avoid reading uninitialized slots because they contain random values. If you use this random value as a pointer, you can expect *lots* of trouble.

When you remove items from indirect vectors by using the function `Detach(...)`, the empty slot that would be left behind is eliminated because indirect vector containers are recompacted after items are removed. When an indirect vector goes out of scope, it deletes the internal storage it had allocated for its pointers, but doesn't delete the objects referenced by the pointers. Listing 9.6 is a short example of using an indirect vector.

Listing 9.6. Using indirect vectors with scalar types.

```
#include <classlib\vectimp.h>
#include <iostream.h>
```

continues

Listing 9.6. continued

```
void main()
{
     // create a local vector
     TIVectorImp<float> a(50);

     // insert a few items
     float x = 1;
     float y = 100;
     float z = 10000;

     a[0] = &x;
     a[1] = &y;
     a[2] = &z;

     // read some data back
     cout << "\nThe first 3 values are:\n"
          << *a[0] << ", "
          << *a[1] << " and "
          << *a[2]
          << endl;
}
```

The output produced by Listing 9.6 is

```
The first 3 values are:
1, 100 and 10000
```

It is also easy to use indirect vectors with class objects. The following listing changes the code in Listing 9.7 to use `string` objects rather than `float`s.

Listing 9.7. Using indirect vectors with class `string`.

```
#include <classlib\vectimp.h>
#include <iostream.h>
#include <cstring.h>

void main()
{
 // create a local vector
 TIVectorImp<string> a(50);

 // insert a few items
 string x("1");
 string y("2");
 string z("3");
```

```
  a[0] = &x;
  a[1] = &y;
  a[2] = &z;

  // read some data back
  cout << "\nThe first 3 values are:\n"
       << *a[0] << ", "
       << *a[1] << " and "
       << *a[2]
       << endl;
}
```

The output produced is the same as for Listing 9.6. The notation to deal with the container elements is identical to the code in Listing 9.6, even though it handles `string` objects rather than `float`s.

Sorted Indirect Vectors

Sorted indirect vectors are similar to simple indirect vectors, but when you insert a pointer into the container, the correct insertion point is determined so that the items pointed at are in sorted order. Removing a pointer from an indirect sorted vector results in the empty slot being squeezed out through array compaction. Listing 9.8 is a short example that uses an indirect sorted vector.

Listing 9.8. Using indirect sorted vectors.

```
#include <classlib\vectimp.h>
#include <iostream.h>

class MyLong {
public:
  long value;
  MyLong(long v) {value = v;}
  int operator==(MyLong l) const
    {return value == l.value ? 1 : 0;}
  int operator<(MyLong l) const
    {return value < l.value ? 1 : 0;}
};

void main()
{
  // create a local vector
  TISVectorImp<MyLong> a(50);
```

continues

Listing 9.8. continued

```
  // insert a few items
  MyLong x = 11;
  MyLong y = -12;
  MyLong z = 1;
  a.Add(&x);
  a.Add(&y);
  a.Add(&z);

  // read the data back
  cout << "\nThe stored items are:\n"
       << a[0]->value << ", "
       << a[1]->value << ", and "
       << a[2]->value << endl;
}
```

The output produced by Listing 9.8 is

```
The stored items are:
-12, 1, and 11
```

The next listing shows how to use the ANSI `string` class with indirect sorted vectors.

Listing 9.9. Using indirect sorted vectors.

```
#include <classlib\vectimp.h>
#include <iostream.h>
#include <cstring.h>

void main()
{
  // create a local vector
  TISVectorImp<string> a(50);

  // insert a few items
  string x("11");
  string y("-12");
  string z("1");
  a.Add(&x);
  a.Add(&y);
  a.Add(&z);

  // read the data back
  cout << "\nThe stored items are:\n"
       << *a[0] << ", "
```

```
        << *a[1] << ", and "
        << *a[2] << endl;
}
```

The output is identical to that of Listing 9.8.

FDS List Containers

The FDS containers support singly-linked and doubly-linked lists. Because both list types have the same basic structure, I limit my discussion to singly-linked FDS lists. As with the FDS vectors, there are both direct and indirect list containers; however, there are no *counted* lists. The fact is that a list is always counted, in the sense that there is always a definable insertion point for lists. Whereas vectors can accept insertions at any arbitrary point, lists have a preferential insertion point, either at the head or tail, depending on the implementation. With FDS list containers, the default insertion point is at the head. The FDS list container hierarchy is organized somewhat like the FDS vector containers, with a parameterized base class. Figure 9.2 shows the complete hierarchy for FDS singly-linked lists.

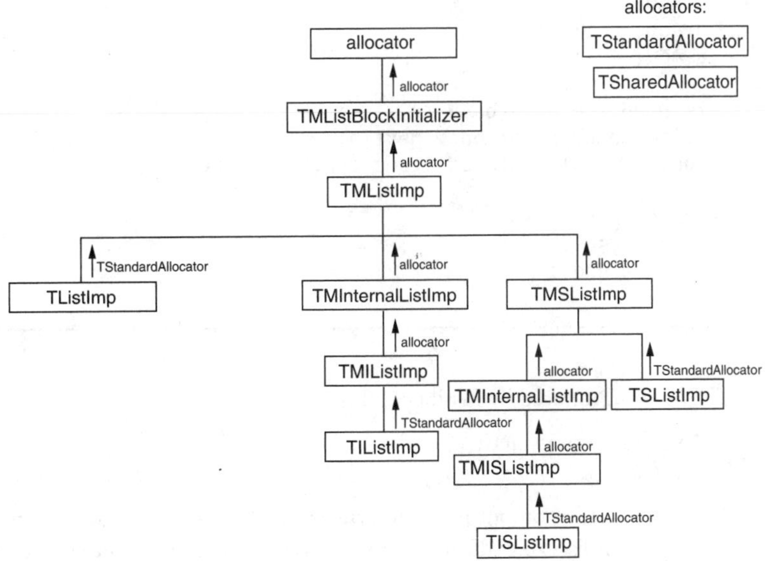

Figure 9.2. The FDS list container class hierarchy.

FDS Lists, like FDS vectors, allow you to specify custom memory allocator classes. See the description in the section “FDS Vector Containers” earlier in this chapter for more information on memory allocators.

Simple Direct Lists

FDS direct lists are flexible and easy to use. In a direct list, you can store scalar data types and user objects. Direct lists don't store the original item you give them, but they store a copy. Because of this, any class object inserted into an FDS direct list must have a copy operator. Because the list manages only copies of items, there are no problems with item ownership. An FDS direct list always owns its internal list items. You can insert objects of any storage type, from local to auto to dynamic, because only a copy of the data is actually stored and managed. Listing 9.10 is a short program that uses `TListImp<T>`.

Listing 9.10. Using direct lists with scalar types.

```
#include <classlib\listimp.h>
#include <iostream.h>

void main()
{
  // create a local list
  TListImp<char> a;

  // insert a few items
  a.Add('A');
  a.Add('B');
  a.Add('C');

  // read the data back
  TListIteratorImp<char> next(a);
  cout << "\nThe stored items are:\n" << next++;

  while (next)
    cout << ", " << next++;
  cout << endl;
}
```

The output produced by Listing 9.10 is

```
The stored items are:
C, B, A
```

The characters are output in the reverse order of insertion because inserting elements at the head of the list causes the list to grow backward. I used an iterator in the example because it isn't possible to read random internal nodes in a `TListImp<T>` container. You can easily change the code in Listing 9.10 to handle class objects, such as ANSI `string` objects. Listing 9.11 shows an example.

Listing 9.11. Using direct lists with ANSI `string` objects.

```
#include <classlib\listimp.h>
#include <iostream.h>
#include <cstring.h>

void main()
{
  // create a local list
  TListImp<string> a;

  // insert a few items
  a.Add("A");
  a.Add("B");
  a.Add("C");

  // read the data back
  TListIteratorImp<string> next(a);
  cout << "\nThe stored items are:\n" << next++;

  while (next)
    cout << ", " << next++;
  cout << endl;
}
```

The output produced is identical to that of Listing 9.10.

Sorted Direct Lists

Linked lists are usually classified as unordered collections because the internal storage order is dependent on the order of insertion rather than on the data inserted. A sorted list is a special breed because it is a list and because it stores data internally in an order that maintains a sorted order. Other than the sort order, direct sorted lists are just like direct lists. You can insert data with a local, auto, static, or dynamic storage class, and you don't have to worry about object ownership problems because only a copy of your data is handled internally. Listing 9.12 is a short example of using a direct sorted FDS list with a scalar data type.

Listing 9.12. Using an FDS direct sorted list with scalar data types.

```
#include <classlib\listimp.h>
#include <iostream.h>

void main()
{
```

continues

Listing 9.12. continued

```
  // create a local list
  TSListImp<int> a;

  // insert a few items
  a.Add(303);
  a.Add(1105);
  a.Add(-102);

  // read the data back
  TListIteratorImp<int> next(a);
  cout << "\nThe stored items are:\n" << next++;

  while (next)
    cout << ", " << next++;
  cout << endl;
}
```

The output produced by Listing 9.12 is

```
The stored items are:
-102, 303, 1105
```

When using direct sorted FDS lists with user class objects, the user class must define the following member functions:

- Default constructor
- `operator<`
- `operator==`
- `operator!=`

Listing 9.13 shows an example of using a user class with a direct sorted list.

Listing 9.13. Using a direct sorted list with user class objects.

```
#include <classlib\listimp.h>
#include <iostream.h>
#include <string.h>

class MyString {

  char* string;

public:
```

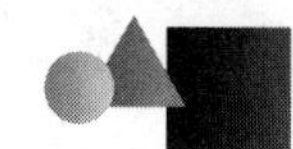

```
  MyString() {string = 0;}
  MyString(char*);
  ~MyString() {if (string) delete string;}
  operator char*() const;
  int operator<(const MyString&) const;
  int operator==(const MyString&) const;
  int operator!=(const MyString&) const;
};

MyString::MyString(char* cp)
{
  string = new char [strlen(cp) + 1];
  strcpy(string, cp);
}

MyString::operator char*() const
{
  if (string)
    return string;
  else
    return " ";
}

int MyString::operator<(const MyString& c) const
{
  return stricmp(string, (char*) c) < 0 ? 1 : 0;
}

int MyString::operator==(const MyString& c) const
{
  return stricmp(string, (char*) c) == 0 ? 1 : 0;
}

int MyString::operator!=(const MyString& c) const
{
  return stricmp(string, (char*) c) != 0 ? 1 : 0;
}

void DoInsert(MyString& str, void* strm)
{
  ostream* os = (ostream*) strm;
  *os << (char*) str << " ";
}

void main()
{
  // create a local list of user class objects
  TSListImp<MyString> a;
```

continues

Listing 9.13. continued

```
    // create a few items
    MyString w("These");
    MyString x("items");
    MyString y("are");
    MyString z("sorted");

    // insert a few items
    a.Add(w); a.Add(x); a.Add(y); a.Add(z);

    // here's a non-destructive iteration
    TSListIteratorImp<MyString> next(a);
    cout << "\nItems using an external iterator:\n";
    while (next)
      cout << (char*) next++ << " ";
    cout << endl;

    // here's another non-destructive iteration
    cout << "\nItems using an internal iterator:\n";
    a.ForEach(DoInsert, &cout);
}
```

The output produced by Listing 9.13 is

```
Items using an external iterator:
are items sorted These

Items using an internal iterator:
are items sorted These
```

Notice the two ways the list is iterated over. The first uses the external iterator object `TSListIteratorImp<MyString>`, the second uses an internal iterator, with the function `TSListImp<MyString>::ForEach()`. The two iteration techniques are equivalent, and produce the same output.

NOTE

When using class objects in sorted FDS containers, be very careful about the way you declare the < and == operators. Make sure they are declared to accept a reference to a `const` object. If you leave out the `const` modifier, the compiler won't always give you errors or warnings, but your code may not work correctly. In the preceding example, leaving out the `const` modifiers will produce an incorrect sort order.

Class MyString was shown only as an example of a generic user class with TSListImp<T>. A better way is to use the ANSI class string. Because of the way the BIDS sorted containers deal with sortable objects, the standard string class will not work directly with TSListImp<T> or the other sorted BIDS containers. You must derive a class from string, and change the < and == operators. The next example shows how to sort string objects with TSListImp<T>.

Listing 9.14. Using a direct sorted list with ANSI string objects.

```
#include <classlib\listimp.h>
#include <iostream.h>
#include <cstring.h>

class MyString: public string {

public:

  MyString() : string("") {}
  MyString(const MyString& s) {string::assign(s);}
  MyString(char* s) {string::assign(s);}
  int operator<(const MyString&) const;
  int operator==(const MyString&) const;
};

int MyString::operator<(const MyString& c) const
{
  return stricmp(c_str(), c.c_str() ) < 0 ? 1 : 0;
}

int MyString::operator==(const MyString& c) const
{
  return stricmp(c_str(), c.c_str() ) == 0 ? 1 : 0;
}

void main()
{
  // create a local list of user class objects
  TSListImp<MyString> a;

  // create a few items
  MyString w("These");
  MyString x("items");
  MyString y("are");
  MyString z("sorted");

  // insert a few items
  a.Add(w); a.Add(x); a.Add(y); a.Add(z);
```

continues

Listing 9.14. continued

```
  // here's a non-destructive iteration
  TSListIteratorImp<MyString> next(a);
  cout << "\nItems using an external iterator:\n";
  while (next)
    cout << next++ << " ";
  cout << endl;
}
```

The notation is slightly simpler than in Listing 9.13 because you can insert objects derived from `string` into an output stream without using the `(char*)` typecast. The output produced by Listing 9.14 is similar to Listing 9.13.

Indirect Lists

When you use an indirect list, you can insert a pointer to any arbitrary data type or user class. User classes are not required to provide any special member functions, such as copy constructors or default constructors, because only pointers-to-objects are managed by the indirect list. Listing 9.15 is a short example that shows how to use an FDS indirect list.

Listing 9.15. Using an indirect list with integers.

```
#include <classlib\listimp.h>
#include <iostream.h>
#include <string.h>

void main()
{
  // create a local list of user class objects
  TIListImp<int> a;

  // create a few items
  int m = 10;
  int n = -100;
  int o = 0;
  int p = -50;

  // insert a few items
  a.Add(&m); a.Add(&n); a.Add(&o); a.Add(&p);

  // iterate over the array using an external
  // iterator object
  TIListIteratorImp<int> next(a);
  cout << "\nList items:\n";
```

```
  while (next)
    cout << *(next++) << " ";
  cout << endl;
}
```

The output produced by Listing 9.15 is

```
List Items:
-50 0 -100 10
```

Inserting items into an indirect list results in the data being stored in the reverse order of insertion. Listing 9.15 also shows the use of an external iterator object to traverse an indirect list.

Sorted Indirect Lists

There are few differences in the way you use an indirect sorted list compared to a plain indirect list. The main difference is that when you read the list elements back, they are in sorted order. Listing 9.16 is a short example showing scalar data types used in an indirect sorted list.

Listing 9.16. Using an indirect sorted list with integers.

```
#include <classlib\listimp.h>
#include <iostream.h>
#include <string.h>

void main()
{
  // create a local list of user class objects
  TISListImp<int> a;

  // create a few items
  int m = 10;
  int n = -100;
  int o = 0;
  int p = -50;

  // insert a few items
  a.Add(&m); a.Add(&n); a.Add(&o); a.Add(&p);

  // iterate over the array using an external
  // iterator object
  TISListIteratorImp<int> next(a);
  cout << "\nSorted list items:\n";
```

continues

Listing 9.16. continued

```
  while (next)
    cout << *(next++) << " ";
  cout << endl;
}
```

The output produced by Listing 9.16 is

```
Sorted list items:
-100 -50 0 10
```

The previous example shows the use of an external iterator object to traverse the objects in the indirect sorted list. When you are using an indirect sorted list with user classes, the classes need to have the same special member functions described for direct sorted lists.

ADT Containers

An *Abstract Data Type* (*ADT*) is a high-level container abstraction that has its low-level implementation based on one of the FDS containers. Borland C++ 4.5 defines the following eight container types as ADTs:

- Array
- Sorted array
- Stack
- Queue
- Deque
- Bag
- Set
- Dictionary

When using an ADT as a class, you must specify which FDS to use for the physical storage of data. For example, arrays are data structures that are randomly accessible. Whether accesses are in constant time (in other words, independent of which element is accessed) depends on how arrays are implemented at the lower level. Stacks provide access only to the *top* element. Queues allow insertions *at the end* and removals *at the front.* Deques allow inserting and removing from both *the end* and *the front.* Bags and sets have no special data ordering. You can't specify an index or other insertion point when you put an item into a bag or set. To remove an item, you just request that a particular item be removed. If the item is found, it is removed.

All the ADTs are capable of using either direct or indirect FDS containers to manage objects. In general, it is more convenient to handle direct objects when the objects are very small, or when the objects are not guaranteed to be dynamically allocated, or if you plan to use heap and non-heap objects together. Objects handled in a direct ADT require a default constructor and a copy operator. If the ADT also supports sorted items, objects are also required to have < and == operators defined.

There are several ways each ADT container is implemented. Each implementation is distinguished by the starting letters of its name, as shown in Table 9.1.

Table 9.1. The ADT container prefixes.

Starting Letters	*Meaning*
TI	Indirect
TC	Counted
TS	Sorted
TM	Managed

Indirect containers store pointers to objects. To avoid having any empty slots, counted containers recompact themselves after you remove an item. Sorted containers require inserted objects to have a default constructor, and the operators < and ==. Managed containers are low-level containers that require you to specify a memory management scheme.

Memory Management with Containers

Containers need to allocate memory for themselves, but allocating memory is not a process that can be determined by the container class library alone. Windows supports different types of memory. There is not only local and global memory, but private and shared memory as well. In addition, applications that make lots of memory allocations may wish to implement a memory sub-allocation scheme, to improve efficiency. Borland has designed the BIDS containers in a way that the allocation of memory is separate from the management of data in a container. Stated differently, the BIDS library has two types of classes: containers and memory allocators.

Each container is associated to something called a *memory allocator*. When a container needs memory, it calls its memory allocator to obtain the memory. Under Windows, memory is allocated often from the global heap, so the BIDS library has a built-in memory allocator called `TStandardAllocator`, which allocates memory from the global heap. All the container classes that are missing the *M* in their name, like TArrayAsVector<T> and TIStackAsList<T>, use TStandardAllocator to get memory. This class has a new operator that simply calls the global new operator, which eventually calls ::GlobalAlloc(). The delete operator for TStandardAllocator calls the global delete operator, which eventually calls ::GlobalFree().

With BIDS containers, you can use a non-standard memory allocator to meet special requirements. All the containers whose names have an *M* near the beginning let you specify a memory allocator. One allocator you will find very useful is class TSharedAllocator, which allocates global memory with the GMEM_DDESHARE flag. This type of allocator must be used with any objects that are allocated in a DLL. Consider an application A that uses a DLL, which in turn allocates memory from the global heap. If more than one application uses the same DLL, there will be a problem when application A terminates, because Windows considers the memory allocated by the DLL to belong to application A, and therefore frees this memory—even though the DLL is still loaded. The next application that calls on the DLL to access the freed memory will cause a GPF. To avoid DLL memory problems, all you need is the GMEM_DDESHARE flag with GlobalAlloc() operations, and that's where TSharedAllocators come into play.

ADT *Arrays*

Direct arrays are probably the most common container abstraction used by C programmers. A simple array of integers is an example of a direct array in C. Although ADT Arrays are bona fide C++ class objects, the BIDS library was designed so that the ADT direct Array can be used with essentially the same syntax as the C array. Borland provides one built-in implementation for ADT Arrays, using an FDS vector to manage its data. Any user class objects inserted into an ADT direct Array must provide the following member functions:

- A default constructor
- An operator==

ADT Arrays and Array iterators are implemented by a series of class hierarchies, shown graphically in Figures 9.3 and 9.4.

It is easy to use ADT direct Array containers because you can often use the same syntax that applies to ANSI C arrays. Listing 9.17 is a short example that uses the template class TArrayAsVector<T>.

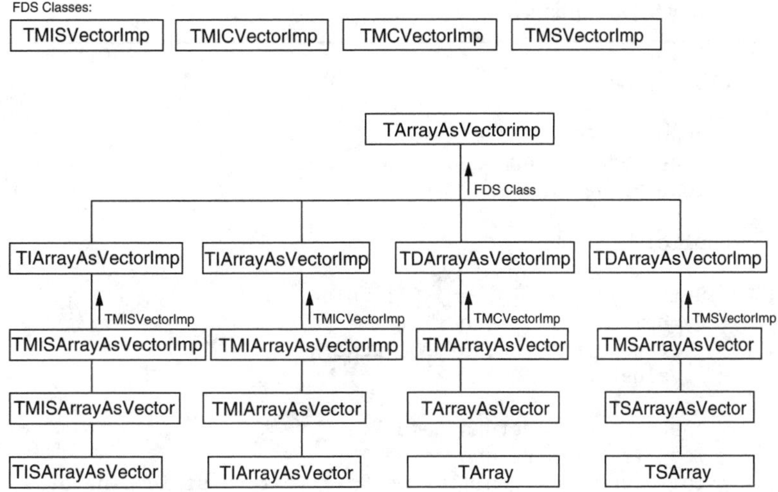

Figure 9.3. The ADT `Array` *classes.*

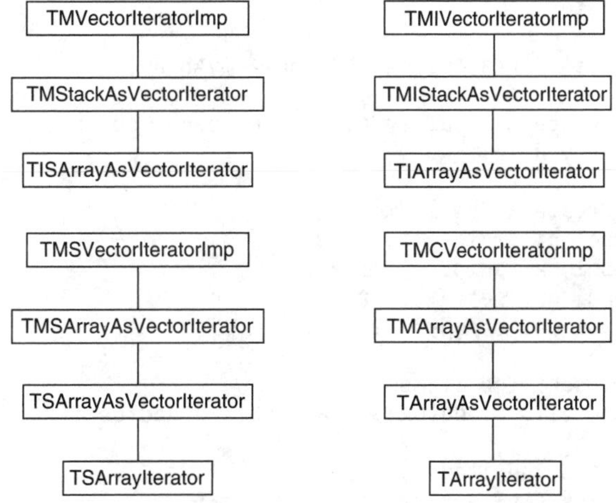

Figure 9.4. The ADT `Array` *iterator classes.*

Listing 9.17. Using an ADT direct `Array` with user objects.

```
#include <classlib\arrays.h>
#include <iostream.h>
#include <string.h>
```

continues

Listing 9.17. continued

```
class Symbol {

  enum {SYMBOL_LENGTH = 40};
  char name [SYMBOL_LENGTH];
  long value;

public:

  Symbol() {name [0] = '\0'; value = 0;}
  Symbol(char* s, long v) {
    strncpy(name, s, SYMBOL_LENGTH);
    value = v;
  }
  char* Name() {return name;}
  long Value() {return value;}
  int operator==(const Symbol& s) {return stricmp(name, s.name) ? 0 :
               1;}
};

void main()
{
  typedef TArrayAsVector<Symbol> myArray;

  // create a local array of user class objects
  myArray a(10);

  // create a few items
  Symbol c1("main", 1010);
  Symbol c2("printf", 4302);
  Symbol c3("setmem", 3086);
  Symbol c4("strcpy", 2446);

  // insert the items
  a.Add(c1); a.Add(c2); a.Add(c3); a.Add(c4);

  // show the items
  cout << "\nSymbol table items:";
  cout << "\na[0] = " << a[0].Name() << ", " << a[0].Value();
  cout << "\na[1] = " << a[1].Name() << ", " << a[1].Value();
  cout << "\na[2] = " << a[2].Name() << ", " << a[2].Value();
  cout << "\na[3] = " << a[3].Name() << ", " << a[3].Value();
  cout << endl;
}
```

The output produced by Listing 9.17 is

```
Symbol table items:
a[0] = main, 1010
a[1] = printf, 4302
a[2] = setmem, 3086
a[3] = strcpy, 2446
```

You can use the template class `TArray<T>`, with its associated iterator `TArrayIterator<T>`, as shorthand notations for `TArrayAsVector<T>` and `TArrayAsVectorIterator<T>`. The best way to handle ADT containers is through a `typedef`, such as

```
typedef TArrayAsVector<Symbol> myArray;
```

This allows you to set up the type `myArray` once and for all in your program. If later you decide to use a different FDS container to manage your `Array`, you need to change only the `typedef`, and then recompile your program. For example, if you decide to use an array that was based on a binary tree FDS, you would change the `typedef` to the following:

```
typedef TArrayAsBinaryTree<Symbol> myArray;
```

You would also need to implement a `BinaryTree` FDS, then define the class template `TArrayAsBinaryTree<T>`, following the implementation of `TArrayAsVector<T>`. When all the changes were in place, you would recompile your entire program.

To use indirect ADT `Arrays` with user objects, you need to provide an == operator in the user class. You don't need a default constructor for user objects used with indirect ADT `Arrays`. Here is a short example that shows user class objects with ADT indirect `Arrays`.

Listing 9.18. Using an ADT indirect `Array` with user objects.

```
#include <classlib\arrays.h>
#include <iostream.h>
#include <string.h>

class Symbol {

  enum {SYMBOL_LENGTH = 40};
  char name [SYMBOL_LENGTH];
  long value;

public:

  Symbol(char* s, long v) {
    strncpy(name, s, SYMBOL_LENGTH);
    value = v;
  }
  char* Name() {return name;}
  long Value() {return value;}
```

continues

Listing 9.18. continued

```
  int operator==(const Symbol& s) const {
    return stricmp(name, s.name) ? 0 : 1;
  }
};

void main()
{
  typedef TIArrayAsVector<Symbol> myArray;

  // create a local array of user class objects
  myArray a(10);

  // don't allow the container to own the
  // elements, because we're putting local
  // objects into the container. If the container
  // is allowed to own its contents (which is
  // the default condition), all objects inserted
  // must by dynamically allocated.

  ///////////////////////////////////////////
  // don't forget this statement
  ///////////////////////////////////////////
  a.OwnsElements(TShouldDelete::NoDelete);

  // create a few items
  Symbol c1("main", 1010);
  Symbol c2("printf", 4302);
  Symbol c3("setmem", 3086);
  Symbol c4("strcpy", 2446);

  // insert the items
  a.Add(&c1); a.Add(&c2); a.Add(&c3); a.Add(&c4);

  // show the items
  cout << "\nSymbol table items:";
  cout << "\na[0] = " << a[0]->Name()
                      << ", "
                      << a[0]->Value();
  cout << "\na[1] = " << a[1]->Name()
                      << ", "
                      << a[1]->Value();
  cout << "\na[2] = " << a[2]->Name()
                      << ", "
                      << a[2]->Value();
  cout << "\na[3] = " << a[3]->Name()
                      << ", "
                      << a[3]->Value();
  cout << endl;
}
```

The output produced by Listing 9.18 is

```
Symbol table items:
a[0] = main, 1010
a[1] = printf, 4302
a[2] = setmem, 3086
a[3] = strcpy, 2446
```

With indirect ADT containers, you have to be very careful about who owns the items that are inserted. By default, the container does. When the container goes out of scope, it will attempt to delete its objects if it owns them. If you place heap objects in the container, there is no problem. If you place static, global, or local objects into the container, you must remove ownership of the objects from the container, using the statement

```
a.OwnsElements(TShouldDelete::NoDelete);
```

ADT Sorted *Arrays*

Sorted direct arrays can be used with both scalar types like `char` and `float`, and with user class objects. When you use ADT direct sorted `Arrays` with user classes, you need to provide the following member functions to handle the sorting:

- Default constructor
- `operator ==`
- `operator <`

The < operator determines the order in which items will be sorted by the ADT `Array`. Listing 9.19 is a short example showing the use of a user class with ADT direct sorted `Arrays`.

Listing 9.19. Using an ADT direct sorted `Array` with user objects.

```
#include <classlib\arrays.h>
#include <iostream.h>
#include <string.h>

class Symbol {

  enum {SYMBOL_LENGTH = 40};
  char name [SYMBOL_LENGTH];
  long value;

public:

  Symbol() {name [0] = '\0'; value = 0;}
```

continues

Listing 9.19. continued

```
  Symbol(char* s, long v) {
    strncpy(name, s, SYMBOL_LENGTH);
    value = v;
  }
  char* Name() {return name;}
  long Value() {return value;}
  int operator==(const Symbol& s) const {
    return stricmp(name, s.name) ? 0 : 1;
  }
  int operator<(const Symbol& s) const {
    return stricmp(name, s.name) < 0 ? 1 : 0;
  }
};

void main()
{
  typedef TSArrayAsVector<Symbol> myArray;
  typedef TSArrayAsVectorIterator<Symbol> myIterator;

  // create a local array of user class objects
  myArray a(10);

  // create a few items
  Symbol c1("peter", 14);
  Symbol c2("cynthia", 35);
  Symbol c3("priscilla", 74);
  Symbol c4("cristina", 29);

  // insert the items
  a.Add(c1); a.Add(c2); a.Add(c3); a.Add(c4);

  myIterator next(a);
  cout << "\nArray contents sorted by name:\n";
  while (next) {
    Symbol s = next++;
    if (strlen(s.Name() ) == 0) continue;
    cout << s.Name() << " " << s.Value() << endl;
  }
}
```

The output produced by Listing 9.19 is

```
Array contents sorted by name:
cristina 29
cynthia 35
peter 14
priscilla 74
```

The items are sorted based on the sort criterion of class `Symbol`. It is easy to change `Symbol` to sort based on the data member `Symbol::value` or any other criterion. With ADT direct sorted arrays, you can insert local, global, static, or heap objects without worrying about object ownership conflicts. Direct containers always store a copy of your data.

ADT Stacks

`Stacks` in the BIDS library are more flexible than `Arrays`, in a certain sense, because they come in two different FDS implementations: as vectors and as lists. ADT `Stacks` are built around a small set of class hierarchies, shown in Figure 9.5.

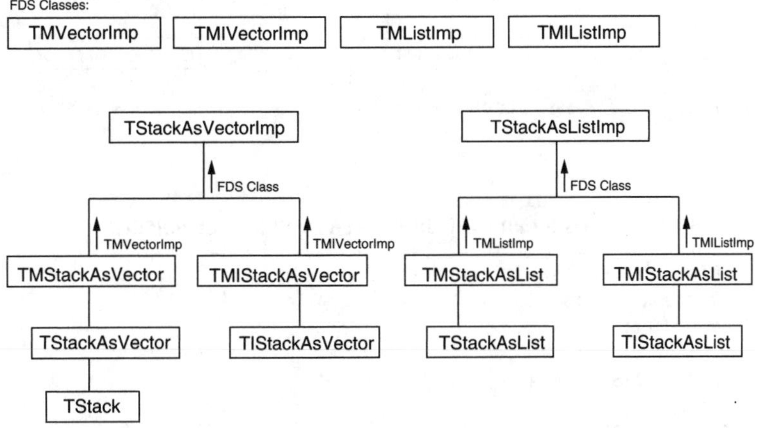

Figure 9.5. The ADT `Stack` *classes.*

The `FDS Class` parameter passed to the base classes `TStackAsVectorImp` and `TStackAsListImp` in Figure 9.5 is a template class, used to declare a data member inside those two base classes. This data member is the low-level container that physically holds the data in an ADT `Stack`.

ADT Direct Stacks

Listing 9.20 is an example of ADT direct stack usage, with an external iterator to traverse the stack.

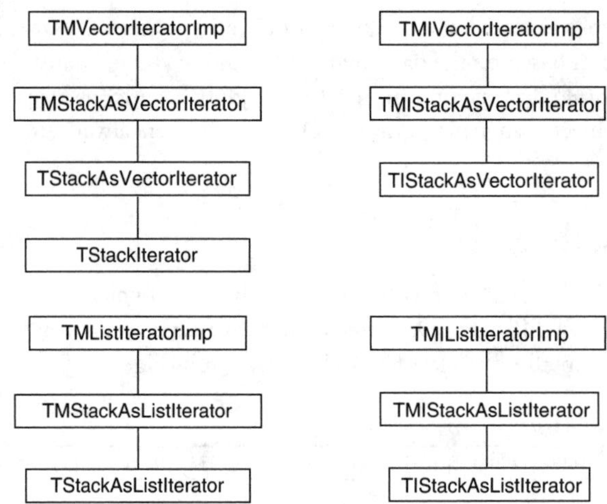

Figure 9.6. The ADT `Stack` *iterator classes.*

Listing 9.20. Using an ADT direct `Stack` with user objects.

```
#include <classlib\stacks.h>
#include <iostream.h>
#include <string.h>

class MyString {

  enum {STRING_LENGTH = 40};
  char name [STRING_LENGTH];

public:

  MyString() {name [0] = '\0';}
  MyString(char* s) { strncpy(name, s, STRING_LENGTH); }
  char* Name() {return name;}
  int operator==(const MyString& s) const {
    return stricmp(name, s.name) ? 0 : 1;
  }
};

void main()
{
  typedef TStackAsVector<MyString> myStack;
  typedef TStackAsVectorIterator<MyString> myIterator;

  // create a local stack of user class objects
  myStack a;
```

```
  // create a few items
  MyString c1("First");
  MyString c2("Second");
  MyString c3("Third");
  MyString c4("Fourth");

  // insert the items
  a.Push(c1); a.Push(c2); a.Push(c3); a.Push(c4);

  // use an external iterator to display the
  // stack contents
  myIterator next(a);
  cout << "\nStack items: ";
  while (next) {
    MyString s = next++;
    if (strlen(s.Name() ) == 0) continue;
    cout << s.Name() << " ";
  }
  cout << endl;
}
```

The output produced by Listing 9.20 is

```
Stack items: First Second Third Fourth
```

From the output produced, you can see that an external stack iterator produces the stack elements in their order of insertion. Using the `Pop()` member function, the stack elements are also produced in the reverse order of their insertion, as shown in Listing 9.21.

Listing 9.21. Popping objects from an ADT direct stack.

```
#include <classlib\stacks.h>
#include <iostream.h>
#include <string.h>

class MyString {

  enum {STRING_LENGTH = 40};
  char name [STRING_LENGTH];

public:

  MyString() {name [0] = '\0';}
  MyString(char* s) { strncpy(name, s, STRING_LENGTH); }
  char* Name() {return name;}
```

continues

Listing 9.21. continued

```
  int operator==(const MyString& s) const {
    return stricmp(name, s.name) ? 0 : 1;
  }
};

void main()
{
  typedef TStackAsVector<MyString> myStack;

  // create a local stack of user class objects
  myStack a;

  // create a few items
  MyString c1("First");
  MyString c2("Second");
  MyString c3("Third");
  MyString c4("Fourth");

  // insert the items
  a.Push(c1); a.Push(c2); a.Push(c3); a.Push(c4);

  // pop the stack objects off
  cout << "\nPopped stack items: ";
  while (!a.IsEmpty() ) {
    MyString s = a.Pop();
    if (strlen(s.Name() ) == 0) continue;
    cout << s.Name() << " ";
  }
  cout << endl;
}
```

The output produced by Listing 9.21 is

```
Popped stack items: Fourth Third Second First
```

ADT Indirect Stacks

Indirect stacks are used in a manner similar to ADT indirect arrays. Attention must be paid to object ownership when you insert a pointer to object into an indirect container. By default, ADT indirect containers are assumed to own the objects they contain. If you put static, local, or global objects into a container, you must be sure to prevent the container from owning its objects, using the following statement:

```
container.OwnsElements(TShouldDelete::NoDelete);
```

If you let a container own local, global, or static objects, be sure to remove all the objects from the container before the container goes out of scope. Only heap objects are allowed to be owned by a container when the container goes out of scope. In Listing 9.22, I show an ADT indirect `Stack`, implemented using FDS lists.

Listing 9.22. Using ADT indirect stacks with user objects.

```
#include <classlib\stacks.h>
#include <iostream.h>
#include <string.h>

class MyString {

  enum {STRING_LENGTH = 40};
  char name [STRING_LENGTH];

public:

  MyString() {name [0] = '\0';}
  MyString(char* s) { strncpy(name, s, STRING_LENGTH); }
  char* Name() {return name;}
  int operator==(const MyString& s) const {
    return stricmp(name, s.name) ? 0 : 1;
  }
};

void main()
{
  // implement the indirect stack using lists
  typedef TIStackAsList<MyString> myStack;

  // create a local stack of user class objects
  myStack a;

  // create a few items
  MyString c1("First");
  MyString c2("Second");
  MyString c3("Third");
  MyString c4("Fourth");

  // insert the items
  a.Push(&c1); a.Push(&c2); a.Push(&c3); a.Push(&c4);

  // pop the stack objects off
  cout << "\nPopped stack items: ";
  while (!a.IsEmpty() ) {
    MyString* s = a.Pop();
```

continues

Listing 9.22. continued

```
    if (strlen(s->Name() ) == 0) continue;
    cout << s->Name() << " ";
  }
  cout << endl;
}
```

The output produced by Listing 9.22 is

```
Popped stack items: Fourth Third Second First
```

ADT Queues and Deques

`Deques` are a generalization of queues. With a queue, you can add objects at the end and remove them from the front. With a deque, you can add and remove objects from both ends. The BIDS library implements both queues and deques using both FDS vectors and FDS doubly-linked lists. Figure 9.7 is a graphical representation of the classes that implement ADT `Deque` containers with FDS vectors. ADT Queue containers have a class hierarchy parallel to `Deque`.

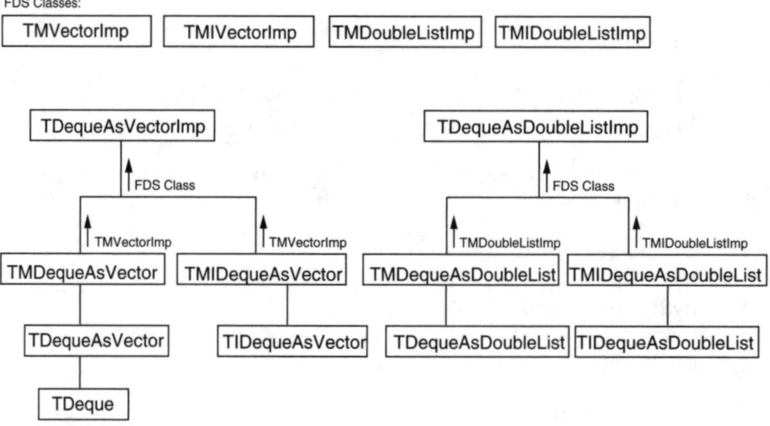

Figure 9.7. The ADT `Deque` *classes.*

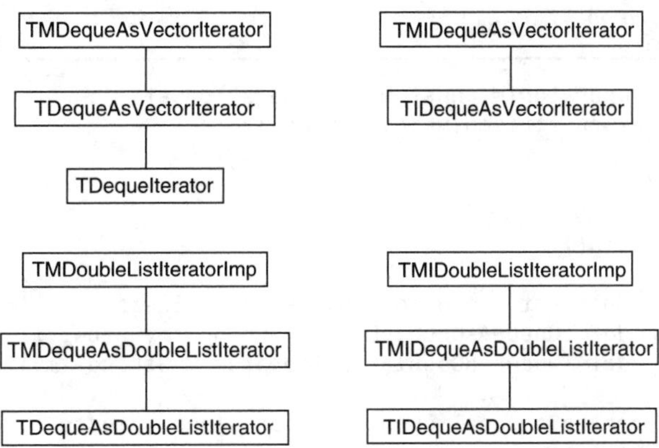

Figure 9.8. The ADT `Deque` *iterator classes.*

The `FDS Class` parameter passed to the base classes `TDequeAsVectorImp` and `TDequeAsDoubleListImp` in Figure 9.7 is a template class, used to declare a data member inside those two base classes. This data member is the low-level container that physically holds the data in an ADT `Deque`. `Deques` are used pretty much the same way as `Queues`. Listing 9.23 is a short example that uses ADT direct `Queues` with a user class. Listing 9.24 shows an example with a `Deque`.

Listing 9.23. Using ADT `Queues` with user objects.

```
#include <classlib\queues.h>
#include <iostream.h>
#include <string.h>

class MyString {

  enum {STRING_LENGTH = 40};
  char name [STRING_LENGTH];

public:

  MyString() {name [0] = '\0';}
  MyString(char* s) {
    strncpy(name, s, STRING_LENGTH);
  }
  char* Name() {return name;}
  int operator==(const MyString& s) const {
    return stricmp(name, s.name) ? 0 : 1;
  }
```

continues

Listing 9.23. continued

```
  int operator!=(const MyString& s) const {
    return stricmp(name, s.name);
  }
};

void main()
{
  // implement the direct queue using lists
  typedef TQueueAsDoubleList<MyString> myQueue;
  typedef TQueueAsDoubleListIterator<MyString> myIterator;

  // create a local queue of user class objects
  myQueue a;

  // create a few items
  MyString c1("First");
  MyString c2("Second");
  MyString c3("Third");
  MyString c4("Fourth");

  // insert the items
  a.Put(c1); a.Put(c2); a.Put(c3); a.Put(c4);

  // remove the queue items from the front
  cout << "\nQueued items: ";
  while (!a.IsEmpty() ) {
    MyString s = a.Get();
    if (strlen(s.Name() ) == 0) continue;
      cout << s.Name() << " ";
  }
  cout << endl;
}
```

The output produced by Listing 9.23 is

```
Queued items: First Second Third Fourth
```

Listing 9.24 shows the usage of an ADT indirect Deque, implemented with FDS vectors.

Listing 9.24. Using ADT indirect `Deques` with user objects.

```
#include <classlib\deques.h>
#include <iostream.h>
#include <string.h>
```

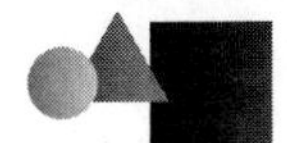

```
class MyString {

  enum {STRING_LENGTH = 40};
  char name [STRING_LENGTH];

public:

  MyString() {name [0] = '\0';}
  MyString(char* s) { strncpy(name, s, STRING_LENGTH); }
  char* Name() {return name;}
  int operator==(const MyString& s) const {
    return stricmp(name, s.name) ? 0 : 1;
  }
  int operator!=(const MyString& s) const {
    return stricmp(name, s.name);
  }
};

void main()
{
  // implement the indirect deque using vectors
  typedef TIDequeAsVector<MyString> myDeque;
  typedef TIDequeAsVectorIterator<MyString> myIterator;

  // create a local queue of user class objects
  myDeque a;

  // create a few items
  MyString c1("First");
  MyString c2("Second");
  MyString c3("Third");
  MyString c4("Fourth");

  // insert the items
  a.PutLeft(&c1); a.PutLeft(&c2);
  a.PutLeft(&c3); a.PutLeft(&c4);

  // remove object ownership from container
  a.OwnsElements(TShouldDelete::NoDelete);

  // remove the queue items from the front
  cout << "\nDeque items: ";
  while (!a.IsEmpty() ) {
    MyString* s = a.GetRight();
    if (strlen(s->Name() ) == 0) continue;
      cout << s->Name() << " ";
  }
  cout << endl;
}
```

The output produced by Listing 9.24 is

```
Deque items: First Second Third Fourth
```

Listing 9.24 inserts pointers to local objects into an ADT indirect deque. When inserting local, global, or static objects into an indirect container of any kind, make sure the container is empty when it goes out of scope, otherwise it will attempt to delete your objects. To explicitly prevent the container from deleting its contents, use the following statement:

```
// remove object ownership from container
a.OwnsElements(TShouldDelete::NoDelete);
```

ADT *Bags* and *Sets*

From a user's perspective, a `Bag` is just an unstructured container that manages a *bunch* of objects. ADT `Bags` can contain multiple occurrences of the same object, whereas ADT `Sets` allow only one copy of the same object to be inserted. ADT `Bags` and `Sets` are implemented with similar classes, and use FDS vectors for the underlying data management. Figure 9.9 is a graphical view of the classes that implement ADT `Bag` containers. Figure 9.10 shows the iterator classes for ADT `Bags`.

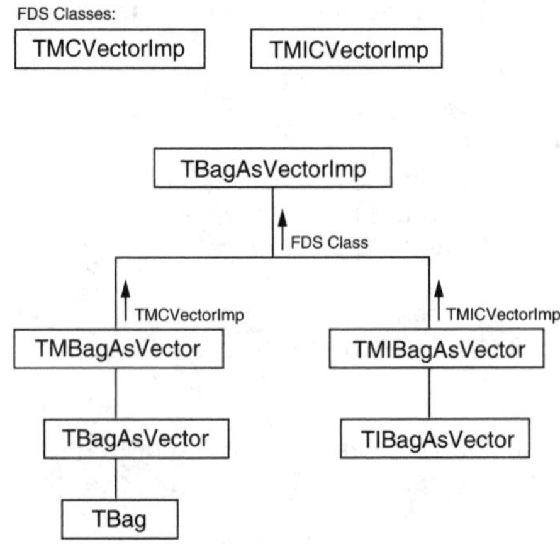

Figure 9.9. The ADT `Bag` *classes.*

There is an equivalent group of classes implementing ADT `Sets`. The `FDS Class` parameter passed to the base class `TBagAsVectorImp` in Figure 9.9 is a template class, used to declare a data member inside that base class. This data member is the low-level container that physically holds the data in an ADT `Bag`. Listing 9.25 is an example of using an ADT direct `Bag` with scalar data types.

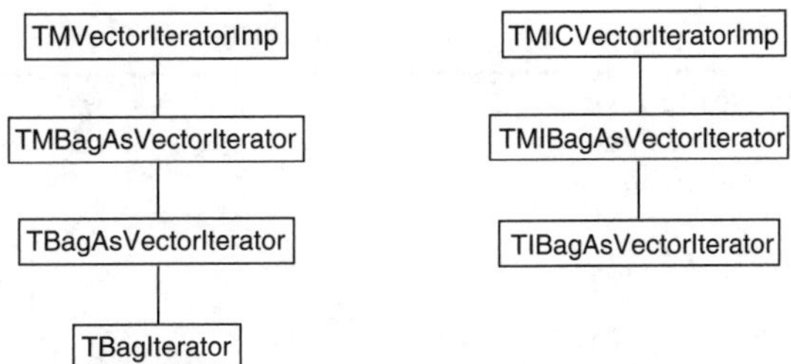

Figure 9.10. The ADT `Bag` *iterator classes.*

Listing 9.25. Using ADT `Bags` with integers.

```
#include <classlib\bags.h>
#include <iostream.h>
#include <string.h>

void main()
{
  // implement the direct bag vectors
  typedef TBagAsVector<int> myBag;
  typedef TBagAsVectorIterator<int> myIterator;

  // create a local bag of scalars
  myBag a;

  // insert some items
  a.Add(100); a.Add(-100); a.Add(0); a.Add(1001);

  // display the bag contents
  cout << "\nBagged items: ";
  myIterator next(a);
  while (next)
    cout << next++ << " ";
  cout << endl;
}
```

The output produced by Listing 9.25 is

```
Bagged items: 100 -100 0 1001
```

It is good practice to *not* rely on the iteration order of the objects in a `Bag`. As you can see, however, the BIDS implementation of ADT `Bags` using FDS vectors maintains objects in the order of their insertion. The order may not be maintained after multiple insertions and removals. Listing 9.26 is a short program that uses ADT indirect `Bags` to store pointers to user objects.

Listing 9.26. Using an ADT indirect `Bag` with user objects.

```
#include <classlib\bags.h>
#include <iostream.h>
#include <string.h>

class MyString {

  enum {STRING_LENGTH = 40};
  char name [STRING_LENGTH];

public:

  MyString() {name [0] = '\0';}
  MyString(char* s) { strncpy(name, s, STRING_LENGTH); }
  char* Name() {return name;}
  int operator==(const MyString s) const {
    return stricmp(name, s.name) ? 0 : 1;
  }
};

void main()
{
  // implement the indirect bag using vectors
  typedef TIBagAsVector<MyString> myBag;
  typedef TIBagAsVectorIterator<MyString> myIterator;

  // create a local bag of user class objects
  myBag a;

  // create a few items
  MyString* c1 = new MyString("First");
  MyString* c2 = new MyString("Second");
  MyString* c3 = new MyString("Third");
  MyString* c4 = new MyString("Fourth");

  // insert the items
  a.Add(c1); a.Add(c2); a.Add(c3); a.Add(c4);

  // display the bag contents
  cout << "\nIndirect bagged items: ";
  myIterator next(a);
  while (next) {
    MyString* s = next++;
    if (strlen(s->Name() ) == 0) continue;
    cout << s->Name() << " ";
  }
  cout << endl;
}
```

The output produced by Listing 9.26 is

```
Indirect bagged items: First Second Third Fourth
```

The previous example inserted pointers to heap objects into an ADT indirect `Bag`. The objects are deleted automatically when the `Bag` container goes out of scope. If you insert pointers to local, global, or static objects, you must remove them before the container tries to delete the referenced objects. To prevent the container from making deletions, use the following statement:

```
bag.OwnsElements(TShouldDelete::NoDelete);
```

ADT `Sets` are very similar to `Bags`, except they allow only one occurrence of a given item to be inserted. Listing 9.27 is an example that is similar to Listing 9.26, using ADT indirect `Sets`.

Listing 9.27. Using ADT indirect `Sets` with user objects.

```
#include <classlib\sets.h>
#include <iostream.h>
#include <string.h>

class MyString {

  enum {STRING_LENGTH = 40};
  char name [STRING_LENGTH];

public:

  MyString() {name [0] = '\0';}
  MyString(char* s) { strncpy(name, s, STRING_LENGTH); }
  char* Name() {return name;}
  int operator==(const MyString& s) const {
    return stricmp(name, s.name) ? 0 : 1;
  }
};

void main()
{
  // implement the indirect set using vectors
  typedef TISetAsVector<MyString> mySet;
  typedef TISetAsVectorIterator<MyString> myIterator;

  // create a local set of user class objects
  mySet a;

  // create a few items
  MyString* c1 = new MyString("First");
```

continues

Listing 9.27. continued

```
  MyString* c2 = new MyString("First");
  MyString* c3 = new MyString("Second");
  MyString* c4 = new MyString("Second");

  // insert the items
  a.Add(c1); a.Add(c2); a.Add(c3); a.Add(c4);

  // display the set contents
  cout << "\nIndirect set items: ";
  myIterator next(a);
  while (next) {
    MyString* s = next++;
    if (strlen(s->Name() ) == 0) continue;
      cout << s->Name() << " ";
  }
  cout << endl;
}
```

The output produced by Listing 9.27 is

```
Indirect set items: First Second
```

The duplicate items are not inserted. The `Set` class template uses your user class' == operator to determine whether two objects are the same. Note that the two `MyString` objects initialized with the same string are two separate objects, as are the pointers `c1` and `c2`, but class `MyString` implements `operator==` to assume equality if two `MyString` objects contain the same characters. The operator `MyString::operator==(const MyString&)` could be changed to discern separate `MyString` objects—even when they had the same string.

Heterogeneous ADT Containers

A heterogeneous container is an object that can store objects of different data types simultaneously. The `Object`-based class library is nice because you can create heterogeneous containers, inserting different items derived from class `Object`. Because only pointers are actually stored in the `Object`-based containers, you can distinguish the contained items using the polymorphic interface of `Object`. Using polymorphic functions frees you from having to know which objects are which, and from using the insidious typecast.

With the BIDS template indirect containers, you can also build heterogeneous containers, as long as you use only items derived from a common ancestor. To illustrate how to handle such containers, I show a short example using an ADT indirect array object.

I insert several different types of items, all derived from class `Object`. When dealing with heterogeneous containers, you must use indirect—rather than direct—containers. Listing 9.28 is a short example.

Listing 9.28. Using ADT indirect containers to store objects of different types.

```
#include <classlib\obsolete\strng.h>
#include <classlib\obsolete\assoc.h>
#include <classlib\obsolete\ldate.h>
#include <classlib\obsolete\ltime.h>
#include <classlib\arrays.h>
#include <iostream.h>

void main()
{
  // implement an indirect array using vectors
  typedef TIArrayAsVector<Object> myArray;
  typedef TIArrayAsVectorIterator<Object> myIterator;

  // create a local array of user class objects
  myArray a(10);

  // create a few items
  a.add(new String("This is a string object") );
  a.add(new Date);
  a.add(new Time);
  String* s = new String("California");
  String* t = new String("population 26 million");
  Association* z = new Association(*s, *t);
  a.add(z);

  // display the array contents
  cout << "\nHeterogeneous array items: ";
  myIterator next(a);
  while (next) {
    Object* obj = next++;
    cout << endl << *obj;
  }
  cout << endl;
}
```

The output produced by Listing 9.28 depends on the system time and date, but will be something like this:

```
Heterogeneous array items:
This is a string object
December 5, 1993
9:51:06.10 pm
```

```
Association { California, population 26 million }
```

To link the previous example, you must add the file TCLASSL.LIB (if you are using the large model) to your project file. This library file is needed only if you're dealing with items derived from class `Object`. Because the Borland distribution disks do not have the `Object`-based library files, you need to build TCLASSL.LIB, following the instructions in the file \BC4\DOC\COMPAT.TXT.

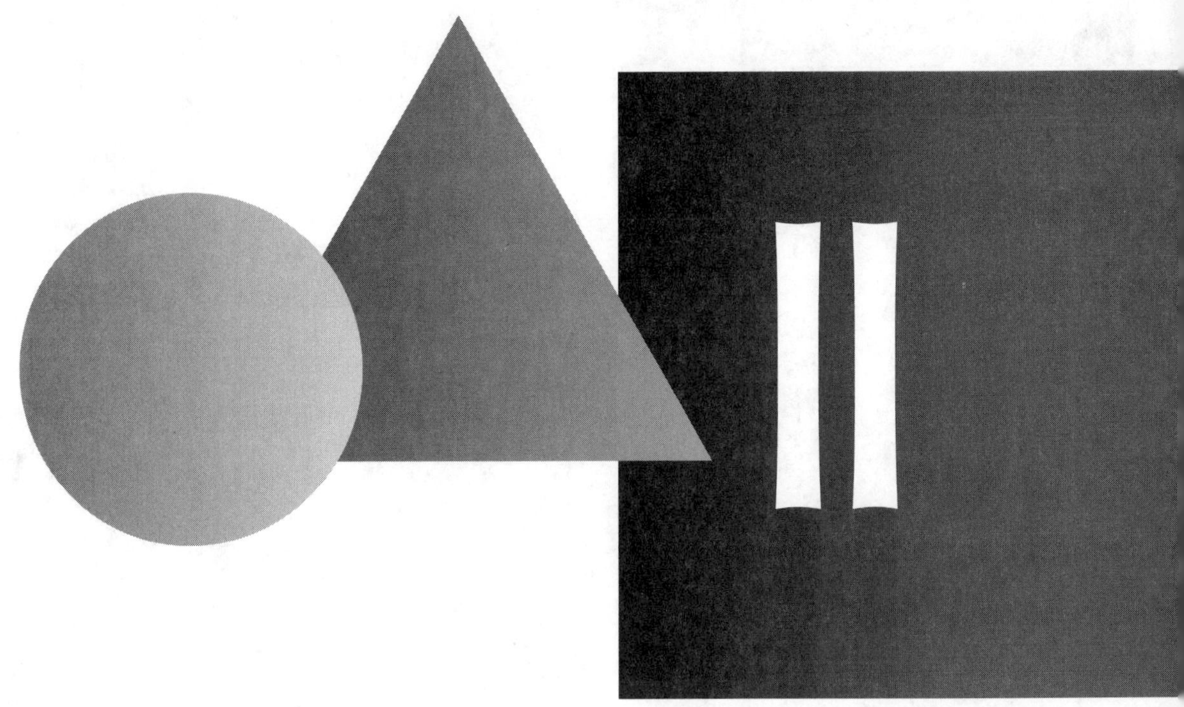

OWL

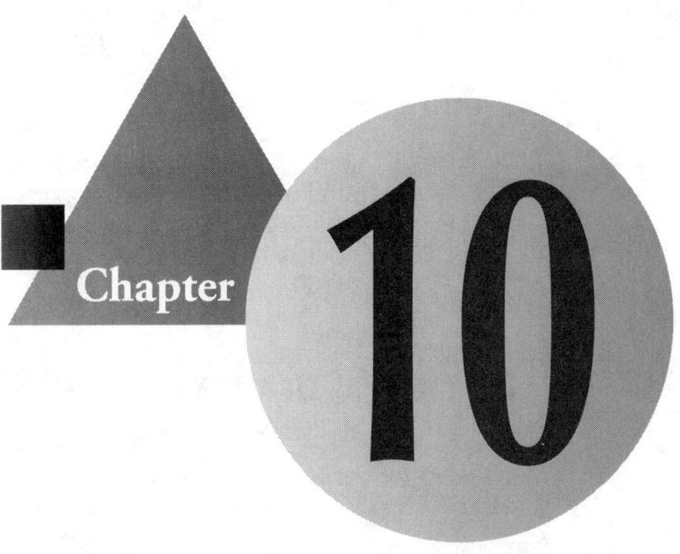

ObjectWindows Library Classes

In this chapter and the following one, I leave behind all remnants of C-style Windows programming and show how to use some of the classes provided in Borland's ObjectWindows Library (OWL). I assume that you are familiar with the basic concepts of OWL and have read the Borland documentation. I try to avoid presenting material that is already covered in the Borland documentation and examples, although some overlap is inevitable.

Before you start using OWL, beware that OWL is basically an all-or-nothing system: If any part of your application uses OWL, the entire application should use OWL. You'll probably have a good deal of trouble trying to use OWL code in one module of source code and non-OWL code elsewhere. Also, if you extend any of the OWL classes, try to preserve the semantics of OWL function names and member variables in your derived classes.

Use the Debugging Version of OWL

Although it is perfectly possible to develop and debug your own code without knowing all the details of what OWL is doing below the surface, I definitely recommend using the debug version of the library, which allows you to step into OWL code with the debugger. On many occasions, you'll find that something doesn't work the way you expect it to, and the best way to figure things out is to step into some OWL code. It's also a good thing to look at the OWL code in general, because it is an excellent guide to how your application code should look. To build the Debug version of OWL, use the make file in the directory \BC45\SOURCE\OWL.

The Entry Point of OWL Applications

OWL was designed to make it possible to create a Windows application with minimal code. The smallest possible OWL program requires only a single function with one line of code. Here is a short but complete OWL program:

```
#include <owl\applicat.h>

int OwlMain(int, char**)
{
  return TApplication().Run();
}
```

The function `OwlMain()` is the OWL equivalent of the function `main()` used in DOS programs. It is the main entry point into an OWL application. OWL calls `OwlMain()` passing two parameters: `argc` and `argv`. The first is the number of command-line arguments, the second a pointer to an array of strings of the command-line arguments. To see the parameters in action, I wrote a trivial OWL program, as shown in Listing 10.1.

Listing 10.1. A short OWL program to display the `OwlMain()` parameters.

```
#include <owl\applicat.h>

int OwlMain(int argc, char** argv)
{
 char buffer [200];
  ostrstream os(buffer, sizeof buffer);
  os << "argc= " << argc << endl;
  for (int i = 0; i < argc; i++)
        os << "argv[" << i << "]= " << argv[i] << endl;
  os << ends;
  MessageBox(NULL, buffer, "Command-Line Arguments", MB_OK);
  return TApplication().Run();
}
```

Running the program from the Windows Program Manager with the `File | Run` command shown in Figure 10.1, the message box in Figure 10.2 is displayed.

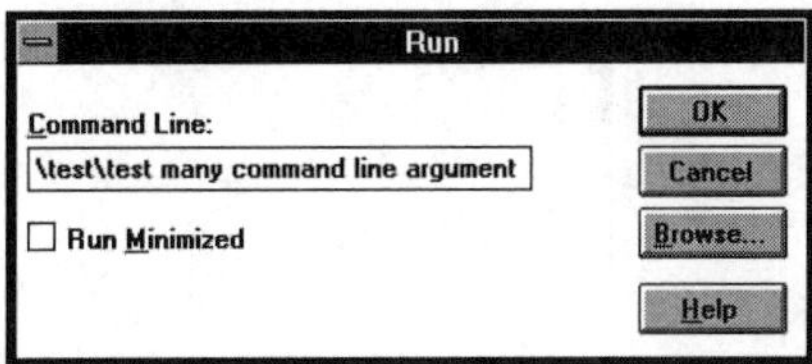

Figure 10.1. The command-line arguments passed to a simple OWL program.

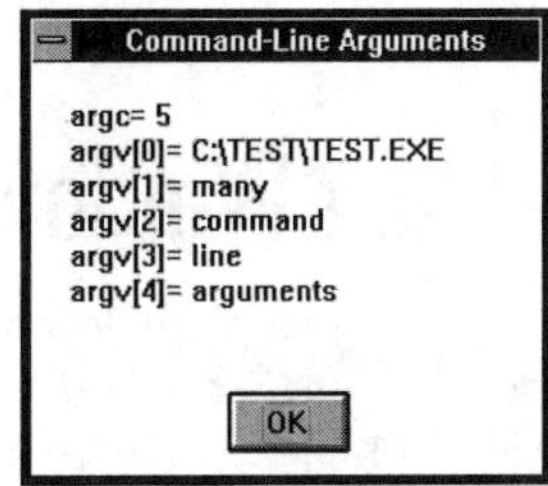

Figure 10.2. The value of the `OwlMain()` *parameters as a result of the command line shown in Figure 10.1.*

Actual OWL programs will derive a class from `TApplication` and add code to create their own specialized windows. You can also create OWL programs that use the traditional `WinMain()` entry point. You might want to do so if you need to obtain the instance parameters that are passed to `WinMain()`. Listing 10.2 shows a trivial OWL program with a `WinMain()` entry point.

Listing 10.2. A short OWL program using `WinMain()` as the entry point.

```
#include <owl\applicat.h>

int PASCAL WinMain(HINSTANCE hInstance, HINSTANCE hPrevInstance,
                   LPSTR cmdLine, int cmdShow)
{
  return TApplication("My Application", hInstance, hPrevInstance,
                      cmdLine, cmdShow).Run();
}
```

The `TApplication` object shows the name of the program on the caption line of the main window. User classes derived from `TApplication` will often add additional information to the caption bar, such as the name of a file being edited or the name of a resource being managed by the program. Note that you don't have to use `WinMain()` just to gain access to the `WinMain()` arguments, because these arguments are stored as data members in classes `TModule` and `TApplication`.

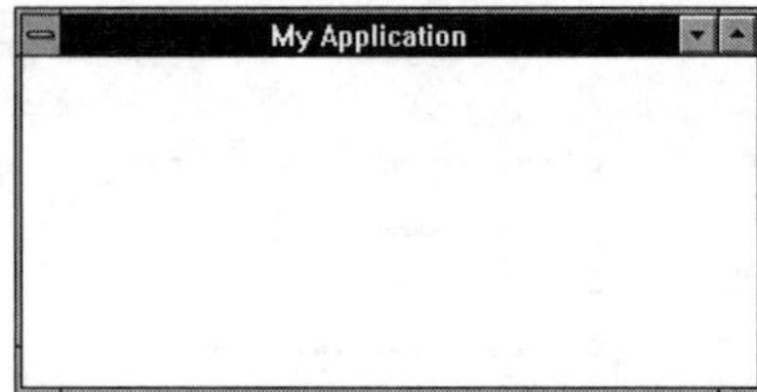

Figure 10.3. The window displayed by the code in Listing 10.2.

Customizing the Main Window

Most Windows programs have a main window. OWL handles many of the details of setting up the main window for you. When you run an OWL program, you instantiate an object of a class derived from `TApplication`. The base class `TApplication` then invokes the virtual member function `TApplication::InitMainWindow()`, which is overridden in your application class to create an instance of the window object that will serve as the application's main window. Listing 10.3 is an example of `TApplication::InitMainWindow()`.

Listing 10.3. Using `TApplication::InitMainWindow()` to create a main window.

```
#include <owl\framewin.h>
#include <owl\applicat.h>

class TMyWindow : public TFrameWindow {...};

class TUserApplication: public TApplication {

public:

  virtual void InitMainWindow()
  {MainWindow = new TMyWindow(NULL, "My App");}

int OwlMain(int, char**)
{
  return TUserApplication().Run();
}
```

If you want to change how the main window—or any other window—looks, you have several options. Some of the attributes changed most frequently are those contained in

the window class registration structure, of type WNDCLASS. This struct contains a variety of items that tell Windows how you want a window class to be created. The struct is declared like this:

```
typedef struct tagWNDCLASS
{
    UINT         style;
    WNDPROC      lpfnWndProc;
    int          cbClsExtra;
    int          cbWndExtra;
    HINSTANCE    hInstance;
    HICON        hIcon;
    HCURSOR      hCursor;
    HBRUSH       hbrBackground;
    LPCSTR       lpszMenuName;
    LPCSTR       lpszClassName;
} WNDCLASS;
```

You can change pretty much any WNDCLASS field except for the `lpfnWndProc` field, because it points to the OWL callback function that controls your window. If you change `lpfnWndProc`, then you'd better be sure you know what you're doing. In fact, if you know that much about OWL, you're probably wasting your time reading this chapter! Table 10.1 shows what each field in the WNDCLASS struct does, and what default value it has.

Table 10.1. The fields of WNDCLASS that affect the appearance of a user window.

Field	*Description*	*OWL Default*
`style`	Class style	`CS_HREDRAW ¦ CS_VREDRAW`
`hIcon`	Icon to use when window is minimized	`LoadIcon(0, IDI_APPLICATION)`
`hCursor`	Cursor handle	`LoadCursor(0, IDC_ARROW)`
`hbrBackground`	Background Brush handle	`HBRUSH(COLOR_ WINDOW + 1)`
`lpszMenuName`	Menu name pointer	`null`

To change one of the fields in the WNDCLASS struct, you need to override two OWL member functions: `TWindow::GetClassName()` and `TWindow::GetWindowClass()`. The former must return a unique string that identifies your window class. The latter is called by OWL, with a reference to a WNDCLASS as a parameter. First, you call the base class

`TWindow::GetWindowClass()` to fill in the default values, and then you can change the fields you want. Listing 10.4 shows an example that changes the background brush to gray and sets the window cursor to a crosshair.

Listing 10.4. An OWL program that modifies the window class registration attributes.

```
#include <owl\framewin.h>
#include <owl\applicat.h>

class TMyWindow : public TFrameWindow {

public:

  TMyWindow(TWindow* parent, const char far* title)
    : TFrameWindow(parent, title)
         { AssignMenu("MENU_MAIN"); }

  LPSTR GetClassName() {return "MyGrayWindow";}
  void GetWindowClass(WNDCLASS&);
};

void TMyWindow::GetWindowClass(WNDCLASS& wndClass)
{
  // always call the base class for proper operation
  TWindow::GetWindowClass(wndClass);

  // now change any class registration fields you want
  wndClass.hCursor       = LoadCursor(0, IDC_CROSS);
  wndClass.hbrBackground = (HBRUSH) GetStockObject(LTGRAY_BRUSH);
}

class TUserApplication: public TApplication {

public:

  virtual void InitMainWindow();
};

void TUserApplication::InitMainWindow()
{
  MainWindow = new TMyWindow(NULL, "My Gray App");
}

int OwlMain(int, char**)
{
  return TUserApplication().Run();
}
```

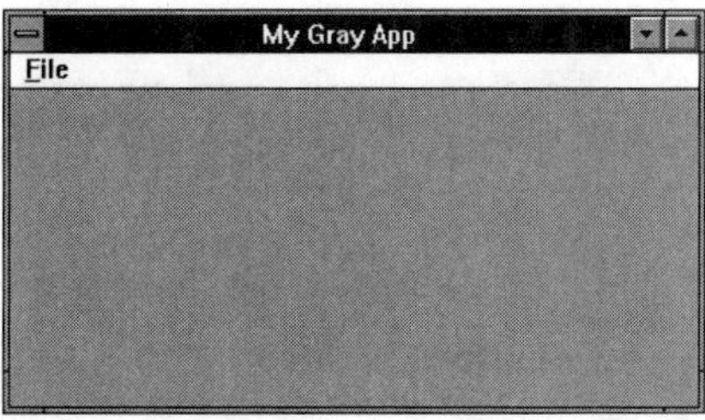

Figure 10.4. The gray window displayed by the code in Listing 10.4.

Any changes you make to the WNDCLASS struct will affect all the instances of that window class, so if you instantiate 10 windows of class `TMyWindow`, they will all be gray. In fact, if another application uses a class with the same name as `TMyWindow(MyGrayWindow)`, then it too will also get gray windows.

OWL Dialog Boxes

Dialog boxes are a standard part of just about every Windows application, and OWL lets you create dialog boxes with great ease: You derive a class from `TDialog`, provide it with member functions to deal with the child control notification messages you need, and add an optional struct to support reading and writing the child control data. In this section I discuss some of the more interesting things you can do with OWL dialog boxes.

Choose Your Dialog Box Style

Most C Windows programmers created dialog boxes that had a plain white background with a flat look, like the one shown in Figure 10.5.

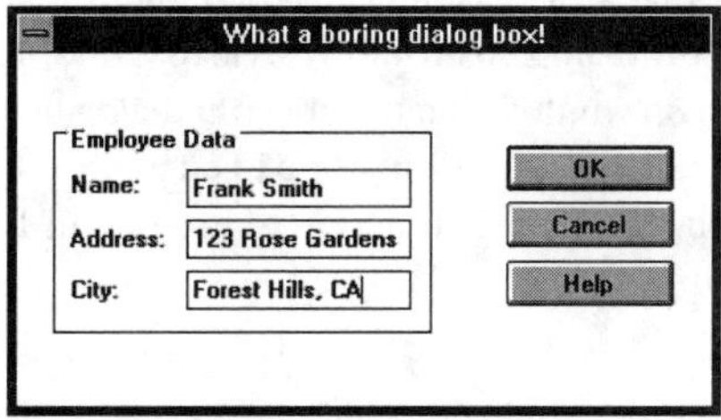

Figure 10.5. The flat dialog boxes used in old C Windows programs.

Most of the new successful Windows programs today have departed from the use of flat dialog boxes, and OWL can make such applications much easier to develop. OWL supports not one but three types of dialog boxes:

- Standard flat dialog boxes
- Gray 3D dialog boxes
- Borland-style dialog boxes

I'll show you how to create both gray 3D and Borland-style dialog boxes in the next two sections.

Gray 3D Dialog Boxes

Gray 3D dialog boxes have been increasing in popularity lately, mainly because they are supported by a small DLL that is available from Microsoft and are therefore easy to incorporate into your programs. The DLL is called CTL3D.DLL, and is contained on the Microsoft Developer's Network CD. Gray 3D dialog boxes use enhanced Windows child controls that have a three-dimensional appearance, as shown in Figure 10.6.

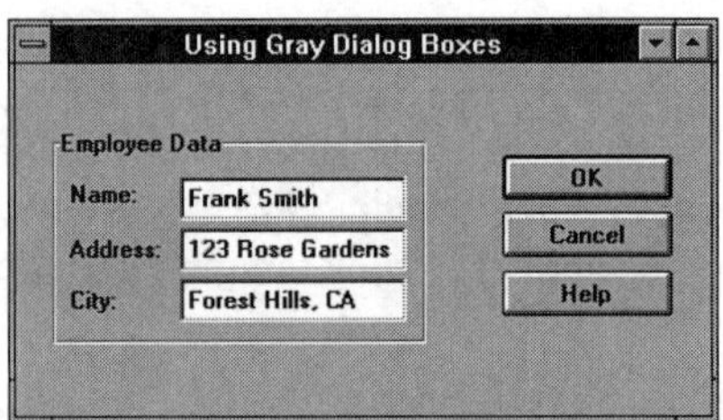

Figure 10.6. An application that uses a gray 3D dialog box as the main window.

I used the same dialog box resource for both Figures 10.5 and 10.6, except that for Figure 10.6 I changed the dialog box window style to Child, so the dialog box would be enclosed by the parent main window. To use gray 3D dialog boxes in an OWL application, all you need to do is call the function `TApplication::EnableCtl3D(BOOL)` inside the `InitMainWindow()` member function. The code in Listing 10.5 was used to create the window in Figure 10.6.

Listing 10.5. An OWL application that uses gray 3D dialog boxes.

```
#include <owl\framewin.h>
#include <owl\dialog.h>
#include <owl\applicat.h>
```

```
class TGrayDialog: public TDialog {

public:

  TGrayDialog() : TDialog(NULL, "DIALOG_GRAY") {}
};

class TUserApplication: public TApplication {

public:

  virtual void InitMainWindow();
};

void TUserApplication::InitMainWindow()
{
  EnableCtl3d(TRUE);
  MainWindow = new TFrameWindow(NULL, "Using Gray Dialog Boxes",
                                new TGrayDialog, TRUE);
}

int OwlMain(int, char**)
{
  return TUserApplication().Run();
}
```

Once you enable gray 3D dialog boxes, all the plain dialog boxes that you create (i.e., all the dialog boxes that aren't Borland-style) will show up with the gray 3D look. Borland style dialog boxes are not affected by enabling gray 3D dialog boxes, but any standard child controls that you place in a Borland-style dialog box (such as an EDIT field) will be replaced by an equivalent 3D control.

Borland-Style Dialog Boxes

Borland developed its proprietary chiseled-steel dialog boxes back in 1991. These stylish dialog boxes not only have a very three-dimensional look to them, but also support a variety of enhanced child controls such as bitmapped buttons, 3D group boxes, and lines. Figure 10.7 shows an example of a Borland-style dialog box, created with the same dialog resource as the two previous figures, and with the code in Listing 10.5, after deleting the line

```
EnableCtl3d(TRUE);
```

in the function `TUserApplication::InitMainWindow()`.

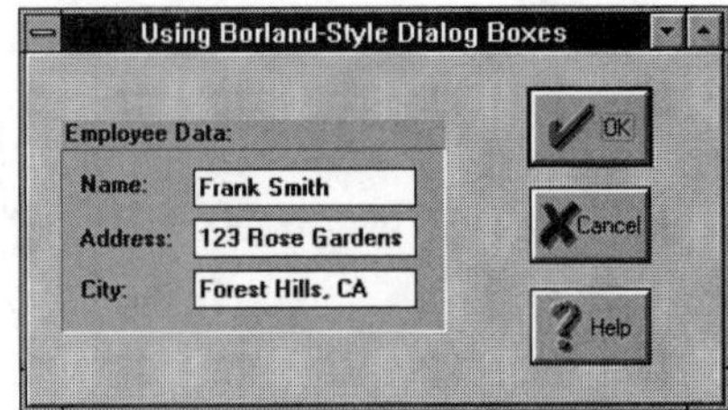

Figure 10.7. A Borland-style dialog box.

All the code for handling the bitmapped and enhanced child controls is hidden away in the file BWCC.DLL, to which your code must have access at runtime.

Bitmaps in Dialog Boxes

Graphics can really increase the overall appeal of a program. Resource Workshop uses graphics extensively to produce a very flashy interface. Windows and OWL cooperate to make it quite straightforward to add bitmapped images to a dialog box. Borland refers to these images as *splashes.* A splash is actually a bitmapped child control, but with no ability to respond to keyboard or mouse events.

Adding splashes requires no code in your application program. OWL uses the file BWCC.DLL to manage splashes with no extra code. To show the details of putting a splash in a dialog box, I wrote a small OWL application called SPLASH that displays a main window with a dialog box that uses a splash bitmap, as shown in Figure 10.8.

Figure 10.8. A splash image displayed in a dialog box.

As I said earlier, there is virtually no code required in your application to support splash images. Listing 10.6 is the code for SPLASH, which displays the dialog box in Figure 10.8.

Listing 10.6. SPLASH, a simple OWL application that displays a bitmapped image in a dialog box.

```
#include <owl\framewin.h>
#include <owl\dialog.h>
#include <owl\applicat.h>

class TAboutDialog: public TDialog {

public:

  TAboutDialog() : TDialog(NULL, "DIALOG_ABOUT") {}
};

class TUserApplication: public TApplication {

public:

  virtual void InitMainWindow();
};

void TUserApplication::InitMainWindow()
{
  MainWindow = new TFrameWindow(NULL, "Using Splash Bitmaps",
                               new TAboutDialog, TRUE);
}

int OwlMain(int, char**)
{
  return TUserApplication().Run();
}
```

Class `TAboutDialog` has only a constructor that invokes the `TDialog` base class with a couple of parameters. Notice that there is no code to support the OK button or to close the dialog box. The base class is capable of taking care of those kinds of details. I created the `DIALOG_ABOUT` resource using Resource Workshop, as usual, and OWL automatically assumed the responsibilities for managing the splash.

The OWL Numbering Scheme for Bitmapped Child Controls

You probably have the impression that something is somehow missing in Listing 10.6. Windows has no support for bitmapped images in dialog boxes, but Listing 10.6 has no code to support the images either. What's going on?

The BWCC.DLL library is quietly working behind the scenes with OWL to make all this possible. Borland resorted to a small stratagem to fit splash images into the Windows framework. The resource name of the child controls used in dialog boxes are used only by Windows for identifying resources when they need to be loaded. A resource name can be either a string (for example, `"DIALOG_ABOUT"`) or an integer value (for example, 1100), but bitmaps are not considered by Windows to be child controls, and therefore have no control ID. Borland introduced a special numbering scheme for resource names that BWCC.DLL can use to keep track of resource types also. Based on the resource name assigned to a child control, BWCC.DLL treats controls differently, allowing the distinction of built-in Windows controls from bitmapped splash images.

Table 10.2 shows how the control ID values are interpreted by BWCC.DLL. High-resolution bitmaps are for VGA or super VGA displays, and low-resolution bitmaps are for EGA displays. A "normal" control is one that is not being pressed and doesn't have the input focus. An active control is one that is being clicked or pressed. A focused control is one that has the input focus but is not being pressed. Normally, a focused control displays a dotted rectangle around the control's legend.

Table 10.2. How BWCC.DLL interprets the resource names of dialog box controls.

Resource Name	*BWCC Interpretation*
0..999	None; the control is a built-in Windows control
1000..1999	High-resolution bitmap for normal controls
2000..2999	Low-resolution bitmap for normal controls
3000..3999	High-resolution bitmap for active controls
4000..4999	Low-resolution bitmap for active controls
5000..5999	High-resolution bitmap for focused controls
6000..6999	Low-resolution bitmap for focused controls

The *thousands* digit in the resource name is only a triggering mechanism for BWCC.DLL. The control ID is assumed to be the value in the three least significant digits of the resource name. For example, the resource file used for Figure 10.8 contains a bitmap with the name 1101. This automatically represents a high-resolution, bitmapped image, but the actual control ID of the bitmap is 101. The dialog box must use the value 101 to indicate the bitmapped image. The BWCC libraries automatically will use the bitmaps 1101, 2101, 3101, 4101, 5101, or 6101 based on the screen resolution and the state of the bitmapped image. Most splash images are prevented from being pressed or receiving the input focus, so only the bitmaps 1101 and 2101 will be required.

Reading and Writing Dialog Box Data

Most dialog boxes are used not only to display static text and pushbuttons but also configuration and user information. Often you need to show the current setting of an option or a default string in an edit control. Traditional Windows programs written in C initialize each pertinent child control while processing the `WM_INITDIALOG` message. With OWL things are a little different and easier: you exploit the built-in data transfer capability of OWL dialog boxes. Consider the dialog box displayed by Resource Workshop when you select the `Bitmap ¦ Size and Attributes` menu command when working with bitmap resources. Figure 10.9 shows this dialog box.

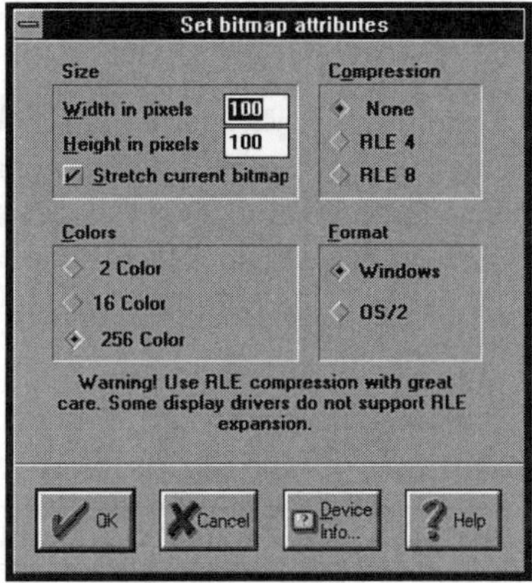

Figure 10.9. A dialog box that uses data transfers to move data in and out of its child controls.

I'll write a short OWL application called TRANSFER to show how easy it is to initialize the various child controls in the dialog box of Figure 10.9. The first thing needed is a dialog class that sets up pointers to the child control objects. I'll call this class `TBitmapAttributesDialog` and show its declaration in Listing 10.7.

Listing 10.7. The declaration of `TBitmapAttributesDialog`, a class that supports the dialog box of Figure 10.9.

```
class TBitmapAttributesDialog: public TDialog {

  TEdit*         widthEdit;
  TEdit*         heightEdit;
  TCheckBox*     resizeCheckBox;
  TRadioButton* colors2RadioButton;
  TRadioButton* colors16RadioButton;
```

continues

Listing 10.7. continued

```
  TRadioButton* colors256RadioButton;
  TRadioButton* windowsRadioButton;
  TRadioButton* os2RadioButton;
  TRadioButton* noneRadioButton;
  TRadioButton* rle4RadioButton;
  TRadioButton* rle8RadioButton;

public:

  TBitmapAttributesDialog(TWindow*);
};
```

The class declares a number of private pointers to child controls. If you study the list carefully, you'll notice that some of the controls displayed in Figure 10.9 are missing. In fact, all the pushbuttons along the bottom of the dialog box are missing from Listing 10.7. You are required to declare only those controls that will send messages to your dialog box or those controls that you need to initialize. Listing 10.8 is the constructor for `TBitmapAttributesDialog`.

Listing 10.8. The constructor for the `TBitmapAttributesDialog` class.

```
TBitmapAttributesDialog::TBitmapAttributesDialog(TWindow* theParent)
                       : TDialog(theParent, "DIALOG_BITMAPATTRIBUTES")
{
  widthEdit            = new TEdit(this, ID_WIDTH, WIDTHSIZE);
  heightEdit           = new TEdit(this, ID_HEIGHT, HEIGHTSIZE);
  resizeCheckBox       = new TCheckBox(this, ID_RESIZE, 0);
  colors2RadioButton   = new TRadioButton(this, ID_2COLORS, 0);
  colors16RadioButton  = new TRadioButton(this, ID_16COLORS, 0);
  colors256RadioButton = new TRadioButton(this, ID_256COLORS, 0);
  windowsRadioButton   = new TRadioButton(this, ID_WINDOWS, 0);
  os2RadioButton       = new TRadioButton(this, ID_OS2, 0);
  noneRadioButton      = new TRadioButton(this, ID_NONE, 0);
  rle4RadioButton      = new TRadioButton(this, ID_RLE4, 0);
  rle8RadioButton      = new TRadioButton(this, ID_RLE8, 0);

  // set up a transfer buffer for moving data in
  // and out of the dialog box controls
  SetTransferBuffer(&Data);
}
```

The constructor dynamically allocates its child controls, and then calls `TWindow::SetTransferBuffer()` to set the transfer buffer pointer to the address of a

buffer containing initialization data for the child controls associated with the dialog box. The `Data` variable is a structure declared like this:

```
// transfer buffer for dialog controls
struct {
  char width [WIDTHSIZE];
  char height [HEIGHTSIZE];
  WORD resize;
  WORD colors2, colors16, colors256;
  WORD windows, os2;
  WORD none, rle4, rle8;
} Data;
```

The structure contains one entry for each child control allocated in the constructor of the `TBitmapAttributesDialog` class. Each control requires its own type of initialization data. This data must appear in the structure `Data` in the same order that the controls are allocated in the dialog constructor. If there is not a perfect one-to-one correspondence between initialization structure and the class constructor controls, the initialization data will be used incorrectly by OWL. Table 10.3 shows the format of initialization data based on control type.

Table 10.3. The data types required in the transfer buffer by each child control that is initialized in a dialog box.

Control	*Initialization Type*
`TButton`	none
`TStatic`	`char []`
`TEdit`	`char []`
`TListBox`	`TListBoxData*`
`TComboBox`	`TComboBoxData*`
`TScrollBar`	`TScrollBarData*`
`TCheckBox`	`WORD`
`TRadioButton`	`WORD`

The transfer buffer is usually a static or global structure. When the dialog box is closed with the OK button, OWL automatically reads the control values into the transfer buffer. Other than the definition and setting up of the transfer buffer fields, your code needs nothing more to read and write data in dialog box controls. Listing 10.9 is the entire source for TRANSFER, an OWL application that uses an initialized dialog box.

Listing 10.9. TRANSFER, an OWL application that initializes the child controls in a dialog box.

```
#include <owl\framewin.h>
#include <owl\dialog.h>
#include <owl\applicat.h>
#include <owl\edit.h>
#include <owl\radiobut.h>
#include <owl\checkbox.h>

// menu commands
const int
  CM_OPTIONSBITMAP = 101,
  CM_HELPABOUT     = 201;

// dialog commands
const int ID_WIDTH      = 101;
const int ID_HEIGHT     = 102;
const int ID_RESIZE     = 103;
const int ID_2COLORS    = 104;
const int ID_16COLORS   = 105;
const int ID_256COLORS  = 106;
const int ID_WINDOWS    = 108;
const int ID_OS2        = 109;
const int ID_NONE       = 110;
const int ID_RLE4       = 111;
const int ID_RLE8       = 112;
const int ID_DEVICEINFO = 156;
const int ID_HELP       = 998;

class TAboutDialog: public TDialog {

public:

  TAboutDialog(TWindow* theParent)
        : TDialog(theParent, "DIALOG_ABOUT") {}
};

const int WIDTHSIZE  = 6;
const int HEIGHTSIZE = 6;

// transfer buffer for dialog controls
struct {
  char width [WIDTHSIZE];
  char height [HEIGHTSIZE];
  WORD resize;
  WORD colors2, colors16, colors256;
  WORD windows, os2;
  WORD none, rle4, rle8;
} Data;
```

```
class TBitmapAttributesDialog: public TDialog {

  TEdit*         widthEdit;
  TEdit*         heightEdit;
  TCheckBox*    resizeCheckBox;
  TRadioButton* colors2RadioButton;
  TRadioButton* colors16RadioButton;
  TRadioButton* colors256RadioButton;
  TRadioButton* windowsRadioButton;
  TRadioButton* os2RadioButton;
  TRadioButton* noneRadioButton;
  TRadioButton* rle4RadioButton;
  TRadioButton* rle8RadioButton;

public:

  TBitmapAttributesDialog(TWindow*);
};

TBitmapAttributesDialog::TBitmapAttributesDialog(TWindow* theParent)
                       : TDialog(theParent, "DIALOG_BITMAPATTRIBUTES")
{
  widthEdit            = new TEdit(this, ID_WIDTH, WIDTHSIZE);
  heightEdit           = new TEdit(this, ID_HEIGHT, HEIGHTSIZE);
  resizeCheckBox       = new TCheckBox(this, ID_RESIZE, 0);
  colors2RadioButton   = new TRadioButton(this, ID_2COLORS, 0);
  colors16RadioButton  = new TRadioButton(this, ID_16COLORS, 0);
  colors256RadioButton = new TRadioButton(this, ID_256COLORS, 0);
  windowsRadioButton   = new TRadioButton(this, ID_WINDOWS, 0);
  os2RadioButton       = new TRadioButton(this, ID_OS2, 0);
  noneRadioButton      = new TRadioButton(this, ID_NONE, 0);
  rle4RadioButton      = new TRadioButton(this, ID_RLE4, 0);
  rle8RadioButton      = new TRadioButton(this, ID_RLE8, 0);

  // set up a transfer buffer for moving data in
  // and out of the dialog box controls
  SetTransferBuffer(&Data);
}

class TProgramWindow : public TFrameWindow {

public:

  TProgramWindow(TWindow* parent, const char far* title);

protected:

    void CmHelpAbout() {TAboutDialog(this).Execute();}
    void CmOptionsBitmap()
      {TBitmapAttributesDialog(this).Execute();}
```

continues

Listing 10.9. continued

```
  DECLARE_RESPONSE_TABLE(TProgramWindow);
};

DEFINE_RESPONSE_TABLE1(TProgramWindow, TFrameWindow)
  EV_COMMAND(CM_OPTIONSBITMAP, CmOptionsBitmap),
  EV_COMMAND(CM_HELPABOUT, CmHelpAbout),
END_RESPONSE_TABLE;


TProgramWindow::TProgramWindow(TWindow* parent, const char far* title)
              : TFrameWindow(parent, title)
{
  AssignMenu("MENU_MAIN");
}

class TUserApplication: public TApplication {

public:

  TUserApplication() : TApplication("My App") {}
  void InitMainWindow();
};

const char* title = "Transferring dialog box data";
void TUserApplication::InitMainWindow()
{
  MainWindow = new TProgramWindow(0, title);
}

int OwlMain(int, char**)
{
  return TUserApplication().Run();
}
```

Running TRANSFER, you can open the `Options ¦ Bitmap` dialog box and set any combination of options. If you close the box and then reopen it, you'll find your settings still there, compliments of the auto-transfer capability of OWL dialog boxes.

OWL Child Controls

OWL has classes that encapsulate all the basic Windows child controls, such as edit boxes, ScrollBars, and ListBoxes. The Borland documentation describes very well how to use these objects to display and interact with controls in dialog boxes, but doesn't go into much detail on how to modify them with derived classes of your own. In the following sections,

I'll be discussing a few interesting ways to extend the basic OWL child controls, and after reading the material, you'll be in a better position to make changes that might suit your own application.

Data Validation

The code in TRANSFER does a great job of moving data in and out of a dialog box, but it has a serious limitation: there is no data checking or validating of any kind. If the user enters -1003 for the bitmap width, the program blindly accepts the value. Data validation is one of the most basic activities you must engage in if you display dialog boxes that users can enter information into. Commercial applications should always check for proper format and range before using data. OWL classes are designed to let you take control over the handling of data when it is to be transferred to or from a dialog box. Each control capable of transferring data has a member function declared like this:

```
virtual UINT Transfer(void* buffer, TTransferDirection direction);
```

This member function is invoked by the parent dialog box when data needs to be transferred in or out of a control. The first argument is a pointer to the control's initialization data, and the second argument indicates whether data is to be read or written to the control. The parameter direction can assume the values `tdGetData`, `tdSetData`, or `tdSizeData`, for reading and writing data or determining the size of the transfer buffer. Data validation is performed when reading data from a control into the transfer buffer.

The traditional way to handle data validation was either to derive a class from `TEdit` and let it check its own data when the member function `TEdit::CanClose()` was called, or to have the parent dialog box check the data entered into the child controls. Both techniques required a lot of coding, especially the former. With OWL 2.5, a new method has been introduced, using a hierarchy of so-called *validator* objects that take care of the most common validation requirements. The hierarchy is shown in Figure 10.10.

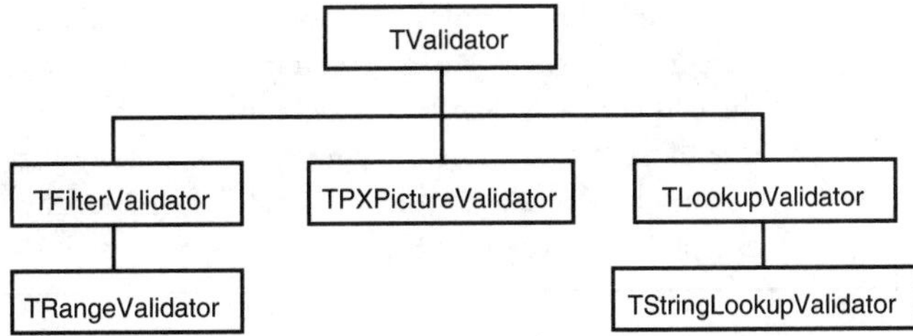

Figure 10.10. The class hierarchy of OWL validator objects.

TValidator is just a seed class that is used only as a base class. It manages some of the items that are common throughout the other validators.

Validator Options

There are a few options you can use with validators. How each option works depends on which specific validator derived from TValidator you are working with. The options are described in Table 10.4.

Table 10.4. The options used by OWL validators.

Option	*Description*
voFill	This option tells OWL to automatically fill in the static (literal) characters in a picture string. With the early release of BC 4.0 that I tested, this option did not work correctly.
voTransfer	When this flag is set, the associated edit control lets the TValidator object attached to it transfer data to and from the edit control's transfer buffer. This may be necessary, for example, if you have a TPXPictureValidator that needs to format the transfer buffer data to match the picture string. For example, the transfer buffer might contain the string "de40", and the picture string might be "&?-##". To make the transfer buffer string conform to the picture string, some processing is necessary inside the function TValidator::Transfer(), so you would derive a class from TPXPictureValidator and override the Transfer() function to convert the string "de40" into the string "De-40". By default, OWL clears this option bit, so if you need voTransfer to be set, you must set it yourself.
voOnAppend	This option tells the validator when to check (validate) the data in the associated edit control. If the option voOnAppend is set, the validator checks the data every time a character is typed. If the option is not set, the edit control's data is checked only when the control is about to lose focus, or you close the parent dialog box by clicking the OK button. By default, all the OWL validators clear the voOnAppend flag, except TPXPictureValidator.

To set an option, you use the function TValidator::SetOption(), like this:

```
TValidator* v = new TPXPictureValidator("#####");
v->SetOption(voFill);
```

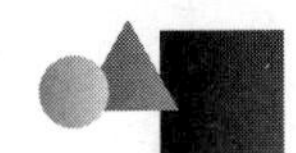

You can set more than one option at a time, like this:

```
v->SetOption(voFill ¦ voTransfer);
```

To clear an option, use the function `TValidator::UnsetOption()`, like this:

```
v->UnsetOption(voFill);
```

To see whether an option is set, use the function `TValidator::HasOption()`, like this:

```
if (v->HasOption(voFill) )
   ...
```

Using *TFilterValidator*

Class `TFilterValidator` takes a character set and checks each character entered into a `TEdit` control against that character set. For example, you might create a `TFilterValidator` using the character set `"A-Za-z.3"` to accept names of people. Note the space character embedded in the set. You could write the following code:

```
TEdit* edit = new TEdit(this, 101, sizeof(editBuffer));
edit->SetValidator(new TFilterValidator("A-Za-z.3 "));
```

You can represent a range of characters using notation like A–Z or 0–9. `TFilterValidator` uses the class `TCharSet` to expand the - into the missing characters. To include the - character in a filter character set, just precede it with a \. For example, you might create the set `"A-Za-z0-9. &#()\-/,"` to accept addresses. Again, note the embedded space, plus the - character.

Using *TRangeValidator*

Class *`TRangeValidator`* is used only with edit fields that accept numeric values. The class constructor takes two **long** values, for the minimum and maximum value acceptable. To create an edit field with a `TRangeValidator`, you would use code like this:

```
TEdit* edit = new TEdit(this, 101, sizeof(editBuffer));
edit->SetValidator(new TRangeValidator(-10, 30) );
```

If you attempt to close the dialog box with an out-of-range number in the edit field, OWL will display the error message in Figure 10.11.

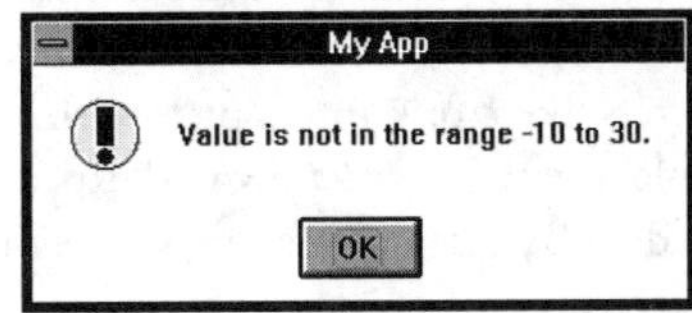

Figure 10.11. The out-of-range error message displayed by `TRangeValidator`.

TRangeValidator doesn't allow you to type anything but the following characters into its associated edit field: the digits 0..9, the + character, and the - character. Everything else is ignored. A range check is performed when the associated edit control loses focus, or when its CanClose() member function is called after you click the dialog box's OK button. An edit control attached to a TRangeValidator is allowed to be empty only if its range includes the value 0. For example, a TRangeValidator with the range (1..49) would not allow an empty edit control, but a TRangeValidator with the range (-10..10) would. The reason is that internally, TRangeValidator equates an empty field to a number with value 0.

Using *TPXPictureValidator*

TPXPictureValidator is a Paradox-compatible picture string validator. A picture string is a template of data that describes the character-level format of data that an edit control expects. There are all kinds of situations in which data is formatted at the character level. For example, U.S. and Canadian telephone numbers are in the format (###) ###-####, where the # character stands for a digit. U.S. Social Security numbers are in the format ###-##-####. TPXPictureValidator accepts a variety of characters in its picture string, telling OWL not only what type of character (digit, letter, or either) to expect, but also how to handle it. Table 10.5 describes the picture characters.

Table 10.5. The picture-string characters used in class `TPXPictureValidator`.

Character	*Description*
#	Digit Only. Decimal points and +- signs not accepted.
?	Letter only, in the range {a..z} and {A..Z}. Punctuation marks and digits not accepted.
&	Letter only. Lowercase letters are converted to uppercase.
@	Any character. This is the most generic picture character, accepting digits, punctuation marks, characters, foreign characters, etc.
!	Any character. If the character is a letter, it is converted to uppercase by the ANSI C function `toupper(char)`.
;	This character is equivalent to the \ character used in C strings. The character following a ; is taken literally, allowing you to insert special characters like # or @ into a picture string of literal characters. For example, the string ";##" would expect the character # followed by a single digit. A ; can appear anywhere inside the picture, except as the last character.
*	Repetition Count. May be followed by one or more digits indicating how many times to repeat the subsequent picture symbol. For example,

Character	*Description*
	the string `"*10&"` is a field that contains 10 letters, to be translated to uppercase. The string `"*5#"` is a field that takes 5 digits. You can follow the `*` character immediately with a mask character, such as `#` or `&`, which will indicate that all the characters in the field are of that type. For example, the string `"*&"` means that only letters are valid, and they will be converted to uppercase. The string `"*#"` means that the field contains all digits.
`[]`	Brackets are used to enclose optional parts of a picture string. For example, a U.S. ZIP code is 5 digits, but may be extended to 9 digits. The picture string `"#####[-####]"` would allow users to enter 5 digits, then an optional `-` character plus 4 more digits. I have not been able to get brackets to work with BC 4.0.
`{}`	The `*` character lets you repeat a given character. What if you want to repeat a series of patterns? The solution is to enclose the characters in {} braces, then the `*` character will repeat the entire sequence. For example, the string `"#*3{#&}"` will accept a digit, then 3 sequences of {digit, letter converted to uppercase}, allowing the user to enter something like `"42R6D8W"`.
,	Separates alternatives. If a field accepts only the character `Y` or `N`, you could use the string `"Y,N"`. If a field accepts only the values 0, 10, 20, you could use the string `"0,10,20"`.
others	All characters that aren't in the set `"#?&!;*[]{}"` are taken literally, meaning that the user must enter that exact character. For example, the string `"#45-D&"` means that the user must enter a digit, the characters "45-D", and a letter.

You pass a picture string to the constructor of class `TPXPictureValidator`. If the string is invalid, the constructor throws a `TPXPictureValidator::TXValidator` exception, which by default displays the error message shown in Figure 10.12.

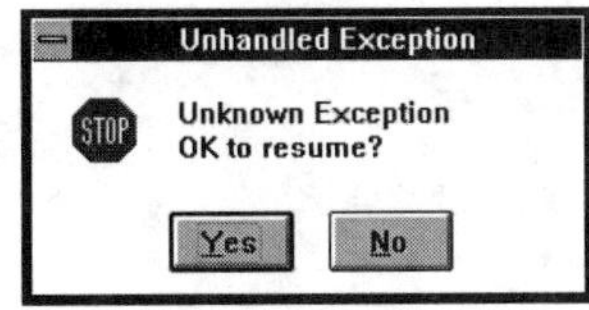

Figure 10.12. The default message box displayed by OWL if you pass an invalid picture string to a `TPXPictureValidator` *object.*

If you click the Yes button, the dialog box (i.e., the parent of the edit control attached to the validator) is not opened, and the application returns to the main message loop to process the next message. Clicking the No button causes the entire application to be shut down.

Using *TStringLookupValidator*

This validator is useful when the data you expect in an edit control must match only certain strings. For example, you might have a data entry application for customer addresses, where the shipping ZIP codes must be in a given set of values. To handle this situation, you use a `TStringLookupValidator` and add the allowable ZIP codes to it, like this:

```
TSortedStringArray* zipCodes = new TSortedStringArray(10, 0, 10);
zipCodes->Add("92713");
zipCodes->Add("92714");
zipCodes->Add("92715");
zipCodes->Add("92718");
zipCodes->Add("92720");

TStringLookupValidator* v = new TStringLookupValidator(zipCodes);
edit->SetValidator(v);
```

The code creates a container called `zipCodes`, whose upper index is initially set to 10 and whose lower index is set to 0. The last parameter in the `TSortedStringArray` constructor is the *delta* value. This indicates the number of entries to add to the array at runtime, should the array overflow. After creating the container, five strings are added to it, and then the container is passed as a parameter to the `TStringLookupValidator` constructor. Finally, the validator is attached to an edit control. If you enter something into this edit control that is not one of the five ZIP codes in the `zipCode` container, OWL will display the error message shown in Figure 10.13.

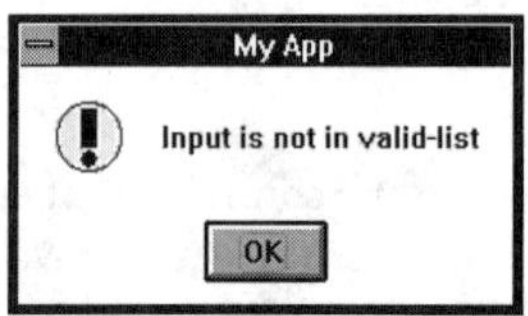

Figure 10.13. The message box displayed by `TStringLookupValidator` *object.*

Customized Controls

One of the greatest visual improvements of Borland-style resources over traditional Windows resources is due to the use of graphically appealing custom controls. Most of the controls used in Resource Workshop are customized, use the dynamic link library

BWCC.DLL, and allow you to incorporate the new enhanced controls into an application very easily.

Without going to the pain of writing your own complete custom control—a rather non-trivial task—there are two other ways to add customized controls to an application: the first requires no code and utilizes the BWCC DLL, the second requires minimal code and requires no DLLs. The first method is usually the best, but is possible only when using Resource Workshop as the resource editing program. The following sections discuss each method.

Using BWCC Custom Controls

I discussed earlier how bitmaps are integrated into dialog boxes by using the resource name as a resource type. BWCC uses the same technique also to support owner-draw controls. Assume that you want to display a dialog box that looks like Figure 10.14.

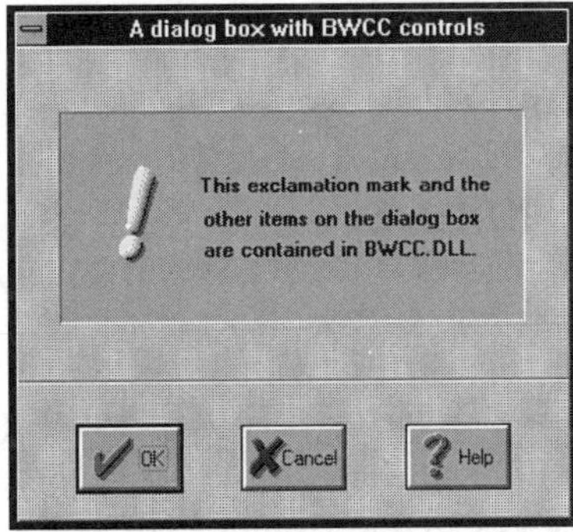

Figure 10.14. A dialog box using BWCC custom controls.

The bitmapped images are of two types: `static` and dynamic. The large *!* character is a `static` child control. Its resource ID value references a bitmapped image contained in the file BWCC.DLL. The custom pushbuttons all use bitmaps contained in BWCC.DLL.

Glyphs

Most of the child controls used in Resource Workshop have a small bitmapped picture accompanied by some text. The picture is usually on the left side of the control and gives a visual mnemonic to the control. Such pictures often are called *glyphs.* The BWCC library contains several glyphs, combined with text, to create ready-made pushbutton bitmaps. Table 10.6 shows the pushbutton bitmaps avaliable in BWCC.DLL, with their resource ID values.

Table 10.6. The pushbutton bitmaps contained in BWCC.DLL.

Bitmap	*ID*	*Resource ID*
	1	IDOK
	2	IDCANCEL
	3	IDABORT
	4	IDRETRY
	5	IDIGNORE
	6	IDYES
	7	IDNO
	998	IDHELP

The first seven resource IDs are declared in the file \BC45\INCLUDE\WINDOWS.H. The last ID (IDHELP) is defined in the file \BC45\INCLUDE\BWCC.H. BWCC.DLL actually contains separate bitmaps for EGA and VGA/superVGA systems. The EGA bitmaps add 2000, 4000, and 6000 to the pushbutton resource ID. The VGA/superVGA bitmaps add 100, 300, and 5000 to the IDs shown in Table 10.6. For example, there are six bitmaps for the OK button in BWCC.DLL: 1001, 2001, 3001, 4001, 5001, 6001.

There are also several other bitmaps in BWCC.DLL. Four of them are generally used in message boxes or dialog boxes. They are shown with their resource IDs in Table 10.7.

Table 10.7. The generic bitmaps contained in BWCC.DLL.

Bitmap	*ID*
	901
	902
	903
	904

The bitmaps in Table 10.7 also come in EGA and VGA/superVGA variations. The EGA bitmaps have the value 2000 added to them. The VGA/superVGA ones have the value 1000 added to them.

Owner-Draw Controls

Using the BWCC library is not an absolute requirement for developing Windows controls that have a special look, but it sure makes the task easier. Using the OWL class hierarchy, you can create your own owner-draw controls that paint themselves on cue from the parent dialog box. OWL owner-draw controls must be derived from class `TControl`. Owner-draw controls send special notification messages to their parent so that the parent can control how and when to display the controls. The parent uses three commands to control the drawing of owner-draw controls, with each command translated into a `virtual` member function call by `TControl`. Table 10.8 shows what the member functions are required to do.

Table 10.8. The `virtual` owner-draw member functions invoked by the `TControl` class.

Function	*Description*
`ODADrawEntire()`	The owner-draw control must display itself in the normal (nonhighlighted) mode.

continues

Table 10.8. continued

Function	*Description*
`ODASelect()`	The owner-draw control must either display itself as pressed or normal, based on the value of an argument passed to it.
`ODAFocus()`	The owner-draw control must either display or hide the focus cue, which typically is a dotted rectangle around the control's legend.

Deriving a generalized owner-draw class from `TControl` is fairly straightforward. I'll develop a class called `TOwnerDrawButton` that will be used as a base class for subsequent user controls. The class constructor will take pointers to three strings. The strings will represent the resource names of the bitmaps to use to display the control in its normal, pressed, and focused state, respectively. The class will use the three pointers to load the associated bitmap images. Listing 10.10 is the code for the `TOwnerDrawButton` class.

Listing 10.10. The implementation of `TOwnerDrawButton`, a general class to support owner-draw controls.

```
class TOwnerDrawButton : public TControl {

  TBitmap* bmNormal;
  TBitmap* bmPressed;
  TBitmap* bmFocused;

  void DrawBitmap(DRAWITEMSTRUCT far&, TBitmap*);

public:

  TOwnerDrawButton(TWindow*, int, char*, char*, char*);
  ~TOwnerDrawButton();

  void SetupWindow() {
    TControl::SetupWindow();
    // disable double clicks
    SetClassWord(GCW_STYLE, GetClassWord(GCW_STYLE) & ~CS_DBLCLKS);
  }

  virtual void ODADrawEntire(DRAWITEMSTRUCT far&);
  virtual void ODASelect(DRAWITEMSTRUCT far&);
  virtual void ODAFocus(DRAWITEMSTRUCT far&);

  virtual void DrawNormal(DRAWITEMSTRUCT far&);
  virtual void DrawPressed(DRAWITEMSTRUCT far&);
  virtual void DrawFocused(DRAWITEMSTRUCT far&);
};
```

```
TOwnerDrawButton::TOwnerDrawButton(TWindow* theParent,
                                   int ResourceId,
                                   char* bm1,
                                   char* bm2,
                                   char* bm3)
                : TControl(theParent, ResourceId)
{
  bmNormal  = new TBitmap(*GetModule(), bm1);
  bmPressed = new TBitmap(*GetModule(), bm2);
  bmFocused = new TBitmap(*GetModule(), bm3);
}

TOwnerDrawButton::~TOwnerDrawButton()
{
  delete bmNormal;
  delete bmPressed;
  delete bmFocused;

}

void TOwnerDrawButton::ODADrawEntire(DRAWITEMSTRUCT far& DrawInfo)
{
  DrawNormal(DrawInfo);
}

void TOwnerDrawButton::ODASelect(DRAWITEMSTRUCT far& DrawInfo)
{
  if (DrawInfo.itemState & ODS_SELECTED)
    DrawPressed(DrawInfo);
  else
    DrawFocused(DrawInfo);
}

void TOwnerDrawButton::ODAFocus(DRAWITEMSTRUCT far& DrawInfo)
{
  if (DrawInfo.itemState & ODS_FOCUS)
    DrawFocused(DrawInfo);
  else
    DrawNormal(DrawInfo);
}

void TOwnerDrawButton::DrawNormal(DRAWITEMSTRUCT far& DrawInfo)
{
  DrawBitmap(DrawInfo, bmNormal);
}

void TOwnerDrawButton::DrawPressed(DRAWITEMSTRUCT far& DrawInfo)
{
```

continues

Listing 10.10. continued

```
  DrawBitmap(DrawInfo, bmPressed);
}

void TOwnerDrawButton::DrawFocused(DRAWITEMSTRUCT far& DrawInfo)
{
  DrawBitmap(DrawInfo, bmFocused);
}

void TOwnerDrawButton::DrawBitmap(DRAWITEMSTRUCT far& DrawInfo,
                                   TBitmap* theBitmap)
{
  int x = DrawInfo.rcItem.left;
  int y = DrawInfo.rcItem.top;

  TDC dc(DrawInfo.hDC);
  TMemoryDC memDC(dc);
  memDC.SelectObject(*theBitmap);
  dc.BitBlt(x, y, theBitmap->Width(), theBitmap->Height(), memDC, 0,
            0);
}
```

By default, mouse double-clicks are enabled for items derived from `TControl`, which uses the preregistered class BUTTON. To make Windows send only `WM_LBUTTONDOWN` messages, even for double-clicks, the window class style bit `CS_DBLCLKS` must be cleared. To do this, I put a couple of lines of code in `TOwnerDrawButton::SetupWindow()`.

The various ODA... member functions are invoked directly by the base class `TControl` when the control is called upon to update itself on the screen. The `private` member function `DrawBitmap()` is used to display an arbitrary bitmap, using a pointer to `TBitmap` as a parameter. To display a bitmap, you need to create a memory DC that is compatible with the display DC, select the `TBitmap` object into it, and then copy the memory bitmap to the screen DC with a `BitBlt()` operation.

To create an owner-draw control using `TOwnerDrawButton` as a base class, you need only to define a very simple class that passes the appropriate string pointers to `TOwnerDrawButton`. Listing 10.11 is an owner-draw OK button implementation.

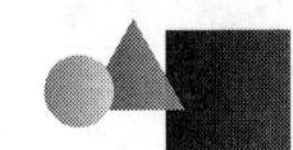

Listing 10.11. An owner-draw OK button.

```
class TOKButton: public TOwnerDrawButton {

public:

  TOKButton(TWindow* theParent, int id)
    : TOwnerDrawButton(theParent, id,
                       "BITMAP_OKNORMAL",
                       "BITMAP_OKPRESSED",
                       "BITMAP_OKFOCUSED") {}
};
```

That's all the code required. Virtually everything is handled through the base classes. The strings used in the constructor reference bitmap resources in the .RES file bound to the application. To show how everything ties in together, Listing 10.12 is a complete OWL application, called OWNER.

Listing 10.12. OWNER, an OWL application that utilizes class `TOwnerDrawButton` to display a variety of owner-draw controls.

```
#include <owl\gdiobject.h>
#include <owl\control.h>
#include <owl\dialog.h>
#include <owl\framewin.h>
#include <owl\applicat.h>

// menu commands
const int IDM_HELPABOUT = 101;

// dialog control IDs
const int
  ID_MYOK     = 101,
  ID_MYCANCEL = 102,
  ID_MYINFO   = 103;

class TOwnerDrawButton : public TControl {

  TBitmap* bmNormal;
  TBitmap* bmPressed;
  TBitmap* bmFocused;

  void DrawBitmap(DRAWITEMSTRUCT far&, TBitmap*);

public:
```

continues

Listing 10.12. continued

```
  TOwnerDrawButton(TWindow*, int, char*, char*, char*);
  ~TOwnerDrawButton();

  void SetupWindow() {
    TControl::SetupWindow();
    // disable double clicks
    SetClassWord(GCW_STYLE, GetClassWord(GCW_STYLE) & ~CS_DBLCLKS);
  }

  virtual void ODADrawEntire(DRAWITEMSTRUCT far&);
  virtual void ODASelect(DRAWITEMSTRUCT far&);
  virtual void ODAFocus(DRAWITEMSTRUCT far&);

  virtual void DrawNormal(DRAWITEMSTRUCT far&);
  virtual void DrawPressed(DRAWITEMSTRUCT far&);
  virtual void DrawFocused(DRAWITEMSTRUCT far&);
};

TOwnerDrawButton::TOwnerDrawButton(TWindow* theParent,
                                   int ResourceId,
                                   char* bm1,
                                   char* bm2,
                                   char* bm3)
                : TControl(theParent, ResourceId)
{
  bmNormal  = new TBitmap(*GetModule(), bm1);
  bmPressed = new TBitmap(*GetModule(), bm2);
  bmFocused = new TBitmap(*GetModule(), bm3);
}

TOwnerDrawButton::~TOwnerDrawButton()
{
  delete bmNormal;
  delete bmPressed;
  delete bmFocused;

}

void TOwnerDrawButton::ODADrawEntire(DRAWITEMSTRUCT far& DrawInfo)
{
  DrawNormal(DrawInfo);
}

void TOwnerDrawButton::ODASelect(DRAWITEMSTRUCT far& DrawInfo)
{
  if (DrawInfo.itemState & ODS_SELECTED)
    DrawPressed(DrawInfo);
```

```
  else
    DrawFocused(DrawInfo);
}

void TOwnerDrawButton::ODAFocus(DRAWITEMSTRUCT far& DrawInfo)
{
  if (DrawInfo.itemState & ODS_FOCUS)
    DrawFocused(DrawInfo);
  else
    DrawNormal(DrawInfo);
}

void TOwnerDrawButton::DrawNormal(DRAWITEMSTRUCT far& DrawInfo)
{
  DrawBitmap(DrawInfo, bmNormal);
}

void TOwnerDrawButton::DrawPressed(DRAWITEMSTRUCT far& DrawInfo)
{
  DrawBitmap(DrawInfo, bmPressed);
}

void TOwnerDrawButton::DrawFocused(DRAWITEMSTRUCT far& DrawInfo)
{
  DrawBitmap(DrawInfo, bmFocused);
}

void TOwnerDrawButton::DrawBitmap(DRAWITEMSTRUCT far& DrawInfo,
                                   TBitmap* theBitmap)
{
  int x = DrawInfo.rcItem.left;
  int y = DrawInfo.rcItem.top;

  TDC dc(DrawInfo.hDC);
  TMemoryDC memDC(dc);
  memDC.SelectObject(*theBitmap);
  dc.BitBlt(x, y, theBitmap->Width(), theBitmap->Height(), memDC, 0,
           0);
}

class TOKButton: public TOwnerDrawButton {

public:

  TOKButton(TWindow* theParent, int id)
    : TOwnerDrawButton(theParent, id,
                        "BITMAP_OKNORMAL",
                        "BITMAP_OKPRESSED",
                        "BITMAP_OKFOCUSED") {}
};
```

continues

Listing 10.12. continued

```
class TCancelButton: public TOwnerDrawButton {

public:

  TCancelButton(TWindow* theParent, int id)
    : TOwnerDrawButton(theParent, id,
                       "BITMAP_CANCELNORMAL",
                       "BITMAP_CANCELPRESSED",
                       "BITMAP_CANCELFOCUSED") {}
};

class TInfoMark: public TOwnerDrawButton {

public:

  TInfoMark(TWindow* theParent, int id)
    : TOwnerDrawButton(theParent, id,
                       "BITMAP_INFO",
                       "BITMAP_INFO",
                       "BITMAP_INFO") {}
};

class TOwnerDrawDialog: public TDialog {

  TOKButton*     okButton;
  TCancelButton* testButton;
  TInfoMark*     infoMark;

public:

  TOwnerDrawDialog();
};

TOwnerDrawDialog::TOwnerDrawDialog()
                 : TDialog(NULL, "DIALOG_OWNERDRAW")
{
  okButton     = new TOKButton(this, ID_MYOK);
  testButton   = new TCancelButton(this, ID_MYCANCEL);
  infoMark     = new TInfoMark(this, ID_MYINFO);
}

LPSTR APPLICATION_NAME = "Using Owner-Draw Controls";

class TUserApplication : public TApplication {

public:

  TUserApplication() : TApplication("My App") {}
  void InitMainWindow() {
```

```
    MainWindow = new TFrameWindow(NULL, APPLICATION_NAME,
                                 new TOwnerDrawDialog, TRUE);
  }
};

int OwlMain(int, char**)
{
  return TUserApplication().Run();
}
```

If you run OWNER, you'll get a main window that incorporates a dialog box in its client area. The dialog box has three owner-draw controls, derived from `TOwnerDrawButton`. The main window is shown in Figure 10.15.

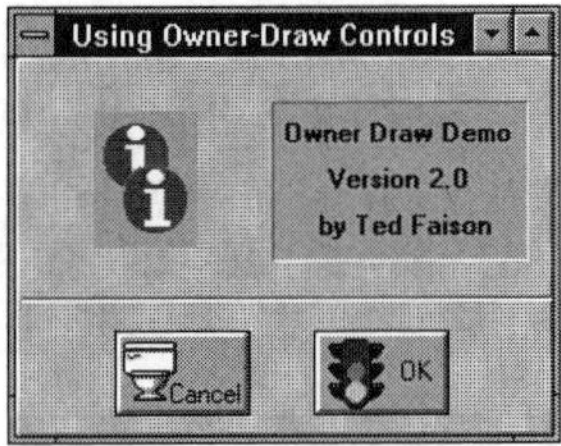

Figure 10.15. The main window of OWNER, showing a number of owner-draw controls derived from class `TOwnerDrawButton`.

The bitmap with the two *i*'s, at the top left of the dialog box in Figure 10.15, was implemented as a BWCC control, but it could have been supported also as a regular Windows bitmap resource. In the latter case, the dialog class `TOwnerDrawDialog` would have had to include code of its own to display the question mark.

Owner-Draw Radio Buttons

Just as you can develop owner-draw pushbuttons, so can you make your own bitmapped radio buttons. Resource Workshop is designed to incorporate bitmapped pushbuttons very easily into your application, but unfortunately, bitmapped radio buttons and check boxes are not supported directly. Nevertheless, developing a custom class to implement owner-draw radio buttons and check boxes isn't too complicated. In this section I'll describe a small OWL application called OWNER1 that illustrates one technique for including owner-draw radio buttons into a program. Check boxes also can be included easily by following the guidelines shown for radio buttons.

Assume that you have an application capable of controlling a Video Cassette Recorder (VCR). Obviously, you could display a dialog box with standard radio buttons, but this is quite boring and doesn't show controls with which users are familiar. OWNER1 will use six owner-draw radio buttons to display a dialog box that looks like Figure 10.16.

Figure 10.16. The owner-draw radio buttons used in OWNER1.

Figure 10.16 shows the Stop button in the pressed state. Not only are owner-draw radio buttons much better looking than traditional radio buttons, but they also can convey more information than a small text legend. Tool palettes, used to select drawing tools in many applications, often use owner-draw radio buttons.

An owner-draw radio button requires a number of bitmaps to display all the possible states it may be in, based on whether it is enabled, focused, or checked. For simplicity, I used only two bitmaps—one for the unchecked state and one for the checked state—but you can easily add any other bitmaps you need. I implemented the owner-draw radio buttons by using a class called `TOwnerDrawRadioButton`, which is declared in Listing 10.13.

Listing 10.13. The declaration of `TOwnerDrawRadioButton`.

```
class TOwnerDrawRadioButton : public TRadioButton {

  TBitmap* bmNormal;
  TBitmap* bmChecked;

  void DrawBitmap(DRAWITEMSTRUCT far&, TBitmap*);

public:

  TOwnerDrawRadioButton(TWindow*, int,
                        TResId normal, TResId pressed);
  ~TOwnerDrawRadioButton();

  virtual void ODADrawEntire(DRAWITEMSTRUCT far&);
  virtual void ODASelect(DRAWITEMSTRUCT far&);
  virtual void ODAFocus(DRAWITEMSTRUCT far&);
```

```
  virtual void DrawNormal(DRAWITEMSTRUCT far&);
  virtual void DrawChecked(DRAWITEMSTRUCT far&);
};
```

The structure is similar to the class `TOwnerDrawButton` used in the program OWNER. The class constructor receives the bitmap resource identifiers, in the form of `TResId` objects. The bitmaps themselves are loaded from the resource file and managed using `TBitmap` objects. When an owner-draw control is manipulated in any way, it sends a `WM_DRAWITEM` message to its parent. Borland-style dialog boxes trap this message and invoke one of the `TControl` `virtual` functions—`ODADrawEntire()`, `ODASelect()`, or `ODAFocus()`—to tell the control how to display itself. Because I support only two possible bitmaps for owner-draw radio buttons, the code is quite simple. Listing 10.14 is the entire code for OWNER1, an OWL application that uses owner draw radio buttons.

Listing 10.14. OWNER1, an OWL application that uses owner-draw radio buttons.

```
#include <owl\gdiobject.h>
#include <owl\radiobut.h>
#include <owl\control.h>
#include <owl\dialog.h>
#include <owl\framewin.h>
#include <owl\applicat.h>

// dialog control IDs
const int
  ID_REWIND       = 101,
  ID_STOP         = 102,
  ID_PLAY         = 103,
  ID_FORWARD      = 104,
  ID_RECORD       = 105,
  ID_PAUSE        = 106;

// bitmap resource IDs for owner-draw radio buttons
const int
  REWIND_NORMAL   = 1101,
  REWIND_PRESSED  = 3101,

  STOP_NORMAL     = 1102,
  STOP_PRESSED    = 3102,

  PLAY_NORMAL     = 1103,
  PLAY_PRESSED    = 3103,

  FORWARD_NORMAL  = 1104,
  FORWARD_PRESSED = 3104,
```

continues

Listing 10.14. continued

```
  RECORD_NORMAL   = 1105,
  RECORD_PRESSED  = 3105,

  PAUSE_NORMAL    = 1106,
  PAUSE_PRESSED   = 3106;


// transfer buffer used to initialize the
// owner draw radio buttons in TDisplayModeDialog
struct {
  WORD rewind;
  WORD stop;
  WORD play;
  WORD forward;
  WORD rec;
  WORD pause;
} InitializationData = {0, 1, 0, 0, 0, 0};


class TOwnerDrawRadioButton : public TRadioButton {

  TBitmap* bmNormal;
  TBitmap* bmChecked;

  void DrawBitmap(DRAWITEMSTRUCT far&, TBitmap*);

public:

  TOwnerDrawRadioButton(TWindow*, int, TResId normal, TResId pressed);
  ~TOwnerDrawRadioButton();

  virtual void ODADrawEntire(DRAWITEMSTRUCT far&);
  virtual void ODASelect(DRAWITEMSTRUCT far&);
  virtual void ODAFocus(DRAWITEMSTRUCT far&);

  virtual void DrawNormal(DRAWITEMSTRUCT far&);
  virtual void DrawChecked(DRAWITEMSTRUCT far&);
};

TOwnerDrawRadioButton::TOwnerDrawRadioButton(TWindow* theParent,
                                             int ResourceId,
                                             TResId normal,
                                             TResId checked)
                     : TRadioButton(theParent, ResourceId)
{
  bmNormal  = new TBitmap(*GetModule(), normal);
  bmChecked = new TBitmap(*GetModule(), checked);
}
```

```
TOwnerDrawRadioButton::~TOwnerDrawRadioButton()
{
  delete bmNormal;
  delete bmChecked;
}

void TOwnerDrawRadioButton::
ODADrawEntire(DRAWITEMSTRUCT far& DrawInfo)
{
  if (GetCheck() & BF_CHECKED)
    DrawChecked(DrawInfo);
  else
    DrawNormal(DrawInfo);
}

void TOwnerDrawRadioButton::
ODASelect(DRAWITEMSTRUCT far& DrawInfo)
{
  if (GetCheck() & BF_CHECKED)
    DrawChecked(DrawInfo);
  else
    DrawNormal(DrawInfo);
}

void TOwnerDrawRadioButton::
ODAFocus(DRAWITEMSTRUCT far& DrawInfo)
{
  if (DrawInfo.itemState & ODS_CHECKED)
    DrawChecked(DrawInfo);
  else
    DrawNormal(DrawInfo);
}

void TOwnerDrawRadioButton::DrawNormal(DRAWITEMSTRUCT far& DrawInfo)
{
  DrawBitmap(DrawInfo, bmNormal);
}

void TOwnerDrawRadioButton::DrawChecked(DRAWITEMSTRUCT far& DrawInfo)
{
  DrawBitmap(DrawInfo, bmChecked);
}

void TOwnerDrawRadioButton::DrawBitmap(DRAWITEMSTRUCT far& DrawInfo,
                                       TBitmap* theBitmap)
{
  int x = DrawInfo.rcItem.left;
  int y = DrawInfo.rcItem.top;
```

continues

Listing 10.14. continued

```
  TDC dc(DrawInfo.hDC);
  TMemoryDC memDC(dc);
  memDC.SelectObject(*theBitmap);
  dc.BitBlt(x, y, theBitmap->Width(), theBitmap->Height(), memDC, 0,
           0);
}

class TVCRControlDialog: public TDialog {

  TOwnerDrawRadioButton* rewind;
  TOwnerDrawRadioButton* stop;
  TOwnerDrawRadioButton* play;
  TOwnerDrawRadioButton* forward;
  TOwnerDrawRadioButton* record;
  TOwnerDrawRadioButton* pause;

public:

     TVCRControlDialog();
};

TVCRControlDialog::TVCRControlDialog()
                  : TDialog(NULL, "DIALOG_VCRCONTROLS")
{
  rewind =
    new TOwnerDrawRadioButton(this, ID_REWIND,
                              REWIND_NORMAL, REWIND_PRESSED);

  stop =
    new TOwnerDrawRadioButton(this, ID_STOP,
                              STOP_NORMAL, STOP_PRESSED);

  play =
    new TOwnerDrawRadioButton(this, ID_PLAY,
                              PLAY_NORMAL, PLAY_PRESSED);

  forward =
    new TOwnerDrawRadioButton(this, ID_FORWARD,
                              FORWARD_NORMAL, FORWARD_PRESSED);

  record =
    new TOwnerDrawRadioButton(this, ID_RECORD,
                              RECORD_NORMAL, RECORD_PRESSED);

  pause =
    new TOwnerDrawRadioButton(this, ID_PAUSE,
                              PAUSE_NORMAL, PAUSE_PRESSED);
```

```
  SetTransferBuffer(&InitializationData);
}

LPSTR APPLICATION_NAME = "Using Owner-Draw Radio Buttons";

class TUserApplication : public TApplication {

public:

  TUserApplication() : TApplication("My App") {}
  void InitMainWindow() {
    MainWindow = new TFrameWindow(NULL, APPLICATION_NAME,
                              new TVCRControlDialog, TRUE);
  }
};

int OwlMain(int, char**)
{
  return TUserApplication().Run();
}
```

If you run OWNER1, you'll notice that the behavior of the owner-draw radio buttons is slightly different from that of standard radio buttons. When you click the radio buttons in OWNER1, nothing seems to happen until you release the mouse button. This is because the `TOwnerDrawRadioButton` class doesn't have a special bitmap to indicate whether the control is focused or not. When you click the left mouse button on a child control, Windows gives the input focus to that control, and normally a dotted rectangle appears around the text for the control. It is relatively easy to extend `TOwnerDrawRadioButton` so that it handles an additional bitmap indicating the focused state. The owner-draw radio buttons in OWNER1 go to the pressed state only when you release the left mouse button. This is different from the way regular pushbuttons work but consistent with standard radio buttons. It isn't too difficult to modify the `TOwnerDrawRadioButton` class so that it goes to the pressed state without waiting for the mouse button to be released.

The `TOwnerDrawRadioButton` class uses a function to draw bitmaps that also was used in the `TOwnerDrawButton` class. The resource file *OWNER1.RES* has all the bitmaps used by the radio buttons. I followed the Borland conventions when assigning resource IDs to the bitmaps. The bitmaps beginning with 1000 are the normal, unchecked versions for VGA displays. The bitmaps beginning with 3000 are the checked versions for VGA displays. If you run OWNER1 on an EGA display, you see only part of the bitmaps.

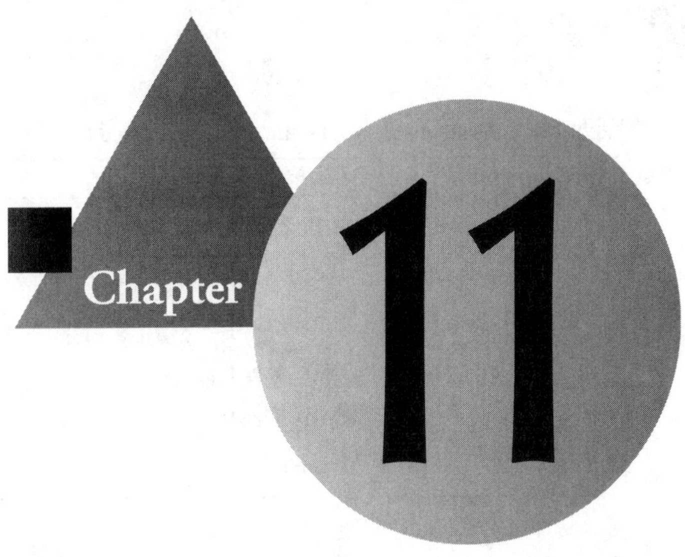

MDI Applications

The Multiple Document Interface (MDI) has not always been a part of Windows. MDI applications were notoriously difficult to develop prior to Windows 3.0, because the developer was responsible for most of the low-level details of MDI. With Windows 3.*x*, MDI messaging and managment were greatly simplified, through the introduction of several new Windows messages, like WM_MDIACTIVATE, WM_MDICREATE, and WM_MDIGETACTIVE. OWL adds additional support, with the result that an MDI OWL application is almost trivial to implement. It isn't an exaggeration to state that you can convert a simple Windows application into an MDI application in a few minutes.

OWL has two basic classes to manage MDI applications: `TMDIFrame` and `TMDIClient`. In most MDI applications, you don't use either class directly, but classes derived from them. The frame window is created with a `TDecoratedMDIFrame` window and the client area is usually a class derived from `TMDIClient`. The individual MDI child windows are derived not from `TWindow` but from `TMDIChild`. `TMDIClient` handles the child window commands. The two OWL classes `TMDIClient` and `TDecoratedMDIFrame` (through its base class `TWindow`) support a number of standard menu commands, as shown in Table 11.1.

Table 11.1. The standard menu commands supported by OWL MDI applications.

Menu Command	*Class*
`Arrange Icons`	`TMDIClient`
`Cascade Windows`	`TMDIClient`
`Tile Windows`	`TMDIClient`
`Close Windows`	`TMDIClient`
`Create new Child`	`TMDIClient`
`Exit`	`TWindow`

In addition to Table 11.1, class `TWindow` supports all the standard system menu commands that are sent via `WM_SYSCOMMAND` messages, like the `SC_CLOSE`, `SC_MOVE`, and `SC_SIZE` commands. To support new application-specific comands, you need to derive a class from `TMDIClient` and provide it with your own handlers. For example, to support a menu command named `Edit ¦ Select All`, you would create a class like this:

Listing 11.1. Adding menu command handlers to MDI applications.

```
#define EDIT_SELECTALL 201

class TMyMDIClient: public TMDIClient {

public:

  TMyMDIClient() : TMDIClient() {}

  void CmEditSelectAll() {}
  // ...

  DECLARE_RESPONSE_TABLE(TMyMDIClient);
};

DEFINE_RESPONSE_TABLE1(TMyMDIClient, TMDIClient)
  EV_COMMAND(IDM_EDIT_SELECTALL, CmEditSelectAll),
END_RESPONSE_TABLE;
```

Class `TMDIClient` has built-in support for the menu commands shown in Table 11.2.

Table 11.2. The MDI commands supported by `TMDIClient`.

MDI Command	*Description*
`CM_ARRANGEICONS`	Arranges MDI icons on parent window
`CM_CASCADECHILDREN`	Arranges open MDI children
`CM_CLOSECHILDREN`	Closes all MDI children
`CM_CREATECHILD`	Opens new MDI child windows
`CM_TILCHILDREN`	Vertically tiles the MDI child windows
`CM_TILECHILDRENHORIZ`	Horizontally tiles the child windows

To use the commands in Table 11.2, you need to include the file OWL\INCLUDE\MDI.RH both in your .RC files and your source code. The command `CM_CREATECHILD` causes `TMDIClient` to invoke the virtual function `TMDIClient::InitChild()`, which by default instantiates a new `TMDIChild` object. You override `TMDIClient::InitChild()` to create derived MDI child windows.

Only one MDI child window can be active at a time. To find the active window, you use the command `TMDIClient::GetActiveChild()`, which returns a pointer to the active child window (if any). You can iterate over the child windows of a `TMDIClient` window using the internal `ForEach()` iterator, as shown in Listing 11.2.

Listing 11.2. Iterating over the children of `TMDIClient`.

```
static void ShowMessageBox(TWindow* child, void*)
{
  char string [200];
  ostrstream os(string, sizeof string);
  os << "This is MDI child " << child->Title << ends;
  ::MessageBox(NULL, string, "Iterating over child windows", MB_OK);
}

void TMyClient::CmIterateOverChildren()
{
  ForEach(ShowMessageBox, 0);
}
```

The function `ShowMessageBox()` is called for each child window of `TMDIClient`. I declared it static to prevent the function name from showing up in the global symbol table, because `ShowMessageBox()` is used only locally.

Window Hierarchies

Windows uses a two-dimensional structure to organize the windows of each application. Every window has four special handles, which can be used to navigate around in the window hierarchy and allow Windows to find parents, child windows, siblings, and so on. The window objects created by OWL in a typical MDI application are directly related to the underlying windows used by Windows. The following figure shows the relationship between the various windows, and how the window handles are set after creating two MDI child windows.

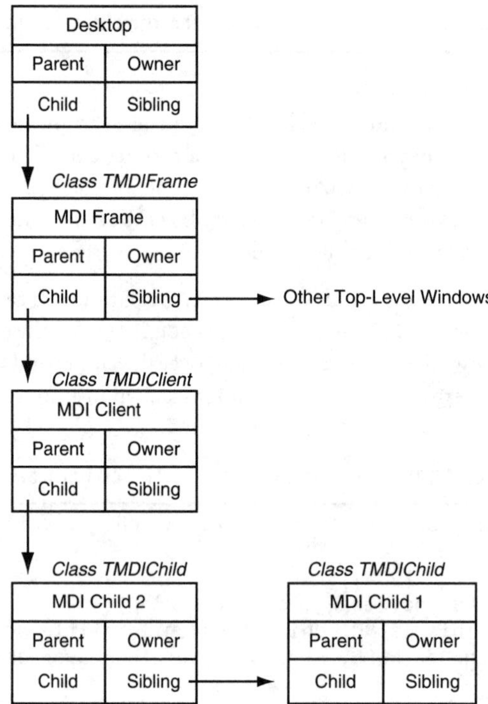

Figure 11.1. The relationship among the various OWL MDI objects.

The MDI Client is a child window of the MDI Frame, and the MDI child windows are children of the MDI Client. The client window has the responsibility of keeping the children objects organized, dispatching messages to them as necessary. For example, when the user selects the standard MDI commands `Tile` and `Cascade`, `TMDIClient` sends the appropriate commands to the children to make them appear tiled or cascaded. There can be only one top-level frame window and one client window in an MDI application.

Each time a new MDI child is created, it is added to the left side of the child list. The new child's sibling handle is then set to reference what had been the first window in the child list, so the list grows in reverse order like a stack. This ordering is normally not an issue, but may be important when iterating over child windows. The leftmost child window in the list is the topmost window in the Z-order. Changing the active MDI child window causes the child windows to be rearranged in the list, so that the topmost window is at the beginning (leftmost) position. The window list is used internally by USER.EXE to figure out which windows are on top of which, and which window to send mouse events to.

Although Windows maintains a list of child windows for its own use, OWL `TWindow` objects also maintain their own child list, referenced by the data member `TWindow::ChildList`. The two lists are equivalent, but OWL uses its own list when a window iterates over its child windows. Note that both Windows and OWL use child lists even for non-MDI windows. OWL `TWindow` objects also maintain a sibling window list, through the data member `TWindow::SiblingList`, that parallels the list maintained by USER.

Customizing the MDI Client Area

Windows handles MDI children using the predefined window class `MDICLIENT`. This class manages commands that affect the MDI children, such as activating or deactivating an MDI child, or minimizing/maximizing an MDI child. OWL puts a wrapper around `MDICLIENT` to make it easier to support MDI features without resorting to low-level Windows API functions. The wrapper is a class called `TMDIClient`.

`TMDIClient` doesn't do much by itself. Most of the time the class just passes messages on to the predefined Windows class `MDICLIENT`. Although `TMDIClient` acts primarily as a liaison, there are a number of things `TMDIClient` does that you might want to change: how MDI child windows are tiled, how they are cascaded, the client background color, how iconized children are arranged, and others. Changing the standard behavior of a `TMDIClient` area is different than changing the behavior of ordinary OWL window objects, because we're dealing with `MDICLIENT`, which is a predefined window class. Predefined Windows classes, such as `EDIT`, `LISTBOX`, and `COMBOBOX` all require a bit of special handling when being customized. The main problem when making changes to a predefined Windows class as a whole is that all the applications running are affected, not just your own. If you change how class `EDIT` handles keyboard input, all applications using `EDIT` controls will be affected. The following section uses class `MDICLIENT` as a basis for discussion of some of the subtleties involved in customizing a predefined Windows class.

Frame and Client Paint Messages

One of the most basic things windows do is to paint themselves. When Windows needs to paint a new frame and client area in an MDI application, it first sends a `WM_ERASEBKGND` to the frame window. When WM_ERASEBKGND is passed to DefWndProc(), which by default calls the API function DefWindowProc(), the frame's client area (which is covered entirely by the MDICLIENT window) is erased using the color or brush indicated in the registration struct WNDCLASS, in field hbrBackground. If no color or brush is found in hbrBackground, the background is erased to the system color COLOR_WINDOW, which normally is a solid white color. After erasing, the frame window receives a WM_PAINT message, to paint the client area.

After the frame window is given the opportunity to erase and paint iself, a WM_ERASEBKGND and a WM_PAINT message are sent to the MDI client window. Any painting that occurs in the client window will cover what was generated by the frame window.

Windows sends the WM_ERASEBKGND and WM_PAINT messages to both the frame and MDI client windows only when the frame needs to be drawn. If you change something in the frame's client window, by moving one of the MDI child windows, or tiling the child windows, the WM_ERASEBKGND and WM_PAINT messages are sent only to the client window—not to the frame. Because Windows automatically uses the brush stored in the hbrBackground field of WNDCLASS, it appears simple to get a custom background color: you just change hbrBackground. Unfortunately, that won't work, for reasons described in the next section.

Changing Attributes of Predefined Windows Classes

Windows defines a number of classes automatically, such as EDIT, SCROLLBAR, and MDICLIENT. These classes are registered for you, and the class names are reserved for use by Windows. If you attempt to register your own class with the name EDIT, the registration will fail. When you want to customize a class that is predefined by Windows, you will need to deviate from the customary OWL procedure of merely deriving a class and adding the necessary member functions.

To change a feature that is part of the window class registration structure, you normally modify a field of the WNDCLASS struct in the member function TWindow::GetWindowClass(). You also need to override the member function TWindow::GetClassName(). For example, to change the cursor for a window, you would write code that looked something like this:

```
LPSTR TMyWindow::GetClassName()
{
  return "TMyWindow";
}
```

```
void TMyWindow::GetWindowClass(WNDCLASS& AWndClass)
{
  // always invoke the base class function first
  TWindow::GetWindowClass(AWndClass);
  AWndClass.hCursor = GetModule()->LoadCursor("IDC_IBEAM");
  // ...
}
```

Windows would then automatically turn the cursor into an I-beam when the mouse was in the client area of `TMyWindow`. The problem with the above code is that it doesn't work when the window class that is being modified is a predefined class, such as `EDIT`, `MDICLIENT`, or `COMBOBOX`. The OWL code that calls `TWindow::GetWindowClass()` is contained in the function `TWindow::Register()`, whose code is shown in Listing 11.3.

Listing 11.3. The OWL code that invokes `TWindow::GetWindowClass()`.

```
BOOL TWindow::Register()
{
  WNDCLASS  windowClass;

  if (!::GetClassInfo(0, GetClassName(), &windowClass) &&
      !GetModule()->GetClassInfo(GetClassName(), &windowClass))
  {
    GetWindowClass(windowClass);
    return ::RegisterClass(&windowClass);
  }

  return TRUE;
}
```

If a class is found to be already registered, `GetWindowClass()` is not called. Net effect: to change the registration attributes of a predefined Windows class, you can't use `GetWindowClass()`, because OWL won't call it. Things aren't as hopeless as they may seem, and there are several ways to change the window cursor—or any other class registration attribute—without using `GetWindowClass()`.

Say that you want to make some kind of change to MDI client windows. One way is to derive a class from `TMDIClient` and override the function `SetupWindow()`, which is called immediately before a window is painted on the screen. Inside `SetupWindow()`, your window has a valid `HWindow` handle, and you can call `TWindow::SetClassWord()` to modify any of the class registration attributes shown in Table 11.3.

Table 11.3. The class registration attributes that can be changed through the API function `SetClassWord()`.

`SetClassWord()` Parameter	*Description*
GCW_HBRBACKGROUND	Handle of the new background brush, used when the window is erased
GCW_HCURSOR	Handle of the window's cursor
GCW_HICON	Handle of the window's icon
GCW_STYLE	Window style bits

If you derived a class called `TMyMDIClient` from `TMDIClient`, here is how its `SetupWindow()` might look to change the window cursor, as shown in Listing 11.4.

Listing 11.4. Changing the cursor for the predefined `MDICLIENT` window class.

```
class TMyMDIClient: public TMDIClient {

  HCURSOR oldCursor;

public:

  void SetupWindow()
  {
    TWindow::SetupWindow();
    HCURSOR cursor = GetModule()->LoadCursor("IDC_IBEAM");
    oldCursor = (HCURSOR) SetClassWord(GCW_HCURSOR, (WORD) cursor);
  }

  // other class declarations...
};
```

The function `TWindow::SetClassWord()` will change the window cursor for all windows of class `MDICLIENT`. The value returned is the previously installed cursor. `SetupWindow()` needs to save this old cursor in order to restore the cursor after the MDI application terminates.

Changing the class registration attributes of a predefined Windows class causes a small problem: once you have altered the registration attributes, all other Windows applications will inherit your changes. For example, if you changed the background color for class `EDIT`, all applications using edit boxes would be affected. This may or may not be desirable. One way to limit the problem is to have the application that modifies the Windows class attributes detect when the user switched to another application. This is easily done by trapping the WM_ACTIVATEAPP message and restoring all Windows attributes to their default state. But then there is still the problem of restoring the old class attribute when your application terminates.

As you can see, modifying class registration attributes might work, but doesn't appear to be an easy solution. Although OWL doesn't have specific code to let you easily change all window class registration attributes, it does offer some support. One of the most commonly changed window class registration attributes is the background color of a window. Let's go back to the WM_ERASEBKGND message again. When Windows needs the predefined `MDICLIENT` window to paint its background, a WM_ERASEBKGND is sent to `TMDIClient`, and it is during the processing of this message that you get the opportunity to change the window color. Under OWL 1.0 you would have needed to derive a class from `TMDIClient`, add a handler for the WM_ERASEBKGND message, and do the painting for your selected color. Let's look at how OWL 2.5 supports colored window backgrounds.

Painting Solid Background Colors

With OWL 2.5, everything is already taken care of for you, and you don't need to add any code at all. If you are creating windows using AppExpert, you can just indicate the color of a window in the AppExpert customization dialog box and the code will be written for you. For windows such as modeless dialog boxes or `TMDIClient` objects, you have to actually write some code yourself.

Class `TWindow`, as implemented in OWL 2.5, has a member function called `SetBkgndColor()`, which you can call to set a window's background color. All you need is one line of code! I wrote a small application program called MDICOLOR to show how simple it is to change the MDI client window's background color.

Listing 11.5. MDICOLOR, an OWL application showing how to change the background color of the MDI client area.

```
// this application shows how to customize the MDI client
// area by deriving a class from TMDIClient

#include <owl\dialog.h>
#include <owl\mdi.h>
#include <owl\applicat.h>

#define IDM_HELPABOUT  101

class TDialogAbout: public TDialog {
```

continues

Listing 11.5. continued

```
public:

  TDialogAbout(TWindow* AParent)
      : TDialog(AParent, "DIALOG_ABOUT") {}
};

class TWindowClient: public TMDIClient {

public:

  TWindowClient() : TMDIClient()
      { SetBkgndColor(RGB(255, 255, 0) ); }

  void CmHelpAbout();
  TMDIChild* InitChild()
  { return new TMDIChild(*this, "Child Window"); }

  DECLARE_RESPONSE_TABLE(TWindowClient);
};

DEFINE_RESPONSE_TABLE1(TWindowClient, TMDIClient)
  EV_COMMAND(IDM_HELPABOUT, CmHelpAbout),
END_RESPONSE_TABLE;


void TWindowClient::CmHelpAbout()
{
  TDialogAbout(this).Execute();
}

class TUserApplication: public TApplication {

public:

  TUserApplication()
      : TApplication("MDI Demo") {}
  virtual void InitMainWindow();
};


void TUserApplication::InitMainWindow()
{
  MainWindow = new TMDIFrame("Coloring the MDI Client area",
                          "MENU_MAIN", *new TWindowClient);
}
```

```
int OwlMain(int, char**)
{
  return TUserApplication().Run();
}
```

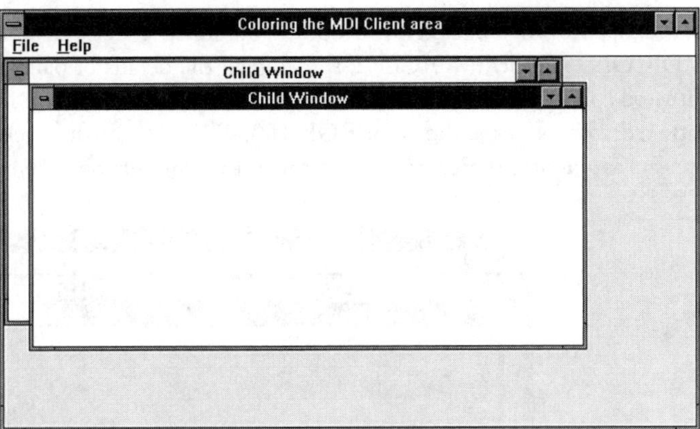

Figure 11.2. The colored MDI client area shown by MDICOLOR.

Although you can't tell from the black and white figure, the MDI client area is actually bright yellow. Typical OWL MDI applications use a class derived from `TMDIClient` to handle the menu commands, so you can just add the one line of code that calls `SetBkgndColor()` to the class constructor code.

Painting Dithered Background Colors

MDICOLOR is limited in the colors it will use to color the MDI client window. OWL paints the window's background in the function `TWindow::EvEraseBkgnd()`, using the function `::ExtTextOut()`. The problem is that `::ExtTextOut()` uses only solid colors. If you specify a color that is not supported directly by your display adaptor, Windows will convert it to the nearest solid color before painting. But what if you really want a particular color, even though it may be painted as a dithered pattern? No problem—just override `TWindow::EvEraseBkgnd()` and do the painting with a GDI function that can handle dithered colors. The function `TDC::FillRect()` is just the ticket. By adding to your MDI client window the member function:

```
BOOL TWindowClient::EvEraseBkgnd(HDC hDC)
{
  if (BkgndColor != NoColor && BkgndColor != NoErase) {
      TDC dc(hDC);
```

```
        TBrush brush(BkgndColor);
        dc.FillRect(GetClientRect(), brush);
        return TRUE;
    }
    return (BOOL)DefaultProcessing();
}
```

you can paint any background color you want. I derived a short program from MDICOLOR, called MDICLR2, showing all the details of painting backgrounds with dithered colors. Figure 11.3 shows how MDICLR2 paints its MDI client window with a dithered color. I chose the color RGB(150, 225, 200) as the background color, which appears as a light dithered green on displays that support only 16 colors.

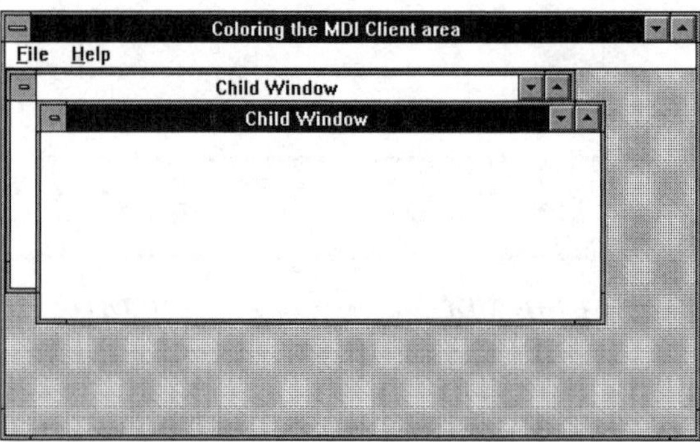

Figure 11.3. The dithered background color used by MDICLR2.

The technique used for MDICLR2 also works with solid colors. Listing 11.6 shows the complete code for MDICLR2.

Listing 11.6. MDICLR2, an OWL MDI application showing how to create windows with dithered background colors.

```
// this application shows how to customize the MDI client
// area by deriving a class from TMDIClient

#include <owl\dialog.h>
#include <owl\mdi.h>
#include <owl\applicat.h>
#include <owl\dc.h>

#define IDM_HELPABOUT  101

class TDialogAbout: public TDialog {
```

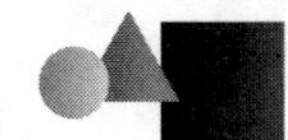

```
public:

  TDialogAbout(TWindow* AParent)
      : TDialog(AParent, "DIALOG_ABOUT") {}
};

class TWindowClient: public TMDIClient {

public:

  TWindowClient() : TMDIClient()
      { SetBkgndColor(RGB(150, 225, 200) ); }

  BOOL EvEraseBkgnd(HDC);
  void CmHelpAbout();
  TMDIChild* InitChild()
  { return new TMDIChild(*this, "Child Window"); }

  DECLARE_RESPONSE_TABLE(TWindowClient);
};

DEFINE_RESPONSE_TABLE1(TWindowClient, TMDIClient)
  EV_COMMAND(IDM_HELPABOUT, CmHelpAbout),
  EV_WM_ERASEBKGND,
END_RESPONSE_TABLE;


void TWindowClient::CmHelpAbout()
{
  TDialogAbout(this).Execute();
}

BOOL TWindowClient::EvEraseBkgnd(HDC hDC)
{
  if (BkgndColor != NoColor && BkgndColor != NoErase) {
      TDC dc(hDC);
      TBrush brush(BkgndColor);
      dc.FillRect(GetClientRect(), brush);
      return TRUE;
  }
  return (BOOL)DefaultProcessing();
}

class TUserApplication: public TApplication {

public:

  TUserApplication()
      : TApplication("MDI Demo") {}
```

continues

Listing 11.6. continued

```
  virtual void InitMainWindow();
};


void TUserApplication::InitMainWindow()
{
  MainWindow = new TMDIFrame("Coloring the MDI Client area",
                      "MENU_MAIN", *new TWindowClient);
}

int OwlMain(int, char**)
{
  return TUserApplication().Run();
}
```

Drag and Drop

Drag and Drop is becoming more and more popular and can be used with both SDI and MDI applications. OWL supports Drag and Drop using a class called `TDropInfo`. To notify Windows that a window is a drag-and-drop receiver, all you have to do is set the WS_EX_ACCEPTFILES bit in the window's `Attr` data member. In an MDI application, you would make either the MDI client or the MDI child windows (or both) drag-and-drop receivers. For the MDI client window, you would declare a class like this:

```
class TMyMDIClient: public TMDIClient {

public:

  TMyMDIClient() : TMDIClient()
      { Attr.ExStyle |= WS_EX_ACCEPTFILES; }

protected:

      void EvDropFiles(TDropInfo dropInfo);

  DECLARE_RESPONSE_TABLE(TMyMDIClient);
};

DEFINE_RESPONSE_TABLE1(TMyMDIClient, TMDIClient)
  EV_WM_DROPFILES,
END_RESPONSE_TABLE;
```

The handler `EvDropFiles()` will be called anytime a filename is dropped into the application MDI client window. The code for `EvDropFiles()` would look like this:

```
void TMyMDIClient::EvDropFiles(TDropInfo dropInfo)
{
  TPoint dropPoint;
  dropInfo.DragQueryPoint(dropPoint);

  int numDropped = dropInfo.DragQueryFileCount();

  char* fileName = new char [255];
  for (int i = 0; i < numDropped; i++) {
      dropInfo.DragQueryFile(i, fileName, 255);
      // handle 'fileName', dropped at point 'dropPoint'
      HandleFile(fileName, dropPoint);
  }
  delete fileName;
  dropInfo.DragFinish();
}
```

The code

```
dropInfo.DragQueryPoint(dropPoint);
```

returns the location at which the files were dropped. The function actually returns the value TRUE if the files were dropped in the client area of the window; otherwise, it returns FALSE. The variable `dropPoint` is a point expressed in window coordinates, so the point (0, 0) is the upper-left corner of the window. When the user drops filenames into an application, you get only one `EvDropFile()` call, regardless of how many files are actually being dropped. You then obtain the number of filenames with the code

```
int numDropped = dropInfo.DragQueryFileCount();
```

You must then repeatedly call the function

```
dropInfo.DragQueryFile(i, fileName, 255);
```

to get one by one the names of the dropped files. The function requires you to pass an array into which Windows copies the name of the next file. When you are done processing the WM_DROPFILES message, you must call the function

```
dropInfo.DragFinish();
```

so that Windows can release the memory it used to hold the names of the dropped files. You can add support for drag and drop to any window, not just to those used in MDI applications as shown in this chapter.

Keyboard Handling

Most applications support the use of the keyboard for accelerator keys, but for various reasons, getting the keyboard to work correctly with MDI child windows was a problem for many OWL 1.0 programmers. One reason was the number of functions that dealt with the keyboard, with little documentation on how they worked or what they were for. Table 11.4 is a list of the main keyboard-related functions in OWL 1.0.

Table 11.4. The OWL 1.0 functions related to keyboard handling.

OWL 1.0 Functions	*Description*
`TApplication::SetKBHandler()`	Established a keyboard handler of a given window in the application
`TWindowsObject::EnableKBHandler()`	Turned on keyboard handling
`TApplication::ProcessAccels()`	Processed accelerator keys for the window that last enabled keyboard handling
`TApplication::ProcessMDIAccels()`	Processed MDI acclerator keys

OWL 1.0 didn't support keyboard handling automatically when you used a dialog box in MDI child windows. In fact, there were several situations in which OWL 1.0 was deficient in keyboard handling, requiring you to add your own code. In contrast, OWL 2.5 has more comprehensive support than OWL 1.0 for keyboard handling and accelerator keys, using the functions shown in Table 11.5.

Table 11.5. The OWL 2.5 functions related to keyboard handling.

OWL 2.5 Functions	*Description*
`TApplication::PumpWaitingMessages()`	Inner message loop
`TApplication::MessageLoop()`	Outer message loop
`TApplication::ProcessAppMsg()`	Traverses the view chain, looking for a window to handle Windows messages
`TFrameWindow::EnableKBHandler()`	Allows a window to enable or disable accelerator key translation
`TFrameWindow::PreProcessMsg()`	Translates dialog box navigation keys and menu accelerator keys
`TMDIChild::PreprocessMsg()`	Translates menu accelerator keys
`TWindow::PreProcessMsg()`	Translates menu accelerator keys
`TMDIClient::PreProcessMsg()`	Translates MDI accelerator keys
`TDialog::PreProcessMsg()`	Translates dialog box navigation keys and menu accelerator keys

Internally, OWL makes use of Windows API functions to process accelerator keys, using the functions shown in Table 11.6.

Table 11.6. OWL functions that call low-level Windows API keyboard handling functions.

Windows API Functions	*Called in OWL Functions*
`IsDialogMessage()`	`TDialog::PreProcessMsg()`
`TFrameWindow::PreProcessMsg()`	
`TranslateMessage()`	`TApplication::PumpWaitingMessages()`
`TWindow::EvLButtonDown()`	
`TranslateMDISysAccelerator()`	`TMDIClient::PreProcessMsg()`
`TranslateAccelerator()`	`TApplication::ProcessAppMsg()`
	`TMDIChild::PreProcessMsg()`
	`TWindow::PreProcessMsg()`

In the following sections I'll describe how OWL handles accelerator keys. Using this information, you will be able to change how accelerators are handled, for those situations in which OWL doesn't do what you want.

The Main Message Loop

Every Windows application has a message loop that receives all the messages Windows sends. The message loop is where keyboard handling (and nearly everything else) starts in a Windows program. Applications written in C usually have a loop that looks like the code in Listing 11.7.

Listing 11.7. The message loop in typical Windows applications written in C.

```
while (GetMessage (&msg, NULL, 0, 0) {
  TranslateMessage(&msg);
  DispatchMessage(&msg);
}
```

OWL applications don't need to create message loops because the base class `TApplication` has a loop that is usually adequate. The loop code is contained inside the member function `TApplication::MessageLoop()`, and looks like that shown in Listing 11.8.

Listing 11.8. The main message loop in `TApplication`.

```
int TApplication::MessageLoop()
{
  long idleCount = 0;

  MessageLoopResult = 0;
  while (!BreakMessageLoop) {
    try {
      if (!IdleAction(idleCount++))
        ::WaitMessage();
      if (PumpWaitingMessages())
        idleCount = 0;
    }
    // catch exceptions...

  BreakMessageLoop = FALSE;
  return MessageLoopResult;
}
```

The message loop is dependent on the variable `BreakMessageLoop`, which can be set to TRUE in the function `PumpWaitingMessages()` when a WM_QUIT message is received. The API function `WaitMessage()` tells Windows to yield control to other applications if there are no messages in the queue. The messages are actually retrieved in the function `TApplication::PumpWaitingMessages()`, as shown in Listing 11.9.

Listing 11.9. The message loop used in OWL applications.

```
BOOL TApplication::PumpWaitingMessages()
{
  MSG  msg;
  BOOL foundOne = FALSE;

  while (::PeekMessage(&msg, 0, 0, 0, PM_REMOVE)) {
    foundOne = TRUE;
    if (msg.message == WM_QUIT) {
      BreakMessageLoop = TRUE;
      MessageLoopResult = msg.wParam;
      ::PostQuitMessage(msg.wParam);  // make sure all loops exit
      break;
    }

    if (!ProcessAppMsg(msg)) {
      ::TranslateMessage(&msg);
      ::DispatchMessage(&msg);
      DeleteCondemned();
      ResumeThrow();
```

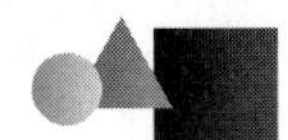

```
    }
  }
  return foundOne;
}
```

PeekMessage() is used to retrieve the next message (if any) from the application queue. The message is handed over to ProcessAppMessage(), which processes accelerator keys. A return value of TRUE indicates that an acclerator key was translated, in which case TranslateMessage() and DispatchMessage() are not called. The function DeleteCondemned() is a function that acts as a garbage collector. When an OWL window is closed, its Windows element is closed but the C++ object is not deleted. It is only marked as *condemned*. Condemned windows are stored in a special container and deleted all at once at the bottom of the message loop by the function DeleteCondemned(). The reason for deleting the windows this way is to avoid certain problems of synchronization between Windows messages and OWL windows when you delete an OWL object.

The Function *TApplication::ProcessAppMessage()*

OWL puts all keyboard-related functions under the care of TApplication::ProcessAppMsg(). This function automatically translates accelerator keys for the main window, pop-up windows, child windows, modal dialog boxes, modeless dialog boxes, and MDI child windows. The value FALSE is returned if a message was not related to keyboard accelerators. ProcessAppMsg() first tries to find a handler for messages. A handler is a window that knows how to translate accelerator keys. OWL looks for a handler by starting with the window a message is destined to. If this window fails to handle the message, OWL gives the message to the window's parent, then to the parent's parent, and so on, until a handler is found. If no handler is found, OWL attempts to translate the main menu's keyboard accelerators. If the message was either processed or translated, the value TRUE is returned. Listing 11.10 shows the code for ProcessAppMessage().

Listing 11.10. The `TApplication` function that searches for a handler for a message.

```
BOOL TApplication::ProcessAppMsg(MSG &msg)
{
  for (HWND hWnd = msg.hwnd; hWnd; hWnd = ::GetParent(hWnd)) {
    TWindow*  win = GetWindowPtr(hWnd);

    if (win && win->PreProcessMsg(msg))
      return TRUE;
  }
```

continues

Listing 11.10. continued

```
  if (HAccTable && MainWindow)
    return ::TranslateAccelerator(MainWindow->HWindow, HAccTable,
&msg);

  return FALSE;
}
```

Windows with Keyboard Handling Enabled

OWL deals with all kinds of windows that can optionally accept accelerator keys. Dialog boxes use the Tab and Shift-Tab keys to move the focus from child control to child control. MDI child windows use Ctrl-F4 to close themselves, and Ctrl-F6 to cycle among child windows. Main windows use accelerator keys to access menu commands. Both dialog boxes and regular windows can use accelerator keys to select child controls. For example, you might select the File Name field of a File Open dialog box by typing Alt-N. Certain accelerator keys are automatically enabled for certain OWL windows. The Tab key works by default in dialog boxes, but not in regular windows. MDI accelerator keys work with MDI child windows, but not with dialog boxes. For unusual situations, OWL may not support the accelerators you want, so you need to understand how accelerators are used in order to get the response you want.

Keyboard handling is taken care of in the function `TFrameWindow::PreProcessMsg()`, which looks like the code in Listing 11.11.

Listing 11.11. The keyboard handling function in `TFrameWindow`.

```
BOOL TFrameWindow::PreProcessMsg(MSG& msg)
{
  if (TWindow::PreProcessMsg(msg))
    return TRUE;

  else if (KeyboardHandling) {
    HWND parent = ::GetParent(msg.hwnd);

    return parent && ::IsDialogMessage(parent, &msg);
  }

  return FALSE;
}
```

Class `TFrameWindow` has a data member called `KeyboardHandling`, which by default is set to FALSE. When `KeyboardHandling` is set to TRUE, OWL gives the frame window's parent a crack at the message. `IsDialogMessage()` gives the parent window the chance to translate the navigation keys used in modal and modeless dialog boxes. `TFrameWindow::PreProcessMsg()` calls the base class `TWindow` to translate accelerator keys. The function `TWindow::PreProcessMsg()` looks like this:

```
BOOL TWindow::PreProcessMsg(MSG& msg)
{
  return hAccel ? ::TranslateAccelerator(HWindow, hAccel, &msg) :
FALSE;
}
```

If the window has a keyboard accelerator, OWL attempts to translate accelerator keys by calling the Windows API function `TranslateAccelerator()`, which returns TRUE if an accelerator key was found and translated. OWL has another class that deals with accelerator keys, called `TMDIChild`. This class is derived from `TFrameWindow`, and overrides `PreProcessMsg()` to process MDI accelerator keys (like Ctrl-F4 and Ctrl-F6). The code looks like this:

```
BOOL TMDIChild::PreProcessMsg(MSG& msg)
{
  if (KeyboardHandling && Parent->PreProcessMsg(msg))
    return TRUE;

  if (hAccel && ::TranslateAccelerator(Parent->Parent->HWindow,
hAccel, &msg))
    return TRUE;

  return TFrameWindow::PreProcessMsg(msg);
}
```

`TMDIChild` tries to handle accelerator keys before calling the base class, because `TFrameWindow` will throw away MDI accelerator key events without actually processing them.

MDI Child Windows with Child Controls

MDI Child windows are not much different from ordinary top-level windows. The main difference is that they are children of `TMDIClient`. Most of the features you associate with MDI child windows, such as tiling and cascading, are not supported by code in the MDI children, because everything is handled behind-the-scenes by `TMDIClient` and its underlying Windows class `MDICLIENT`. When you develop an MDI child window class in OWL, you normally don't have to deal with any MDI details, so code written for an OWL MDI child window is essentially indistinguishable from code written for an ordinary OWL window.

This homogeneity in code typically allows you to develop code much faster, without worrying about low-level details; unfortunately, however, there are times when you do need to write code specifically for MDI child windows, especially when you want to change some basic window feature or when you add child controls with keyboard support.

Sometimes you may want to have not one, but a whole series of child controls to a window. Using MDI, you have basically two options: you can add the child controls to a `TMDIChild` window, or you can add them to a dialog box using Resource Workshop. The advantage of using MDI windows over dialog boxes is that when you open multiple windows, Windows takes control over the organization of the MDI children, allowing the main menu to be used seamlessly with each MDI child. The advantage of using dialog boxes is that you can develop the window using Resource Workshop, positioning each child control precisely, setting tab sequences, and testing the entire resource, without writing a line of code. In the next few sections I'll discuss how to incorporate child controls into MDI child windows, using two techniques:

1. Modifying the basic MDI child window, adding keyboard support for child controls, and changing the background colors.
2. Filling the interior of the MDI child window with a dialog box, having the dialog box control the child controls.

Changing the Background of an MDI Child Window

Before adding child controls to a `TMDIChild` window, I need to show how to make `TMDIChild` paint its background to make it look like a Borland dialog box. When you develop dialog boxes with BCW and Resource Workshop, you have the option of creating the well-known *chiseled-steel* windows, which use a special bitmap for their background. All you have to do is give a dialog box the class name **`bordlg`** and the rest is taken care of for you. The chiseled-steel background looks much more appealing than a flat white or gray one, and gives child controls a much more dramatic, three-dimensional effect.

Windows sends the message WM_ERASEBKGND to a window in order to erase the background of all or part of the client area of the window. If you don't process WM_ERASEBKGND, it is passed to `DefWndProc()`, which paints the background with a system color, usually solid white.

To give a custom background to a window, you must intercept the WM_ERASEBKGND and paint the background with a suitable brush. Borland uses an 8-x-8-pixel brush to create the chiseled-steel look for the Borland-style dialog boxes. Figure 11.4 shows what the brush pattern looks like.

Figure 11.4. The bitmap used to create the chiseled-steel background in Borland-style dialog boxes.

I used an 8-x-8-pixel brush to create a background for the MDI child windows, but just to be a little different, I have created a bitmap with a slight bluish dominant, to give windows what you might call a *chiseled-cobalt* look.

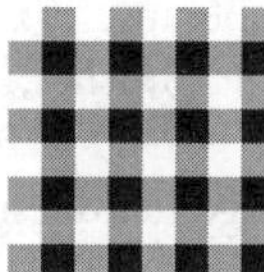

Figure 11.5. The 8-x-8-brush bitmap to create a chiseled-cobalt background.

I wrote a small MDI application called MDIBACK that uses the chiseled-cobalt pattern. MDIBACK displays empty MDI child windows with the new background color. Figure 11.6 shows how MDIBACK looks after opening a few MDI child windows.

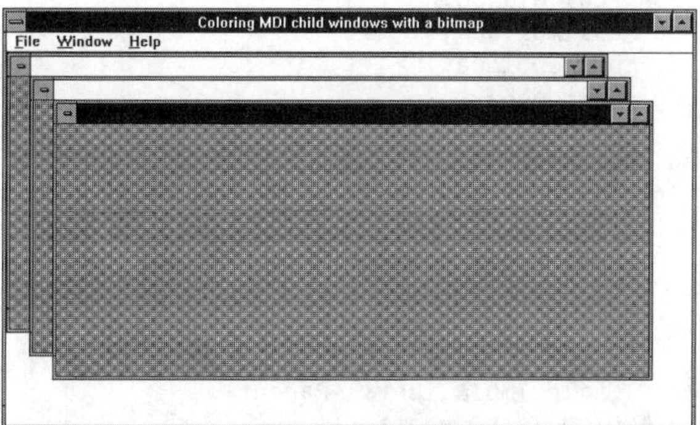

Figure 11.6. The chiseled-cobalt MDI child windows displayed in MDIBACK.

All the work for creating the background pattern is in the function `EvEraseBkgnd()`, which looks like this:

```
BOOL TBlueMDIChild::EvEraseBkgnd(HDC hDC)
{
  // load the bitmap resource
  TBitmap bitmap(*GetModule(), "BITMAP_CHISELEDCOBALT");

  // paint the background
  TDC dc(hDC);
  dc.SelectObject(TBrush(bitmap) );
  dc.PatBlt(GetClientRect() );
  return TRUE;
}
```

`EvEraseBkgnd()` makes use of some of the new GDI objects available in OWL 2.5, such as `TBitmap`, `TDC`, and `TBrush`. `TDC` creates an object-oriented counterpart for a Windows device context. `TDC` is smart because it knows how to automatically deselect and delete GDI objects such as pens and brushes, helping your code avoid GDI memory leaks. `EvEraseBkgnd()` returns the value TRUE to Windows to indicate that it processed the WM_ERASEBKGND message and doesn't want Windows to do anything more. Listing 11.12 shows the source code for MDIBACK.

Listing 11.12. The source code for MDIBACK, an MDI application that uses MDI child windows with a custom background pattern.

```
// this application demonstrates how to achieve a
// 'chiseled-cobalt' effect in MDI child windows

 #include <owl\dialog.h>
#include <owl\mdi.h>
#include <owl\applicat.h>
#include <owl\dc.h>

// menu commands
const int IDM_HELPABOUT = 201;

class TBlueMDIChild: public TMDIChild {

public:

  TBlueMDIChild(TMDIClient& AParent)
      : TMDIChild(AParent) {}

protected:

  BOOL EvEraseBkgnd(HDC);
  DECLARE_RESPONSE_TABLE(TBlueMDIChild);
};
```

```
DEFINE_RESPONSE_TABLE1(TBlueMDIChild, TMDIChild)
  EV_WM_ERASEBKGND,
END_RESPONSE_TABLE;

BOOL TBlueMDIChild::EvEraseBkgnd(HDC hDC)
{
  // load the bitmap resource
  TBitmap bitmap(*GetModule(), "BITMAP_CHISELEDCOBALT");

  // paint the background
  TDC dc(hDC);
  dc.SelectObject(TBrush(bitmap) );
  dc.PatBlt(GetClientRect() );
  return TRUE;
}

class TDialogAbout: public TDialog {

public:

  TDialogAbout(TWindow* AParent)
      : TDialog(AParent, "DIALOG_ABOUT") {}
};

class TMyClient : public TMDIClient {

protected:

  TMDIChild* InitChild();
  void CmHelpAbout();
  DECLARE_RESPONSE_TABLE(TMyClient);
};

DEFINE_RESPONSE_TABLE1(TMyClient, TMDIClient)
  EV_COMMAND(IDM_HELPABOUT, CmHelpAbout),
END_RESPONSE_TABLE;

TMDIChild* TMyClient::InitChild()
{
  return new TBlueMDIChild(*this);
}

void TMyClient::CmHelpAbout()
{
  TDialogAbout(this).Execute();
}

class TUserApplication: public TApplication {
```

continues

Listing 11.12. continued

```
public:

  TUserApplication()
      : TApplication("MDIChildBitmap") {}
  void InitMainWindow()
  { MainWindow = new TMDIFrame("Coloring MDI child windows with a
bitmap",
                               "MENU_MAIN", *new TMyClient);
  }
};

int OwlMain(int, char**)
{
  return TUserApplication().Run();
}
```

Handling Child Controls in an MDI Child Window

Now that we have a good-looking background, we can add some child controls to an MDI child window, making something that will look just like a dialog box. There are a few differences between the controls used in dialog boxes and those used in MDI child windows, but it isn't difficult to make both sets of controls look and act the same.

When using controls in a dialog box, you create OWL objects only for those child controls that generate notification messages, such as pushbuttons and edit boxes. You don't generally create OWL objects for controls such as static text fields, group boxes, or vertical and horizontal *bump* lines. On the other hand, when creating child controls for use in a window, you have to create each and every control that you want to have displayed, regardless of whether the control generates any messages. Moreover, creating controls this way is a bit more tedious because you must tell OWL information that would ordinarily be contained in a resource file.

Two Constructors for Child Controls

Child control objects in OWL are designed to be used both in dialog boxes and in ordinary windows. All OWL control objects therefore have two different constructors: one used when the control is defined in a resource file, and one when the control is created on the fly, with no resource file. Consider, for example, the process of constructing the OWL control for a dialog box's pushbutton. The pushbutton is defined in the application's resource file, and the constructor for the control is called like this:

```
TButton* button = new TButton(this, ID_BUTTON);
```

The position and size of the control are not passed to the constructor because the resource file contains the full definition for the control. When creating a control on the fly in a window, there is no resource file specification for the control, so a different constructor must be used, to which the missing information is passed. Here is how you would create a pushbutton inside a regular window:

```
TButton* button = new TButton(this, IDBUTTON, "", 126, 172, 64, 40,
TRUE);
```

I'll refer to this kind of constructor as the *long form*. The four integers are the origin and size of the button, and the last parameter indicates whether the pushbutton is a default button or not. If so, a thick rectangle is drawn around the control.

Differences Between the Two Constructors

When you create child controls using the long form constructor, the resulting child controls have different default settings from child controls created from resource files. The main difference is that the long form constructors don't set the WB_TRANSFER bit, which means that the child controls have their transfer buffers disabled. To enable them, you must call `EnableTransfer()` like this:

```
childControl->EnableTransfer();
```

Radio buttons and checkboxes normally are used in groups. The Tab key should move the focus from one group to the next. For the Tab key to work correctly, use the WS_GROUP style bit with the first radio button or checkbox in each group. The long form constructor turns off the WS_GROUP style for each control, so you will need to turn the style bit on for controls that start a new group. To turn the bit on, just use the following code:

```
childControl->Attr.Style |= WS_GROUP;
```

Using Resource Workshop to create resource-based controls, you can set the WS_GROUP bit directly, using the property dialog box for each control.

A Complete Example

To show all the details of adding child controls to MDI child windows, I wrote a complete example program called MDICTL, which is available on the companion disk. MDICTL creates MDI child windows that are almost indistinguishable from Borland-style dialog boxes created with Resource Workshop. Other than the color of the background brush pattern, the only differences are the border style used in the MDI child windows and the presence of the minimize and maximize buttons on the caption bar. Figure 11.7 shows an MDI child window displayed by MDICTL.

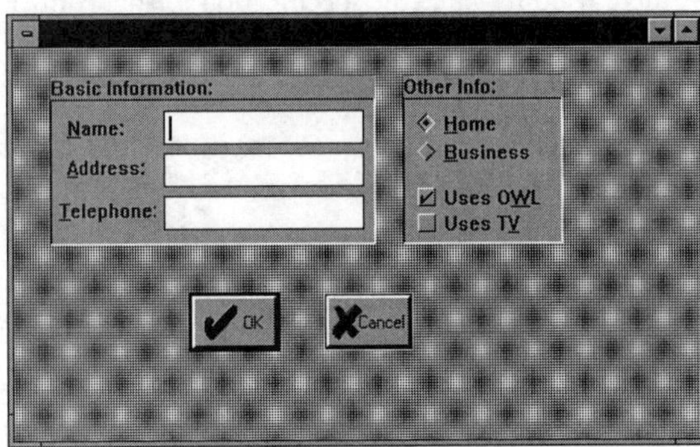

Figure 11.7. The MDI child windows created in MDICTL.

The child controls function exactly as if they were in a dialog box, but a little extra work needs to be done to support keyboard navigation keys, which I'll discuss in a moment. First, here is the complete source code for MDICTL, as shown in Listing 11.13.

Listing 11.13. MDICTL, an MDI application that uses child controls in MDI child windows.

```
// this application demonstrates how to add child
// controls to MDI child windows

#include <owl\dialog.h>
#include <owl\mdi.h>
#include <owl\applicat.h>
#include <owl\dc.h>
#include <owl\static.h>
#include <owl\edit.h>
#include <owl\groupbox.h>
#include <owl\button.h>
#include <owl\radiobut.h>
#include <owl\checkbox.h>
#include <string.h>

// menu commands
const int IDM_HELPABOUT = 201;
```

```
// MDI window child control IDs
const int
  WIDTH         = 20,
  IDC_NAME      = 101,
  IDC_ADDRESS   = 102,
  IDC_TELEPHONE = 103,
  IDC_HOME      = 104,
  IDC_BUSINESS  = 105,
  IDC_USESOWL   = 106,
  IDC_USESTV    = 107;

// a class to handle and initialize the transfer buffer
struct TMyChildTransferBuffer {

  char nameBuffer      [WIDTH];
  char addressBuffer   [WIDTH];
  char telephoneBuffer [WIDTH];
  WORD home;
  WORD business;
  WORD usesOWL;
  WORD usesTV;

  TMyChildTransferBuffer::TMyChildTransferBuffer()
  {
     // initialize the transfer buffer
     strcpy(nameBuffer, "");
     strcpy(addressBuffer, "");
     strcpy(telephoneBuffer, "");
     home = business = usesOWL = usesTV = FALSE;
  }
};

// the actual transfer buffer
static TMyChildTransferBuffer buffer;

class TMyChild: public TMDIChild {

  TEdit*        name;
  TEdit*        address;
  TEdit*        telephone;
  TRadioButton* home;
  TRadioButton* business;
  TCheckBox*    usesOWL;
  TCheckBox*    usesTV;

public:

  TMyChild(TMDIClient&);
```

continues

Listing 11.13. continued

```
protected:

  BOOL EvEraseBkgnd(HDC);
  void EvSetFocus(HWND);
  void CmOk();
  void CmCancel();

  DECLARE_RESPONSE_TABLE(TMyChild);
};

DEFINE_RESPONSE_TABLE1(TMyChild, TMDIChild)
  EV_WM_ERASEBKGND,
  EV_WM_SETFOCUS,
  EV_COMMAND(IDOK, CmOk),
  EV_COMMAND(IDCANCEL, CmCancel),
END_RESPONSE_TABLE;

TMyChild::TMyChild(TMDIClient& AParent)
      : TMDIChild(AParent, "")
{
  // create a few child controls
  new TStatic(this, -1, "Basic Information:",
              26, 20, 234, 16, WIDTH);
  new TGroupBox(this, -1, "", 26, 36, 234, 102);


  new TStatic(this, -1, "&Name:", 38, 48, 52, 18, WIDTH);
  name = new TEdit(this, IDC_NAME, buffer.nameBuffer,
                   108, 44, 144, 24, WIDTH, FALSE);
  name->EnableTransfer();


  new TStatic(this, -1, "&Address:", 38, 76, 58, 16, WIDTH);
  address = new TEdit(this, IDC_ADDRESS, buffer.addressBuffer,
                      108, 74, 144, 24, WIDTH, FALSE);
  address->EnableTransfer();


  new TStatic(this, -1, "&Telephone:", 32, 106, 70, 20, WIDTH);
  telephone = new TEdit(this, IDC_TELEPHONE, buffer.telephoneBuffer,
                        108, 104, 144, 24, WIDTH, FALSE);
  telephone->EnableTransfer();

  new TStatic(this, -1, "Other Info:", 280, 20, 114, 16, WIDTH);
  new TGroupBox(this, -1, "", 280, 36, 114, 102);


  home = new TRadioButton(this, IDC_HOME, "&Home",
                          290, 44, 64, 20, NULL);
```

```
  home->Attr.Style |= (WS_TABSTOP | WS_GROUP);
  home->EnableTransfer();


  business = new TRadioButton(this, IDC_BUSINESS, "&Business",
                              290, 64, 85, 20, NULL);
  business->Attr.Style |= WS_TABSTOP;
  business->EnableTransfer();


  usesOWL = new TCheckBox(this, IDC_USESOWL, "Uses O&WL",
                          290, 96, 88, 20, NULL);
  usesOWL->Attr.Style |= (WS_TABSTOP | WS_GROUP);
  usesOWL->EnableTransfer();


  usesTV = new TCheckBox(this, IDC_USESTV, "Uses T&V",
                         290, 114, 88, 20, NULL);
  usesTV->Attr.Style |= WS_TABSTOP;
  usesTV->EnableTransfer();


  new TButton(this, IDOK, "",     126, 172, 64, 40, TRUE);
  new TButton(this, IDCANCEL, "", 222, 172, 64, 40, FALSE);


  // make the TAB, shift-TAB and other dialog
  // accelerator keys work on the child controls
  EnableKBHandler();

  // enable transfer buffers
  SetTransferBuffer(&buffer);
}

BOOL TMyChild::EvEraseBkgnd(HDC hDC)
{
  // load the bitmap resource
  TBitmap bitmap(*GetModule(), "BITMAP_CHISELEDCOBALT");

  // paint the background
  TDC dc(hDC);
  dc.SelectObject(TBrush(bitmap) );
  dc.PatBlt(GetClientRect() );
  return TRUE;
}

void TMyChild::EvSetFocus(HWND)
{
  DefaultProcessing();
```

continues

Listing 11.13. continued

```
  ::SetFocus(name->HWindow);
}

void TMyChild::CmCancel()
{
  // close the window without reading
  // data into the transfer buffer
  CloseWindow();
}

void TMyChild::CmOk()
{
  // read data into the transfer buffer
  TransferData(tdGetData);
}

class TDialogAbout: public TDialog {

public:

  TDialogAbout(TWindow* AParent)
    : TDialog(AParent, "DIALOG_ABOUT") {}
};

class TMyClient : public TMDIClient {

protected:

  TMDIChild* InitChild();
  void CmHelpAbout();
  DECLARE_RESPONSE_TABLE(TMyClient);
};

DEFINE_RESPONSE_TABLE1(TMyClient, TMDIClient)
  EV_COMMAND(IDM_HELPABOUT, CmHelpAbout),
END_RESPONSE_TABLE;

TMDIChild* TMyClient::InitChild()
{
  return new TMyChild(*this);
}

void TMyClient::CmHelpAbout()
{
  TDialogAbout(this).Execute();
}

class TUserApplication: public TApplication {
```

```
public:

  TUserApplication()
      : TApplication("MDI Window Controls") {}
  void InitMainWindow()
  { MainWindow = new TMDIFrame("Using controls in MDI child windows",
                              "MENU_MAIN", *new TMyClient);
    EnableBWCC();  // so groups show up as gray
  }
};

int OwlMain(int, char**)
{
  return TUserApplication().Run();
}
```

MDICTL demonstrates the use of a transfer buffer with an MDI child window. The variable `buffer` defines a transfer field for each control that will participate in transfer operations. The transfer buffer is initialized in the constructor for `TMyChildTransferBuffer`. The intialization is performed only once, when the program is started, not every time a dialog box is opened. Note that every item displayed in the MDI child is created explicitly, including objects of type `TGroupBox` and `TStatic`, which are ordinarily defined only in resource files, with no OWL C++ counterparts. Child controls created inside OWL windows that aren't dialog boxes have their transfer buffering mechanism disabled by default. To enable it, the function `EnableTransfer()` must be called for each child control that has a field defined for it in the transfer buffer.

Objects derived from `TWindow` do not have keyboard handling enabled by default. Because the MDI child windows in MDICTL are derived from`TWindow`, the Tab and Arrow keys are ignored unless keyboard handling is enabled. To enable keyboard handling, the function `EnableKBHandler()` is called in the constructor for `TMDIChild`.

When the MDI child window receives the input focus, the focus must be passed to the first control in tab order whose WS_TABSTOP bit is set. The edit box titled Name is the first control. To pass the focus to the edit box, the WM_SETFOCUS message is processed with the code

```
void TMyChild::EvSetFocus(HWND)
{
  DefaultProcessing();
  ::SetFocus(name->HWindow);
}
```

The function `DefaultProcessing()` is called to allow default processing of the WM_SETFOCUS message, and then the focus is transferred to the Name edit box.

When the Cancel button is clicked, the MDI child window is closed without updating the transfer buffer. When the OK button is clicked, the child control data is copied to the transfer buffer without closing the window, like this:

```
void TMyChild::CmOk()
{
  // read data into the transfer buffer
  TransferData(tdGetData);
}
```

The function `TransferData()` iterates over all the child windows of the given window. For each child window that has its transfer buffering mechanism enabled, the transfer buffer is updated. Figure 11.8 shows how MDICTL looks after opening a few MDI child windows:

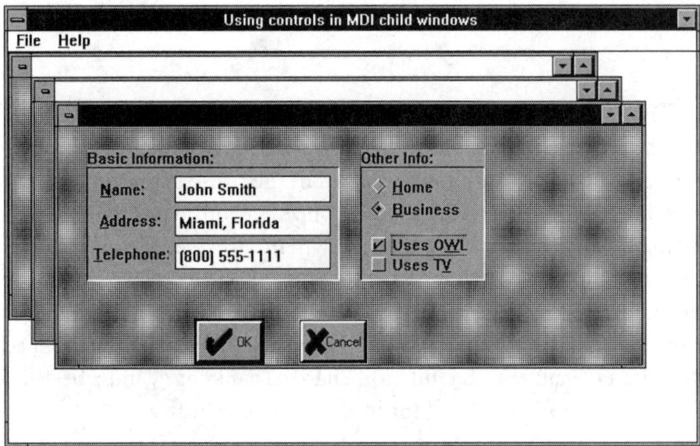

Figure 11.8. How MDICTL looks after opening a few child windows.

When you click the OK button, the transfer buffer is updated. Because all the MDI child windows in MDICTL use the same transfer buffer, any other MDI child windows you open will have the same data as the transfer buffer.

Using a Dialog Box as an MDI Child

Developing MDI child windows with controls, as shown in the previous section, is not convenient when you need to deal with many controls, primarily because the exact position of each control must be determined empirically, by compiling and running a program. A dialog box is much easier to develop because you can use Resource Workshop to quickly draw and adjust all the child controls without having to write any code.

OWL 2.5 supports the use of dialog boxes as client windows of frame windows. MDI child windows are encapsulated in class `TMDIChild`, which is derived from `TFrameWindow`. To make MDI child windows out of dialog boxes, you create a `TMDIChild` window and pass a pointer to the client dialog box, using code like this:

```
class TMyDialog : public TDialog {};
class TMyClient : public TMDIClient {};

// assume MyMDIClient points to a TMyClient object
return new TMDIChild(*MyMDIClient, "My Caption", new TMyDialog(NULL),
TRUE);
```

The first parameter to `TMDIChild` is a reference to the MDI client window in your application. The second parameter is the title of the MDI child window. The third parameter is a pointer to the dialog box that will fill the client area of the MDI child window. The last parameter tells OWL to make the MDI child window shrink down to the size of the client dialog box.

Dialog boxes used inside `TMDIChild` (or any other type of frame windows) are passed a NULL pointer for the parent window. The problem is that when you create a frame window like a `TMDIChild`, you must pass a pointer to the dialog box to use for the client area, but because you're inside the constructor for the frame window, you don't yet have a pointer to it that you can pass to the child dialog box. Passing a NULL parent pointer to the dialog box doesn't mean the dialog box has no parent. As it turns out, OWL goes and determines the actual parent window of the dialog box, and then sets the dialog's parent to be the `TMDIChild` window.

The dialog used in the client area of MDI child windows (and also of ordinary frame windows) must have the WS_CHILD style. The caption of the dialog box is ignored, and OWL uses the title string of the `TMDIChild` window for the caption. I wrote a short application called MDIDLG that demonstrates how to use dialog boxes in MDI child windows. Figure 11.9 shows the properties of the dialog box used in MDIDLG.

You can use both regular and Borland-style dialogs to fill the child window. OWL ignores the border style bits specified for the dialog box, and always displays the dialog box in an enclosing frame window that has a thick frame and a caption bar. The dialog's font settings are not important here, and can be set to anything you want. The dialog box is created as a child window to make Windows clip the dialog to the client area of the parent window and to make the dialog box track the parent if the parent is resized or moved. Make sure that you set the turn on the Visible attribute for the dialog box, otherwise you'll get MDI child windows that have nothing inside them.

Running MDIDLG, you get MDI child windows shown in Figure 11.10.

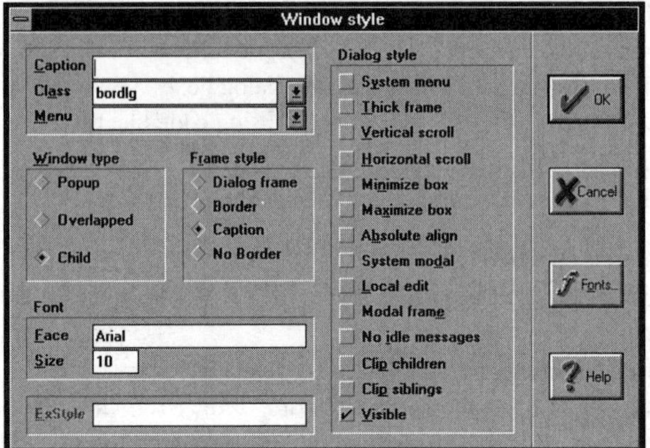

Figure 11.9. The properties of the dialog box used in MDIDLG.

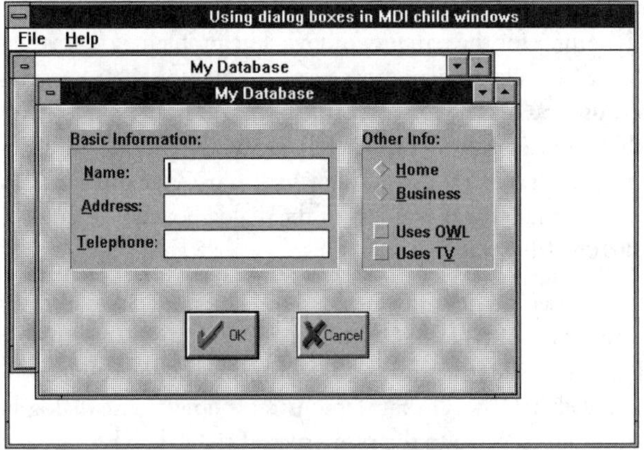

Figure 11.10. The dialog boxes used in MDI child windows with MDIDLG.

Listing 11.14 shows the complete code for MDIDLG.

Listing 11.14. The complete code for MDIDLG, an OWL application showing how to use dialog boxes as MDI child windows.

```
// this application demonstrates the use a dialog box as
// an MDI child window

#include <owl\dialog.h>
#include <owl\mdi.h>
#include <owl\applicat.h>
```

```
#include <owl\edit.h>
#include <owl\button.h>
#include <owl\radiobut.h>
#include <owl\checkbox.h>

// menu commands
const int IDM_HELPABOUT = 201;

// Dialog box child control IDs
const int
  IDC_NAME      = 101,
  IDC_ADDRESS   = 102,
  IDC_TELEPHONE = 103,
  IDC_HOME      = 104,
  IDC_BUSINESS  = 105,
  IDC_USESOWL   = 106,
  IDC_USESTV    = 107;

const int EDITLENGTH   = 80;

class TDialogPhone : public TDialog {

  TEdit*        name;
  TEdit*        address;
  TEdit*        telephone;
  TRadioButton* home;
  TRadioButton* business;
  TCheckBox*    usesOWL;
  TCheckBox*    usesTV;

public:

  TDialogPhone(TWindow*);
  BOOL PreProcessMsg(MSG& msg) {
    // translate MDI accelerator keys
    if (Parent->Parent->PreProcessMsg(msg) )
      return TRUE;
    // translate ordinary accelerator keys
    return TDialog::PreProcessMsg(msg);
  }
};

TDialogPhone::TDialogPhone(TWindow* parent)
            : TDialog(parent, "DIALOG_DATAENTRY")
{
  name      = new TEdit(this, IDC_NAME, EDITLENGTH);
  address   = new TEdit(this, IDC_ADDRESS, EDITLENGTH);
  telephone = new TEdit(this, IDC_TELEPHONE, EDITLENGTH);
```

continues

Listing 11.14. continued

```
  home      = new TRadioButton(this, IDC_HOME, NULL);
  business  = new TRadioButton(this, IDC_BUSINESS, NULL);
  usesOWL   = new TCheckBox(this, IDC_USESOWL, NULL);
  usesTV    = new TCheckBox(this, IDC_USESTV, NULL);
}

class TDialogAbout: public TDialog {

public:

  TDialogAbout(TWindow* AParent)
      : TDialog(AParent, "DIALOG_ABOUT") {}
};

class TMyClient : public TMDIClient {

protected:

  TMDIChild* InitChild();
  void CmHelpAbout();
  DECLARE_RESPONSE_TABLE(TMyClient);
};

DEFINE_RESPONSE_TABLE1(TMyClient, TMDIClient)
  EV_COMMAND(IDM_HELPABOUT, CmHelpAbout),
END_RESPONSE_TABLE;

TMDIChild* TMyClient::InitChild()
{
  return new TMDIChild(*this, "My Database", new TDialogPhone(NULL),
TRUE);
}

void TMyClient::CmHelpAbout()
{
  TDialogAbout(this).Execute();
}

class TUserApplication: public TApplication {

public:

  TUserApplication() : TApplication("MDI Window Controls") {}
  void InitMainWindow()
  { MainWindow = new TMDIFrame("Using dialog boxes in MDI child
windows",
                                "MENU_MAIN", *new TMyClient);
  }
};
```

```
int OwlMain(int, char**)
{
  return TUserApplication().Run();
}
```

OWL takes care of most keyboard handling details for you. If you run MDIDLG, you'll see that the Tab key, the Arrow keys, and the other dialog box accelerator keys all work as you would expect them to. If you type Alt-N, the focus moves to the Name field. Typing Alt-H moves the focus to the Home radio button, and checks it. I didn't put any code to support reading and writing the child controls in the dialog boxes, to avoid cluttering up the code with details.

There is one important thing to note about dialog boxes put inside `TMDIChild` windows: the standard OWL keyboard handling for dialog boxes doesn't translate MDI accelerator keys, like Ctrl-F4 and Ctrl-F6. To make a dialog box translate these keys correctly, you need to override the base class function `TDialog::PreProcess()` with a new function, as follows:

```
BOOL TMyDialog::PreProcessMsg(MSG& msg)
{
  // translate MDI accelerator keys
  if (Parent->Parent->PreProcessMsg(msg) )
     return TRUE;
  // translate ordinary accelerator keys
  return TDialog::PreProcessMsg(msg);
}
```

The function calls the parent's `PreProcessMsg()` function. For a dialog box used inside the client area of a `TMDIChild` window, the parent is the `TMDIChild` window, and the parent's parent is the `TMDIClient` window. The `PreProcessMsg()` member function of `TMDIClient` attempts to translate MDI accelerator keys. If it is successful, it returns a TRUE value to prevent further keyboard handling. If no MDI accelerator keys were found to translate, you need to call the keyboard handling function `TDialog::PreProcess()`. This function translates both normal accelerator keys (for menu commands and dialog box controls) and dialog box navigation keys.

If you open a few MDI child windows in MDIDLG, you can experiment a bit with the menu commands, the mouse, and the keyboard. The dialog box navigation keys, such as Tab and Shift-Tab, work normally. The dialog accelerator keys are also correctly translated.

There is a small note to add about the Windows dialog box manager and accelerator keys used in MDIDLG. When you press Alt-N, the dialog box manager looks for a child control whose WS_TABSTOP bit is set and whose caption has an &N in it. If it finds such a control, it gives the focus to it. Because static controls are not allowed to have the input focus, the manager looks for the next child control in tab order with the WS_TABSTOP bit set. The child right after the static field Name is the edit box right next to it, so Windows gives the focus to the edit box.

Menus in MDI Applications

Menus are usually used to enter commands, such as `File ¦ New`, `Edit ¦ Cut`, and so on, but menus aren't always limited to input. Windows allows you to change menu items, by adding check marks, bitmaps or highlights, to allow menus to provide status information. For example, MDI applications have a pull-down menu called Window, under which a list of MDI open child windows is shown. The active child window is indicated by a check mark. In addition to checking or graying menu items, you also have the option of adding or deleting menu commands and of replacing entire menus. There are two ways MDI child windows can change the main window menu: by replacing the main menu entirely with a new one, and by merging a menu to the existing one. I'll discuss each method separately.

Replacing the Main Menu

When the user switches between MDI child windows using the mouse or the keyboard, Windows sends WM_MDIACTIVATE messages to the MDI children, indicating which window is being deactivated and which activated. It is a simple matter to intercept the WM_MDIACTIVATE message and make changes to the menu based on the MDI child window being activated. OWL has the function `TFrameWindow::AssignMenu()`, which allows you to change the menu of the main window. I wrote a short application called MDIMENU to demonstrate the process. The program allows you to open a series of MDI child windows. The main menu looks like Figure 11.11.

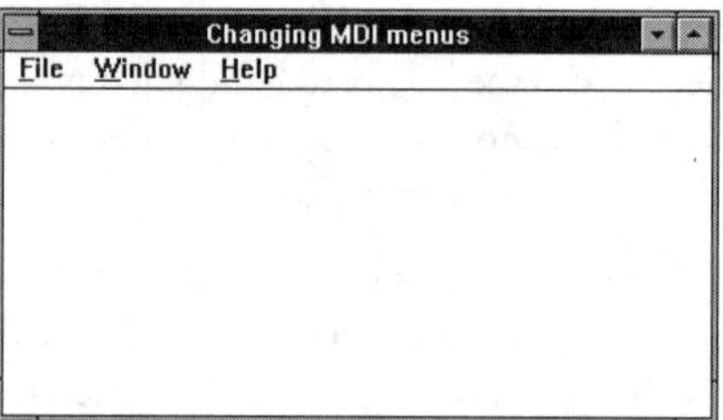

Figure 11.11. The main menu of MDIMENU before opening child windows.

MDIMENU has two types of child windows. After opening a child window of type 1, the main menu is changed to look like Figure 11.12.

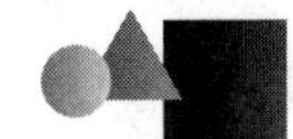

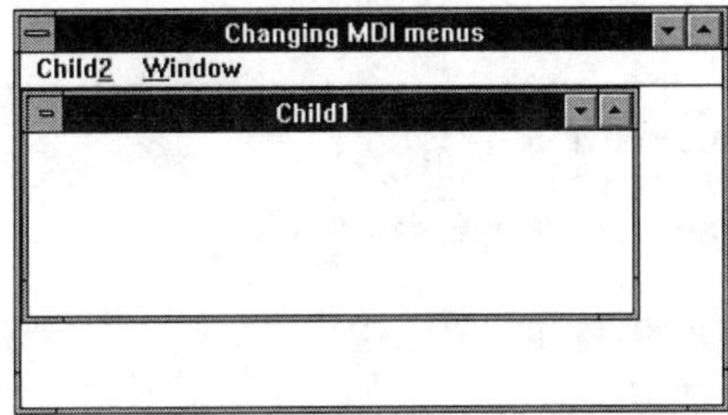

Figure 11.12. The main menu of MDIMENU after opening a type 1 child window.

After opening a child window of type 2, the main menu is changed to look like Figure 11.13.

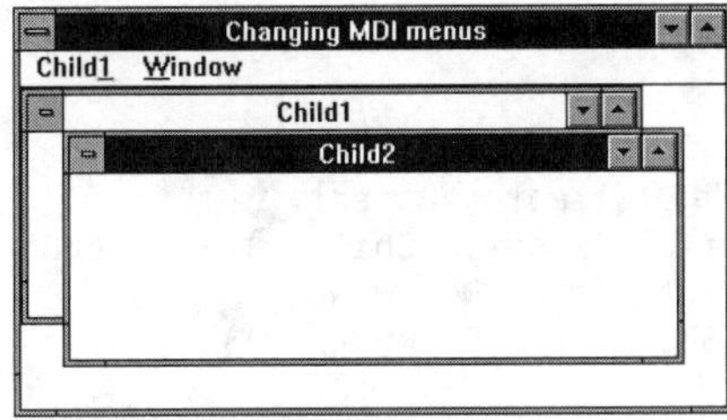

Figure 11.13. The main menu of MDIMENU after opening a type 2 child window.

If you change the active child window, the main menu is also changed. Closing all child windows makes the menu revert to the original menu, shown in Figure 11.11. The code is contained on the companion disk, in the file MDIMENU.CPP, which looks like that shown in Listing 11.15.

Listing 11.15. The code for MDIMENU, an application whose MDI child windows load their own main menus.

```
// this application demonstrates how MDI child
// windows can replace the main menu.

#include <owl\dialog.h>
#include <owl\mdi.h>
#include <owl\applicat.h>

// menu commands
const int
```

continues

Listing 11.15. continued

```
  IDM_FILENEWCHILD1 = 101,
  IDM_FILENEWCHILD2 = 102,
  IDM_HELPABOUT     = 201;

class TDialogAbout: public TDialog {

public:

  TDialogAbout(TWindow* AParent)
    : TDialog(AParent, "DIALOG_ABOUT") {}
};

class TMyChild1: public TMDIChild {

  char* oldMenu;

public:

  TMyChild1(TMDIClient& AParent)
    : TMDIChild(AParent, "Child1") {oldMenu = 0;}
  void EvMDIActivate(HWND, HWND);
  DECLARE_RESPONSE_TABLE(TMyChild1);
};

DEFINE_RESPONSE_TABLE1(TMyChild1, TMDIChild)
  EV_WM_MDIACTIVATE,
END_RESPONSE_TABLE;

void TMyChild1::EvMDIActivate(HWND activated, HWND)
{
  TFrameWindow* frame = TYPESAFE_DOWNCAST(Parent->Parent,
TFrameWindow);
  PRECONDITION(frame);

  if (HWindow == activated) {
    // window is being acivated
    oldMenu = strnewdup(frame->Attr.Menu);
    frame->AssignMenu("MENU_CHILD1");
  }

  else {
    CHECK(oldMenu);
    frame->AssignMenu(oldMenu);
    delete oldMenu;
  }
}

class TMyChild2: public TMDIChild {
```

```
  char* oldMenu;

public:

  TMyChild2(TMDIClient& AParent)
      : TMDIChild(AParent, "Child2") {oldMenu = 0;}
  void EvMDIActivate(HWND, HWND);
  DECLARE_RESPONSE_TABLE(TMyChild2);
};

DEFINE_RESPONSE_TABLE1(TMyChild2, TMDIChild)
  EV_WM_MDIACTIVATE,
END_RESPONSE_TABLE;


void TMyChild2::EvMDIActivate(HWND activated, HWND)
{
  TFrameWindow* frame = TYPESAFE_DOWNCAST(Parent->Parent,
TFrameWindow);
  PRECONDITION(frame);

  if (HWindow == activated) {
    // window is being acivated
    oldMenu = strnewdup(frame->Attr.Menu);
    frame->AssignMenu("MENU_CHILD2");
  }

  else {
    CHECK(oldMenu);
    frame->AssignMenu(oldMenu);
    delete oldMenu;
  }
}

class TWindowClient: public TMDIClient {

public:

  void CmHelpAbout();
  void CmFileNewChild1();
  void CmFileNewChild2();

  DECLARE_RESPONSE_TABLE(TWindowClient);
};

DEFINE_RESPONSE_TABLE1(TWindowClient, TMDIClient)
  EV_COMMAND(IDM_FILENEWCHILD1, CmFileNewChild1),
  EV_COMMAND(IDM_FILENEWCHILD2, CmFileNewChild2),
  EV_COMMAND(IDM_HELPABOUT, CmHelpAbout),
END_RESPONSE_TABLE;
```

continues

Listing 11.15. continued

```
void TWindowClient::CmFileNewChild1()
{
  TWindow* window = new TMyChild1(*this);
  window->Create();
}

void TWindowClient::CmFileNewChild2()
{
  TWindow* window = new TMyChild2(*this);
  window->Create();
}

void TWindowClient::CmHelpAbout()
{
  TDialogAbout(this).Execute();
}

class TUserApplication: public TApplication {

public:

  TUserApplication()
    : TApplication("MDI Demo") {}
  virtual void InitMainWindow()
    { MainWindow = new TMDIFrame("Changing MDI menus",
                                 "MENU_MAIN",
                                 *new TWindowClient);
    }
};

int OwlMain(int, char**)
{
  return TUserApplication().Run();
}
```

MDIMENU uses the WM_MDIACTIVATE message to switch menus, using the code in Listing 11.16.

Listing 11.16. The code that changes the main menu in the child windows of MDIMENU.

```
void TMyChild1::EvMDIActivate(HWND activated, HWND)
{
  TFrameWindow* frame = TYPESAFE_DOWNCAST(Parent->Parent,
TFrameWindow);
  PRECONDITION(frame);
```

```
  if (HWindow == activated) {
    // window is being acivated
    oldMenu = strnewdup(frame->Attr.Menu);
    frame->AssignMenu("MENU_CHILD1");
  }

  else {
    CHECK(oldMenu);
    frame->AssignMenu(oldMenu);
    delete oldMenu;
  }
}
```

The name of the menu being replaced is saved, so the menu can be restored when the MDI child window is deactivated or closed. The code that actually changes menus is:

```
frame->AssignMenu("MENU_CHILD1");
```

`AssignMenu()` is a member function of `TFrameWindow` and takes a resource identifier (either an integer or a string) as a parameter. The function discards any previously assigned menus, destroying the menu resource. You don't have to redraw the menu after an `AssignMenu()` call, because OWL updates the menu for you.

Merging Menus

Often MDI applications have a default menu that is displayed before any child windows are opened. For example, in Resource Workshop, the default menu has only the File and Help pop-up menus. Opening the Dialog Box editor, additional pop-up menus appear. OWL has built-in code to allow you to handle situations like these through a process of menu merging, used also in OLE 2.0.

OLE 2.0 Menu Merging

Before describing the OWL menu-merging mechanism, you need to know a few concepts of OLE 2.0 menu handling. With OLE 2.0, you can have OLE containers and OLE embedded objects. Containers are applications that use embedded OLE objects. For example, Word for Windows is an OLE container, and MS Draw is an OLE miniserver object that you can embed inside a Word for Windows document. OLE 2.0 has a mechanism called *in-place activation*, which refers to an embedded object being activated without opening its own window, but right in the middle of the container application's window. When an embedded object is in-place activated, it makes changes to the container application's menu bar, adding commands that are supported by the embedded object.

For example, activating an MS Draw object in a Word for Windows document results in pull-down menus like Draw and Colors appearing on the Word for Windows menu bar. These menus are added through the OLE 2.0 in-place activation menu-merging commands.

For the purposes of menu merging, OLE 2.0 organizes pop-up menus into groups, where each group can contain one or more menus. OLE uses the following six standard groups:

1. The File Group, which contains standard commands like `New`, `Open`, and `Exit`.
2. The Edit Group, with commands like `Cut`, `Copy`, and `Paste`.
3. The Container group, which includes all the non-standard pop-up menus used in container applications. For example, Word for Windows, which is a container application, has the following pop-up menus: `File`, `Edit`, `View`, `Insert`, `Format`, `Tools`, `Table`, `Window`, `Help`. The menus `View`, `Insert`, `Format`, `Tools`, and `Table` all belong to the Container Group. The others belong to other Groups.
4. The Object Group, which includes pop-up menus that an in-place, activated, embedded object can merge with the menu items of the container application. Using the Word for Windows example again, activating an MS Draw object results in the `Draw` and `Colors` pop-up menus being merged with the Word for Windows menu bar. The `Draw` and `Colors` pop-up menus belong to the Object Group.
5. The Window Group, which includes commands like `Tile`, `Cascade`, and `Close All`.
6. The Help Group, with commands like `Index`, `Context`, and `About`.

Container applications create their own menu bar, typically using the File, Edit, Container, and Help groups. The container group is where all the container-specific menus are placed. Embedded OLE objects can merge their own menus into the container menu's Object group, which the container doesn't use. In-place activated OLE objects can not only merge menus into the container's menu bar, but also change or even remove items from the container's menu.

How OWL Merges Menus

OWL is not OLE, but it does support an equivalent menu merging mechanism, based on the OWL class `TMenuDescr`, which encapsulates menus. To get menus to merge, you need to create the main menu and the child menus using code like this:

```
SetMenuDescr(TMenuDescr("MENU_NAME", 0, 1, 0, 0, 0, 0));
```

The parameters passed to `TMenuDescr` indicate a menu name and a number of menu fields. Each of the six integers references an OLE 2.0 menu group. The first integer is for the File Group, the second for the Edit Group, and so on. The value of the integer indicates how many pop-up menus MENU_NAME wants to merge in at a given position. Table 11.7 shows the menu groups indicated by each integer parameter.

Table 11.7. The Menu groups indicated by the integer parameters passed to `TMenuDescr`.

Integer Parameter	*Menu Group*
1	File Group
2	Edit Group
3	Container Group
4	Object Group
5	Window Group
6	Help Group

To see how the `TMenuDescr` parameters work, assume that you have the menu called MENU_NAME, defined as shown in Listing 11.17.

Listing 11.17. A sample menu to be used with `TMenuDescr`.

```
MENU_NAME MENU {
 POPUP "Child&2" {
  MENUITEM "&New", 102
 }

 POPUP "&Options"{
  MENUITEM "Option &1", 110
  MENUITEM "Option &2", 111
 }
}
```

Assume that the main menu was defined as shown in Listing 11.18.

Listing 11.18. The main menu used in a menu merge.

```
MENU_MAIN MENU {
 POPUP "&File" {
  MENUITEM "New Child&1", 101
  MENUITEM "New Child&2", 102
```

continues

Listing 11.18. continued

```
  MENUITEM "E&xit", 24310
 }

 POPUP "&Help" {
  MENUITEM "&About...", 201
 }
}
```

The main menu would be set up in the MDI frame window with the code:

```
MainWindow->SetMenuDescr(TMenuDescr("MENU_MAIN", 1, 0, 0, 0, 0, 1));
```

The code shows that the menu has one pop-up menu to be inserted at the first location (where the File Group normally is), and a second pop-up to be inserted as the Help menu. If a child window uses the code

```
SetMenuDescr(TMenuDescr("MENU_NAME", 0, 2, 0, 0, 0, 0));
```

to install its menu, then OWL will merge the two pop-up menus in MENU_NAME into MENU_MAIN, so that there are two pop-up menus from MENU_NAME that appear where the Edit menu normally is. I wrote a short application called MERGEMN that shows how menu merging works. The complete code for MERGEMN.CPP is shown in Listing 11.19.

Listing 11.19. MERGEMN, an application demonstrating merged menus.

```
// this application demonstrates how to merge MDI child
// menus with the main menu.

#include <owl\dialog.h>
#include <owl\mdi.h>
#include <owl\applicat.h>

// menu commands
const int
  IDM_FILENEWCHILD1 = 101,
  IDM_FILENEWCHILD2 = 102,
  IDM_OPTION1       = 110,
  IDM_OPTION2       = 111,
  IDM_HELPABOUT     = 201;

class TDialogAbout: public TDialog {

public:
```

```
  TDialogAbout(TWindow* AParent)
      : TDialog(AParent, "DIALOG_ABOUT") {}
};

class TMyChild1: public TMDIChild {

public:

  TMyChild1(TMDIClient& AParent)
      : TMDIChild(AParent, "Child1")
      { SetMenuDescr(TMenuDescr("MENU_CHILD1", 0, 2, 0, 0, 0, 0)); }
};

class TMyChild2: public TMDIChild {

public:

  TMyChild2(TMDIClient& AParent)
      : TMDIChild(AParent, "Child2")
      { SetMenuDescr(TMenuDescr("MENU_CHILD2", 0, 1, 0, 0, 0, 0)); }
};

class TWindowClient: public TMDIClient {

public:

  void CmHelpAbout();
  void CmFileNewChild1();
  void CmFileNewChild2();

  void CmOption1()
      { MessageBox("You selected option 1", "Menu Selection"); }
  void CmOption2()
      { MessageBox("You selected option 2", "Menu Selection"); }

  DECLARE_RESPONSE_TABLE(TWindowClient);
};

DEFINE_RESPONSE_TABLE1(TWindowClient, TMDIClient)
  EV_COMMAND(IDM_FILENEWCHILD1, CmFileNewChild1),
  EV_COMMAND(IDM_FILENEWCHILD2, CmFileNewChild2),
  EV_COMMAND(IDM_OPTION1, CmOption1),
  EV_COMMAND(IDM_OPTION2, CmOption2),
  EV_COMMAND(IDM_HELPABOUT, CmHelpAbout),
END_RESPONSE_TABLE;

void TWindowClient::CmFileNewChild1()
{
  TWindow* window = new TMyChild1(*this);
```

continues

Listing 11.19. continued

```
  window->Create();
}

void TWindowClient::CmFileNewChild2()
{
  TWindow* window = new TMyChild2(*this);
  window->Create();
}

void TWindowClient::CmHelpAbout()
{
  TDialogAbout(this).Execute();
}

class TUserApplication: public TApplication {

public:

  TUserApplication()
      : TApplication("MDI Demo") {}
  virtual void InitMainWindow();
};


void TUserApplication::InitMainWindow()
{
  MainWindow = new TMDIFrame("Merging child menus",
                        "MENU_MAIN", *new TWindowClient);
  MainWindow->SetMenuDescr(TMenuDescr("MENU_MAIN", 1, 0, 0, 0, 0, 1));
}

int OwlMain(int, char**)
{
  return TUserApplication().Run();
}
```

The initial main menu displayed by MERGEMN looks like Figure 11.14.

MERGEMN allows you to open two kinds of MDI child windows, each with a different menu. Opening the first type of MDI child results in the main menu looking like Figure 11.15.

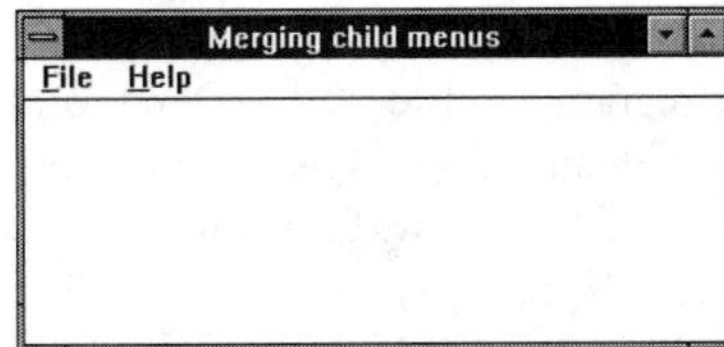

Figure 11.14. The menu shown in MERGEMN when no child windows are open.

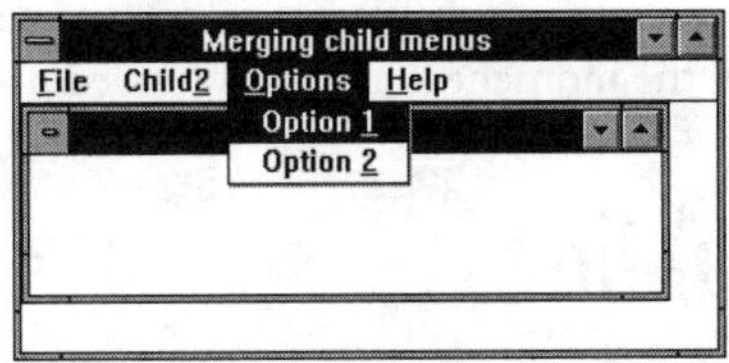

Figure 11.15. The menu shown in MERGEMN when one of the MDI child windows is open.

Figure 11.15 shows one of the pop-up menus merged into the main menu by the MDI child window. Opening the second type of MDI child produces the main menu in Figure 11.16.

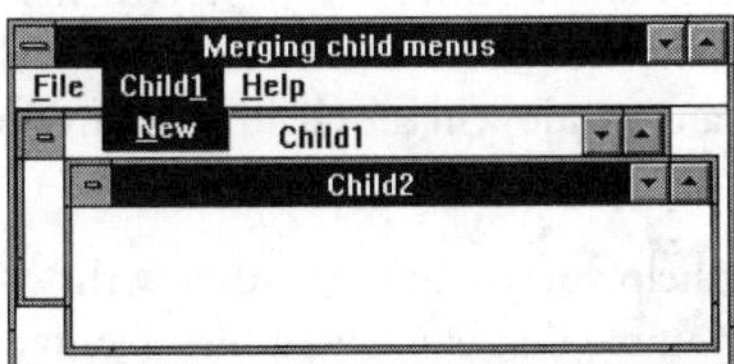

Figure 11.16. The menu shown in MERGEMN when the second MDI child window type is opened.

Figure 11.16 shows the pop-up menu merged by the MDI child window into the main menu. All your application code has to do to support menu merging is create menus using `TMenuDescr` objects and use the function `SetMenuDescr()`. OWL automatically merges the menus when necessary, deletes unused menus, and handles the switching of menus when MDI child windows are activated.

Changing the State of Menu Items

Menus are often used to convey status information to the user. By checking an item, an application is telling the user the state of variable, or a mode the system is in. By graying menus items out, the user is informed about which commands are inaccessible in the current mode of the program. Consider an MDI editor, like BCW, whose Edit pop-up menu contains the items Cut and Copy. These items need to be grayed out when no text is selected in the active child window. Opening a new window should show the Edit menu items initially grayed. If the user types into the window, then selects some text, the Edit menu items should be enabled. If the user opens multiple child windows and switches among them, the Edit menu items should reflect only the state of the active child. Given the multitude of ways users can switch among child windows, select text, open and close windows, and so on, it is much simpler to defer any decisions about the state of the Edit menu items until the moment the menu is pulled down.

Command Enabling

OWL handles the enabling and disabling of menu commands through a built-in process that uses events response tables and objects of class `TCommandEnabler`. When the user selects a menu using the keyboard or the mouse, Windows sends a WM_INITMENUPOPUP message to the main window of your application, which is an object derived from class `TFrameWindow`. OWL searches the current *command chain* for handlers for each entry in the menu. The command chain is the chain of windows leading from the main window down to the active window. OWL enables menu items for which handlers are found. For the others, a WM_COMMAND_ENABLE message is sent down the command chain. WM_COMMMAND_ENABLE is a message generated by OWL, not Windows. If any window in the chain contains a handler for this message, the handler is called to allow it to explicitly enable or disable a menu item.

An example may help you to understand how the WM_COMMAND_ENABLE message is handled. Assume that you have a menu item called Edit | Cut. If you have an edit window open, it will have a handler for the Edit | Cut command, so OWL would find this handler and automatically enable the Edit | Cut menu command. Your application may want to override this default behavior and disable the Edit | Cut menu command if no text is selected in the editor window. If your editor class was a class called `TMyWindow`, it would be declared something like this:

```
class TMyWindow : public TWindow {

  // ...

protected:

  void      CmEditCut();
  void      CmEditCutEnable(TCommandEnabler& commandHandler);

  DECLARE_RESPONSE_TABLE(TMyWindow);
};
```

```
DEFINE_RESPONSE_TABLE1(TMyWindow, TWindow)
  // ...
  EV_COMMAND(CM_EDITCUT, CmEditCut),
  EV_COMMAND_ENABLE(CM_EDITCUT, CmEditCutEnable),
END_RESPONSE_TABLE;
```

The same menu command, CM_EDITCUT, is associated with two different entries in the response table. The `CmEditCut()` handler would do the actual cutting of text to the clipboard. It would have code looking something like this:

```
void TMyWindow::CmEditCut()
{
  if (text_selected)
      // cut the text to the clipboard
}
```

The command enabler handler would look something like this:

```
void TMyWindow::CmEditCutEnable(TCommandEnabler& commandHandler)
{
  if (text_selected)
      commandHandler.Enable(TRUE);
  else
      commandHandler.Enable(FALSE);
}
```

Command enabling affects not only entries in your application's main menu but also items on the toolbar created with class `TControlBar`. After all, toolbars are simply bitmapped accelerators for menu commands.

Adding Checkmarks to Menu Commands

With OWL, it is extremely easy to add or remove checkmarks to menu commands. The best way is to use a `TMenu` object. You can create a `TMenu` object for the menu of a `TFrameWindow`-derived class using the code

```
TMenu menu(*this);
```

Using the `TMenu`, you can call its member function `CheckMenuItem()`. Assume that you had the menu item Font | Bold, which selected a bold font in an MDI editor application. You might want to gray the command out if the editor was running a spell checker. You would also want to toggle a checkmark next to the Bold menu command each time the user selected it. If you used a class `TMyWindow`, it would be declared like this:

```
class TMyWindow : public TMDIFrame {

  BOOL fontBold;
  // ...
```

```
protected:

  void      CmFontBold();
  void      CmFontBoldEnable(TCommandEnabler& commandHandler);

  DECLARE_RESPONSE_TABLE(TMyWindow);
};

DEFINE_RESPONSE_TABLE1(TMyWindow, TWindow)
  // ...
  EV_COMMAND(CM_FONT_BOLD, CmFontBold),
  EV_COMMAND_ENABLE(CM_FONTBOLD, CmFontBoldEnable),
END_RESPONSE_TABLE;
```

the code would look like this:

```
void TMyFrameWindow::CmFontBold()
{
  TMenu menu(*this);
  fontBold = !fontBold;
  menu.CheckMenuItem(CM_FONTBOLD, fontBold ? MF_CHECKED :
MF_UNCHECKED);
  DrawMenuBar();
}
```

After adding or removing checkmarks, remember to call `DrawMenuBar()`, otherwise your changes won't show up on the menu! Many OWL MDI applications handle main menu commands in a class derived from `TMDIClient`, which is not derived from `TFrameWindow`. With `TMDIClient`-derived classes, you must use the parent `TMDIFrame` window to construct the `TMenu` object. Assume that you had a class `TMyClient` declared like this:

```
class TMyClient : public TMDIClient {

protected:

  void CmFontBold();
  DECLARE_RESPONSE_TABLE(TMyClient);
};

DEFINE_RESPONSE_TABLE1(TMyClient, TMDIClient)
  EV_COMMAND(CM_FONTBOLD, CmFontBold),
END_RESPONSE_TABLE;
```

Then, inside the member function `TMyClient::CmFontBold()` you would create the `TMenu` object like this:

```
void TMyClient::CmFontBold()
{
  TMenu menu(*(this->Parent) );
  // ...
}
```

I started this chapter by stating that MDI applications are almost trivial to create under OWL. By looking at the examples throughout the chapter, you can see how little code is actually required. `AppExpert` will often create 90 percent of the code needed in simple programs. Switching an application from SDI to MDI is an easy task under OWL. In many cases, all you need to do is the following:

1. Derive the main frame window from `TMDIFrame` rather than `TFrameWindow`.
2. Derive the window used to fill the client area from `TMDIChild` rather than `TWindow`.

Most applications use a tool bar and status bar, requiring the main frame window to be derived from `TDecoratedMDIFrame` rather than `TMDIFrame`. Switching an application from MDI to SDI is usually a bit more complicated than going from SDI to MDI, because the MDI application will often have code that is designed to deal with multiple child windows—something that is inapplicable to SDI programs.

Variations on a ListBox

ListBoxes are extremely useful child controls that are often used to present arrays of strings. The standard Windows ListBox shows the strings in a single vertical column, with a vertical scroll bar to browse through the strings, should they not all be visible in the ListBox. There are situations in which a standard ListBox is inadequate for displaying information. Here are just a few:

- The information has an inherent structure to it, requiring some kind of formatted output.
- Multiple columns of data are required.
- Horizontal and vertical scrolling are required.

In this chapter, I'll show ways to modify the standard ListBox, giving it the flexibility needed to solve problems frequently encountered. Following the techniques shown, you can add additional customizations to fit your own needs.

Tab Stops

Often data is presented in tabular format. The items on an invoice and the names in a telephone directory are examples of tabular data. It is relatively easy to create a ListBox to display data in tabular format, with the data in each column separated by tab characters. I wrote a short application called TABLIST to show the details. TABLIST displays a dialog box that displays the items of an invoice, using a multicolumn ListBox, as shown in the following figure:

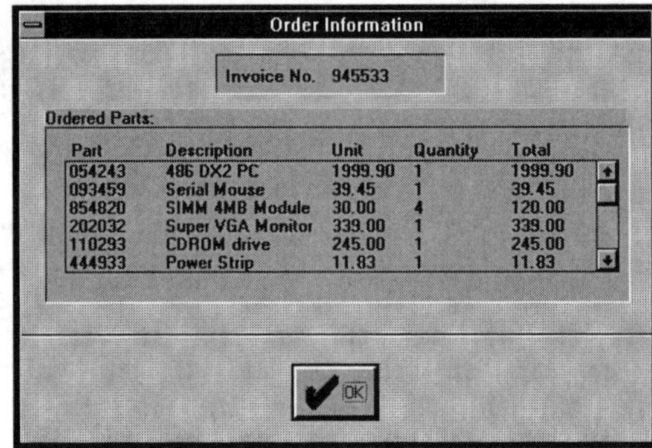

Figure 12.1. The multicolumn ListBox displayed by the OWL application TABLIST.

To create a multicolumn ListBox, you need to add tab stops to the control. Assuming that the dialog box is developed using Resource Workshop, you need to click the Tab Stops check box on the property dialog box for the ListBox. If creating the control without a resource file, you need to set the `LBS_USETABSTOPS` style bit for the ListBox.

Setting the Tab Stops

Once tab stops have been enabled, the next step is to set up an array of integers, indicating the positions of the tab stops to be used in the ListBox. Each integer entry must be a tab stop position expressed in units known as *horizontal dialog units.* A horizontal dialog unit is 1/4 of a dialog base unit, which in turn is the width of the average character in the font selected for the dialog box. The easiest way to determine the tab stop positions is to use Resource Workshop. Using the `Options | Preferences` menu, select Dialog Units for the status line. Doing so, you can position the title string for each ListBox column, and simply read the starting coordinate for each column off the status line. That's how I created the TABLIST application. Changing the font for the dialog box will require you to change all the tab stop values in the tab array, so select a dialog box first, then position the title strings and plug the column starting coordinates into the tab array.

Having created an array of tab stops, you must tell the ListBox to use the tabs, with an `LB_SETTABSTOPS` message. Assuming that you created an OWL `TListBox` object, pointed to by the variable ListBox, you would set the tab stops using the code:

```
WPARAM wParam = sizeof(tabStops) / sizeof(int);
int okay = info->SendMessage(LB_SETTABSTOPS, wParam,
(LPARAM) &tabStops);
```

The value returned by `SendMessage()` is nonzero if all the tab stops were set, and zero otherwise. The entries in the tab array must be in ascending order.

A Short Example

Having shown the basics of tab setting, here is the source code for the application TABLIST, which illustrates all the details together:

Listing 12.1. The source code for TABLIST, an application using ListBoxes with tab stops.

```
// this application demonstrates how to support
// tabs in listboxes

#include <owl\framewin.h>
#include <owl\dialog.h>
#include <owl\applicat.h>
#include <owl\static.h>
#include <owl\listbox.h>

#include <bwcc.h>
#include <stdio.h>

// menu commands
const int
  IDM_ORDERSNEW = 101,
  IDM_HELPABOUT = 201;

// tab stops in dialog units
const int
  TAB_DESCRIPTION = 42,
  TAB_UNITPRICE   = 112,
  TAB_QUANTITY    = 146,
  TAB_TOTAL       = 187;

// dialog box child control IDs
const int
  IDC_INVOICE = 101,
  IDC_INFO    = 102;
```

continues

Listing 12.1. continued

```
class TDialogAbout: public TDialog {

public:

  TDialogAbout(TWindow* AParent)
    : TDialog(AParent, "DIALOG_ABOUT") {}
};

class TDialogOrders: public TDialog {

  TStatic*  invoice;
  TListBox* info;

public:

  TDialogOrders(TWindow*);
  void SetupWindow();
};

TDialogOrders::TDialogOrders(TWindow* AParent)
                    : TDialog(AParent, "DIALOG_ORDERS")
{
  invoice = new TStatic(this, IDC_INVOICE, 10);
  info = new TListBox(this, IDC_INFO);
}

void TDialogOrders::SetupWindow()
{
  int tabStops [] = {
    TAB_DESCRIPTION,
    TAB_UNITPRICE,
    TAB_QUANTITY,
    TAB_TOTAL
  };

  TDialog::SetupWindow();

  invoice->SetText("945533");

  WPARAM wParam = sizeof(tabStops) / sizeof(int);
  int okay = info->SendMessage(LB_SETTABSTOPS,
               wParam, (LPARAM) &tabStops);

  if (!okay) {
    BWCCMessageBox(NULL,
               "There was an error setting the tab "
               "stops in the ListBox.",
               "Error",
               MB_ICONEXCLAMATION ¦ MB_OK);
```

```
    return;
  }

  // initialize the listbox with tabbed strings
  char string [200];
  sprintf(string, "%s\t%s\t%s\t%s\t%s",
       "054243", "486 DX2 PC", "1999.90", "1", "1999.90");
  info->AddString(string);

  sprintf(string, "%s\t%s\t%s\t%s\t%s",
       "093459", "Serial Mouse", "39.45", "1", "39.45");
  info->AddString(string);

  sprintf(string, "%s\t%s\t%s\t%s\t%s",
       "854820", "SIMM 4MB Module", "30.00", "4", "120.00");
  info->AddString(string);

  sprintf(string, "%s\t%s\t%s\t%s\t%s",
       "202032", "Super VGA Monitor", "339.00", "1", "339.00");
  info->AddString(string);

  sprintf(string, "%s\t%s\t%s\t%s\t%s",
       "110293", "CDROM drive", "245.00", "1", "245.00");
  info->AddString(string);

  sprintf(string, "%s\t%s\t%s\t%s\t%s",
          "444933", "Power Strip", "11.83", "1", "11.83");
  info->AddString(string);

  sprintf(string, "%s\t%s\t%s\t%s\t%s",
          "559644", "2400 Bd Int. Modem", "79.95", "1", "79.95");
  info->AddString(string);
}

class TWindowMain : public TFrameWindow {

public:

  TWindowMain();

protected:

  void CmOrdersNew();
  void CmHelpAbout();
  DECLARE_RESPONSE_TABLE(TWindowMain);
};

DEFINE_RESPONSE_TABLE1(TWindowMain, TFrameWindow)
  EV_COMMAND(IDM_ORDERSNEW, CmOrdersNew),
```

continues

Listing 12.1. continued

```
  EV_COMMAND(IDM_HELPABOUT, CmHelpAbout),
END_RESPONSE_TABLE;

TWindowMain::TWindowMain()
                 : TFrameWindow(NULL, "Tab Stops with ListBoxes")
{
  AssignMenu("MENU_MAIN");
}

void TWindowMain::CmOrdersNew()
{
  TDialogOrders(this).Execute();
}

void TWindowMain::CmHelpAbout()
{
  TDialogAbout(this).Execute();
}

class TUserApplication: public TApplication {

public:

  TUserApplication()
      : TApplication("Listboxes") {}
  void InitMainWindow()
  { MainWindow = new TWindowMain; }
};

int OwlMain(int, char**)
{
  return TUserApplication().Run();
}
```

The data member `TDialogOrders::info` points to a `TListBox` object, whose `LBS_USETABSTOPS` style bit is set. The tab stops are passed to the ListBox in the function `TDialogOrders::SetupWindow()`, because only at this point is there a valid Windows element associated with the OWL ListBox object.

Tab Stop Overruns

The application TABLIST is very short and shows how simple it is to add tab stops to an application. If you play with TABLIST, you'll see that it works okay, but there is a problem. If you add strings to the ListBox that extend past the next tab stop, all the subsequent

fields will be aligned incorrectly. TABLIST didn't have problems with tab stops because all the strings to be added were fixed at compile time, so their widths were known. In general, ListBoxes deal with strings that are known only at runtime, such as the list of files in a directory, or the names of employees in a database.

Windows doesn't clip strings if they are too long to fit into a column, so you have to prevent tab overruns yourself. To prevent overruns, you can clip strings that are too long, or you can adjust the tab stops to accommodate the longest string. Both methods are relatively difficult to implement, due to the way ListBoxes handle tab stops and the many different ways overruns can occur.

Simulating Tab Stops with Multiple ListBoxes

Windows automatically clips any text you add to a ListBox, so why not use a separate ListBox for each column of data, effectively simulating tab stops? Any text exceeding the width of a column would be clipped without any intervention on behalf of the application program. If each ListBox had its own border, then you could have a vertical line at the beginning and end of each column. By carefully positioning the adjacent ListBoxes, you could make the left border of one overlap the right border of the other. I recreated the dialog box used in TABLIST, using multiple ListBoxes. Figure 12.2 shows how it looks.

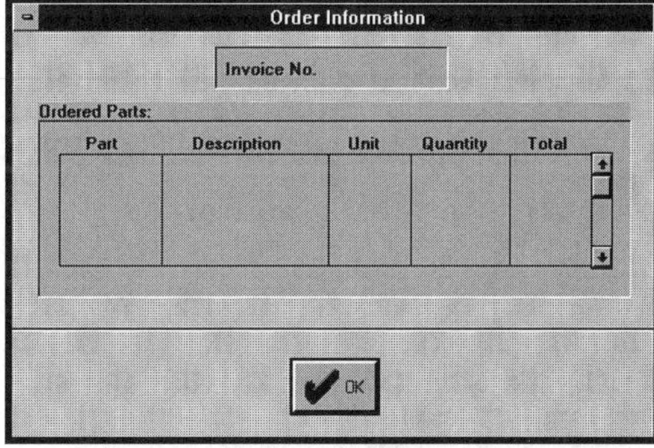

Figure 12.2. Using multiple ListBoxes to create tabular output.

By looking at the figure, you can't really tell that there are multiple ListBoxes. ScrollBars are not used in the ListBoxes, because a single ScrollBar on the right is used to scroll all the ListBoxes together. If you don't want the vertical lines between the fields, you can turn off the `WS_BORDER` style bit for the ListBoxes. Disabling the border has the side effect of removing ALL the border lines from the ListBoxes, including those that should surround the group of ListBoxes. To create a group border, you can use a Borland-style group object, resulting in a dialog box that looks like Figure 12.3.

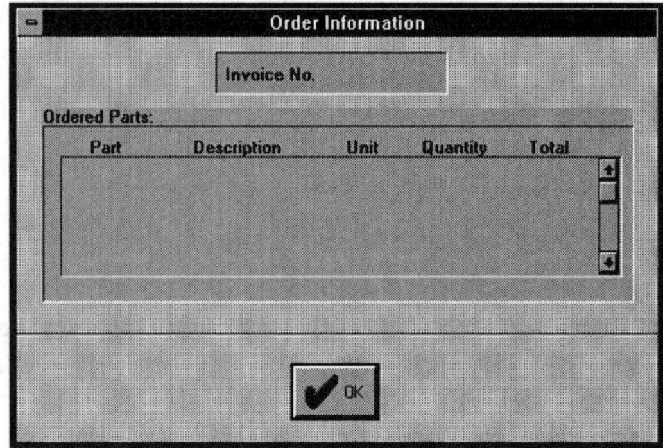

Figure 12.3. Using ListBoxes without a border.

Whether to have vertical separator lines between the fields or not is obviously application dependent. Using multiple ListBoxes instead of one means that rather than inserting tabbed-text strings into a ListBox, you have to insert text into each of the ListBoxes individually. If you put the ListBoxes into a container, you can simplify the management of the ListBoxes. For example, if you had an `Array` container called `listBoxes` that contained pointers to all the ListBoxes, you would add a tabbed-text string to the ListBoxes as shown in Listing 12.2.

Listing 12.2. Adding tabbed text to the multiple ListBoxes.

```
void TDialogOrders::AddTabbedString(LPSTR string)
{
  LPSTR tempString = _fstrdup(string);
  LPSTR subString = _fstrtok(tempString, "\t");
  int i = 0;
  while (subString && (i < listBoxes.GetItemsInContainer() ) ) {

      // add a word to the next ListBox
      TNewListBox* nextListbox = listBoxes [i++];
      nextListbox->AddString(subString);

      // find the next word
      subString = _fstrtok(NULL, "\t");
  }
}
```

The code in Listing 12.2 parses a string containing tabs, extracting tab-delimited substrings. Each substring is then added to a separate listbox.

Moving the ListBox Selection Bars

When the user clicks an item of a regular ListBox, the item becomes selected and is highlighted. With multiple ListBoxes emulating a single control, clicking on an item in one of the ListBoxes should cause all the items on the same line in the other ListBoxes to also become selected. By keeping the ListBoxes in a container, only the following few lines of code shown in Listing 12.3 are necessary.

Listing 12.3. Moving all the ListBox selection bars simultaneously.

```
void SetSelection(TNewListBox& listBox, void* R)
{
  int* index = (int*) R;
  listBox.SetSelIndex(*index);
}

LRESULT TDialogOrders::EvListBoxClicked(WPARAM index, LPARAM)
{
  // select the same line for all List boxes
  listBoxes.ForEach(SetSelection, &index);
  return 0;
}
```

The `forEach()` iterator function is used to call `SetSelection()` once for each ListBox in the container.

There is only one problem left to solve: when to call `TDialogOrders::EvListBoxClicked()`. ListBoxes send an `LB_SELCHANGE` notification message to the parent when a change in selection is made, but the notification message is sent just *after* the newly selected item is highlighted. Using the notification message to trigger `TDialogOrders::EvListBoxClicked()`, the user would see the selection bar move only on the ListBox that was clicked. When the mouse button was released, `EvListBoxClicked()` would be called, making all the other ListBoxes move their selection bar. This behavior isn't acceptable, because all selection bars need to move at the same time. What is needed is a notification message occurring when a `WM_LBUTTONDOWN` event occurs in a ListBox.

The easiest way to have the ListBoxes send a message to the parent when a `WM_LBUTTONDOWN` message is received is to derive a class from `TListBox`, which I called `TNewListBox`, and intercept the `WM_LBUTTONDOWN` message. The code is shown in Listing 12.4.

Listing 12.4. The parent notification member function to indicate mouse clicks in a ListBox.

```
void TNewListBox::EvLButtonDown(UINT, TPoint& point)
{
  // find the index of the top line
  int top = GetTopIndex();

  // see how big a listbox entry is
  TRect rect;
  GetItemRect(top, rect);

  // determine which row in the listbox was clicked
  int index;
  if (rect.bottom != 0)
    index = point.y / rect.bottom;
  else
    index = 0;
  index += top;

  // notify the parent
  Parent->SendMessage(UM_LBCLICKED, index, 0);
}
```

The user message `UM_LBCLICKED` is passed to the parent dialog box when the left mouse button is clicked in the ListBox. In order for the parent to handle ListBox selection changes, it needs to know which item was selected. To compute the selected line, `TNewListBox` uses an `LB_GETITEMRECT` message to find the dimensions of each item rectangle. Knowing these dimensions and the coordinates of the mouse click, the index of the clicked item is computed.

The parent dialog box traps the `UM_LBCLICKED` message and invokes `TDialogOrders::EvListboxClicked()`, making all the ListBoxes change their selection simultaneously. The end result on the screen is that all the ListBoxes behave as one.

A Complete Example

I wrote a small application, called TABLIST1, to show how the multiple ListBoxes work. TABLIST1 displays a small dialog box, showing the tabulated items of an invoice. Figure 12.4 shows how the dialog box looks on the screen.

TABLIST1 consists of the three source files DLGORDER.CPP, NEWLBOX.CPP, and TABLIST1.CPP. The dialog box is implemented in DLGORDER.CPP, with a class called `TDialogOrders`. Listing 12.5 is the declaration of `TDialogOrders`.

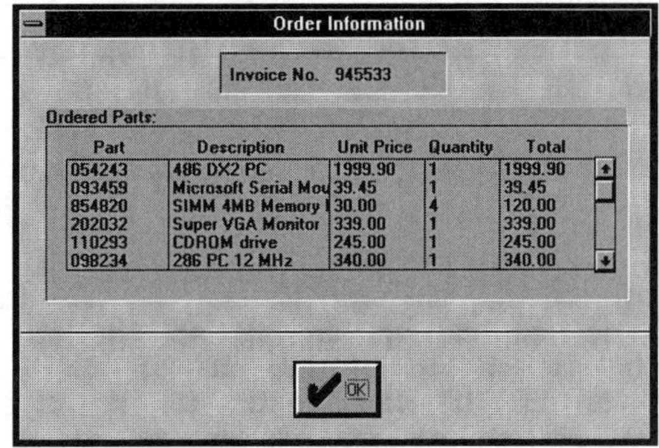

Figure 12.4. The dialog box displayed by TABLIST1.

Listing 12.5. The declaration of `TDialogOrders`.

```
#ifndef __DLGORDER_HPP
#define __DLGORDER_HPP

#include <owl\dialog.h>
#include <owl\static.h>
#include <owl\scrollba.h>
#include <stdio.h>
#include <classlib\arrays.h>

#include "newlbox.hpp"

// dialog box child control IDs
const int
  IDC_INVOICE     = 101,
  IDC_INFO        = 102,
  IDC_DESCRIPTION = 103,
  IDC_UNITPRICE   = 104,
  IDC_QUANTITY    = 105,
  IDC_TOTAL       = 106,
  IDC_SCROLLBAR   = 107;

class TDialogOrders: public TDialog {

  int itemCount;
  TStatic*    invoice;
  TScrollBar* scrollBar;

  typedef TIArrayAsVector<TNewListBox> ListBoxArray;
  ListBoxArray& listBoxes;
```

continues

Listing 12.5. continued

```
public:

  TDialogOrders(TWindow*);
  ~TDialogOrders();

  void SetupWindow();
  void AddTabbedString(LPSTR);

  LRESULT EvListBoxClicked(UINT, LONG);
  void EvVScroll(UINT, UINT, HWND);
  DECLARE_RESPONSE_TABLE(TDialogOrders);
};

#endif
```

The implementation of `TDialogOrders` is shown in Listing 12.6.

Listing 12.6. The code for `TDialogOrders`, used in TABLIST1.

```
#include "dlgorder.hpp"

DEFINE_RESPONSE_TABLE1(TDialogOrders, TDialog)
  EV_WM_VSCROLL,
  EV_MESSAGE(UM_LBCLICKED, EvListBoxClicked),
END_RESPONSE_TABLE;

TDialogOrders::TDialogOrders(TWindow* AParent)
                     : TDialog(AParent, "DIALOG_ORDERS"),
                       listBoxes(*new ListBoxArray(20, 0, 20) )
{
  invoice = new TStatic(this, IDC_INVOICE, 10);

  // don't let the container delete the ListBoxes,
  // because the dialog box will delete them
  listBoxes.OwnsElements(FALSE);

  // create the ListBoxes, and add them to the container
  listBoxes.Add(new TNewListBox(this, IDC_INFO) );
  listBoxes.Add(new TNewListBox(this, IDC_DESCRIPTION) );
  listBoxes.Add(new TNewListBox(this, IDC_UNITPRICE) );
  listBoxes.Add(new TNewListBox(this, IDC_QUANTITY) );
  listBoxes.Add(new TNewListBox(this, IDC_TOTAL) );

  // create a stand-alone scrollbar
  scrollBar = new TScrollBar(this, IDC_SCROLLBAR);
}
```

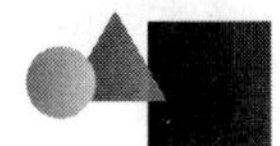

```
TDialogOrders::~TDialogOrders()
{
  delete &listBoxes;
}

// Tabbed strings to put into the ListBoxes
static char* data [] = {
  "054243\t486 DX2 PC\t1999.90\t1\t1999.90",
  "093459\tMicrosoft Serial Mouse\t39.45\t1\t39.45",
  "854820\tSIMM 4MB Memory Module\t30.00\t4\t120.00",
  "202032\tSuper VGA Monitor\t339.00\t1\t339.00",
  "110293\tCDROM drive\t245.00\t1\t245.00",
  "098234\t286 PC 12 MHz\t340.00\t1\t340.00",
  "884984\tMouse Systems Mouse\t29.95\t1\t29.95",
  "902908\tTrack Ball with 3 buttons\t10.00\t3\t30.00",
  "034503\t3.5 Floppy Disk Drive\t26.55\t1\t26.55",
  "093240\tCGA Monitor 240 Volts\t85.00\t1\t\t85.00",

  // add the same strings again, to fill up the ListBoxes
  "054243\t486 DX2 PC\t1999.90\t1\t1999.90",
  "093459\tMicrosoft Serial Mouse\t39.45\t1\t39.45",
  "854820\tSIMM 4MB Memory Module\t30.00\t4\t120.00",
  "202032\tSuper VGA Monitor\t339.00\t1\t339.00",
  "110293\tCDROM drive\t245.00\t1\t245.00",
  "098234\t286 PC 12 MHz\t340.00\t1\t340.00",
  "884984\tMouse Systems Mouse\t29.95\t1\t29.95",
  "902908\tTrack Ball with 3 buttons\t10.00\t3\t30.00",
  "034503\t3.5 Floppy Disk Drive\t26.55\t1\t26.55",
  "093240\tCGA Monitor 240 Volts\t85.00\t1\t\t85.00",

  // ... and again
  "054243\t486 DX2 PC\t1999.90\t1\t1999.90",
  "093459\tMicrosoft Serial Mouse\t39.45\t1\t39.45",
  "854820\tSIMM 4MB Memory Module\t30.00\t4\t120.00",
  "202032\tSuper VGA Monitor\t339.00\t1\t339.00",
  "110293\tCDROM drive\t245.00\t1\t245.00",
  "098234\t286 PC 12 MHz\t340.00\t1\t340.00",
  "884984\tMouse Systems Mouse\t29.95\t1\t29.95",
  "902908\tTrack Ball with 3 buttons\t10.00\t3\t30.00",
  "034503\t3.5 Floppy Disk Drive\t26.55\t1\t26.55",
  "093240\tCGA Monitor 240 Volts\t85.00\t1\t\t85.00"
};

void TDialogOrders::SetupWindow()
{
  TDialog::SetupWindow();


  invoice->SetText("945533");
```

continues

Listing 12.6. continued

```
  // initialize the ListBoxes with strings
  itemCount = sizeof(data) / sizeof(char*);
  for (int i = 0; i < itemCount; i++)
      AddTabbedString(data [i]);

  // see how many lines of text fit in a ListBox
  TNewListBox* lb = listBoxes [0];
  TRect rect;
  lb->GetClientRect(rect);
  int linesPerPage = rect.bottom / lb->GetItemHeight(0);

  // setup the scrollbar accordingly
  scrollBar->PageMagnitude = linesPerPage + 1;
  scrollBar->SetPosition(0);
  scrollBar->SetRange(0, itemCount - linesPerPage);
}

// break a string into words, and add a word to each
// of the ListBoxes in the group
void TDialogOrders::AddTabbedString(LPSTR string)
{
  LPSTR tempString = _fstrdup(string);
  LPSTR subString = _fstrtok(tempString, "\t");
  int i = 0;
  while (subString && (i < listBoxes.GetItemsInContainer() ) ) {

      // add a word to the next ListBox
      TNewListBox* nextListbox = listBoxes [i++];
      nextListbox->AddString(subString);

      // find the next word
      subString = _fstrtok(NULL, "\t");
  }
}

void SetSelection(TNewListBox& listbox, void* R)
{
  int* index = (int*) R;
  listbox.SetSelIndex(*index);
}

LRESULT TDialogOrders::EvListBoxClicked(WPARAM index, LPARAM)
{
  // select the same line for all ListBoxes
  listBoxes.ForEach(SetSelection, &index);
  return 0;
}
```

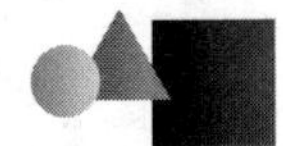

```
void ScrollTo(TNewListBox& listbox, void* R)
{
  int* firstItem = (int*) R;
  listbox.SetTopIndex(*firstItem);
}

void TDialogOrders::EvVScroll(UINT scrollCode, UINT thumbPos, HWND)
{
  int firstItem = scrollBar->GetPosition();
  switch (scrollCode) {

       case SB_PAGEDOWN:
           firstItem += scrollBar->PageMagnitude;
           break;

       case SB_PAGEUP:
           firstItem -= scrollBar->PageMagnitude;;
           break;

       case SB_LINEDOWN:
           firstItem++;
           break;

       case SB_LINEUP:
           firstItem—;
           break;

       case SB_TOP:
           firstItem = 0;
           break;

       case SB_BOTTOM:
           firstItem = itemCount - 1;
           break;

       case SB_THUMBPOSITION:
       case SB_THUMBTRACK:
           firstItem = thumbPos;
           break;
     }

     firstItem = (firstItem >= itemCount) ? itemCount - 1 : firstItem;
     firstItem = (firstItem < 0) ? 0 : firstItem;

     scrollBar->SetPosition(firstItem);
     listBoxes.ForEach(ScrollTo, &firstItem);
}
```

A BIDS container of type `TIArrayAsVector<TNewListBox>` is used to manage the group of ListBoxes, allowing simple `forEach()` iterators to call all the ListBoxes. A stand-alone child ScrollBar is created to scroll all the ListBoxes. The ScrollBar sends `WM_VSCROLL` messages to the parent dialog box when the user moves the thumb position, or when the user clicks and holds the mouse button on the ScrollBar.

The member function `AddTabbedString()` parses a string that contains tab characters, and adds the parsed substrings to the individual ListBoxes.

In `SetupWindow()`, the ScrollBar is initialized by setting its thumb position and its range. The range is set after computing the number of items added to the ListBoxes. The variable `linesPerPage` is computed, because the ScrollBar needs to scroll by that amount when the user clicks the area above or below the thumb position, causing a page up or page down command. Listing 12.7 shows the .RC file that describes the dialog box.

Listing 12.7. The .RC resource describing the dialog box shown by `TDialogOrders`.

```
DIALOG_ORDERS DIALOG 26, 48, 267, 177
STYLE DS_MODALFRAME | WS_POPUP | WS_CAPTION | WS_SYSMENU
CLASS "bordlg"
CAPTION "Order Information"
FONT 8, "MS Sans Serif"
BEGIN
     CONTROL "Button", 1, "BorBtn", 1 | WS_CHILD | WS_VISIBLE |
     WS_TABSTOP,  115, 143, 37, 23
     CONTROL "", 102, "LISTBOX", LBS_NOTIFY | WS_CHILD | WS_VISIBLE |
     WS_BORDER,   20, 54, 42, 54
     CONTROL "", 103, "LISTBOX", LBS_NOTIFY | WS_CHILD | WS_VISIBLE |
     WS_BORDER,   63, 54, 67, 54
     CONTROL "", 104, "LISTBOX", LBS_NOTIFY | WS_CHILD | WS_VISIBLE |
     WS_BORDER,   30, 54, 40, 54
     CONTROL "", 105, "LISTBOX", LBS_NOTIFY | WS_CHILD | WS_VISIBLE |
     WS_BORDER,   171, 54, 31, 54
     CONTROL "", -1, "BorShade", 1 | WS_CHILD | WS_VISIBLE, 11, 39,
     246, 77
     LTEXT "Ordered Parts:", -1, 11, 31, 245, 8
     LTEXT "Part No.", -1, 31, 44, 25, 8
     LTEXT "Description", -1, 74, 44, 39, 8
     LTEXT "Unit Price", -1, 133, 44, 34, 8
     LTEXT "Quantity", -1, 172, 44, 32, 8
     LTEXT "Total", -1, 213, 44, 22, 8
     CONTROL "", -1, "BorShade", 2 | WS_CHILD | WS_VISIBLE, -3, 130,
     271, 3
```

```
LTEXT "Invoice No.", -1, 88, 12, 38, 8
LTEXT "", 101, 132, 12, 42, 8
CONTROL "", -1, "BorShade", 1 ¦ WS_CHILD ¦ WS_VISIBLE, 84, 7, 96,
18
SCROLLBAR 107, 242, 53, 9, 51, SBS_VERT ¦ WS_CHILD ¦ WS_VISIBLE
CONTROL "", 106, "LISTBOX", LBS_NOTIFY ¦ WS_CHILD ¦ WS_VISIBLE ¦
WS_BORDER, 202, 54, 40, 54
END
```

`TDialogOrders` uses the derived ListBox called `TNewListbox`, whose code is shown in Listing 12.8.

Listing 12.8. The code for `TNewListbox`, a class that allows tab stops to be emulated through the use of multiple ListBoxes.

```
#ifndef __NEWLBOX_HPP
#define __NEWLBOX_HPP

#include <owl\listbox.h>

const int UM_LBCLICKED = WM_USER + 1001;

class TNewListBox: public TListBox {

public:

  TNewListBox(TWindow* AParent, int id, TModule* module = NULL)
      : TListBox(AParent, id, module) {}

  void EvLButtonDown(UINT, TPoint&);
  DECLARE_RESPONSE_TABLE(TNewListBox);
};

#endif

#include "newlbox.hpp"

DEFINE_RESPONSE_TABLE1(TNewListBox, TListBox)
  EV_WM_LBUTTONDOWN,
END_RESPONSE_TABLE;

void TNewListBox::EvLButtonDown(UINT, TPoint& point)
{
  // find the index of the top line
  int top = GetTopIndex();
```

continues

Listing 12.8. continued

```
    // see how big a listbox entry is
    TRect rect;
    GetItemRect(top, rect);

    // determine which row in the listbox was clicked
    int index;
    if (rect.bottom != 0)
      index = point.y / rect.bottom;
    else
      index = 0;
    index += top;

    // notify the parent
    Parent->SendMessage(UM_LBCLICKED, index, 0);
}
```

When a `WM_LBUTTONDOWN` message is received, `TNewListbox` determines the index of the clicked item, and simply tells the parent. The parent takes care of moving the selection bar of all the ListBoxes at the same time.

Listing 12.9 shows the code for TABLIST1, which is a small OWL program that uses `TDialogOrders` and `TNewListbox`.

Listing 12.9. The source code for TABLIST1, an application that demonstrates how multiple ListBoxes can be used to emulate one ListBox with tab stops.

```
// this application demonstrates how to simulate
// tab stops using multiple ListBoxes

#include "dlgorder.hpp"

#include <owl\framewin.h>
#include <owl\applicat.h>

// menu commands
const int
  IDM_ORDERSNEW = 101,
  IDM_HELPABOUT = 201;

class TDialogAbout: public TDialog {

public:

  TDialogAbout(TWindow* AParent)
      : TDialog(AParent, "DIALOG_ABOUT") {}
};
```

```
class TWindowMain : public TFrameWindow {

public:

  TWindowMain();

protected:

  void CmOrdersNew();
  void CmHelpAbout();
  DECLARE_RESPONSE_TABLE(TWindowMain);
};

DEFINE_RESPONSE_TABLE1(TWindowMain, TFrameWindow)
  EV_COMMAND(IDM_ORDERSNEW, CmOrdersNew),
  EV_COMMAND(IDM_HELPABOUT, CmHelpAbout),
END_RESPONSE_TABLE;

TWindowMain::TWindowMain()
  : TFrameWindow(NULL, "Simulating Tab Stops with Multiple ListBoxes")
{
  AssignMenu("MENU_MAIN");
}

void TWindowMain::CmOrdersNew()
{
  TDialogOrders(this).Execute();
}

void TWindowMain::CmHelpAbout()
{
  TDialogAbout(this).Execute();
}

class TUserApplication: public TApplication {

public:

  TUserApplication()
      : TApplication("Listboxes") {}
  void InitMainWindow()
  { MainWindow = new TWindowMain; }
};

int OwlMain(int, char**)
{
  return TUserApplication().Run();
}
```

User-Customizable Display Formats

Often users need to be able to alter the default information display. Consider a report generator for a data base. Some user may not be interested in all the information generated, whereas others may want to change the way the information is presented on the screen. The old way of customizing data was to have a programmer modify the source code of an application to support customer requirements. Today this approach is unacceptable. Users needs to be able to customize their reports without having to be programmers, and without knowledge of how a system works internally.

A good solution to this problem is to use a third-party, database-aware spreadsheet custom control that is compatible with Resource Workshop. You can then change the format of your data by changing the custom control properties with Resource Workshop. In the next section, I'll show how to use Resource Workshop to customize a dialog box that uses multiple listboxes to display tabular information.

Changing Column Widths

The dialog box shown in Figure 12.4 is a good example of a typical report. Some users may have description strings that consistently get clipped. To enlarge the column used for description strings, one would be tempted to modify the .RES file of TABLIST1 and then relink the application, but there is a better approach. If users have access to Resource Workshop, they can modify the dialog box resource directly in the .EXE file, with no need to recompile. For example, by widening the Description column, TABLIST1 displays data like that shown in Figure 12.5.

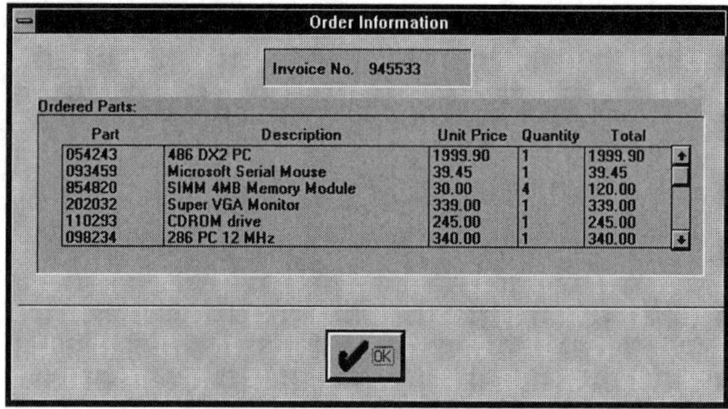

Figure 12.5. Changing the way information is displayed by TABLIST1, without recompiling any code.

The only tool used to produce the dialog box in Figure 12.5 was Resource Workshop, to change the .EXE file of TABLIST1. Any changes made to the .EXE file are permanent, unless the application code is regenerated by relinking.

Rearranging Columns

There are quite a few things users can do to change how information is displayed. For example, they can not only widen columns (without touching a line of code!), but also rearrange the order in which the columns are displayed, as shown in Figure 12.6.

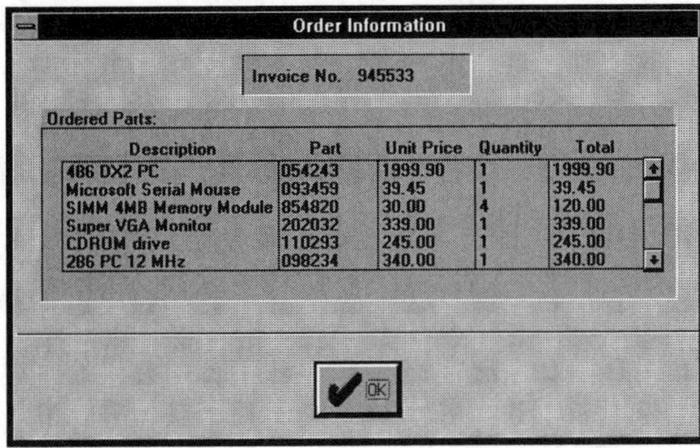

Figure 12.6. Changing the column orders.

Again, the changes in Figure 12.6 were made exclusively using Resource Workshop on the .EXE file for TABLIST1. All the controls of the dialog box continue to function correctly. Only the position of displayed data has been changed.

Deleting Unnecessary Columns

Some users may not want to have all the columns displayed. Can you delete a column from the screen without needing to change any source code? Almost. The trick is to use Resource Workshop on the .EXE file: don't delete anything from the dialog box, just move undesired fields off the dialog box. For example, assume that you didn't want the `UnitPrice` field to be displayed. Using Resource Workshop to modify the display, the result is a dialog box like that shown in Figure 12.7.

Here again, no code was modified, recompiled, or linked. To create the dialog box in Figure 12.7, I dragged the `UnitPrice` legend and column off the dialog box—without deleting anything—and rearranged the remaining columns. Here is how the dialog box looks under Resource Workshop:

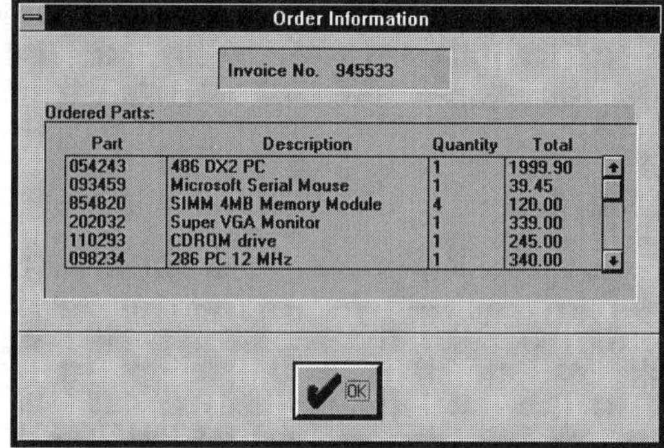

Figure 12.7. How TABLIST1 appears after editing the .EXE file.

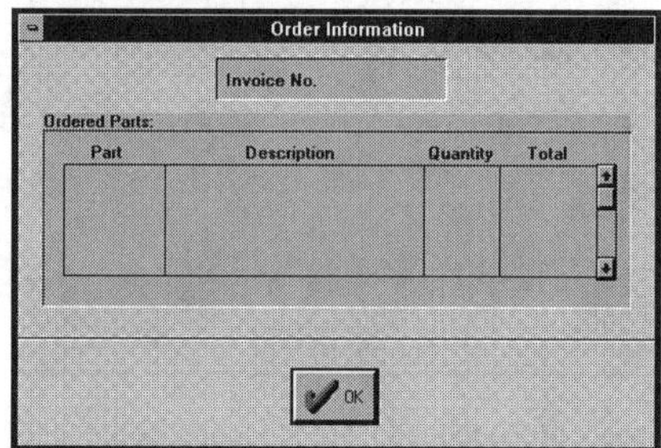

Figure 12.8. The dialog box displayed by Resource Workshop.

Notice the string `"Unit Price"` and the rectangle under it, at the bottom left of the screen. The rectangle is the `UnitPrice` ListBox, and the string is a static text field. It doesn't matter where you drag controls, for hiding purposes, as long as the controls are completely off the dialog box. Because the controls are child windows of the dialog box, Windows will clip any part of them that extends beyond the client area of the dialog box.

Horizontal ScrollBars

ListBoxes are typically used with ScrollBars to facilitate the management of long lists of items. Windows automatically manages a vertical ScrollBar for you, should a ListBox have more items than will fit in the ListBox client area.

Horizontal ScrollBars are another matter. Although there are Windows style bits and messages that refer to horizontal ScrollBars, it is up to the application to provide a significant amount of support code to make horizontal ScrollBars work. A horizontal scollbar is useful when the strings in a ListBox are too long to fit entirely. Figure 12.9 shows how a horizontal ScrollBar looks in a Borland-style ListBox.

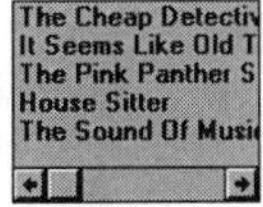

Figure 12.9. The horizontal ScrollBar displayed in a ListBox.

The main difference between a Borland-style ListBox and a standard Windows ListBox is the color of the background. Borland uses a solid light gray, and Windows normally uses white.

The first step in creating a horizontally scrollable ListBox is to set the WS_HSCROLL style. If you are using Resource Workshop, click the Horizontal Scroll Bar check box. Setting the style bit doesn't tell Windows to display a horizontal ScrollBar in the ListBox, but merely that the ListBox *can* have a horizontal ScrollBar. To make the ScrollBar actually appear on the screen, you need to do some additional work.

The Horizontal ListBox Extent

Before you can even think about displaying a horizontal ScrollBar, you need to determine whether you need one in the first place. If the strings added to a ListBox are all short enough to be fully displayed, you don't need the ScrollBar. To determine whether a string fits in the ListBox, you must compare the string's extent with the ListBox's. If any string added exceeds the ListBox's extent, you must display the ScrollBar.

To determine the extent of a string, you need first to select a device context, then select the font being used into that context, and then call `GetExtExtent()`, using code like that shown in Listing 12.10.

Listing 12.10. Determining the extent of a string in a ListBox.

```
TClientDC dc(HWindow);
HFONT hfont = GetWindowFont();
dc.SelectObject(hfont);
TSize extent = dc.GetTextExtent(AString, _fstrlen(AString) );
```

In the preceding code, it is assumed that `HWindow` is the window handle of the ListBox. The extent of the ListBox needs to be set to the extent of the longest string in the ListBox. The horizontal extent of a ListBox is used to set the range of the horizontal ScrollBar. You set a ListBox's horizontal extent with the `LB_SETHORIZONTALEXTENT` message, using code like this:

```
SendMessage(HWindow, LB_SETHORIZONTALEXTENT, stringExtent, 0);
```

You can also use the LB_GETHORIZONTALEXTENT to determine the extent of a ListBox. Don't confuse the horizontal extent with the width of a ListBox.

When you have a bunch of strings in a ListBox and you delete one, you need to check whether the longest string was deleted. If so, you need to find the next longest string, and see whether it also exceeds the ListBox's extent. If so, you leave the horizontal ScrollBar displayed, and set the ListBox's extent to the extent of the longest string. If not, you need to make Windows hide the ScrollBar.

Hiding the ScrollBar is relatively easy. You just need to set the ListBox horizontal extent to zero, using the code:

```
SendMessage(HWindow, LB_SETHORIZONTALEXTENT, 0, , 0);
```

If a ListBox was scrolled to the right—even by one pixel—when you set the extent to zero, Windows will not hide the ScrollBar. In all other cases it will, so just before setting the horizontal extent, you need to move the ScrollBar thumb all the way to the left by sending the ListBox a WM_HSCROLL message like this:

```
SendMessage(HWindow, WM_HSCROLL, SB_TOP, 0);
```

HWindow is assumed to be the window handle of the ListBox.

Keeping Track of String Extents

When the longest string of a ListBox is deleted, you need to find the extent of the next-longest string and set the ListBox's extent accordingly. In traditional C Windows code, determining the extent of next-longest string required a lot of user code, but with OWL, a standard sorted container provides a simple solution. If you store the extents for all of a ListBox's strings in a container sorted in ascending order, the last item will be the largest.

The next issue is where to put the container. A TListBox object has no place for user containers, so you need to derive a class from TListBox. Let's call the class THorizontalListBox, and declare a data member to reference an indirect sorted container of type TISArrayAsVector<int>. The items in the container will be pointers to integers, representing text extents for the strings in the ListBox.

Adding Strings to the ListBox

When a new string is added or inserted into the ListBox, a new int object is allocated from the heap and a pointer to it is added to the container. Then the horizontal extent of the ListBox is updated, using the value of the last extent stored, which is guaranteed to be the extent of the largest string in the ListBox. The code in Listing 12.11 is called each time a string is added or inserted into a ListBox.

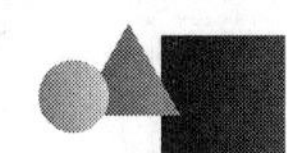

Listing 12.11. Updating the horizontal extent of a ListBox when a new string is added.

```
// allocate a new int from the heap
int* length = new int;

// determine the extent of the string
*length = TextExtent(AString);

// add the new extent to the container
textExtents.Add(length);

// get the extent of the largest string in the Listbox
int lastElement = textExtents.GetItemsInContainer() - 1;
int greatestExtent = *textExtents[lastElement];

// set the new listbox extent
SendMessage(HWindow, LB_SETHORIZONTALEXTENT, greatestExtent, 0);
```

The container will delete the pointers added to it when items are removed from the listbox.

Deleting Strings from the ListBox

When a string is deleted, we need to remove the string's extent from the container, so that each extent in the container is associated with some string in the ListBox. To remove an item from a container, the following code will work:

```
// remove the text extent from the container
int* length = new int;
*length = TextExtent(string);
textExtents.Detach(length, TShouldDelete::Delete);
delete length;
```

The member function `TISArrayAsVector<T>::Detach(T*, DeleteType)` is used to detach an item from the `textExtents` container. The `T*` parameter must point to an integer. If a pointer is found that points to that value, the pointer is detached and deleted; otherwise, no action is taken. After updating the container, the horizontal extent of the ListBox needs to be set to the longest item remaining in the ListBox. With a sorted container holding the extents, all we have to do is look at the value of the last item in the container, and then use that value to set the new horizontal extent. Listing 12.12 is an example of code showing how to set the horizontal extent for a ListBox.

Listing 12.12. Setting the new horizontal extent for a ListBox, after deleting a string.

```
// find the extent of the longest string in the
// ListBox, and set the horizontal extent accordingly
```

continues

Listing 12.12. continued

```
int lastElement = textExtents.GetItemsInContainer() - 1;
int greatestExtent = *textExtents[lastElement];

// set the extent
SendMessage(HWindow, LB_SETHORIZONTALEXTENT, greatestExtent, 0);
```

With OWL, the `LB_SETHORIZONTALEXTENT` message is handled by the member function `TListBox::SetHorizontalExtent(int)`.

Clearing the ListBox

To clear all the strings from a ListBox in OWL, you use the member function `TListbox::ClearList()`. Class `THorizontalListbox` needs to override this function in order to clear all the extents from the extent container and also to remove the ScrollBar. The code required is shown in Listing 12.13.

Listing 12.13. Clearing all the strings from a ListBox.

```
void THorizontalListBox::ClearList()
{
  // delete all the text extents in the container
  textExtents.Flush();

  // update the ListBox horizontal extent
  UpdateHorizontalExtent();

  // Call DeleteString, to force Windows 3.0 to remove the
  // horizontal scrollbar. Windows 3.1 doesn't need this call
  DeleteString(0);

  // clear out the remaining strings in the ListBox
  TListBox::ClearList();
}
```

The function `UpdateHorizontalExtent()` looks up the extent of the largest string in the ListBox and sets the ListBox's extent accordingly. Because no strings are left, the extent is set to zero. The call to `DeleteString()` is not required under Windows 3.1, because the ScrollBar is hidden automatically if the ListBox extent is set to zero and the ScrollBar thumb is completely to the left—as it will be after `UpdateHorizontalExtent()` is called with an empty extent container.

Under Windows 3.0, to make the horizontal ScrollBar disappear, you need to add or delete a string from the ListBox. Setting the extent to zero is not sufficient by itself.

The final operation is to call the base class `TListBox` to delete all the ListBox strings.

A Complete Example

Adding horizontal ScrollBars turned out to require quite a bit of work, so I'll write a complete OWL application to show how all the various pieces fit together. The application is called HLIST and displays a dialog box that might be used in a video store to keep track of items that need to be ordered. Figure 12.10 shows the dialog box displayed in HLIST.

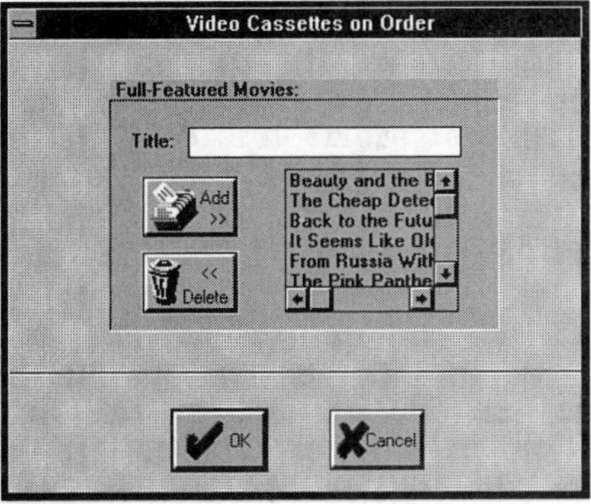

Figure 12.10. The horizontally scrollable ListBox displayed by HLIST.

The dialog box has a ListBox showing the items that need to be ordered. It also has a couple of extra controls to add or remove items from the list. The Add button will take text entered into the Title edit control and place the text into the ListBox. The Delete button will remove the selected item from the ListBox. Each time an item is added or deleted, the ListBox ScrollBar is updated. When the ListBox contains strings whose extents are all smaller than the ListBox width, the horizontal ScrollBar is removed.

HLIST is implemented with three source files: DLGVORD.CPP, which manages the dialog box controls; HLBOX.CPP, which contains the code for `THorizontalListbox`; and HLIST.CPP, which has the main application code. All the files are available on the companion disk. Listing 12.14 shows the header file used by DLGVORD.

Listing 12.14. The header file for `TDialogOrders`.

```
#ifndef __DLGVORD_HPP
#define __DLGVORD_HPP
```

continues

Listing 12.14. continued

```
#include <owl\dialog.h>
#include <owl\edit.h>

#include "hlbox.hpp"

// dialog box child control IDs
const int
  IDC_ADD    = 101,
  IDC_DELETE = 102,
  IDC_TITLE  = 201,
  IDC_ORDERS = 202;

// miscellaneous
const int EDIT_LENGTH = 80;

class TDialogOrders: public TDialog {

  TEdit*              title;
  THorizontalListBox* orders;

public:

  TDialogOrders(TWindow*);
  void SetupWindow();
  void Add();
  void Delete();

  DECLARE_RESPONSE_TABLE(TDialogOrders);
};

#endif
```

The class `TDialogOrdersInitializer` is used to initialize the controls in the dialog box. A static object of class `TDialogOrdersInitializer` is defined in the source file, guaranteeing that its constructor will be called before `WinMain()` is called. Listing 12.15 shows the source code for DLGVORD.

Listing 12.15. The source code for class `TDialogOrders`.

```
#include "dlgvord.hpp"

DEFINE_RESPONSE_TABLE1(TDialogOrders, TDialog)
  EV_BN_CLICKED(IDC_ADD, Add),
  EV_BN_CLICKED(IDC_DELETE, Delete),
END_RESPONSE_TABLE;
```

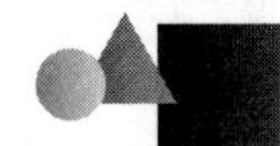

```
TDialogOrders::TDialogOrders(TWindow* AParent)
          : TDialog(AParent, "DIALOG_ORDERS"),
               TWindow(AParent)
{
  title  = new TEdit(this, IDC_TITLE, EDIT_LENGTH);
  orders = new THorizontalListBox(this, IDC_ORDERS);
}

void TDialogOrders::SetupWindow()
{
  TDialog::SetupWindow();

  orders->AddString("Beauty and the Beast");
  orders->AddString("The Cheap Detective");
  orders->AddString("Back to the Future");
  orders->AddString("It Seems Like Old Times");
  orders->AddString("From Russia With Love");
  orders->AddString("The Pink Panther Strikes Again");
  orders->AddString("Terminator");
  orders->AddString("House Sitter");
  orders->AddString("Cinderella");
  orders->AddString("Psycho");
  orders->AddString("The Sound Of Music");
}

void TDialogOrders::Add()
{
  char string [EDIT_LENGTH];
  title->GetLine(string, sizeof string, 0);
  if (title->GetLineLength(0) == 0)
      // no title to add
      return;

  orders->AddString(string);
  title->Clear();
}

void TDialogOrders::Delete()
{
  int selection = orders->GetSelIndex();
  if (selection < 0)
      // no selections
      return;

  orders->DeleteString(selection);
}
```

When the Add button is clicked, the Title edit control is checked to see whether it contains any characters. If so, the string is added to the ListBox. When the Delete button is clicked, the ListBox is checked to see whether any items are selected. If so, the item is removed from the ListBox.

Most of the code in HLIST is contained in class `THorizontalListbox`. Listing 12.16 shows its header file.

Listing 12.16. The header file for class THorizontalListbox.

```
#ifndef __HLBOX_HPP
#define __HLBOX_HPP

#include <owl\listbox.h>
#include <classlib\arrays.h>

class _OWLCLASS THorizontalListBox: public TListBox {

  typedef TISArrayAsVector<int> SortedIntegers;
  SortedIntegers& textExtents;

public:

  THorizontalListBox(TWindow*, int, TModule* = NULL);
  ~THorizontalListBox();

  int AddString(const char far*);
  int InsertString(const char far*, int);
  int DeleteString(int);
  void ClearList();
  int TextExtent(const char far*);

  void UpdateHorizontalExtent();
  int SetItemData(int, DWORD);
};

#endif
```

Listing 12.17 shows the source code for `THorizontalListbox`.

Listing 12.17. The source code for THorizontalListbox.

```
#include "hlbox.hpp"
#include <owl\dc.h>
```

```
THorizontalListBox::THorizontalListBox(TWindow* AParent,
                                        int id,
                                        TModule* module)
                    : TListBox(AParent, id, module),
                      textExtents(*new SortedIntegers(20, 0, 20) )
{
}

THorizontalListBox::~THorizontalListBox()
{
  delete &textExtents;
}

int THorizontalListBox::AddString(const char far* AString)
{
  // store the extent of each string in sorted
  // order in a container
  int* length = new int;
  *length = TextExtent(AString);
  textExtents.Add(length);

  // update the ListBox horizontal extent
  UpdateHorizontalExtent();

  return TListBox::AddString(AString);
}

int THorizontalListBox::InsertString(const char far* AString,
int Index)
{
  // store the extent of each string in sorted
  // order in a container
  int* length = new int;
  *length = TextExtent(AString);
  textExtents.Add(length);

  // update the ListBox horizontal extent
  UpdateHorizontalExtent();

  return TListBox::InsertString(AString, Index);
}

int THorizontalListBox::DeleteString(int Index)
{
  // find the text extent of the string to be deleted
  char string [256];
  GetString(string, Index);
```

continues

Listing 12.17. continued

```
  int* length = new int;
  *length = TextExtent(string);
  textExtents.Detach(length, TShouldDelete::Delete);
  delete length;

  // update the ListBox horizontal extent
  UpdateHorizontalExtent();

  return TListBox::DeleteString(Index);
}

void THorizontalListBox::ClearList()
{
  // delete all the text extents in the container
  textExtents.Flush();

  // update the ListBox horizontal extent
  UpdateHorizontalExtent();

  // Call DeleteString, to force Windows 3.0 to remove the
  // horizontal scrollbar. Windows 3.1 doesn't need this call
  DeleteString(0);

  // clear out the remaining strings in the ListBox
  TListBox::ClearList();
}

// find the extent of a ListBox string
int THorizontalListBox::TextExtent(const char far* AString)
{
  TSize extent;

  // select the ListBox into the device context
  TClientDC dc(HWindow);

  HFONT hfont = GetWindowFont();

  if (hfont) {
      // non-system font being used: select it into the
      // ListBox's device context before calling GetTextExtent
      dc.SelectObject(hfont);
      extent = dc.GetTextExtent(AString, _fstrlen(AString) );
  }

  else {
      // system font in use: no font selection necessary,
      // because GetTextExtent will use the system font
      // by default
```

```
        extent = dc.GetTextExtent(AString, _fstrlen(AString) );
    }

    return extent.cx;
}

void THorizontalListBox::UpdateHorizontalExtent()
{
    int greatestExtent;

    // find the extent of the longest string in the
    // ListBox, and set the horizontal extent accordingly
    int lastElement = textExtents.GetItemsInContainer() - 1;

    if (lastElement < 0)
        // no more strings in the ListBox
        greatestExtent = 0;
    else
        greatestExtent = *textExtents[lastElement];

    // add a small amount of space, to that when the
    // ListBox is completely scrolled to the right,
    // the last character is completely visible
    TClientDC dc(HWindow);
    greatestExtent += (dc.GetTextExtent("X", 1)).cx;

    // if the longest string fits completely in the ListBox,
    // then scroll the box completely to the left, so
    // Windows will hide the scrollbar
    TRect rect;
    GetClientRect(rect);

    int listWidth = rect.right - rect.left;
    if (listWidth >= greatestExtent)
        HandleMessage(WM_HSCROLL, SB_TOP, 0);

    // set the extent
    SetHorizontalExtent(greatestExtent);
}

int THorizontalListBox::SetItemData(int index, DWORD itemData)
{
    int value = TListBox::SetItemData(index, itemData);

    // update the ListBox horizontal extent
    UpdateHorizontalExtent();
    return value;
}
```

Notice the initialization of the reference data member textExtents, using the code

```
textExtents(*new SortedIntegers(20, 0, 20) )
```

just before the body of the class constructor. The array is declared to have an upper index of 20, a lower index of 0, and a delta value of 20. The delta value is used by the array when its size needs to be expanded dynamically at runtime to accommodate more items.

The member functions `THorizontalListBox::AddString()` and `THorizontalListBox::InsertString()` call the base class to perform the actual string adding or inserting. In addition, the extent container is used to keep the horizontal ScrollBar updated with the extent of the longest string in the ListBox.

The member function `TextExtent(LPSTR)` determines the extent (in pixels) of a string, using the font selected by the ListBox.

The member function `UpdateHorizontalExtent()` looks up the extent of the longest string in a ListBox, and then adds a small increment before setting the ListBox extent. The small addition is necessary, because without it, scrolling the longest string all the way to the right side would show the last character partially covered by the right border of the ListBox.

Listing 12.18 shows the code for HLIST, an OWL application using class `THorizontalListBox`.

Listing 12.18. HLIST, an OWL application demonstrating the use of class `THorizontalListBox`.

```
// this application demonstrates how to implement horizontal
// scrollbars in single-column ListBoxes

#include <owl\framewin.h>
#include <owl\dialog.h>
#include <owl\applicat.h>
#include <owl\static.h>
#include <owl\listbox.h>

#include <bwcc.h>
#include <stdio.h>
#include "dlgvord.hpp"

// menu commands
const int
  IDM_ORDERSNEW = 101,
  IDM_HELPABOUT = 201;

class TDialogAbout: public TDialog {
```

```
public:

  TDialogAbout(TWindow* AParent)
      : TDialog(AParent, "DIALOG_ABOUT") {}
};

class TWindowMain : public TFrameWindow {

public:

  TWindowMain();

protected:

  void CmOrdersNew();
  void CmHelpAbout();
  DECLARE_RESPONSE_TABLE(TWindowMain);
};

DEFINE_RESPONSE_TABLE1(TWindowMain, TFrameWindow)
  EV_COMMAND(IDM_ORDERSNEW, CmOrdersNew),
  EV_COMMAND(IDM_HELPABOUT, CmHelpAbout),
END_RESPONSE_TABLE;

TWindowMain::TWindowMain()
          : TFrameWindow(NULL, "ListBoxes with Horizontal
               Scrollbars")
               {
                 AssignMenu("MENU_MAIN");
}

void TWindowMain::CmOrdersNew()
{
  TDialogOrders(this).Execute();
}

void TWindowMain::CmHelpAbout()
{
  TDialogAbout(this).Execute();
}

class TUserApplication: public TApplication {

public:

  TUserApplication()
      : TApplication("HorizontalListboxes") {}
  void InitMainWindow()
  { MainWindow = new TWindowMain; }
};
```

continues

Listing 12.18. continued

```
int OwlMain(int, char**)
{
  return TUserApplication().Run();
}
```

Class `THorizontalListBox` is designed to be easily reusable, and can be used as is in your own applications. You can use the standard `TListBox` OWL functions with it, and you never even need to know what a horizontal ScrollBar is or how it works, thanks to OWL and C++.

Multicolumn ListBoxes

By default, Windows displays the strings in a ListBox as a vertical list. If there are too many strings to fit in the client area of the ListBox, a vertical ScrollBar appears on the right side of the control. The ScrollBar allows you to move up or down the list of strings.

ListBoxes also offer a different way to present list of strings: in side-by-side columns. Strings are added from top to bottom until the bottom of the client area is reached. Additional strings are added to the next column, beginning from the top line and progressing downwards. The columns are laid out as newspaper columns, from left to right. There is currently no way to change this ordering. International users whose languages read from right to left are stuck with left-to-right column order. Although there is an `LB_SETCOLUMNWIDTH` message to change the column spacing, it doesn't let you reverse the column layout. Figure 12.11 shows how a Borland-style multicolumn ListBox looks on the screen.

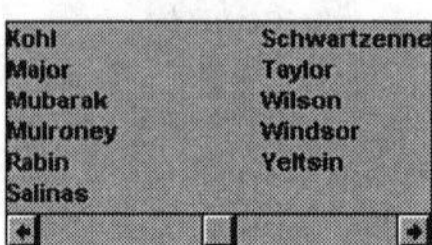

Figure 12.11. A Borland-style, multicolumn ListBox.

The strings shown are sorted using the `LBS_SORT` style with the ListBox. The strings are sorted from top to bottom in each column. The main difference between Borland-style, multicolumn ListBoxes and standard Windows ListBoxes is the color of the background. Borland uses a solid gray, whereas Windows normally uses white. The horizontal ScrollBar appears only if there are more columns than will fit in the ListBox.

The thumb position doesn't move in pixel increments in multicolumn ListBoxes. If you drag the thumb just a short distance, it will jump back to its original position when you release it. Clicking the page up or page down portion of the ScrollBar makes all the columns scroll. For example, scrolling by pages to the right will make the second column become the first column, and so on. The left and right arrows on the ScrollBar also behave as page up and page down commands.

The `LBS_NOINTEGRALHEIGHT` style has no effect for multicolumn ListBoxes. Strings are added to each column until there is not enough room to completely display the next string, and then the next column to the right is started.

Column Overruns

By default, the width of each column in a multicolumn ListBox is 120 pixels, which is enough to display about 15 characters in the system font, and about 20 characters in Arial 8 bold. If you add a string that is wider than the column, you'll have a column overrun. When a column overrun occurs, Windows clips the string, leaving zero pixels between the end of the clipped string and the beginning of the string in the column next to it. Figure 12.12 shows a multicolumn ListBox with column overruns.

Figure 12.12. A multicolumn ListBox with column overruns.

The ListBox in Figure 12.12 has no horizontal ScrollBar, because all the columns of data fit in the ListBox.

To change the column spacing, you can use the `LB_SETCOLUMNWIDTH` message, using a statement like this:

```
// set the column width to 50 pixels
SendMessage(HWindow, LB_SETCOLUMNWIDTH, 50, 0);
```

The `HWindow` parameter is assumed to be the handle of the multicolumn ListBox. The value passed as the `WPARAM` parameter is expressed in pixels. There is no equivalent message called `LB_GETCOLUMNWIDTH` to determine the current column width of a control. Instead, you can use the `LB_GETITEMRECT` message, which returns the bounding rectangle of an element, like this:

```
RECT rect;
SendMessage(HWindow, LB_GETITEMRECT, 0, (LPARAM) &rect);
```

`HWindow` is again assumed to be the handle of the multicolumn ListBox control.

A Short Example

I wrote a short example, called HLIST1, that demonstrates the use of a multicolumn ListBox. The program displays the dialog box shown in Figure 12.13.

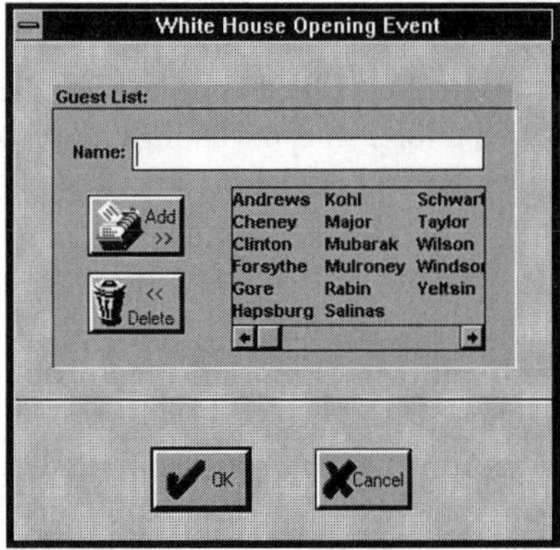

Figure 12.13. The multicolumn ListBox displayed by HLIST1.

The Add and Delete buttons can be used to insert or remove items to or from the ListBox. HLIST1 uses a class called `TDialogGuests`, whose header file looks like that shown in Listing 12.19.

Listing 12.19. HLIST1, an OWL application demonstrating the use of class `THorizontalListBox`.

```
#ifndef __DLGGUEST_HPP
#define __DLGGUEST_HPP

#include <owl\dialog.h>
#include <owl\edit.h>
#include <owl\listbox.h>

// dialog box child control IDs
const int
  IDC_ADD    = 101,
  IDC_DELETE = 102,
  IDC_NAME   = 201,
  IDC_GUESTS = 202;

// miscellaneous
const int EDIT_LENGTH = 80;
```

```
// initializer class for the Guests dialog box
class TDialogGuestsInitializer {

public:

  struct {
      char name [EDIT_LENGTH];
      TListBoxData guests;
  } Data;

     TDialogGuestsInitializer();
};

class TDialogGuests: public TDialog {

  TEdit*    name;
  TListBox* guests;

public:

  TDialogGuests(TWindow*);
  void SetupWindow();

  void Add();
  void Delete();
  DECLARE_RESPONSE_TABLE(TDialogGuests);
};

#endif
```

Class `TDialogGuestsInitializer` is used to initialize the transfer buffer for `TDialogGuests`. The initialization occurs only once, when the program is started. Subsequent changes made by the user are kept in the transfer buffer. Listing 12.10 shows the source code for `TDialogGuests`.

Listing 12.20. The source code for `TDialogGuests`.

```
#include "dlgguest.hpp"

// initializer for the dialog box controls
static TDialogGuestsInitializer buffer;

TDialogGuestsInitializer::TDialogGuestsInitializer()
{
  _fstrcpy(Data.name, "");
  Data.guests.AddString("Mulroney");
```

continues

Listing 12.20. continued

```
  Data.guests.AddString("Clinton");
  Data.guests.AddString("Yeltsin");
  Data.guests.AddString("Gore");
  Data.guests.AddString("Kohl");
  Data.guests.AddString("Major");
  Data.guests.AddString("Schwartzenneger");
  Data.guests.AddString("Taylor");
  Data.guests.AddString("Wilson");
  Data.guests.AddString("Cheney");
  Data.guests.AddString("Windsor");
  Data.guests.AddString("Forsythe");
  Data.guests.AddString("Hapsburg");
  Data.guests.AddString("Andrews");
  Data.guests.AddString("Rabin");
  Data.guests.AddString("Mubarak");
  Data.guests.AddString("Salinas");
}

DEFINE_RESPONSE_TABLE1(TDialogGuests, TDialog)
  EV_BN_CLICKED(IDC_ADD, Add),
  EV_BN_CLICKED(IDC_DELETE, Delete),
END_RESPONSE_TABLE;

TDialogGuests::TDialogGuests(TWindow* AParent)
             : TDialog(AParent, "DIALOG_GUESTS")
{
  name  = new TEdit(this, IDC_NAME, EDIT_LENGTH);
  guests = new TListBox(this, IDC_GUESTS);

  TransferBuffer = &buffer.Data;
}

void TDialogGuests::SetupWindow()
{
  TDialog::SetupWindow();

  // change the ListBox column width
  guests->SetColumnWidth(60);
}

void TDialogGuests::Add()
{
  char string [EDIT_LENGTH];
  name->GetLine(string, sizeof string, 0);
  if (name->GetLineLength(0) == 0)
      // no name to add
      return;
```

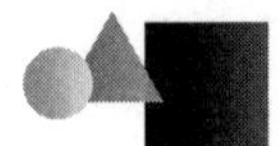

```
  guests->AddString(string);
  name->Clear();
}

void TDialogGuests::Delete()
{
  int selection = guests->GetSelIndex();
  if (selection < 0)
      // no selections
      return;

  guests->DeleteString(selection);
}
```

The dialog box changes the default column width, by sending an `LB_SETCOLUMNWIDTH` to the ListBox. The message must be sent after calling `TDialog::SetupWindows()`, in order for there to be a valid `HWindow` handle for the data member guests. The Add and Delete buttons work the same way as in the previous example, HLIST.

Owner-Draw ListBoxes

Most of the time, ListBoxes are used to display strings, but there are occasions when you have lists of items that are better described with pictures or other non-standard methods. When you run into situations like these, you need an owner-draw ListBox. Word for Windows uses owner-draw ListBoxes in the `Tools | Options` dialog box, shown in Figure 12.14.

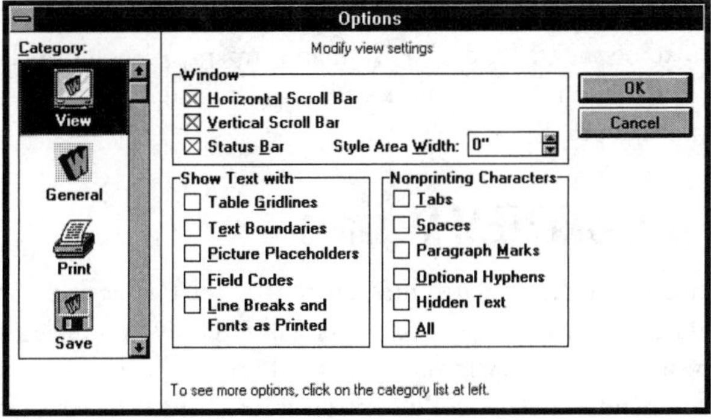

Figure 12.14. The `Tools | Options` *dialog box in Word for Windows, showing an owner-draw ListBox.*

When a ListBox is declared owner-draw, the parent window becomes responsible for drawing the control. Windows sends a number of different messages to the parent to determine which items to draw and how to draw them. The parent assumes the task of actually painting inside the owner-draw ListBox.

The *LBS_HASSTRINGS* Style

Owner-draw ListBoxes are not restricted to graphical items—they can also manage text items. When doing so, they offer you the option of managing the text and text pointers used in the ListBox. The `LBS_HASSTRINGS` style bit is what you use to tell an owner-draw ListBox that you want it to manage the strings and string pointers for you. When `LBS_HASSTRINGS` is set (which is the default case for non-owner-draw controls), you can use the `LB_GETTEXT` message to get the text of a given item in the ListBox. If the `LBS_HASSTRINGS` bit is not set, then an `LB_GETTEXT` message will return the data that was set for the given item with an `LB_SETITEMDATA` message.

Windows checks for the `LBS_HASSTRINGS` bit when it sends `WM_MEASUREITEM` and `WM_DRAWITEM` messages to the owner of an owner-draw ListBox. If the bit is set, then the `itemData` field of the `MEASUREITEMSTRUCT` and `DRAWITEMSTRUCT` structures will contain the `LPARAM` parameter used in the last `AddString()` or `InsertString()` call for the given item. If the `LBS_HASSTRINGS` bit is not set, the `itemData` field of the two structures will contain the `LPARAM` parameter used in the last `LB_SETITEMDATA` message for the given item. See the following sections for a description of the `WM_MEASUREITEM` and `WM_DRAWITEM` messages.

Displaying Icons

Owner-draw ListBoxes are often used to display bitmaps or icons. Given the similarity between how these two resources are handled, I'll describe only the use of icons, which happen to be slightly easier to use than bitmaps. Although I describe only owner-draw ListBoxes, most of the techniques are also applicable to owner-draw ComboBoxes with minimal changes.

The *WM_MEASUREITEM* Message

The first owner-draw-related message sent to the owner of an owner-draw control is the `WM_MEASUREITEM` message. The owner will typically be a dialog box. `WM_MEASUREITEM` is sent even before `SetupWindow()` is called for the dialog box, meaning that there are no `HWindow` handles for the child controls at the time. Owner-draw ListBoxes can contain items that are all the same size or items that are of different sizes. In the first case, you use

the LBS_OWNERDRAWFIXED style; in the latter case, you use the LBS_OWNERDRAWVARIABLE style. When you create an owner-draw control using Resource Workshop, you click the Fixed or Variable radio buttons on the ListBox properties dialog box.

The WPARAM parameter with the WM_MEASURITEM message contains an identifier for the control that needs an item to be measured. For owner-draw menus, the value is zero. For edit controls in owner-draw comboboxes, the value is -1. In all other cases, the WPARAM value is the control ID (not the window handle!) of the child being measured.

The LPARAM parameter is a far pointer to a MEASUREITEMSTRUCT struct, whose declaration is shown in Listing 12.21.

Listing 12.21. The structure pointed at by the LPARAM parameter in the WM_MEASUREITEM message.

```
typedef struct tagMEASUREITEMSTRUCT {
    UINT   CtlType;
    UINT   CtlID;
    UINT   itemID;
    UINT   itemWidth;
    UINT   itemHeight;
    DWORD  itemData;
} MEASUREITEMSTRUCT;
```

The CtlType field identifies the type of control requiring measurement. Possible values are as follows:

```
ODT_BUTTON
ODT_COMBOBOX
ODT_LISTBOX
ODT_MENU
```

The CtlID field contains the ID of the child control. CtlID will have the same value as the WPARAM parameter, except for owner-draw menus, in which case the CtlID field is not used.

The itemID field is used only with variable-sized, owner-draw controls; otherwise, it is left unitialized. With variable-sized controls, Windows sends a WM_MEASUREITEM message for each item in the control. For a ListBox, the first item has an itemID of 0, the next a value of 1, and so one.

The itemWidth field must be filled in by your application only if the WM_MEASUREITEM message regards an owner-draw menu; otherwise, itemWidth can be left unitialized.

The itemHeight field must always be filled by your application code, and indicates the height of an item in a ListBox, ComboBox, or menu. The value is expressed in pixels.

The itemData field contains valid data only if the MM_MEASUREITEM was sent as a result of something being added to a variable owner-draw ListBox or ComboBox using one of the following messages:

```
CB_ADDSTRING
CB_INSERTSTRING
LB_ADDSTRING
LB_INSERTSTRING
```

In such cases, itemData will contain the LPARAM argument that was passed to these messages.

The *WM_DRAWITEM* Message

This message is sent to the owner of an owner-draw control every time something in the control needs to be repainted, due to a change in the focus status, the selection status, or other. When WM_DRAWITEM is sent to the owner, the child control is guaranteed to have a valid HWindow.

The WPARAM parameter sent with the WM_DRAWITEM message contains the child ID of the control that sent the message, or zero if the control is a menu.

The LPARAM parameter contains a far pointer to a DRAWITEMSTRUCT, which is declared as shown in Listing 12.22.

Listing 12.22. The structure pointed at by the LPARAM parameter in the WM_DRAWITEM message.

```
typedef struct tagDRAWITEMSTRUCT {
    UINT  CtlType;
    UINT  CtlID;
    UINT  itemID;
    UINT  itemAction;
    UINT  itemState;
    HWND  hwndItem;
    HDC   hDC;
    RECT  rcItem;
    DWORD itemData;
} DRAWITEMSTRUCT;
```

The CtlType field specifies the type of control that sent the WM_DRAWITEM message, as for WM_MEASUREITEM messages. Possible values are:

```
ODT_BUTTON
ODT_COMBOBOX
ODT_LISTBOX
ODT_MENU
```

The `CtlID` field specifies the child ID of the control, unless the control is a menu, in which case `CtlID` is not used.

The `itemID` field is the identifier of the menu, or the item to draw in a ListBox or ComboBox. The first item in a ListBox or ComboBox has an `itemID` of zero, the next item has an `itemID` of 1, and so on.

The `itemAction` field tells the owner what type of drawing is required to update the owner-draw control. Possible values are an `OR` combination of the values in Table 12.1.

Table 12.1. The drawing actions indicated by the `itemAction` field of a `WM_DRAWITEM` message.

Value	*Description*
`ODA_DRAWENTIRE`	The entire item needs to be drawn. Typically, this entails erasing the background, and then painting the item.
`ODA_FOCUS`	The item has either gained or lost focus. Typically, you will need to draw or hide a focus rectangle. The `ODA_FOCUS` tells you only that a change in the focus status has occurred. You must look at the `itemState` field to determine whether the item has gained or lost the focus.
`ODA_SELECT`	The item has either been selected or deselected. The `ODA_SELECT` bit tells you only that a change in the selection status has occurred. To find out the item's actual state, look at the `itemState` field. For example, when an item in a ListBox is selected, you might want to erase the background to solid black, then paint some text in white. If the item is deselected, you might erase the background to solid white and paint the text in black.

The `itemState` field indicates the current state of a control. The field can contain an `OR` combination of the values in Table 12.2.

Table 12.2. The states indicated by the `itemAction` field of a `WM_DRAWITEM` message.

Value	*Description*
ODS_CHECKED	This bit is valid only for menu items. If the bit is set, then the menu item is to be drawn with a check mark.
ODS_DISABLED	The item to draw is disabled. If the item has text, you might want to paint the text as grayed out.
ODS_FOCUS	The item to paint has the input focus. Typically, you will want to paint a focus rectangle around some portion of the item. Note that a focused item may be either selected or not selected.
ODS_GRAYED	This bit applies only to owner-draw menus. If the bit is set, the menu item is to be drawn as grayed out to indicate that the menu item is not enabled.
ODS_SELECTED	This indicates that an item is to be drawn in the selected state. Note that a selected item doesn't necessarily have the input focus.

The next field in the `DRAWITEMSTRUCT` structure is the `hwndItem` field, which contains the window handle of the control that needs to be drawn. For menus, `hwndItem` contains the menu handle. If you use OWL objects to manage your child controls, you can convert a window handle into a pointer to a `TWindow` using the function `GetWindowPtr(HWND)`, like this:

```
// convert a window handle into an OWL
// TWindow object (if one exists)
TWindow*  window = GetWindowPtr(hWnd);
```

The function `GetWindowPtr(HWND)` is defined in \BC4\SOURCE\OWL\OWL.CPP. If there is no `TWindow` object with the given window handle, `GetWindowPtr(HWND)` will return a NULL.

The `hDC` field of the `DRAWITEMSTRUCT` is the device context to be used when drawing the owner-draw control. If you select any resources into this context, such as fonts, brushes, or other, you *must* be sure to deselect them before returning from the `WM_DRAWITEM` message.

The `rcItem` field indicates the boundary in which the owner-draw control can be painted.

The `itemData` field contains the data associated with the item to be drawn. This data is typically assigned to ListBoxes or ComboBoxes with `LB_SETITEMDATA` or `CB_SETITEMDATA` messages. For controls with the `LBS_HASSTRINGS` or `CBS_HASSTRINGS` style set, the

itemData will be the value passed to the control with LB_ADDSTRING, LB_INSERTSTRING, CB_ADDSTRING, or CB_INS ERTSTRING messages.

An Example

I wrote a short application called ODLIST to show some of the details of owner-draw ListBoxes. Owner-draw ComboBoxes mostly follow the same rules as ListBoxes, with a few exceptions. ODLIST reads the icon's resources out of a DLL, and displays them in an owner-draw ListBox. Figure 12.15 shows the ListBox.

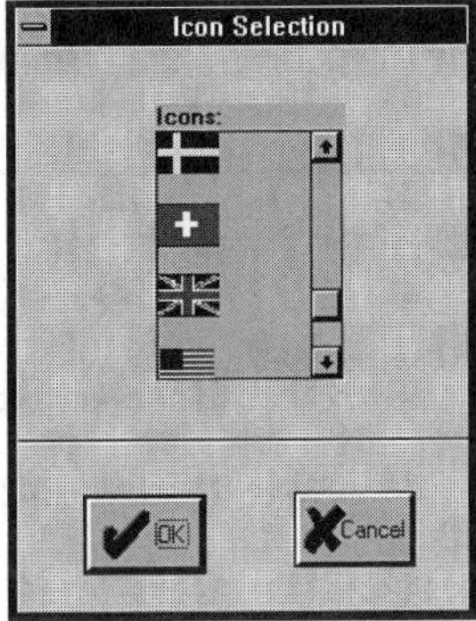

Figure 12.15. The owner-draw ListBox displayed in ODLIST.

The icons are national flags and are stored in a .DLL I created called ODICONS.DLL. The source code for ODICONS is trivial and looks like that shown in Listing 12.23.

Listing 12.23. The source code for the ODICONS.DLL.

```
#include <owl.h>

// DLL entry point
int FAR PASCAL LibMain(HINSTANCE, WORD, WORD, LPSTR)
{
  return TRUE;
}
```

The icons to the DLL were added using Resource Workshop. ODLIST extracts the icons out of the DLL using the API function

```
HICON ExtractIcon(HINSTANCE, LPCSTR, UINT);
```

The first parameter is the instance handle of your application. Windows uses it to free the memory allocated to any icons extracted, when the application terminates.

The LPCSTR parameter is a pointer to the name of the .EXE, .ICO, or .DLL file containing the icons to be extracted.

The UINT parameter tells `ExtractIcon()` the index of the icon you wish to extract. The first icon in the file has an index of zero, the second an index of one, and so on. To determine the number of icons in the file, use the value -1.

ODLIST extracts the icons from a file, and inserts them into an owner-draw ListBox with the code in Listing 12.24.

Listing 12.24. Extracting the icons from a resource file and putting them into an owner-draw ListBox.

```
HINSTANCE hinstance = *GetModule();
const int GET_ICON_COUNT = -1;

// see how many icons are in file ODICONS.DLL
int iconCount = (int) ExtractIcon(hinstance,
                                  "ODICONS.DLL",
                                  GET_ICON_COUNT);

// extract all the icons from the file and
// insert them into the owner-draw ListBox
for (int i = 0; i < iconCount; i++) {
  HICON icon = ExtractIcon(hinstance, "ODICONS.DLL", i);
  country->AddString( (LPSTR) icon);
}
```

The variable country is assumed to be a pointer to an OWL `TListBox` object. The ListBox used in ODLIST uses a fixed size for each item. The parent dialog box handles the `WM_MEASUREITEM` message as shown in Listing 12.25.

Listing 12.25. How ODLIST responds to the `WM_MEASUREITEM` message.

```
void TDialogCountry::EvMeasureItem(UINT, MEASUREITEMSTRUCT far& mis)
{
  int height = GetSystemMetrics(SM_CYICON);
  mis.itemHeight = height + height / 8;
}
```

The height of icon resources is fixed in Windows. The height (in pixels) is determined by a call to `GetSystemMetrics()` with the parameter SM_CYICON. I added a small fraction to the icon height to guarantee a small amount of empty space between adjacent items in the ListBox. Most of the space between the items in Figure 12.15 shown previously is due to the fact that the icons in ODICONS.DLL do not utilize all the vertical space allocated to icons.

Most of the code to support the owner-draw ListBox in ODLIST is in the function that handles the `WM_DRAWITEM` message in the dialog box. Listing 12.26 shows the code used in ODLIST.

Listing 12.26. The code that handles the `WM_DRAWITEM` for the owner-draw ListBox in ODLIST.

```
void TDialogCountry::EvDrawItem(UINT, DRAWITEMSTRUCT far& dis)
{
  // compute the size of the focus rectangle
  TRect rect;
  rect.top = dis.rcItem.top;
  rect.left = dis.rcItem.left;
  rect.bottom = rect.top + GetSystemMetrics(SM_CYICON);
  rect.right= rect.left + GetSystemMetrics(SM_CXICON);

  TDC dc(dis.hDC);
  if (dis.itemAction & (ODA_DRAWENTIRE | ODA_SELECT) ) {

    HBRUSH background;
    if (dis.itemState & ODS_SELECTED)
      background = (HBRUSH) GetStockObject(BLACK_BRUSH);
    else
      background = (HBRUSH) GetStockObject(LTGRAY_BRUSH);

    dc.FillRect(dis.rcItem, background);
    dc.DrawIcon(dis.rcItem.left, dis.rcItem.top,
                (HICON) dis.itemData);

    if (dis.itemState & ODS_FOCUS)
      dc.DrawFocusRect(rect);
  }

  else if (dis.itemAction & ODA_FOCUS)
    // toggle the focus rectangle
    dc.DrawFocusRect(rect);
}
```

The function draws a black background under icons that are selected. A smaller focus rectangle is drawn, which is big enough only to surround an icon. Each call to `DrawFocusRect()` toggles the focus rectangle because an `XOR` raster operation is used.

The function in Listing 12.26 doesn't check the ID of the control to be drawn because the dialog box contains only one owner-draw control. If you have several owner-draw controls in the same dialog box, then you'll have to check the child ID in `dis->CtlID`, and act accordingly.

Listing 12.27 shows the complete code for ODLIST.

Listing 12.27. The complete source code for ODLIST, an application demonstrating owner-draw ListBoxes.

```
// this application demonstrates how to implement
// owner-draw listboxes that display icons

#include <owl\framewin.h>
#include <owl\applicat.h>
#include <owl\dialog.h>
#include <owl\listbox.h>
#include <owl\gdiobjec.h>
#include <shellapi.h>

// menu commands
const int
  IDM_COUNTRYNEW = 101,
  IDM_HELPABOUT  = 201;

// dialog box child control IDs
const int
  IDC_COUNTRY = 101;

class TDialogAbout: public TDialog {

public:

  TDialogAbout(TWindow* AParent)
      : TDialog(AParent, "DIALOG_ABOUT") {}
};

class TDialogCountry: public TDialog {

  TListBox* country;

public:

  TDialogCountry(TWindow*);
  void SetupWindow();
```

```
  void EvDrawItem(UINT, DRAWITEMSTRUCT far&);
  void EvMeasureItem(UINT, MEASUREITEMSTRUCT far&);

  DECLARE_RESPONSE_TABLE(TDialogCountry);
};

DEFINE_RESPONSE_TABLE1(TDialogCountry, TDialog)
  EV_WM_DRAWITEM,
  EV_WM_MEASUREITEM,
END_RESPONSE_TABLE;

TDialogCountry::TDialogCountry(TWindow* AParent)
                      : TDialog(AParent, "DIALOG_COUNTRY")
{
  country = new TListBox(this, IDC_COUNTRY);
}

void TDialogCountry::SetupWindow()
{
  TDialog::SetupWindow();

  HINSTANCE hinstance = *GetModule();
  const int GET_ICON_COUNT = -1;

  // see how many icons are in file ODICONS.DLL
  int iconCount = (int) ExtractIcon(hinstance,
                                    "ODICONS.DLL",
                                    GET_ICON_COUNT);

  // extract all the icons from the file and
  // insert them into the owner-draw ListBox
  for (int i = 0; i < iconCount; i++) {
    HICON icon = ExtractIcon(hinstance, "ODICONS.DLL", i);
    country->AddString( (LPSTR) icon);
  }
}

void TDialogCountry::EvDrawItem(UINT, DRAWITEMSTRUCT far& dis)
{
  // compute the size of the focus rectangle
  TRect rect;
  rect.top = dis.rcItem.top;
  rect.left = dis.rcItem.left;
  rect.bottom = rect.top + GetSystemMetrics(SM_CYICON);
  rect.right= rect.left + GetSystemMetrics(SM_CXICON);

  TDC dc(dis.hDC);
  if (dis.itemAction & (ODA_DRAWENTIRE ¦ ODA_SELECT) ) {
```

continues

Listing 12.27. continued

```
    HBRUSH background;
    if (dis.itemState & ODS_SELECTED)
      background = (HBRUSH) GetStockObject(BLACK_BRUSH);
    else
      background = (HBRUSH) GetStockObject(LTGRAY_BRUSH);

    dc.FillRect(dis.rcItem, background);
    dc.DrawIcon(dis.rcItem.left, dis.rcItem.top,
                (HICON) dis.itemData);

    if (dis.itemState & ODS_FOCUS)
      dc.DrawFocusRect(rect);
  }

  else if (dis.itemAction & ODA_FOCUS)
    // toggle the focus rectangle
   dc.DrawFocusRect(rect);
}

void TDialogCountry::EvMeasureItem(UINT, MEASUREITEMSTRUCT far& mis)
{
  int height = GetSystemMetrics(SM_CYICON);
  mis.itemHeight = height + height / 8;
}

class TWindowMain : public TFrameWindow {

public:

  TWindowMain();

protected:

  void CmCountryNew();
  void CmHelpAbout();
  DECLARE_RESPONSE_TABLE(TWindowMain);
};

DEFINE_RESPONSE_TABLE1(TWindowMain, TFrameWindow)
  EV_COMMAND(IDM_COUNTRYNEW, CmCountryNew),
  EV_COMMAND(IDM_HELPABOUT, CmHelpAbout),
END_RESPONSE_TABLE;

TWindowMain::TWindowMain()
                  : TFrameWindow(NULL, "Using Owner-Draw ListBoxes")
{
  AssignMenu("MENU_MAIN");
}
```

```
void TWindowMain::CmCountryNew()
{
  TDialogCountry(this).Execute();
}

void TWindowMain::CmHelpAbout()
{
  TDialogAbout(this).Execute();
}

class TUserApplication: public TApplication {

public:

  TUserApplication()
      : TApplication("Owner-Draw ListBoxes") {}
  void InitMainWindow()
  { MainWindow = new TWindowMain; }
};

int OwlMain(int, char**)
{
  return TUserApplication().Run();
}
```

The include file SHELLAPI.H is necessary to use the API function `ExtractIcons()`. When running ODLIST, be sure the DLL ODICONS is available and in the same directory, otherwise no icons will show up in the ListBox. The icons are extracted from the DLL in `TDialogCountry::SetupWindow()` and added to the ListBox. The ListBox was created without the `LBS_HASSTRINGS` style because the control is used to manage non-textual information.

Using Icons and Strings Together

ODLIST displays only a series of icons. Often you may have to display an icon or bitmap, but also show some kind of text as a description field, as shown in Figure 12.16.

The icons in ODLIST were not sorted. To support items in sorted ListBoxes, the owner of the control must respond to the `WM_COMPAREITEM`, which is sent every time Windows tries to locate items in the ListBox. If you display strings alongside icons or bitmaps in the ListBox, you may want to sort the graphical items according to the alphabetical order of the associated strings.

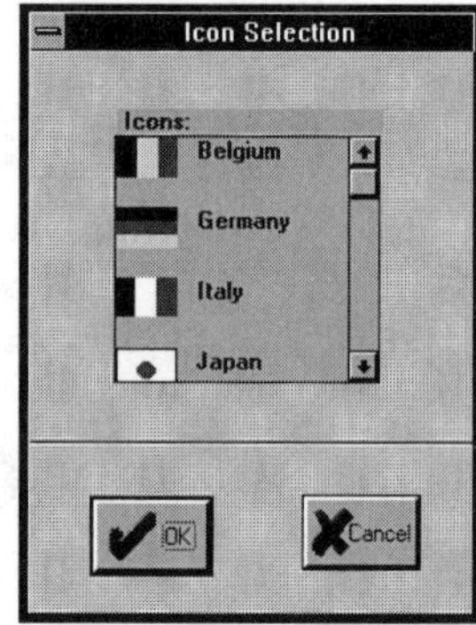

Figure 12.16. Displaying icons and text together.

Standard ListBoxes are not capable of storing two items at the same index, much less displaying them. The owner-draw ListBox I'll develop in this section uses the following structure to manage its data:

```
struct ListboxData {
  HICON icon;
  LPSTR description;
};
```

Each entry in the ListBox uses an icon handle and a pointer to a text string. Because I won't be handling strings directly in the ListBox, I didn't set the `LBS_HASSTRINGS` style. To add icon/text combinations to the ListBox, the `AddString()` member function can be used like this:

```
// initialize an item to be added to the Listbox
static ListBoxData item [] = {
  { GetModule()->LoadIcon("ICON_FLAG_UK"), "UK" };

// add the icon and string to the Listbox
country->AddString( (LPSTR) &item);
```

To retrieve the struct stored at each index in the ListBox, you can use the `LB_GETITEMDATA` message (which is encapsulated in the member function `TListBox::GetItemData()`) like this:

```
ListboxData* lbdp = (ListBoxData*) listBox->GetItemData(index);
```

where `listBox` is the window handle of the ListBox and `index` is the index of the item whose data you're looking up. Several of the owner-draw-related messages provide structures that have an `itemData` field in them. For example, the `WM_COMPAREITEM` message passes a pointer to a `COMPAREITEMSTRUCT`, which OWL converts into a reference, allowing the item data to be accessed like this:

```
ListboxData* lbdp = (ListboxData*) cis.itemData1;
```

where `cis` is a reference to a `COMPAREITEMSTRUCT` struct.

Drawing the Icon and Text

Now that we can access `ListboxData` items in the owner-draw ListBox, it is straightforward to paint the items in the ListBox. Windows sends a `WM_DRAWITEM` to the owner of the ListBox each time a new item needs to be redrawn. The `WM_DRAWITEM` messages carries with it a pointer to a `DRAWITEMSTRUCT` in the `LPARAM` parameter. OWL converts the pointer into a reference. This structure has all the information you need to paint a new entry. You don't really need that much information to determine how to paint items. You need to know where to draw, which item to draw, and the selection/focus status of that item.

Conventionally, selected items are drawn on a black background. Text appears in white. When an item has the input focus, a dotted rectangle is painted around it. The code in Listing 12.28 does the job.

Listing 12.28. Painting an icon and a string in an owner-draw ListBox.

```
void TDialogCountry::EvDrawItem(UINT, DRAWITEMSTRUCT far& dis)
{
  // compute the size of the focus rectangle
  TRect rect;
  rect.top = dis.rcItem.top;
  rect.left = dis.rcItem.left;
  rect.bottom = rect.top + GetSystemMetrics(SM_CYICON);
  rect.right= rect.left + GetSystemMetrics(SM_CXICON);
  int iconWidth  = rect.right - rect.left;
  TDC dc(dis.hDC);

  if (dis.itemAction & (ODA_DRAWENTIRE | ODA_SELECT) ) {

    HBRUSH background;
    if (dis.itemState & ODS_SELECTED) {
      background = (HBRUSH) GetStockObject(BLACK_BRUSH);
      const COLORREF WHITE = RGB(255, 255, 255);
      dc.SetTextColor(WHITE);
    }
    else {
      background = (HBRUSH) GetStockObject(LTGRAY_BRUSH);
      const COLORREF BLACK = RGB(0, 0, 0);
      dc.SetTextColor(BLACK);
    }
```

continues

Listing 12.28. continued

```
    dc.FillRect(dis.rcItem, background);
    ListBoxData* data = (ListBoxData*) dis.itemData;

    // display the icon
    dc.DrawIcon(dis.rcItem.left, dis.rcItem.top, data->icon);

    // display the text
    dc.TextOut(dis.rcItem.left + iconWidth + 10,
               dis.rcItem.top, data->description,
               _fstrlen(data->description) );

    if (dis.itemState & ODS_FOCUS)
      dc.DrawFocusRect(rect);
  }

  else if (dis.itemAction & ODA_FOCUS)
    // toggle the focus rectangle
    dc.DrawFocusRect(rect);
}
```

The drawing function doesn't have to worry at all about the order in which items are displayed in the ListBox, because ordering is taken care of elsewhere—with a `WM_COMPAREITEM` message.

The focus rectangle is drawn by `EvDrawItem()` to enclose only the icon. The rectangle is painted with the call

```
dc.DrawFocusRect(rect);
```

which uses an `XOR` raster operation to paint an unfilled rectangle with a dotted border. Calling `DrawFocusRect()` twice with the same rectangle will cause the drawing and undrawing of the focus rectangle.

`EvDrawItem()` displays selected items by painting them on a black background, as shown in Figure 12.17.

Note the dotted focus rectangle around the selected icon. The items are spaced vertically according to the value set in response to a `WM_MEASUREITEM` message. I set the spacing to be a little larger than the size of an icon.

The *WM_COMPAREITEM* Message

When a ListBox is designated as sorted, using the `LBS_SORT` style, Windows sends the owner of an owner-draw control a barrage of `WM_COMPAREITEM` messages. In response to

such messages, your code must return a value indicating how the two items passed to you compare. Given the two items, item1 and item2, your code must have the values in Table 12.3.

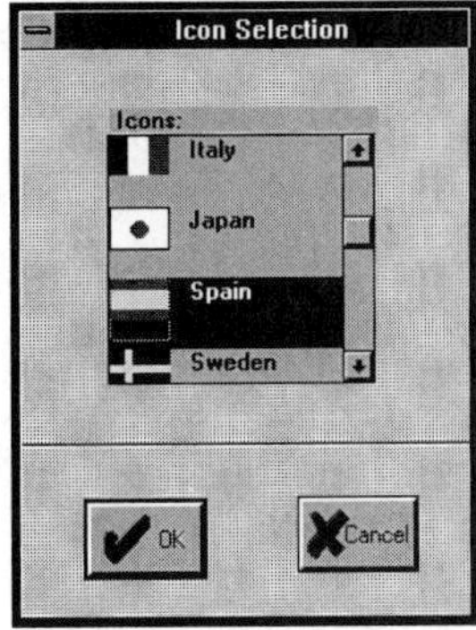

Figure 12.17. How `EvDrawItem()` *displays a selected item using a black background.*

Table 12.3. The return values for a `WM_COMPAREITEM` message.

Condition	*Return Value*
item1 < item2	-1
item1 == item2	0
item1 > item2	1

When handling strings, you should use the Windows function `lstrcmp()`. This function compares strings, using the sort order defined for the language selected.

When determining the sort order of two non-textual items, your application can make any assumptions it wants. For example, you could sort icons based on their handle values. You might sort bitmaps based on their size or the number of colors used. How you decide to have objects sorted is entirely up to you.

A Complete Example

I wrote a short application called ODLIST1 that displays the icons shown in Figure 12.17. Listing 12.29 presents the complete code.

Listing 12.29. ODLIST1, an OWL application using owner-draw ListBoxes to display icons with text.

```
// this application demonstrates how to implement
// owner-draw listboxes that display icons, sorted according
// to text strings describing the icons

#include <owl\framewin.h>
#include <owl\applicat.h>
#include <owl\dialog.h>
#include <owl\listbox.h>
#include <owl\gdiobjec.h>
#include <shellapi.h>

// menu commands
const int
  IDM_COUNTRYNEW = 101,
  IDM_HELPABOUT  = 201;

// dialog box child control IDs
const int
  IDC_COUNTRY = 101;

// structure used in the owner-draw ListBox
struct ListBoxData {
  HICON icon;
  LPSTR description;
};

class TDialogAbout: public TDialog {

public:

  TDialogAbout(TWindow* AParent)
    : TDialog(AParent, "DIALOG_ABOUT") {}
};

class TDialogCountry: public TDialog {

  TListBox* country;

public:

  TDialogCountry(TWindow*);
  void SetupWindow();
  LRESULT EvCompareItem(UINT, COMPAREITEMSTRUCT far&);
  void EvDrawItem(UINT, DRAWITEMSTRUCT far&);
  void EvMeasureItem(UINT, MEASUREITEMSTRUCT far&);

  DECLARE_RESPONSE_TABLE(TDialogCountry);
};
```

```
DEFINE_RESPONSE_TABLE1(TDialogCountry, TDialog)
  EV_WM_COMPAREITEM,
  EV_WM_DRAWITEM,
  EV_WM_MEASUREITEM,
END_RESPONSE_TABLE;

TDialogCountry::TDialogCountry(TWindow* AParent)
              : TDialog(AParent, "DIALOG_COUNTRY")
{
  country = new TListBox(this, IDC_COUNTRY);
}

void TDialogCountry::SetupWindow()
{
  TDialog::SetupWindow();

  static ListBoxData data [] = {
    { GetModule()->LoadIcon("ICON_FLAG_UK"),          "UK" },
    { GetModule()->LoadIcon("ICON_FLAG_BELGIUM"),     "Belgium" },
    { GetModule()->LoadIcon("ICON_FLAG_SWEDEN"),      "Sweden" },
    { GetModule()->LoadIcon("ICON_FLAG_SPAIN"),       "Spain" },
    { GetModule()->LoadIcon("ICON_FLAG_ITALY"),       "Italy" },
    { GetModule()->LoadIcon("ICON_FLAG_GERMANY"),     "Germany" },
    { GetModule()->LoadIcon("ICON_FLAG_USA"),         "USA" },
    { GetModule()->LoadIcon("ICON_FLAG_JAPAN"),       "Japan" },
    { GetModule()->LoadIcon("ICON_FLAG_SWITZERLAND"), "Switzerland" }
  };

  // add some icons and strings to the ListBox
  int itemCount = sizeof(data) / sizeof(ListBoxData);
  for (int i = 0; i < itemCount; i++)
    country->AddString( (LPSTR) &data [i]);
}

LRESULT TDialogCountry::EvCompareItem(UINT, COMPAREITEMSTRUCT far&
cis)
{
  LPSTR text1 = ( (ListBoxData*) cis.itemData1)->description;
  LPSTR text2 = ( (ListBoxData*) cis.itemData2)->description;

  return lstrcmp(text1, text2);
}

void TDialogCountry::EvDrawItem(UINT, DRAWITEMSTRUCT far& dis)
{
  // compute the size of the focus rectangle
  TRect rect;
  rect.top = dis.rcItem.top;
  rect.left = dis.rcItem.left;
```

continues

Listing 12.29. continued

```
  rect.bottom = rect.top + GetSystemMetrics(SM_CYICON);
  rect.right= rect.left + GetSystemMetrics(SM_CXICON);
  int iconWidth  = rect.right - rect.left;
  TDC dc(dis.hDC);

  if (dis.itemAction & (ODA_DRAWENTIRE ¦ ODA_SELECT) ) {

    HBRUSH background;
    if (dis.itemState & ODS_SELECTED) {
      background = (HBRUSH) GetStockObject(BLACK_BRUSH);
      const COLORREF WHITE = RGB(255, 255, 255);
      dc.SetTextColor(WHITE);
    }
    else {
      background = (HBRUSH) GetStockObject(LTGRAY_BRUSH);
      const COLORREF BLACK = RGB(0, 0, 0);
      dc.SetTextColor(BLACK);
    }

    dc.FillRect(dis.rcItem, background);
    ListBoxData* data = (ListBoxData*) dis.itemData;

    // display the icon
    dc.DrawIcon(dis.rcItem.left, dis.rcItem.top, data->icon);

    // display the text
    dc.TextOut(dis.rcItem.left + iconWidth + 10,
               dis.rcItem.top, data->description,
               _fstrlen(data->description) );

    if (dis.itemState & ODS_FOCUS)
      dc.DrawFocusRect(rect);
  }

  else if (dis.itemAction & ODA_FOCUS)
    // toggle the focus rectangle
    dc.DrawFocusRect(rect);
}

void TDialogCountry::EvMeasureItem(UINT, MEASUREITEMSTRUCT far& mis)
{
  int height = GetSystemMetrics(SM_CYICON);
  mis.itemHeight = height + height / 8;
}

class TWindowMain : public TFrameWindow {

public:

  TWindowMain();
```

```
protected:

  void CmCountryNew();
  void CmHelpAbout();
  DECLARE_RESPONSE_TABLE(TWindowMain);
};

DEFINE_RESPONSE_TABLE1(TWindowMain, TFrameWindow)
  EV_COMMAND(IDM_COUNTRYNEW, CmCountryNew),
  EV_COMMAND(IDM_HELPABOUT, CmHelpAbout),
END_RESPONSE_TABLE;

TWindowMain::TWindowMain()
           : TFrameWindow(NULL,
             "Sorted Owner-Draw ListBoxes with Icons and Text")
{
  AssignMenu("MENU_MAIN");
}

void TWindowMain::CmCountryNew()
{
  TDialogCountry(this).Execute();
}

void TWindowMain::CmHelpAbout()
{
  TDialogAbout(this).Execute();
}

class TUserApplication: public TApplication {

public:

  TUserApplication()
      : TApplication("Owner-Draw ListBoxes") {}
  void InitMainWindow()
  { MainWindow = new TWindowMain; }
};

int OwlMain(int, char**)
{
  return TUserApplication().Run();
}
```

ODLIST1 sorts the icons by their description text, processing the `WM_COMPAREITEM` message as shown in Listing 12.30.

Listing 12.30. Sorting the icons based on the description strings.

```
LRESULT TDialogCountry::EvCompareItem(UINT, COMPAREITEMSTRUCT far&
cis)
{
  LPSTR text1 = ( (ListBoxData*) cis.itemData1)->description;
  LPSTR text2 = ( (ListBoxData*) cis.itemData2)->description;

  return lstrcmp(text1, text2);
}
```

Columnar Data without Tab Overruns

The sample program TABLIST, described at the beginning of this chapter, displayed tabbed text in a standard ListBox. After adding tab stops to a ListBox, TABLIST added tabbed strings to the control. A possibly annoying problem with TABLIST is that it doesn't handle tab overruns. If you add text that extends beyond a tab stop, the rest of the tabbed positions become misaligned and the data doesn't line up correctly in the ListBox. It isn't completely trivial to fix tab overruns in a standard ListBox, but it is relatively easy to create an owner-draw ListBox that can handle tabbed text and paint the text without allowing tab stop overruns.

I created a short application called ODLIST2 to demonstrate an owner-draw ListBox that supports tabbed strings. The ListBox uses a data structure that defines the starting and ending coordinates of each column. Tab characters in strings determine which column text is displayed in. The advantage of columns over tab stops is that a column has both a starting and an ending coordinate. Tab stops have only a single starting coordinate. With two coordinates, you can lay out columns so that there is empty space between them, allowing your data to be easier to read—especially when handling strings that need to be truncated due to excessive length.

Figure 12.18 shows how the owner-draw ListBox appears on the screen.

Long Strings Are Truncated

When a string is encountered that doesn't fit in a column, the ListBox doesn't just clip off the part that doesn't fit. Clipping occurs on a pixel boundary, and clipping text this way would result in odd-looking character fragments at the end of a clipped string. Instead of just clipping text arbitrarily, ODLIST2 determines the largest number of characters of a string that will fit into a column and truncates the string accordingly. As a result, no par-

tial characters appear on the screen. The strings are painted in the owner-draw controls inside the member function `DisplayMailingList()`, which is called by the parent dialog box during the processing of a `WM_DRAWITEM` message. Listing 12.31 shows the code.

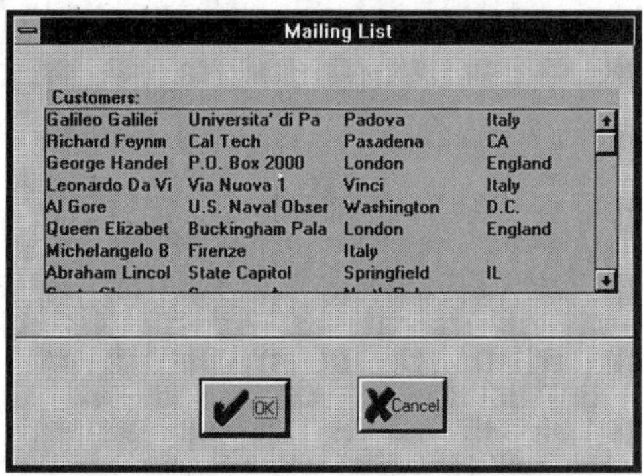

Figure 12.18. A multicolumn, owner-draw ListBox that prevents tab stop overruns.

Listing 12.31. How text is displayed in each column after truncating the text to make it fit.

```
void TDialogMailingList::DisplayMailingText(LPSTR text,
                                            TRect rect,
                                            TDC& dc)
{
  // use a local copy of the string for parsing
  char* string = _fstrdup(text);

  // parse the string for tabs
  LPSTR subString = _fstrtok(string, "\t");
  int i = 0;

  while (subString) {

    // compute the clipping rectangle for the next
    // column of text
    rect.left = Columns [i]. start;
    rect.right = Columns [i]. end;

    // truncate any characters that don't fit in the column
    for (int length = _fstrlen(subString); length > 0; length--) {
      int extent = dc.GetTextExtent(subString, length).cx;
      if (extent <= rect.Width() ) {
```

continues

Listing 12.31. continued

```
        // display the next column of text, showing only
        // those characters that fit completely in the column
        dc.ExtTextOut(rect.left, rect.top, ETO_CLIPPED,
                      &rect, subString, length, NULL);
      break;
      }
    }

    subString = _fstrtok(NULL, "\t");
    i++;
    if (i == sizeof(Columns) / sizeof(ColumnData) )
      break;
  }
  delete string;
}
```

The text parameter passed to `DisplayMailingList()` represents a tabbed-delimited string to paint. The individual substrings are parsed out of the string using the function `_fstrtok()`, which is equivalent to the standard `strtok()` function except that it handles far pointers.

Painting the Text

After parsing out a tab-delimited substring, `TDC::GetTextExtent()` is used to find the largest string that will fit into the column. The coordinates for all the ListBox columns are stored in pixels, in the global array `Columns`. After determining the longest string that will fit, `ExtTextOut()` is used to actually paint the string. `ExtTextOut()` takes a clipping rectangle as a parameter.

The clipping rectangle is set to correspond to the column in which text is to be painted, as is derived from the rect parameter passed to `DrawMailingText()`. The parameter rect is a rectangle whose top and bottom values delimit the item to draw, but whose left and right fields go all the way from the left to the right side of the ListBox's client area. The left and right coordinates of the text clipping rectangle are obtained from the `Columns` array.

The ListBox in ODLIST2 displays text in a manner compatible with standard ListBoxes. When an item is focused, a dotted focus rectangle is drawn around it. When an item is selected, the item is displayed in white text on a black background. The selection and focus cues are displayed by the `EvDrawItem()` member function, as shown in Listing 12.32.

Listing 12.32. The code that determines how text is to be painted.

```
void TDialogMailingList::EvDrawItem(UINT, DRAWITEMSTRUCT far& dis)
{
  HBRUSH background;

  TDC dc(dis.hDC);
  if (dis.itemAction & (ODA_DRAWENTIRE ¦ ODA_SELECT) ) {

    if (dis.itemState & ODS_SELECTED) {
      background = (HBRUSH) GetStockObject(BLACK_BRUSH);
      dc.SetTextColor(TColor::White);
    }
    else {
      background = (HBRUSH) GetStockObject(LTGRAY_BRUSH);
      dc.SetTextColor(TColor::Black);
    }

    dc.FillRect(dis.rcItem, background);
    char itemText [255];
    ::SendMessage(dis.hwndItem, LB_GETTEXT, dis.itemID, (LPARAM)
                &itemText);
    DisplayMailingText(itemText, dis.rcItem, dc);

    if (dis.itemState & ODS_FOCUS)
      dc.DrawFocusRect(dis.rcItem);
  }

  else if (dis.itemAction & ODA_FOCUS)
    // toggle the focus rectangle
    dc.DrawFocusRect(dis.rcItem);
}
```

`EvDrawItem()` doesn't actually paint any text. It just determines the colors of the text and the background, and calls `DisplayMailingText()` to paint the text.

A Complete Example

To show how all the various parts fit together, I'll show the complete source code for ODLIST2, which is also available on the companion disk. Listing 12.33 shows the code.

Listing 12.33. ODLIST2, an OWL application that uses an owner-draw ListBox to display data in columns.

```
// this application demonstrates how to support
// tabs in listboxes, using owner-draw controls to
// prevent tab overruns

#include <owl\framewin.h>
#include <owl\applicat.h>
#include <owl\dialog.h>
#include <owl\listbox.h>
#include <owl\gdiobjec.h>
#include <stdio.h>

// menu commands
const int
  IDM_MAILINGLIST = 101,
  IDM_HELPABOUT   = 201;

// columns coordinates in pixels
const int
  NAME_START    = 0,
  NAME_END      = 90,
  ADDRESS_START = 100,
  ADDRESS_END   = 200,
  CITY_START    = 210,
  CITY_END      = 300,
  STATE_START   = 310,
  STATE_END     = 400;

struct ColumnData {
  int start;
  int end;
} Columns [] = {
  NAME_START,    NAME_END,
  ADDRESS_START, ADDRESS_END,
  CITY_START,    CITY_END,
  STATE_START,   STATE_END
};

// dialog box child control IDs
const int
  IDC_CUSTOMERINFO = 101;

class TDialogAbout: public TDialog {

public:

  TDialogAbout(TWindow* AParent)
      : TDialog(AParent, "DIALOG_ABOUT") {}
};
```

```
class TDialogMailingList: public TDialog {

  TListBox* customerInfo;

public:

  TDialogMailingList(TWindow*);
  void SetupWindow();

  void EvDrawItem(UINT, DRAWITEMSTRUCT far&);
  void EvMeasureItem(UINT, MEASUREITEMSTRUCT far&);

  void DisplayMailingText(LPSTR, TRect, TDC&);
  DECLARE_RESPONSE_TABLE(TDialogMailingList);
};

DEFINE_RESPONSE_TABLE1(TDialogMailingList, TDialog)
  EV_WM_DRAWITEM,
  EV_WM_MEASUREITEM,
END_RESPONSE_TABLE;

TDialogMailingList::TDialogMailingList(TWindow* AParent)
                  : TDialog(AParent, "DIALOG_MAILINGLIST")
{
  customerInfo = new TListBox(this, IDC_CUSTOMERINFO);
}

void TDialogMailingList::SetupWindow()
{
  TDialog::SetupWindow();

  // initialize the listbox with tabbed strings
  char string [200];
  sprintf(string, "%s\t%s\t%s\t%s",
       "Galileo Galilei", "Universita' di Padova", "Padova", "Italy");
  customerInfo->AddString(string);

  sprintf(string, "%s\t%s\t%s\t%s",
       "Richard Feynman", "Cal Tech", "Pasadena", "CA");
  customerInfo->AddString(string);

  sprintf(string, "%s\t%s\t%s\t%s",
       "George Handel", "P.O. Box 2000", "London", "England");
  customerInfo->AddString(string);

  sprintf(string, "%s\t%s\t%s\t%s",
       "Leonardo Da Vinci", "Via Nuova 1", "Vinci", "Italy");
  customerInfo->AddString(string);
```

continues

Listing 12.33. continued

```
  sprintf(string, "%s\t%s\t%s\t%s",
       "Al Gore", "U.S. Naval Observatory", "Washington", "D.C.");
  customerInfo->AddString(string);

  sprintf(string, "%s\t%s\t%s\t%s",
       "Queen Elizabeth II", "Buckingham Palace", "London",
       "England");
  customerInfo->AddString(string);

  sprintf(string, "%s\t%s\t%s",
       "Michelangelo Buonaroti", "Firenze", "Italy");
  customerInfo->AddString(string);

  sprintf(string, "%s\t%s\t%s\t%s",
       "Abraham Lincoln", "State Capital", "Springfield", "IL");
  customerInfo->AddString(string);

  sprintf(string, "%s\t%s\t%s",
       "Santa Claus", "Snowman Ave", "North Pole");
  customerInfo->AddString(string);
}

void TDialogMailingList::EvDrawItem(UINT, DRAWITEMSTRUCT far& dis)
{
  HBRUSH background;

  TDC dc(dis.hDC);
  if (dis.itemAction & (ODA_DRAWENTIRE | ODA_SELECT) ) {

    if (dis.itemState & ODS_SELECTED) {
      background = (HBRUSH) GetStockObject(BLACK_BRUSH);
      dc.SetTextColor(TColor::White);
    }
    else {
      background = (HBRUSH) GetStockObject(LTGRAY_BRUSH);
      dc.SetTextColor(TColor::Black);
    }

    dc.FillRect(dis.rcItem, background);
    char itemText [255];
    ::SendMessage(dis.hwndItem, LB_GETTEXT, dis.itemID, (LPARAM)
                &itemText);
    DisplayMailingText(itemText, dis.rcItem, dc);

    if (dis.itemState & ODS_FOCUS)
      dc.DrawFocusRect(dis.rcItem);
  }
```

```
  else if (dis.itemAction & ODA_FOCUS)
    // toggle the focus rectangle
    dc.DrawFocusRect(dis.rcItem);
}

void TDialogMailingList::DisplayMailingText(LPSTR text,
                                            TRect rect,
                                            TDC& dc)
{
  // use a local copy of the string for parsing
  char* string = _fstrdup(text);

  // parse the string for tabs
  LPSTR subString = _fstrtok(string, "\t");
  int i = 0;

  while (subString) {

    // compute the clipping rectangle for the next
    // column of text
    rect.left = Columns [i]. start;
    rect.right = Columns [i]. end;

    // truncate any characters that don't fit in the column
    for (int length = _fstrlen(subString); length > 0; length--) {
      int extent = dc.GetTextExtent(subString, length).cx;
      if (extent <= rect.Width() ) {

        // display the next column of text, showing only
        // those characters that fit completely in the column
        dc.ExtTextOut(rect.left, rect.top, ETO_CLIPPED,
                      &rect, subString, length, NULL);
        break;
      }
    }

    subString = _fstrtok(NULL, "\t");
    i++;
    if (i == sizeof(Columns) / sizeof(ColumnData) )
      break;
  }
  delete string;
}

void TDialogMailingList::EvMeasureItem(UINT, MEASUREITEMSTRUCT far&
mis)
{
  mis.itemHeight = 15;
}
```

continues

Listing 12.33. continued

```
class TWindowMain : public TFrameWindow {

public:

  TWindowMain();

protected:

  void CmMailingList();
  void CmHelpAbout();
  DECLARE_RESPONSE_TABLE(TWindowMain);
};

DEFINE_RESPONSE_TABLE1(TWindowMain, TFrameWindow)
  EV_COMMAND(IDM_MAILINGLIST, CmMailingList),
  EV_COMMAND(IDM_HELPABOUT, CmHelpAbout),
END_RESPONSE_TABLE;

TWindowMain::TWindowMain()
           : TFrameWindow(NULL,
       "Tab Stops without Overruns, Using Owner-Draw ListBoxes")
{
  AssignMenu("MENU_MAIN");
}

void TWindowMain::CmMailingList()
{
  TDialogMailingList(this).Execute();
}

void TWindowMain::CmHelpAbout()
{
  TDialogAbout(this).Execute();
}

class TUserApplication: public TApplication {

public:

  TUserApplication()
      : TApplication("Owner-Draw ListBoxes") {}
  void InitMainWindow()
  { MainWindow = new TWindowMain; }
};

int OwlMain(int, char**)
{
  return TUserApplication().Run();
}
```

Storing the Column Table Inside the ListBox

The ListBox in ODLIST2 uses a global structure to store the column data. To avoid using globals, it is possible to store the column stops inside the ListBox. Emulating how tab stops are handled by standard ListBoxes, you could derive a class from `TListbox` and pass it a pointer to the column array, doing something like the code shown in Listing 12.34.

Listing 12.34. A derived `TListbox` class to manage column data without the need for global data structures.

```
#include <owl\listbox.h>

struct ColumnData {
  int start;
  int end;
};

class TColumnListbox: public TListbox {

  HGLOBAL hColumns;

public:

  TColumnListbox(TWindow* parent, int ID)
    : TListbox(parent, ID) {hColumns = 0;}

  ~TColumnListbox() {if (hColumns) GlobalFree(hColumns);}
  void SetColumns(int, ColumnData*);
};

void TColumnListbox::SetColumns(int count, ColumnData* columns)
{
  // de-allocate previously allocated memory — if any
  if (hColumns)
    GlobalFree(hColumns);

  // copy the column data into memory managed
  // internally by the Listbox
  int size = count * sizeof(ColumnData);
  hColumns = GlobalAlloc(GMEM_MOVEABLE, size);
  if (!hColumns)
    return;

  void far* pointer = GlobalLock(hColumns);
  _fmemcpy(pointer, columns, count);
  GlobalUnlock(hColumns);
}
```

continues

Listing 12.34. continued

```
class TMyDialog: public TDialog {

  TColumnListbox* listBox;

public:

  TMyDialog(TWindow* parent)
    : TDialog(parent, "DIALOG_SAMPLE")
    {listBox = new TColumnListbox(this, 100);}

  void SetupWindow();
};


void TMyDialog::SetupWindow()
{
  TDialog::SetupWindow();

  const int
    NAME_START    = 0,
    NAME_END      = 90,
    ADDRESS_START = 100,
    ADDRESS_END   = 200,
    CITY_START    = 210,
    CITY_END      = 300,
    STATE_START   = 310,
    STATE_END     = 400;

  ColumnData columns [] = {
    NAME_START,    NAME_END,
    ADDRESS_START, ADDRESS_END,
    CITY_START,    CITY_END,
    STATE_START,   STATE_END
  };

  int count = sizeof(columns) / sizeof(ColumnData);
  listBox->SetColumns(count, columns);
}
```

Class `TColumnListbox` allocates a block of memory from the global heap and copies the column data into it. The memory is released in the class destructor. I omitted the details of owner drawing, but class `TMyDialog` is responsible for drawing the `TColumnListbox` and should have the same drawing functions described in ODLIST2.

ListBoxes are among the most flexible and useful of Windows child controls. The standard Windows way to draw nontextual items in ListBoxes is to use owner drawing, in which the parent window is responsible for drawing the items in the ListBox. But having a control delegate its own painting to the parent window is a technique that is not object-oriented, and is also messy and unnecessarily complicated. The object-oriented approach is to derive a class from `TListBox` and make it handle the painting of whatever items are stored in the listbox.

I have discussed both the owner-draw (see example ODLIST) and the derived class approach (see example TABLIST1) in this chapter. The elegance and simplicity of the latter method should be apparent, making owner drawing a technique that is best left to old C programs.

OLE Programming with OWL

With the release of OLE 2.0 in 1993, an important technology was unleashed to the masses. OLE is not just an extension to Windows, it is a change in programming philosophy that will profoundly affect the way developers write code. Although OLE is to be considered only an extension to Windows 3.1, with Windows 95 it is a basic part of the system. OLE is not one of those short lived buzzwords that no one will remember next year: OLE is here to stay, and will be an increasingly important part of every Windows developer's life.

In this chapter I'll discuss briefly what OLE is, and how Borland added OLE support to OWL. Unless otherwise noted, I'll use the term OLE to indicate OLE 2.0. I'll try not to duplicate information that can be found in the Borland documentation, so I won't waste a lot of space showing how to use AppExpert and ClassExpert to create OLE servers and containers. I'll discuss some of the design issues Borland faced in adding OLE support to their product, and will emphasize some of the more interesting aspects of OLE implementation. The emphasis will be on the classes and class hierarchies Borland developed, and how everything ties together.

Why OLE?

Creating applications for Windows is not trivial. Although Windows 3.*x* internally managed objects for things like brushes, modules and tasks, it didn't use objects that any object-oriented programmer could use directly. Sure, when Windows sends you a message, you get an `HWND` as a parameter, but the parameter is really only a handle to a struct with some data in it. You can't derive a C++ class from this struct, or invoke member functions for the struct. *Objects* in Windows 3.*x* are just parcels of data. Windows 3.*x* had some of the right ingredients, but real objects were missing.

As Windows applications became more complex, the cries increased for a simpler software development model—a system that would let programmers concentrate more on application details and less on Windows internals. One of the keys in simplifying software development is reusability. If you have an application that knows how to handle spreadsheets and you need spreadsheet capabilities in another app, it makes sense for the second app to use the services of the first. In the early Windows days, DDE was the method used to connect apps. DDE is conceptually similar to a serial communication link between applications on the same machine—with all of the pitfalls. One problem was error recovery. If one app tried to connect via DDE to an app that wasn't running, the situation had to be dealt with. When sending messages, error messages or unexpected responses could come back—all of which had to be explicitly dealt with. DDE worked, but was very brittle and took a lot of development time to be usable.

Another problem was the lack of standards for DDE. There was no such thing as runtime discovery of capabilities. If you wanted to connect app `A` to app `B`, you had to know exactly what DDE messages `B` supported, and what responses could be generated. DDE did achieve the goal of connecting apps together, but the lack of standards, robustness and generality were insurmountable barriers to its widespread popularity.

OLE is an object-based solution that in one pass (two actually—it was only with OLE 2.0 that the standard started to take off) solved all the problems of DDE, and then solved a whole slew of problems DDE hadn't even addressed. Table 13.1 lists the major features supported by OLE.

Table 13.1. The major features supported by OLE.

Feature	*Description*
Linking	OLE objects can be linked to a container application. The container doesn't actually store the linked objects, only the links. If the linked objects are updated, the container application will see the changes automatically.
Embedding	OLE objects can be inserted directly into a container application. Saving the application to disk results in the embedded objects

Feature	*Description*
	also being saved. If you embed an object into a container, a copy of the object is made and embedded. Changes to the original object have no effect on the object embedded in the container.
Clipboard Operations	OLE objects can be cut, copied and pasted using standard Clipboard operations. Pasting an OLE object from the clipboard doesn't merely place a picture of something into your app, it brings in a complete OLE object. You can click on this object to activate it and perform operations that were available to the original object. If you special paste a Word object, then activating it launches the entire Word for Windows application, assuming Word is available on your system.
Drag-and-Drop	You can drag OLE objects around with the mouse and drop them into OLE container applications. The dropped objects remain full-blown OLE objects, with the in-place activation logic discussed under Clipboard Operations.
Compound Files	Saving documents that contain embedded objects results in a file that contains the documents with all their embedded objects. OLE uses compound files to create files that are internally structured into files (called streams) and directories (called storages). Documents are stored in their own separate storage.
Automation	Applications can make certain properties and methods available to be invoked from other applications. Rather than sending messages as in DDE, automation allows functions to be called directly, pretty much like a regular member function call in C++. Automation is the technology built into OLE that allows functionality to be exposed by one application, and used by another.
Localization	Objects that are automated, linked or embedded may wind up in an application that uses a different locale (such as language) from the one it was developed in. OLE makes it easy to internationalize objects by making available a number of standards for dealing with language and other locale-dependent issues.
Dynamic Querying	One of the most powerful features of OLE is the ability to discover at runtime the features of an OLE object. With DDE, you needed to know life, death and works of the app you wanted to connect to. With OLE, you don't need to know anything a priori. Using the `QueryInterface` function that is supported by all OLE objects, you can explore an object's features at runtime.

OLE is novel in many ways, but isn't the only object-based technology in the world. Mac users have a standard called OpenDoc, OS/2 programmers have DSOM/SOM, and other systems are being developed for Unix users. Microsoft didn't invent all the technologies that are part of OLE, and many ideas about how objects should work and be handled are still in the research phase.

OLE was basically invented to solve the problem of *binary interoperability*. Developers needed a way for applications to talk to each other and to be used as building blocks inside other applications. The interfaces between these apps had to be standardized and not be dependent on the language or environment used to create the apps.

Drawbacks of OLE

From what you just read, you might be tempted to believe that OLE is the solution for all the problems in software development. After all, you can drop objects into your applications, store them in files, call exposed functions of automated objects. To bring OLE into perspective, it is necessary to show not only its strengths, but also its limitations, as seen from a C++ perspective.

No Support for Distributed Objects

Objects are self-contained entities. In a distributed environment, objects could be stored anywhere. An OLE object on one node of a network should be usable from any other node in the network, the way files are. Such a distributed object model is not currently supported by OLE. To combine OLE objects together into an application, all the objects need to be on the same computer. Microsoft is currently addressing this limitation of OLE, and future versions of OLE will definitely support distributed objects.

No Direct Support for Inheritance

C++ programmers are used to reusing functionality through inheritance. Inheritance lets you specify a class that you want to reuse, and specify the member functions you want to change. By default, derived classes inherit all the functionality of the base class. OLE doesn't support this model of inheritance. Given an OLE object of type A, you can't create a new OLE object of type B that inherits (in the C++ sense) the capabilities of A.

But all isn't lost. Although OLE doesn't support C++ style inheritance, it does support two techniques that let you use one object inside another. The inner object is essentially encapsulated by the second, and from the outside users see only a single object with the functionality of both objects. The techniques are called *object containment* and *object aggregation*. Using these techniques, described later in the chapter, you can create objects that appear to inherit capabilities from one or more base classes.

OLE Uses Objects

Windows internally supports the concept of object. Programmers are used to dealing with entities like `HBRUSH`, `HWND`, and `HMODULE`. The handles really only access structs that contain information on a given item. In OOP, data is not stored by itself, but is combined with functionality, in the form of methods or member functions. When Microsoft decided to add support for real objects, it decided that the objects would have to be language-neutral. The objects had to have a specific binary interface so that anyone could use them, regardless of which language an application was written in. The Component Object Model (COM) was born.

The Component Object Model

COM objects are binary objects that support certain basic features. The basis for Microsoft's Component Object Model is the interface. Every COM object has one or more interfaces, and each interface contains functions that are callable. A COM object interface is really a pointer to a table of functions, just like the `VPTR` pointer in a C++ class that uses virtual functions.

In C++ you handle objects through pointers or references. Using these pointers or references, you can manipulate all the public data members of an object. With COM interfaces, you can call functions, but you never can access the object's data. Interfaces contain only functions, not data. To enable users of a COM object to access an internal variable, the object needs to have the appropriate access functions that read or write the variable.

So structurally, a COM object is a binary object that has one or more interfaces. The only interface that a COM object *must* support is `IUnknown`. This interface has three functions: `QueryInterface`, `AddRef`, and `Release`. The first function returns pointers to other interfaces supported by the COM object. The second increases the object's internal reference count, indicating the number of users of the object. The last function, `Release`, decreases the reference count for a COM object. When the count drops to zero, the object removes itself from memory.

Interfaces of OLE Objects

All OLE objects are COM objects. It follows that all OLE objects support the `IUnknown` interface. What distinguishes an OLE object from a simple COM object is a certain amount of added functionality that the OLE object has, in the form of new interfaces. While COM simply indicates the structure of an object, OLE indicates a certain functionality, built into a binary object with the COM architecture. OLE objects support one or more of the features shown in Table 13.1. An OLE object need not support all of those features. Each feature is supported through one or more interfaces, like `IPersist`, `IViewObject`, `IDataObject`, `IDropTarget`, and others.

How OLE Objects Talk to Each Other

Having defined the basic characteristics of OLE objects, the next question is *how does an application talk to an embedded or linked OLE object, and vice-versa?* From the preceding discussion, it should be clear that the only possible way is through calls to functions contained in OLE interfaces. An application wishing to embed or link OLE objects must be an OLE object itself, often called an *OLE container*. Containers support a number of interfaces through which the embedded or linked objects can talk to them. For example, a container object that lets you drag-and-drop OLE objects onto it will support the `IDropTarget` interface (and probably several others as well). The object being dragged and dropped will need to support the `IDataObject` interface (and probably several other interfaces as well). When one object wants to talk to the other, it simply calls one of the functions contained in one of the object's interfaces. Both objects must be OLE objects, because one object was linked or embedded in the other.

There is also another scenario when applications can talk to OLE objects, in which the application doesn't link or embed the OLE object. Say you have an application, and you have a financial calculator implemented as an OLE object. If your application needs to make some computations that the calculator knows how to do, you would like to be able to some how connect your app to the calculator and request it to do the calculations. In the old days you would have solved the situation using DDE: The calculator would support certain DDE commands, and you would write some DDE code into your app to transfer data to and from the calculator. That was in the old days. With OLE, you *automate* the calculator and call it from the application. No DDE involved. Automating an OLE object means adding a number of special interfaces like `IDispatch`, `ITypeLib` and `ITypeInfo`. These interfaces *expose* certain methods of the OLE object, and allow you to call those methods from other applications. The beauty is that the calling applications are not required to link or embed the automated objects they use, so there is very little overhead required.

Borland's Approach to OLE

Obviously there is a lot to OLE, and what developer's need is a reasonably easy way to incorporate OLE features into their programs. In C++ programs you often add new features by deriving classes from base classes that do the complicated stuff. The overall task of creating all the necessary base classes may not be simple, but inheriting from those classes is easy. The recommended technique to empower an application with OLE functionality is to use an application framework that supports OLE. Microsoft added support for OLE to Visual C++ by adding OLE code directly to MFC. They wrote something like 20,000 lines of code to encapsulate OLE in MFC. The details are obviously hideous, but the result is that users can simply create an OLE application by deriving a class from an MFC class.

Microsoft's end result might seem reasonable on the surface, but it does have its problems. For one thing, putting OLE code directly into MFC makes MFC much more complex. Second, to add OLE functionality to a Visual C++ program you are now required to use MFC. Third, if you have an application that you simply want to add OLE functionality to, you're up the proverbial creek.

Borland doesn't do things like Microsoft (that's the understatement of the year!). For one thing, Borland doesn't have access to near-unlimited resources for brute-force development and debugging (which MFC certainly required). Even if they did, they just don't do things that way. The Borland developers sat back and watched Microsoft introduce OLE on a few applications, like Word, Visual C+, and Access. Studying the pros and cons of the Microsoft approach, they later decided on an implementation strategy.

The very first observation they made was that OLE was too tedious and low-level, so they created a wrapper around the basic OLE API. There are lots of high level operations that recur in applications, like dealing with documents and views. They identified these high level operations, and created interfaces for them. The code containing these interfaces was put into a DLL, and used to OLE-enable applications like Quattro Pro for Windows and Paradox. The DLL was called BOCOLE, and is described in the next section.

The second major decision Borland made was not to add direct OLE function calls into OWL. As a result, they created a brand new application framework for OLE programming, and called it Object Components Frameworks (OCF). OCF has all kinds of classes to connect application objects like views and documents to OLE. To add OLE support to OWL, all they did was add some OCF data members here and there in OWL, and invoke them at the right time, so OWL changed very little. Figure 13.1 shows the relationship between OWL, OCF, and BOCOLE.

Figure 13.1. The relationship between OWL, OCF, and BOCOLE.

There are no direct calls into the OLE API in OWL. OWL talks to OCF and knows nothing about OLE details. OCF is the OLE guru, and knows a lot about OLE. OCF calls high-level interfaces created by BOCOLE, and also makes direct low-level calls into the OLE API.

A fall-out from the decision to put all OLE dependencies into OCF instead of OWL is that OCF can now be used to add OLE support to applications written in Visual C++.

The process is relatively straightforward, involving the sprinkling of a few OCF classes at strategic points in the app. Borland has numerous examples showing how to use OCF with C++ programs without OWL.

The BOCOLE Engine

As mentioned previously, BOCOLE (for *Borland Object Components OLE*) is a wrapper DLL that creates a number of medium and high-level interfaces to OLE. The idea is that operations that occur frequently from the application side should map directly into some kind of BOCOLE interface. Applications deal with such entities as views, documents, linked and embedded objects, so Borland added equivalent interfaces to BOCOLE, like `IBDocument`, `IBWindow` and `IBPart`. Figure 13.2 is a schematic representation of how BOCOLE looks from the application side.

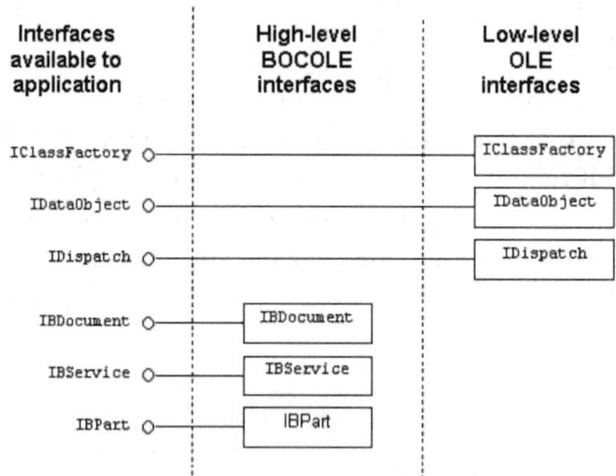

Figure 13.2. An application's perspective of how BOCOLE extends the low-level OLE API.

Figure 13.2 shows only a few sample interfaces available in the OLE and BOCOLE layers. Following the OLE standard, interfaces are represented as *jacks*, and are depicted as a line ending with a circle. Which interfaces are actually callable for a given OLE object will obviously depend on what kind of object it is. Figure 13.3 shows a complete hierarchy of the high-level interfaces made available by BOCOLE.

Calling functions in the high-level interfaces results in one or more calls to low level OLE interfaces. Much of the processing inside BOCOLE is delegated to internal C++ objects called *helpers*. These helpers connect to the high-level interfaces and help to manage collections of OLE objects. Table 13.2 is a list of the high-level BOCOLE helper classes.

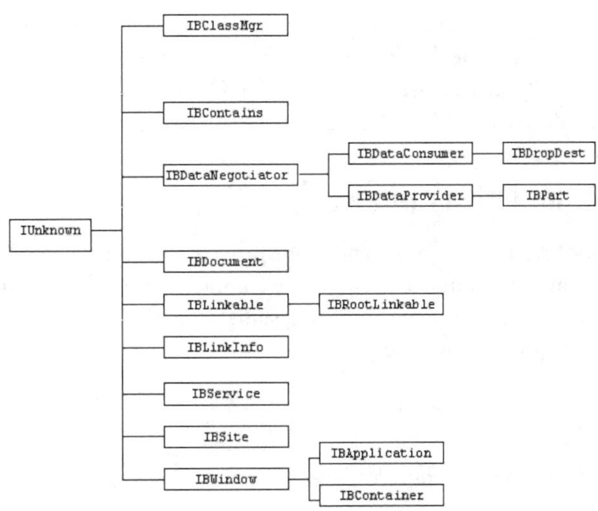

Figure 13.3. The high-level interfaces implemented in BOCOLE.

Table 13.2. The main BOCOLE helper classes.

`BOleClassManager`
`BOleComponent`
`BOleContainer`
`BOleData`
`BOleDocument`
`BOleFact`
`BOleInProcServer`
`BOlePart`
`BOleService`
`BOleSite`

Each of the classes in Table 13.2 supports one or more of the high-level interfaces shown in Figure 13.3. For example, the high level interface `IBDocument` declares the function `UpdateLinks()`. Class `BOleDocument` has the member function `UpdateLinks()` that is called through the `IBDocument` interface. The function iterates over the objects embedded or linked in the document, and updates their links through low-level OLE API calls. All you really see from the outside of BOCOLE are the interfaces. The helper objects hidden inside are accessible.

ObjectComponents Framework

Borland created OCF as a stand-alone piece of software that could provide OLE capabilities to any application. The classes are completely decoupled from OWL, and in fact you can use OCF with Visual C++ if you want. OCF is a complex class hierarchy and supports the following OLE features:

- Linking
- Embedding
- Clipboard Operations
- Drag-and-Drop
- Compound Files
- OLE Servers
- OLE Containers
- Automation
- Type Library Creation
- Server registration
- Localization

Because of its excellent design, OCF is relatively easy to use. To add support for an OLE feature, you normally just derive your class from an OCF class, or embed an OCF object in your class. OCF completely envelopes the OLE API, presenting to developers a clean and object-oriented facade. You don't have to worry about OLE problems, like memory management, registration attributes or type libraries. You use familiar C++ notation to derive classes from OCF, and that's it. In fact normally you don't even do that, because OLE applications are normally generated using AppExpert, leaving little or no additional OLE-dependent code to write.

OCF Messages

When you invoke a function of an OLE object, the call leads to code inside the OLE object. If the OLE object was created with OCF, eventually OCF code will get called. For certain basic operations (like showing or hiding an embedded object), OCF can handle the call by itself. Most of the time, however, OCF will need to call your application code to handle the call. OCF doesn't have any knowledge of how your application code was written, nor

should it. Rather than attempting to call a function in your code, OCF uses the Windows standard of sending you a notification message. OCF can send quite a few different kinds of notifications, but all of them have the message type `WM_OCEVENT`. `WPARAM` carries the notification parameter and `LPARAM` holds additional optional information. Table 13.3 is a list of the OCF notification messages that OCF can send.

Table 13.3. The types of OCF notification messages.

Notification Code	*Description*
`OC_APPBORDERSPACEREQ`	Requests a container for border space to display a frame.
`OC_APPBORDERSPACESET`	Sets the amount of border space used to display a frame.
`OC_APPDIALOGHELP`	Help button was pressed on a standard OLE dialog box.
`OC_APPFRAMERECT`	Gets the inner rectangle of the main window.
`OC_APPINSMENUS`	Inserts menus of embedded/linked object into main menu.
`OC_APPMENUS`	Sets main menu of the application.
`OC_APPPROCESSMSG`	Processes accelerator key messages.
`OC_APPRESTOREUI`	Eliminates the toolbar and menu items added to the application for an activated linked/embedded object.
`OC_APPSHUTDOWN`	Closes the main window.
`OC_APPSTATUSTEXT`	Sets the text on the status line.
`OC_VIEWATTACHWINDOW`	Server attaches itself to an owner window.
`OC_VIEWBORDER REQ`	Requests border space in view.
`OC_VIEWBORDER SET`	Sets border space in view.
`OC_VIEWBREAKLINK`	Server breaks a link to an item.
`OC_VIEWCLIPDATA`	Server renders its data in a given format.
`OC_VIEWCLOSE`	Server closes its remote view in the container view space.
`OC_VIEWDRAG`	A linked/embedded object is being dragged. Give feedback to the container application and the user.
`OC_VIEWDROP`	An object is being embedded into a container by a drop operation.
`OC_VIEWGETITEMNAME`	Server names its contents or selection.
`OC_VIEWGETPALETTE`	Server returns the palette used to draw its view.

continues

Table 13.3. continued

Notification Code	*Description*
OC_VIEWGETSCALE	Asks a container for view scaling information.
OC_VIEWGETSITERECT	Asks a container for the bounding rectangle of the view site.
OC_VIEWINMENUS	Server inserts its own menus in the container's menu bar.
OC_VIEWLOADPART	Server loads its document data.
OC_VIEWOPENDOC	Asks a container to open an existing document.
OC_VIEWPAINT	Server paints itself in the container's view space.
OC_VIEWPARTINVALID	A linked/embedded object was invalidated.
OC_VIEWPARTSIZE	Requests the view extent of a linked/embedded object.
OC_VIEWSAVEPART	Server saves itself in a compound file.
OC_VIEWSCROLL	Requests a linked/embedded object to scroll its view.
OC_VIEWSETLINK	Server establishes a link to an item.
OC_VIEWSETSCALE	Servers sets up scaling information.
OC_VIEWSETSITERECT	Requests a container to set the size of the bounding rectangle of the view of a linked/embedded object.
OC_VIEWSETTITLE	Sets the window title.
OC_VIEWSHOWTOOLS	Server displays its toolbar in the container's view space.
OC_VIEWTITLE	Requests the window title of a view.

To handle a notification message, you process `WM_OCEVENT` messages and check the notification parameter. The notifications messages can be grouped into two categories: those sent to an application, and those sent to individual windows in an application. The notifications that start with `OC_APP...` designate messages sent to applications. Notifications that start with `OC_VIEW...` are destined for specific windows in an application.

OCF Connector Objects

OLE is built on a myriad of low-level interfaces. Applications are built with windows containing views and documents. OLE supports operations at a much lower level, dealing for example with the mechanics of drag-and-drop, or pasting objects from the clipboard. Between low-level OLE and a typical application there is what might be called *a mismatch in*

impedance, an expression borrowed from electrical engineering that indicates an interconnection problem caused by internal differences in the objects being connected. OCF has the dual task of hiding the low-level OLE mess, and offering to applications an interface that has classes that parallel those used in the application.

An OCF connector class is a C++ class that is connected on one side to the application and on the other to an OLE object. Table 13.4 shows the four basic connector classes in OCF.

Table 13.4. The OCF connector classes.

Connector Class	*Description*
`TOcApp`	Handles application-level OLE functionality, like accelerator key translation and OLE server registration.
`TOcView`	Handles the painting of OLE container windows that contain linked or embedded objects.
`TOcRemView`	Handles the painting of linked or embedded server objects in the container's view (considered a *remote view*).
`TOcPart`	Used to represent any linked or embedded object. Handles actions that containers perform on these objects.

OCF has all kinds of classes that deal with OLE. The connector classes are the highest level classes, as seen from application programs. The following sections will discuss each connector class in a little more detail.

TOcApp

The highest level class in any application is the user application class, which handles the Windows message pump, performs accelerator key translations, and dispatches messages. OCF has a similar class, called `TOcApp`, and its purpose is to handle features that regard the user's application. The following sections discuss the main areas which `TOcApp` objects help out in.

Accelerator Key Translation

One feature `TOcApp` handles is the translation of accelerator keys for linked/embedded objects that are active. In order for accelerator keys to be handled correctly, `TOcApp` must be called inside the user application message loop. In response to accelerator keys, `TOcApp` may send one of more messages to other windows in the OLE object it is part of.

Menu Merging

TOcApp also performs menu merging. When you activate a linked or embedded server object by clicking in it, the menu commands built into the server are merged with the menu commands of the container application. If the server has the menus Format, Tools, and Table, and the container has the menus File, Edit, and Help, the overall menu will contain the items File, Edit, Format, Tools, Table, and Help.

I'll make an ultra-fast digression on menu merging, since it's a technique new to OLE which C++ programmers may not be familiar with. OLE containers and servers build menus using special menu descriptors. One descriptor is used for each popup menu displayed on the main menu bar. Descriptors are organized into six groups under OLE, described in Table 13.5.

Table 13.5. The six functional groups into which menus are divided, for OLE menu merging.

Menu Group	*Description*
File Group	This is the first pop-up menu displayed on the left side of the main menu bar. Normally it contains File commands, like Open, Close, Save, Print, and Exit.
Edit Group	This is the second popup from the left on the main menu bar. It contains standard commands like Cut, Copy, and Paste, and also the OLE commands Insert Object and Paste Special.
Container Group	This group contains popup menus that are displayed only when an OLE object is being used as a container. If the object is run as a server (assuming it can be), then the menus in the Container Group are not shown.
Object Group	This group contains all those commands that an object supports when it is run as an embedded or linked server.
Window Group	This group contains MDI window commands like Tile, Cascade, and Arrange All.
Help Group	This contains the Help-related commands like Index, Contents, and About.

Each group can contain one or more popup menus, so the use of OLE functional groups by no means limits you to six popup menus. Using the server example above, the popup menus Format, Tools, and Table would be built with Menu Descriptors for the Object Group.

View Site Support

When an OLE container links or embeds a server object, there needs to be a way for the server to display itself on the screen. There is some negotiating that goes on between the container and the server, and the result is a rectangle in which the server paints itself. Basically, the negotiation starts with the container telling the server how big the container's overall client area is, taking into account toolbars and status bars, if any. The server takes this information, and decides whether to paint itself with scaling or not. The server can display its own toolbar in the container view space, and also control the text shown in the container's status bar.

When a linked/embedded server is deactivated, everything the server did that affected the container view needs to be undone. `TOcApp` takes care of all these details, like restoring old toolbars, status bars and menus.

TOcView

An OLE container has the ability to link or embed server objects in its windows. Each window that can hold or embed server objects must use a `TOcView` OCF class. `TOcView` keeps a list of the servers in a container, and manages these objects as necessary. For example, if you scroll a window with linked or embedded objects in it, the container not only needs to repaint itself, but also tell each of the servers it holds to repaint themselves. `TOcView` keeps track of which linked/embedded objects are active, and helps out in clipboard operations as well.

Each of the linked or embedded server objects in a container is represented by an object of type `TOcPart`, as shown in Figure 13.4.

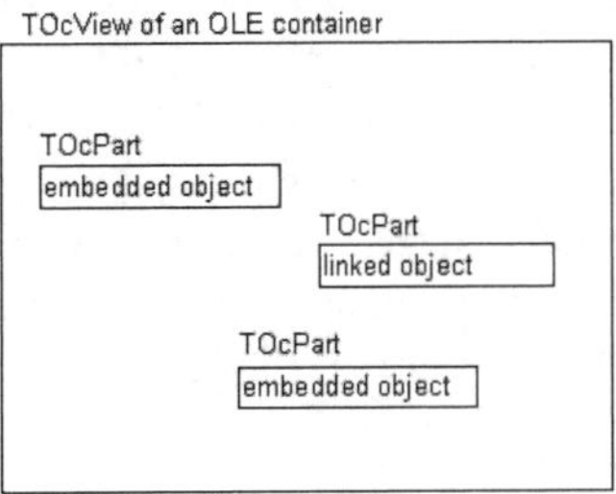

Figure 13.4. `TOcViews` *and* `TOcParts`.

TOcRemView

When a server is linked or embedded in a container, the server paints itself in a rectangle contained in the container's view space. This rectangle—along with all associated drawing characteristics—is called a *remote view*, and is handled by the OCF class `TOcRemView`. When a control needs to paint itself in a remote view, OLE creates a metafile device context in the container's view space. The server paints itself into this metafile, and the drawing commands are stored. With all the commands stored, OLE containers can repaint linked or embedded servers without server involvement. Obviously, anytime the server needs to modify the way it appears on the screen, it will have to update the content of its OLE metafile. Figure 13.5 shows the relationship between a container's view space, remote views and their metafile.

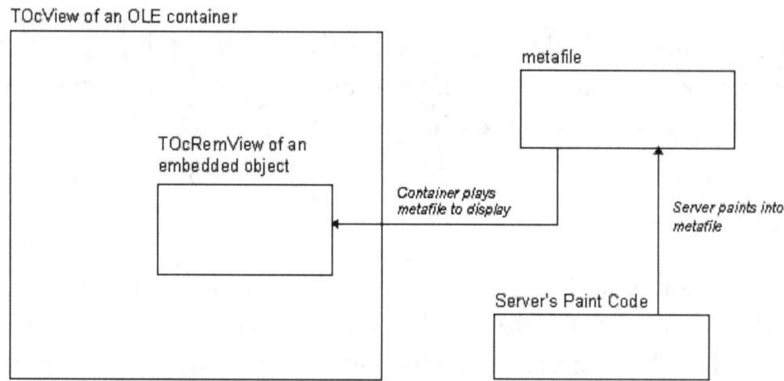

Figure 13.5. The relationship between `TOcRemView`*, metafiles and container views.*

TOcPart

Embedding or linking a server object inside an OLE container requires lots of communication between the container and server. The container has to coordinate all the actions that affect the various servers it contains. OCF has the class `TOcPart` that represents each embedded or linked object. When you develop an OLE server, on the inside it looks like an application. From the outside, when that server is put into a container, it looks like a `TOcPart`. Class `TOcPart` makes linked or embedded OLE servers look like regular C++ objects to their surrounding container app. `TOcPart`s support direct member function calls like `Activate()`, `Show()`, `Draw()`, allowing the container code to manipulate servers with ease.

OWL and OCF

OCF was designed to encapsulate as much OLE functionality as possible, allowing applications to acquire OLE functionality with relative ease. As a result, Borland didn't have to make very many changes to OWL, and OLE applications created with OWL have a structure very similar to non-OLE applications.

When you develop OWL applications, you deal mainly with objects derived from `TWindow`. The main window is a frame window supporting optional items like toolbars and status bars. In OWL parlance, such windows are *called decorated windows*. SDI applications derive their main window from class `TOleFrame`, MDI apps from class `TOleMDIFrame`.

A Window for Each OLE Object

An essential feature of decorated windows is their ability to handle child windows automatically. This is important in OLE, because OLE containers will create one child window (managed by class `TOcPart`) for each linked or embedded object in them. The decorated window needs to store objects in separate windows, because it may need to move items around at certain times. For example, if you activate an embedded object that has its own toolbar, the container will have to make room for it if a toolbar wasn't already shown. The same for the status bar, or any other decorations the object uses that weren't used by the container, such as floating palettes. When the container inserts a toolbar, the size of the frame window's client area is reduced, and some of the windows containing linked/embedded objects may need to be repainted, moved or scaled. Keeping each linked/embedded object in its own window makes everything easier to handle. Figure 13.6 shows the classes involved in an SDI application whose main window contains one linked and one embedded object.

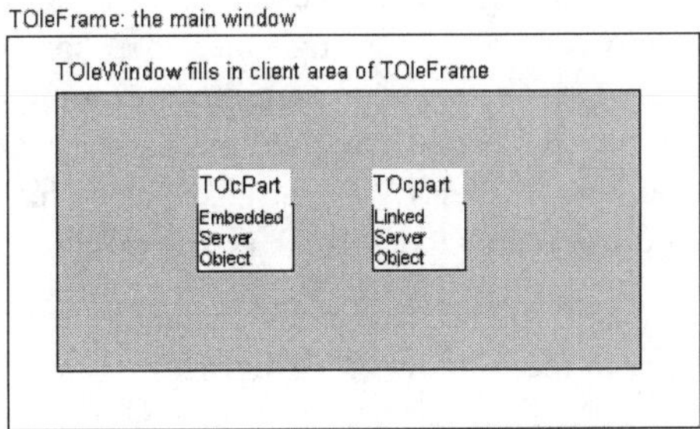

Figure 13.6. The classes used in an SDI application with one linked and one embedded object.

Usually the main window in an SDI app is not a `TOleWindow`, but a class derived from `TOleWindow`. The derived class has handlers for your application's main menu commands.

In MDI applications, the main window is derived from class `TOleMDIFrame`, and each child window is of type `TMDIChild`, and the client area of each child is occupied by objects derived from class `TOleWindow`. Figure 13.7 shows the various classes.

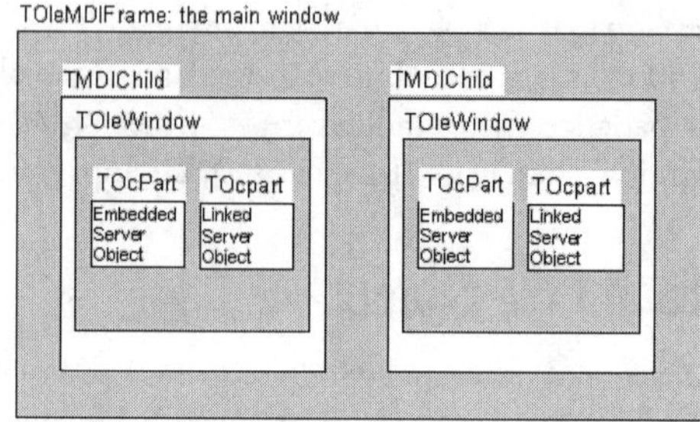

Figure 13.7. Two MDI child windows each containing linked and embedded objects.

Handling OCF Messages

When OWL needs to tell an OCF object to do something, it calls an OCF member function. For example, to make an embedded object show itself, OWL calls the code

```
part->Show(true);
```

When OCF wants to tell your application to do something, it can't simply invoke a member function. OCF has no idea what member functions are in your application, and doesn't even assume you are using OWL. The standard way for information to travel around in the Windows environment is through messages, so OCF sends your application an `WM_OCEVENT` message. The message carries a notification parameter in `WPARAM`, as shown previously in Table 13.3. To handle these messages, you add event handlers to your windows' Event Response Tables (EVTs), just like you do for regular Windows messages. For each OCF notification message, there is a corresponding member function to handle it.

I'll give an example. If you want a window to handle the `OC_VIEWPAINT` notification, then you add an entry to the window's EVT like this:

```
DEFINE_RESPONSE_TABLE1(TMyWindow, TOleWindow)
  EV_OC_VIEWPAINT,
END_RESPONSE_TABLE;
```

Corresponding to the `EV_OC_VIEWPAINT` EVT entry, there is the member function

```
bool TMyWindow::EvOcViewPaint(TOcViewPaint far& vp)
```

that must be added to the window. Every OCF notification message is handled the same way. OWL has default handlers for all the OCF notifications, but there are some (like `EvOcViewPaint`) that normally will be overridden. The important thing is that if you don't provide handlers for all the necessary OCF notifications during development time, your application will still do something (without crashing!).

Inserting an OLE Object into a Container

There are three fundamental ways for a user to insert linked or embedded objects into a container application:

- using the `Insert Object` from the `Edit` menu
- drag-and-drop
- pasting an object from the clipboard

I'll discuss each method, and the OWL/OCF code involved, in the following sections.

Using the Insert Object Command

On the `Edit` menu for every OLE container application is the command `Insert Object`. Clicking this command brings up a standard OLE dialog box, showing the names of all the types of OLE servers registered in the system. The dialog box looks like this:

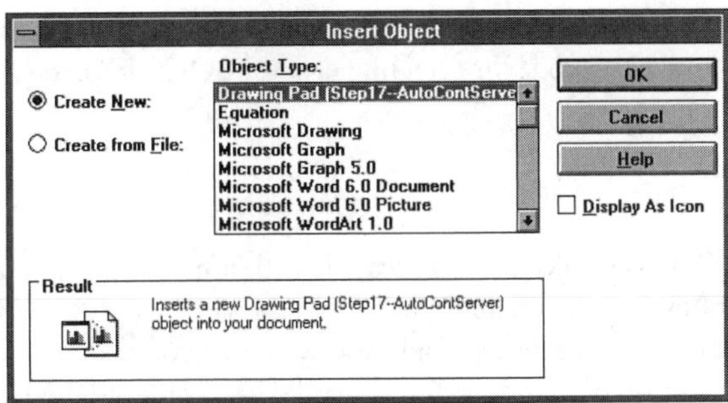

Figure 13.8. The standard OLE Insert Object dialog box.

The code that OWL uses to bring this dialog box up is contained in class `TOleWindow`, and looks something like Listing 13.1.

Listing 13.1. The OWL code that displays the OLE Insert Object dialog box.

```
void TOleWindow::CmEditInsertObject()
{
  TOcInitInfo initInfo(OcView);

  if (OcApp->Browse(initInfo)) {
    TRect rect;
    GetInsertPosition(rect);
    SetSelection(new TOcPart(*GetOcDoc(),
                             initInfo, rect));
```

continues

Listing 13.1. continued

```
    OcView->Rename();
    InvalidatePart(invView);
  }
}
```

The call `OcApp->Browse()` causes the dialog box to appear. If the user closes the dialog box with the OK button, then the parameter `initInfo` returns with information regarding the class ID of the selected server type. This information is then passed to the constructor of `TOcPart`. `TOcPart` loads the server, starts it running, and attaches itself to it. The call

```
InvalidatePart(invView);
```

only does something if the container is itself linked or embedded in another container, in which case the server repaints its remote view. After the `TOcPart` is created and inserted into the container, all future operations on the OLE server go through `TOcPart`. There is no low-level OLE code, or even higher-level BOCOLE code in OWL to deal with OLE objects.

Drag-and-Drop

To drag a server object, you activate it with a mouse click and move/copy it to either a new window or to a different position in the same window. Dragging can be used also to move/copy objects between applications. When you release the mouse, the object figuratively *drops* into the window directly under it. In order for you to be able to drag and drop an object, two things must be true: the object must be draggable and the window it's dropped on must support dropped objects. OLE applications developed with OWL can do both things, but I'll focus my discussion on the dropping action.

When you drag an OLE object over a window, the object asks the window if it accepts drops. The type of object is passed in the request. If the window accepts that kind of object to be dropped, it answers affirmatively. This simple dialog is handled by the OCF notification message `OC_VIEWDROP`. `TOleWindow` has a default handler that looks like this:

```
bool TOleWindow::EvOcViewDrop(TOcDragDrop far& ddInfo)
{
  return true;
}
```

which indicates that any type of OLE object can be dropped. Your applications might be more restrictive, so you would override the `EvOcViewDrop()` handler in a derived class, and check the type of object being dropped in the `ddInfo` parameter.

When the user releases the mouse button, the object is dropped, and a flurry of OLE events are set into motion. All the small details are handled by BOCOLE, the rest by OCF. There is no OWL code involved at all! The most important result of the drop operation is that the dropped object shows up in the destination window. The OCF class `TOcView` implements this magic with code that looks something like Listing 13.2.

Listing 13.2. The code that embeds a new object following a drop operation.

```
HRESULT TOcView::Drop(TOcInitInfo far* initInfo,
                      TPoint far* where,
                      const TRect far* objPos)
{
  initInfo->Container = this;
  TPoint awhere(*where);
  TRect  aobjPos(*objPos);
  TOcDragDrop dd = {
    (TOcInitInfo far*)initInfo, &awhere, &aobjPos
  };

  // Make sure that the view will accept this drop
  if (!ForwardEvent(OC_VIEWDROP, &dd))
   return HR_FAIL;

  // Create part now that view approved
  new TOcPart(OcDocument, *dd.InitInfo, aobjPos);
  Rename();
  return HR_NOERROR;
}
```

The code isn't too different than the code used to handle the `Insert Object` dialog box. The embedding of a new object occurs when the constructor for class `TOcPart` is called. Just before embedding a new object, the code sends an `OC_VIEWDROP` notification message to the destination window, to check that drops are accepted.

Pasting an Object from the Clipboard

You can paste OLE objects into an application the same way you paste text, using the `Edit | Paste` command. OWL has code to handle this command in `TOleWindow`, which delegates the command to the OCF class `TOcView`. The member function `TOcView::Paste(bool)` handles the command. The parameter passed indicates whether the object being pasted is to be embedded or linked. The code looks something like that shown in Listing 13.3.

Listing 13.3. The code to insert an object into an OLE container using the Edit | Paste command.

```
bool TOcView::Paste(bool linking)
{
  SetLink(linking);
  TOcInitInfo init(this);
  bool result = OcApp.Paste(init);
  if (result) {
    result = HRSucceeded(Drop(&init, &TPoint(5,5),
                              &TRect(0,0,100,100)));
  }

  init.ReleaseDataObject();
  return result;
}
```

The code initializes a `TOcInitInfo` object with information about the object being pasted. The information is then used to simulate a Drop operation, making the object appear in the rectangle whose upper-left corner is at the position (5, 5). The dropped object is painted in a window 100 pixels wide and 100 pixels high. The object's view can subsequently be moved and resized in the container window.

Painting an OLE Object

Painting something on the screen basically involves calling some GDI functions. When you embed a server into a container application, the sequence of GDI calls doesn't change, compared to a non-embedded server, but there is a lot of code that needs to be added to synchronize the painting activities of the container and server.

Let's assume you have embedded an OLE server object in your application. If the server's data is changed, the changes must show up on the screen in the container application's view space. At the lowest OLE level, the server notifies the container of changes by invoking the `OnViewChange()` function in the container's `IAdviseSink` interface. If the server is implemented using OCF, then all it needs to do is invoke the function `TOleWindow::InvalidatePart()`, which calls the remote view's function `TOcRemView::Invalidate()`. Ultimately, the `OnViewChange()` OLE function is invoked. OLE then sends a `WM_PAINT` message to the server, resulting in the actual painting. OLE servers developed in OCF actually get an `OC_VIEWPAINT` notification with a device context to use for painting. The server doesn't need to know whether it is painting itself as a stand-alone application or as a linked/embedded object: in both cases it receives an `OC_VIEWPAINT` message.

Figure 13.9 shows a graphical depiction of the OLE activities that occur when a server wishes to update its view in a container.

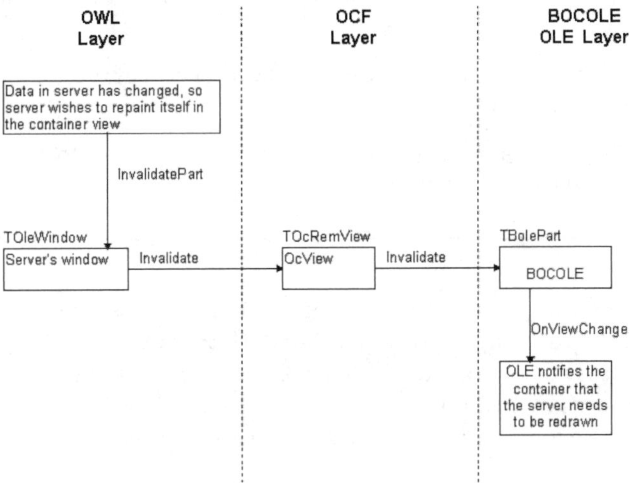

Figure 13.9. How the server tells its container about changes.

After the container is notified of changes in the server's data, the container invalidates the server's view, which then causes the server to receive an `OC_VIEWPAINT` notification. The message carries the device context of a metafile. The server paints itself into this metafile. The container later takes the metafile and plays it into the view occupied by the server. At this point you're probably thinking, "*It would have taken me weeks to figure all that out!*" You're right. The simple description I just gave barely begins to give you an idea of what's going on. Under the covers, there is a sea of OLE interfaces and function calls that need to be called in exactly the right order.

Selecting an OLE Object

When you link/embed a server OLE object, the server can be in several states: inactive, selected, open, and so forth. Clicking on an object selects it, and a focus rectangle is drawn around the object, with handles to let you resize the object's view. Let's take a quick look at what OLE activities are involved in the simple process of selecting an OLE object. When you click the mouse on the object, the mouse event is handled by the container's window, since the server paints itself into a reserved area of the container's window. The function `TOleWindow::EvLButtonDown()` handles the event, with code that looks something like that shown in Listing 13.4.

Listing 13.4. A simplified version of the code that handles a mouse click on a linked or embedded object.

```
void TOleWindow::EvLButtonDown(uint flags, TPoint& point)
{

  // Deactivating any objects there were active
  Deactivate();

  // go and select the object
  Select(flags, point);
}
```

The function `TOleWindow::Select()` locates the `TOcPart` object over which the mouse was clicked, then calls `SetSelection(TOcPart*)` with a pointer to the clicked object. `SetSelection()` invokes the function `TOcPart::Select()`, which enables the part to change its internal state to `selected`, then invalidates the object's rectangle, causing the view to repaint itself with the focus rectangle and handles.

Toolbar Negotiation and Placement

When you activate a linked or embedded object by double-clicking on it, the object has the option of merging some of its menus with the container's menus. I discussed how OWL handles menu merging in MDI applications in Chapter 11. OLE supports menu merging in a similar fashion, and goes beyond. If an activated server uses a toolbar, it can also replace the container's toolbar with its own. The server can display its toolbar even if the container doesn't have one—providing the container allows this.

The process of objects showing their own toolbar in the container's view space is controlled by a negotiation process. The container knows if it has a toolbar, and whether it allows in-place active objects to display their own toolbar. What the container doesn't know is what the toolbars of active objects might look like, or how much space they might take. The object itself knows this part. The negotiation enables the container to combine its knowledge of toolbars with the in-place object, and reach come kind of agreement. At one extreme, the container may not allow objects to display a toolbar. The object then has the option of either creating the toolbar as a floating window, or to not run at all. At the other extreme, the container might indicate that the server can display a toolbar anywhere on the screen. Let's take a look at how the toolbar negotiation process works in OWL and OCF.

The object being in-place activated first requests the area in which the toolbar will be displayed by the parent container. The OLE function `GetBorder()`, in the `IOleInPlaceUIWindow` interface of a `BOleDocument` BOCOLE object, returns the entire client area of the container. Then BOCOLE invokes the member function `TOcRemView::ShowTools(true)`, where the toolbar space negotiation takes place. Listing 13.5 shows a fragment of the code.

Listing 13.5. Negotiation for toolbar space in `TOcRemView`.

```
HRESULT TOcRemView::ShowTools(bool show)
{
  // initialize a helper object
  TOcToolBarInfo far& tbi = ToolBarInfo;

  // Let the remote view create/destroy its toolbar
  // return the toolbar's HWND in 'tbi.HTopTB'
  ForwardEvent(OC_VIEWSHOWTOOLS, &tbi))
  HWND hwndToolBar = tbi.HTopTB;

  if (show) {

    // Get the bounding rect of the our toolbar
    // we'll assume the toolbar is always display at the
    // top of the client area
    TRect border(...);

    // see if the container will grant us this space
    BAppI->RequestBorderSpace(&border);

    // use the border the container agreed to,
    // and allocate the space for the toolbar
    BAppI->SetBorderSpace(&border);

    // move the toolbar to the location we agreed
    // to with the container
    TRect contFrameR;
    BAppI->GetWindowRect(&contFrameR);
    ::MoveWindow(tbi.HTopTB, -1, -1,
                 contFrameR.Width()+2, ttbr.Height(), false);

    // make the toolbar a child of the container's frame window
    ::SetParent(hwndToolBar, BAppI->GetWindow();

    // display the toolbar finally
    ::ShowWindow(hwndToolBar, SW_NORMAL);
  }

  else {
    // make the toolbar a child of the server's frame window
    ::SetParent(hwndToolBar, OcApp.GetWindow();

    // dife the toolbar
    ::ShowWindow(hwndToolBar, SW_HIDE);
  }
  return HR_NOERROR;
}
```

The ForwardEvent() call sends an OC_VIEWSHOWTOOLS notification to the window that manages the server's view. I'll talk about the notification handler in a moment. TOcRemView::ShowTools() is called both to show and hide the toolbar. If it needs to create the toolbar, it negotiates with the container using RequestBorderSpace() and SetBorderSpace(). It then takes the toolbar created by the server in response to the OC_VIEWSHOWTOOLS notification, and displays it in the container view, at the location that was agreed upon by the server and container. Also, the toolbar is reparented, making it a child window of the container's frame window.

If the toolbar is being destroyed, meaning the server is being deactivated, the toolbar is reparented, making it a child window of the server's frame window. The window is then hidden, but not destroyed. If the server is later activated, it already will have a toolbar, so it won't need to create a new one.

Now it's time to show how the server code handles the OC_VIEWSHOWTOOLS message. The server's window will need to have a handler for this message, in which it creates a toolbar, with code that does something like that shown in Listing 13.6.

Listing 13.6. The server's code that create a new toolbar.

```
// define a handler for OC_VIEWSHOWTOOLS notifications
DEFINE_RESPONSE_TABLE1(TMyServerView, TOleView)
  EV_OC_VIEWSHOWTOOLS,
END_RESPONSE_TABLE;


bool TMyServerView::EvOcViewShowTools(TOcToolBarInfo far& tbi)
{
  if (tbi.Show) {
    // create a new toolbar
    TWindow* window = GetApplication()->GetMainWindow();
    TOleFrame* frame = TYPESAFE_DOWNCAST(window, TOleFrame);
    ToolBar = new TControlBar(frame->GetRemViewBucket() );
    TButtonGadget* b1;
    TButtonGadget* b2;
    b1 = new TButtonGadget(CM_1, CM_2, ButtonGadget::Command);
    b2 = new TButtonGadget(CM_1, CM_2, ButtonGadget::Command);
    ToolBar->Insert(*b1);
    ToolBar->Insert(*b2);
    ToolBar->Create();
    tbi.HTopTB = (HWND)*ToolBar;
  }
  else {
    // destroy the toolbar
    ToolBar->Destroy();
    delete ToolBar;
    ToolBar = 0;
  }
  return true;
}
```

And there you have it: toolbars with OLE functionality. If you think the code I showed you was bad, you haven't looked at the OLE SDK documentation. It goes into gyrations with stuff like `IOleInPlaceUIWindow` interfaces or conversions of view space coordinate systems.

Invoking an Automated Object

One of the less-touted, but more useful features of OLE is *automation*. Linking and Embedding objects are simplistic ways to add functionality to an application. Once an object is embedded or linked to an app, it can be activated and used, but there is really no connection between the container app and the activated server object. Say you want the user to embed a spreadsheet in your app. Let's say you want to let the user select a cell in the spreadsheet, and use its contents in the container app. You're out of luck, because the spreadsheet and container don't know how to talk to each other, in terms of transferring the contents of selected cells. Drag-and-drop might be a solution, but is not a programmatic one. What you need is a way for the container to tell the server what to do. You need to basically have a way of invoking methods stored inside the server, and a way of retrieving the results (if any).

Enter OLE Automation, which is considerably more flexible than linking or embedding objects. Using Automation, the object providing the automation services doesn't even have to be linked or embedded in the application using the object. But let me standardize my notation before going too far. When an application A sends automation commands to another application B, I'll call A the automation controller, or simply controller. I'll call application B the automated object, or simply the object.

Let's say you create a simple calculator application. The user can click its buttons to perform normal calculations. In order for other programs to be able to click the calculator's buttons, you need to automate the calculator. If you have a financial application that needs to use the calculator's capabilities, you would like to manipulate the calculator with code like this:

```
TMyCalculator calculator;
calculator.Bind("Calc.Application");
calculator.Press("3.14");
calculator.Press("*");
calculator.Press("2");
double result = calculator.Result();
```

Now all the smarts for calculating are in one application, and all the knowledge of what calculations to perform are in another. The two applications have little in common. In fact the automated controller doesn't even now your financial application exists.

To make the preceding code possible, the calculator must expose a number of methods and properties to OLE. I won't describe the process of actually creating the automation object and automation controller, since the Borland documentation does an eminent job of that. What I will focus on are the details of how OWL and OCF connect the controller to the object, allowing such an elegant notation to be used.

The Proxy Object

The class called `TMyCalculator` above was not defined in the calculator application. The class was created by the Borland utility `AUTOGEN`, which used all sorts of information stored in the calculator's type library. Class `TMyCalculator` is called a *proxy* class, and automation controllers access automated objects through proxy objects. The steps for generating a proxy class are the following: first you create your automated server, with special macros to expose methods and properties; then you generate a Type Library for the object, by executing the automated application with the command line option `-TypeLib`. Once you have the Type Library, you run `AUTOGEN` and pass it the name of the Type Library to use. `AUTOGEN` creates both the declaration and definition of the proxy class.

Binding the Proxy Object to an OLE Automated Object

In the code of your automation controller, you first declare the proxy object like this:

```
TMyCalculator calculator;
```

Before you can invoke any of the exposed methods or properties of the automated object, you need to connect the object to a physical OLE automated application, using the code:

```
calculator.Bind("Calc.Application");
```

The parameter passed to `Bind()` is the program ID of an OLE automated application. Let's take a look at what happens when you call `Bind()`. All proxy classes are derived from the OWL class `TAutoProxy`, which has several `Bind()` member functions that take various argument types. The code above invokes a chain of `Bind()` functions, the first of which looks something like this:

```
void TAutoProxy::Bind(const char far* progid)
{
  GUID guid;
  CLSIDFromProgID(progid, &guid);
  Bind(guid);
}
```

So one `Bind()` calls another `Bind()`, after converting an automated application's program ID (which is a string), into a globally unique identifier (`GUID`) of the automated application The second `Bind()` function looks something like this:

```
void TAutoProxy::Bind(const GUID& guid)
{
  IUnknown* unk;
  HRESULT stat;
```

```
  stat = ::CoCreateInstance(guid, 0, CLSCTX_SERVER,
                            IID_IUnknown,
                            (void FAR*FAR*)&unk);
  char guidBuf[60];
  TClassId copy(guid);
  lstrcpy (guidBuf, copy);
  Bind(unk);
}
```

This function calls the OLE function `CoCreateInstance()` to create an object with the given `GUID`. The newly created object is not an automated object yet. All we have of the object is a pointer to its `IUnknown` interface, which is subsequently passed to yet another `Bind()` function, that looks something like this:

```
void TAutoProxy::Bind(IUnknown* unk)
{
  IDispatch* dsp;
  HRESULT stat;
  stat = unk->QueryInterface(IID_IDispatch, (void**) &dsp);
  unk->Release();
  Bind(dsp);
}
```

The function obtains a pointer to the OLE object's `IDispatch` interface. Every OLE automated object is required to have an `IDispatch` interface. There is some error code in the original `Bind()` functions which I didn't show in the code snippets above, in order to concentrate on the flow of events. `Bind()` calls `Release()` to decrement the internal reference counter of `unk`, after the `QueryInterface()` call incremented it. So now we have a pointer to an `IDispatch` interface for an OLE object. That's all we need to control the object through automation.

Invoking Proxy Member Functions

Now comes the interesting part. We have a C++ object of type TAutoProxy connected to an OLE automated object. Let's see what happens when the controller application executes the code:

```
calculator.Press("3.14");
```

The proxy class `TMyCalculator` has a member function `Press()`, declared like this:

```
class TMyCalculator : public TAutoProxy {
public:

  //...
 void Press(TAutoString keys);
};
```

The code for this function looks something like this:

```
void TMyCalculator::Press(TAutoString keys)
{
  AUTONAMES0("Press")
  AUTOARGS0();
  AUTOCALL_METHOD1V(keys)
}
```

The function contains three macros. The macros work off of information in a table and a command stack. Arguments are pushed onto this stack, and later passed to the automation method. The proxy object knows which OLE method in the bound OLE object corresponds to the `Press()` member function. The `AUTOGEN` utility generated that information from data contained in the `DECLARE` and `DEFINE_AUTOCLASS` macros.

Inheritance and OLE

Inheritance is a basic C++ feature that allows you to build classes that use the code of base classes. Because C++ gives you the option of calling base class functions in derived classes, the latter can both extend and restrict the features of a base class. By default, all the base class features are inherited in a derived class. The C++ inheritance model works well in the context of software development, but is not well-suited for use in OLE. The following sections discuss some of the pros and cons of C++ inheritance.

Advantages of Inheritance in C++

Probably the nicest feature of C++ inheritance is the ease with which one class can derive from another. To create a class `B` that inherits from class `A`, all you have to write is

```
class B: public A {
  // ...
};
```

With this simple declaration, ALL the features of `A` are inherited by `B`. The only code necessary in class `B` is code that changes the way a member function works in the base class `A`.

Another attractive feature of C++ inheritance is that a class is written without any need to know about its subsequent use as a base class. Any class can be used as a base class, no special code is required in a class to make this possible. You could say that a C++ class is by default an inheritable class. Actually, C++ classes do support a certain level of security from derived classes, using the access specifier `protected`. Access specifiers are really a way of protecting an object's internal data from users, and derived classes are simply one kind of user of a class.

Disadvantages of C++ Inheritance

The purpose of inheritance is to allow code to be reused. Ideally, you would want to be able to take a class developed by anyone and use it as a base class. In C++, this is not always entirely possible. The main problem is that C++ supports compile-time inheritance only. You can't dynamically inherit code at runtime. Because inheritance is a compile-time feature, to inherit from a class means the class must have a C++ declaration. If a base class uses anything that is vendor-specific (which is typical in class hierarchies like OWL and MFC), your compiler may not know how to compile in your base classes. In a nutshell, C++ inheritance is not only language-specific (requiring C++ base classes), but also vendor-specific.

An additional problem is non-standardized name mangling. If you have some C++ objects stored in a DLL, you may want to derive new classes from them. The names of the exported functions in the DLL are mangled, and use the name mangling scheme of the compiler used to build the DLL. If you are using a compiler that uses a different name mangling scheme, then the compiler will not know how to access the functions in the DLL. C++ and Windows DLLs just don't mix well.

The OLE Approach to Reusability

Because OLE is a technology whose purpose is to guarantee object interoperability at the binary level, any scheme to support the reuse of code had to work regardless of internal object implementation details, compiler types and vendors. In OLE there are two techniques that support code reuse: object containment and object aggregation. I'll examine both in some detail.

Containment

As the word indicates, the *Object Containment* technique relies on the nesting of one OLE object inside another. Actually, the inner object doesn't even have to be an OLE object, just a Windows COM object. Assume you have an OLE object of type `Furniture`, containing an interface called `IDimensions` that lets you set/change the length, width and height. If you need to create an OLE object of type `Chair`, you would want to reuse the code of `Furniture` somehow. Figure 13.10 shows a schematic representation of how you might contain the `Furniture` object inside the `Chair` object.

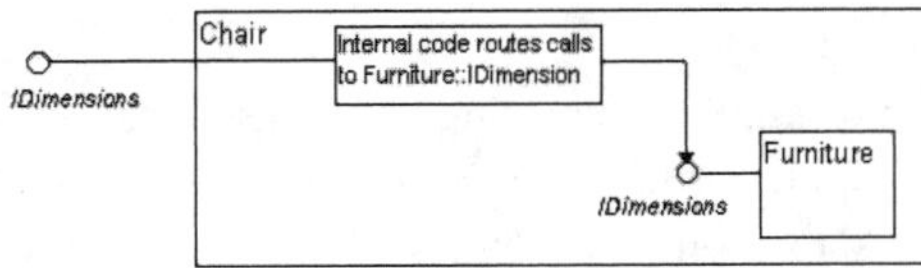

Figure 13.10. Using containment to let one OLE object reuse the code of another.

The code contained inside the `Furniture` object needs to be wired to the interface presented to the outside world by the enclosing `Chair` object. If the user of `Chair` invokes a function in the `Chair::IDimension` interface, you need to intercept the call inside `Chair`, and redirect the call to the internal `Furniture::IDimension` interface. This works correctly, except under one condition: when the `Chair` user calls the function `QueryInterface()` through the `Furniture::IDimension` interface. Calls to `Chair's` `QueryInterface()` must never be routed into `Furniture`, because `Furniture` doesn't know the interfaces of its enclosing object `Chair`. Object containment in OLE looks a lot like a C++ class that has another C++ class as a data member. In C++, you might have code as it appears in Listing 13.7.

Listing 13.7. An example of object containment in C++.

```
class Furniture {
  float height;
public:
  Furniture() {height = 0;}
  void Height(float h) {height = h;}
  float Height() {return height;}
};

class Chair {
  Furniture furniture;
public:
  void Height(float h) {furniture.Height(h);}
  float Height() {return furniture.Height();}
};
```

OLE Object Containment is convenient when you want to reuse a small number of functions of another object, but also make some changes in the functionality of the contained object. If there are dozens or hundreds of contained functions, then the code required to redirect the calls to the contained object becomes substantial. Object Containment is also good when you don't want to reuse all the functions of a contained object—only some. Containment gives you complete control over which functions you reuse and which ones you don't.

Aggregation

Another OLE technique supporting code reuse is called *Object Aggregation.* On the surface, this technique is similar to Containment, but taking a closer look, you'll see that Aggregation is quite a bit more complex In Containment, using the `Chair::IDimension` interface required code that delegated `Chair::IDimension` interface calls to the `Furniture::IDimension` interface. With Aggregation, the `Furniture::IDimension` interface is exposed directly by `Chair`, so `Furniture` and `Chair` share the same `IDimension` interface.

With aggregation, Chair doesn't get involved in calls to the Furniture::IDimension interface, so the technique is valid when you want to reuse code verbatim. Chair has no way to intercept calls made to the IDimension interface, because Furniture is connected to that interface. So how do you make one OLE object share an interface with another object? That's what is described in the next section.

The Controlling Unknown

OLE has built-in hooks that support aggregation. When you create an OLE object with the IClassFactory::CreateInstance() call, you have the option of passing it a special pointer. This pointer points to the outer class, which in my example is a pointer to class Chair. The declaration for CreateInstance() looks something like this:

```
HRESULT IClassFactory::
CreateInstance(IUnknown* controllingIUnknown,
               REFIID riid,
               LPVOID FAR * ppvObj);
```

The controllingIUnknown parameter is a pointer to the IUnknown interface of the Chair object. The Furniture object created by the call to CreateInstance() must store the pointer to its outer class for subsequent use. On the other hand, the call to CreateInstance() above will return a pointer to the IUnknown interface of Furniture. This pointer will need to be stored inside the Chair object.

I still haven't shown how the IDimension interface of class Furniture is exposed directly as an interface of class Chair. The explanation is pretty simple. To get interfaces for Chair, you call Chair::IUnknown::QueryInterface(), and request the IDimension interface. All class Chair needs to do is have a special QueryInterface() function. The function first checks to see if the requested interface is part of Chair. If the interface is not found, the Chair::IUnknown::QueryInterface() delegates the call to Furniture::IUnknown::QueryInterface(). Calling Chair::IUnknown::QueryInterface() for IDimension will result in Furniture::IUnknown::QueryInterface() getting called, and returning a pointer to Furniture::IDimension. The whole process is shown schematically in Figure 13.11.

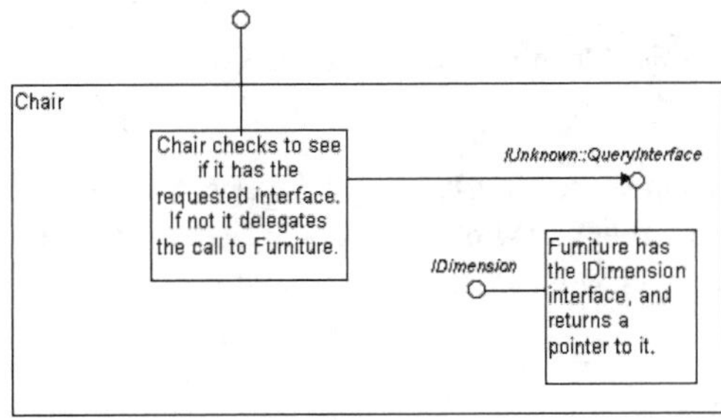

Figure 13.11. How aggregate objects expose inner functionality.

Users of class `Chair` have no way of telling whether an interface like `IDimension` was returned from `Chair` or from an object aggregated inside `Furniture`. Note that OLE aggregation is recursive: aggregated objects may contain aggregated objects. Any number of objects can be aggregated inside another, and to any level. When more than more object is contained inside another, the situation is reminiscent of multiple inheritance, and the parent object decides the delegation order of the contained objects. For example, if object `A` contains two aggregated objects `B` and `C`, when the user queries `A` for an interface it doesn't know, then `A` must delegate the `QueryInterface()` call first to one object (for instance, `B`) then to the other (such as `C`). The order of delegation (first `B`, then `C` or vice-versa) may be significant if both `B` and `C` know the requested interface.

Class *TUnknown*

OCF defines the class `TUnknown` to encapsulate a generic COM object. The only interface supported directly by `TUnknown` is `IUnknown`. If an object supports other interfaces, those interfaces will be obtainable by calling `IUnknown::QueryInterface` of the `TUnknown` object. `TUnknown` uses a nested class called `TUnknownI` (the `I` is for *inner*) to represent aggregated objects inside it. Class `TUnknown` knows how to delegate interface requests to inner objects, and the inner objects know how to find their outer objects. Class `TUnknown` allows only one object to be nested inside another, but nesting can occur to any depth. Because each object can only contain one nested object, `TUnknown` supports a model similar to C++ single inheritance. Class `TUnknown` is used to encapsulate the basic functionality of OLE objects that may or may not use aggregation, as shown in Figure 13.12.

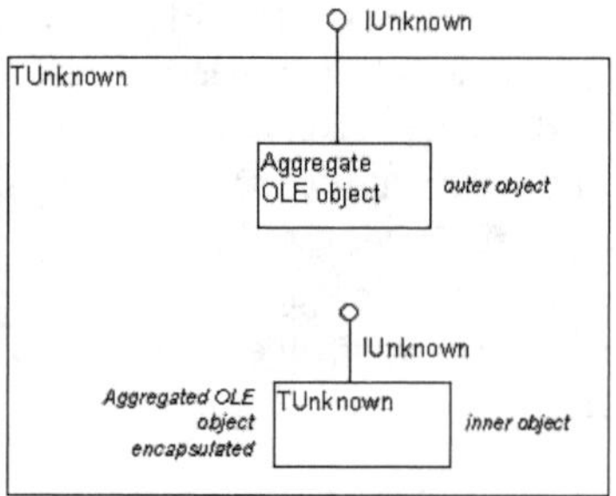

Figure 13.12. How `TUnknown` *encapsulates OLE objects.*

Class `TUnknown` is used in OCF as a base class for classes that use aggregation to inherit capabilities of other COM objects. A little later I'll describe class `TOcView`, a class derived from `TUnknown`. Class `TUnknown` is declared in a manner shown by Listing 13.8.

Listing 13.8. The declaration of class `TUnknown`.

```
class TUnknown {

  // class TUnknownI is a nested class
  TUnknownI I;
  friend class TUnknownI;

protected:

  TUnknown();
  virtual ~TUnknown();

  IUnknown& ThisUnknown() {return I;}
  virtual HRESULT QueryObject(const GUID& iid, void** pif);

  IUnknown* Outer;

public:

  operator IUnknown&();
  operator IUnknown*();
  IUnknown* SetOuter(IUnknown* outer = 0);
  IUnknown* GetOuter();
  unsigned long GetRefCount();
  IUnknown& Aggregate(TUnknown& inner);

};
```

Although the preceding code doesn't show it, class `TUnknownI` is not only a friend class, but a nested class that encapsulates the OLE `IUnknown` interface of a `TUnknown` object. I separated the declarations of `TUnknown` and `TUnknownI` to simplify my discussion.

The constructor for `TUnknown` is protected, restricting the use of `TUnknown` only as a base class. The constructor sets up the data member `Outer` to point at the data member `I`, which represents the object's `IUnknown` interface.

The protected function `ThisUnknown()` enables derived classes to get access to a `TUnknown` object's `IUnknown` interface.

The next protected function, `QueryObject()`, is designed to be overridden in derived classes. The function is called to find interfaces that were requested by calling `TUnknown::IUnknown::QueryInterface()`. The function iterates over all the BOCOLE interfaces and objects, until the desired interface is located (or none is found). The order in which the BOCOLE interfaces and objects are examined is fixed for each object type. For example, class `TOcRemView`, derived from `TUnknown`, has the code shown in Listing 13.9.

Listing 13.9. How `TOcRemView` searches for OLE interfaces in `QueryObject()`.

```
TOcRemView::QueryObject(const IID& iid, void** iface)
{
  // check BOCOLE interfaces first
  //
     SUCCEEDED(hr = IBPart_QueryInterface(this, iid, iface))
  || SUCCEEDED(hr = IBDataProvider_QueryInterface(this, iid, iface))

  // check TOcRemView base classes
  || SUCCEEDED(hr = TOcView::QueryObject(iid, iface))

  // then check the BOCOLE helper objects
  || (BSite && SUCCEEDED(hr = BSite->QueryInterface(iid, iface)));

  return hr;
}
```

The function delegates first to BOCOLE interfaces, then to OCF base classes, then to BOCOLE helper objects.

Class `TUnknown` has two operators related to `IUnknown`: one returns a pointer to an `IUnknown`, the other returns a reference. When you obtain a pointer to the `IUnknown` interface of an object, OLE requires that you increment the usage count of that object by calling `AddRef()`. This technique of having users of an object control the internal variable of that object is what might be called anti-OOP. OLE is supposed to be the vehicle for new object-oriented programming with Windows, but it itself contains un-OOP features. Borland patched the problem with the operator `IUnknown*()`. When you get a pointer to the `IUnknown` interface of a `TUnknown` object, the operator itself increments the reference count for the object. The user doesn't have to get involved. The other operator, `IUnknown()`, returns a reference to the `IUnknown` interface, without incrementing the reference count. Be careful when you use this operator. If you assign its returned value to an `IUnknown&` variable, there is a possibility that the object referenced won't exist at some later time.

The are a few more functions to describe in `TUnknown`. The functions `SetOuter()` and `GetOuter()` let you set/get the OLE object wrapped up by a `TUnknown` object. Using the C++ inheritance model, this object is equivalent to the most derived object in a single inheritance hierarchy.

The function `GetRefCount()` returns the reference count of an object. In the absence of object aggregation, the reference count is easy to determine: calls to `AddRef()` increment it and calls to `Release()` decrement it. With aggregation you have a problem, because there is more than one OLE object involved. Who's reference count do you use? `TUnknown` uses the simple algorithm: It returns the reference count of the most nested aggregated object, which is guaranteed to be equal to or greater than the reference count of all its outer objects.

The last function of TUnknown, Aggregate(), takes a pointer to a TUnknown object and nests that object inside another TUnknown object. If you have two TUnknown object pointers A and B, calling A->Aggregate(B) will result in the situation shown in Figure 13.13.

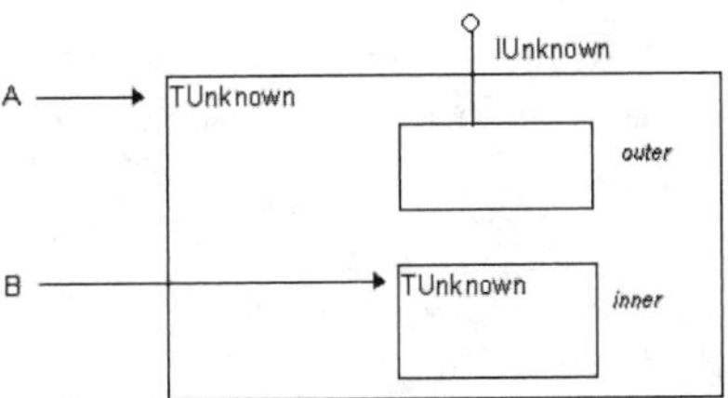

Figure 13.13. The result of calling A->Aggregate(B).

Using TUnknown::Aggregate() to insert one TUnknown object inside another results updates the reference count of the inner object (pointed at by B in the previous example).

The Nested Class *TUnknownI*

After seeing all the details of the controlling class TUnknown, let's take a look at the nested class TUnknownI. The class' main purpose is to encapsulate a generic OLE object, with links for aggregation. The IUnknown interface exposed by TUnknown is actually just a pointer to a TUnknownI class. The layout of the first three member functions of TUnknownI, QueryInterface(), AddRef(), and Release(), matches the order dictated by the Component Object Model precisely.

The nested class TUnknownI is declared in a manner shown in Listing 13.10.

Listing 13.10. The declaration of class TUnknownI.

```
class TUnknownI : public IUnknown {

public:

  HRESULT QueryInterface(const GUID& iid, void** pif);
  unsigned long AddRef();
  unsigned long Release();
  TUnknownI();
  ~TUnknownI();
  unsigned  RefCnt;
  TUnknown* Inner;

private:

  TUnknown& Host();
};
```

QueryInterface() calls the outer object's QueryObject() member function, which in turn iterates over interfaces, TUnknown base classes and BOCOLE helper objects to locate the desired interface, as shown previously. AddRef() and Release() control the object's reference count.

The variable Inner maintains a link to the TUnknown object aggregated inside the outer TUnknown object, resulting in a structure depicted in Figure 13.14.

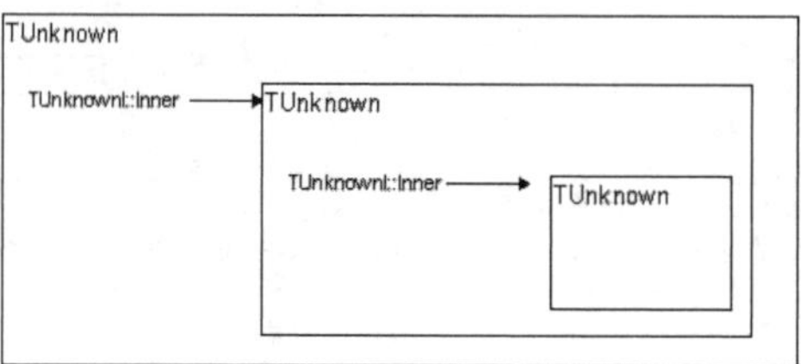

Figure 13.14. The recursive nesting of TUnknown *objects through the* TUnknownI::Inner *pointer.*

TUnknown objects form a chain, whose nodes are connected by TUnknownI::Inner pointers. TUnknown objects can be nested to any arbitrary depth.

The last member of TUnknownI, the private member function Host(), returns a reference to the TUnknown object enclosing a given TUnknownI object.

Using Class *TUnknown*: Class *TOcView*

Class TUnknown doesn't do anything useful by itself, except to establish a framework to support OLE object aggregation and QueryInterface() delegation. Class TUnknown can't be used directly, but only as a base class. To ensure this, its constructor was made protected. To see the class in action, you need to see how a derived class looks and works. There are several OCF classes derived from TUnknown, as shown in Figure 13.15.

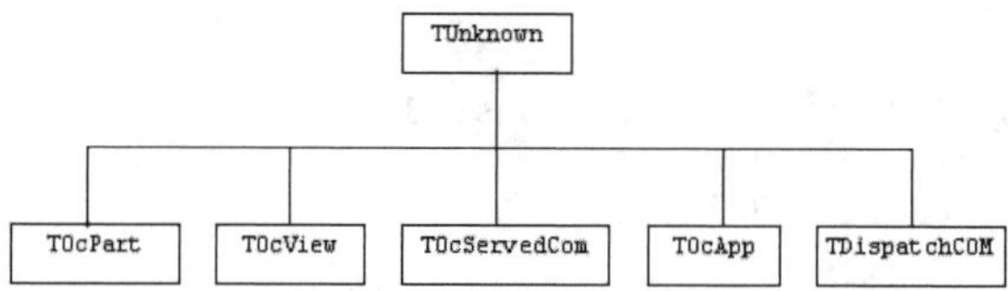

Figure 13.15. The OCF classes derived from TUnknown.

The classes shown in Figure 13.15 all have other base classes besides TUnknown. The base class TUnknown is required to allow OCF objects to support OLE aggregation. Let's take a look at the details of the class TOcView, to see how TUnknown is used. TOcView supports several OLE interfaces, as shown in Figure 13.16.

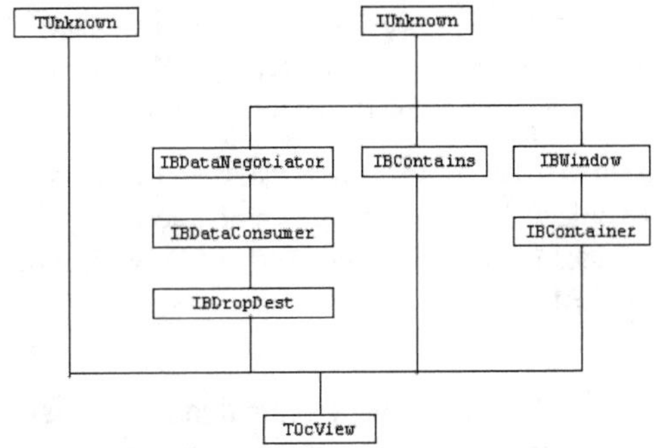

Figure 13.16. The class hierarchy of `TOcView`.

Objects of type `TOcView` know how to draw the view of a document. If the document contains linked or embedded objects, then the views of those objects must also be drawn. `TOcViews` must therefore support the BOCOLE `IBContainer` and `IBContains` interfaces. Because users can drag-and-drop new objects into a `TOcView`, the BOCOLE `IDropDest` interface is also supported.

So where does `TUnknown` fit into this picture? Class `TOcView` doesn't contain aggregated OLE objects, but it does have a number of OLE interfaces and BOCOLE helper objects. `TUnknown` establishes a uniform procedure for `QueryInterface()` delegation, through the virtual function `QueryObject`. Users of `TOcView` objects call `TOcView::IUnknown::QueryInterface()` to obtain interfaces. This call is handled internally by the base class `TUnknown`. The code for `TUnknownI::QueryInterface()` looks the code in Listing 13.11.

Listing 13.11. The implementation of `TUnKnownI::QueryInterface()`.

```
HRESULT TUnknown::TUnknownI::QueryInterface(const GUID& iid, void**
pif)
{
  *pif = 0;
  if (iid.Data1 == 0) { // IID_IUnknown.Data1
    CmpGuidOle(this, iid, pif);
    if (*pif)
      return NOERROR;
  }
  if (Host().QueryObject(iid, pif) == NOERROR)
    return NOERROR;
  if (Inner)
    return Inner->ThisUnknown().QueryInterface(iid, pif);
  else
    return ResultFromScode(E_NOINTERFACE);
}
```

The function first checks to see if an `IUnknown` interface was requested. If so, the current object is returned through the parameter `pif`. Note that a pointer to a `TUnknownI` object is equivalent to a pointer to an `IUnknown` interface.

If the requested interface is not `IUnknown`, then the request is first delegated to the enclosing `TUnknown` object, then down the chain of objects aggregated inside the `TUnknown` object. `TOcView` overrides `TUnknown::QueryObject()`, with code that looks something like that shown in Listing 13.12.

Listing 13.12. The `QueryObject()` function in TOcView.

```
HRESULT TOcView::QueryObject(const IID& iid, void** iface)
{
   HRESULT hr;

  // delegate to BOCOLE interfaces first

  SUCCEEDED(hr = IBContainer_QueryInterface(this, iid, iface))
  || SUCCEEDED(hr = IBContains_QueryInterface(this, iid, iface))
  || SUCCEEDED(hr = IBDataConsumer_QueryInterface(this, iid, iface))
  || SUCCEEDED(hr = IBDropDest_QueryInterface(this, iid, iface))
  || SUCCEEDED(hr = IBDataNegotiator_QueryInterface(this, iid, iface))

  // then delegate to BOCOLE helper objects

  || (BContainer && SUCCEEDED(hr = BContainer->QueryInterface(iid,
iface)))
  || (BDocument && SUCCEEDED(hr = BDocument->QueryInterface(iid,
iface)));

  return hr;
}
```

As you can see, the query is delegated first to the BOCOLE interfaces supported by `TOcView`, then to the BOCOLE helper objects managed internally by `TOcView`. If an interface request is received that can't be honored by `TOcView::QueryObject()`, then the function `TUnknownI::QueryInterface()` will automatically search the chain of aggregated objects (if any).

Compound Files

OLE introduces the ability for one document to contain others. When that document is saved, all embedded documents are also saved, creating a compound file that contains documents embedded inside each other in a hierarchy. Microsoft often touts this ability to produce compound files as a new technology, but OWL programmers have been creating compound files for years.

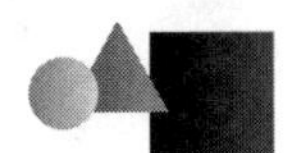

When you create a streamable object in OWL, that object becomes capable or reading and writing itself to a stream. The object also controls the reading and writing of all objects contained in it. If an OWL `TWindow` contains other child `TWindows`, then the parent window reads/writes the child windows. A streamed `TWindow` object produces a file that is very similar to an OLE compound file. Practically all OWL classes are streamable, but the objects saved in files are OWL objects. To create an compound file, OLE requires that all objects stored be OLE objects, supporting certain interfaces, so Borland extended the notion of streamability to include the OCF classes that encapsulate OLE objects.

In OLE compound files, you can store documents inside documents. For each embedded document, OLE defines a storage compartment, similar to a DOS directory, called a *storage*. Within its own storage, a document is free to set up partitions, called *streams*, that are the functional equivalent to DOS files. An OLE Compound File stores data as shown schematically in Figure 13.17.

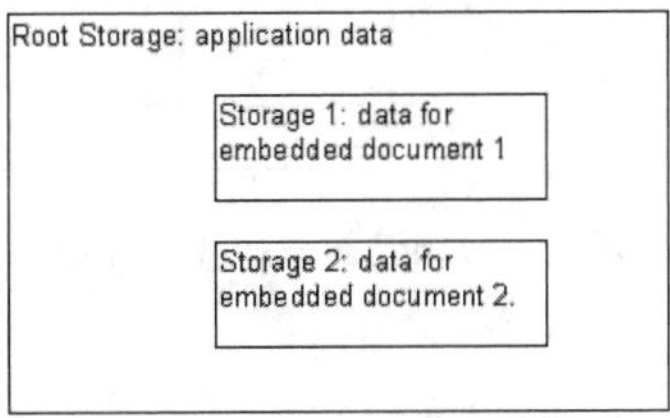

Figure 13.17. The structure of a compound file with two storages.

An application has full control over the number of storages it creates. Theoretically it could even store all the embedded data in the root storage of a file, but OLE conventions call for one storage to be created for each embedded document. If an embedded document contains embedded documents itself, then sub-storages will be needed. The following sections will discuss briefly how Borland added support for Compound Files to OWL and OCF.

Class *TOleWindow*

In OLE, the interfaces that deal with a document's data are completely separate from those that deal with the way the document appears on the screen. The OLE notion of documents deals with data, and documents display themselves through views. This all sounds very much like the Doc/View model supported already by OWL. While the concepts of documents and views are similar in OLE and OWL, the implementations are vastly different. As a result, OWL has classes for its internal Doc/View model, and classes for OLE's document and view interfaces.

Anytime you create an OLE SDI application with OWL, you must derive the main window from `TOleWindow`. If you're creating an MDI app, then the child windows will need to have their client area occupied by a TOleWindow-derived window. Figure 13.18 shows the structure of an SDI application. Figure 13.19 shows the case for an MDI application.

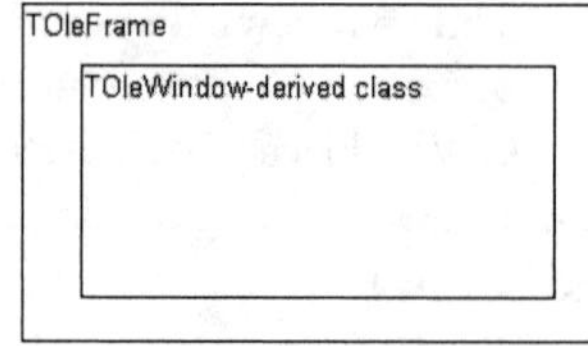

Figure 13.18. The use of `TOleWindow` *in an SDI application.*

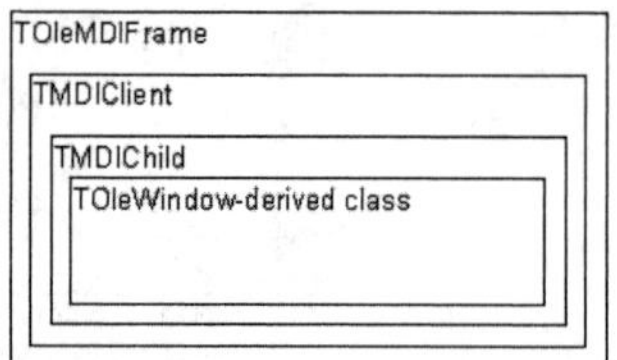

Figure 13.19. The use of `TOleWindow` *in an MDI application.*

`TOleWindow` is the highest level OWL class that deals with OCF and OWL. The class handles the OLE operations on the data for each window using a `TOcDocument` object. `TOleWindow` also manages a `TOcView` object, with OLE interfaces for drawing documents, supporting drag-and-drop, and a few other things.

The Document-Management Classes

There are two classes that deal with documents. One is called `TOleDocument`, the other is `TOcDocument`. Don't confuse the two. The former is an OWL Doc/View class that manages the C++ stream into which data is written or read. `TOleDocument` creates new storages in compound files for each document. The class has member functions to open and close files, to commit or revert transacted data and to read/write properties into compound files.

Class `TOcDocument` is a lower-level OCF class that supports the actual reading and writing of embedded objects into a given storage previously created by `TOleDocument`. The member function `TOcDocument::SaveParts()` iterates over the embedded documents and saves them. The member function `TOcDocument::LoadParts()` reads the data for all the objects embedded in a document.

Conclusion

In this chapter I have tried to describe some of the more important OLE-related implementation issues of OWL and OCF. One chapter is barely enough to get started, but hopefully I have shown you enough to show one thing: Borland has really done a spectacular job of merging OLE functionality into OWL, without upsetting the internal structure of OWL. They were able to do this by creating two layers of insulation software—OCF and BOCOLE. OLE is a technology that will doubtless evolve considerably over the next few years. Borland has positioned itself to be able to accommodate substantial changes and extensions to OLE with minimal impact on OWL itself, because nearly all the OLE-dependent code in a typical Borland C++ application is outside of OWL. Microsoft's approach to OLE support was quite different, involving the addition of low-level OLE API calls directly to MFC classes.

We look at OLE as a rather arcane technology today, but soon it will just be another one of the technologies we use routinely. OLE promises to take us closer to the goal of component-based programming, in which developers can use off-the-shelf objects from a toolbox to create entire applications. There will always be glue code, like the glue circuitry used in hardware today to connect the VLSI and ULSI chips in a system. What the industry needs to come up with is a standard or series of standards for high-level software interfaces, so the amount of software glue is truly minimal.

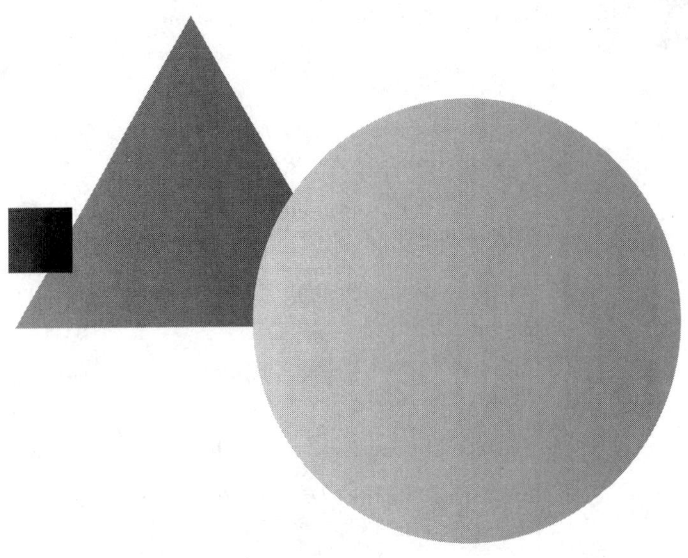

Bibliography

Books

Atkinson, Lee, and Mark Atkinson. *Using Borland C++*. 2nd ed. Indianapolis, IN: Que Corporation, 1992.

Booch, Grady. *Object-Oriented Design with Applications.* Redwood City, CA: Benjamin/Cummings Publishing Co. Inc, 1991.

Conger, James L. *Windows API Bible*. Waite Group Press, 1992.

Cox, Brad. *Object-Oriented Programming, an Evolutionary Approach.* Reading, MA: Addison Wesley, 1987.

Ellis, Margaret, and Bjarne Stroustrup. *The Annotated C++ Reference Manual.* Reading, MA: Addison Wesley, 1990.

Faison, Ted. *Graphical User Interfaces with Turbo C++*. Indianapolis, IN: SAMS, 1990.

Knuth, Donald E. *The Art of Computer Programming, Vol. 1–Fundamental Algorithms.* Reading MA: Addison Wesley, 1968.

Knuth, Donald E. *The Art of Computer Programming, Vol. 3–Searching and Sorting.* Reading MA: Addison Wesley, 1973.

LaLonde, Wilf, and John Pugh. *Inside Smalltalk, Vol. 1.* Englewood Cliffs, NJ: Prentice Hall, 1990.

LaLonde, Wilf, and John Pugh. *Inside Smalltalk, Vol 2.* Englewood Cliffs, NJ: Prentice Hall, 1991.

Meyer, Bertrand. *Object-Oriented Software Construction.* Englewood Cliffs, NJ: Prentice Hall, 1988.

Petzold, Charles. *Programming Windows.* 2nd ed. Redwood, WA: Microsoft Press, 1990.

Stroustrup, Bjarne. *The C++ Programming Language.* 2nd ed. Reading, MA: Addison Wesley, 1991.

Schildt, Herbert. *Turbo C/C++: The Complete Reference.* Berkeley, CA: Osborne McGraw-Hill, 1990.

Tello, Ernest. *Object-Oriented Programming for Windows.* New York: John Wiley & Sons, 1991.

The Whitewater Group. *Actor User's Manual.* Evanston, IL: The Whitewater Group Inc., 1991.

Articles

Bonneau, Paul. "List Boxes with tab stops." Windows Q & A, *Windows/DOS Developer's Journal,* May, September, December, 1992.

Brockschmidt, Kraig and Kyle Marsh. "Considerations for Horizontal Scroll Bars in ListBoxes." *Microsoft Developer Technology Group Notes,* March, 1992.

Burk, Ron. "Building a Better Boolean with C++." *The C Users Journal* April 1990: pp. 57–66.

Clark, David. "A Date Object in C++." *The C Users Journal.* June, 1990: pp. 57–69.

Eckel, Bruce. "Taking Control to Task." *Computer Language.* Feb., 1991: pp. 38–51.

Felice, Bob. "Implementing the CCITT Cyclic Redundancy Check." *The C Users Journal* Sept. 1990: pp. 61–64.

Finnegran, Fran. "Editing in ListBoxes." Windows Questions and Answers, *Windows Systems Journal,* Vol. 8, No. 4: pp. 67–75.

Koenig, Andrew. "Decoupling Application Libraries from Input-Output." *The C++ Journal* Fall 1990: pp. 15–19.

Provenzano, Tom. "A Hash Table Manager in C++." *The C Users Journal* Nov. 1989: pp. 83–95.

Welch, Kevin. "Using Object-Oriented Methodologies in Windows Applications." *Microsoft Systems Journal* May 1990: pp. 63–66.

White, Eric. "OOP as a Programming Style." *The C Users Journal* Feb. 1990: pp. 43–57.

Williams, Kent. "Smart Searching with C++." *Computer Language* Sept. 1990: pp. 45–56.

Public Domain Software

Gorlen, K.E. *NIH Class Library*. National Institutes of Health, Computer Systems Laboratory, Division of Computer Research and Technology, Bethesda, MD.

Index

Symbols

A

B

C

D

F

G

H

I-J-K

L

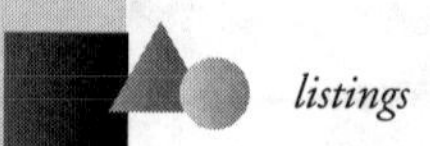

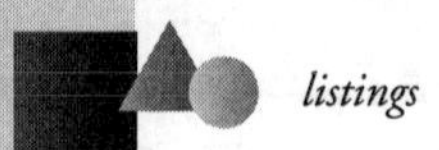

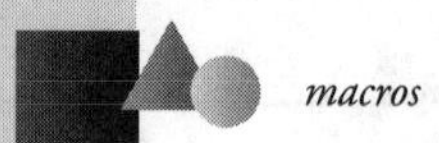

M

O

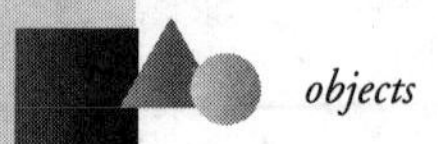

Q

R

S

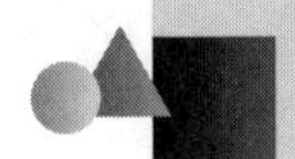

V

Book ISBN 0-672-30605-0

What's on the Disk

The companion disk contains the source code for all the complete programs presented in the text.

Installing the Floppy Disk

The software included with this book is stored in a compressed form. You cannot use the software without first installing it to your hard drive. The installation program runs from within Windows.

> **NOTE**
>
> To install the files on the disk, you'll need at least 800K free space on your hard drive.

1. From File Manager or Program Manager, choose **R**un from the **F**ile menu.
2. Type `<drive>INSTALL` and press Enter, where `<drive>` is the letter of the drive that contains the installation disk. For example, if the disk is in drive B:, type `B:INSTALL` and press Enter.

Follow the on-screen instructions in the installation program. The files will be installed in the \BC45OOP directory, unless you chose a different directory during installation. When the installation is complete, be sure to read the file INSINFO.TXT This file contains information on the files and programs that were installed.